"Keep the Damned Women Out"

"CONFUSED—of course, I'm confused! I have a son at Vassar and a daughter at Yale!"

"Keep the Damned Women Out"

The Struggle for Coeducation

Nancy Weiss Malkiel

PRINCETON UNIVERSITY PRESS

PRINCETON & OXFORD

Published by Princeton University Press,
41 William Street, Princeton, New Jersey 08540
In the United Kingdom: Princeton University Press,
6 Oxford Street, Woodstock, Oxfordshire OX20 1TR
press.princeton.edu

Jacket design by Amanda Weiss

Library of Congress Cataloging-in-Publication Data

Names: Malkiel, Nancy Weiss, author.
Title: Keep the damned women out : the struggle for coeducation /
    Nancy Weiss Malkiel.
Description: Princeton : Princeton University Press, [2016] | Includes
    bibliographical references and index.
Identifiers: LCCN 2016008822 | ISBN 9780691172996 (hardcover :
    acid-free paper)
Subjects: LCSH: Women—Education, Higher—United States—
    History—20th century. | Women—Education, Higher—Great
    Britain—History—20th century. | Coeducation—United
    States—History—20th century. | Coeducation—Great Britain—
    History—20th century. | Universities and colleges—United States—
    Administration—History—20th century. | Universities and colleges—
    Great Britain—Administration—History—20th century. | College
    administrators—United States—History—20th century. | College
    administrators—Great Britain—History—20th century.
Classification: LCC LC1756 .M26 2016 | DDC 371.822—dc23
    LC record available at https://lccn.loc.gov/2016008822

British Library Cataloging-in-Publication Data is available

This book has been composed in Sabon LT Std and Milano

Printed on acid-free paper. ∞

Printed in the United States of America

10 9 8 7 6 5 4 3 2 1

To Burt and Piper

Contents

Part V

TAKING STOCK

Illustrations

Frontispiece: BERRY'S WORLD © 1967 James Berry. Used by permission of UNIVERSAL UCLICK for UFS. All rights reserved. Image courtesy of Princeton University Library: Office of the Provost Records, William G. Bowen, AC195, Box 19, Folder 2, Princeton University Archives, Department of Rare Books and Special Collections, Princeton University Library.

Following page 166

"Princeton, did you say? How interesting. I'm a Yale man myself." Carl Rose/The New Yorker Collection/The Cartoon Bank.

Elizabeth Cary Agassiz. George M. Cushing photograph. W350728, Schlesinger Library, Radcliffe Institute, Harvard University.

Nathan Marsh Pusey. W355244, Schlesinger Library, Radcliffe Institute, Harvard University.

Mary Ingraham Bunting. W351260, Schlesinger Library, Radcliffe Institute, Harvard University.

Matina Souretis Horner and Mary Ingraham Bunting. E. B. Boatner photograph. W352076, Schlesinger Library, Radcliffe Institute, Harvard University. Reproduced by permission of E. B. Boatner.

Derek Bok. Jane Reed photograph. W356656, Schlesinger Library, Radcliffe Institute, Harvard University.

Matina Souretis Horner and Linda S. Wilson. Lilian Kemp photograph. W356653, Schlesinger Library, Radcliffe Institute, Harvard University. Reproduced by permission of Lilian Kemp.

Mary Maples Dunn, Nancy-Beth Gordon Sheerr, Linda S. Wilson, and Neil Rudenstine. W356907, Schlesinger Library, Radcliffe Institute, Harvard University.

Alfred Whitney Griswold. Larry Willard photograph. MADID image 8176, Office of Public Affairs, Yale University, Photographs of Individuals (RU 686), Manuscripts and Archives, Yale University Library.

Kingman Brewster, Jr. MADID image 3559, Office of Public Affairs, Yale University, Photographs of Individuals (RU 686), Manuscripts and Archives, Yale University Library.

Hanna Holborn Gray. Office of Public Affairs, Yale University, Photographs of Individuals (RU 686), Manuscripts and Archives, Yale University Library.

Elga Wasserman. Charles Alburtus photograph, Yale University News Bureau. Office of Public Affairs, Yale University, Photographs of Individuals (RU 686), Manuscripts and Archives, Yale University Library. Reproduced by permission of the Yale University Library.

Henry Chauncey, Jr. Images of Yale Individuals (RU 684), Manuscripts and Archives, Yale University Library.

"Guys and Dolls." Yale University News Bureau. MADID image 3814, Yale Events and Activities Photographs (RU 690), Manuscripts and Archives, Yale University Library. Reproduced by permission of the Yale University Library.

Robert F. Goheen. Office of the President Records, Robert F. Goheen, AC193, Box 563, Folder 2, Princeton University Archives, Department of Rare Books and Special Collections, Princeton University Library.

William G. Bowen. Office of the President Records, William G. Bowen, AC187, Box 451, Princeton University Archives, Department of Rare Books and Special Collections, Princeton University Library.

Gardner Patterson. Historical Photograph Collection, Campus Life Series, AC112, Box FAC76, Princeton University Archives, Department of Rare Books and Special Collections, Princeton University Library.

Arthur J. Horton. Historical Photograph Collection, Campus Life Series, AC112, Box FAC50, Princeton University Archives, Department of Rare Books and Special Collections, Princeton University Library.

Halcyone H. Bohen. Office of Communication Records, AC168, Box 231, Princeton University Archives, Department of Rare Books and Special Collections, Princeton University Library.

Suzanne Keller with students. Historical Photograph Collection, Campus Life Series, AC112, Box FAC54, Princeton University Archives, Department of Rare Books and Special Collections, Princeton University Library.

John Sloan Dickey. Image 12-60-62, Photographic Records Collection, Rauner Special Collections Library. Courtesy of Dartmouth College Library.

John G. Kemeny. Image 12-74-1027, Photographic Records Collection, Rauner Special Collections Library. Courtesy of Dartmouth College Library.

Keep Sage All Male. Image 3-74-1001, Photographic Records Collection, Rauner Special Collections Library. Courtesy of Dartmouth College Library.

Following page 358

Alan Simpson. Image Ph.f8.47, Archives and Special Collections Library, Vassar College.

Elizabeth Daniels. Image Ph.f6.31, Archives and Special Collections Library, Vassar College.

Dining in Dorms, 1970s. Archives and Special Collections Library, Vassar College.

Thomas C. Mendenhall. Richard Fish photograph. Smith College Archives, Smith College.

Ely Chinoy. Carol Studios photograph, Lynbrook, NY. Smith College Archives, Smith College.

Ruth M. Adams. Photograph by Bradford F. Herzog, courtesy of the Wellesley College Archives.

Philip Phibbs. Photograph by Bradford F. Herzog, courtesy of the Wellesley College Archives.

Lord Robbins (Lionel Robbins). From the London School of Economics Library's collections, IMAGELIBRARY/386.

Lord Franks (Oliver Franks). Image 224141, painting in the collection of Worcester College, Oxford. Reproduced by permission of the Provost and Fellows of Worcester College, Oxford.

Lord Bridges (Edward E. Bridges). Allan Gwynne-Jones portrait, University of Reading (Ref: UAC/10004). Reproduced by permission of Bridgeman Art Library, London.

R. H. Tizard. Churchill Archives Centre, Churchill College, CCPH/1/7.

Sir William Hawthorne. Julia Hedgecoe photograph. Churchill Archives Centre, Churchill College, CCPH/3/1/6. Photograph © Julia Hedgecoe. Reproduced by permission of Julia Hedgecoe.

Edmund Leach. Photograph by Robert Le Rougetel, ARPS. Archive Centre, King's College, Cambridge, Coll Ph 1313. Reproduced by permission of Robert Le Rougetel, ARPS.

Sir Eric Ashby. Official college portrait, Clare College. Reproduced by permission of the Master, Fellows, and Scholars of Clare College, Cambridge.

Hrothgar John Habakkuk. Painting of Principal Habakkuk, Jesus College, Oxford. Reproduced by permission of Jesus College, Oxford.

Maurice Bowra. Portrait by Henry Lamb, Wadham College, Oxford. Reproduced by permission of the Warden and Fellows of Wadham College, Oxford.

Stuart Hampshire. Portrait by Lawrence Gowing, Wadham College, Oxford. Reproduced by permission of the Warden and Fellows of Wadham College, Oxford.

Allan Bullock. St. Catherine's College Archives. Reproduced by permission of the Master and Fellows of St. Catherine's College.

Sir Noel Frederick Hall. Walter Bird photograph. NPG x168068. © National Portrait Gallery, London.

Geoffrey Warnock. Portrait by Humphrey Ocean, Hertford College, Oxford. © 2016 Artists Rights Society (ARS), New York/DACS, London.

Preface

The 1960s marked a major turning point in elite higher education in the United States and the United Kingdom. As the decade opened, colleges and universities closely resembled the institutions they had been in the 1950s and earlier. By end of the 1960s, so much had changed. The familiar contours of college and university life had been upended and reshaped in profoundly important ways: in the composition of student bodies and faculties, structures of governance, ways of doing institutional business, and relationships to the public issues of the day. That coeducation should come in the context of those many changes is both understandable as part of the larger enterprise of institutional transformation and, at the same time, worthy of special attention and analysis.

This book focuses on the actions of a small number of the most elite private institutions of higher education in the United States and the United Kingdom, actions taken almost simultaneously in a very brief window of time. Beginning in 1969 and mainly ending in 1974, there was a flood of decisions for coeducation on both sides of the Atlantic Ocean. This book addresses these questions: Why did very traditional, very conservative, very elite institutions decide to embark on such a fundamental change? Why did so many schools act in the late 1960s and early 1970s? How was coeducation accomplished in the face of strong opposition? What was the role of institutional leadership? And, with the admission of students of the opposite sex to formerly single-sex schools, what happened? In other words, how well did coeducation work in its early incarnations?

The story begins with Harvard, Yale, and Princeton. It addresses the unusual circumstances of Harvard and Radcliffe—coordinate institutions for three quarters of a century but hamstrung in their efforts to move to formal coeducation. It focuses next on the decisions for coeducation at Yale and Princeton, which were the prime movers, first competing with one another for advantage at every turn, then inspiring a wave of decisions at other institutions that watched them closely, learned from their reasoning and research, and responded to their actions. The book turns then to Vassar, the most prominent women's college to embark on coeducation, and looks also at Vassar's Seven Sisters peers, Smith and Wellesley, which investigated admitting men during this period but decided to remain single-sex. The book moves next to Dartmouth, where coeducation came slightly later than at Yale and Princeton and was accompanied by a ferocious reaction that made Dartmouth distinctive for highly problematic behavior toward women students. It then crosses the Atlantic to examine the advent of coeducation at the University of Cambridge, where the first three men's colleges—Churchill, Clare, and King's—admitted women in 1972, and the University of Oxford, where the first five—Brasenose, Hertford, Jesus, St. Catherine's, and Wadham—followed suit in 1974.

This is a transatlantic study, for multiple reasons. First, universities on both sides of the Atlantic were strongly influenced by upheavals of the 1960s, especially the antiwar movement, the student movement, and the women's movement, and it is important to understand how these movements led to fundamental changes in so many of the basic structures and assumptions of university life. Second, decisions for coeducation on both sides of the Atlantic were being taken at the same time, and we need to make sense of their similarities and differences. Third, as we shall see, explicit connections existed between American and British universities and their leaders. What was happening in the United States, particularly at Princeton and Yale, had some influence on what was happening in Oxford and Cambridge, and we need to understand how and why.

Above all, this book is a study in institutional decision-making. It seeks to demonstrate how colleges and universities came to embrace a particular kind of institutional transformation and to take stock of the consequences of their decisions. Therefore, it is important to be clear at the outset that the contexts in and processes by which those decisions were made in the United States were different from those in the United Kingdom. American and British colleges and universities had unique institutional structures that profoundly affected the process of change. Those structures were embedded in their respective histories. In American colleges, from the earliest colonial times, "there was no established base of faculty on whom anyone could rely." In the absence of an established faculty, authority resided importantly in external lay boards of trustees. In turn, those boards sought to appoint strong presidents to provide the necessary institutional leadership. These presidents reported to the board, not to the faculty. In contrast, the United Kingdom had a long history of strong faculty governance, with weak authority on the part of college leaders and "the absence of strong external boards." In short, in British colleges, the faculty was in charge.[1]

In the United States, then, college and university presidents played critical roles in the coming of coeducation. Presidents needed to convince their boards to embrace coeducation. They had to harness faculty support; they needed to deal with alumni who had very strong views about coeducation; they needed to mobilize the internal planning and execution to make coeducation happen; and they then needed to find the necessary resources. In the United Kingdom, the situation was different. In the main, decision-making was done college by college rather than in the universities of Cambridge or Oxford as a whole. Leadership on the part of certain principals, wardens, provosts, or masters, as the heads of colleges were variously titled, was certainly important in hastening the advent and effectiveness of coeducation. Nevertheless, some colleges went coed despite the hesitation, or even outright opposition, of their leaders. Such decisions rested with the college fellows, and the 1960s saw notable generational shifts in college fellowships as a younger cohort, newly appointed in that decade, often took the lead in encouraging their colleges to go mixed. There were no trustees to convince, and the role of alumni in Britain was much less consequential than in the United States. These fundamental differences shape the narratives that follow.

---

1 William G. Bowen and Eugene M. Tobin, *Locus of Authority: The Evolution of Faculty Roles in the Governance of Higher Education* (Princeton, NJ: Princeton University Press, 2015), pp. 14, 15, 18–20.

Why focus on elite higher education rather than higher education more generally? Elite institutions are not more important than other institutions, but what happens at elite institutions has an outsized influence on other institutions. It would be too simple to say that elite institutions lead and everybody else falls in line. But certainly in the United States, for better or not, many colleges and universities watch closely what goes on at Harvard, Yale, and Princeton (and, more recently, Stanford) and seek to model their own programs and initiatives on those institutions. The same is true in the United Kingdom, where Oxford and Cambridge set a tone and provide a model that profoundly influences other institutions.

The book could have addressed the decisions in this same time period of other colleges and universities—in the United States, for example, leading liberal arts colleges like Amherst, Williams, and Wesleyan or universities like Georgetown, Johns Hopkins, and the California Institute of Technology. In some instances the sources are limited—in the case of Williams, for example, neither the president's papers nor the records of the board of trustees are yet available to scholars. In other instances the issue of influence is determinative. Although additional histories might deepen and enrich our understanding, the colleges and universities themselves did not have the shaping effect on their peers of the institutions chosen for this study.

Important common themes run throughout the book. One key theme is leadership as a fundamental element in institutional change. The more skillful the president—or the warden, master, provost, or principal, in the British cases—the easier it was to imagine, and then move the institution to embrace, a different future. Put the other way, the less effective the leader, the easier it was for the many forces of opposition to throw sand in the gears. The second theme is process. The more an institution invested in careful analysis and planning, the more likely it was to contain the opposition and introduce coeducation reasonably smoothly. In the absence of adequate process, newcomers—especially women—had a more difficult time. The third theme is self-interest—not only the strategic self-interest of institutions that saw coeducation as a means to shore up a first-rate applicant pool and enrolled student body but also the self-interest of fathers and grandfathers who realized that their own daughters and granddaughters might be the beneficiaries of coeducation. The fourth theme is the complexity of institutional change—how difficult it was to anticipate the needs and desires of the newly admitted students; how hard it was, even with the best intentions, to plan properly for their academic and non-academic lives; how easy it was to make decisions that proved untenable and needed to be changed; and how important it was to be flexible enough, nimble enough, and indeed humble enough to regroup.

As we proceed, we will also contemplate the nature of the transformations wrought by coeducation. In a section of his 1968 report laying out the case for coeducation at Princeton, Gardner Patterson made the statement that "Princeton would have to avoid graduating a group of 'little men.'"[2] We do not know exactly what Patterson meant, but suggestive observations by others speak to what appears to have been his point. Robin Herman, a Princeton student in the class of 1973, wrote, "The 170 women who pioneered a 'new Princeton' . . . left school [after their first year at the university] with a definite feeling that Princeton had changed them more than they had changed Princeton and its 222-year masculine tradition."[3] That tradition was deeply rooted. As Debra Orenstein, a woman in the class of 1983, reflected later, "There's an element—and I think it's especially strong at Princeton, where traditions are so strong—that says, 'We have these 200-year-old traditions. Sorry you've been kept out for 199 years, but now that you're in, join us and shut up.' The expectation is that nothing about Princeton will have to change as a result of your being here, nothing about you will have to change, you will come in and fit the mold and be a Princetonian."[4]

To mark the twentieth anniversary of the admission of women to King's College, Cambridge, the college organized a celebration

2 "'The Education of Women at Princeton': A Special Report," *Princeton Alumni Weekly* 69 (Sept. 24, 1968): 19.

3 Robin Herman, "In the Wink of an Eyelash, Swish of a Skirt, Traditions Fall and Women Conquer Princeton," *Daily Princetonian*, June 20, 1970, p. 45.

4 Debra Orenstein, in Kirsten Bibbins, Anne Chiang, and Heather Stephenson, eds., *Women Reflect about Princeton* (Princeton University, 1989), p. 162.

around the theme "Is King's still a male college admitting women?" To mark the event, a woman named Lara McClure designed a mural depicting an imaginary woman at King's, "a monument to all Kingswomen," which was then painted by a number of women in the King's community. "To my mind, this was an entirely appropriate way to celebrate twenty years of women at King's," McClure said. "It was an entirely honest statement on how life as a woman here is viewed, in what many still perceive to be a male environment reluctantly admitting us as honorary men."[5] Decades later, reflecting on the coming of coeducation at Hertford College, Oxford, history fellow Christopher Tyerman made a similar point. "It seems to me clear," he observed, that the institutions at Oxford that admitted women

> didn't really change at all beyond the installation of a few more lavatories and sinks and . . . some full length mirrors for the "girls." Structurally and culturally the old men-only colleges altered their social habits and administrative and academic procedures and conventions not or hardly at all. The women . . . de facto had to conform to what they found—i.e. to become in a sense honorary men, playing the same sports, games; going to the same bars; doing student politics the same way, doing the work/essays/exams the same as always etc. etc. The consciences of the men were salved . . . but it was hardly a feminist or even feminine triumph or one for genuinely coeducation with equal attention paid to each gender interest.[6]

These observations bear on one final point that will become clear to readers but merits special emphasis at the outset. The protagonists in this story are men. With the exception of Mary Ingraham Bunting, the president of Radcliffe College, every strategist, every decision-maker, everyone leading the charge for coeducation was male. This is not a story of women banding together to demand

---

5 Lara McClure, "Emulsion and Emotion," in *"Is King's Still a Male College Admitting Women?" For the Record: '20 Years On'; A Celebration*, Mar. 13, 1993, from the private collection of Melissa Lane.

6 E-mail, Christopher Tyerman to Nancy Weiss Malkiel, July 17, 2013.

opportunity, to press for access, to win rights and privileges previously reserved for men. As appealing as it might be to imagine the coming of coeducation as one element in the full flowering of mid- to late twentieth-century feminism, such a narrative would be at odds with the historical record. Coeducation resulted not from organized efforts by women activists but from strategic decisions taken by powerful men.

As we explore the coming of coeducation at these elite institutions of higher education, then, we need to keep some fundamental questions in mind: Coeducation for whom? For what purposes? And with what results? We need also to remember that although decisions for coeducation were hotly contested, they were debated civilly, and they were taken without any of the rancor we have seen more recently in such highly publicized educational controversies as the decision to charge tuition at the historically free Cooper Union or the decision to close the all-female Sweet Briar College, controversies that led, among other things, to the firing or resignation of presidents and to the wholesale resignations of board members. Complicated as it was, coeducation may have had an element of inevitability about it; transformative as it was, transformation occurred within significant limits. How these factors bore on the nature of the debate and decisions is worth contemplating as we go forward.[7]

Before we do that, two additional points need to be made. As will be very clear, Princeton occupies more space in this book than any other college or university. That is true for two reasons. The first is that the Patterson report was extremely important not only to Princeton but to Yale, to other American colleges and universities, and to Oxford and Cambridge. Addressing that report in detail is essential to the accounts that follow. The second reason is that Princeton has richer archival materials than any other institution, and some of those are materials to which I have unique access. The Princeton materials yield stories that deserve to be told and that illustrate themes that are equally applicable to peer colleges and universities.

---

7 I am indebted to William G. Bowen for these observations.

The second point is personal. This book is a work of history, not a memoir. And yet Nancy Weiss Malkiel, author, also appears in these pages from time to time as Nancy Weiss, participant. As we go forward together, the reader should be aware of—but I hope not discomfited by—this double role.

Acknowledgments

A question from then-Princeton president Shirley M. Tilghman—
"Would you be interested in writing a history of coeducation at
Princeton?"—planted the seed for this book. She and her provost,
now Princeton's president, Christopher L. Eisgruber, generously
provided the time and resources to support my research. (She also
saw to it that Princeton's fifty-year rule governing access to key
records was changed to a forty-year rule, a modification essential to completing this project.) Opportunities to present my early
work in local forums—the American Studies Program at Princeton, the Shelby Cullom Davis Center for Historical Studies, and
the Friends of the Princeton University Library—showed me that
there were bigger, more interesting questions to be addressed than
I had first imagined.

I have depended on the generosity and expertise of so many
archivists and librarians: in the United States, at Dartmouth, Harvard, Princeton, the Schlesinger Library at Radcliffe, Sarah Lawrence, Smith, Vassar, Wellesley, and Yale; in the United Kingdom,
at Churchill, Clare, and King's Colleges at the University of Cambridge and at Brasenose, Hertford, Jesus, St. Catherine's, and Wadham Colleges, as well as the Bodleian Library, at the University of
Oxford. I hope it will not seem invidious to single out a subset of
these individuals who have been especially helpful: Daniel J. Linke
and Christa Cleeton at Princeton; Diana Carey, Alissa Link, and
Ellen Shea at the Schlesinger Library; Michael Frost and Claryn
Spies at Yale; Sarah Hartwell and Laura Schieb at Dartmouth;
Dean Rogers at Vassar; Nanci Young at Smith; Jane Callahan and
Ian Graham at Wellesley; Abby Lester at Sarah Lawrence; Natalie
Adams, Gillian Booker, and Sophie Bridges at Churchill; Robert
Athol and Alexandra Browne at Clare; Peter Monteith and Patri-
cia McGuire at King's; Elizabeth Boardman and Georgie Edwards

at Brasenose; Christopher Tyerman and Alice Roques at Hertford; the late Christopher Jeens and Owen McKnight at Jesus; Renée Prud'Homme and Barbara Costa at St. Catherine's; and Clifford S. L. Davies and Tim Kirtley at Wadham. Charlotte Brewer, senior tutor and professor of English at Hertford, outdid herself in providing access to materials and individuals there.

Many people who participated in the history chronicled here were extremely generous with their time and insights in personal interviews and correspondence. Their names appear in the list of interviews and throughout the footnotes. I record here my gratitude for their willingness to help me understand the story I needed to tell.

Two undergraduate research assistants—Natalie Sargent at Smith and Colleen Baker at Princeton—tracked down a wealth of important sources. Dov Weinryb Grohsgal, a graduate student research assistant turned valued colleague at Princeton, taught me to take digital photographs in the archives and helped me find frustratingly elusive information.

For ideas, contacts, opportunities, and materials of various sorts, I am indebted to Neal Abraham, Russell Adair, Victoria Austin-Smith, Caroline Benson, Carol Black, John W. Boyer, Mark Burstein, Nichole Calero, Alan Chimacoff, Lizabeth Cohen, Nancy Cott, Darcy A. Cotton, Erin Driver-Linn, Alison Finch, Estelle Freedman, Joan S. Girgus, Emma Goodrum, Rowena Gosling, Polly Winfrey Griffin, Ann Halliday, Hendrik A. Hartog, Kate Higgins, Daniel Horowitz, Helen Lefkowitz Horowitz, Melissa S. Lane, Jonathan R. LeBouef, Julia Lee, Jane A. Levin, Richard C. Levin, Linda K. Lorimer, Christopher McCloskey, Kristina Miller, Mary Miller, Christopher Morley, Evangeline Morphos, Philip G. Nord, Gilda G. Paul, Jill Pellew, Ben Primer, Eve Hart Rice, Adele Smith Simmons, Emma Smith, Gregory Smith, Jill Symons, Elizabeth Taylor, Miles Taylor, Sheila Tobias, Toni Turano, Scott C. VanderVeer, Jacqueline Winston-Silk, and Jeremy Zullow. Judith L. Hanson, Debora L. Macy, Max G. Siles, and Carla M. Zimowsk of the Department of History at Princeton provided practical support of many kinds.

I owe an extraordinary debt to William G. Bowen, David Cannadine, Carol T. Christ, Hanna Holborn Gray, and Nannerl O.

Keohane, friends and colleagues who have been hugely generous in reading some or all of this manuscript at various stages and giving me the great benefit of their advice and wisdom.

Peter J. Dougherty, director of Princeton University Press, supported this project enthusiastically from the moment he first heard about it. His unwavering encouragement and keen editorial judgment made this book possible, and his confidence and gift of always seeing the upside buoyed my spirits. He is an incomparable editor and a great friend, and I could not be more grateful.

One of Peter's many contributions was to engage Steven Rigolosi, an editor of good taste and great skill, who helped to shape up and slim down the manuscript. A highly accomplished team at Princeton University Press shepherded the book from manuscript to publication, especially Terri O'Prey, associate managing editor and production editor *extraordinaire*; Samantha Nader, editorial associate; Dimitri Karetnikov, illustration manager; and Amanda Weiss, book designer. Marilyn Martin contributed copyediting, Stephanie Sakson proofreading, and Tobiah Waldron indexing.

My husband, Burton G. Malkiel, has made inestimable contributions to this project. He read draft after draft, improving every chapter, every page, through his excellent judgment and sharp insights. On so many fronts, he went out of his way to create optimal conditions for me to work, indeed, insisted that I work while he took care of the mundane tasks of daily life. His love and partnership are the joy of my life.

Last year, Burt included Piper in the dedication of the eleventh edition of *A Random Walk Down Wall Street*. I could do no less.

Princeton, New Jersey
July 2016

Introduction

1

Setting the Stage: The Turbulent 1960s

The decisions to embrace coeducation at elite private colleges and universities by no means represent the beginning of coeducation in institutions of higher education in the United States and the United Kingdom, and it is important to start here with the earlier history.

Early Experiments with Coeducation

At Oberlin, the first private college in the United States to become coeducational (in 1837), women students took on sex-segregated roles for the college community that mirrored their eventual familial responsibilities, like laundry, sewing, and dishwashing.[1] Coeducation was the norm at the many state universities founded in the mid- to late nineteenth century.[2] But the initial enthusiasm for it at some of the leading universities, like Berkeley, Cornell, and Michigan, waned in the face of experience. Too many women students were enrolling, and they were doing too well academically; the fear was that they might feminize, even overrun, their universities. In response, the institutions separated men and women in

1 Ronald W. Hogeland, "Coeducation of the Sexes at Oberlin College: A Study of Social Ideas in Mid–Nineteenth Century America," *Journal of Social History* 6 (1972–73): 160–76.

2 Thomas Woody, *A History of Women's Education in the United States*, vol. 2 (Science Press, 1929; reprint New York: Octagon Books, 1966), ch. 5. The outliers were Louisiana and Georgia, which went coed in the 1900s and 1910s, respectively; North Carolina and Florida, in the 1940s; and Virginia, the last of the state universities to enroll women, in 1970.

many spheres of campus life, a separation finally reversed only in the 1960s.[3]

There was also an impulse for separation at private universities. In the 1930s, Duke and the University of Pennsylvania established women's colleges that persisted as separate entities until the 1970s. Although small numbers of women had been enrolled earlier at Duke, the women's college was founded in 1930 as a coordinate college occupying a geographically distinct campus. Initially, classes for freshmen and sophomores were segregated by sex, a practice that ended by the 1960s. In 1972 the university merged the men's and women's colleges.[4] At the University of Pennsylvania, the college of liberal arts for women was founded in 1933, when the university first offered a four-year liberal arts degree program to women. In 1954 Penn opened the undergraduate programs of the school of engineering and applied science and the Wharton school to women, the last programs at the university to exclude them. In 1975 the college of liberal arts for women merged with the college of arts and sciences for men.[5]

At Chicago, founded as a coeducational university in 1892, the impulse for separation resulted from the success of the first cohorts of women students. In 1892 women comprised 24 percent of the enrollment in the college. By 1900 that number had increased to 52 percent, and in the decade 1892–1902 women accounted for more than 56 percent of elections to Phi Beta Kappa. President William Rainey Harper feared that being identified as a predominantly female institution would alienate the benefactors on whom the new university depended. His solution was

3 Charlotte Williams Conable, *Women at Cornell: The Myth of Equal Education* (Ithaca, NY: Cornell University Press, 1977); Ruth Bordin, *Women at Michigan: The "Dangerous Experiment," 1870s to the Present* (Ann Arbor: University of Michigan Press, 1999); Lynn D. Gordon, *Gender and Higher Education in the Progressive Era* (New Haven, CT: Yale University Press, 1990), pp. 52–84.

4 "Historical Note," *Guide to the Woman's College Records, 1928–1974*, Duke University Libraries, http://library.duke.edu/rubenstein/findingaids/uawomans/#historicalnote, accessed July 14, 2014.

5 Mark Frazier Lloyd, "Women at Penn: Timeline of Pioneers and Achievements," updated 2004, University Archives and Records Center, University of Pennsylvania, http://www.archives.upenn.edu/histy/features/women/chrontext.html, accessed July 14, 2014.

to introduce sex-segregated instruction in required introductory courses in the university's junior college for freshmen and sophomores. Despite protests from college alumnae, educators elsewhere, and representatives of national women's organizations, the policy went into effect in the winter of 1903. But the planned separation was only partially effective, affecting just half of the students in the junior college by 1906–7. After that, the scheme disappeared. Harper died in 1906, and his successor, Harry Pratt Judson, had a mandate from the trustees to bring the budget under control. Separate instruction had been extremely expensive, with duplication of faculty effort and increased instructional costs. The sex-segregation plan may have been abandoned in the interest of saving money.[6]

Typically, decisions to limit opportunities for women students were made by men. Stanford was different. The university was established by Leland Stanford, a railroad magnate, U.S. senator, and former California governor, and his wife, Jane, as a memorial to their son, Leland Stanford, Jr., who died of typhoid fever in 1884 at the age of fifteen. The founding grant from the Stanfords, dating to 1885, specified that the university, which opened in 1891, would be coeducational, with "equal facilities" and "equal advantages" for both sexes. Initially, women accounted for 25 percent of the students, but that number grew quickly, reaching 40 percent by 1899. Jane Stanford feared that women would overrun the university, making it less attractive to male students and no longer a fitting memorial to her son. In 1899, after Leland Stanford's death, Jane Stanford added to the founding grant the legal requirement that "the number of women attending the University as students shall at no time ever exceed five hundred." The cap on women remained in effect until 1933, when enrollments were low because of the Great Depression. The Stanford trustees then reinterpreted

6 Gordon, *Gender and Higher Education in the Progressive Era*, pp. 85–120; Janel M. Mueller, "Coeducation at Chicago—Whose Aims?," Sept. 26, 1994, in *The Aims of Education: The College of the University of Chicago* (University of Chicago, 1997), pp. 120, 123–24, 126; e-mail, John W. Boyer to Nancy Weiss Malkiel, Nov. 13, 2014. I am indebted to Dean Boyer for pointing me to the Mueller essay.

the quota to mean an undergraduate male-female ratio of 3 to 2, which remained in place until 1973.[7]

The most extreme reaction came at Wesleyan, founded in 1831, which had embarked on coeducation as an experiment beginning in 1872. With too many women enrolling and women succeeding too well in their academic work, male graduates feared that the college's masculine image was threatened. Worried, too, that women graduates would not be generous donors, the trustees decided in 1909 to make Wesleyan a college for men beginning in 1912. Wesleyan alumnae responded by spearheading the effort that led to the founding of Connecticut College for Women in 1911. Wesleyan resumed coeducation in 1970.[8]

Just as coeducation was instituted over the nineteenth and early twentieth centuries at many public and private institutions in the United States, the same was true in Canada. Queen's University in Kingston, Ontario, admitted women in 1880; McGill University in Montreal and the University of Toronto followed suit in 1884. Women were enrolled at the University of British Columbia from its earliest years on its new campus in Vancouver, which opened in 1915.[9] And in the United Kingdom, by the mid-twentieth century, coeducation was the established mode at virtually every institution except Cambridge and Oxford.

---

7 Professor of History Estelle Freedman, "Women and Education," lecture notes, Stanford University, transmitted in an e-mail, Freedman to Nancy Weiss Malkiel, May 29, 2013; *Stanford University: The Founding Grant with Amendments, Legislation, and Court Decrees* (Stanford University, 1987), http://sul-derivatives.stanford.edu/derivative?CSNID= 00003895&mediaType=application/pdf, accessed July 14, 2014; "Jane Stanford: Timeline," *Jane L. Stanford: The Woman Behind Stanford*, Stanford University, http://janestanford .stanford.edu/timeline.html#c3, accessed July 14, 2014; "Court Action Begun to End the 'Ratio,'" *Stanford Observer*, Oct. 1972, clipping in Brewster II, Box 258, Folder 1.

8 David B. Potts, *Wesleyan University, 1831–1910: Collegiate Enterprise in New England* (New Haven, CT: Yale University Press, 1992), chs. 4, 6.

9 Sara Z. Burke, "New Women and Old Romans: Co-education at the University of Toronto, 1884–95," *Canadian Historical Review* 80 (June 1999): 219–41; Sarah Battat, "The Advent of Coeducation at McGill University," paper written for Freshman Seminar 149, Jan. 14, 2014, Princeton University, in the possession of Nancy Weiss Malkiel. For some of the principal published sources on coeducation in Canada, see Lynne Marks and Chad Gaffield, "Women at Queen's University, 1895–1905: A 'Little Sphere' All Their Own?," *Ontario History* 78 (Dec. 1986): 331–49; Anne Rochon Ford, *A Path Not Strewn with Roses: One Hundred Years of Women at the University of Toronto, 1884–1984* (Toronto: University of Toronto Press, 1985); Lee Stewart, *"It's Up to You": Women at UBC in the Early Years* (Vancouver: University of British Columbia Press, 1990).

But at the most elite, most prestigious private colleges and universities on both sides of the Atlantic, the norm was single-sex education. Understanding why those institutions embraced coeducation is the focus of this book. Before we turn to the individual college and university experiences, however, we need to understand the political and social changes in the 1960s that created the context for such important institutional transformation.

A Context for Change: Political and Social Movements

In politics and society, the world of 1960 was profoundly different from the world of 1970 in both the United States and the United Kingdom. By 1970, transformative social and political movements had challenged and reshaped the basic processes that had governed political discourse and mechanisms for effecting social change. The civil rights movement, the student movement, the antiwar movement, and the women's movement set an important context for the flood of decisions for coeducation.

THE CIVIL RIGHTS AND STUDENT MOVEMENTS

In the face of deeply entrenched racial segregation and discrimination against black Americans, the civil rights movement in the United States focused both on changing the law to guarantee the same rights to all citizens and on the mobilization of civil disobedience to ensure that the new laws were enforced. After decades of suits by the National Association for the Advancement of Colored People (NAACP) and others, the U.S. Supreme Court outlawed segregation in the public schools in *Brown v. Board of Education* in 1954. Staunch white southern resistance to the court's decision led to nonviolent direct-action protests throughout the South to secure equal access for black Americans to public accommodations, employment, education, and voting rights. Bus boycotts, sit-ins, and Freedom Rides challenged the established order in local communities; massive nonviolent demonstrations in the southern cities of Birmingham, Montgomery, and Selma met with extreme violence on the part of whites, including local authorities.

Responding to violence perpetrated on nonviolent protesters seeking their fundamental rights, Presidents John F. Kennedy and Lyndon B. Johnson pressed the U.S. Congress to pass civil rights bills of major consequence. Thanks to the Civil Rights Act of 1964 and the Voting Rights Act of 1965, the law of the land now protected black voting rights and promised black Americans equal access to employment and to places of public accommodation. Under the sustained pressure of nonviolent direct action, white Americans in communities across the South began slowly to change longstanding practices of segregation and discrimination.[10]

College students, male and female, black and white, northern and southern, participated actively in the direct-action movement, an experience that profoundly affected their views about one another, about their universities, and about the society in which they lived. The engine for the student movement of the 1960s was the "New Left" organization Students for a Democratic Society (SDS), founded in 1960 in New York in association with the socialist League for Industrial Democracy. Striking out on its own, SDS held a national convention in the summer of 1962 at Port Huron, Michigan. The Port Huron Statement, a manifesto drafted by Tom Hayden, former editor of the University of Michigan *Daily*, offered an "agenda for a generation" of student activists "looking uncomfortably to the world we inherit." American society was replete with "complicated and disturbing paradoxes": racial inequality, poverty amidst plenty, the role of U.S. economic and military investments in perpetuating the Cold War, the threat of nuclear destruction, the "sapping of the earth's physical resources," and the many "isms" that imperiled the world order, such as colonialism,

---

10 On the civil rights movement, see, e.g., Harvard Sitkoff, *The Struggle for Black Equality, 1954–1980* (New York: Hill and Wang, 1981); Robert Weisbrot, *Freedom Bound: A History of America's Civil Rights Movement* (New York: W. W. Norton, 1990); Taylor Branch, *Parting the Waters: America in the King Years, 1954–63* (New York: Simon & Schuster, 1988); Branch, *Pillar of Fire: America in the King Years, 1963–65* (New York: Simon & Schuster, 1998); Branch, *At Canaan's Edge: America in the King Years, 1965–68* (New York: Simon & Schuster, 2006); Clayborne Carson, *In Struggle: SNCC and the Black Awakening of the 1960s* (Cambridge, MA: Harvard University Press, 1981); August Meier and Elliott Rudwick, *CORE: A Study in the Civil Rights Movement, 1942–1968* (New York: Oxford University Press, 1973).

imperialism, and totalitarianism. SDS was committed to "the search for truly democratic alternatives" and to "social experimentation with them."

The universities were implicated in the paradoxes and stasis of the old order: "Our professors and administrators sacrifice controversy to public relations; their curriculums change more slowly than the living events of the world; their skills and silence are purchased by investors in the arms race; passion is called unscholastic." In the main, the college campus was "a place of private people . . . a place of commitment to business-as-usual, getting ahead, playing it cool . . . a place of . . . mass reluctance toward the controversial public stance," a place characterized by pointless rules, intransigent bureaucracy, and irrelevant scholarship. Students were passive and disengaged from the public issues of the day; there were no big goals, no moral commitments of consequence, no engagement in the key challenges of the times.[11] Hayden's solution: "participatory democracy" whereby students would take control of their own lives in the academic communities in which they lived and, together with faculty members, "wrest control of the educational process from the administrative bureaucracy." Students could then act as agents of more comprehensive change by joining in a broad-based, transformative movement to reconstruct American democracy.[12]

SDS made its first big splash in the biggest of all university contexts: the 27,000-student University of California at Berkeley. Clark Kerr, the president of the University of California (UC) system and a former chancellor of Berkeley, identified the seedbed for protest at Berkeley as the changing relationship between faculty and students. Senior faculty members, increasingly engaged in research, were less attentive to and engaged with undergraduates than had been the case historically and thus were no longer well placed to play interpretive, mediating roles between students and the university.

11 Students for a Democratic Society, "The Port Huron Statement," in Ronald Lora, ed., *America in the 60's: Cultural Authorities in Transition* (New York: John Wiley, 1974), pp. 259–70.

12 Hayden, quoted in Allen J. Matusow, *The Unraveling of America: A History of Liberalism in the 1960s* (New York: Harper & Row, 1984), p. 313.

If the retreat of the research-driven faculty from undergraduate life laid the groundwork, the flashpoint for the emergence
of protest was the move to restrict student political activity on
the twenty-six-foot strip of brick sidewalk outside the university's main gate on Bancroft Way at the intersection of Telegraph
Avenue, where student organizations displayed their literature, recruited supporters, and solicited funds. In the face of increasingly
aggressive student political activity in the fall of 1964, the university announced that it was closing the Bancroft–Telegraph strip to
groups engaged in activities involving off-campus issues, a policy
then modified so that students could set up their tables but could
not engage in any fund-raising, recruitment, or advocacy.

Students quickly began flouting the new regulation, and on
September 30, five students were called to the dean's office for
disciplinary action. One of them, a graduate student in philosophy named Mario Savio, brought along a group of five hundred
students who claimed that they had all broken the rules by staffing unauthorized tables and should be subject to punishment. The
group occupied the administration building, Sproul Hall, through
the night. At midnight the chancellor of the Berkeley campus, Edward Strong, announced that the five original students, plus three
others who had led the march on Sproul Hall, were being suspended. On October 1, a former graduate student in mathematics,
Jack Weinberg, was arrested for soliciting funds for the Congress
of Racial Equality (CORE) at a table on the sidewalk. A large
group of students immobilized the police car that had come to take
Weinberg away. A legacy of the event was Weinberg's exclamation
"Don't trust anyone over thirty"—a statement quickly adopted as
the shorthand slogan of the student movement.

The next day, speaking for the UC system, Kerr declared, "The
rules will not be changed in the face of mob action." A thousand police officers came to the campus, but after a day of tense negotiations
a compromise was reached to avert violent confrontation. The next
two months saw a political struggle between the students—now
represented by a radical faction organized as the Free Speech Movement (FSM)—and the university, with campus authorities, the president of the university system, and the university regents divided over

which regulations should be enforced and how discipline should be meted out. After weeks of negotiations over disciplinary action for the eight suspended students, the university decided to reinstate the students, with the suspensions noted on their records. Savio and three other students were ordered to appear before the regents to answer charges that they had committed acts of violence against the police during the demonstrations in October.

On December 2, six thousand people assembled for a rally outside Sproul Hall. Savio declared, "There's a time when the operation of the [university] machine becomes so odious, makes you so sick at heart, that you can't take part, you can't even tacitly take part. And you've got to put your bodies upon the gears, and upon the wheels, upon the levers, upon all the apparatus, and you've got to make it stop." More than a thousand people then entered the building. During the night, Governor Edmund "Pat" Brown sent in a huge force of police in full riot gear to clear the building. In the end, some eight hundred people were arrested, about six hundred of them students. A student strike followed, interrupting classes and other university functions. The faculty rallied to back the students, voting 824 to 115 on December 8 to support the demands of the FSM. Going forward, there would be no restrictions on political activity on campus beyond those that applied in the community at large.[13]

Inspired by the events at Berkeley, student protests erupted at campuses around the country, beginning in the spring of 1965 and continuing through the decade. Students challenged the university's right to stand in loco parentis, and they pushed successfully

13 Godfrey Hodgson, *America in Our Time* (Garden City, NY: Doubleday, 1976), pp. 288–96; Irwin Unger, *The Movement: A History of the American New Left, 1959–1972* (New York: Dodd, Mead, 1974), pp. 62–75 (the Weinberg and Savio quotes are in Unger); Matusow, *The Unraveling of America*, pp. 316–18; Verne A. Stadtman, *The University of California, 1868–1968* (New York: McGraw Hill, 1970), pp. 443–67. The Kerr quote is in Clark Kerr, "Toward a Nationwide System of Higher Education?," 47th Annual Meeting, American Council on Education, Oct. 2, [1964,] ark.cdlib.org/ark:/13030/kt258001wp, accessed Mar. 23, 2016. A discussion of Kerr's mistakes in handling the crisis is in William G. Bowen and Eugene M. Tobin, *Locus of Authority: The Evolution of Faculty Roles in the Governance of Higher Education* (Princeton, NJ: Princeton University Press, 2015), pp. 231–33, and Clark Kerr, *The Gold and the Blue: A Personal Memoir of the University of California, 1949–1967*, vol. 2: *Political Turmoil* (Berkeley: University of California Press, 2003), passim.

for the liberalization or elimination of such restrictions as parietals (regulations concerning visitation by the opposite sex in dormitory rooms) and for a stronger hand in governing their own residential and social lives. They challenged the rigid, faculty-imposed structure of academic life, and they pushed successfully for curricular reforms: the abolition or liberalization of requirements, the elimination of what they considered to be irrelevant courses, the institution of pass-fail grading and self-scheduled examinations. Their protests resulted in the creation of new institutions of academic governance with greater student representation.

Student protests also went beyond day-to-day campus matters, with protesters often decrying universities as morally repugnant, integral parts of the establishment, noting universities' ties to the military-industrial complex and accusing them of actively perpetuating racism and imperialism. Student protesters pointed to recruitment on campus by the military, the Central Intelligence Agency (CIA), and the Dow Chemical Company; university sponsorship of Reserve Officers' Training Corps (ROTC) programs; and some of the research done by faculty members—research related to national defense and intelligence operations, research in biological warfare, and research under the covert sponsorship of the CIA. They objected to university investments in companies doing business in South Africa and to the encroachment of some urban universities on neighboring black communities. They argued for intensive recruitment of minority students, a diminution of the military presence on campus, and social responsibility with regard to investment policies and urban universities' surrounding communities.

Although the majority of students involved in the protests were peaceful, other students occupied campus buildings, terrorizing teachers and other students, vandalizing public and private property, burning books, defacing buildings, and committing acts of violence. Students had moved well beyond accepted channels for seeking social and institutional change.[14]

14 William E. Leuchtenburg, *A Troubled Feast: American Society Since 1945* (Boston: Little, Brown, 1973; updated ed., 1983), p. 231; Arthur Marwick, *The Sixties: Cultural Revolution in Britain, France, Italy, and the United States, c. 1958–c. 1974* (Oxford: Oxford University Press, 1998), p. 665.

THE ANTIWAR MOVEMENT

The third major movement of the 1960s, the antiwar movement, was intimately intertwined with the student movement. A large part of the impetus for the student movement came from the war in Vietnam. Many students were deeply disturbed by American involvement in a war in which it was difficult to discern a clear national interest, a war in which their contemporaries—indeed, their friends and classmates—were being drafted and killed, a war in which repeated American bombing was killing untold numbers of noncombatants and destroying so much of the countryside in Vietnam and later in Cambodia.

Campus opposition to the war was first expressed in faculty teach-ins, starting at the University of Michigan in March 1965 and spreading to colleges and universities across the country. Every time President Johnson escalated American engagement, campuses erupted in response. Revelations of episodes of horrific fighting, like the Tet offensive against American and South Vietnamese troops conducted by the Vietcong in January and February 1968, or of atrocities committed by the United States, like the My Lai massacre of unarmed civilians in South Vietnam in March, stoked the anger of students and faculty. Students joined faculty members to stage antiwar protests on campus; beginning in the spring of 1965 and continuing through the decade, they also took part in massive demonstrations in Washington, D.C., New York, and San Francisco.[15]

Unlike their elders, most male students were subject to the draft for service in a war that many of them deplored. Students personalized their protests, burning their draft cards, fleeing across the border to Canada to avoid military service (or, in some cases, refusing induction and going to jail), and chanting, at public demonstrations in Washington and elsewhere, "One, Two, Three, Four, We Don't Want to Go to War."[16]

15 Matusow, *The Unraveling of America*, pp. 318–30.
16 Todd Gitlin, *The Sixties: Years of Hope, Days of Rage* (New York: Bantam Books, 1987), pp. 247–55, 291–94.

Following the "Cambodian incursion," or invasion, announced by President Richard M. Nixon on April 30, 1970, and the fatal shooting of four student antiwar protesters at Kent State University on May 4 by Ohio national guardsmen, campuses around the country exploded in protest, with student strikes at hundreds of colleges and universities. Other schools, though not formally on strike, ended the academic year abruptly, with final examinations postponed or cancelled. Ten days after Kent State, two black students were killed at Jackson State University in Mississippi under circumstances similar to those at Kent State.[17]

The violence in Cambodia and at Kent State and Jackson State significantly widened support for the antiwar movement, and moderate and even conservative students joined in the outrage of their more liberal peers. The events were deeply disturbing in their own right, but they were compounded by the words of President Nixon, who publicly derided student protesters "blowing up the campuses" as "bums."[18]

THE WOMEN'S MOVEMENT

The fourth movement of the 1960s that influenced the coming of coeducation to elite colleges and universities was the women's movement, a movement closely related to and yet different in important ways from the civil rights movement. By 1960 it had been four decades since women had established what they perceived to be an adequate legal basis for equality: the right to vote. But suffrage had left a great many issues unsettled, and a number of factors made the 1960s a propitious time to take them on.

Giving women the right to vote did not affect the range of sex discrimination that was built into the fabric of American society. It did not give women equal employment opportunities; it did not require equal pay for equal work. Adjusting for education,

17 Jonathan Schell, *The Time of Illusion* (New York: Alfred A. Knopf, 1976), pp. 90–102; Leuchtenburg, *A Troubled Feast*, pp. 244–46; Unger, *The Movement*, pp. 185–88; John Morton Blum, *Years of Discord: American Politics and Society, 1961–1974* (New York: W. W. Norton, 1991), pp. 367–70.

18 Nixon is quoted in Schell, *The Time of Illusion*, p. 97.

experience, skills, and field, women in 1960 were earning 61 percent of men's wages (a drop of 3 percent since 1955), though the situation improved slightly by 1970, when women earned 70 percent of male wages. Moreover, no matter what the industry, there was a ceiling on how far women could go.[19] The vote did not give women the same educational opportunities as men, especially in graduate and professional schools. It did not give women agency to make their own decisions: It did not give them access to credit in their own name. It did not entitle them to terminate an unwanted pregnancy. It did not affect cultural and personal expectations about women's subordinate role: that it was women's responsibility to maintain the home and raise the children; that the husband's needs and wishes should take precedence over his wife's; that biology and nature made women suited to supportive, nurturing roles.

The broad source of the women's movement lay in the discrepancy between the socially prescribed ideal of woman as homemaker and helpmate and the more complicated reality of woman's role as wife, mother, college graduate, and member of the labor force. Education made it hard to accept the 1950s version of the cult of domesticity. America told women that home and family were the sources of all happiness. Yet for the woman who had so recently studied Proust or Kant, it was hard to find fulfillment in a suburban carpool and an all-electric kitchen. Employment patterns, too, contradicted the cultural ideal as more women entered the workforce. The gap between the male sphere and the female sphere was narrowing. Adolescent girls, growing up with the role model of a working mother, changed their expectations accordingly.

And the media began to pay attention, reporting on the "trapped housewife." Articles in the mass media of the 1950s had rhapsodized about women as superwomen—*Life*, for example, had

19 Ruth Rosen, *The World Split Open: How the Modern Women's Movement Changed America* (New York: Viking Penguin, 2000), p. 26; Burton G. Malkiel and Judith A. Malkiel, "Male-Female Pay Differentials in Professional Employment," *American Economic Review* 63 (Sept. 1973): 693–705; Ronald L. Oaxaca, "Male-Female Wage Differentials in Urban Labor Markets," *International Economic Review* 14 (Oct. 1973): 693–709; Ronald Oaxaca, "Sex Discrimination in Wages," in Orley Ashenfelter and Albert Rees, eds., *Discrimination in Labor Markets* (Princeton, NJ: Princeton University Press, 1973), pp. 124–51.

described an exemplary housewife as "Home Manager, Mother, Hostess, and Useful Civic Worker." Now the media focused, in the words of one *Newsweek* cover story, on "Young Wives with Brains: Babies, Yes—But What Else?"[20] The typical American woman, the media reported, was bored, restless, isolated, overeducated, and underemployed.

Federal and state commissions on the status of women began to document the problems inherent in women's position in American society—and, in so doing, provided "a platform from which inequities could be publicized and the need for women's rights put forth."[21] The commission reports were candid in their descriptions but moderate in tone. Less moderate was the book that came to serve as the manifesto for the new women's movement. In *The Feminine Mystique*, published in 1963, Betty Friedan laid out a brilliant, biting portrait of the "problem that has no name," indicting the American home as a "comfortable concentration camp" and describing the woman in it as a bored, restless, unhappy prisoner of domesticity.[22] Here was an emerging basis for a public questioning of women's roles.

The women's movement of the 1960s took shape on two related but distinct levels. One level sought equality for women in the public sphere through equal access to jobs, equal pay for equal work, and legal prohibitions against discrimination on the basis of sex. This part of the movement was conceived and led primarily by professional women who had worked with the governmental commissions on the status of women. Its principal vehicle, the National Organization of Women (NOW), was founded in 1966 "to bring women into full participation in the mainstream of American society *now*, exercising all the privileges and responsibilities thereof in truly equal partnership with men." There were other organizations as well, the Women's Equity Action League (WEAL) and the National Women's Political Caucus among them, all designed to end

---

20 Sara Evans, *Personal Politics: The Roots of Women's Liberation in the Civil Rights Movement and the New Left* (New York: Alfred A. Knopf, 1979), pp. 5, 16.

21 Ibid., p. 17.

22 Betty Friedan, *The Feminine Mystique* (New York: W. W. Norton, 1963).

sex discrimination in employment and education and to promote the equal participation of women in the nation's public life.[23]

The civil rights movement gave feminism an ideology that asserted the importance of equality and human rights. NOW and WEAL were modeled on the NAACP, and they learned about legal activism and lobbying from the NAACP's example. The "rights" level of the new women's movement piggybacked on the civil rights movement in other ways as well. The Civil Rights Act of 1964 gave women an additional legal basis for equality. Title VII of that act prohibited employment discrimination on the basis of sex as well as race. Introduced as an amendment to the civil rights bill by Howard W. Smith (the powerful Virginia Democrat who chaired the House Rules Committee) to demonstrate the folly of the proposed legislation, Title VII provided women with a powerful legal weapon to take on discrimination in hiring and promotion.[24] The civil rights movement also provided the women's movement with the conceptual basis for an attack on sex discrimination; the precedents in civil rights demonstrated that a legal remedy was available for discrimination on the basis of sex.

The second level of the women's movement focused on the status of women in the private realm. Why were women treated as sex objects? Why was it assumed that women would change the diapers and clean the house? Why were men the spokespeople and leaders, women the typists and cooks? Why assume that the female nature was particularly suited to domesticity and motherhood? Such questions struck at societal expectations about women's roles in a more fundamental way than did the push for equality in the public sphere. It was one thing to say that women should have equal access to employment opportunities; it was much more threatening to social norms to claim that carpools and baby-tending were the responsibility of the husband as well as the wife. The implication was clear: Gender no longer determined automatic social roles.

---

23 Evans, *Personal Politics*, pp. 16–21; Christine Stansell, *The Feminist Promise: 1792 to the Present* (New York: Modern Library, 2010), pp. 204–16; Gloria Steinem, "After Black Power, Women's Liberation," *New York Magazine*, Apr. 4, 1969, http://nymag.com/news/politics/46802/, accessed Apr. 3, 2013 (source of the quote).

24 Stansell, *The Feminist Promise*, pp. 207–8.

The questioning of women's inequality in the private sphere came about in large part on the initiative of young women who were vitally involved in the civil rights and student movements of the 1960s. Simply by getting involved—going south, joining civil rights demonstrations, living in and organizing black communities, picketing and occupying buildings at colleges and universities, exposing themselves to physical danger—these young women had broken with established cultural norms. At war with their own culture on so many counts, they were ripe to question assumptions about sex roles as well. Their experiences showed them that women could and did do many things dramatically different from playing conventional social roles. But even in the civil rights and student movements, women were usually consigned to traditional female roles—typing, cooking, housekeeping, providing sexual companionship. How could supposedly egalitarian movements replicate such unequal sex roles? When women in the radical civil rights organization the Student Non-Violent Coordinating Committee (SNCC), angry at being excluded from decision-making and leadership positions and angry at assumptions of male superiority, raised the issue at a SNCC conference in 1964, it was treated as a joke.[25]

If SNCC seemed increasingly inhospitable to women, SDS was even more strongly dominated by males. Here again, women ran up against galling contradictions. Vitally involved in the grueling work of community organizing among the poor in northern cities, women were nevertheless excluded from the inner circle of SDS, exploited sexually by their male colleagues, and expected to handle housekeeping chores. After 1965, when SDS turned its attention to the war, women's auxiliary status in the movement was even more forcibly underscored. For men, resisting the draft meant a personal risk of going to jail. Women could only offer support.[26]

Steeped in the egalitarianism of movements against the oppression of blacks and poor people, trained in organizing and collective action, and pushed out of important roles in SNCC and SDS, a number of young women activists began to exchange views on

25 Rosen, *The World Split Open*, pp. 96–110; Evans, *Personal Politics*, pp. 57, 60–82.
26 Rosen, *The World Split Open*, pp. 115–24.

female oppression. They took on questions that Betty Friedan and NOW had not confronted: How do women differ from men? Are those differences biologically or culturally determined? Why devalue the feminine but exalt the masculine? Attempting to raise the issue of female oppression at the New Left's National Conference for New Politics in 1967, women delegates, including Shulamith Firestone, co-founder of radical feminist groups such as Redstockings, were patronized and ridiculed. "Move on, little girl," said the conference chair, patting Firestone on the head. "We have more important issues to talk about here than women's liberation."[27]

Now women activists were ready to break with the movements in which they had been trained and to concentrate exclusively on women's issues. In 1967 they launched the women's liberation movement. Within a year, the movement had spread like wildfire across the country. It made its public debut with a flamboyant display of guerrilla theater at the Miss America pageant in Atlantic City in August 1968. Young women activists "crowned a live sheep to symbolize the beauty pageant's objectification of female bodies, and filled a 'freedom trashcan' with objects of female torture— girdles, bras, curlers, issues of *Ladies' Home Journal*." A woman "auctioned off an effigy of Miss America: 'Gentlemen, I offer you the 1969 model. She walks. She talks. She smiles on cue. *And* she does housework.'"[28]

In February 1969, women's liberation groups disrupted bridal fairs in San Francisco and New York. In New York, members of the Women's International Terrorist Conspiracy from Hell (WITCH) sang, in a take-off on "Here Comes the Bride," "Here Comes the Slave, Off to Her Grave."[29] Female activists forced their way into male bars and clubs; they sat in at *Newsweek* and *Ladies' Home Journal*; they stormed meetings of professional associations to demand equal employment opportunities.[30] Media

27 Quoted in ibid., p. 129.
28 Evans, *Personal Politics*, p. 214.
29 Rosen, *The World Split Open*, p. 205.
30 William H. Chafe, *The American Woman: Her Changing Social, Economic, and Political Roles, 1920–1970* (New York: Oxford University Press, 1972), pp. 226–27; Stansell, *The Feminist Promise*, pp. 239, 243; Rosen, *The World Split Open*, p. 207.

coverage, derogatory as it often was, "provoked a massive influx of new members into all branches of the feminist movement."[31]

Still to come were the signal public victories of the women's movement: the passage by the U.S. Congress in 1972 of the Equal Rights Amendment (which nevertheless later failed to win ratification in a sufficient number of states for it to become law) and the 1973 U.S. Supreme Court decision in *Roe v. Wade* that a woman's right to privacy under the due process clause of the Fourteenth Amendment made abortion in the first three months of pregnancy a medical matter to be decided by a woman and her doctor.[32] As well, Title IX, part of the Education Amendments Act of 1972, prohibited discrimination on the basis of sex in federally funded educational programs and activities, enlarging opportunities for women students in coeducational institutions.[33]

The confluence of the public-sphere women's rights movement and the private-sphere movement for women's liberation provided the context in which elite colleges and universities began to consider the possibility of educating young women alongside young men. Like men, women were profoundly influenced by the major social disruptions of the 1960s: the assassinations of President John F. Kennedy, Senator Robert F. Kennedy, and civil rights icon Martin Luther King, Jr.; the wave of race riots that swept American cities; the antiwar demonstrations; the often violent protests on college campuses, with their deeply unsettling effects on personal property and perceptions of physical safety. Sharing these searing experiences made it increasingly difficult to imagine pursuing separate, sheltered college educations.

Moreover, the introduction of birth control pills in the United States in 1960 enabled a sexual revolution wherein young women could have sex with young men without risking pregnancy. Separating sex from fear of pregnancy resulted in a vast change in female expectations and behavior. Women could now experiment

31 Evans, *Personal Politics*, p. 214.
32 Ibid., p. 217.
33 Overview of Title IX of the Education Amendments of 1972, https://www.justice.gov/crt/overview-title-ix-education-amendments-1972-20-usc-1681-et-seq, accessed Dec. 22, 2015.

with their sexuality in ways that had not been possible before; sex could now be for them, as it had always been for men, a source of fun, a source of pleasure. By transforming the possibilities for sexual activity, the pill also paved the way for new social arrangements that brought male and female students into regular, easy contact. Going to college together was part and parcel of these changes.

Moving toward Coeducation: The Slow Evolution of Sex Roles

Even to imagine coeducation required a dramatic shift in the way men at elite colleges and universities thought about and interacted with women. In their attitudes toward women, college men of the early 1960s were very much like their older brothers of the 1950s. In 1955 *Time* magazine commissioned interviews with graduating seniors at twenty colleges and universities, asking them what they expected their lives to be like fifteen years hence. The sociologist David Riesman, who examined the transcripts, reported on some of the most striking findings. Witness what three seniors in the class of 1955 said about their future wives: "She shouldn't be submissive," a Harvard man said. "She can be independent on little things, but the big decisions will have to go my way . . . the marriage must be the most important thing that ever happened to her." A Princeton student said that his wife would be "vivacious and easy with people. And she will belong to everything in sight too—especially the League of Women Voters." Another Princeton student said that his wife would be "the Grace Kelly, camel's-haircoat type. Feet on the ground, and not an empty shell or a fake. Although an Ivy League type, she will also be centered in the home, a housewife. Perhaps at forty-five, with the children grown up, she will go in for hospital work and so on. . . . And improving herself culturally and thus bringing a deeper sense of culture into our home will be one of her main interests."[34]

The views of male college students in the 1950s were consistent with their elders' perceptions of women's roles. Publicists and

34 Quoted in David Riesman, "The Found Generation," *American Scholar* 25 (Autumn 1956): 430–32. The description of the interviews is on pp. 422–23.

educators alike celebrated women as homemakers and helpmates. The muckraking critic Agnes Meyer in 1950 called women "the cement of society," with motherhood their only proper vocation.[35] In his commencement address at Smith College in 1955, Illinois governor and unsuccessful Democratic presidential candidate Adlai E. Stevenson told the graduating seniors that he could "wish [them] no better vocations than [motherhood and marriage]." By raising good western children, these young women would help to defend American society against totalitarianism and authoritarianism. Through their role as "wives and mothers," they would "influence [man and boy] and [thereby] play a direct part in the unfolding drama of our free society."[36] Writing in *Saturday Review* in 1958, the anthropologist Ashley Montagu reinforced Stevenson's point: "Being a good wife, a good mother, in short a good homemaker is the most important of all the occupations in the world."[37] Editors of *Mademoiselle*, analyzing hundreds of questionnaires, concluded that young women shared their elders' views; they "wanted to be well-rounded rather than to excel, viewed the family as 'the ultimate measure of success,' and looked forward to relaxed, uneventful marriages 'of thoroughly barbecued bliss.'"[38]

Male presidents of women's colleges joined the chorus. The president of Mills College, Lynn Townsend White, Jr., said that women's colleges should "shake off their subservience to masculine values" and create a "distinctively feminine curriculum," including ceramics, textiles, weaving, leatherwork, and flower arranging, that reflected rather than denied the differences between the sexes. James Madison Wood, the president of Stephens College, touting the college's programs in home economics, child development, and interior decorating, said, "If [homemaking] roles are to be played with distinction, the college years must be rehearsal periods for the major performance."[39]

35 Quoted in Chafe, *The American Woman*, p. 206.
36 Quoted in Thealexa Becker, "The Journey from Housewife to Having It All: A History of Smith College Commencement Speeches," Jan. 28, 2011, pp. 13–15, Smith College Archives.
37 Quoted in Chafe, *The American Woman*, pp. 206–7.
38 Leuchtenburg, *A Troubled Feast*, p. 74.
39 Quoted in Chafe, *The American Woman*, pp. 207–8.

Female presidents of women's colleges sounded similar themes. The president of Sweet Briar College, Anne Parnell, declared that "the task of creating a good home and raising good children" should be "raised to the dignity of a profession and made the primary purpose of women's colleges."[40] Hanna Holborn Gray (later provost and acting president of Yale and president of the University of Chicago), a member of the class of 1950 at Bryn Mawr, remembered a talk there by the president of Wellesley, Mildred McAfee Horton, about "how the graduates of women's colleges would make better mothers, helping educate their children at a higher level, imbuing them with respect for civilized values" while at the same time contributing their leadership skills to parent-teacher associations and "bringing their knowledge and taste to service on museum boards." This message was particularly galling at Bryn Mawr, the one women's college with a full-fledged graduate school from the outset, a college with a strong emphasis on "high scholarship and the training of women for scholarly pursuits, intellectual fulfillment, and personal independence."[41] A chapel talk a half century earlier by the college's second president, the formidable M. Carey Thomas, was still the stuff of legend at Bryn Mawr when Gray was a student. According to Thomas's written script, she declared, "Our failures only marry." As students remembered it, their president slipped, as she often did in chapel addresses, and said, instead, "Only our failures marry."[42]

These themes were not simply artifacts of the 1950s. Even into the 1960s, the president of Smith College, Thomas Corwin Mendenhall, spoke to his students about futures in which they would play multiple roles: wives, mothers, community volunteers, civic leaders, and professionals in various fields. And women students behaved accordingly. From World War II into the late 1950s, the median age of first marriages for women was under twenty-one, by far the lowest in the twentieth century (it had been twenty-three in

40 Ibid.

41 Hanna Holborn Gray, "Bryn Mawr College," draft autobiographical chapter, Nov. 10, 2014, typescript courtesy of Hanna Holborn Gray.

42 Thomas, quoted in Helen Lefkowitz Horowitz, *The Power and Passion of M. Carey Thomas* (New York: Alfred A. Knopf, 1994), p. 385.

1940 and would be twenty-one by 1960, then over twenty-two by 1970).[43] Sixty percent of college women dropped out of school to marry. The birth rate for third children doubled from World War II into the early 1960s, and the rate for fourth children tripled. There was an exodus to the suburbs, and interior decorating, sewing, child care, and parent-teacher associations filled the lives of women recently absorbed in collegiate study.[44]

Changing expectations about the roles women would assume in American society had a powerful effect on the way college women saw their opportunities, as well as on the way college men began to perceive college women. So did the new ways in which college men and college women began interacting in the 1960s. In the struggle for civil rights, college men and college women marched together, picketed together, and sat in together, and they worked together to register black voters in the Mississippi Freedom Summer of 1964. Once the wave of antiwar protests began, college men and college women demonstrated together to express their fierce opposition to the policies of the Johnson and Nixon administrations in the war in Southeast Asia.[45] With interactions of these kinds, it became increasingly untenable to assume that single-sex institutions were the proper way to educate college men and college women. And with traditional relationships between students and their institutions altered as a result of the student movement, traditional single-sex elite higher education seemed increasingly anachronistic.

Paving the Way for Coeducation: Other Forces

Although the civil rights movement was a distinctly American phenomenon, the women's movement, the antiwar movement, and the student movement were felt powerfully in Europe, affecting

43 U.S. Decennial Census, 1890–2000, www.census.gov/hhes/socdemo/marriage/data /acs/ElliottetalPAA2012figs.pdf, accessed July 14, 2014.

44 Rosalind Rosenberg, *Divided Lives: American Women in the Twentieth Century* (New York: Hill and Wang, 1992), p. 147; Stansell, *The Feminist Promise*, p. 183.

45 On the participation of Smith students in protests against the Vietnam War and against the draft, often together with Amherst students, see Nancy Weiss, "This Year's Graduates," *Smith Alumnae Quarterly* 59 (Aug. 1968): 15–16.

expectations at Cambridge and Oxford about the ways men and women were to be educated. As the American historian Richard Hofstadter observed in his commencement speech at Columbia in the spring of 1968, "Not only in New York and Berkeley, but in Madrid and Paris, in Belgrade and Oxford, in Rome, Berlin and London, and on many college and university campuses throughout this country, students are disaffected, restive and rebellious."[46] Sir Eric Ashby, the master of Clare College, Cambridge, remarked on the "sustained gale-force wind of change" in British colleges and universities, with "sit-ins, protests, and assaults on the Establishment" part of the normal order of the day.[47] But Ashby was quick to point out that there was nothing uniquely British about the "movement of discontent among undergraduates with all that is traditionally involved in the concept of being *in statu pupillari*" (in the status of students). Rather, he said, it was part of "a world-picture of student self-assertion, visible from California to Indonesia."[48]

Other steps taken in the 1960s by colleges and universities paved the way, even if unintentionally, for coeducation. The first was the deliberate effort to diversify the student bodies of the most elite single-sex institutions. In the United States, efforts to increase diversity meant recruiting beyond traditional feeder schools and shifting the balance from independent day schools and boarding schools to public high schools. It meant admitting fewer legacies and more students from families of more modest means, students on scholarship, more Catholics and Jews, and even, by the end of the decade, some African Americans. In the United Kingdom, Cambridge and Oxford colleges began to look to grammar schools and state schools to supplement their traditional constituency of students from private boarding schools (in their terms, public schools) like Eton and Harrow. As student bodies on both sides of

---

46 Richard Hofstadter, "Columbia University Commencement Address for the 214th Academic Year," *American Scholar* 37 (Autumn 1968): 587. I am indebted to William G. Bowen for pointing me to this speech.

47 Eric Ashby, "Notes from the Master," *Clare Association Annual*, 1966, p. 23 ("gale-force wind"), and 1968, p. 16 ("sit-ins"), both in Clare, CCCS/4/5.

48 Ibid., 1966, p. 23.

the Atlantic became more diverse, it became increasingly anachronistic to draw the line at admitting women. Diversity in terms of gender followed logically from diversity of other kinds.[49]

In the 1960s, colleges and universities also began to diversify their faculties. For generations the faculties of Harvard, Yale, and Princeton had been populated by graduates of Harvard, Yale, and Princeton. Increasingly, elite colleges and universities hired faculty with Ph.D.s from the great state universities, like Berkeley, Wisconsin, and Michigan.[50] These new faculty had direct experience with coeducation and were more open to the possibility of teaching women as well as men in their own classrooms. In some cases the pressure for coeducation came from the faculty; in others, faculty members responded enthusiastically to the prospect when it was raised by administrators and students. At Oxford and Cambridge, colleges that took the lead in embracing coeducation had typically appointed new cohorts of young fellows in the 1960s, some of them with direct experience with coeducation, virtually all of them more open-minded and progressive than many of their elders.

Amidst the profound social and political transformations of the 1960s, coeducation came to be instituted at very traditional, very conservative institutions, some of them centuries old, seemingly all at once, and over an astonishingly brief period of time. Given the social and political movements of the 1960s and the other steps colleges and universities were taking to diversify, it would have been remarkable if single-sex institutions had emerged from the

---

49 On diversification of student bodies in the 1960s in the United States, see, e.g., Jerome Karabel, *The Chosen: The Hidden History of Admission and Exclusion at Harvard, Yale, and Princeton* (Boston and New York: Houghton Mifflin, 2005); Marcia Graham Synnott, *Student Diversity at the Big Three: Changes at Harvard, Yale, and Princeton since the 1920s* (New Brunswick, NJ: Transaction Publishers, 2013). For the United Kingdom, see Joseph A. Soares, *The Decline of Privilege: The Modernization of Oxford University* (Stanford, CA: Stanford University Press, 1999); Carol Dyhouse, *Students: A Gendered History* (London and New York: Routledge, 2006).

50 At Princeton, e.g., while the number of faculty hired from Harvard, Yale, and Princeton stayed constant from the 1950s to the 1960s, the number of faculty hired from public universities increased by 68 percent. These data are derived from trustee minutes and faculty personnel records in the Princeton University Archives, Department of Rare Books and Special Collections, Princeton University Library. I am indebted to Daniel J. Linke for making the data available to me and to Jeremy Zullow for compiling them.

decade unchanged. No matter how powerful the influence of the times, however, the coming of coeducation was not a smooth, easy, uncontested process. Nor was it the same at different colleges and universities. It varied, institution by institution, on the basis of institutional culture, structure, and leadership. The people in charge, the quality and effectiveness of their leadership, made a critical difference in propelling or holding back institutional change. In the main, these people were men, in most cases leading colleges and universities established by and administered over many centuries for men. Although this book is about coeducation, and thus inevitably about women, it is primarily about those men: the decisions they made, the leadership they demonstrated, and the ways in which they harnessed the power of their institutions to meet the challenges of the times. Understanding how all of that happened takes us to the histories of the individual institutions that grappled with coeducation in the years from 1969 through 1974.

Part I

The Ivy League:
Harvard, Yale, and
Princeton

2

Harvard-Radcliffe: "To Be Accepted by the Old and Beloved University"

As a matter of chronology and influence, the story of the coming of coeducation begins with the Ivy League. Harvard, Yale, and Princeton took the lead among elite private colleges and universities in embracing coeducation in the late 1960s, and their actions bore importantly on decisions taken by other institutions. By all rights, Harvard should have been the first mover. The circumstances were propitious: Radcliffe was a half-mile up the street from Harvard, with students whose academic qualifications fully matched those of Harvard students. Radcliffe women had been taking classes with Harvard men since the 1940s. The colleges had merged most of their extracurricular activities in the 1950s. The presidents of both institutions were enthusiastic. But realizing coeducation in Cambridge turned out to be a surprisingly complicated endeavor.

A Proposal of Marriage

In April 1961, Nathan Marsh Pusey, a classical scholar completing his eighth year as president of Harvard University, approached his colleague, Mary Ingraham Bunting, a microbiologist just beginning her second year as president of Radcliffe College, with the equivalent of a proposal of marriage: "The Harvard Corporation [the university's governing board] have asked me to ascertain from you and the Governing Boards of Radcliffe College whether Radcliffe would be interested in exploring the possibility of becoming fully a part of Harvard University."[1]

Bunting, known as Polly, had come to Radcliffe from the deanship of Douglass College, the women's college at Rutgers University in New Brunswick, New Jersey. She and Pusey had gotten off to a good start from the moment of her arrival in Cambridge. At her inauguration, Pusey said that "people were always asking him to explain the Harvard-Radcliffe relationship, that he never felt he understood it, but that he knew he liked it." To Bunting, Pusey's open-mindedness provided an excellent foundation for their relationship: "I thought . . . that's wonderful, he hasn't built any fences around us; he's left it all wide open." She went on to say, "Fuzziness can be useful in lots of situations," and fuzziness was what Pusey had given her. She was "not going to ask him to clarify anything, at least not until there is a pressing need. We'll just see what we can do under existing conditions and how well we can work together."[2]

In fact, Pusey's invitation in April 1961 came as a result of a proposal from Bunting, who had quickly figured out how she thought the relationship between the two institutions should evolve. Following a conversation between the two presidents in January 1961, Pusey recorded in handwritten notes that Bunting "want[ed] the Harvard Corporation to invite Radcliffe to become part of Harvard College." Her plan was "first to reorganize their College on a House basis . . . then give up the Grad School, join the Colleges, have their board become a visiting committee if necessary, etc." Harvard "would take on the whole responsibility" for women's education, and Radcliffe would function as "an undergraduate college on an equal basis" with Harvard College.[3]

Following that roadmap turned out to be much more difficult than Bunting or Pusey might have imagined. Although functional coeducation would be realized by 1972, the formal merger between

---

1 Nathan M. Pusey to Mary I. Bunting, Apr. 7, 1961, Bunting, Box 7, Folder 114.
2 Bunting oral history, interview no. 8, Oct. 5, 1978, p. 226.
3 Nathan Marsh Pusey, handwritten notes, Jan. 30, 1961, Pusey, Box 246, Folder Radcliffe, 1961–62.

Harvard and Radcliffe was not to be concluded until 1999. Understanding the long, often tortuous path to merger requires reckoning with the deep investment of Radcliffe trustees and alumnae in the history and prestige of their college. Relinquishing any part of that—indeed, compromising the institution's fundamental independence—was not to be undertaken lightly.

The Founding of Radcliffe

The Bunting-Pusey exchange came nearly seventy years after the founding of Radcliffe, with a unique set of arrangements that made Harvard and Radcliffe the most prominent example of co-ordinate education in the United States. After the Civil War, as women's colleges began to be established and as some universities began admitting women, Harvard made plain that it would not follow suit. In his inaugural address in 1869, President Charles W. Eliot declared that Harvard had no intention of admitting women to the college or to any of the professional schools that required nearby residence. "The difficulties involved in a common residence of hundreds of young men and women of immature character and marriageable age are very grave," Eliot said. The world knew "next to nothing about the natural mental capacities of the female sex"; it would take "generations of civil freedom and social equality" to be able to "obtain the data necessary for an adequate discussion of women's natural tendencies, tastes and capabilities." Eliot opined, "Upon a matter concerning which prejudices are deep and opinion inflammable and experience scanty, only one course is prudent or justifiable when such great interests are at stake—that of cautious and well-considered experiment."[4]

Harvard tried two experiments to give women access to non-credit lectures given by Harvard professors, but they failed to gain traction.[5] Things changed when a group of educated women in

4 Typescript, Inaugural Address of Charles W. Eliot as President of Harvard, Oct. 19, 1869, Bunting, Box 44, Folder 714.

5 On the University Lectures (1863–72), see Sally Schwager, "Taking up the Challenge: The Origins of Radcliffe," in Laurel Thatcher Ulrich, ed., *Yards and Gates: Gender in Harvard and Radcliffe History* (New York: Palgrave Macmillan, 2004), pp. 89–90. On the

Boston and Cambridge, unwilling to let Harvard off the hook in terms of what they considered its responsibility for the education of women, formed the Woman's Education Association of Boston in 1872. Wives, mothers, daughters, and sisters of Harvard men, many of them were writers or scholars in their own right; a number of them had studied privately with members of the Harvard faculty. They invited Eliot to a meeting to discuss "women's access to the College." The president denied their request; few women had sought instruction at Harvard, he said, so the demand was not there. Moreover, there was no space for women, because lower-level courses at Harvard were overcrowded. The women proposed that Harvard give degrees to women who educated themselves and passed examinations required of Harvard men. Initially supportive of the idea, Eliot changed course and, backed by the corporation, declared the plan unworkable. A Harvard degree required time in residence. Moreover, the university had no intention of awarding degrees to women.[6]

By the end of the 1870s, a new plan was put in place for Harvard faculty to teach women students. It came about at the initiative of two Cambridge residents, Arthur and Stella Gilman, who had a daughter approaching college age and who wanted to create what they considered an appropriate educational opportunity for her and her contemporaries. Classes at the so-called Harvard Annex began in September 1879 for twenty-seven local women students. The annex became incorporated in 1882 as the Society for the Collegiate Instruction of Women, and Elizabeth Cary Agassiz, widow and biographer of Louis Agassiz, the first professor in Harvard's Lawrence Scientific School, and herself the director of the Agassiz School for Girls in Cambridge in the late 1850s and early 1860s, was named president. The society's purpose was to "promot[e] the education of women with the assistance of the instructors in Harvard University." In 1893, the Harvard corporation agreed to a formal institutional link whereby the corporation

---

University Courses of Instruction, announced by Eliot in his inaugural address but disbanded after two years, see ibid., p. 91, and typescript, Inaugural Address of Charles W. Eliot.

6 Schwager, "Taking up the Challenge," pp. 92–94.

would approve faculty appointments but the society would see to matters of organization, business affairs, and discipline. Diplomas, to be countersigned by Harvard's president, "would bear the Harvard seal, and the Annex would take the name 'Radcliffe College.'" In 1894, by act of the Massachusetts State Legislature, Radcliffe was chartered as a degree-granting institution.[7] The purpose of the countersignature by the president of Harvard, in Eliot's words, was to attest that "the degrees given by Radcliffe College to its own graduates shall be equivalent in all respects to the degrees given to the graduates of Harvard College."[8] Thereafter, in each degree-granting season, the president of Radcliffe would forward to the president of Harvard a list of candidates for degrees to be approved by the Harvard corporation.[9] Two months after Radcliffe was chartered, the Harvard board of overseers resolved that the university would not give bachelor's degrees to women "under any circumstances."[10]

Agassiz had wanted to avoid "drift[ing] into building up another female college, distinct from the University."[11] There was no profit, she thought, in seeking to replicate Vassar, Smith, or Wellesley; the point was to take advantage of the intellectual resources of Harvard, with all of its "traditions of learning and experience," "its relation to the intellectual world outside, its maturity of thought and method; its claim on cultivated minds everywhere."[12] Radcliffe

7 Hugh Hawkins, "Elizabeth Cabot Cary Agassiz," in Edward T. James, Janet Wilson James, and Paul S. Boyer, eds., *Notable American Women, 1607–1950: A Biographical Dictionary*, vol. 1 (Cambridge, MA: Belknap Press of Harvard University Press, 1971), pp. 23–24 ("Harvard seal," p. 24); Articles of Incorporation of the Society for the Collegiate Instruction of Women, Aug. 16, 1882 and An Act to Change the Name of the Society for the Collegiate Instruction of Women and to Extend Its Powers, Mar. 21–22, 1894, typescripts in Bunting, Box 44, Folder 714.

8 President Eliot's Interpretation of Relationship, Aug. 4, 1921, typescript in Conant, Box 235, Folder Radcliffe College, 1942–43.

9 See, e.g., Ada L. Comstock to James Bryant Conant, Oct. 3, 1942, Feb. 26 and May 24, 1943, Conant, Box 235, Folder Radcliffe College, 1942–43.

10 Schwager, "Taking up the Challenge," p. 105.

11 Typescript, Elizabeth Cary Agassiz to Arthur Gilman, Mar. 24, 1882, quoted in Lucy Allen Paton, *Elizabeth Cary Agassiz: A Biography* (Boston: Houghton Mifflin, 1909), pp. 205–6, in Bunting, Box 44, Folder 714.

12 Typescript, Mrs. Agassiz's report on the early days of the Annex, 1884, quoted in Paton, *Elizabeth Cary Agassiz*, pp. 211–17, in Bunting, Box 44, Folder 714.

was not aiming for full coeducation; rather, the idea was to benefit from proximity to Harvard to secure a rigorous education for women.[13] As Agassiz declared to the Radcliffe graduating class in 1894, "We have all longed . . . to be accepted by the old and beloved University, under whose shadow we ventured to begin our work, hoping for final recognition. Today that recognition is ours. Harvard has consented to receive our college as her ward—has made herself responsible for our education and has given us her signature and her seal as guarantee thereunto. . . . Perhaps no University opens a nobler course of instruction to women, than Harvard offers to her Radcliffe students of today."[14]

Agassiz's successor as president of Radcliffe, Le Baron Russell Briggs, a Harvard English professor who served simultaneously as dean of the Harvard faculty of arts and sciences, described Radcliffe as springing "from the conviction that Harvard College might and must do for women something of what, for centuries long, it had done for men; that the ideals and teaching of Harvard College would find response in earnest, right-minded, able girls; that there were some women in America to whom a degree certified by Harvard College as equivalent to its own would mean more than any other degree in the world."[15] Later he declared, "This college differs from any other college for women in the world. . . . This college exists to give girls as much of what for centuries has meant so much to Harvard men, that is to say, Radcliffe is, so far as possible, a girls' Harvard, an uncoeducational girls' Harvard."[16]

That said, both Briggs and Eliot had a clear vision of the purposes of the education offered at the "girls' Harvard." The point, in Eliot's words, was to "fit [women] to make family life and social life more intelligent, more enjoyable, happier, and more productive."

---

13 Typescript, Elizabeth Cary Agassiz to E. W. Hooper, Apr. 1893, quoted in Paton, *Elizabeth Cary Agassiz*, pp. 234–35, in Bunting, Box 44, Folder 714.

14 Typescript, Commencement Speech by Mrs. Agassiz, 1894, quoted in Paton, *Elizabeth Cary Agassiz*, pp. 261–63, in Bunting, Box 44, Folder 714.

15 Typescript, Le Baron Russell Briggs, speech to Radcliffe students, Sept. 30, 1909, Bunting, Box 44, Folder 714.

16 Typescript, Le Baron Russell Briggs, registration day speech, Sept. 23, 1913, Bunting, Box 44, Folder 714.

In other words, higher education would make women students better wives and mothers.[17]

The engine for the "girls' Harvard" was the Harvard faculty members who traveled the short distance up Brattle Street or Garden Street from Harvard Yard to repeat their classes for Radcliffe women. The teaching arrangements were negotiated by Radcliffe, and faculty members were paid by Radcliffe—a salary supplement of real consequence—until the administrative arrangements between Harvard and Radcliffe were revised in 1943. Under the new arrangement Radcliffe paid a lump sum to Harvard—set initially at 82 to 85 percent of the tuition monies collected, later raised to 88 percent—and Harvard assumed official responsibility for delivering instruction to Radcliffe students. The new agreement was signed by James Bryant Conant, president of Harvard, and Ada Louise Comstock, president of Radcliffe.

The 1943 agreement allowed for a more rational, planned curriculum for Radcliffe, with greater certainty about the courses that would be taught and the faculty members who would be teaching them. The agreement recognized that Harvard had a responsibility for the education of women and provided, in the words of historian Paul Buck, dean of the Harvard faculty of arts and sciences, a more "dignified basis" for the relationship between the two institutions. But it had nothing to do with convictions at Harvard about the virtues of coeducation. Under the pressures of wartime, with many Harvard students away from the campus, Harvard needed revenue to replace lost tuition dollars, and faculty members began to grumble about the inefficiency of repeating less than fully enrolled courses for Radcliffe women. Radcliffe tuition dollars would stabilize the university's revenue. And by combining Harvard and Radcliffe teaching responsibilities, Buck could increase faculty salaries at a time when wage stabilization rules would otherwise have complicated, if not precluded, a rise in compensation.

Once the war ended, Comstock, now retired, worried that the university might return to segregated classes. Conant countered

17 Eliot, quoted in Schwager, "Taking up the Challenge," p. 106. For Briggs's similar view, see p. 107.

that the Harvard faculty liked the new arrangements too much to consider changing them. Mixed-sex classrooms—the official label was "joint instruction"—were formalized for upperclass students in 1947 and for freshmen in 1950.[18]

Lingering Differences

When Bunting took up the presidency of Radcliffe, she quickly found that there was much more to be done to make the education of Radcliffe women equivalent to the education of Harvard men. As dean at Douglass, Bunting had acquired ample experience in providing a first-rate education for women students. A graduate of Vassar, she knew full well the aspirations and accomplishments of the premier women's colleges in the United States. With the example of Harvard close at hand, there was no mistaking where Radcliffe fell short. Bunting said later, "One of the things that surprised me most . . . was the realization that it was precisely in those aspects of student lives for which Radcliffe was responsible, that one found the greatest discrepancies." The most obvious defects had to do with dormitories, financial aid, athletics, and what Bunting called "collegial life."[19]

As for housing, the Radcliffe dormitories suffered from serious overcrowding. Unlike the Harvard houses, there were few suites and no small common rooms in which "to relieve the pressure."

18 In Bunting, Box 44, Folder 714, see typescript, Final Annual Report of President Comstock, 1942–43. In Conant, Box 235, Folder Radcliffe College, 1942–43, see Paul H. Buck to the President and Fellows of Harvard College, Feb. 24, 1943; Memorandum of Remarks Made by Dean Buck at the Faculty Meeting of Mar. 2, 1943, in Regard to the Proposed Plan to Regulate Harvard-Radcliffe Relations ("dignified basis"); Docket, Faculty of Arts and Sciences, Mar. 16, 1943; minutes, meeting of the President and Fellows of Harvard College, Apr. 5, 1943; minutes, meeting of the Faculty of Arts and Sciences, Apr. 6, 1943; Agreement between President and Fellows of Harvard College and Trustees of Radcliffe College, Apr. 16, 1943; and "Harvard-Radcliffe Agreement," Joint Harvard-Radcliffe News Release, Apr. 18, 1943. In Bunting, Box 48, Folder 775, see Amendments to Agreement between President and Fellows of Harvard College and Trustees of Radcliffe College, Action by Radcliffe Council, Sept. 8, 1947, and Feb. 6, 1950. See also Dunlop oral history, p. 2; Morton Keller and Phyllis Keller, *Making Harvard Modern: The Rise of America's University*, updated ed. (New York: Oxford University Press, 2007), p. 55, and telephone interview with Matina Horner, Feb. 9, 2015. All personal interviews (as distinct from oral history interviews) cited in the book were conducted by the author.

19 Bunting oral history, interview no. 6, Oct. 3, 1978, p. 136.

Students had little privacy, little "space in which to work at their own pace," little opportunity to set their own schedules for study and sleep. The overcrowding significantly magnified the pressures experienced by students at a college as demanding as Radcliffe.

As for financial aid, Radcliffe matched Harvard "in the scholarship funds available per needy student" but lagged Harvard in terms of the "proportion of [needy students] in [the] student body." The lag reflected differences in national attitudes about daughters and sons going to college, Bunting thought, more than it did differences in institutional admission policies. "It was another example," she said, of what she labeled "that climate of unexpectation" with respect to women's roles in American society. In athletics, Radcliffe also lagged Harvard in facilities and "budgets for intramural or intercollegiate sports."

In terms of "collegial life," the differences between the two colleges were stark. The Harvard house system was "designed and maintained to foster closer relationships between faculty and students and between students from different backgrounds," Bunting explained.

> It involved leisurely meals in large dining halls where a group of tutors and faculty associates could get to know a group of students; and opportunities for spontaneous groups of students to work together on a wide variety of projects. It was seen as an important part of the education of Harvard men, the principal means of providing informal counsel and putting students in touch with distinguished visitors from the outside world. It was one of the many ways in which Harvard demonstrated . . . that there was more to education than doing well in courses.

Radcliffe offered meager opportunities of that sort. Bunting summed up, "Radcliffe students were commuting to Harvard classes, commuting from crowded barracks; they were not part of the collegial life of the University."[20] There was much work to be

20 Ibid., pp. 136–40.

done to move Radcliffe closer to the Harvard model, work that would not engage the politically explosive question of merger.

But the question of the relationship between the two institutions was front and center almost from the moment Bunting took up her responsibilities. Seemingly simple matters—how to accommodate both Harvard and Radcliffe in university directories, how to describe Radcliffe in the university's general catalogue—raised for Bunting the question "as to whether Radcliffe's position in the university ought to be more carefully defined than it is." In her mind, Radcliffe was clearly "part of Harvard University," and she wanted to say so directly. At the same time, she wanted Harvard to more candidly "admit the co-educational nature of the joint enterprise in Cambridge." Bunting favored greater clarity and a more explicit description of the relationship between the two institutions, an approach on which she and Pusey, in the words of his assistant, saw "very much eye to eye."[21]

Bunting moved deliberately, first toward improving the educational experience of Radcliffe undergraduates, then by testing the waters with respect to the fuller integration of Radcliffe into the larger university. Her first step was to create a house plan at Radcliffe so that the Radcliffe residential experience might play a role similar to that of the Harvard houses. Existing dormitories in the Radcliffe quadrangle, together with a new complex to be built, would comprise four houses, each led by faculty masters, with graduate students in residence. The four houses would share a new undergraduate library with faculty offices, study space, and facilities for tutorials and seminars. The houses would also provide relief from the serious overcrowding in the existing Radcliffe dormitories by providing more numerous and more commodious living spaces, as well as common rooms and recreational spaces. And—again, as at Harvard—there would be faculty families in residence, providing as role models women who had "found ways of combining a creative home life with continued intellectual development and usefulness."

21 Memorandum, William Bentinck-Smith to Nathan Marsh Pusey, Sept. 8, 1960, and Bentinck-Smith to Oscar M. Shaw, Sept. 19, 1960 (source of the quotes), Pusey, Box 217, Folder Radcliffe College, 1960–61.

Informal faculty-student gatherings would take place in the houses, and decanal advising, student government, recreational programs, and other activities would be reorganized on a house basis.[22] Three of the houses could be created in the near term; the fourth would depend on fund-raising for new construction. Bunting secured a public endorsement of her plan from Pusey.[23]

Radcliffe: Becoming a Part of Harvard, Not an Appendage

Bunting made plain to Pusey her "growing conviction of the importance to Radcliffe and to Harvard of considering this college a part rather than an appendage of the University."[24] How to bring about the fuller integration of Radcliffe into the larger university required creative thinking and political savvy. The first test case came with the Radcliffe graduate school. Although the Harvard faculty provided graduate instruction to women, Radcliffe had been enrolling women graduate students from the time of its founding, and the graduate school had been established in 1934. Pusey was eager to open the Harvard graduate school of arts and sciences to women, and he wanted to know Radcliffe's position on the matter.

Bunting was very clear about what she thought. Graduate instruction would continue to be the province of Harvard. Women would apply to Harvard, which would make admission decisions and award scholarships. Radcliffe would assign scholarship money to women graduate students. Diplomas would be awarded by Harvard, with due note of the relationship to Radcliffe. All of these arrangements would fit into Bunting's larger ambitions. As the dean

22 Mary I. Bunting to Nathan M. Pusey, Apr. 27, 1961, Pusey, Box 217, Folder Radcliffe College, 1960–61 (source of the quote); Bunting, Speech at the Opening of College, Sept. 24, 1961, Bunting, Box 16, Folder 258; Bunting oral history, interview no. 6, Oct. 3, 1978, pp. 141–42, 144–45, 152, 160; "Radcliffe to Create House System for Undergraduates," *Radcliffe Quarterly* 45 (May 1961): 4–5.

23 Mary I. Bunting to Nathan Pusey, Apr. 27 and May 26, 1961, Pusey, Box 217, Folder Radcliffe College, 1960–61; Pusey to Bunting, with attached Statement on Radcliffe Houses, May 22, 1961, Bunting, Box 7, Folder 114.

24 Mary I. Bunting to Nathan Pusey, May 26, 1961, Pusey, Box 217, Folder Radcliffe College, 1960–61.

of the graduate school at Harvard interpreted it, Bunting preferred that "Radcliffe College on the one hand retain its historic identity but on the other hand become part of Harvard University." As a Harvard lawyer told it, Bunting was "eager to accomplish" the formal recognition of Radcliffe "as a part of Harvard University while continuing to maintain its separate corporate identity and to own and manage its own endowment."[25]

But what was clear to Bunting was much less clear to the Radcliffe board. The proposal that Radcliffe cease to admit women to graduate study, with women candidates eligible instead for admission directly to Harvard, did not sit well with them; the trustees thought that it would be inappropriate for Radcliffe fellowship funds and the Radcliffe graduate center to be devoted to students who were not registered at Radcliffe.

The Radcliffe trustees finally concluded that instead of focusing exclusively on the graduate school, they ought to be "think[ing] of the College as a complete unit" and asking Harvard to grant Harvard degrees to *all* Radcliffe students.[26] Radcliffe was already "functioning as a college within the University"; having Harvard award all degrees to Radcliffe students would make the relationship "evident." Radcliffe would maintain its identity and manage its funds. It would still administer the undergraduate college for women, taking responsibility for "its physical plant, the financial condition of the College, and the admission, guidance, and housing of undergraduate women." Radcliffe "would simply suspend its right to grant degrees to its students."[27] With the approval of the Harvard faculty and the governing boards of both institutions, this version of the new arrangement, with Harvard granting diplomas

25 J. P. Elder [Harvard dean] to Nathan M. Pusey, Dec. 5, 1961, and O. M. Shaw [Harvard lawyer], Memorandum for Mr. Coolidge, Dec. 4, 1961, both in Pusey, Box 246, Folder Radcliffe, 1961–62.

26 In Bunting, Box 12, Folder 191, see minutes, Council of Radcliffe College, Nov. 6 and Dec. 4, 1961, and Mar. 5, 1962 (source of the quotes). In Bunting, Box 13, Folder 203, see minutes, President and Fellows of Harvard College, Nov. 20, 1961; memorandum, Mary I. Bunting to President Pusey, Feb. 6, 1962; and Bunting to the Members of the Board, Mar. 15, 1962.

27 Mary I. Bunting to the Members of the Board, Mar. 15, 1962, Bunting, Box 13, Folder 203.

to all Radcliffe students, graduate and undergraduate, and with all women admitted to the Harvard graduate school also being enrolled at Radcliffe, went into effect in 1962–63.[28]

Even then, though, the political sensitivities surrounding these moves were still acute, and symbolism mattered hugely to the Radcliffe trustees. As Pusey recorded in a note to the file in June 1962, "Mrs. Bunting said that it would greatly help her relationship with her Trustees, who would otherwise conclude that she had in some way sold the institution down the river, if for the time being we permitted the tuition of women graduate students who will be admitted to our Graduate School of Arts and Sciences to be paid to Radcliffe." Radcliffe would then transmit the tuition revenue to Harvard. In a year or two, Bunting told Pusey, it should be possible for Radcliffe to agree to "have this responsibility passed to the Harvard business office." Pusey noted that he had "agreed to this arrangement."[29]

Bunting began her talk at the opening of college in September 1962 by emphasizing the significance of what had been accomplished: "This is the year," she said, "that Radcliffe quietly takes its place as an acknowledged and integral part of Harvard University. . . . This is the year that all degrees earned by Radcliffe students will be awarded by Harvard and the educational arrangements in operation since 1943 finally and officially sanctioned."[30] In short, Radcliffe was now acknowledged, de facto, as the undergraduate women's college of Harvard University, in effect the coordinate partner of Harvard College.[31]

28 In Pusey, Box 246, Folder Radcliffe, 1961–62, see Mary I. Bunting to Nathan M. Pusey, Mar. 26, 1962; Pusey to the Members of the Corporation, Apr. 12, 1962; and minutes, President and Fellows of Harvard College, Apr. 16, 1962. In Bunting, Box 13, Folder 203, see Graduate School: Corporation Vote, Council Vote of June 4, 1962, and minutes, President and Fellows of Harvard College, June 13, 1962. In Bunting, Box 12, Folder 191, see minutes, Council of Radcliffe College, June 4, 1962. A sample diploma awarded to an undergraduate woman is pictured in Dorothy Elia Howells, *A Century to Celebrate: Radcliffe College, 1879–1979* (Radcliffe College, 1979), p. 32.

29 Memorandum, Nathan Marsh Pusey to the File, June 6, 1962, Pusey, Box 246, Folder Radcliffe, 1961–62.

30 Excerpts from Mrs. Bunting's Opening of College Talk, Sept. 23, 1962, Bunting, Box 19, Folder 320.

31 Statement of the Radcliffe Council, Feb. 4, 1963, attached to Nathan M. Pusey to Mary I. Bunting, Feb. 19, 1963, Bunting, Box 18, Folder 301.

A Lunch in Bar Harbor—and Resistance from the Board

The question of the formal incorporation of Radcliffe College into Harvard University remained on the table. Bunting had continued to think seriously about the relationship of the two undergraduate colleges during a year away from Radcliffe in 1964–65, when she was in Washington serving as a member of the Atomic Energy Commission. Upon her return, she found that in the course of fund-raising for Radcliffe, some trustees were being asked to explain the "relationship" between the two colleges. They asked her to draft a paper on the subject.

In the course of drafting, Bunting determined that it might be time to try to fix the relationship rather than "try to explain it in its present form. . . . If we could put the undergraduate Colleges together, it might be traumatic for a short period but in the end everyone would benefit."[32] Bunting decided that she "had better talk [the idea] over with Mr. Pusey before I said a word to anyone else. If he was not receptive, there was no use muddying the waters at Radcliffe." Pusey was, as usual, spending the summer in Bar Harbor, Maine. Bunting phoned and asked if she could come up to talk. Pusey invited her to lunch.

"Was it possible," Bunting asked Pusey, "that the time had come to incorporate Radcliffe within Harvard"? Pusey was immediately receptive; he said that "he would like nothing better than to have that happen." Pusey asked Bunting "what the reaction would be at Radcliffe." Bunting said that she would like to broach the idea with the trustees in the fall. If things went well, the next step would be to appoint a small committee to examine "the pros and cons."[33]

But things did not go well. By coincidence, in a committee meeting the morning before the November board meeting, a new member of the board had raised the question of exploring the possibility of a merger. "His questions," Bunting said, "had raised hackles, and when I introduced the same idea later, some trustees wondered whether there was a plot."[34] The trustees were concerned espe-

32 Bunting oral history, interview no. 8, Oct. 5, 1978, pp. 229–30.
33 Ibid., p. 230.
34 Ibid., p. 231.

cially about fund-raising. Some trustees believed that it would help fund-raising if the college were "recognized as part of Harvard"; others thought that Radcliffe's "case and its cause would be weakened by any closer identification with Harvard." Some feared that even discussing the issue would "cause confusion which would hurt fund-raising."[35]

Bunting was not ready to give up the idea, and she wrote to Pusey in the wake of the trustees' discussion: "A great university in a great democracy can not focus on just one half of the problem. Women's education can not be properly managed without concern for its special features." Radcliffe's "special mission" would be accomplished most effectively when it was "incorporated as a distinctive unit within Harvard University, or, to say it the other way, when Harvard cares enough about the education of women to want to see it carried forward as effectively as possible." Bunting wrote that she could not imagine a more consequential impact on women's education in the United States "than to have Harvard believe that women's education is too important to leave to women."[36]

As was so often the case, Bunting was well ahead of her board. Her longtime board chair, Helen Homans Gilbert, who generally saw things the same way Bunting did, later described their relationship this way: Bunting "just plunged" ahead with whatever she wanted to pursue. "I always felt," Gilbert said in reference to a different issue, "I was sort of hanging on her by the coattail."[37] Insofar as the Harvard-Radcliffe relationship was concerned, the Radcliffe trustees preempted Bunting by setting up their own committee "to study the question." As Bunting told the story, the committee met, "talked things over, and, without inviting me to make any presentation, decided that the time was not right for anything like merger to occur."[38]

That precluded the appointment of a joint exploratory committee. As Pusey told Gilbert, there was too much division of opinion, too many "serious misgivings," among the Radcliffe trustees. "Ultimately," he believed, "it will be to Radcliffe's best interest to become a part of Harvard." But "it would be folly to endeavor to

35 Mary I. Bunting to Nathan M. Pusey, Nov. 29, 1965, Bunting, Box 30, Folder 473.
36 Ibid.
37 Gilbert oral history, pp. 38 ("coattail"), 39 ("she just plunged").
38 Bunting oral history, interview no. 8, Oct. 5, 1978, pp. 231–32.

press toward this goal until the Trustees of Radcliffe are fully convinced and request the move."[39]

It was not that Pusey had changed his mind about the advisability of "making Radcliffe an integral part of the University," he told Bunting. The issue had to do with timing and circumstance. "From the beginning of my involvement in this matter," he wrote her, "it has seemed to me that we should not attempt finally to unite the two institutions until those to whom Radcliffe's governance is entrusted are fully persuaded that union will be a good thing, actively press for it, and wish fully to entrust their responsibility to Harvard. I have been quite certain in any case that Harvard should not take the lead in urging further change in the present relationship." Although it had seemed in the summer of 1965 that the time might have come "to move forward," evidence of "considerable differences of opinion" among the Radcliffe trustees made him less sure. He was worried that some people would interpret the formal establishment of a committee to mean that "the decision to unite had already been taken." The results might be to turn "what are now amorphous, weak, negative opinions actively hostile." He and Bunting "should now simply continue to talk informally about the problem, looking for a more propitious time or waiting until we are confronted with an urgent occasion to move ahead."[40]

In the meantime, new administrative arrangements further integrated the two undergraduate colleges. In one visible step, the Harvard registrar's office took over Radcliffe undergraduate registration, including course enrollments, maintenance of academic records, and issuance of transcripts, effective in the summer of 1966.[41] Less visible was the decision to allow Radcliffe to make purchases through Harvard's purchasing office.[42]

---

39 Nathan M. Pusey to Helen Homans Gilbert, Dec. 10, 1965, Bunting, Box 35, Folder 542.

40 Nathan M. Pusey to Mary I. Bunting, Dec. 10, 1965, Bunting, Box 30, Folder 473.

41 Mary I. Bunting to Franklin L. Ford, Oct. 8 and Dec. 15, 1965; Ford to Bunting, Oct. 14 and Dec. 21, 1965; Robert Shenton to [J.] Boyd Britton, Nov. 1, 1965; memoranda, Bunting to Britton, Nov. 1 and 18, 1965; memorandum, Britton to Bunting, Nov. 30, 1965; Britton to Shenton, Nov. 26, 1965; Britton to Robert I. Hunneman, Nov. 30, 1965; Hunneman to Britton, Dec. 3, 1965; and minutes, President and Fellows of Harvard College, June 6, 1966, all in Bunting, Box 32, Folder 494.

42 Bunting oral history, interview no. 6, Oct. 3, 1978, p. 168.

Most important to undergraduates' daily lives were two decisions with respect to libraries, one at Radcliffe, the other at Harvard. The construction of a new undergraduate library for Radcliffe had been planned to follow completion of a new house, but the combination of strong interest on the part of undergraduates and the desires of the donor, Susan Morse Hilles, led to a change in priorities. In September 1966, the college opened Hilles library at the Radcliffe quadrangle. The student columnist for the *Radcliffe Quarterly* called the new library "breathtaking." It not only served the needs of Radcliffe women for library and study purposes but also immediately attracted large numbers of Harvard men. As Bunting commented, there were "generally more men than women in the building." One staff member remarked, "Radcliffe is no longer an appendage; Hilles has tied the College to the University."[43]

Equally important to Radcliffe undergraduates was the decision in the spring of 1967 to open Lamont, Harvard's undergraduate library, to women students, who had been excluded from the facility on the grounds that they would distract Harvard men from their studies. The *Harvard Crimson* announced the news with the headline "Lamont Will Open to Cliffies after Twenty Celibate Years." Noting that the move would have been "inconceivable" when Lamont first opened, the student columnist for the *Radcliffe Quarterly* described it as "the crumbling of but one more male bastion in Harvard Yard."[44]

In the meantime, the Radcliffe trustees continued to consider the question of merger. A small ad hoc group met in late January 1966 to explore the pros and cons.[45] Although no formal conclusions were reached, the group sensed that the case for merger had not yet been made in a compelling fashion and that it was not

43 Radcliffe College, *Report of the President, 1961–1964*, pp. 9–10; Radcliffe College, *Report of the President, 1965–1967*, pp. 5–6 (the quotes from Bunting and the staff member are on p. 6); Linda J. Greenhouse, "On Campus," *Radcliffe Quarterly* 50 (Nov.–Dec. 1966): 11 ("breathtaking").

44 Linda J. Greenhouse, "On Campus," *Radcliffe Quarterly* 51 (Feb.–Mar. 1967): 20 (source of the quotes); Marcia G. Synnott, "The Changing 'Harvard Student': Ethnicity, Race, and Gender," in Ulrich, ed., *Yards and Gates*, p. 205.

45 Minutes of meeting of ad hoc group, Jan. 27, 1966, and The Report of the Ad Hoc Committee on Merger, 1st draft, n.d., both in Bunting, Box 35, Folder 542.

the time to act on such a proposal.[46] Gilbert sent the first draft
of the ad hoc committee's report to Bunting for advice on what
might be reported to the board. Bunting expressed disappointment
in the results of the discussion. She had imagined that the purpose of the committee was "to decide what the arrangement would
or could be if Radcliffe was incorporated within Harvard." What
would be lost? What would be gained? How would incorporation
best be accomplished? She could accept the committee's conclusion
that "the time was [not] ripe" for incorporation, but she would be
sorry if the matter were allowed to drop without trustees "either
listening to a proponent or clarifying the possibilities."[47]

In the fall of 1966, Bunting took a more measured approach
with the Radcliffe trustees. She had hoped to come to them with a
plan for consummation of a marriage between Harvard and Radcliffe, to be accomplished by the time of Radcliffe's hundredth anniversary in 1979. But with "pressing fund-raising plans at both
Harvard and Radcliffe," she recognized that the time was not
right to open the question of reorganization. "The engagement
is progressing happily," she said, "and although I would not wish
to prolong it indefinitely there are valid reasons for not pressing
now. The time to give serious consideration to reorganization will
come later."[48]

The Student Movement and the Push for Coresidence

In fact, the matter was dropped for the next three years. For their
part, Radcliffe students, like their counterparts at Harvard, were
preoccupied with other matters.

In November 1966, Secretary of Defense Robert S. McNamara,
the cabinet member most closely identified with the Vietnam War,

46 Thaddeus R. Beal to Helen Gilbert, Feb. 7, 1966; Robert Gardiner to Gilbert, Feb. 8,
1966; and W. J. Bender to Gilbert, Feb. 9, 1966, all in Bunting, Box 35, Folder 542.

47 Memorandum, Helen Homans Gilbert to Mary I. Bunting, [Feb. 1966,] and
Bunting, handwritten notes in response to Gilbert, Feb. 27, 1966, both in Bunting, Box 35,
Folder 542.

48 Mary I. Bunting remarks, dinner meeting of the Radcliffe Board of Trustees, Nov. 16,
1966, Gilbert, Box 1, Folder 6.

came to the Harvard campus to address students. Some hundred men and women from Harvard and Radcliffe surrounded Mc-Namara's car outside Quincy House, rocking the vehicle back and forth as they shouted protests and obscenities. Narrowly escaping injury, McNamara re-entered the house and made his way to Harvard Yard through an underground tunnel.

In May 1967, twenty-three Radcliffe students began a hunger strike to protest the college's policy of allowing only a few seniors to live off campus. In October of the same year, protesting the use of chemicals in the war in Vietnam, several hundred Harvard and Radcliffe students barricaded recruiters from Dow Chemical Company inside a laboratory building at Harvard where they had been conducting interviews.

In December 1968, some twenty African American women sat in the hallway outside the president's office at Radcliffe to protest the college's record in enrolling African American students and hiring African Americans in the admission office. And in December, too, some two hundred Harvard and Radcliffe students, many of them members of SDS, forced their way into a Harvard faculty meeting to protest the ROTC's presence on campus.[49]

It was in this context that the issue of the relationship between Harvard and Radcliffe resurfaced in quite specific form. In January 1969 a proposal was put forth for a trial exchange of students to take up residence in dormitories on each other's campuses. The proposal grew out of the work of the student Harvard-Radcliffe Policy Committee (HRPC), which observed that the two institutions were "essentially coeducational" with respect to classes and extracurricular activities but not at all coeducational in terms of dining and residence, the two venues where "the presence or absence of coeducation has the greatest effects upon students' lives." It was difficult for Harvard men to develop informal relationships with women; indeed, it was hard for them even to meet women. Women were primarily "dating partners"; they were "seen as something different,

49 Elaine Yaffe, *Mary Ingraham Bunting: Her Two Lives* (Savannah, GA: Frederic C. Beil, 2005), ch. 22; Keller and Keller, *Making Harvard Modern*, pp. 307–14; Linda J. Greenhouse, "On Campus," *Radcliffe Quarterly* 52 (Feb.–Mar. 1968): 20–21; Anne de Saint Phalle, "On Campus," *Radcliffe Quarterly* 53 (Mar. 1969): 25–26.

something fundamentally apart from men, something unusual and separate." As a result, the committee said, "Men do not have a chance to really get to know women as people, to be exposed to the different point of view and perspective that women often have." Radcliffe students, too, had trouble developing informal relationships with the opposite sex, rarely interacting with them in settings other than weekend dates, often seeing them as "unusual and different." Ultimately, "permanent coeducational housing" should be instituted "on a college-wide basis." For the short run, a trial exchange should be instituted for the fall of 1969.[50]

The student leaders of the HRPC were stunned to learn from Pusey that Harvard would not consider taking on oversight responsibility for Radcliffe students in residence until the larger question of the relationship of Harvard and Radcliffe could be settled. He told the students that "Harvard was very willing to merge with Radcliffe, but would consider such a step only at such time as Radcliffe College requested that Harvard do so." The corporation, he said, saw "total de facto administrative responsibility as a pre-requisite to considering residential coeducation, even at the experimental level." Among other things, Radcliffe and Harvard students were under the authority of separate deans and separate administrative boards, which handled matters of discipline and determined satisfactory academic progress. It would be difficult, if not impossible, to make the coresidence system work under those circumstances. Pusey later confirmed to the *Harvard Crimson* that "as things stand, with divided authority, Harvard could not take on the responsibility of overseeing Cliffies."[51] At the same time, Pusey rejected on the same grounds a proposal for coeducational housing from the faculty masters of Winthrop House at Harvard and Currier, the new house under construction at Radcliffe. Mixed

50 Harvard-Radcliffe Policy Committee, Report on Coeducation at Harvard and Radcliffe, Jan. 5, 1969, May, Box 10, Folder 152. For a fine study of the campaign for coresidence, see Marie Hicks, "The Price of Excellence: Coresidence and Women's Integration at Oxford and Harvard Universities, 1964–1977" (unpublished senior thesis, Harvard University, Mar. 23, 2000), Radcliffe College Archives.

51 Mary K. Tolbert to Mary I. Bunting, Jan. 15, 1969, Bunting, Box 42a, Folder 656; *Harvard Crimson*, Jan. 16, 1969, clipping in Bunting, Box 40, Folder 624.

housing would have to wait until Radcliffe was administratively part of Harvard.[52]

Pusey wanted to accomplish merger. Encouraging students to lobby for it was likely to help his cause. As Bunting said, "Student pressures provided the leverage . . . to make us all take another look at the merger question." The presidents agreed to take up the question again with their respective boards. As Bunting told the *Radcliffe Quarterly*, "Mr. Pusey responded to students' inquiries about coeducational living by saying that there could be no experiments as long as Radcliffe and Harvard were under separate managements and that if merger were to occur, Radcliffe must ask. This was . . . an invitation, one that I thought we could not ignore."[53]

After two students presented arguments for coeducational housing at a meeting in February 1969 of the Radcliffe council, the group of administrators and trustees responsible for setting policy for the college, Bunting called a special meeting of the Radcliffe board of trustees to consider the question.[54] In the meantime, the Radcliffe alumnae association revived discussions about what merger would mean for the Radcliffe name and identity, for Radcliffe alumnae, for representation of women on decision-making boards at Harvard, and for attention to the needs of women alumnae and graduate students.[55] With Yale and Princeton embarking on coeducation, the president of the association wrote to alumnae,

52 *Harvard Crimson*, Jan. 20, 1969, clipping in Bunting, Box 40, Folder 624.

53 Bunting oral history, interview no. 8, Oct. 5, 1978, pp. 232–34 ("the leverage"— the quote is on p. 234); "Would You Answer Some Questions about the Merger, President Bunting?," *Radcliffe Quarterly* 53 (Mar. 1969): 2.

54 *Harvard Crimson*, Feb. 6, 1969, clipping in Bunting, Box 40, Folder 624. For some student views, see, e.g., Marcy Weintraub and Martha F. Miller to Mary I. Bunting, Feb. 18, 1969; Christine P. Almy to Bunting, Feb. 19, 1969; Judith Seligson to Bunting, Feb. 20, 1969; and Eleanor B. Emmons to Bunting, Feb. 21, 1969, all in Bunting, Box 42a, Folder 656. See also "Do You Know . . . What Merger Will Mean? What Coeducational Living Will Mean?," typescript distributed by students to Radcliffe trustees, Feb. 1969, Bunting, Box 42a, Folder 655.

55 Special Concerns of Radcliffe Alumnae Association Board about the Future, attached to Ruth G. Wright to Mary I. Bunting, Jan. 23, 1969, and Radcliffe College Alumnae Association, Committee on Recommendations to the President, Preliminary Statement on Projected Harvard-Radcliffe Merger, Feb. 14, 1969, both in Bunting, Box 40, Folder 618; "The Question of Merger," *Radcliffe Quarterly* 53 (Aug. 1969): 21–23.

there was "reason to believe that Harvard also is now ready to assume full responsibility for undergraduate women." And there was "an indication that Harvard would welcome us to full membership as part of Harvard."[56]

Radcliffe and Harvard students lobbied for merger. "Harvard Radcliffe merger now please," a telegram from a group of students read.[57] A Harvard freshman bemoaned the lack of "opportunity for me to normally sit down and talk with a bunch of girls as I can with a bunch of boys."[58] One of his classmates spelled out the "social, intellectual and personal" gains that would be realized by adding women to the Harvard houses.[59] Three Harvard men wrote to ask the Radcliffe trustees to "eliminate the outmoded and unnecessary barriers to coeducation" so that Harvard and Radcliffe could "keep pace with the other progressive institutions."[60] And from four Radcliffe seniors came a letter calling for full merger: "We want to go to Harvard, ought to go to Harvard, and go to Harvard as much as we can at present. We wanted to go to <u>Harvard</u>; we came to Radcliffe because it was then as close as we could get. Radcliffe's primary raison d'être has always been to let girls go to Harvard as much as possible." Division by sex in housing and dining, they argued, was "artificial and unhealthy" for both sexes. "Since we academically <u>do</u> go to Harvard, and since virtually all of our outside activities are centered there, the remaining barriers to our full participation in the Harvard community are annoying anomalies."[61]

As the news of merger discussions made the national press, Radcliffe alumnae began to weigh in. There were strong views on both sides. A member of the class of 1949 in Princeton Junction, New Jersey, sent a telegram calling merger "inevitable and desirable."[62]

56 Ruth G. Wright to Radcliffe Alumna, Feb. 20, 1969, Bunting, Box 40, Folder 618.

57 Telegram, Marian Petrides et al. to Mary I. Bunting, Feb. 21, 1969, Bunting, Box 42a, Folder 656.

58 Daniel A. Gensler to Mary I. Bunting, Feb. 20, 1969, Bunting, Box 42a, Folder 656.

59 Stephen A. Schifferes to Mary I. Bunting, Feb. 20, 1969, Bunting, Box 42a, Folder 656.

60 Garrison Bliss et al. to Trustees, Feb. 20, 1969, Bunting, Box 42a, Folder 656.

61 Judith Anderson et al. to the Trustees of Radcliffe College, Feb. 21, 1969, Bunting, Box 42a, Folder 656.

62 Telegram, Jennifer Selfridge Macleod to Mary I. Bunting, Feb. 19, 1969, Bunting, Box 42a, Folder 656.

From a graduate in the class of 1937 in Westwood, Massachusetts, came a letter voicing vehement "objection to any move on the part of Radcliffe's trustees which would mean the eventual disappearance of Radcliffe College." As for coeducational housing, the alumna wrote, "Why should Radcliffe cheapen itself and bow to the tide of what amounts to immoral and/or amoral innovation in regard to housing, merely to be 'up-to-date'?"[63]

On Saturday, February 22, 1969, after a six-hour meeting, the Radcliffe trustees voted by a substantial majority to ask the Radcliffe council "to initiate discussion with the President and Fellows of Harvard College with a view to merging the two institutions." The council voted later that day to implement the trustee recommendation.[64] The *Harvard Crimson*, publishing a special edition on Sunday, declared in a banner headline, "'Cliffe Finally Proposes Marriage to Ten Thousand Men of Harvard." Merger negotiations, the newspaper said, were set to begin when the Harvard corporation met on March 3. "The union of the two schools," the paper opined, was "inevitable, but the wedding day may still be some time away."[65]

When the national press announced the same news, students, alumnae, and others wrote to register their views, for and against. Bunting made plain where she stood. "For a long time," she wrote to one correspondent, "I have felt that it would be advantageous to women students to be full members of Harvard. . . . I see the move as fulfillment for Radcliffe."[66]

---

63 Marie L. Paraboschi to Mary I. Bunting, Feb. 19, 1969, Bunting, Box 42a, Folder 656.

64 Minutes, Radcliffe College Board of Trustees, Feb. 22, 1969, Gilbert, Box 1, Folder 6; minutes, Council of Radcliffe College, Feb. 22, 1969, Bunting, Box 41, Folder 629; Mary I. Bunting to Nathan M. Pusey, Feb. 24, 1969, Bunting, Box 41, Folder 646.

65 *Harvard Crimson*, Feb. 23, 1969, clipping in Bunting, Box 42a, Folder 655.

66 Mary I. Bunting to Elizabeth L. Cless, Feb. 24, 1969, Bunting, Box 42a, Folder 656.

3

Yale: "Girls Are People, Just Like You and Me"

Yale University had been educating women graduate students in the arts and sciences and in the professional schools for almost a century before undergraduate coeducation was ever contemplated. The school of fine art admitted its first degree candidates in 1869 and awarded the first Yale degree to a woman in 1891. Women had been attending classes in the graduate school of arts and sciences for some time before the corporation—the university's governing board—voted in 1892 to admit women to candidacy for the doctoral degree. The first Yale doctorates were awarded to women in 1894, and by 1900 Yale led all universities in the United States in the number of Ph.D.s awarded to women.

Yale's school of nursing was exclusively female during its first three decades and was the first unit of the university to have a female dean. The Yale corporation voted in the spring of 1916 to admit women to the medical school, pending the acquisition of funding for necessary physical alterations. The first women matriculated that fall after the father of one of the applicants—a Yale economics professor—donated funds to build women's bathrooms. The law school admitted women to degree candidacy in 1919, and the divinity school admitted them in 1932.[1]

---

1 Shilpa Raval, "Introducing Women to Yale," in Yale University Women Faculty Forum, *Gender Matters: Women and Yale in Its Third Century* (Yale University, [2002?]), pp. 26–27; Henry W. Farnam to Arthur T. Hadley, Mar. 31, 1916 [re bathrooms at the medical school], in Steering Committee on the 40th Anniversary of Coeducation,

Undergraduate Coeducation: The Opening Salvo

Undergraduate coeducation was another matter: more complicated, trickier to contemplate, not to be hurried. The first formal mention of the prospect came from Yale's dean of admission, Arthur Howe, Jr., in September 1956. Presenting his annual report to the faculty, Howe characterized all-male schools as "outmoded"—"harmful, academically and socially." He said that a good number of students he would have liked to attract to Yale—"the brightest and best" in the secondary schools he visited—"did not apply or considered Yale their second choice because it was single-sex." They had the feeling, he said, "that co-educational institutions were more natural, more realistic, more progressive." Losing strong prospects on those grounds, often to "lesser" institutions, was hard to stomach. Yale should think about admitting women.[2]

Someone gave the story to a local radio station, and the *New York Times* reported the next day that Yale was considering coeducation. Yale's president, A. Whitney Griswold, declared that Yale was "far from being convinced that it would be the right course of action. There is not the remotest possibility of its taking place at Yale within the foreseeable future."[3] When Griswold attended a meeting with McGeorge Bundy, a Yale graduate then serving as dean of the faculty of arts and sciences at Harvard, Bundy teased him about the Howe proposal; Griswold, in turn, penned a humorous response:

Reflections on Coeducation: A Critical History of Women at Yale (Yale College, 2010), p. 37. The last school to admit women—forestry and environmental studies—did so in 1967.

2 Howe, quoted in three sources: *New York Times*, Sept. 29, 1956, reprinted in Pamela Geismar, Eve Hart Rice, and Joan O'Meara Winant, eds., *Fresh Women: Reflections on Coeducation and Life after Yale, 1969, 1989, 2009* (New Haven, CT: Privately published, 2010), p. 140 ("outmoded"); Tony Reese, "When Yale Needed 'Girls,'" *New Journal* 17 (Mar. 1, 1985): 9, in Heller, Box 1, Folder 5 ("did not apply"); and Jerome Karabel, *The Chosen: The Hidden History of Admission and Exclusion at Harvard, Yale, and Princeton* (Boston and New York: Houghton Mifflin, 2005), p. 417 ("harmful," "brightest and best," "more natural," "lesser").

3 Griswold quoted in *New York Times*, Sept. 30, 1956, reprinted in Geismar, Rice, and Winant, eds., *Fresh Women*, p. 141.

By keeping in step with the male,
We proceed at the pace of a snail,
Said the Dean of Admissions,
Let's shift our positions
And get some fast women at Yale.[4]

The *Yale Daily News* welcomed Griswold's denial. "Oh save us!" the paper exclaimed: "Oh save us from the giggling crowds, the domestic lecture, and the home economics classes of a female infiltration. . . . We will not spend our 25th reunion drinking with overweight matrons and their husbands who went to Hofstra. And the library stacks will not be an indoor lovers lane, and Mory's on Friday afternoons will not be the scene of chattering bridge parties."[5]

"I think the way it got out did more than anything to postpone coeducation by 10 years," Howe later reflected. "The President's Office was swamped with letters from disgruntled alumni. The only significant development that came out of my suggestion was an increased awareness of the possibility."[6]

The Yale faculty first expressed support for the admission of undergraduate women in the unanimous adoption in April 1962 of the report of the president's committee on the freshman year, which said that coeducation should be part of Yale's future. Yale had "a national duty, as well as a duty to itself, to provide the rigorous training for women that we supply for men."[7] Getting there, however, was to be a slow, non-linear process that reflected the evolving thinking of the new president of the university, Kingman

4 Griswold, quoted in Reuben A. Holden, *Profiles and Portraits of Yale University Presidents* (Freeport, ME: Bond Wheelwright, 1968), p. 136, n. 5.

5 Editorial, *Yale Daily News*, Sept. 30, 1956, reprinted in Geismar, Rice, and Winant, eds., *Fresh Women*, p. 143.

6 Howe, quoted in Reese, "When Yale Needed 'Girls,'" 11.

7 *The Report of the President's Committee on the Freshman Year* (New Haven, CT: Yale University Press, April 1962), p. 12, quoted in Elga R. Wasserman, "Coeducation Comes to Yale College," *Educational Record* (Spring 1970): 144, in Wasserman I, Box 35, Folder 1029 (source of the quote); Yale University news release, Proposal for Coeducation in Yale College, presented by President Kingman Brewster, Jr., of Yale to the faculty on Nov. 14, 1968, Brewster I, Box 222, Folder 14.

Brewster, Jr., and took an unexpected detour through Poughkeep-sie, New York.

The Brewster Imperatives

Brewster, a graduate of Yale in the class of 1941, had been well known as an undergraduate: chairman of the *Yale Daily News*; a founder of the Yale chapter of America First, the student-initiated organization committed to keeping the United States out of the war in Europe; a student who had turned down membership in the most prestigious of Yale secret societies, Skull and Bones, in objection to the secrecy that went along with its exclusiveness. After renouncing his non-interventionist commitments and serving in the U.S. Navy from 1942 to 1946, Brewster enrolled at Harvard Law School, where he then taught from 1950 to 1960. He returned to Yale in 1960 at Griswold's invitation to become provost of the university. When Griswold died in 1963, the corporation, after a national search, elected Brewster president, a position he held until 1977, when President Jimmy Carter named him U.S. ambassador to the Court of St. James's.[8]

It was clear from the start of his presidency that Brewster recognized the imperative to bring undergraduate women to New Haven, but he felt that a stronger imperative needed to be attended to first. Yale's student body had been exceptionally homogeneous: white, Anglo-Saxon, Protestant, often the sons of alumni, predominantly from private preparatory schools, especially the boarding schools of New England and the Middle Atlantic states. Brewster understood that to continue to fulfill its mission as one of the world's leading institutions of higher education, Yale would have to diversify. In 1965 he appointed a new admission dean, R. Inslee ("Inky") Clark '57, with a mandate to modernize Yale admissions.[9]

---

8 Geoffrey Kabaservice, *The Guardians: Kingman Brewster, His Circle, and the Rise of the Liberal Establishment* (New York: Henry Holt, 2004), passim; Holden, *Profiles and Portraits of Yale University Presidents*, pp. 147–48.

9 On the evolution of admission policy and practice at Yale in the Brewster years, see Joseph A. Soares, *The Power of Privilege: Yale and America's Elite Colleges* (Stanford, CA: Stanford University Press, 2007), ch. 4.

Just eight years out of college, Clark was a surprising choice. He had taught at the Lawrenceville School after his graduation from Yale; he had joined the admission office in 1961 as the junior member of the staff, and he was serving in a part-time post as dean of Trumbull College, one of Yale's twelve undergraduate residential colleges. A public-school graduate whose father had not gone to college, Clark had been a member of Skull and Bones and president of the inter-fraternity council. To some people on campus who wanted to see changes in undergraduate admissions— including the university chaplain, William Sloane Coffin—Clark was an Old Blue, "too Yale . . . traditional Yale," which made him an unlikely agent of change.[10]

Yet Clark moved decisively to make change happen. He hired new staff in the admission office—public-school graduates, non-Yale people, a black man (the first in the office), younger men—the sorts of people who would embrace the new "mission of going out and talent searching and finding and digging, as opposed to going to where the [applicants] had always come from."[11] As Clark explained later, "I wanted to strengthen and deepen the applicant pool to secure stronger representation from groups not traditionally in it." Brewster put it this way: "Inky beat the bushes in areas Yale had not really approached before." The result was a significant increase in the number of public-school, ethnic minority, Catholic and Jewish, and non–East Coast students. To take one example: In the class of 1963, 44 percent of Yale students had graduated from public schools; in the class of 1971, the number had risen to 61 percent.[12] By the time Clark left his post in 1970 to take up the headmastership of the Horace Mann School in New York City, Yale looked very different than it had when he had taken over as dean of admission. For all the gains in diversification, however, there were also costs, because prep-school students and alumni sons appeared to be at a disadvantage in a process that had previously favored them.[13]

10 Clark oral history, Apr. 8, 1993, pp. 2, 29 (Coffin quote), and May 13, 1993, p. 26.
11 Ibid., Apr. 8, 1993, p. 34.
12 Clark and Brewster, quoted in Reese, "When Yale Needed 'Girls,'" 11; Clark oral history, Apr. 8, 1993, pp. 35–45.
13 Haskins oral history, p. 34.

An encounter in the spring of 1966 between Clark and members of the Yale corporation illustrated how wrenching these moves were for many Old Blues. Clark had been summoned to report on the changes he was implementing. As Geoffrey Kabaservice tells the story:

Clark . . . described the process leading up to the admission of his first class . . . and the new emphasis he had placed on talent spotting, merit, and diversity. One of the Corporation members . . . finally said, "Let me get down to basics. You're admitting an entirely different class than we're used to. You're admitting them for a different purpose than training leaders." . . . Clark responded that in a changing America, leaders might come from nontraditional sources, including public high school graduates, Jews, minorities, and even women. His interlocutor shot back, "You're talking about Jews and public school graduates as leaders. Look around you at this table"—he waved a hand at Brewster, [John] Lindsay, [Paul] Moore, Bill Bundy. . . . "These are America's leaders. There are no Jews here. There are no public school graduates here."

The implication was plain: The Yale establishment, committed to producing leaders, believed that the goal could best be accomplished by replicating the Yale establishment.[14]

The rapidity of change in the composition of the student body helped to stoke alumni discontent with Brewster. Harold Howe II, U.S. commissioner of education in the administration of President Lyndon Johnson and later vice president for education at the Ford Foundation, a corporation member who was the brother of Clark's predecessor as dean, later remarked that Arthur Howe "always argued that he was launched on a slow, gradual change" in the mix of students admitted to Yale "and that a very high proportion of the alumni's discontent with Kingman might have been avoided if that

14 Kabaservice, *The Guardians*, p. 259. I am indebted to William G. Bowen for underscoring the significance of this passage.

process had not been so rapidly moved by Inky Clark, who became a cheerleader for it, and was egged on by Kingman." Harold Howe said that Arthur thought that "by going at it five to ten years more slowly, they would have avoided the disturbance of the alumni about their kids not getting in, because it was happening gradually."[15]

Other members of the corporation thought that Clark was the problem. William P. Bundy, who served in the CIA during the Eisenhower administration and in the defense and state departments during the Kennedy and Johnson administrations, said that Clark was "a drastic change man" with "a real radical streak" who had not been straightforward in his dealings with the corporation. He "had a rather disruptive influence," Bundy concluded, "not because his ideas were wrong, but because his way of executing them was peremptory and really unconstitutional to a degree."[16] J. Richardson Dilworth, a financier and philanthropist who was head of the family office and senior adviser to the Rockefeller family, as well as a member of the corporation from 1959 to 1986, the last thirteen of those years as senior fellow, "kept the pressure on" Brewster to recognize the trouble Clark was causing. "It took [Brewster] about two years," Dilworth said later, "to get it clear in his mind that Clark was not only a menace but a real complication in terms of his subsequent efforts at fund raising—not so much because of what Clark was trying to do, but rather the arrogance and his way of doing it."[17]

Competition Kicks In

It was against the background of significant change in the composition of the undergraduate student body that Brewster began to address the question of women at Yale. He did so for three

15 Howe oral history, p. 32.

16 WP Bundy oral history, May 10, 1991, pp. 34–35 ("change man," "radical streak"), and Apr. 24, 1992, p. 13 ("disruptive influence"); Bundy obituary, *New York Times*, Oct. 7, 2000, http://www.nytimes.com/2000/10/07/us/william-p-bundy-83-dies-advised-3 -presidents-on-American-policy-in-Vietnam.html, accessed Jan. 1, 2015.

17 Dilworth oral history, p. 17; Dilworth obituary, *New York Times*, Dec. 31, 1997, www.nytimes.com/1997/12/31/arts/j-richardson-dilworth-81-philanthropist.html, accessed Jan. 1, 2015.

reasons. The first was competitive. Yale wanted its share of the best high school students, and Yale's single-sex status, Brewster said, was becoming "a real handicap in getting the best men." Second, there were "a lot of good [women] students" in the high schools, and "there was a growing sense" that Yale was missing out on them. Third, "the whole life of the place was less civilized than it would be if women were not considered a weekend freak, but were taken for granted as part of the landscape."[18]

Competitiveness was the key issue. Yale had been accustomed to going head to head with Harvard in competing for the most compelling applicants. Even as late as 1960, Harvard, Yale, and Princeton were drawing reasonably evenly among cross-admits. The presidency of a charismatic young Harvard man, John F. Kennedy, had begun to stir increasing interest in Harvard, but the growing desire of high school boys to go to college with girls skewed the balance decisively toward Cambridge.[19] By 1965, as Jerome Karabel has noted, "Harvard lost only one admit in seven to other institutions, but Yale lost one in three. Even more disturbing, Yale was losing 86 percent of students admitted to both institutions." When Yale asked students admitted to the class of 1969 to explain why they were not coming to New Haven, the students pointed to "proximity to girls' colleges" and "coeducational undergraduate programs" as reasons to matriculate elsewhere. These factors were especially influential in explaining decisions to choose Harvard over Yale.[20] Coeducation was an obvious remedy.

Bringing undergraduate women to Yale as a matter of principle was one thing. How to do it, however, was more complicated. In the beginning, Brewster strongly preferred something other than straightforward coeducation, and he first imagined establishing a coordinate college for women. He addressed the prospect in fits and starts, with some initiatives that, once started, did not seem to accomplish very much; with others that, though more fully explored, were unsuccessful; and finally, with a decision for coeducation that

---

18 Brewster oral history, pp. 16–17. On the theme of the need to admit women in order to continue to attract first-rate male students, see also Kernan oral history, p. 33.

19 Telephone interview with Derek Bok, Jan. 21, 2015.

20 Karabel, *The Chosen*, p. 416.

appeared hasty and precipitous rather than the result of a careful, orderly process.

The Yale corporation first took up the question of women undergraduates in March 1966, when it received the report of the committee on Yale College of the university council, an alumni advisory body established during the Griswold presidency. Among other recommendations, the report advocated the admission of women to Yale College. Brewster made plain that he opposed reducing the number of male students to make room for women or increasing the size of the student body; instead he "favored a separate but coordinate college whose students would be able to attend Yale classes." After discussion, "the sense of the meeting was that the Corporation favored a study of the possibilities of a coordinate college, but opposed the introduction of women at the expense of men."[21]

The next day, the corporation approved the following resolution: "The Corporation recognizes the need for high quality education for women, and is interested in exploring how Yale might contribute to meeting this need. . . . The Corporation would not favor admitting women if it required reducing the number of men in Yale College. . . . The Corporation would prefer a Coordinate College approach rather than the expansion of Yale College to accommodate women."[22]

News of the corporation's action stirred up predictable reactions from alumni, who defended their all-male education in spirited letters to the *Yale Alumni Magazine*. "There is a glory to tradition," one alumnus wrote from Washington, D.C. He continued,

> I think of the girl filled weekend—the cocktail party, the dances, the plays . . . the big football game. Then there is the adventure of . . . journeying to the girls' colleges. . . . And gentlemen—let's face it—charming as women are—they get to be a drag if you are forced to associate with them

21 Minutes, Committee of the Whole, Yale Corporation, Mar. 11, 1966, Vassar-Yale, Box 4, Folder 30.

22 Corporation statement concerning the admission of women as undergraduate students at Mar. 12, 1966, meeting, Brewster I, Box 4, Folder 5.

each and every day. Think of the poor student who has a steady date—he wants to concentrate on the basic principles of thermodynamics, but she keeps trying to gossip about the idiotic trivia all women try to impose on men.[23]

"The word 'Yale,'" a 1926 graduate opined, "has . . . a meaning of its own in which the element of masculinity is clearly dominant. . . . The turtleneck sweater, the curved pipe, the bulldog shoes may bring a laugh, but underneath it all lies a pride that every Yale man understands."[24]

Exploring a Yale-Vassar Affiliation

Alumni need not have worried in mid-1966 that coeducation was going to disrupt their treasured male sanctuary. It was very clear, as Brewster later wrote, that Yale could not "afford to divert substantial . . . resources to this cause." The assumption of the corporation was that "the greater part of the financing of a new women's college would have to come from sources which would not otherwise be likely to help Yale meet [its pressing] needs"— from those "more interested in this development than in anything else they might do to support the institution."[25]

There were no such prospects then, but a fortuitous suggestion gave Brewster an opening. Julius Stratton, chairman of the Ford Foundation, former president of the Massachusetts Institute of Technology, and a trustee of Vassar College, set up a meeting between Brewster and the president of Vassar, Alan Simpson, to discuss the possibility of a relationship between Yale and Vassar. It was not a new idea; Brewster's and Simpson's predecessors, Griswold and Sarah Gibson Blanding, had had a conversation about it in 1961, followed by a meeting of some Yale and Vassar trustees, but nothing had come of it. Simpson, a British-born, Oxford-educated

23 Conrad Yung-Kwai, letter to the editor, *Yale Alumni Magazine* 29 (July 1966): 3.

24 Quoted in "'On the Advisability and Feasibility of Women at Yale': The Coeducation Debate at Yale College," *Yale Alumni Magazine* 73 (Sept.–Oct. 2009): 45.

25 Kingman Brewster, Jr., *Report of the President, Yale University: 1966–67* (Nov. 1967), pp. 2, 34.

historian, had been dean of the college at the University of Chicago when he was named president of Vassar in 1964. Initially committed to Vassar's future as a small liberal arts college for women, he changed his mind in the face of difficulties in faculty recruitment, concerns about Vassar's competitiveness in admissions, and reports of student dissatisfaction with Vassar's geographical isolation from men's colleges. Simpson was interested in alternative options for Vassar's future. Stratton thought a conversation between the two men might be productive.[26]

Moreover, Brewster and Simpson had personal connections that reinforced the potential wisdom of Stratton's idea. Brewster's wife, Mary Louise, had been a member of Vassar's class of 1943. When she left Vassar in her senior year to marry Kingman, he had remarked to Griswold, "If I can't offer her as much as Vassar, what the hell good am I?"[27] The Brewsters had already visited the college during Simpson's tenure, and the two couples had struck up a friendship.[28] There were other ties between the two institutions as well. They shared a trustee, Harold Howe. And another Vassar trustee, Kate Hadley, was the wife of Morris Hadley, a member of the Yale corporation.[29]

Brewster and Simpson met on December 4, 1966. Within less than two weeks, the Yale corporation and the Vassar board of trustees had approved a study of "the possibilities of cooperation by the two institutions, including the desirability and feasibility of relocating Vassar College in New Haven as an independent coordinate college."[30] For Vassar, the prospect of "such a brilliant partnership," as Simpson put it, had the potential to address his concerns by providing "a wider field for [the college's] modern

26 Elizabeth A. Daniels and Clyde Griffen, *"Full Steam Ahead in Poughkeepsie":*
The Story of Coeducation at Vassar, 1966–1974 (Vassar College, 2000), pp. 16–23; "A
Visit with Miss Sarah Gibson Blanding," *Vassar Chronicle*, Apr. 1976, p. 3. On Stratton's
enthusiasm for the idea, see Miller oral history, p. 13.

27 Kingman Brewster, Jr., to A. Whitney Griswold, Dec. 23, 1942, quoted in Kabaservice, *The Guardians*, p. 294.

28 Reese, "When Yale Needed 'Girls,'" 11; interview with Henry Chauncey, Jr., Apr. 13,
2012, New Haven, CT; Vassar trustees (E), Mar. 15, 1966, pp. 10–11.

29 Howe oral history, pp. 13, 20.

30 Vote of the Board of Trustees of Vassar College, Dec. 14, 1966, and Vote of the Yale
Corporation, Dec. 16, 1966 (source of the quote), both in Vassar-Yale, Box 4, Folder 30.

mission than its historic home."[31] For Yale, in Brewster's words, the opportunity offered "the simplest and clearest way to carry out the intention of the Corporation" expressed in its March vote while at the same time making clear that "the interest is in hospitality to another institution, not 'coeducation' in any sense that would interfere with Yale['s] ancient purposes and the seeking of support for them."[32]

A joint committee of trustees of the two institutions, chaired by the two presidents, set the course for the study at an initial meeting in January 1967. The plan was to undertake a thorough analysis of the physical, financial, legal, and educational considerations involved in a possible move for Vassar from Poughkeepsie to New Haven. The work was to be carried out by the presidents, members of their administrative staffs, and members of their faculties.[33]

Funded by the Carnegie and Ford Foundations, the Vassar-Yale study unfolded over the next ten months. Many of the topics investigated were fundamentally educational: Which colleges and universities around the country provided good models of coordinate or other close inter-institutional relationships? How would the institutions deal with the different statures of the Vassar and Yale faculties and the different salary scales? Which Yale departments could absorb more students without having to add more faculty members? What would be appropriate opportunities for Vassar-specific instruction by Vassar faculty members? The study group explored more practical issues as well: Vassar had a beautiful campus in Poughkeepsie with a profusion of stately trees; where would a new Vassar campus in New Haven be built? (Yale thought that the best plan might be to relocate the divinity school.)[34]

31 Alan Simpson, quoted in Joint Announcement of Vassar College and Yale University, Dec. 18, 1966, Vassar-Yale, Box 10, Folder 96.

32 Typescript, Kingman Brewster, Jr., letter, n.d. [Dec. 1966], Vassar-Yale, Box 4, Folder 30.

33 Agenda for Meeting of the Joint Trustee–Fellow Committee, Jan. 17, 1967, Vassar-Yale, Box 8, Folder 66; Joint Public Announcement, Vassar College and Yale University, Jan. 20, 1967, Vassar-Yale, Box 10, Folder 96.

34 Minutes, Meeting of Vassar-Yale Study Group, Feb. 3, 9, 13, 20, 23, and 27, Mar. 3 and 9, Apr. 13 and 21, and June 1, 1967, Vassar-Yale, Box 8, Folder 72. On the trees, see Reese, "When Yale Needed 'Girls,'" 11; Chauncey interview. On the Carnegie and

Brewster was personally enthusiastic about the possible move. In February 1967 he told more than a thousand Yale alumni and wives gathered in New Haven for the annual alumni day luncheon that the relocation would have substantial benefits for Yale. Yale, he said, could make "a crucial contribution to higher education in the United States" by helping to meet "the demand for first rate collegiate education for women." But altruism was not the overriding motive. "Our concern," Brewster was quick to point out, "is not so much what Yale can do for women but what can women do for Yale." Yale had been underutilizing academic resources that could be well used by women at a neighboring college. Including women in courses with Yale students would "enrich and enlarge the variety of interests, points of views, and values taken into consideration" in class discussions and stimulate "a higher level of performance" on everyone's part. And having "a first-rate women's undergraduate college in close proximity to the Yale campus," Brewster said, "would substantially raise the moral quality of the four undergraduate Yale College years" by encouraging the development of "a more normal social atmosphere" with "responsible relationships" between the sexes in place of Yale's typical "'here-today-and-gone-tomorrow' social life" of mixers, road trips, and big weekends.[35]

In September 1967, in a preliminary report to the joint trustee committee, Brewster reiterated his case. "The social and moral value of having two thousand college girls of outstanding intellectual and personal qualifications resident in New Haven is apparent," he said. Yale was "at a serious disadvantage" without them. "The crash week-end, the degrading form of social activity known as the Mixer, have been . . . a most unhealthy and unnatural part of the four Yale undergraduate years. Such an environment is not conducive to the development of a considerate, mature, and normal relationship among the sexes." In "the absence of a first-rate women's college," many of Yale's "best potential freshman candidates" were "choos[ing] to go elsewhere."

Ford funding, see Kingman Brewster, Jr., to Alan Pifer, Feb. 16, 1967, and Alan Simpson to Pifer, Feb. 18, 1967, Vassar-Yale, Box 10, Folder 96.

35 Text of remarks of President Kingman Brewster, Jr., Alumni Day Luncheon, Feb. 18, 1967, Brewster II, Box 258, Folder 5.

The advantages of bringing Vassar to New Haven were much more than social. There would likely be curricular innovations and opportunities that would benefit male and female students. "Mixed classes" would "provide a greater variety of views and perspectives and result in livelier and more highly motivated student work," and "the presence of the opposite sex" would enhance intellectual motivation and engagement, not distract from it. Moreover, the profusion of opportunities for cultural, political, and social activity outside the classroom would "be more normal and much richer" if "shared by women students of the first rank."[36]

The Vassar-Yale report laid out the basic assumptions undergirding the proposed partnership. The plan would be for "a coordinate arrangement rather than a merger or complete coeducation." Vassar would retain its corporate identity, trustees, administrators, and faculty; it would set its own degree requirements and issue its own degrees. Vassar faculty would be appointed to the Yale faculty "with full rights . . . on all matters except appointments and promotions." The same would be true of Yale faculty appointed to the faculty at Vassar. Committees would coordinate offerings and programs of study of the individual academic departments and make recommendations for junior faculty appointments, and a joint committee would make recommendations about appointment and promotion to the senior professorial ranks. Vassar faculty members might be invited to teach in the Yale graduate school or professional schools. Every attempt would be made to equalize teaching responsibilities and to bring Vassar faculty salaries up to the level of Yale's.[37]

As for curriculum, the operating assumption was that much of the introductory-level teaching would be done separately, that more advanced courses would generally be mixed, and that senior seminars and theses would be handled mainly on the home campus. Most of Vassar's classes would be accommodated in Yale

---

36 Kingman Brewster, Jr., "Yale's Perspective on the Vassar Affiliation," in *Vassar-Yale Report from the Joint Study Committee*, Sept. 1967, pp. 3–9, Manuscripts and Archives, Yale University Library.

37 *Vassar-Yale Report from the Joint Study Committee*, pp. 23, 31–44.

classrooms, though some classrooms would be constructed on the new Vassar campus.[38]

Outside the classroom, Vassar would continue to have its own student government and to set its own social rules. Some extracurricular activities would be conducted separately "to provide opportunities for leadership and participation for the largest possible number of undergraduate women," but many student activities would be merged. The two institutions would maintain their own residential and dining facilities. Yale, however, might take on certain functions for Vassar, including purchasing, human resources, housekeeping, maintenance and repairs, security, food services, mail and telephone services, and utilities.[39]

Simpson shared Brewster's enthusiasm for the proposed venture. "The education of undergraduate women in isolation from men has outlived its historical justification," he said in a brief introduction to the preliminary report. Yale and Vassar were "brilliant anachronisms." In that context, "the responsibility of those charged with the education of women is to see that their special needs—the elevation of their goals, the planning of their different lifespans, the fulfillment of their potentialities as human beings— are met within the context of either coordinate education or co-education." Affiliation with Yale would meet those needs while allowing Vassar "to concentrate . . . on our historic mission—the enlargement of the range of opportunities for educated women."[40]

The rhetoric of the two presidents notwithstanding, the proposed Vassar-Yale collaboration was a tough sell. Alvin Kernan, associate provost at Yale, who had principal operating responsibility there for the study, said later that the idea struck him as unrealistic. "It looked to me," he told an interviewer, "like it was a loser's game from the beginning."

I couldn't see why Vassar would want to move. I could see why Yale would like to bring Vassar down to New Haven,

38 Ibid., pp. 51–62, 93–96.
39 Ibid., pp. 68–69, 74–78. The quote is on pp. 68–69.
40 Alan Simpson, "Vassar's Perspective on the Yale Affiliation," in ibid., pp. 11–17.

and bring its endowment along with it, and its traditions, and a first-rate group of female students. But it seemed to me that there was nothing much to be gained for Vassar. . . . I used to go up frequently to Poughkeepsie to meet with various groups of faculty, and their questions were always, "What do you want us for?" and "What would it be like for us? Wouldn't we just be submerged when we went down to New Haven by the Yale faculty?" . . . I had to try to find some convincing arguments to give them. . . . I did my best, but it was uphill all the way.[41]

Harold Howe, the Vassar trustee who served simultaneously on the Yale corporation, echoed Kernan's skepticism. "Yale never gave Vassar a decent proposal," he reflected years later. "Kingman really waffled on that one. If he wanted Vassar to come down there, he had to crack the nut of trusting the Vassar faculty to be good people and to achieve some kind of tenure at Yale. He wouldn't do that. . . . The Yalies were never willing to make an offer of equality in the marriage. They were going to make an offer of second-hand citizenship. What's more, they were not even going to be generous with real estate."[42]

Not surprisingly, the proposed collaboration met with strong opposition from a significant proportion of Vassar's faculty and alumnae. Leaving aside the complexities of combining two institutions with different faculties and different academic standards, Vassar had a beautiful campus in Poughkeepsie, which had a powerful hold on alumnae. Early expectations that the buildings might be sold to IBM failed to be realized, and the impracticality of Vassar abandoning its century-old home to build a new campus in New Haven was apparent to most observers. Early on, opposition to relocation became so vocal that Simpson was forced to authorize simultaneous exploration of alternatives in Poughkeepsie for Vassar's future.

As the discussions proceeded, the intensity of alumnae discontent made plain to the Vassar trustees that a move to New Haven

41 Kernan oral history, p. 32.
42 Howe oral history, p. 22.

would be a mistake. The Vassar board held out some hope for a compromise position—perhaps Vassar might develop an experimental college in New Haven while the main Vassar campus remained in Poughkeepsie—but the Yale corporation was not interested in anything short of full relocation. In mid-November, Simpson met privately with Brewster to report that his board was ready to terminate the Vassar-Yale study. On November 20, before the report of the study had been circulated publicly, the Vassar trustees announced to the Vassar community that the college, "commit[ted] to the education of women" and determined to be "mistress in [its] own house," would "remain in its birthplace" and explore imaginative new designs for the future on-site in Poughkeepsie.[43] Disappointed though he may have been, Simpson reversed course and declared enthusiastically, "Full Speed Ahead in Poughkeepsie." At first the future seemed to hold the prospect of establishing a coordinate college for men near the Vassar campus, but in May 1968 the Vassar faculty voted overwhelmingly for full coeducation, a direction that the Vassar trustees endorsed in July, with the first male students slated to enroll in the fall of 1969.[44]

Brewster, too, was disappointed, but without missing a beat, he announced a change of direction for Yale. If Vassar would not become Yale's partner, Yale would look into founding a coordinate women's college in New Haven. Yale would not be starting from scratch; the Vassar study had provided a wealth of information that could be applied to plans for a new women's college. Such a college, Brewster said, would "promise an imaginative contribution to undergraduate education in general and the liberal education of women in particular."[45]

43 Daniels and Griffen, *"Full Steam Ahead in Poughkeepsie,"* pp. 26–48; A Proposal to Establish a Branch of Vassar College in New Haven, Nov. 6, 1967, and Alan Simpson to Kingman Brewster, Nov. 9, 1967, both in Brewster I, Box 218, Folder 13; A Statement by the Trustees of Vassar College, Nov. 20, 1967 (source of the quotes), Vassar-Yale, Box 10, Folder 96.

44 Daniels and Griffen, *"Full Steam Ahead in Poughkeepsie,"* pp. 46 (source of the quote), 50–52.

45 President Brewster's statement re Vassar's decision to remain in Poughkeepsie, Nov. 20, 1967, Brewster I, Box 218, Folder 13 (source of the quote); transcript, President Brewster press conference, Nov. 20, 1967, Vassar-Yale, Box 10, Folder 96.

After the Vassar Decision: A New Coordinate College for Yale?

In December 1967 Brewster established an advisory committee to aid in planning the new women's coordinate college. Its members were Rosemary Park, vice chancellor for educational planning and programs at the University of California, Los Angeles, a former president of Barnard and of Connecticut College for Women; Thaddeus R. Beal, a Yale alumnus of the class of 1939, president of the Harvard Trust Company in Cambridge, Massachusetts, and a trustee of Radcliffe; and Janet Brewster Murrow, a trustee of Mount Holyoke, widow of Edward R. Murrow (the iconic radio and television commentator), and Brewster's first cousin.[46]

Although the deliberations of the advisory committee were not recorded, we know from Brewster's writings that he imagined a range of possibilities for the education of women in New Haven. A "Vassar-type institution affiliated with Yale" with a traditional four-year program of study in the liberal arts was one option, but there were others. One of them, Brewster wrote in May 1968 in a discursive document that he shared with the advisory committee, was to break the four-year pattern and concentrate either on the first two years of college or on the last two. A second was to create interdisciplinary programs that would take advantage of special curricular strengths in Yale College and the professional schools in areas that might be of particular interest to women, including the direction, administration, and management of arts and culture; the delivery of health care; and urban and neighborhood planning, policy, and administration. And there was an opportunity to consider a more flexible program of study instead of the highly regimented four consecutive years of study expected of undergraduate men.[47] As Brewster noted later, the advisory committee issued no formal report, but "papers generated by its discussions" (principally

46 Yale University news release, Dec. 15, 1967, and Kingman Brewster, Jr., to Janet Murrow, Dec. 14, 1967, both in Brewster I, Box 222, Folder 16; Brewster to Murrow, Jan. 15, 1968, Brewster I, Box 222, Folder 17.

47 Kingman Brewster, Jr., to Janet Murrow, Jan. 15, 1968, Brewster I, Box 222, Folder 17 (source of the quote); Kingman Brewster, Jr., An Institution for University Women at Yale: A Proposal, May 13, 1968, Brewster I, Box 222, Folder 13.

papers he authored) "became a supplement to the Vassar study as background for the consideration of the Yale Corporation."[48]

Brewster had two reasons for pursing "the 'coordinate' rather than the coeducational route," he explained later to the president of Amherst, John William Ward. The first reason was his "respect for alumni concerns." The second had to do with his "feeling that perhaps the distinctive needs of women might be insufficiently attended to if they were admitted directly to Yale College." But he ultimately "changed [his] mind" and supported full coeducation, attributing the change of heart to the influence of members of the corporation.[49]

Brewster did not say to Ward that he was influenced also by the publication in September 1968 of the Patterson report, a study commissioned fifteen months earlier by Princeton President Robert F. Goheen and the university's trustees to examine the question of the education of women at Princeton. Despite the retrospective disavowal of the importance of the Princeton study—Brewster's assistant, Henry Chauncey, Jr., said years later that it was of no consequence to Yale[50]—the documentary record points in a different direction. Gardner Patterson, the Princeton economist who carried out the study, sent Chauncey a copy of the finished report on September 13; at that time, Chauncey recorded his view that Patterson's work was "<u>truly</u> impressive."[51] The report, Brewster later told his faculty, "whetted" Yale's "sense of competitive rivalry." He added, "More important, the thoughtful and exhaustive study . . . provided additional data and argumentation which was quite pertinent to the Yale situation."[52]

48 Proposal for coeducation in Yale College, presented by President Kingman Brewster, Jr., of Yale to the faculty on Nov. 14, 1968, Brewster I, Box 222, Folder 14.

49 John William Ward to Kingman Brewster, Jr., Nov. 3, 1972, and Brewster to Ward, Nov. 17, 1972, both in Brewster II, Box 258, Folder 1. Ward, having advocated coeducation for Amherst, had written to Brewster at the behest of his trustees to ask about Yale's experience in terms of alumni reaction.

50 Chauncey interview.

51 Gardner Patterson to Henry Chauncey, Jr., Sept. 13, 1968, and Chauncey to Patterson, Sept. 23, 1968, both in Brewster I, Box 222, Folder 17. See also Chauncey to William H. Timbers, Sept. 10, 1969, Brewster II, Box 258, Folder 7: "The study by the Patterson Committee at Princeton is a superb report and outlines financial information which, as far as I know, is not documented anywhere."

52 Proposal for coeducation in Yale College, presented by President Kingman Brewster, Jr., of Yale to the faculty on Nov. 14, 1968, Brewster I, Box 222, Folder 14.

By September 23, Brewster was ready to disseminate his interpretation of what the Princeton report meant for Yale. Patterson's discussion of the "merits of coeducation" added little to "conclusions already reached at Yale." But the report's detailed analysis of finances and of arguments for and against various forms of coeducation and coordinate education were "far more thorough than anything developed at Yale," and its consideration of the likely effect of coeducation on alumni support seemed directly applicable to Yale.[53]

Brewster's response to the report focused on three options: complete coeducation, as at Stanford; Radcliffe-type coordinate education; and "cluster coordinate" education, which meant the establishment of "two or more institutions for women's education which use one or more of the divisions and their related professional fields as the organizing principle for women's education at Yale." Complete coeducation was the preferred choice of the Yale faculty and student body and would be the most feasible financially. The Radcliffe-type arrangement would involve separate trustees, administrative leadership, admissions, and possibly even degrees, but there would be no separate faculty. That arrangement might lead to the highest-quality leadership of the new enterprise and to the most effective focus on successful institution-building; it might afford the most attractive opportunity for a donor; and it would likely "minimize the dilution or dissipation of the corporate tradition of Yale College." The cluster coordinate approach would allow for the creation of residential neighborhoods of women of all ages, grouped around related disciplines and professions, as Brewster had imagined back in May.[54] Yale had no option but to do something, and to do it quickly. If Yale failed to act, Brewster said, "We thought we'd be left out of the parade."[55]

By mid-November, with minimal process, the choice was made. Brewster drafted a proposal for coeducation in Yale College, presented it to the corporation for approval, and took it to the

---

53 Kingman Brewster, Jr., Higher Education for Women at Yale, Sept. 23, 1968, Brewster I, Box 222, Folder 13.

54 Ibid.

55 Brewster, quoted in Reese, "When Yale Needed 'Girls,'" 13.

faculty, which voted enthusiastically to approve it at a meeting on November 14.[56]

The Corporation's Approval of Coeducation for Yale

That was Brewster's style: impulsive, free-wheeling, given to acting, acting quickly, and acting with little process when he believed in the bet he was making. According to Hanna Holborn Gray, a member of the Yale corporation who became Brewster's provost, Brewster was "consultative but informal." He talked to people constantly, both individually and in small groups. He was "constantly absorbing conversations," listening to and learning from "other people's ideas." But when he acted, Gray said, he had "a tendency to plunge a little quickly." She added, "His plunges worked out very well most of the time."[57]

In the absence of process and careful planning, how did Brewster manage to pull off such a momentous decision? Brewster had close and comfortable associations with members of the faculty, and they were enthusiastic about coeducation. He also had good relationships with members of the corporation, a group of sixteen fellows who met monthly during the academic year. That small size enabled the corporation to act de facto as a committee of the whole. Important issues were discussed thoroughly when the corporation first convened in the corporation room in Woodbridge Hall, the main administration building, on Friday afternoons; votes were taken in formal session the next morning, after members had a chance to absorb the afternoon's discussion and, not incidentally, to talk informally among themselves on Friday nights.[58]

It was not as easy to sell coeducation to the corporation as it was to the faculty. Not all of the fellows were on board at the outset. Some of the more conservative among them preferred Brewster's original path toward a coordinate college for women, and some were reluctant about changing Yale at all. And there were

---

56 Yale University news release, Nov. 14, 1968, Brewster I, Box 222, Folder 14.
57 Interview with Hanna Holborn Gray, Nov. 18, 2014, New York City.
58 Ibid.; Howe oral history, part 2, pp. 8–10.

many questions: How would the alumni react? How would co-education be financed? What would need to be done with respect to facilities?

The night before the corporation convened to address the matter, Brewster asked for a meeting with two influential members. One was John Hay ("Jock") Whitney, who had been, variously, venture capitalist, philanthropist, editor-in-chief and publisher of the *New York Herald Tribune*, and U.S. ambassador to the Court of St. James's and would, the next year, become senior fellow of the corporation. The other was J. Irwin Miller, chairman of Cummins Engine Company, a thoughtful centrist with liberal inclinations, a man who, like Whitney, had established a close personal relationship with Brewster. Brewster had great respect for both men. He would say later of Whitney, "Jock was the voice of reason. He never panicked. He was always thinking things out—worrying about their implications. . . . In the later 1960s, there were many tensions among Yale's trustees about the university's policies, and Jock was very good at finding common ground on which they could all comfortably stand."[59]

Miller was already on record as being comfortable with—indeed, favoring—institutional change. Speaking to alumni in June 1967, he said, "Yale is a great place now precisely because it is changing radically and creatively in response to a wildly changing environment." There was, he said, an increasing sentiment among young men "that says 'We want an educational experience that is somehow comparable to the experience in the world outside.'" If coeducation were not adopted by Yale and Princeton, he said, it would mean "a long, slow decline" in the quality of those student bodies.[60]

"Among Yale's trustees at the time," Brewster said later, "Jock and Irwin Miller did the most to change the university from being excessively homogeneous and dominated by an inherited elite to achieving greater diversity. Co-education, of course, was a major

59 Brewster, quoted in E. J. Kahn, Jr., *Jock: The Life and Times of John Hay Whitney* (Garden City, NY: Doubleday, 1981), p. 299.

60 Miller, quoted in Karabel, *The Chosen*, p. 418.

aspect of that." The two men, Brewster said, were "sort of the Old Turks of the Corporation." In the conversation on the eve of the corporation meeting, Brewster asked Whitney and Miller, "Will Yale get more financial support by first going co-educational and then asking for approval, or by asking first and then doing it?" According to Brewster, "They both said, 'Do it, then ask.' That was gutsy. They knew I was talking about *them*. That made me bite the bullet and put the issue up to the Corporation."[61]

When the corporation took up the issue in October 1968, leading members, including Whitney, Miller, and William W. Scranton, former governor of Pennsylvania, worked both in formal afternoon discussions and in informal evening conversations to bring other members around. Paul Moore, Jr., an Episcopal bishop then presiding at the Cathedral of St. John the Divine in New York City, was a clear ally. So were John V. Lindsay, mayor of New York City, and J. Richardson Dilworth. Cyrus Vance, who had served recently as secretary of the army and deputy secretary of defense in the Kennedy and Johnson administrations and would go on to be secretary of state in the Carter administration, was another influential member who had Brewster's ear and the respect of his peers, though his overall progressivism was tempered with some Yale-specific traditionalism (he would admit later to some sadness when his secret society, Skull and Bones, finally admitted women). William McChesney Martin, Jr., chairman of the board of governors of the Federal Reserve, was an important convert; although he was probably not disposed to change, he was open to listening to his colleagues. Once Martin had been convinced, other members of the corporation were persuaded to come along as well.[62]

The corporation agreed unanimously that "coeducation would improve the quality of Yale College and Yale's ability to attract the students it most wants." There should be flexibility for the future, and women students should be "treated at least as well as men students" in terms of facilities and programs. The administration was

61 Brewster, quoted in Kahn, *Jock*, p. 300.

62 Scranton oral history, pp. 17–25; Gray interview; Howe oral history, pp. 23–25; Lindsay oral history, pp. 17–18; Dilworth oral history, p. 32.

instructed to come back to the corporation with a plan to meet these general requirements.[63]

Members of the corporation understood that they were proceeding with a minimum of process. "We really rushed it," William P. Bundy said of the decision. "My impression was that [Brewster] kind of rammed that one through."[64] Miller, fully appreciating the irony of what the corporation was doing, commented that the university had "selected the wrong road after great study [referring to Vassar-Yale and its aftermath] and embarked on the right road in one impulsive meeting without really counting the cost."[65]

Part of the reasoning behind proceeding to full coeducation had to do with what was right and sensible for Yale. But part of it had to do with competitive rivalry with Princeton. Although the Princeton trustees had not yet taken a decision, the Patterson report pointed toward coeducation, and Yale had every interest in getting out ahead of Princeton and winning every possible advantage. As Elga Wasserman, who would be appointed one of the administrative co-leaders of Yale's planning efforts, stated the following spring, "Traditional rivalry with Princeton probably helped to give Yale the final push it needed to abandon its 267-year-old, all-male tradition."[66]

Yale students had been actively pressuring the administration for coeducation. The *Yale Daily News* had begun campaigning in the spring of 1966, when it ran a twenty-part series of essays on the question of whether Yale should admit women undergraduates. This "coeducation forum" featured Yale faculty members and administrators, college and university presidents, and other public figures, many of whom strongly advocated bringing undergraduate women to Yale. The paper also presented case studies of coordinate education at other institutions, and it conducted a poll of

63 Proposal for coeducation in Yale College, presented by President Kingman Brewster, Jr., of Yale to the faculty on Nov. 14, 1968, Brewster I, Box 222, Folder 14.

64 WP Bundy oral history, Apr. 24, 1992, p. 16.

65 Miller, quoted in Stanley E. Flink, "Kingman Brewster's Death, at 69, Cut Short a Lifetime of Devotion to Yale and Its Mission," in *Kingman Brewster: Remembrances* (Yale University, 1997), p. 28.

66 Wasserman, "Coeducation Comes to Yale College," p. 145.

faculty and students about coeducation and coordinate education. It also began running editorials in favor of coeducation. In cooperation with Dwight Hall, Yale's student-run center for public service and social justice, the paper sponsored open forums and panel discussions about coeducation.[67] In early November 1968, the paper published a white paper on coeducation, making a strong case for admitting women.[68]

By the fall of 1968, coeducation became the battle cry of the Yale chapter of SDS, which hoped to use it to mobilize the Yale campus.[69] More moderate students took a different approach, sponsoring a coeducation week that brought seven hundred women students from twenty-two eastern colleges and universities to Yale for the first week in November.[70] The head of the student steering committee, Aviam Soifer, a senior, told the *New York Times*, "The idea is to take the male-female relationship out of the absurdly pressured situation of a weekend date. . . . A lot of the guys think of women simply as objects, or dumb broads, but they're human beings too."[71] The women went to classes, ate in dining halls, and stayed in dormitory rooms vacated by their usual male residents. There were speeches, teach-ins on the subject of coeducation, parties, concerts, and film showings. Yale Hillel held a bagel and lox brunch, and SDS invited the women to join their demonstration on Election Day.[72] The main idea, Soifer said, was for men and

67 In *Yale Daily News*, for the Coeducation Forum, see, e.g., Apr. 11, 13, 20, and 25 and May 5 and 11, 1966; on the case studies of coordinate education, May 9 and 12, 1966; on the poll of faculty and students, May 18, 1966. For the newspaper's editorials, see Jan. 26, Mar. 14, and May 25, 1966. On the forums and panel discussions sponsored with Dwight Hall, see Apr. 11 and 29 and May 6, 1966.

68 *Yale Daily News*, "The Coeducation White Paper: Everything You Need to Know," Nov. 7, 1968, Brewster I, Box 222, Folder 18.

69 Kabaservice, *The Guardians*, pp. 365–68; *Yale Daily News*, Oct. 16, 1968.

70 *Yale Daily News*, Oct. 21, 23, 24, 25, 28, 29, and 30 and Nov. 1 and 4, 1968; Proposal for coeducation in Yale College, presented by President Kingman Brewster, Jr., of Yale to the faculty on Nov. 14, 1968, Brewster I, Box 222, Folder 14; "The Eli Girls," *Time*, Nov. 22, 1968, p. 55, clipping in Heller, Box 1, Folder 4; Soifer oral history, pp. 1–33.

71 Quoted in *New York Times*, Nov. 5, 1968, reprinted in Geismar, Rice, and Winant, eds., *Fresh Women*, p. 156.

72 *Yale Daily News*, Nov. 1, 4, 6, and 7, 1968; Janet Lever and Pepper Schwartz, *Women at Yale: Liberating a College Campus* (Indianapolis, IN: Bobbs-Merrill, 1971), pp. 31–34.

women "to meet over coffee, over lunch, or whatever, and just get accustomed to each other."[73]

Anticipating "a seven-day mixer," as a Smith woman put it, the group of sixty Smith students who "went south to New Haven" found that after the first day, "the atmosphere was more natural, and it seemed almost as if we girls had always been at Yale."[74] The *Yale Daily News* sampled student reactions. Another Smith woman said that she might prefer "to return to my 'Exclusive Eastern Women's College' where at least I am mistress of my own environment." But others had a different view. "Coming from an all-girls' school, I didn't mind being appreciated all week long," a Wellesley woman wrote. "This is one girl . . . who would like to transfer to Yale. Next fall. Next week." Yale men commented about their guests, "They've really brightened this place up" and "The place smells nicer." Some said the week had reminded them of the artificiality of single-sex schooling. "What happens when you go to a men's school is you forget how really good [girls] can be. You get entangled in a weekend-to-weekend existence, and you become a product of it. You lose sight of the simple fact that girls are people, just like you and me. Instead they become things to play with on allotted days. Things."[75]

As for faculty members, reporters for the *Yale Daily News* turned up general support but occasional dissenting or condescending comments. A professor of art history said, "Having undergraduate women in classes would make Yale better—better in that there would be a greater sense of wholeness and completeness in the human reactions to what is going on." A professor of Chinese history said that he found coeds "very decorative, well groomed, and a bit bland." A psychology professor, remarking on the "sex-boundedness in the air" in his class on deviant behavior, said that he favored teaching coeducational classes because, "to a degree, there are certain outlooks that are sexually determined,

73 Quoted in *New York Times*, Nov. 5, 1968, reprinted in Geismar, Rice, and Winant, eds., *Fresh Women*, p. 157.
74 Linne Mooney, "Yalettes, Yalies View Election Returns, March to Brewster for Coeducation," *Sophian*, Nov. 14, 1968, Box 17, Smith College Archives.
75 Quoted in Lever and Schwartz, *Women at Yale*, pp. 33–34.

and are important in making a more provocative and titillating class discussion." A literature professor remarked that his students were "much more anxious to talk with girls in the class." In contrast, an unidentified faculty member said that he liked Yale just the way it was: "I feel a greater sense of accomplishment when I direct my efforts towards those who will one day have a greater role in society—men."[76]

At the same time, Brewster asked administrative colleagues to develop refined estimates of the costs of adding fifteen hundred women students to the college. They estimated that it would take about $55 million to provide residential facilities and financial aid for the women students.[77] They assumed that other operating costs would be covered by tuition and fees.

Acknowledging that Yale had no practical experience in figuring out the best arrangements for undergraduate women, Brewster said that the corporation had decided to eschew further study and planning and "to proceed at once to bring to Yale a sufficient number of women undergraduates so that their experience and their views and interests may provide a basis for the evolution of full coeducation."[78] Brewster later acknowledged, "I was slow to come around to the notion that just admitting women to Yale College would be as good as having a women's college. I was wrong and happily I changed my mind, but I did so slowly."[79]

76 Quoted in *Yale Daily News*, Nov. 8, 1968.

77 Proposal for coeducation in Yale College, presented by President Kingman Brewster, Jr., of Yale to the faculty on Nov. 14, 1968, Brewster I, Box 222, Folder 14.

78 Ibid.

79 Brewster, quoted in Reese, "When Yale Needed 'Girls,'" 14.

4

Princeton: "Coeducation Is Inevitable"

Princeton University was an unlikely venue, and Robert F. Goheen an unlikely standard-bearer, for the transformation of elite higher education in the 1960s. A member of the class of 1940 at Princeton, Goheen had joined the faculty as an assistant professor of classics in 1950. When he took office as Princeton's sixteenth president in 1957, he was only thirty-seven years old. The university was still very much an undergraduate college. The graduate school was very small, and Princeton had not yet claimed its place as a research university of the first rank. The student body had long been made up mainly of graduates of private day and boarding schools; the inclusion of significant numbers of students from public schools and families of more moderate means had just begun. Heavily Protestant, overwhelmingly white, Princeton had not yet shaken its reputation for prejudice on grounds of religion and race.[1]

"The Pleasantest Country Club in America"

In so many ways Princeton gave off the aura popularized in the famous novel by F. Scott Fitzgerald, *This Side of Paradise*. Fitzgerald, who had matriculated in the class of 1917 but failed

---

1 James Axtell, *The Making of Princeton University: From Woodrow Wilson to the Present* (Princeton, NJ, and Oxford: Princeton University Press, 2006), ch. 3; Jerome Karabel, *The Chosen: The Hidden History of Admission and Exclusion at Harvard, Yale, and Princeton* (Boston and New York: Houghton Mifflin, 2005), chs. 8, 10; Marcia Graham Synnott, *The Half-Opened Door: Discrimination and Admissions at Harvard, Yale, and Princeton, 1900–1970* (Westport, CT: Greenwood Press, 1979), ch. 6; Marcia Graham Synnott, *Student Diversity at the Big Three: Changes at Harvard, Yale, and Princeton since the 1920s* (New Brunswick, NJ: Transaction Publishers, 2013), passim.

to graduate, called Princeton "the pleasantest country club in America," an image reinforced in campus social life, which was dominated by the eating clubs, the private facilities where juniors and seniors ate, drank, and partied. The clubs projected social prestige (some called it snobbery) and gentility. In their study of American higher education, published in 1968, Christopher Jencks and David Riesman chose Princeton as an example of "stag undergraduate institutions" that were "prone to a kind of excess" and were "notable for athletic overemphasis and for a narrow Philistine pragmatism." As Jencks and Riesman noted, "These stag institutions preserve earlier collegiate styles, like the Jazz Age pride in holding hard liquor one can still find at the University of Virginia [and] the teen-age muscularity only now disappearing at Princeton."[2]

That said, Princeton provided undergraduates with compelling educational opportunities inside and outside the classroom. Goheen had taken excellent advantage of everything Princeton had to offer. He was an exceptional student in classics and the special program in the humanities, a star of the varsity soccer team, and a campus leader—president of the intramural athletic association, president of his eating club, Quadrangle, and an active participant in the undergraduate student government. In his senior year he was awarded the M. Taylor Pyne Honor Prize, the highest general distinction the university confers on an undergraduate.

In attitudes toward women, Goheen's Princeton accepted, indeed was built around, prevailing societal views about women's place. Goheen also knew from his own family that single-sex education was the norm for able women in the United States. His wife, Margaret Skelly Goheen, had graduated from Vassar in 1941. She said that she delighted in her college experience; it had never occurred to her that she and her classmates lacked for male companionship.[3] Goheen's account matched hers, with just a touch of

---

2 Fitzgerald, quoted in Axtell, *The Making of Princeton University*, p. 117 (see also p. 119); Christopher Jencks and David Riesman, *The Academic Revolution* (Garden City, NY: Doubleday, 1968), p. 300.

3 Interview with Margaret Skelly Goheen, Mar. 9, 2012, Princeton, NJ.

irony added: "My wife," he said later, "seemed to have experienced Vassar without dire consequences."[4]

The assumptions about the appropriateness of single-sex education for women extended also to the Goheens' four daughters. The eldest, Anne, followed her mother to Poughkeepsie. Trudi, the second daughter, chose to go to Bryn Mawr. The third, Megan, also went to Vassar, and the youngest, Elizabeth, graduated from Douglass. Goheen remarked later, "I had noticed no serious warping in my wife and . . . daughters for their having all graduated from women's colleges."[5] Through the 1950s and early 1960s, there was no discussion at the Goheen home about women being able to study at Princeton.[6] Nor was there any challenge to the message imparted at women's colleges: Women were being educated to be wives and mothers, community volunteers, helpmates to the men who would claim leadership positions in business and the professions.

For all of his experience, however, Goheen was a man of open mind and great thoughtfulness, and he began to see that the world around him was changing. As he reflected years later, "I saw that women were playing an increasingly influential role in this world, an increasingly more outspoken one. And it became . . . quite clear that Princeton had fallen behind in this respect. We just were not in touch with this whole segment of our society that were going to be influential players in this society."[7] Goheen came to understand that accepted models for women's roles were being challenged, perhaps even becoming outmoded. By the mid-1960s, he later acknowledged, "the claims of women to a fairer, fuller place in business, education, the professions and public affairs were gaining wide credence and acceptance. Even I could not miss that, and the women of my family did not fail to bring it home."[8]

4 Robert F. Goheen, "A President Recalls Coeducation," *Daily Princetonian*, Apr. 13, 1989.

5 Robert F. Goheen, "Reminiscence on the Coeducating of Princeton," 20th Anniversary of Coeducation, Keynote Event, Mar. 31, 1989, typescript in the possession of Nancy Weiss Malkiel.

6 Margaret Skelly Goheen interview.

7 Goheen oral history, Oct. 26, 2004, p. 5.

8 Goheen, "A President Recalls Coeducation."

Goheen also recognized important changes in the competitive environment in which Princeton operated. He traveled frequently, visiting secondary schools during the trips he made to speak to alumni, and he listened to members of the admission staff. He learned, to his surprise, that "increasing numbers of the ablest seniors in both the public and private schools that had been Princeton's biggest feeders were choosing not to come here because of our monasticism."[9] Some of them applied but, once admitted, chose to go elsewhere; others "were not applying to Princeton simply because it was not coeducational." Princeton took seriously its self-appointed role of educating leaders—"the future movers and shakers of the country." That some of them "just refused to come and be educated here for that reason" was "a great shock."[10]

First Steps toward Coeducation

Goheen had also taken some steps as president that—unintentionally—laid some groundwork for undergraduate coeducation. The first had to do with the graduate school. Goheen had first become aware of the exclusion of women from candidacy for graduate degrees in the spring of 1957, when, as president-designate, he traveled to India to attend the centenary celebrations of the University of Calcutta. There he met Kay Bracken, a political officer in the American consulate who, he learned, had taken many courses in Near Eastern studies at Princeton but had, by university policy, been denied the opportunity to qualify for a Princeton degree. "That seemed to me," he said later, "both wasteful and improper." But, as Goheen readily acknowledged, his attention to the issue essentially stopped there.[11]

Bracken was not a singular case. Goheen was probably unfamiliar with the request shortly before he became president from Marina von Neumann Whitman to be admitted to Princeton's Ph.D. program in economics. Whitman, daughter of the legendary

9 Ibid.
10 Goheen oral history, Oct. 26, 2004, p. 5.
11 Goheen, "A President Recalls Coeducation."

mathematician John von Neumann, one of the first members of the permanent faculty at the Institute for Advanced Study, had grown up in Princeton. After graduating at the top of her class from Radcliffe, she was back in town, living in university housing with her husband, an assistant professor of English. Goheen's predecessor, Harold W. Dodds, had told her that she could not be admitted to degree candidacy because the university had no facilities to accommodate women graduate students. Like Bracken, Whitman was allowed to take graduate seminars at Princeton, but she was obliged to enroll elsewhere—in her case, Columbia—to earn her Ph.D.[12]

In the winter of 1960–61, Polly Bunting, who had just left the deanship of Douglass College to become president of Radcliffe, urged Princeton to admit Sabra Follett Meservey, an instructor in history at Douglass, to the Ph.D. program in oriental studies. Goheen called Meservey "an ideal candidate to let us override what I call the 'Bracken limitation.'" She was the wife of a nuclear physicist on the research staff at Princeton's Plasma Physics Laboratory, and she lived in Princeton. The dean of the graduate school, Donald R. Hamilton, supported her candidacy. Goheen took the issue to the board of trustees. Despite some trustees' concern that in admitting Meservey the university might be letting "the camel get its nose under the tent," the board agreed that women might be admitted to the graduate school in cases "where Princeton offered their academic interests and qualifications a strong fit."[13]

Meservey was an excellent fit. Princeton admitted her, Hamilton said, because she was "such an outstanding person . . . and her reasons for wanting to come here were so good, that we hated to turn her down." She wanted to study in a field—Turkish history and language—in which Princeton was "particularly strong." Indeed, she wanted "to study subjects that she can do better with here than

12 Telephone conversation with William J. Baumol, Oct. 3, 2010; Marina von Neumann Whitman, *The Martian's Daughter: A Memoir* (Ann Arbor: University of Michigan Press, 2012), pp. 88, 94–95.

13 Goheen, "A President Recalls Coeducation"; *Newark News*, Apr. 23, 1961, clipping in Patterson, Box 376, Folder 1.

at almost any place else."[14] Although Princeton might admit "other women in the future as special cases," it did not plan to offer admission to women more generally because it had "no residential facilities for women students."[15]

In 1962–63, eight more women were enrolled in the graduate school. In 1964, Meservey earned a master's degree, and the first Princeton Ph.D. awarded to a woman was earned by biochemist T'sai-Ying Cheng.[16] But the university—unique among its peers—held to its policy of admitting women to graduate degree candidacy in only the most exceptional cases. In 1969–70, with undergraduate coeducation beginning, the graduate school finally relaxed the constraints, and enrollment grew to 200 women and 1,300 men—an increase of 150 women since 1967.[17]

More disruptive to Princeton's all-male status quo than the admission of women graduate students was the enrollment of a limited number of women undergraduates through the new critical languages program. First instituted in 1963–64 with funding from the Carnegie Corporation, the program brought a small number of undergraduates from other colleges and universities to Princeton for one or two years of intensive study of Arabic, Chinese, Japanese, Persian, Russian, and Turkish, languages not taught on an advanced level at their home campuses, along with related regional studies courses in the social sciences and humanities. The students were to return to their own colleges for the senior year.[18]

In the first year of the program, five of the fourteen "critters" (as the students were known) were women. Their reception by Princeton undergraduates, many of whom had little experience with women as students, was less than gracious. One male student's

14 Quoted in *New York Herald Tribune*, Apr. 23, 1961, clipping in Patterson, Box 376, Folder 1.

15 Quoted in Princeton University news release, Apr. 23, 1961, Patterson, Box 376, Folder 1.

16 *Princeton Herald*, Sept. 26, 1962; *Princeton Packet*, Jan. 29 and May 27, 1964, clippings in Patterson, Box 376, Folder 1.

17 Luther Munford, "Coeducation at Princeton: The Struggle of an Idea at a University in Transition," *Daily Princetonian*, Oct. 21, 1969, p. 13. On the uniqueness of Princeton's position, see Jencks and Riesman, *The Academic Revolution*, p. 298.

18 Princeton University news release, Sept. 22, 1963, Patterson, Box 376, Folder 1.

comments typified the problem: "It disgusts me to be in competition with girls," he told the *Daily Princetonian*. "If I had wanted to go to classes with girls, I would have gone to Stanford."[19] Male students were not reluctant to express their displeasure; the presence of the women students was called "a travesty," "a crime."[20] It did not help that the first group of women came from public colleges, like the City College of New York and Douglass College at Rutgers; nor was it lost on Princeton men that four of the first five women were Jewish. The 1964 yearbook, the *Bric-a-Brac*, made the point in a snide aside: "The Princeton Chapter of Hadassah sent out a welcome wagon."[21]

In the second year of the program, 1964–65, women accounted for ten of the twenty-six students. In the third year, twelve out of twenty-four students were women.[22] By 1967–68, the number of women had grown to fifteen.[23] Beginning in the second year, the program included students from elite private colleges, including the Seven Sisters, who met a more welcome reception from Princeton men, who could imagine taking them to meals at eating clubs and inviting them on dates.[24]

To many Princetonians, female "critters" were at best curiosities, at worst interlopers. A woman from Goucher reported an encounter in the library: "Get out of here!" exclaimed a man whom she had never seen before. "I can't concentrate when you're in this carrel."[25] A United Press International (UPI) reporter, writing about the program as its second year drew toward a close, said that "the girls estimate that the majority of Princeton undergraduates don't want girls in their classes." One woman told the reporter, "Sometimes when I'm walking to class I overhear someone say,

19 *Daily Princetonian*, Sept. 23, 1963.
20 *Trenton Times*, Sept. 27, 1963, clipping in Patterson, Box 376, Folder 1.
21 Patience Haggin, "Pioneering Women: The 50th Anniversary of Princeton's First Female Undergraduate Students," *Daily Princetonian*, May 30, 2014.
22 David H. Blair, Jr., to University Offices Concerned, Sept. 16, 1964, and Critical Language Students, 1965–66, both in ODUS, Box 7, Folder 28; Martha L. Lamar, "Problems of Critical Languages," *Princeton Alumni Weekly* 66 (Nov. 16, 1965): 10.
23 John V. Dippel, "On the Campus," *Princeton Alumni Weekly* 68 (Oct. 17, 1967): 6.
24 Haggin, "Pioneering Women."
25 Quoted in Lamar, "Problems of Critical Languages," 12.

'There goes one of them,'" adding that she found the experience "unnerving." Another student told a story expressing the loneliness of being on a campus of 3,200 not-very-accepting men: "Boys come up and say, 'My great-grandfather went to Princeton and it was a men's school, my grandfather went here and it was a men's school, my father went here and my sons are going here and it will still be a school for men.'"[26]

By 1968–69, however, some of the barriers were starting to crumble. It was not that the sixteen women on campus were warmly received. Martha Hirshfield, a student from Wellesley who was studying Chinese, said, "You walk around campus and the guys look at you like you're trees. They look right through you." Sue Jean Lee, who had come from the City College of New York also to study Chinese, reported that "in the first meeting of one of her classes, the boys all stared at her, and two of them stood in the back rather than sit in the empty seats beside her. 'Sit down, she won't bite,' the professor snapped." Lynn Nagasako from Reed College, who made the mistake of saying "orgasm" instead of "organism," was "pointed out all over campus as 'the one who said "orgasm" in class.'"[27]

How does one reconcile the apparent contradiction between the growing interest in undergraduate coeducation on the part, at least, of the *Daily Princetonian* and the student government and, on the other hand, the compelling anecdotes about male resistance to female "critters" on campus? The early and mid-1960s were still quite early in the evolution of student views on coeducation; welcoming women to the campus was an idea that took some time to take root. Moreover, there was a difference between imagining that Princeton might someday enroll a significant number of undergraduate women and actually interacting on a daily basis with a very small handful of women visitors who had come briefly from somewhere else and, therefore, did not really belong.

26 "Will Your Daughter Go to Princeton?," unidentified clipping, Mar. 21, 1965, Subject Files Princeton, Coeducation, Box 376, Folder 1.
27 Jane Steinberg, "214 to 1: Junior Year at Princeton Can Be More Exciting Than Paris or Madrid . . . If You Happen to Be a Girl," *Mademoiselle*, Apr. 1969, clipping in Subject Files Princeton, Coeducation, Box 376, Folder 3.

The experience of the "critters" improved over time. They wrote for the *Princetonian* and participated in the Triangle club, student government, chapel choir, Theatre Intime, and some of the eating clubs. Involvement in campus activities made the women feel as though they belonged at Princeton and provided "a common ground for substantial and lasting friendships."[28] In 1969–70, eight women earned A.B. degrees from Princeton. They had come the previous year as critical languages students and had applied to stay on as regular degree candidates.[29]

Goheen's Evolving Views

Goheen's views about Princeton and coeducation were also evolving under the influence of the powerful new advocate joining him in Nassau Hall. In the spring of 1966, Goheen invited the labor economist William G. Bowen to become the university's first full-time provost, effective in July 1967. Bowen was a Princeton Ph.D. who had joined the faculty in 1958 as an assistant professor of economics. He had been promoted to associate professor in 1961 and to professor of economics and public affairs in 1965. Since 1964 he had been directing the graduate program in the Woodrow Wilson School of Public and International Affairs.

Bowen's position on coeducation was clear: Princeton needed to admit women undergraduates, and needed to do it sooner rather than later, or the university would risk becoming an educational anachronism. Bowen himself had been an undergraduate at Denison University, and he knew about coeducation from personal experience. But he also had a clear-eyed view of Princeton: It had to become coeducational to remain a great university, to retain excellent faculty and attract excellent students. Bowen told Goheen that he "wasn't sure it was workable to have someone in the provost position . . . who was known to have such a different view on the

28 *Daily Princetonian*, Sept. 30, 1968; Steinberg, "214 to 1" (source of the quote); Edward R. Weidlein III '68, "On the Campus," *Princeton Alumni Weekly* 68 (Oct. 10, 1967): 4; Sue Jean Lee for the Critical Language Girls, *Bric-a-Brac*, 1969, p. 75.

29 Princeton University news release, June 9, 1970, Subject Files Princeton, Coeducation, Box 376, Folder 4.

very sensitive . . . issue of co-education." Goheen responded, "You should do your best to persuade me and . . . I'll do my best to persuade you and we'll just see how it comes out." Bowen recalled that he smiled and said, "Bob, if I just give up on you I can always quit."[30]

The second influence on Goheen's evolving views about co-education came from students. In January 1965 the *Daily Princetonian* published a long article by James M. Markham '65 diagnosing in detail the "social illness" that resulted at Princeton from the absence of easy interaction with women. Demonstrating in compelling detail that Princeton students were miserably unhappy, Markham argued for "a sister college across the lake" to remedy the glaring deficiencies in undergraduate social life.[31]

The official reaction to Markham's piece was strongly negative. The dean of the faculty, J. Douglas Brown '19, accused the *Princetonian* of having "'grossly exaggerated' the problem 'in order to make an issue.'" History professor Joseph R. Strayer '26 said, "Things would be a lot healthier around here if you guys didn't complain so much."[32] And Goheen himself declared that Princeton did not have "any 'social' problems that coeducation would cure." Coeducation *was* "the solution for Princeton's social illness," the *Princetonian* retorted. The issue was not simply related to social life. "There is good reason to believe," the newspaper said, "that the development of a young man's mind is . . . enhanced by normal contact with women."[33] Goheen commented that "coeducation would solve some problems, but it would also create many."[34]

The Markham piece got Goheen's attention. As he said later, "When thoughtful students like Jim Markham needled me, I began to think about it. Before that, coeducation was an aberration, a whacky idea to kick around."[35] But Goheen was still not ready to address the subject. In December 1966, in a conversation to mark the tenth year of his presidency, he said, "In the best of all possible

---

30 Bowen oral history, June 9, 2009, pp. 21, 14.
31 *Daily Princetonian*, Jan. 8, 1965.
32 Munford, "Coeducation at Princeton," p. 6.
33 Editorial, *Daily Princetonian*, Jan. 8, 1965.
34 Quoted in *New York Times*, Feb. 8, 1965, clipping in Patterson, Box 376, Folder 1.
35 Munford, "Coeducation at Princeton," p. 7.

worlds, there would be a good coordinate college for women nearby . . . but it doesn't seem to me or the trustees that we should divert substantial resources at this point to accommodate a lot of nice young ladies, brilliant though they may be."[36]

Still, the world was changing around Goheen, and he understood that Princeton would have to change with it. On May 17, 1967, the *Daily Princetonian* carried a front-page story with the banner headline: "Goheen: Coeducation Is Inevitable." The reporter, Robert K. Durkee '69, quoted Goheen: "It is inevitable that, at some point in the future, Princeton is going to move into the education of women. The only questions now are those of strategy, priority and timing." The principal motivation, the president observed, "won't and shouldn't be that Princeton's social life is warped. This is certainly one consideration, but a greater consideration is what Princeton could offer to women in higher educational opportunity and what women could bring to the intellectual and the entire life of Princeton." Speaking personally, he said, he was "persuaded that in mixed classes you get a fuller range of sensitivities and points of view than when girls or boys study alone." The administration, he said, was committed to studying the situation with care. The course ahead was one of "gradualism—full discussion yet with some degree of urgency."[37] The next day, the *New York Times* repeated the *Princetonian*'s account.[38]

Goheen had never intended to make any such announcement. He had imagined that he was having a wide-ranging, off-the-record conversation as background for a series of articles about student life scheduled for publication in the fall. It had not occurred to him to exact a promise from Durkee not to publish without his approval.[39]

36 William McCleery, "An Informal Call on Princeton's Robert F. Goheen in His 10th Year as President," *University Magazine*, Winter 1966–67, in *Princeton Alumni Weekly* 67 (Dec. 6, 1966): 19–20.

37 *Daily Princetonian*, May 17, 1967.

38 *New York Times*, May 18, 1967, clipping in Goheen, Box 93, Folder 4.

39 Minutes of a Stated Meeting of the Executive Committee, May 19, 1967, p. 2, Princeton trustees, Series 1, Vol. 65; Robert F. Goheen, The Education of Women at Princeton: Notes for a Presentation to the Board, June 1967, Goheen, Box 93, Folder 4; Goheen oral history, Nov. 4, 2004, p. 1.

The public announcement of the inevitability of coeducation was embarrassing to Goheen because it appeared before the trustees could formally consider the question. Nonetheless, the trustees had been expecting to address the subject at their June meeting, and Goheen had planned to ask the board to authorize "a serious, systematic study of the options."[40] He had been preparing the trustees for the conversation, and the board was well aware of his views. In January he had reported that Yale was engaged in an effort to persuade Vassar to move to New Haven. That news, he said, should give the board "food for serious thought, since Princeton in a few years might find itself the only major university not significantly engaged in the education of women." Goheen had raised the question of the feasibility of Princeton "remain[ing] alone in not providing the educational experience that many young women are asking for today," and he had underscored his concern about remaining competitive with Harvard and Yale in admissions if Princeton were to remain "monastic."[41]

The competitive issue was a serious concern. Princeton's acting director of admission, John T. Osander '57, who would be named director at the January board meeting, had that same week corroborated Goheen's view. As Osander told the *Daily Princetonian*, Princeton "'would definitely suffer' in competition with Yale if the proposal to move Vassar to New Haven were carried out." Students admitted to both Princeton and Yale had typically been divided about evenly in the choices they made about where to enroll; if Vassar were to affiliate with Yale, Osander predicted, it would "tip the balance in favor of Yale." Osander noted, too, that a "large number of students . . . reject Princeton acceptances because of the better social life at other schools."[42]

Harvard was a case in point. As Jerome Karabel has pointed out, Princeton's standing relative to Harvard was on the decline: "In 1955, Harvard lost 85 students to Princeton; by 1965, the number had dropped to 32. Meanwhile, 124 students admitted to

40 Robert F. Goheen to Gardner Patterson, May 26, 1967, Patterson, Box 3, Folder 3.
41 Minutes of Meeting of the Board of Trustees, Princeton University, Jan. 14, 1967, p. 8, Princeton trustees, Series 1, Vol. 65.
42 *Daily Princetonian*, Jan. 9, 1967.

both . . . [schools] chose Harvard—a ratio of almost 4 men to 1. Overall, Harvard's yield rate in 1965 was 86 percent; Princeton's was a comparatively weak 68 percent. Yet just ten years earlier, Princeton had enjoyed a slight edge in overall yield: 62 vs. 61 percent."[43] Osander's predecessor, E. Alden Dunham II '53, who had left the admission office in July 1966 to join the Carnegie Corporation, told the *Princetonian* in January 1967 that some three-quarters of the students admitted to both Harvard and Princeton typically chose to go to Cambridge.[44]

Goheen and the trustees agreed to begin a serious discussion of coeducation at the June 1967 board meeting.[45] In the meantime, with the authorization of the executive committee, Goheen pursued what he hoped might be an opportunity to bring a women's college to Princeton in some coordinate relationship with the university.

Exploring a Coordinate Relationship with Sarah Lawrence

From 1887 until 1897, there had been a small college for women, Evelyn College, just off Nassau Street, about a mile east of the center of Princeton. Its board included Princeton faculty, administrators, and trustees. The college depended on Princeton faculty members for its instruction. Evelyn students were permitted to use the Princeton library and museums on a limited basis. Princeton students sought out Evelyn students for social companionship, and the women showed up regularly at football games and parties in the eating clubs. The college enrolled nearly fifty students at its peak, mainly daughters of university and Princeton Theological Seminary faculty members and sisters of Princeton undergraduates, but enrollment declined to fourteen students in the college's final year. Never financially robust, the college fell on hard times during the depression following the Panic of 1893 and closed in 1897.[46]

---

43 Karabel, *The Chosen*, p. 428.

44 *Daily Princetonian*, Jan. 9, 1967.

45 Minutes of Meeting of the Board of Trustees, Princeton University, Apr. 15, 1967, p. 11, Princeton trustees, Series 1, Vol. 65.

46 In *Harper's Bazaar*, see "Women's Colleges—Evelyn College," 21 (Nov. 17, 1888): 781, and Adaline W. Sterling, "Evelyn College," 29 (Sept. 26, 1896): 806–7. In *Daily*

Now Goheen was looking for a more substantial relationship. Yale's attempt to persuade Vassar to move to New Haven had led Princeton to search for a potential partner of its own. Goheen had heard rumors that Sarah Lawrence might be receptive to affiliating with Princeton, and he had embarked in the late winter of 1967 on conversations with the college's president, Esther Raushenbush, about the two institutions "lashing up together."[47] Suppose Sarah Lawrence were to move to Princeton and build a new campus near the university; what would be the potential for a fruitful relationship? Sarah Lawrence was attractive to Goheen for several reasons. The college's focus on intensive faculty-student interaction and tutorial-style teaching fit well with Princeton's preceptorials and independent work, and its programs in the creative and performing arts and in "community and sociological studies" would bring opportunities to Princeton undergraduates that Goheen was eager to cultivate.[48]

Raushenbush was sufficiently intrigued to explore the proposition—"our little flirtation with Princeton," she called it later[49]—but she worried that even the slightest hint that the college was considering such a possibility would prove to be explosive in the board and among faculty, students, and alumnae. Princeton's resources could expand the educational opportunities and physical facilities available to Sarah Lawrence students and faculty; at the same time, Princeton's reputed conservatism seemed at odds with Sarah Lawrence's distinctive character. Would enough be gained to offset

---

Princetonian, see Nov. 16, 1960, p. 5; Mar. 22, 1963, pp. 1, 5; Feb. 25, 1966, p. 5; and Dec. 9, 1968, pp. 1, 5. See also "Evelyn College for Women," in Alexander Leitch, *A Princeton Companion* (Princeton, NJ: Princeton University Press, 1978), pp. 170–71; Frances Patricia Healy, "A History of Evelyn College for Women, Princeton, New Jersey, 1887 to 1897" (Ph.D. dissertation, Ohio State University, 1967, University Microfilms, Ann Arbor, MI); Caroline Hearst, "A 'Dangerous Experiment' in Finances: The Story of Evelyn College, Princeton's Insolvent Coordinate College," paper written for History 487, Jan. 14, 2014, Princeton University, in the possession of Nancy Weiss Malkiel.

47 Goheen oral history, Oct. 26, 2004, p. 5; Gregory Vlastos to Robert F. Goheen, Jan. 27, 1967, Goheen, Box 93, Folder 4; Munford, "Coeducation at Princeton," p. 7.

48 Esther Raushenbush to David Riesman, May 4, 1967, Raushenbush, Box 2, Folder 7. Raushenbush's account of Goheen's interest in Sarah Lawrence can be found in fuller detail in Executive Session, Board of Trustees Meeting, May 10, 1967, Sarah Lawrence trustees. For Goheen's version, see, e.g., *Daily Princetonian*, June 8, 1967.

49 Raushenbush oral history, interview no. 9, Mar. 26, 1973, p. 286.

the losses of identity and location? The question was not whether to commit to Princeton but simply whether to embark on a study.

In April 1967 Raushenbush convened a small group of faculty members to consider the proposal. They were strongly negative. With its "intensely established character" and "academic conventionalism," Princeton would not be "congenial to the nature" of Sarah Lawrence. It would be difficult for Sarah Lawrence to protect its identity and go "its own way" in Princeton. The college would be best served by making its own independent plans for the future.[50]

When the idea was aired formally in the Sarah Lawrence board in May, it was quashed immediately. Although a small number of trustees thought it unwise to reject Princeton's proposal without studying the possibility, the overwhelming consensus was that Princeton had everything to gain and Sarah Lawrence everything to lose. The board voted unanimously to "inform Princeton that . . . our best interest would not be served by our moving to Princeton."[51]

To Goheen, Raushenbush wrote, "The discussion was long and serious; and the outcome was that [the board] took a strong position supporting the college's continued, unaffiliated existence, here at Bronxville, at least for the foreseeable future." Were the college to move, it would likely lose its independence and flexibility in planning for the future. No matter what the two schools' intentions, Princeton's strength would simply "come to govern" Sarah Lawrence's "educational decisions." Moreover, the board expressed concern that "both women students and faculty would slowly shift in character to suit the mode of Princeton," losing some of the distinctive qualities that gave Sarah Lawrence "its special character."[52] In correspondence with Sarah Lawrence trustees, Raushenbush added that the board believed that "even bringing it

50 Notes on a Meeting of the General Committee, Apr. 13, 1967, to Discuss Project S, General Committee Records, Box 1, Sarah Lawrence College Archives.

51 Executive Session, Board of Trustees Meeting, May 10, 1967, Sarah Lawrence trustees.

52 Esther Raushenbush to Robert F. Goheen, May 11, 1967, Raushenbush, Box 2, Folder 7.

[the contemplated move] into open discussion" would "seriously endanger" the college's current efforts to raise funds.[53] In fact, she never favored the move. As she acknowledged later, "There was no point when I felt we should do this. I just felt it would be the end of Sarah Lawrence."[54]

On June 3, the *New York Times* reported that Sarah Lawrence had rebuffed Princeton's overtures; the college would remain in Bronxville and explore coeducation on its own terms.[55] Sarah Lawrence admitted men in 1969. In October 1968, following the circulation of the Patterson report recommending coeducation for Princeton, Raushenbush wrote to Goheen, "I have thought from the beginning that this should be your direction."[56]

Goheen Goes to the Princeton Board

As the Sarah Lawrence conversations unfolded, there were new internal pressures at Princeton for coeducation. Campaigning in student elections had not been permitted previously, but in the spring of 1967 there was a new student government organization, and for the first time, candidates would be campaigning for positions. Coeducation was a natural platform. The student campaigners distributed polls to undergraduates and faculty members; both groups strongly supported coeducation. A coeducation panel discussion featured undergraduate political candidates, together with women from Vassar, Wellesley, and Radcliffe. The candidates in favor of coeducation won their elections; coeducation had "proven its worth as an issue."[57]

It was in this context that Goheen presented the case for coeducation to the board in June. It could "no longer be reckoned to Princeton's advantage," Goheen said, "to postpone entry into the

53 Esther Raushenbush to Bernhard M. Auer, May 25, 1967, Raushenbush, Box 2, Folder 7.

54 Raushenbush oral history, interview no. 9, Mar. 26, 1973, p. 287.

55 *New York Times*, June 3, 1967, clipping in Goheen, Box 93, Folder 4.

56 Esther Raushenbush to Robert F. Goheen, Oct. 8, 1968, Goheen, Box 94, Folder 2.

57 Munford, "Coeducation at Princeton," p. 7 (source of the quote); *Daily Princetonian*, Apr. 26 and May 1 and 2, 1967.

education of women on a significant scale." The first reason had to do with admissions: There was some evidence that Princeton was "beginning to become <u>comparatively</u> less attractive to some applicants whom we would like to have because of lack of girls here."[58] Everyone was sensitive to Princeton's standing among applicants, especially with respect to its chief competitors, Harvard and Yale. Goheen read a letter he had received in May from the president of the Westminster Schools in Atlanta, William L. Pressley, who alerted Goheen to "a change here . . . which I suspect is also taking place in other secondary schools." When college admission officers visited Westminster, Pressley wrote, "our boys asked this question: 'Are girls on the campus or do the boys have to wait until the weekend and import girls?'" It was, he said, "the most frequently asked question," and "the answer made a difference, for our seniors chose the colleges where the girls are." From the first graduating class at Westminster a dozen years earlier, the school had averaged three students a year in the entering class at Princeton. For the class of 1971, no one would be enrolling. Although Princeton had extended offers to "the best" of the Westminster candidates, those students had opted for their first-choice colleges, "and these colleges have girls."[59] Goheen acknowledged that the Pressley testimony was "not conclusive evidence." But, he added, "active interest in coeducation at <u>Yale</u>, <u>Wesleyan</u>, <u>Williams</u>, and <u>Hamilton</u>, and the new <u>MIT-Wellesley</u> linkage will increase the problem for us. Measured against them, Princeton is likely to seem increasingly deficient to many good applicants."

Goheen's second reason for believing that Princeton needed to embrace the education of women was "what women can add to the intellectual and cultural life of the University." His third reason was "the more extensive and active role of women in the modern world and their rising need for the best in higher education." Given that the status of women would likely continue to evolve, an

58 Robert F. Goheen, The Education of Women at Princeton: Notes for a Presentation to the Board, June 1967, Goheen, Box 93, Folder 4.
59 William L. Pressley to Robert F. Goheen, May 3, 1967, Goheen, Box 93, Folder 4.

all-male institution would simply be "anachronistic" twenty years thence.

Goheen asked the board to authorize a "careful and hard-headed" study of Princeton's options. What choices did Princeton have? How much would each one cost? How would admitting women stack up against "other high priority concerns"?[60] Such questions would need to be answered in great detail. And if Goheen were to have any hope of selling coeducation to the doubters in the Princeton community, hard facts and painstaking analysis would be essential.[61] As Bowen said, "The only way we were going to bring the trustees to a thoughtful conclusion . . . was with real evidence," presented through "a major research project" that would "examine both the desirability and the feasibility . . . of co-education."[62]

Goheen told the board that Gardner Patterson, an economist on the faculty of the Woodrow Wilson School, was available to conduct such a study. Goheen concluded, "A university with so profound a sense of obligation to the world can no longer, I believe, ignore the educational needs of one half the human race." Careful not to overstep, he quickly added, "But I ask for no such large and binding agreement from the Board today on this matter. I ask only that you take the issue to be a pressing one, worth your most sober and prayerful consideration; and that you empower the administration to proceed with the study that I have recommended."[63]

Trustees familiar with other educational institutions spoke of the benefits to education when men and women studied together. Others spoke about coeducation as the "'wave of the present' in higher education." To continue "to be a great university," Princeton would need to enroll women. Trustees spoke about children and grandchildren who profited from, indeed preferred, going to coeducational schools. A trustee with nine granddaughters said

60 Goheen, The Education of Women at Princeton: Notes for a Presentation to the Board.

61 Goheen oral history, Oct. 26, 2004, p. 5.

62 Bowen oral history, June 9, 2009, p. 20.

63 Goheen, The Education of Women at Princeton: Notes for a Presentation to the Board.

that he would "be pleased to have [them] attend Princeton." Even trustees who were not prepared to opine on the merits of the case supported an "open-minded," "thorough," "objective," "careful," "critical" study.[64] Although the minutes do not record the dissenters, some trustees were at least cautiously skeptical, or even outright opposed, as subsequent correspondence with Goheen makes plain.[65]

During the lunch recess, the president and the chairman of the executive committee, James F. Oates, Jr., '21, chairman of the board of the Equitable Life Assurance Society, drew up a proposed announcement of the board's authorization of the study, which was approved unanimously when the trustees reconvened.[66] The president announced the authorization the next day at the university commencement in remarks entitled "Nassau Hall: Constancy and Change." As he told the graduating seniors and their guests, "I would ask you to look on Nassau Hall" not just as "the embodiment of a stiff and unchanging institution" but as "a symbol of change—of change as one of the few constants in the life of any vital institution." He called attention to the decision to undertake a study of the possibility of coeducation at Princeton, an apt example of his general point.[67]

The Patterson Methodology

Goheen's next task was to form the committee to conduct the study. He had already lined Patterson up to lead the effort. A native Iowan, Patterson had earned his A.B. degree from the University of Michigan in 1938 and his M.A. there the following year. In 1949,

---

64 Minutes of Meeting of the Board of Trustees, Princeton University, June 12, 1967, pp. 11–12, Princeton trustees, Series 1, Vol. 65.

65 See, e.g., Donald Danforth to Robert F. Goheen, June 14, 1967; Goheen to Danforth, June 30, 1967; Harvey Molé to Goheen, June 9 and Aug. 18, 1967; and Goheen to Molé, June 30, 1967, all in Goheen, Box 93, Folder 4. See also the strongly negative Donold B. Lourie to Arthur J. Horton, Nov. 16, 1967, and John Stuart to Lourie, Nov. 16, 1967, both in Horton, Box 1, Folder 6.

66 Minutes of Meeting of the Board of Trustees, Princeton University, June 12, 1967, p. 13, Princeton trustees, Series 1, Vol. 65.

67 Princeton University news release, June 14, 1967, Goheen, Box 93, Folder 4.

the same year that he earned his Ph.D. in economics from Harvard, he joined the Princeton faculty. From 1958 through 1964, he held the directorship (a position later called dean) of the Woodrow Wilson School, drawing on the resources of a newly endowed foundation, later identified as the Robertson Foundation, to inaugurate a graduate program to train students for careers in the public arena, especially international affairs.

Although international finance at Princeton was well staffed with theorists, Patterson was a policy expert, and he had ample practical experience in the field. Over the course of his career, he had served on numerous government assignments abroad. Most recently, in February 1966, he had taken leave from the university to serve as assistant director-general for trade policy and intelligence at the General Agreement on Tariffs and Trade (GATT) Conference in Geneva.[68]

Patterson clearly had the stature, broad respect on campus, organizational ability, and analytic expertise to carry out the study. He was also available, because the GATT position, initially intended to last through the first semester of the next academic year, was ending early, by Patterson's own choice. The Kennedy Round of trade negotiations had ended in the late spring of 1967, and it appeared to Patterson that the remaining work at GATT would be relatively routine, no longer at the level of complexity and urgency that had justified his permission to be away for two years. He would be returning to Princeton in September without teaching obligations for the fall, so he would be free to focus on the assignment Goheen was asking him to undertake.[69] One other factor weighed in Patterson's appointment. As Goheen said, "I also had a sense that he did not have any passionate convictions on coeducation."[70]

The primary task, Goheen told Patterson, was to sort out and carefully assess "the educational and financial implications of the

68 Biographical Information, Dr. Gardner Patterson, n.d., Horton, Box 1, Folder 6; Princeton University faculty personnel records, accessed via a staff member in the office of the dean of the faculty.

69 Patterson took another leave in 1969–70 and resigned officially from Princeton as of June 30, 1970, to become GATT's director-general for trade policy, effective August 1, 1969. Princeton University faculty personnel records.

70 Quoted in Munford, "Coeducation at Princeton," p. 8.

various possible ways Princeton might try to move into coeducation." It would be important to draw on the best experience of other institutions. The goal would be "to work toward answers that are manageable without being unimaginative." With Patterson's "analytical abilities" and "good judgment," Goheen thought he was the right man for the job.[71]

Bowen sent a note encouraging Patterson to accept the president's invitation. "I have been convinced for some time now that what the University does (or does not do) with regard to the education of women will have profound effects on the future of this place," he wrote. "It is absolutely clear to me that you are the right person, in terms of ability, sense, status—and the presence of a daughter—to serve as chairman of a faculty group to explore this issue."[72]

By the time Bowen's letter arrived in Geneva, Patterson had already posted a letter back to Goheen accepting his invitation. In a note to Bowen, Patterson called it "an easy decision" because of "the importance of the matter."[73] To Goheen he wrote, "I would be glad to try my hand" at the study. "My heart will be in it, too."[74] Patterson explained later, "It's the sort of problem that interests a man trained in economics—coeducation is a matter of how to balance off at the margins, to weigh a series of benefits and costs, advantages and disadvantages."[75]

After consulting with Bowen and others, Goheen named faculty members and administrators to the study committee that Patterson would chair. In his letter of invitation, he described the work at hand. There were "thorny fiscal problems and many other issues to be weighed and discussed." The investigation was to be "sober" and "objective," giving "no less attention to the cons than the pros."[76]

The Patterson committee first convened in the president's office on September 22, 1967. Goheen and Bowen spoke about "priorities

---

71 Robert F. Goheen to Gardner Patterson, May 26, 1967, Patterson, Box 3, Folder 3.

72 William G. Bowen to Gardner Patterson, May 29, 1967, Patterson, Box 3, Folder 3.

73 Gardner Patterson to William G. Bowen, June 1, 1967, Patterson, Box 3, Folder 3.

74 Gardner Patterson to Robert F. Goheen, June 1, 1967, Patterson, Box 3, Folder 3.

75 Quoted in John V. Dippel, "The Coeducation Study," *Princeton Alumni Weekly* 68 (Dec. 5, 1967): 6.

76 Robert F. Goheen to Michael N. Danielson, July 25, 1967, Patterson, Box 3, Folder 3.

for the committee," and Patterson told his colleagues how he saw the work ahead. He would be "solely responsible for the report"; the committee would serve in an advisory capacity to him.[77] That condition had been important to Patterson; as he later told a reporter for the *Daily Princetonian*, "after negotiating for a year and a half with international diplomats," he had no interest in taking on "the burden of getting seven or eight academicians to agree with each other."[78] A small advisory committee of students would work alongside the Patterson committee as the project went forward.[79]

The principal link between the committee and the president would be the provost, who would be taking a role that was not so much officially assigned as enacted in practice and almost naturally assumed. Bowen was fully engaged, meeting frequently with Patterson, conferring on matters of substance as well as strategy, offering advice, reporting to Goheen on the work of the committee, and inviting the president's reactions and suggestions.[80]

Although the committee met periodically, Patterson carried out the lion's share of the work. He set out systematically to inform himself about the experience of coeducation and coordinate education at other colleges and universities. He made campus visits, gathering relevant materials, talking to administrators and faculty members, and taking copious notes, reporting his findings to his committee and to the provost.[81] In addition, he corresponded with faculty members and administrators at other institutions with something to say about, or some interest in contemplating, coeducation and coordinate education. He collected data, reviewed internal studies and reports, and borrowed good ideas where he found them.[82]

77 *Daily Princetonian*, Sept. 26, 1967. See also William G. Bowen to Robert F. Goheen, Sept. 11, 1967, Goheen, Box 93, Folder 4.

78 Munford, "Coeducation at Princeton," p. 8.

79 Robert F. Goheen to Undergraduate Assembly President Marc E. Lackritz, Sept. 14, 1967, and Lackritz to Goheen, Sept. 21, 1967, both in Goheen, Box 93, Folder 4.

80 See, e.g., William G. Bowen to Robert F. Goheen, Oct. 12, 1967, Goheen, Box 93, Folder 4.

81 William G. Bowen to Robert F. Goheen, Nov. 14, 1967, Patterson, Box 1, Folder 3. The many detailed reports on these campus visits can be found in Patterson, Box 1, Folder 3, and Box 2, Folders 2, 3, 6, 9.

82 These interactions are documented in plentiful correspondence in Patterson, Box 1, Folders 19, 20, 21, 22; Box 2, Folders 5, 8; and Box 4, Folder 9.

The experiences of other institutions provided useful guide-posts. What were the pros and cons of coeducation and coordinate education? What was the best ratio of men to women? How did patterns of course selection differ by gender? What about the choices of concentrations? What of attrition rates by gender? What happened to dynamics in the classroom when women were added? Did women require any special curricular arrangements? Would women engage in independent study in the same fashion that men did, or would they require greater supervision? Did the costs of residential arrangements for women differ from those for men? Did women require any all-female spaces beyond their dormitory rooms? How did coeducation affect women students' health and well-being? What administrative costs attended the incorporation of women into the student body? Were administrators needed for the dedicated oversight and care of women students? Did women require different levels of financial aid than men? What were patterns of alumni giving among women and men?[83]

Beyond what could be learned by visiting other institutions, there was a clear need for data. Patterson and his colleagues wanted to know what high school students planning to go to college thought about single-sex versus coeducational versus coordinate institutions and how their opinions varied, if at all, depending on such variables as academic standing and likely area of study. They wanted to know what Princeton undergraduates thought: How did they appraise the Princeton social scene? Where did they stand on coeducation? And if Princeton were to remain all-male, would they recommend it to their younger brothers?[84]

The results of the poll of secondary school students were as follows: 78 percent of males and females favored coeducational colleges, and the percentage "increased with a student's class rank.

---

83 See, e.g., Gardner Patterson memorandum for file, Course Selections: Harvard-Radcliffe, Oct. 3, 1967; David N. Kershaw to Robert Shenton, Oct. 18, 1967; Questions to Be Asked at Radcliffe and Harvard by Professor Patterson and Dr. Berry on October 30 and 31 and November 1, 1967; and draft, Memorandum for the Files, Discussions at Harvard and Radcliffe, October 30 and 31 and Nov. 2, 1967, all in Patterson, Box 2, Folder 3; Patterson to Richard W. Lyman, Nov. 1, 1967, and Memorandum for the Files, Visit to Stanford, November 15, 16, 17, and 20, 1967, both in Patterson, Box 2, Folder 9.

84 William G. Bowen to Robert F. Goheen, Oct. 17 and Nov. 14, 1967, Goheen, Box 93, Folder 4; *Daily Princetonian*, Oct. 13 and Nov. 15, 1967.

Only five per cent said they favored a one-sex college." The results of the undergraduate poll were equally striking: "83 per cent [of the respondents] favored coeducation; 90 per cent said it would help the classroom atmosphere." Only 18 percent "characterized the present social system as 'satisfactory.'" To the question of whether they would advise an academically qualified younger brother to choose an all-male Princeton, the students' disinclination to do so increased with their experience at Princeton. The answer was "No from 22 per cent of the freshmen, 41 per cent of the sophomores, 50 per cent of the juniors and 56 per cent of the seniors."[85]

Patterson and his colleagues wanted to know, too, what members of the Princeton faculty thought about single-sex versus coeducational classrooms. They distributed a detailed questionnaire. What did faculty members think about the prospect of teaching coeducational, as opposed to all-male, classes? If both sexes were represented in the classroom, what would be the effect on "the willingness of students to ask questions and engage in discussion with the instructor and other students," on "the variety of viewpoints" and "methods of tackling problems," and, "more generally, on full and free discussion"? Would faculty members prefer to send their sons to coeducational or single-sex institutions? Where would they prefer to send their daughters? What would be the effect of coeducation on faculty recruitment? On attracting the best high school students to Princeton? In sum, what did members of the faculty think about the importance of admitting women to Princeton?[86] The results of the poll were clear: "91 per cent of the entire faculty, and 98 per cent of the faculty under 30 favored coeducation."[87]

The committee was also interested in the views of faculty members who had taught at coeducational institutions or who had taught classes at Princeton that included women in the critical languages program. What difference did having men and women

---

85 Munford, "Coeducation at Princeton," p. 9.

86 Memorandum, "Education of Women at Princeton," Faculty-Administration Committee on Education of Women at Princeton to Members of the Faculty, Oct. 27, 1967, Goheen, Box 93, Folder 4.

87 Munford, "Coeducation at Princeton," p. 9.

in the classroom make in terms of class participation? Was there any validity to the "oft-repeated assertion that bright girls 'play dumb'" in classes with men? Did coeducation increase the level of men's participation so that *they* would avoid appearing dumb in front of the women? Was "a greater variety of approaches and viewpoints" voiced in coeducational classes? How did the presence of students of both sexes affect student preparation, instructor preparation, and the quality of teaching? Were men reluctant to enroll in, or attracted to, classes with substantial numbers of women? And what of women's inclinations with respect to classes with substantial numbers of men? Were women more demanding than men of time in office hours?[88]

Part of the committee's task, then, was to draft and disseminate its own surveys and collect and analyze response data. Some of that effort was accomplished with the clear understanding that Princeton was asking for the information. In the case of the survey of high school students, the decision was made to undertake the effort in collaboration with Smith College, where a faculty committee was studying the question of coeducation. The questionnaire, developed in partnership between the two institutions, was disseminated anonymously, making no mention of who was asking the questions, and embedding questions about coeducation in a wide-ranging set of other questions so that the motive for the survey would not be apparent.[89]

Along with these efforts, David Kershaw, the Woodrow Wilson School administrator staffing the committee, and associate provost Paul Benacerraf, on loan from his professorship in philosophy, undertook the laborious job of collecting and analyzing data about Princeton—patterns of course enrollments, numbers of departmental concentrators, numbers of faculty members, class sizes,

88 Draft, Gardner Patterson to Professor [Fritz] Mote, Sept. 20, 1967, Bowen provost, Box 18, Folder 1; Patterson to Professor Martin B. Dickson, Sept. 29, 1967; Charles E. Townsend to Patterson, Oct. 3, 1967; Mote to Patterson, Oct. 5, 1967; and Norman Itzkowitz to Patterson, Oct. 13, 1967, all in Patterson, Box 4, Folder 1. The quotes are in the memos from Patterson.

89 Draft Questionnaire to High School Students Planning to Attend College, Sept. 1967, Goheen, Box 93, Folder 4; Special Questionnaire on Seniors' Attitudes toward College, n.d., Bowen provost, Box 18, Folder 7.

physical facilities—to determine the university's capacity for adding more undergraduates. What could be learned about likely patterns of course and major selection among women students? Where did Princeton have excess capacity to fill? Where would capacity need to be increased? What new facilities would be required? Would more faculty be needed? What impact, if any, would coeducation have on modes of instruction? What additional staffing would university offices require? What would be the relative costs of adding women to the undergraduate student body in a fully coeducational mode, compared with building a coordinate women's college? To complement the Princeton data, Patterson asked for data from the federal government and an array of educational organizations.[90]

Gathering the views of Princeton alumni proved to be the thorniest challenge. Goheen, Bowen, and Patterson agreed that surveying alumni would be a mistake. Alumni opinions about Princeton were typically grounded in sentiment and history. Princeton needed to look forward, not back. The committee needed to understand the views of current and future students, who would populate the student body going forward; and it needed to understand the views of the faculty who would be teaching future generations of undergraduates. Alumni were tricky; they were very likely to express strong views based on their own experience, but they had little or no expertise about or claim on the future. And if they were polled without having important information about the pros and cons of coeducation, they were likely to dig themselves into a position—undoubtedly negative—from which it would be difficult to extricate themselves. Moreover, because attitudes were changing and younger alumni were more receptive to coeducation, any poll of older alumni would skew the results. At the same time, alumni could not understand why they were not being asked for their views. If the committee was surveying high school students, undergraduates, and faculty members, why not also solicit the

90 Gardner Patterson to Bernard Sisco, Sept. 22, 1967; George P. Berry to John Stalnaker, Oct. 19, 1967; Berry to Henry Chauncey, Oct. 19, 1967; and Patterson to Gilmore Stott, Feb. 26, 1968, all in Patterson, Box 2, Folder 1; Minutes of Meeting of the Board of Trustees, Princeton University, Oct. 20, 1967, p. 10, Princeton trustees, Series 1, Vol. 66.

opinions of alumni, who knew more about and had more invested in Princeton than any other constituency?

The issue needed to be handled carefully. In October, Patterson and Bowen briefed the leaders of the alumni council about the mandate of the Patterson committee, its work thus far, and its plans going forward so that the alumni council could discuss the matter in a knowledgeable way with other alumni. The next step— following a suggestion made by the council chair—was to arrange more formally to inform alumni of the committee's work by way of an interview with Patterson in the *Princeton Alumni Weekly* (*PAW*). The goal of the interview was to help alumni to "understand the complexity of the issues involved and the systematic way in which the University [was] attempting to sort out the various alternatives," Bowen told Goheen. Appreciating the thoroughness and care of the Patterson investigation might go a long way to heading off "irresponsible alumni criticism." Done well, Bowen believed, the interview "should disabuse some people of the idea that this is an easy question to be decided simply on the basis of how one feels about girls and should also allay the fears of some others that the University is moving precipitously into coeducation without having considered all of the implications." It was much better to tell alumni in detail what the committee was doing, and to invite thoughtful discussion of the issues, than to seem "to keep the alumni in the dark."[91]

The interview with Patterson appeared in the December 5, 1967, issue of the *PAW*. Patterson reassured alumni that the university's enduring commitments would not change: "Our assumption is that the fundamental mission of the university—to provide an excellent education to capable students and to maintain an extensive program of research—continues unchanged." Patterson continued, "But we must also keep abreast of the times, and decide how best to fulfill these tasks in the environment in which we are now living. . . . The composition of the student body, and the question

---

91 William G. Bowen to Robert F. Goheen, Oct. 17, 1967; T. Henry Dixon to John Davies, Oct. 18, 1967; and Goheen to Dan D. Coyle, Nov. 7, 1967, all in Goheen, Box 93, Folder 4.

of women in it, is a major issue that every major university, including Princeton, has to face." Patterson's interviewer then reviewed the committee's approach to its work and the activities Patterson and his colleagues were undertaking. The interview closed with an invitation from Patterson to alumni to let him know what they thought.[92]

In mid-January 1968, Patterson reported to the board of trustees on the work done to that point. The board asked questions, offered suggestions, and urged that alumni be kept fully informed.[93] Some specific actions ensued from the board discussion. In January the Patterson committee sent a questionnaire to Princetonians involved in education; in March Patterson followed suit with a letter and questionnaire to members of the alumni schools committees. In late February Goheen prepared a letter to all alumni to accompany a transcript of the interim report that Patterson had made to the trustees. Both were published in the *PAW*.[94]

Of all communications from alumni, the most telling came from Paul Swain Havens, the president of the all-female Wilson College, a member of the Princeton class of 1925:

> I am struck by the nearly complete absence in your questionnaire of any interest in the program or welfare or opportunities <u>for women</u> who might one day be Princeton undergraduates. The emphasis is everywhere on what might be good, bad, or indifferent for Princeton or its male students. But women are not to be regarded as merely tools of the welfare and comfort of Princeton and her male students. Their

92 Dippel, "The Coeducation Study," 6, 11, 12. The quote is from p. 6.
93 Transcript of Report to the Board of Trustees by Professor Gardner Patterson, Jan. 13, 1968, Patterson, Box 4, Folder 9; Minutes of Meeting of the Board of Trustees, Princeton University, Jan. 13, 1968, pp. 6–9, Princeton trustees, Series 1, Vol. 66.
94 In Goheen, Box 93, Folder 5, see Robert F. Goheen to Gardner Patterson, Jan. 15, 1968. In Bowen provost, Box 18, Folder 7, see Patterson to Princeton Alumnus [in the field of education], Jan. 17, 1968, and Patterson to Princeton Schools Committee Member, Mar. 27, 1968. In Horton, Box 1, Folder 5, see Goheen to John D. Davies, Feb. 22, 1968, and Goheen to Princeton Alumnus, Feb. 22, 1968, with attached Report (Interim) to the Trustees of Princeton University—Presented at the January Meeting by Professor Gardner Patterson. See also Patterson, "Coeducation—An Interim Report," *Princeton Alumni Weekly* 68 (Mar. 12, 1968): 6–8, 11.

education must be seen to be as important as that of Princeton men; and unless Princeton gives serious and conscientious thought to what it has to offer women, to planning for their growth—intellectual, spiritual, and social—as carefully as for the growth of the male students, then Princeton should abandon all thoughts of co-education.[95]

Patterson responded, "I must in all frankness acknowledge that from time to time we do slip into the mistake of considering certain aspects of this problem primarily from their possible effects on the welfare of . . . male students. . . . Indeed, the risk that Princeton might short-change women if they were to be admitted is one that has bothered me a great deal."[96] Goheen agreed, adding, "We who are responsible for this current study are as interested in what Princeton can and should do for the higher education of women, as in what women could do to improve the education of Princeton men."[97]

Did Princeton really have the needs and concerns of women in mind? Or was coeducation primarily a strategic move, a way of retaining competitive advantage by strengthening the quality and educational experience of male students? Those big, abstract, theoretical questions were not on Princeton's agenda in 1968. The immediate concern was more practical: to finish the Patterson report and sell it to the board of trustees.

95 Paul Swain Havens to Gardner Patterson, Jan. 30, 1968, Patterson, Box 1, Folder 19.
96 Gardner Patterson to Paul Swain Havens, Feb. 8, 1968, Patterson, Box 1, Folder 19.
97 Robert F. Goheen to Paul S. Havens, Feb. 8, 1968, Goheen, Box 93, Folder 5.

5

Princeton: "A Penetrating Analysis of Far-Reaching Significance"

Unexpectedly, one of the biggest obstacles to the timely completion of the Patterson report was a member of the Patterson committee, Arthur J. ("Jerry") Horton, the director of development, a member of the Princeton class of 1942.[1]

Jerry Horton Slams on the Brakes

Horton believed that Princeton had long thrived as a college for men; adding women to the mix would spoil the uniqueness, the special ambiance, that made the university so successful. Moreover, it would depress alumni giving. Surely it was wrong to imagine that the best boys would not consider an all-male Princeton; Horton knew personally of fine young men who wanted more than anything to enroll. Although the director of admission, John T. Osander, had told the Patterson committee that the absence of coeducation loomed as a serious issue for admissions, Horton knew that some members of the admission staff, along with alumni schools committee volunteers, believed otherwise. Moreover, Horton knew

1 Horton joined the annual giving staff in 1954. He became director of annual giving in 1959 and was promoted to director of development in the summer of 1967. With the appointment in the summer of 1969 of the university's first vice president for development, Henry E. Bessire '57, Horton was no longer fully in charge of the development office, but he continued to hold his directorship until 1976, when he was named recording secretary of the university, the post he held at the time of his death from a heart attack in April 1980. *New York Times*, Apr. 19, 1980; Princeton University administrative personnel records, accessed via an administrative staff member.

from friends at other institutions that having men and women on campus together was a recipe for trouble: more sexually transmitted diseases, more unplanned and unwanted pregnancies, more diversion from serious engagement in study, more frivolous partying, with all the imagined consequences.

While professing his loyalty as a university citizen, Horton engaged in a rear-guard action to challenge, even subvert, the committee's work. In memo after memo, he raised questions and objections about the committee's thinking and mode of proceeding. And he offered suggestions, some constructive, some less so, about better ways of communicating with alumni.[2]

When Gardner Patterson asked heads of administrative offices about the likely effect on their operations of the enrollment of women, Horton wrote:

> In time . . . we may have to consider Girl Agents . . . and maybe someone in AGO [the annual giving office]—a girl?—to handle them; . . . we will run headlong into a huge problem (as any coed place will confirm)—that of the surnames (i.e., when alumna Joyce Jones becomes Mrs. John P. Smith . . . whether he is alumnus or not). This IS a problem and would require more indexes and cross references and, of course, just plain more of everything in the record-keeping world. Plus a <u>lot of confusion</u>.[3]

In his response to the questionnaire to alumni in education, Horton laid out his objections to introducing coeducation to Princeton. He had concerns about the expense; how could the university contemplate finding tens of millions of dollars for coeducation when more than a hundred million dollars of unmet fund-raising objectives were already on the table?[4] He had concerns, too, about

---

2 In Bowen provost, Box 18, Folder 12, see Arthur J. Horton to Gardner Patterson, Feb. 13, 1968. In Horton, Box 1, Folder 5, see Horton, memorandum to the file, "Education of Women," Dec. 22, 1967, and Horton to William G. Bowen, Jan. 26, 1968.

3 Arthur J. Horton to Leslie L. Vivian, Mar. 22, 1968, Horton, Box 1, Folder 5.

4 Arthur J. Horton to Gardner Patterson, Feb. 13, 1968, Bowen provost, Box 18, Folder 12. On the money issue, see also Horton to William Bowen, Mar. 19, 1968, Horton, Box 1, Folder 5.

the impact of women on a Princeton education. Women would be distracting; their presence would interfere with the educational experience of Princeton men. "<u>Very</u> difficult for me to think that young men can gain as much from Princeton experience while spending time with girls 7 days a week as they can now," Horton said. "It's fun to become immersed in a problem, paper, thesis; just beyond my comprehension that boys could become <u>as</u> absorbed if they were plotting dates for coke, movies, etc as a regular daily thing."[5] (Later, he also began worrying how any woman could write a senior thesis with all the social pressure she would be under.[6]) Having women around all the time "couldn't help but cut down on time now devoted to studies and other pursuits" and would surely interfere with "a lot of the outside-the-classroom 'education' which boys now receive." Moreover, it was not clear that a Princeton education would be good for women. If he had a qualified daughter, Horton said, he would likely prefer to have her go elsewhere. Princeton was just "too 'intellectual'" for women, who should be in training to become "a good wife, mother & family person [rather] than a whiz kid."[7]

But Horton's objections were grounded in one question, "Why at Princeton?" He wrote to Patterson, "Princeton, the Princeton experience, is different—in a good way. Why do we want to change our character so markedly . . . ? The fact that others are doing it doesn't hold much water with me." He summed up, "I'm not against females, not against the idea of higher education for them, not against their role in the country. I just don't see why <u>we</u> feel we should necessarily concern ourselves with educating a few of them . . . at the very real risk of spoiling the esprit which has been responsible . . . for a large part of Princeton's successes in the past."[8]

Horton became the intake point for the opinions of alumni concerned about coeducation, and he collected many hundreds

5 Arthur J. Horton, Questionnaire to Undergraduate and Graduate Alumni Active in the Field of Education, Feb. 11, 1968, attached to Horton to Gardner Patterson, Feb. 13, 1968, Bowen provost, Box 18, Folder 12.

6 Arthur J. Horton to Gardner Patterson, Mar. 29, 1968, Horton, Box 1, Folder 5.

7 Horton, Questionnaire to Undergraduate and Graduate Alumni Active in the Field of Education.

8 Arthur J. Horton to Gardner Patterson, Feb. 13, 1968, Bowen provost, Box 18, Folder 12.

of letters, cards, and notes from disgruntled graduates.[9] These he shared, selectively, with Patterson and the provost, William Bowen, and, later, with trustees whom he believed were also likely to be opposed to coeducation. Sometimes he encouraged his alumni correspondents to write directly to those individuals; sometimes he passed along particular concerns and questions; sometimes he and his staff helped alumni craft their letters of objection and their answers to responses from Patterson.[10] When he got word of major donors who were put off by the possibility of coeducation, he made sure to pass the information along.[11] Horton also collected data to support his point of view. From F. Dana Payne, Jr., a dean at Cornell, for example, he solicited "data" on unwanted pregnancies and wrote, after Payne confirmed that Cornell had a number of them, "Keep us in mind if you've any more dope. The more <u>factual</u> the better. They love statistics (if they are in the right direction!). Anything you can release on that venereal disease problem? Rather touchy, I will admit. But if there are figures we'd sure like."[12] Throughout, Horton professed innocence to Patterson and Bowen. He was not "running around the countryside rallying forces against the project." He hadn't solicited the testimony. He wasn't trying to stir up trouble. It was just coming his way, and he was passing the information along.[13]

9 All of these he assembled in what is now the Arthur J. Horton Collection on Co-education, comprising four boxes in the Princeton University Archives. On each of the documents, doubtless to tell his secretary how he wanted the filing done, Horton had penciled, "Ladies."

10 For an example of correspondence with an alumnus whom Horton and colleagues helped in framing arguments and whom they directed to a particular trustee, see Theodore E. McAlister to Harold H. Helm, Feb. 26, 1968; Gardner Patterson to McAlister, Mar. 6, 1968; McAlister to Arthur J. Horton, Mar. 13, 1968; and Horton to McAlister, Mar. 29, 1968, all in Horton, Box 1, Folder 6.

11 See, e.g., Arthur J. Horton to Robert F. Goheen, May 29, 1967, Goheen, Box 93, Folder 4, in which Horton reports that Mrs. Edgar Palmer was "upset about 'all this coeducation talk'" and was threatening to change her will. See also Horton to Gardner Patterson, Feb. 28, 1968, Horton, Box 1, Folder 5, about a "top prospect" who was "quite sour" on Princeton because of the consideration of admitting women undergraduates.

12 In Horton, Box 1, Folder 5, see F. Dana Payne, Jr., to Arthur J. Horton, Mar. 16, 1968. In Horton, Box 1, Folder 6, see Horton to Payne, Mar. 29, 1968 (source of the quote). In Horton, Box 2, Folder 1, see Payne to Horton and Joseph L. Bolster, Jr., Apr. 13, 1968; Horton to Gardner Patterson, Apr. 14, 1968; and Horton to Payne, Apr. 17, 1968.

13 The quote comes from Arthur J. Horton to Gardner Patterson, Feb. 13, 1968, Bowen provost, Box 18, Folder 12. On Horton's protestations of innocence, see also,

Bowen and Patterson responded methodically to Horton's charges and suggestions. Bowen took on the policy questions; Patterson took on some of the more specific charges, using evidence to refute them. They kept trying to marshal data to show Horton where his allegations and assumptions were unfounded.[14] But Horton was unimpressed, and he continued to argue his case. In early April of 1968, for example, Osander reported to Bowen that he had "seven memos on my desk from Jerry Horton," all accumulated in the past week or so. "On this general question of coeducation the collected memos give the appearance of some sort of nervous twitch."[15]

Horton claimed that he had tried hard to listen, to read, to talk to others, and he had "done <u>much</u> soul-searching." But he decided that he would be unable to endorse the report. He sought Patterson's advice about what to do.[16] Patterson had hoped to be able to say that although individual committee members might have chosen their own wording, they found themselves "in agreement with the major findings and in support of the recommendations as well as with the thrust of the entire document." That was no longer possible, and he and Horton would have to work together on the "exact wording" to convey that Horton remained unconvinced.

As he had throughout, Patterson handled Horton with remarkable graciousness. If he was frustrated by Horton's repeated challenges, he declined to show it. "Your criticisms and the doubts have been of great help to me," he wrote, ". . . because you have

---

e.g., Horton to Patterson, Jan. 3, 1968, Horton, Box 1, Folder 6: "I received the enclosed letter . . . in yesterday's mail. . . . His blast, for the record, was entirely unsolicited by me—although it seems to echo many of the concerns which I have been trying to put forth to you in my various memos of recent dates."

14 In Bowen provost, Box 18, Folder 12, see W. G. Bowen to A. J. Horton, Feb. 5, 1968, responding to Horton to Bowen, Jan. 26, 1968, and Horton to Bowen, Feb. 12, 1968. In Horton, Box 1, Folder 5, see Gardner Patterson to Horton, Mar. 29, 1968; Patterson to Horton and Bowen, Mar. 26, 1968; Horton to Patterson, Feb. 27 and Mar. 1, 1968; Horton to Scott McVay, Mar. 19, 1968; and Patterson to Horton, Mar. 29, 1968. In Bowen provost, Box 19, Folder 3, see Bowen to E. Alden Dunham, Mar. 11, 1968, and Dunham to Bowen, Mar. 18, 1968.

15 Arthur J. Horton to Gardner Patterson, Apr. 11, 1968, and John T. Osander to William G. Bowen, Apr. 11, 1968, both in Bowen provost, Box 18, Folder 12.

16 Arthur J. Horton to Gardner Patterson, Apr. 18, 1968, Horton, Box 2, Folder 1. See also Horton to Patterson, May 28, 1968, Patterson, Box 1, Folder 9.

brought to my attention many points that I would otherwise certainly have overlooked. I have the sense now that no one can surprise me because you have been so diligent in probing the issue."[17]

The Trustees Organize to Consider the Patterson Report

In June 1968, Patterson made a second interim report to the Princeton trustees. Not only was it important to acquaint the board with the direction of the report; as Bowen had noted, because "the financial consequences" were "much less grim" than many members of the board had anticipated, having the information might lead the board to be more favorably disposed to the report as a whole.[18] On July 12, President Goheen informed the trustees that the report was finished and would be distributed to them shortly, and that it had his "firm endorsement." He said that a special committee of the board had been constituted under the leadership of Harold H. Helm '20 to give the report "close scrutiny" and provide its views to the full board in the fall.[19]

Lining up Helm had been critically important to Goheen. Helm had chaired the executive committee, he now chaired the finance committee, and he commanded wide respect among his colleagues. On July 8, Goheen went to visit him at his office at Chemical Bank New York Trust Company. He was taking a gamble. Helm was by no means a supporter of coeducation, but Goheen needed his backing to have a shot at winning over the trustees. When Goheen asked Helm to chair the study committee, he demurred: "But I don't believe in it!"[20] Helm told Goheen, "Bob, you've got the wrong man. I'm not sure at all I favor it, and I've got special doubts about the . . . report on finances."[21] Surely there was someone else better suited to lead the group. "Harold, I didn't ask you to believe in it," Goheen replied. "I asked you to study it."[22]

---

17 Gardner Patterson to Arthur J. Horton, Apr. 22, 1968, Patterson, Box 1, Folder 9.
18 W. G. Bowen to R. F. Goheen, May 13, 1968, Goheen, Box 93, Folder 5.
19 Robert F. Goheen to the Trustees, July 12, 1968, Goheen, Box 93, Folder 5.
20 Goheen oral history, Oct. 26, 2004, p. 6.
21 Luther Munford, "Coeducation at Princeton: The Struggle of an Idea at a University in Transition," *Daily Princetonian*, Oct. 21, 1969, p. 11.
22 Goheen oral history, Oct. 26, 2004, p. 6.

As a counterweight to Helm, Laurance S. Rockefeller '32, president of the Rockefeller Brothers Fund, was named vice chairman. Rockefeller had made plain that he was "deeply interested" in coeducation and ready to provide some tangible financial support for it.[23] The other members of the committee were Stephen Ailes '33, former secretary of the army and a lawyer at Steptoe & Johnson in Washington; William H. Attwood '41, editor-in-chief at Cowles Communications in New York; James I. Armstrong '41, president of Middlebury College; John B. Coburn '36, an Episcopal bishop serving as dean of the Episcopal Theological School in Cambridge, Massachusetts; Richard R. Hough '39, a vice president of American Telephone & Telegraph Company in New York; Donald B. Kipp '28, a lawyer at Pitney, Hardin, and Ward in Newark; William H. Rea '34, a steel company executive and civic leader in Pittsburgh; and Henderson Supplee, Jr., '26, of Philadelphia, who had retired as chairman of the board at ARCO. The group was well balanced in terms of age, length of service, and views on coeducation.[24]

The Helm committee met for the first time on July 23 at the Princeton Club in New York. Trustees offered advice on strengthening the report. They believed that Horton ought to be urged to write a dissenting statement so that people who had "misgivings about the education of women at Princeton" would see "evidence that opposing views were presented and discussed." The committee heard about plans for the rollout once the report was ready for public dissemination: a special meeting of the board on September 13, followed by a series of regional alumni meetings in the fall, as well as discussion among faculty and students. The group then went through the report, page by page, making a number of editorial suggestions.[25]

There was considerable discussion, again, about costs. Some trustees expressed skepticism about the financial data Patterson presented. Ricardo Mestres '31, financial vice president and

23 Ricardo Mestres to Robert F. Goheen, Apr. 24, 1968, Goheen, Box 93, Folder 5.

24 Robert F. Goheen to the Trustees, July 12, 1968, Goheen, Box 93, Folder 5; The Trustees of Princeton University, 1968–69, Horton, Box 1, Folder 3.

25 The Trustees of Princeton University, Committee to Consider the Report on the Education of Women, First Meeting, July 23, 1968, Goheen, Box 94, Folder 3.

treasurer of the university, spoke in support of Patterson's analysis. Mestres said he was persuaded by the finding "that the teaching resources of the University are so far from being fully used that women could be educated for a relatively low additional cost." Helm dealt with the unease over the cost projections by appointing a subcommittee on the financial aspects of the report, which would report back to the full committee at a subsequent meeting.[26]

In the wake of the meeting, both Helm and Goheen reached out to Horton. Helm asked Horton to meet him and Rockefeller for lunch in New York to give his views. Horton would then meet later in the day with the full committee. Goheen told Horton that the trustees felt that he "couldn't disagree and let it go at that without explanation." Horton was "completely free to say what was on [his] mind." But he really needed to explain himself.[27]

Goheen knew that coeducation was going to be a difficult proposition to sell. Horton's dissent, the likely firestorm among alumni when the report was released, the intense focus of some trustees on the reliability of the projected costs, and the challenge of raising money for coeducation led him to continue looking for alternate paths. He had a personal preference for coordinate education, and it was difficult for him to let go of the idea completely. As late as the end of August, Goheen was soliciting senior administrators' views about the feasibility of coordinate arrangements for women under a scheme he labeled "Stockton College."[28]

As appealing as coordinate education might be, the Patterson report, with its clear advocacy of coeducation, was on the table when the board of trustees met on September 13, 1968, at the University Club in New York. In attendance were twenty-eight of the thirty-four current trustees, along with six emeritus trustees and senior administrators. Helm read a statement summarizing the

26 Ibid. For Mestres's earlier skepticism on costs, see, e.g., Ricardo A. Mestres to Gardner Patterson, June 25, 1968, Goheen, Box 93, Folder 5.

27 Arthur J. Horton, memorandum to the file, "Summary of activities following the last meeting of Committee on Education of Women," Sept. 3, 1968, Horton, Box 4, Folder 5.

28 Robert F. Goheen to Those Designated, Aug. 29, 1968; J. P. Moran to Goheen, Sept. 10, 1968; Neil L. Rudenstine to Goheen, Sept. 12, 1968; and Richard A. Lester to Goheen, Sept. 16, 1968, all in Goheen, Box 96, Folder 3.

work of the special committee. Describing the Patterson report as "thorough and persuasive," the committee recommended that it be made widely available for discussion.[29]

Trustees raised many questions. What would be the trade-offs if women were admitted? What other important university objectives would be precluded? Suppose men were to be added instead—what would be the educational gains and losses, and what would be the relative costs? Would raising funds for coeducation damage efforts to raise funds for other priorities?[30]

Helm read a letter from Robert C. Tyson '27, chairman of the finance committee of the U.S. Steel Corporation, and reported a conversation with Donold B. Lourie '22, chairman of the board of the Quaker Oats Company. Both, unable to attend the meeting, had expressed "strong reservations" about Patterson's conclusions.[31]

Patterson's Calculations Prove Controversial

The report's financial estimates drew the most intense criticism; they were so low that trustees could not trust them. Helm also read a letter from an emeritus trustee, Dean Mathey '12, a partner in the Wall Street firm Dillon, Read & Co. and the longtime chairman of the board's finance committee, expressing his deep reservations. The estimate of additional expenses that would be incurred, Mathey wrote, "is, in my opinion, one of the most fantastically understated estimates that a responsible committee could possibly present to the Trustees." Mathey added, "If the Board were to accept the recommendations of the Patterson report without prayerfully reviewing the financial consequences of its acts, I believe it would be doing the greatest disservice possible to the University which we all love and have served over the years."[32]

29 Princeton University, Minutes of Special Meeting of the Board of Trustees, Sept. 13, 1968, pp. 2–3, Princeton trustees, Series 1, Vol. 67. Emeritus trustees received notice of all meetings and were invited to attend but had no vote.

30 Ibid., pp. 3–5.

31 Ibid., p. 4; Robert C. Tyson to James F. Oates, Jr., Sept. 10, 1968, Goheen, Box 93, Folder 6.

32 Dean Mathey to James F. Oates, Sept. 10, 1968, Goheen, Box 93, Folder 6.

Goheen had already told Mathey that although he was sympathetic to Mathey's "concern and anxiety," he thought that Mathey was "much harder on those calculations [the financial estimates in the report] than is warranted." To Donald Kipp, who also expressed serious reservations about the report, especially on financial grounds, Goheen wrote, "There are, of course, difficult financial questions, and they must be faced squarely. At the same time, I think that this is the kind of fundamental issue which has to be resolved first on its intrinsic merits and then dealt with in terms of its practicalities."[33]

What these trustees thought coeducation would or should cost is not known. Nor is it clear that their objections rested exclusively on financial grounds. As Mestres later observed in a confidential letter to Helm, "It is not very reassuring after sixteen years in this position to experience what I am convinced are emotional objections to the program cloaked under the vague and unspecified questions of economic viability."[34]

What the Patterson report said—using figures scrupulously reviewed, checked, and rechecked by Mestres, Bowen, and others—is that the effect on the operating budget of the admission of a thousand women (at 1968–69 prices) would be a net increase of between $215,000 and $380,000 a year—in other words, $215 to $380 per student—and that the capital costs (again at 1968–69 prices) incurred would be between $24.2 and $25.7 million. The report acknowledged that the figures were "surprisingly low," so low that "they may strain the credulity of many of those acquainted with the financing of education at Princeton," and it took some care to explain the numbers. With respect to the operating budget, at issue were "the differences between marginal costs and average costs." With a thousand additional students, it would be possible to make better use of existing faculty and other resources, which would actually enable a reduction in the per-student costs for the current undergraduate student body. In other words, Princeton

33 Robert F. Goheen to Dean Mathey, Sept. 11, 1968, and Goheen to Donald B. Kipp, Sept. 24, 1968, both in Goheen, Box 93, Folder 6.

34 Ricardo A. Mestres to Harold H. Helm, Oct. 28, 1968, Goheen, Box 95, Folder 5.

could add a thousand women undergraduates "for much less than a proportional increase in costs."

The opportunity presented itself at that moment, the report said, because of "four interrelated considerations." The first was that significant growth in the graduate program since World War II had created capacity that was not being fully utilized and could be made available to undergraduates. The second was Princeton's decision to provide strong academic departments across the arts and sciences, which meant that certain fields, like the languages and literatures and the arts, had capacity beyond what the existing student body was utilizing. The third consideration was that Princeton had intentionally built up a senior faculty adequate to carry out graduate instruction and scholarship in all fields; that growth could redound to the benefit of a larger undergraduate student population. Put differently, "considerably more under-graduate[s]" might "benefit from the presence of more or less the same senior faculty and graduate student populations." The fourth consideration was that Princeton had built many new buildings and renovated others over the past decade, with room for future growth in student numbers incorporated into those additions to the campus footprint.[35]

The report devoted more than two-fifths of its text to a close analysis of the projected costs. In addition, the provost did his own careful review of the committee's financial estimates. But with the intensity of the skepticism expressed by some of their number, the trustees believed that it would be wise to commission an outside study to assess the reliability of the financial data, an endeavor they later enlisted the Ford Foundation to carry out.[36]

The board endorsed the administration's proposals to disseminate the Patterson report through the *Princeton Alumni Weekly*

---

35 "'The Education of Women at Princeton': A Special Report," *Princeton Alumni Weekly* 69 (Sept. 24, 1968): 31–32ff.

36 For the Bowen review, see William G. Bowen to Members of the Trustee Sub-committee on the Education of Women, Sept. 9, 1968, Princeton trustees, Series 5, Box 58, Folder 22. On the outside study by the Ford Foundation, see Princeton University, Minutes of a Stated Meeting of the Executive Committee, Sept. 27, 1968, p. 2, Princeton trustees, Series 1, Vol. 67.

and to discuss it in meetings with alumni around the country.[37] At lunch following the meeting, trustees stressed, among other points, "the importance of the crossroads decision being faced by the Board." At the conclusion of his minutes, the board's clerk, Donald Kipp, recorded a telling point: "It was observed that in recent decades there has been radical change in attitude toward women in education, as in business and in the professions, and that a future Board may wonder why the present decision seemed difficult."[38]

At a press conference following the board meeting, Helm called the report a "penetrating analysis" that would be of "far-reaching significance to Princeton and . . . to all colleges and universities" in the United States. The report would be disseminated and discussed broadly. The trustees cautioned that it would take some time to reach a decision about how to proceed.[39]

The Patterson Report Is Released

The Patterson report was released on September 16, 1968, in the form of a special issue of the *Princeton Alumni Weekly*, dated September 24, which was mailed to all alumni, faculty members, students, and others.[40] The report offered an unambiguous endorsement of coeducation: "Princeton would be a better university if women were admitted to the undergraduate college." The undergraduate student body should consist "of not less than 25 percent" women, with a preferred target of not fewer than a thousand; the inclusion of women should be accomplished by increasing the total number of students. As for format, coeducation was far preferable to coordinate education. And the fiscal obstacles to

---

37 Princeton University, Minutes of Special Meeting of the Board of Trustees, Sept. 13, 1968, p. 5, Princeton trustees, Series 1, Vol. 67.

38 Ibid.

39 Princeton University news release, "Harold H. Helm: Statement at Press Conference on the Education of Women at Princeton, Sept. 13, 1968," Sept. 16, 1968, Admission Office, Box 11; *Daily Princetonian*, Sept. 17, 1968.

40 Dan D. Coyle, Memorandum: "'The Education of Women at Princeton': A Special Report," Sept. 11, 1968, Goheen, Box 93, Folder 6; "'The Education of Women at Princeton': A Special Report."

such a move—real though they were—were "far less" than had been imagined and clearly "feasible to overcome."[41]

Recommending the addition of a thousand women undergraduates was an important strategic decision. Substituting women for men would have been much more explosive politically. Princeton was in the business of producing leaders—*male* leaders—and alumni had a strong investment in the young men who matriculated at the university, whether they were sons or grandsons of alumni or excellent students from schools and communities to which alumni were deeply attached. Any move to decrease the number of undergraduate men would have been much riskier than the course of action proposed in the report.

As the report made plain, the stakes for Princeton were unusually high: "This is a momentous issue for Princeton; the most important question the University as a community has faced for many decades. Nationally, Princeton's response may well determine her ability to remain in the front rank of American educational institutions. Internally, no part of the University will remain unaffected." If Princeton chose not to seize the opportunity, "within a decade, if not sooner, Princeton's competitive position for students, for faculty, and for financial support, would be less strong than it now is."[42] Princeton's competitiveness was a crucial point. As Bowen noted later, "The decision on this issue would tell us whether Princeton was prepared to evolve in a thoughtful way . . . or whether it would just be 'stuck in the mud.'" (A decision against coeducation, Bowen told Goheen, would lead him to "leave Princeton, having given up on its capacity to evolve.")[43] What the report did not say—but Patterson, the administration, and the trustees knew—was that Princeton's competitive position would change because a raft of previously all-male colleges and universities were in the thick of their own deliberations about coeducation and had already announced, or would shortly be announcing, their future plans.[44]

41 "'The Education of Women at Princeton': A Special Report," 52–53.
42 Ibid., 52.
43 I am indebted to William G. Bowen for these reflections.
44 See, e.g., Robert F. Goheen to John C. Leslie, Nov. 5, 1968, Goheen, Box 95, Folder 5; Harold H. Helm to Members of the Executive Committee and Committee on

"Princeton is confronted with the challenge of adapting herself to fundamental changes in secondary education and in the nation's values and mores," the report continued. "Women are rapidly assuming all the rights and obligations that their many talents—including powerful intellectual ones—warrant. . . . Segregation of the sexes was fully consistent with our social institutions only a generation ago; but now, in the late 1960s, it is, quite simply, seen as anachronistic by most college students."[45] And, as Bowen noted later, single-sex education was also seen as anachronistic "by faculty and administrators, as well as by many forward-looking alumni."[46]

As the report pointed out, students in the late 1960s expected college to afford them opportunities to learn "from persons who have different combinations of qualities—intellectual, emotional, social." Men and women had much to learn from one another; they brought "different approaches, different angles of vision, [and] different viewpoints to many subject matters. . . . Bringing them together in the classroom improves the education of both."[47]

A coeducational Princeton would attract stronger and better students. Although Princeton was drawing a great many very good male applicants, it was attracting too few who were absolutely first-rate. And too many of the most compelling students admitted were choosing to enroll at other schools. Overall, Princeton lost 39 percent of the total number of men admitted in the spring of 1968 to the class of 1972, but it lost 56 percent of the admitted students rated as "truly outstanding both academically and non-academically." In the preceding year, for the class of 1971, Princeton had lost only 47 percent of that exceptional group. The absence of women students played a strong role in these students' decisions to enroll at other institutions. The data for the admitted

---

the Education of Women, Nov. 25, 1968, Goheen, Box 93, Folder 6. Helm transmitted an excerpt from an article in the Nov. 15, 1968, issue of *Higher Education and National Affairs* (pp. 4–5), indicating that twenty-six men's schools and thirty-six women's colleges had "recently elected to accept both men and women as students."

45 "'The Education of Women at Princeton': A Special Report," 52.
46 I am indebted to William G. Bowen for this comment.
47 "'The Education of Women at Princeton': A Special Report," 52.

class of 1972 spoke to the point: Princeton lost 132 men to Harvard, 127 to Yale, and 35 each to Stanford and MIT (a total of 329 men)—all first-rate institutions, and all currently or likely soon to be coed.[48] Among students admitted to the class of 1971, 149 had gone to Harvard, 110 to Yale, and 21 to Stanford (a total of 280 men).[49] Coeducation would bear importantly on Princeton's ability to compete for the most talented high school men.[50]

The report found no grounds to support the argument that having men and women on campus together "distracts students from the essential business of a university." It pointed out that current circumstances, requiring a considerable investment of time on the part of men to secure the company of women, involved a substantial distraction of another sort. There was no reason to believe that a coeducational Princeton would tip the existing balance of intellectual and social activity. And the report dismissed out of hand "the notion that a coeducational Princeton would be simply a husband-hunting ground for many of the women, and a source of social and sexual convenience for the men."[51]

The report demonstrated, on the basis of extensive data, that women were well equipped, by virtue of high school preparation and achievement, to participate fully in Princeton's intellectual life. It cited the testimony of undergraduates as well as secondary school students that the quality of classroom discussion would be enhanced by the participation of both sexes. It drew on testimony from faculty members at coeducational institutions, who attested to the salutary influence of women on the intellectual vitality of their classes, the diversity of viewpoints expressed by their students, and the intellectual engagement of men in class discussions. It concluded that "the quality of intellectual life at Princeton would be improved by the presence of both men and women, assuming both were of roughly equal ability."[52]

---

48 Robert K. Durkee, "On the Campus," *Princeton Alumni Weekly* 69 (Mar. 4, 1969): 4.
49 *Daily Princetonian*, June 15, 1967.
50 "'The Education of Women at Princeton': A Special Report," 7–10.
51 Ibid., 52.
52 Ibid., 10–13.

Moreover, the admission of women would bring desirable changes in student course enrollments and choices of majors, with the likely effect of making better use of the university's faculty and curricular resources. Departments in the languages and literatures, art and music, anthropology and psychology—currently less heavily enrolled—would likely benefit. Drawing on the experience of coeducational institutions, the report offered reassurance that the enrollment of women would not drive men out of fields in which women had the greatest interest.[53]

The report argued, too, that women were increasingly participating actively in the labor force and using their education in important ways. That trend would continue. Far from wasting a Princeton education on individuals who would not use it, admitting women would "enable Princeton to contribute to the education of a sector of our population containing many individuals whose responsibilities outside the home are increasing rapidly."[54]

The report was Patterson's. The task of the committee had been "to advise and consult." Members of the committee had "reviewed drafts of all the chapters and discussed them thoroughly" with Patterson, but the prose was his. Noting in a statement appended to the report that "no large group of people could be expected to be of one mind on every element of so complex an issue as the education of women at Princeton," the committee, save for one of its members, offered its enthusiastic endorsement of Patterson's "findings and recommendations."[55]

Horton added a separate statement, explaining his "fundamental disagreement with the conclusions reached" in the report. The education of women was not a priority for Princeton, he wrote. There were already so many other claims on Princeton's resources "to sustain the momentum of her programs of teaching and research"; it would be a mistake to divert funds from those important efforts. Asking for support from alumni and friends of the university for existing long-range commitments as well as for the

53 Ibid., 13–14.
54 Ibid., 14.
55 Statement of the Faculty-Administration Committee, in ibid., 55.

education of women would, by "over-extend[ing] our demands" upon loyal supporters, "have a damaging effect on our overall fund-raising efforts." Moreover, increasing the size of the undergraduate student body threatened to "dilute the very core of what we cherish"—precepts, seminars, independent work, close interaction of faculty and students. Adding women to the student body risked diminishing the "ardor" of alumni for the university; "as a result, the charisma which has distinguished Princeton, indeed placed her in an enviable position, could be dissipated, undermining one of her great assets."[56]

The Patterson Report Draws Mixed Reactions

Heavily grounded in data, the Patterson report presented a complicated analysis. Some writers for national publications took the trouble to study it and offered thoughtful accounts of what it said and why it was important. Bonnie Barrett Stretch, assistant education editor of the *Saturday Review*, devoted a full page in the magazine to an intelligent summary of the report under the title "It's Better Together."[57] But the report was also easily mischaracterized, even caricatured, if writers were so inclined. In an editorial on September 17, the *New York Times* said: "Ever since [its founding Princeton] has generally been regarded as one of the more conservative centers of learning. That it should now be ready to consider such a tradition-shattering move [as coeducation] will undoubtedly stir older alumni to apoplexy, or at least denunciatory letters to The Alumni Weekly." The editorial continued, whether or not tongue in cheek, "The [Patterson] committee found, in effect, that if Princeton wants to continue to attract the highest type of young men to its campus it has to offer them the delights of feminine companionship as well as the delights of learning."[58] Patterson fired off a letter to the editor to set the record straight. "What a lot

56 Statement of Mr. Horton, in "'The Education of Women at Princeton': A Special Report," 55–56.

57 Bonnie Barrett Stretch, "It's Better Together," *Saturday Review*, Nov. 16, 1968, p. 109, attached to W. G. Bowen to R. F. Goheen, Nov. 14, 1968, Goheen, Box 93, Folder 6.

58 Editorial, "Nassau's Sons—and Daughters," *New York Times*, Sept. 17, 1968, p. 46.

of work my colleagues and I could have saved had we thought that providing such 'delights' for our male students would be a sufficient justification for urging our trustees and president to overturn a 225-year-old tradition and to incur substantial financial obligations to boot." In fact, the committee had made its case for admitting women on, "of all things, educational grounds."[59]

Whether or not Princeton alumni took the trouble to study the Patterson report, it made a lot of them very angry. "This pisses me off so much I'm writing you right back on this," an alumnus in the class of 1947 penned to the executive director of the alumni council, William D'O. Lippincott. "I'm enraged over this! Let 1000 Alumni sons or other well qualified guys in FIRST—their livelihood depends on a University education. Women's DON'T!" If Princeton went ahead with coeducation, he said, he would "IMMEDIATELY" stop the work he had been doing on behalf of annual giving— "you'll find me cancelling OUT."[60]

That coeducation would irrevocably change—indeed, destroy— Princeton was a pervasive theme. An alumnus from the class of 1929, "bitterly opposed to the integration of sexes at Princeton," declared that "the changes proposed would terminate the University which has meant much to me, since the Princeton I know would no longer exist."[61] A member of the class of 1932 wrote from Cleveland, "If Princeton goes coeducational . . . my alma mater will have been taken away from me, and PRINCETON IS DEAD."[62] From Palm Beach, Florida, came a simple proposal: "What is all this nonsense about admitting women to Princeton?

59 Gardner Patterson, "Women at Princeton," letter to the editor, *New York Times*, Oct. 26, 1968, clipping in Patterson, Box 4, Folder 6.

60 Geoff Doyle to William D'O. Lippincott, handwritten note on T. Henry Dixon and Lippincott to the Alumni Council, Class and Regional Club Presidents & Secretaries, Sept. 13, 1968, Horton, Box 3, Folder 1.

61 W. Frank Morris to Harvey E. Molé, Oct. 18, 1968, Goheen, Box 93, Folder 6. On the same theme, using similar language, see John K. Jenney '25, in Letters on Coeducation: Selected Excerpts, Sept. 15–Dec. 6, 1968, p. 15, Goheen, Box 93, Folder 6; Winston Smith, Jr., letter to the editor, *Princeton Alumni Weekly* 69 (Nov. 26, 1968): 5.

62 Warren Daane to Edward J. Hawkins, Jr., Nov. 14, 1968, attached to Supplement, Report on Alumni Meeting re Coeducation, Cleveland, Ohio, Oct. 25, 1968, Goheen, Box 94, Folder 7.

A good old-fashioned whore-house would be considerably more efficient, and much, much cheaper."[63]

After reading the report, an alumnus in the class of 1951 from Alabama wrote, "My imagination was stirred and I could see Nassau Street circa 1975. Langrocks [the venerable men's clothing store] has given way to a branch of Bergdorf Goodman, Jack Honore's barbershop has had to add a beauty parlor to compete with the new Elizabeth Arden salon down the street, and Skirm's [Smoke Shop] has put in a Maidenform bra counter."[64] A member of the class of 1913 from Florida responded in verse:

> So, to the nutty notions
> Which feed the campus squirrels,
> Let's add the last, which takes the prize,
> And let in all the girls.[65]

Coeducation was "being inevitably crammed down the throats of the alumni," complained a member of the class of 1930 from Pittsburgh.[66] Alumni objected to permitting "the ill-conceived desires of uninformed secondary school students" to dictate a "major policy change," to allowing "the fancies of some immature, undisciplined, pampered young men" to "influence the future course of Princeton" in place of the views of "mature, experienced, reasonable alumni."[67]

They objected, too, to what they believed was Goheen's outsized influence in setting the university's direction. The president had made clear what he wanted to achieve, critics said, and there was little room for Patterson or the trustees to navigate independent

---

63 A Princeton Alumnus, letter to the editor, *Princeton Alumni Weekly*, Sept. 29, 1968, Goheen, Box 94, Folder 7.

64 George H. Deyo, letter to the editor, *Princeton Alumni Weekly*, Sept. 28, 1968, Horton, Box 3, Folder 1.

65 Francis C. Lowthorp '13, letter to the editor, *Princeton Alumni Weekly* 69 (Nov. 26, 1968): 5.

66 John A. Metz, Jr., to Charles Baton, Dec. 4, 1968, Goheen, Box 95, Folder 2.

67 Kenneth G. Preston, Jr., to William D'O. Lippincott, Nov. 8, 1968 ("ill-conceived desires"), and Glenn G. Anderson to Lippincott, Nov. 15, 1968 ("fancies"), both attached to Supplement, Report on Alumni Meeting re Coeducation, Cleveland, Ohio, Oct. 25, 1968, Goheen, Box 94, Folder 7.

of his influence. An alumnus in the class of 1930, who considered the report "slanted and biased," wrote from Chicago to Mestres, "The constant feeling I get is that Bob [Goheen] set the goal and Patterson built the road to get there without much regard for the materials used."[68]

In Princeton, in an editorial broadcast on radio station WHWH, the president of Nassau Broadcasting Company, Herbert W. Hobler '44, slammed the report as "thoroughly incomplete," "completely biased and one-sided," seriously lacking because of its failure to present "all of the negative aspects of women at Princeton," and "a great embarrassment to qualified research personnel."[69] Provoked, the normally even-keeled Goheen retorted that Hobler's attack was "highly intemperate" and simply wrong; Patterson had amply satisfied the mandate of the trustees, and all the negative arguments had been presented and assessed. Moreover, Goheen stated, Patterson's work was first-rate—experts in higher education and educational economics had attested to the "competence and high caliber" of the report.[70] For example, Alan Pifer, president of the Carnegie Corporation of New York (which had helped to support the costs of the study), had called the report "extraordinarily interesting"—"a first-class piece of work." Joseph Kershaw, program officer for higher education and research at the Ford Foundation, one of the outside experts who had evaluated the report, said, "I've never seen as conscientious and thorough analysis of educational problems and costs anywhere. . . . It was a pioneering report. No one who thinks about coeducation could afford to be without it."[71]

68 Tilden Cummings to Ricardo A. Mestres, Nov. 18, 1968, Goheen, Box 95, Folder 2.

69 Herbert W. Hobler, "The Patterson Report on Princeton University Co-Education," editorial, Sept. 23, 1968, broadcast over WHWH Princeton seven times, Sept. 23–24, Goheen, Box 94, Folder 3. That the report was "biased and slanted" was a common theme among critics; see, e.g., Arthur C. Burns '45 in Letters on Coeducation: Selected Excerpts, Sept. 15–Dec. 6, 1968, p. 1.

70 Robert F. Goheen to Herbert W. Hobler, Sept. 27, 1968, Goheen, Box 95, Folder 4.

71 Alan Pifer to Robert F. Goheen, Oct. 16, 1968, Patterson, Box 3, Folder 10; Kershaw, quoted in Munford, "Coeducation at Princeton," p. 12. See also Charles Fried '56 in Letters on Coeducation: Selected Excerpts, Sept. 15–Dec. 6, 1968, p. 1: "In my work I have seen many, many recommendations for policy changes made to governments, institutions, legislatures, and the like. The Princeton report on coeducation is perhaps the very best argued and documented such recommendation I have seen."

The litany of objections from alumni critics continued. Educating women would diminish Princeton's contribution to the nation's service. As an alumnus in the class of 1955 put it, "A woman
cannot use her education and talents in public service to the same
extent as a male who spends full time at his profession unless she
abdicates the role of bearing and <u>personally</u> raising children. For
every woman admitted to Princeton, a man would be denied that
opportunity."[72] Moreover, bringing women into Princeton classrooms would destroy "the unique student-teacher relationship
that only a Princeton-type educational system can provide," another graduate in the class of 1955 asserted.[73] Less substantive but
still strongly felt were the views of the alumnus in the class of 1936
who said that coeducation would dilute "Princeton's sturdy masculinity with disconcerting, mini-skirted young things cavorting on
its playing fields" or those of the alumnus in the class of 1958 who
said that women are "too distracting."[74]

More broadly, many alumni believed that there had to be a place
in higher education for Princeton as it was currently constituted.
From a graduate in the class of 1923: "I think there is definitely a
place in our scheme of things for an all-male college and Princeton
has been great both in tradition and the loyalty of its graduates,
and I am afraid that a coeducational set-up would dilute this."[75]
Being "an all-male college" was integral to "the Princeton spirit,"
an alumnus in the class of 1955 argued. "I find it inconceivable,"
he said, "that there is not room in this country for one all-male
first-class institution."[76]

---

72 David H. Fulmer '55 to Harold H. Helm, Jan. 8, 1969, Goheen, Box 95, Folder 3.

73 Kenneth G. Preston '55, in Letters on Coeducation: Selected Excerpts, Sept. 15–
Dec. 6, 1968, p. 5.

74 Elleard B. Heffern '36 to R. Manning Brown, Dec. 11, 1968, Goheen, Box 95,
Folder 4; Roland D. Zimany '58 to Gardner Patterson, June 16, 1968, Patterson, Box 1,
Folder 18. For more on the questionable effects of mixing young men and young women
at this stage of life, see David M. Davis, M.D. '07, letter to the editor, *Princeton Alumni
Weekly* 68 (May 28, 1968): 5, 18.

75 C. E. Fyles '23, in Letters on Coeducation: Selected Excerpts, Sept. 15–Dec. 6,
1968, p. 8.

76 Richard S. Dillon '55, in Letters on Coeducation: Selected Excerpts, Sept. 15–Dec. 6,
1968, p. 6. See also Gordon G. Evans '42 to Robert F. Goheen, Aug. 11, 1967, Patterson,
Box 1, Folder 17.

And, of course, there was the ultimate threat from alumni: Coeducation would bring a cessation of financial support. That prospect had not been addressed in the Patterson report. The report had talked about the distinctive alumni loyalty that Princeton had been fortunate to enjoy. It had made an effort to characterize the sources of that loyalty, and it had expressed confidence that it could be nourished effectively in the future in the context of a coeducational institution. Indeed, given that support for coeducation among Princeton alumni involved in education increased markedly as the respondents grew younger, the report suggested that "it would be rash to assume that, if Princeton were to remain all-male, it would be able in the future to maintain the present high levels of alumni support."[77]

But some alumni thought otherwise. From a member of the class of 1933: "If Princeton becomes coeducational I will cease permanently all contributions to Annual Giving." A member of the class of 1957 declared that he would continue his "support of the University" only up to the point where "Princeton goes coed."[78] From an alumnus in the class of 1937: "I do not intend to give one red penny to support a coeducational program I feel is all wrong for Princeton."[79] And from a member of the class of 1941, who recorded "zero" as the amount of his gift to annual giving, came a broad-scale indictment of Princeton's evolving admission policy, including the university's "racist" efforts to enroll black students, its willingness (so he claimed) to readmit "convicted draft-dodgers," and, worst of all, the "financially irresponsible intent to admit 1000 additional females for the edification of these so called

77 "'The Education of Women at Princeton': A Special Report," 17–18. Yale took a similar view, according to a report from their provost to Bowen. See W. G. Bowen to Gardner Patterson, Apr. 16, 1968, Patterson, Box 1, Folder 3.

78 Franklin H. Williams '33 (p. 14) and George White, Jr., '57 (p. 12), in Letters on Coeducation: Selected Excerpts, Sept. 15–Dec. 6, 1968. For further examples of promised withdrawal of financial support, see John Johns '24 and Alan Crawford '15, in Letters on Coeducation: Selected Excerpts, Sept. 15–Dec. 6, 1968, p. 14.

79 Handwritten note from Swagar Sherley '37 to John F. Maloney, Chairman of Annual Giving, on Maloney to Dear Fellow Princetonian, Nov. 18, 1968, Horton, Box 3, Folder 4. For Sherley's objections to the trustees' decision to authorize a study of coeducation without even polling the alumni, see Sherley's letter to the editor, *Princeton Alumni Weekly* 68 (Sept. 26, 1967): 5.

'best boys,' thus giving the lie to perennial insistence on equating smallness of size with quality education." As he wrote to his class fund agent, "Please count me <u>out</u>!"[80]

Sentiments of this sort led the annual giving staff to forecast a decline in participation and a failure to reach the desired dollar goal for the 1968–69 campaign and—were coeducation to be implemented—reduced levels of annual giving in the future. As we shall see later, these fears turned out to be groundless.[81]

The potential impact went beyond annual giving. Still willing to make a "token" contribution to avoid spoiling the percentage of his class supporting annual giving, an alumnus in the class of 1916 wrote to his class agent, "I don't want any part of a damn co-ed outfit. . . . Until recently, my wife and I, who have no children or near relatives, have named Princeton . . . as the ultimate beneficiary in our wills; but we have now taken it out entirely."[82] While the loudest protestations often came from alumni who had been modest donors, the threats sometimes came from men whose support really mattered. A case in point: H. Norris Love '26, who had given $100,000 to the $53 Million Campaign of 1959–62, told his friend Donold B. Lourie, "If Princeton goes co-ed, they'll not get a ___ cent more from me."[83]

Coexisting with such dire threats was significant alumni support for coeducation. As a "living organism," the university needed to "adapt to its times and environment," said an alumnus in the class of 1939.[84] Enrolling women would make the educational experience at Princeton "a richer one," opined a graduate in the class of 1964.[85] And not admitting women was out of the question. From an alumnus in the class of 1963: Remaining all-male would mean that Princeton would "inevitably fall behind."[86] From a 1909

80 Robert Leibowitz to "Dear Sam," Dec. 6, 1968, Horton, Box 3, Folder 6.

81 Annual Giving and the Education of Women, attached to J. L. Bolster, Jr., to Robert F. Goheen, Jan. 6, 1969, Goheen, Box 94, Folder 1. For Annual Giving results in 1968–69 and thereafter, see p. 190.

82 J. H. Shepherd to Ebe [J. Ebert Butterworth], Dec. 30, 1968, Horton, Box 3, Folder 5.

83 Donold B. Lourie to Harold H. Helm, Dec. 16, 1968, Horton, Box 3, Folder 7.

84 Frederick L. Redpath '39, in Letters on Coeducation: Selected Excerpts, Sept. 15–Dec. 6, 1968, p. 7.

85 Kenneth A. Goldman to Robert F. Goheen, Oct. 25, 1968, Goheen, Box 94, Folder 2.

86 John W. Douglas '63, in Letters on Coeducation: Selected Excerpts, Sept. 15–Dec. 6, 1968, p. 8.

graduate: "Unless Princeton chooses to admit a thousand smart girl students as soon as possible, it will become one of the few conceited 'hair on the chest' institutions which will ultimately fade out of the picture."[87] From a member of the class of 1954: "There was once a time when there was a need for a great University that accepted only Christians. There was once a time when there was a need for a great University that accepted only white men. Princeton realized in the past that the search for knowledge was the exclusive right of all men. The dialogue was enhanced when the barriers were dropped. The only barrier that remains is the sex barrier. When that is removed Princeton will take its rightful place in the 20th century."[88]

From Charles S. Robertson '26, who, with his wife, Marie, had several years earlier anonymously endowed the foundation to support the graduate program of the Woodrow Wilson School, there came congratulations to Patterson and the members of his committee "on an outstanding job exceedingly well done." Acknowledging that he had a fifteen-year-old daughter who might benefit from a coeducational Princeton, Robertson added, "The truth of the matter is that Marie and I sincerely believe that girls are here to stay and that the sooner Princeton welcomes them as students the better University it will be."[89] Other alumni confessed to similar self-interest. "I have a particular interest in seeing this done," one wrote, "because it now appears that my sixteen-year-old granddaughter may realize her ambition to go to Princeton as did her father and both grandfathers."[90]

For the first time in fourteen years, the *Princeton Alumni Weekly* published an editorial, which enthusiastically supported coeducation. That the magazine chose to take a stance, the editor, John Davies '41, wrote, was an indication of *"the urgency of the issue."* He continued, "For any friend of Princeton . . . to oppose

87 William H. Zinsser to Ralph K. Ritchie, Oct. 1, 1968, Horton, Box 3, Folder 2.

88 Jeremiah Ford III '54 to Robert F. Goheen, Nov. 25, 1968, Goheen, Box 95, Folder 3.

89 Charles S. Robertson to Gardner Patterson, Sept. 26, 1968, Goheen, Box 95, Folder 6.

90 Edward L. Clifford to Livingston T. Merchant, Jan. 24, 1969, Goheen, Box 95, Folder 2. On the same theme, see Lancelot L. Farrar, Jr., '54, letter to the editor, *Princeton Alumni Weekly* 68 (Nov. 28, 1967): 5.

coeducation . . . is the equivalent of a Ford Motor Company director advocating 'Let's Bring Back The Edsel!'"[91]

The on-campus reactions to the Patterson report were straightforward: students and faculty in favor; the administration, save for the development office, in enthusiastic support. On October 25, the faculty advisory committee on policy sent the faculty a resolution "firmly endors[ing] the major conclusions and recommendations" of the Patterson report, acknowledging that there might need to be "temporary adjustments and postponements in other programs" and expressing the willingness of the faculty "to bear its share of these burdens" in the interest of the "long-term benefit to the University."[92] On October 30, the undergraduate assembly adopted a similar resolution of support.[93] On November 4, at an unusually well-attended meeting, the faculty "overwhelmingly approved" by voice vote the resolution circulated earlier.[94]

As for the administration, members of the admission office staff now joined the director, John T. Osander '57, in vocally expressing support for coeducation.[95] In the development office, however, the opposition hardened and the Horton machine swung into action. Alumni as well as members of the administrative staff opposed to coeducation congratulated him on taking a courageous stand in opposition to the report. It would likely be said someday that Horton had, "almost singlehandedly, subdued the infidels and saved the very life of his (and our) beloved Princeton," wrote an

91 John Davies '41, "Coeducation—A Self-Evident Conclusion," *Princeton Alumni Weekly* 69 (Nov. 26, 1968): 11.

92 Faculty Advisory Committee on Policy and the President to Members of the Faculty, Oct. 25, 1968, Bowen provost, Box 18, Folder 6.

93 William G. Bowen to Messrs. Goheen, Mestres, Sullivan, and Rudenstine, Oct. 29, 1968, Goheen, Box 93, Folder 6; UGA Resolution on the Patterson Report on the Education of Women at Princeton, Oct. 30, 1968, Goheen, Box 94, Folder 2.

94 Resolution of the University Faculty on the Education of Women at Princeton, adopted Nov. 4, 1968, distributed to Trustees' Executive Committee, Nov. 15, 1968; Princeton University news release, Nov. 11, 1968 (source of the quote); and William G. Bowen to Clerk of the Faculty, Nov. 6, 1968, all in Goheen, Box 93, Folder 6. The *Daily Princetonian*, Nov. 5, 1968, reported that 175 faculty members had voted in favor, with "only a handful of 'nays.'"

95 W. G. Bowen to President R. F. Goheen, Nov. 13, 1968, Goheen, Box 94, Folder 6.

alumnus in the class of 1943 in a representative comment.[96] Apparently oblivious to the inappropriateness of resisting what was clearly meant to be the university's future path, Horton explained the position of his staff this way: "In a way, you might say we are Butter & Egg men, finding out fairly suddenly that we are also peddling Cheese. We have more to learn about the new product."[97] And Horton continued personally to correspond with like-minded alumni and to supply data, correspondence, and reports of conversations to administrators and trustees he considered to be sympathetic to his cause.[98]

But Horton was tilting at windmills. Although much discussion would ensue, and many views would be expressed, pro and con, the Patterson report, not its opponents, would claim center stage going forward.

96 Robert S. Creadick '43, in Letters on Coeducation: Selected Excerpts, Sept. 15-Dec. 6, 1968, p. 2. See also Stu[art] Carothers to [Arthur] J. Horton, n.d. [Sept. 1968]; Horton to Carothers, Sept. 23, 1968, both in Horton, Box 3, Folder 1.

97 Arthur J. Horton to Leslie L. Vivian, Oct. 10, 1968, Goheen, Box 93, Folder 6.

98 In Horton, Box 4, Folder 7, see Arthur J. Horton to Richard R. Hough, Sept. 23, 1968. In Horton, Box 3, Folder 1, see Horton to Robert C. Miller, Sept. 23, 1968. In Goheen, Box 94, Folder 7, see Horton to Jeremiah A. Farrington, Sept. 23 and Oct. 9, 1968, and Horton to Leslie L. Vivian, Oct. 24, 1968. In Horton, Box 3, Folder 4, see Horton to Farrington, Nov. 25, 1968. In Goheen, Box 94, Folder 6, see Horton, Aide Memoire, Nov. 14, 1968, and Horton to Farrington, Nov. 26 and 27, 1968. For the flavor of some of the correspondence Horton received from alumni, see Van Cleaf Bachman '61 to Horton, Sept. 21, 1968, Horton, Box 3, Folder 1; John H. Boyd '42 to Horton, Oct. 1, 1968, Horton, Box 3, Folder 2.

6

Yale: "Treat Yale as You Would a Good Woman"

In November 1968, fully mindful of Princeton's consideration of the Patterson recommendations, the Yale corporation authorized the president, Kingman Brewster, to present to the faculty a plan to admit 250 women freshmen in the fall of 1969. The women would be housed in one of the smaller residential colleges, with the college's male residents reassigned to other colleges. The housing plan was intended to avoid a host of problems that might ensue if women were distributed among the twelve colleges, including asking women to live in dormitories with men, establishing badly skewed ratios of men to women, and investing in physical renovations in many colleges without having any idea of what residential arrangements women would prefer. The plan also called for admitting up to 250 women transfer students, who would be housed off campus but affiliated with the residential colleges.

"A Late and Somewhat Precipitate Decision"

Brewster acknowledged that Yale was getting a late start and that little or no advance planning had taken place, but he advocated going forward instead of postponing. Relying on "experience and experimentation" instead of "further abstract study" might enable Yale to "evolve a pattern for learning and for living . . . more in tune with the needs of tomorrow's students" than the arrangements at any of Yale's "major institutional rivals." There were "risks and burdens" in taking such a "late and somewhat precipitate" decision, but even though everything would have to be put in place "in a frightful hurry," Brewster thought it was worth taking the plunge.[1] The plan won the overwhelming approval of the faculty on November 14 (there was just one dissenter).[2]

Deciding to proceed "at an admittedly awkward double trot in preference to a graceful amble," as Marie Borroff, a tenured professor of English, put it, meant not having had the opportunity to attend thoughtfully to a raft of details.[3] Brewster's hastily drawn plans needed to be revised almost immediately. Despite the president's personal plea—"I come here to request that the men of Trumbull make the gallant gesture of vacating their rooms for at least a year"—the men of Trumbull objected strenuously to being asked to move out.[4] Other students agreed: If women were coming to Yale, they needed to be fully integrated into the Yale experience. Forty-one freshmen in Jonathan Edwards expressed themselves in elegant calligraphy: "We . . . hereby express our emphatic disapproval of the co-education plan as set forth by President Kingman Brewster. We are opposed to the evacuation of Trumbull College, or any other college or colleges for the purposes of co-education."[5] Three Morse freshmen sent a less elegant communication: "What is this <u>bullshit</u> about Trumbull? The girls belong at Yale as full-fledged Yalies, on the O[ld] C[ampus] as freshmen, in the colleges as upperclassmen. . . . If you segregate 250 women in Trumbull, you will just be creating a Yale-sanctioned whorehouse. The whole point of coeducation is that women are no different than men."[6]

1 Proposal for coeducation in Yale College, presented by President Kingman Brewster, Jr., of Yale to the faculty on Nov. 14, 1968, Brewster I, Box 222, Folder 14.

2 *New York Times*, Nov. 15, 1968, reprinted in Pamela Geismar, Eve Hart Rice, and Joan O'Meara Winant, eds., *Fresh Women: Reflections on Coeducation and Life after Yale, 1969, 1989, 2009* (New Haven, CT: Privately published, 2010), p. 162; *Yale Daily News*, Nov. 15, 1968.

3 Marie Borroff to Kingman Brewster, Jr., Nov. 17, 1968, Brewster I, Box 222, Folder 17.

4 Typescript, Kingman Brewster, Jr., remarks at Trumbull College, n.d. [Nov. 14, 1968], Brewster I, Box 222, Folder 18.

5 Declaration by Jonathan Edwards College freshmen, Nov. 18, 1968, attached to ? [college master] to Kingman Brewster, Jr., Nov. 19, 1968, Brewster I, Box 222, Folder 14.

6 Richard Probst, Michael R. Reich, and Rod E. Harris to Kingman Brewster, Jr., postcard postmarked Nov. 15, 1968, Brewster I, Box 60, Folder 14. See also William Shapiro and Frederick Utley (officers of the Pierson college council) to Brewster, n.d., Brewster I, Box 222, Folder 14.

Within days, the administration changed course: The freshman women would be housed in a dormitory on the old campus, like other Yale freshmen. Like other freshmen, they would be affiliated with residential colleges, where they would take up residence after the freshman year, though the number of colleges would be kept relatively small so that the women would not find themselves "hopelessly outnumbered."[7] But limiting women students to a small number of colleges met strong objection from undergraduates. At a meeting of more than a hundred students in Silliman College, for example, it was argued emphatically that, "both on principle and because the girls will want it that way, the freshmen girls should be treated like freshmen, eating in Commons and affiliated with all the colleges." Transfer students, too, should be affiliated with all twelve colleges. Any other arrangements, the college master reported to Brewster, would be "contrived and unnatural" and distort the college system for years to come.[8]

Staffing up to handle applications from women, the admission office added two women admission officers. The office would be "looking for the same academic ability, talent, and diversity which marks the men at Yale," a goal Inky Clark, the dean of admission, was sure they could meet. He was confident that the admitted women would be impressive in every respect: "Brains and looks are not mutually exclusive." Alumni schools committee interviewers were encouraged to point out to "young ladies considering Yale" that the first female matriculants would help to "shape plans for the life style which will characterize the Yale Woman."[9]

Brewster delegated leadership for coeducation planning to two colleagues. Elga R. Wasserman, assistant dean of the graduate school, an alumna of Smith College with a Ph.D. in chemistry from Radcliffe, the wife of Yale chemistry professor Harry Wasserman, would relinquish her deanship to head a new planning committee

7 Kingman Brewster, Jr., to the Masters of the Residential Colleges, Nov. 18, 1968 (source of the quote), Brewster I, Box 222, Folder 17; Yale University news release, Nov. 19, 1968, Brewster I, Box 222, Folder 13.

8 Elias Clark to Kingman Brewster, Jr., Nov. 19, 1968, Brewster I, Box 222, Folder 14.

9 Coeducation at Yale, Yale Alumni Schools Committee Memo, Special Edition, Nov. 26, 1968, Brewster I, Box 60, Folder 16.

on coeducation. Henry Chauncey, Jr., '57, would take a leave from his position as assistant to the president to take charge of administrative planning.[10] Wasserman would take the lead on matters concerning the education of women, including admissions and residential policies, and Chauncey would take the lead on matters concerning facilities and financial planning, but they would work together at every turn.

Wasserman had hoped to carry the title "assistant dean of the college" to parallel the position she held at the graduate school, but Brewster declined; other deans in the college office had told him that they would feel demeaned if a woman carried the title. Whether that was true—and Wasserman had some doubts—she stepped up to the challenge. She called herself "a change agent for Brewster." Brewster told her, "I want you to make Yale a good place for women."[11]

The planning committee on coeducation, composed of administrators, faculty, and students, met almost weekly from December 1968 through May 1969. The agendas focused initially on admissions and financial aid, housing and dining, security and campus safety, but soon expanded to include advising and counseling, as well as likely course enrollments and distribution of majors among women students.[12] The committee agreed that freshman women would be housed in Vanderbilt, a dormitory on the old campus, with women students in the graduate and professional schools living among them as freshman counselors.[13] The committee drew

10 Typescript, Kingman Brewster, Jr., remarks at Trumbull College, n.d. [Nov. 14, 1968], Brewster I, Box 222, Folder 18.

11 Elga Wasserman, in DVD "Coeducating the Male-Only Ivies: A Retrospective," Wesleyan University, Oct. 12, 2013; Wasserman, in DVD "40th Anniversary of Coeducation Celebration," Yale University, Jan. 30, 2010 (source of the quotes).

12 In May, Box 10, Folder 152, see minutes, Planning Committee on Coeducation, Dec. 9 and 16, 1968, and Jan. 6 and 20 and Feb. 3 and 28, 1969, and Elga Wasserman to Georges May, Jan. 10, 1969. In Brewster I, Box 60, Folder 16, see Henry Chauncey, Jr., to Spencer F. Miller, Feb. 5, 1969; George Langdon, Jr., to President Brewster et al., Feb. 25, 1969; and Report of the Chairman of the Planning Committee on Coeducation, 1968–1969, May 29, 1969. In Wasserman I, Box 29, Folder 972, see minutes, Planning Committee on Coeducation, Feb. 14, 1969. In May, Box 10, Folder 153, see minutes, Planning Committee on Coeducation, Apr. 25, 1969.

13 Minutes, Coeducation Planning Committee, Dec. 9, 1968, May, Box 10, Folder 152; Elga Wasserman to Members of the Yale College Faculty, Apr. 1969, May, Box 10, Folder 153.

up a housing plan whereby each of the twelve colleges would have fifty women members (thirty of them in residence) in 1969–70, and all colleges would have women in each of the four classes by 1970–71. Freshman women would be affiliated with each of the colleges in groups of about twenty students, a pattern mirroring normal arrangements for freshman men.[14] Operating costs of the first year of coeducation would be covered by tuition and room fees paid by the women students.[15]

Nearly 2,850 women applied for admission to the freshman class; 1,100 completed applications for transfer admission.[16] The applications were read by admission staff members and also by Wasserman or Chauncey and faculty members from the planning committee on coeducation.[17] Clark said that the admitted women needed to be "academically very strong," because they would be "coming into a very, very male-oriented place." And they needed to be "strong emotionally so as to be able to handle this kind of situation."[18] Chauncey said that he was looking for "stability" and "strength," as well as "a certain toughness, a pioneer quality."[19]

Wasserman echoed Chauncey: "We knew that this would be a pioneer class facing pioneer-type problems." Agreeing that they were looking for students who "had the toughness to survive," she told Clark and his staff that the women "have to be strong people. They can't be fragile. Once we're coed for a while, we can take the kinds of risks in those areas that we would with men. But in this first batch, they're going to be just 250 undergraduate women

14 Planning Committee on Coeducation, Plans for Housing Women at Yale for 1969–70, Wasserman II, Box 1; Residential Facilities for Women Undergraduates, typescript sent to Yale Press for printing, Mar. 25, 1969, Wasserman I, Box 29, Folder 971; Elga Wasserman to Members of the Yale College Faculty, Apr. 1969, May, Box 10, Folder 153.

15 Report of the Chairman of the Planning Committee on Coeducation, 1968–69, May 29, 1969, Brewster I, Box 60, Folder 16.

16 Yale College Class of 1973, typescript, Sept. 26, 1969, May, Box 10, Folder 154.

17 Elga Wasserman to Members of the Yale College Faculty, Apr. 1969, May, Box 10, Folder 153; Summary Report of the Chairman of the Planning Committee on Coeducation, 1968–69, June 17, 1969; and Yale University news release, Fact Sheet on Yale Co-eds, Sept. 10, 1969, all in Wasserman II, Box 1.

18 Clark oral history, May 13, 1993, p. 32.

19 Chauncey, quoted in Tony Reese, "When Yale Needed 'Girls,'" *New Journal* 17 (Mar. 1, 1985): 15 ("stability," "strength"), in Heller, Box 1, Folder 5; Chauncey, quoted in Jonathan Lear, "How Yale Selected Her First Coeds," *New York Times Magazine*, Apr. 13, 1969, clipping in Brewster II, Box 258, Folder 5.

coming into that all-male pool."[20] Wasserman reassured male students nervous about the superwomen joining them on campus that there would not be "too many . . . girls who are both really bright and really aggressive"—exceptionally bright, yes, but more likely to be quiet than overly assertive.[21]

In the end, 284 women were admitted to the freshman class of 1973, and 375 women, from eighty-six colleges and universities, were admitted as transfer students. Of those students, 230 women accepted offers of admission to the freshman class, as did 358 transfer students entering the sophomore and junior classes. With changes of mind among some transfer students, 576 undergraduate women matriculated in the fall of 1969.[22]

Brain Drain from the Women's Colleges

The announcement in the late fall of 1968 that coeducation was coming had raised the antennae of women's college presidents. The president of Connecticut College, Charles Shain, spoke for many of them when he wrote to Brewster "expressing his concern lest Yale rob us all blind."[23] Wasserman wrote the presidents in December to allay fears that Yale was "planning to 'raid' our neighboring institutions." Yale intended to draw transfer students from many colleges and universities; the plan was "to limit severely the number of girls we admit from any one school" and to admit few, if any, transfer students after the first year.[24]

20 Wasserman, quoted in Reese, "When Yale Needed 'Girls,'" p. 15 ("pioneer class"); Wasserman oral history I, p. 15 ("toughness to survive"); Wasserman oral history II, p. 62; Wasserman, quoted in Clark oral history, May 13, 1993, p. 33.

21 Wasserman, quoted in Lear, "How Yale Selected Her First Coeds."

22 Summary Report of the Chairman of the Planning Committee on Coeducation, 1968–69, June 17, 1969, Wasserman II, Box 1; Elga Wasserman to the Women of the Yale College Classes of 1973, 1972, and 1971, Aug. 1969, Wasserman I, Box 29, Folder 971; Yale College Registrar / IPEDS Fall Headcount Surveys, Yale University Office of Institutional Research.

23 Quoted in Thomas C. Mendenhall to Elga Wasserman, Dec. 10, 1968, Wasserman I, Box 38, Folder 1071. Whether Shain actually put the case that way or that was Mendenhall's slightly freewheeling interpretation is not clear; the relevant letter from Shain to Brewster was considerably more temperate, although the point was the same. See Charles E. Shain to Kingman Brewster, Nov. 15, 1968, Mendenhall, Series 8, Box 2.

24 Elga Wasserman to Thomas C. Mendenhall, Dec. 6, 1968, Wasserman I, Box 38, Folder 1071; Wasserman to Ruth M. Adams, Dec. 6, 1968, May, Box 10, Folder 152; *Yale*

Although Wasserman's promises provided "comforting" news to the presidents in December, the comfort dissipated when transfer admission offers were made in April. Large numbers of offers went to students at Smith (forty-eight) and Wellesley (fifty), to the consternation of those colleges' respective presidents. Writing "more in sorrow than in anger," the president of Smith, Thomas C. Mendenhall, told Brewster that Yale's action was "an unfriendly, unwise, and anti-social act"—certainly contrary to what he had been led to expect, which would have been the loss of no more than ten to fifteen students from any college. Mendenhall had been a history professor and master of Berkeley College at Yale before taking up the presidency at Smith in 1959, and he felt wounded by Yale's betrayal. As he penned in a personal note to Brewster, "I really think this was below the belt!"[25]

Ruth Adams, the president of Wellesley, wrote Brewster a terse note conveying a similar message. Taking such a large group of students from Wellesley seemed at odds with assurances that Yale would limit its admissions from any single school. "We assume," Adams said, that Yale's decision to take so many Wellesley students "was intended as a compliment." She continued, "Pleasant though compliments are, this one seems overly generous. I doubt that Yale has honored its commitment to neighboring institutions."[26] (Telling the story years later, Adams was less constrained: "Brewster creamed off my junior and senior class . . . Barnard's junior and senior class. Cleaned up Holyoke's junior and senior class." Brewster's response: "But, Ruth, if they really want to come, I can't say, no."[27])

Wasserman responded for Yale. There had been no bad faith, no promises violated. Yale had exercised appropriate restraint, had made no effort to recruit or interview at neighboring colleges. "I

Daily News, Feb. 10, 1970, and Dec. 2, 1971. In fact, given the overcrowding in undergraduate housing, no transfer students were accepted in 1970 or 1971.

25 Thomas C. Mendenhall to Elga Wasserman, Dec. 10, 1968, Wasserman I, Box 38, Folder 1071 ("comforting"); Mendenhall to Kingman Brewster, Apr. 22, 1969, Wasserman II, Box 1.

26 Ruth M. Adams to Kingman Brewster, Apr. 25, 1969, Wasserman I, Box 38, Folder 1074.

27 Adams oral history, p. 5.

realize that we accepted relatively large numbers of students from a few Eastern schools," she wrote to Adams. "Had we accepted fewer students from these schools we would have been forced to turn down outstanding applicants who were far superior to applicants whom we accepted from other institutions. This . . . would not be a fair procedure." To Mendenhall she wrote, "I am sorry that Yale's decision to coeducate is causing problems at Smith. I do not believe, however, that we can solve your problems by refusing to accept qualified students who have expressed a desire to leave Smith College."[28] Brewster told Mendenhall: "We did not 'recruit' transfers. . . . It just happened that a disproportionate number of Smith girls applied, and an even greater proportion were superior. As long as we were not 'drumming' I think that the ultimate choice has to be the girl's, if she merited the choice."[29]

Preparations over the remainder of the spring and summer ranged from painting and furnishing Vanderbilt Hall to outfitting and preparing signage for restrooms for women to augmenting campus lighting and installing locks on doors.[30]

"Goldfish in a Bowl": Women Undergraduates Arrive

The arrival of the women students in September 1969 created the anticipated splash. Reporters and photographers from national newspapers and magazines descended on the campus. *Time* was there; so were *Mademoiselle* and *Women's Wear Daily*. "The fuss over coeds," the *Washington Post* said, was "higher education's big freak show."[31] Wasserman echoed the *Post*'s formulation: It was as if "some breed of freaks had arrived here." Amy Solomon, the first freshman woman to register, moved into her room on the

28 Elga Wasserman to Ruth Adams, May 1, 1969, Wasserman I, Box 38, Folder 1074; Wasserman to Thomas Mendenhall, Apr. 25, 1969, Wasserman II, Box 1.

29 Kingman Brewster, Jr., to Thomas C. Mendenhall, May 15, 1969, Mendenhall, Series 8, Box 2.

30 In Wasserman I, Box 29, Folder 971, see Elga Wasserman to the Women of the Yale College Classes of 1973, 1972, and 1971, Aug. 1969, and Wasserman, Coeducation—A Progress Report, Nov. 17, 1969. In Brewster I, Box 60, Folder 16, see Wasserman to Lewis S. Beach, Sept. 2, 1969.

31 B. J. Phillips, "The Yale Girls," *Washington Post*, Sept. 22, 1969, p. B1.

fifth floor of Vanderbilt Hall, trailed by a photographer from the *Hartford Courant,* who climbed the five flights to find her.[32] Solomon's roommate, Cindy McCain, said of registration, "Talk about freak shows. There were photographers lined up like it was the Miss America Pageant. You had to walk between rows of them to register. They ask, 'Are you a girl? Are you a Yale girl?'"[33] One newly arrived woman student told a television reporter, "It feels like we're in a goldfish bowl."[34]

For women graduate students, who had been studying at Yale for years, there was considerable irony in the fuss about the new arrivals. The intense focus on women undergraduates conveyed the message that women graduate students were not important. Phil's Barber Shop, on York Street adjacent to the campus, hung a large poster in its window welcoming women students to Yale. The poster featured a woman in a barber's chair. The caption read: "The first woman at Yale to have her hair cut at Phil's." A woman graduate student mused, "I had been having my hair cut at Phil's for over a year. Didn't I count? It's as if I haven't been here until now. Until the arrival of women at Yale College—an event which seems to have generated more excitement and received more publicity than the arrival of men on the moon—there have been no women at Yale. Until now, I haven't been a woman at Yale."[35]

The campus police festooned the old campus with banners saying, "Welcome to the Guys and Dolls of '73."[36] Wasserman greeted the new freshmen with a hopeful message: "I would like to see you here as Yale students rather than as Yale women."[37] Welcoming the freshmen at the traditional assembly in September, Brewster focused on "the temptations to cynicism" rather than on the arrival of Yale's first undergraduate women, but he noted in passing the importance

---

32 Julie Pimsleur, "Boola Boola . . . Yale Goes Coed," 1990, Film Study Center, Yale University.

33 Phillips, "The Yale Girls."

34 Pimsleur, "Boola Boola."

35 Elizabeth Davis, "Changing Identities: When Yale's 'First' Women Arrived," *Yale Alumni Magazine* 43 (Oct. 1979): 21.

36 Lucy L. Eddy, "In the Blue," *Yale Alumni Magazine* 33 (Apr. 1970): 24.

37 Elga Wasserman, statement for the <u>Eli Book</u>, Class of 1973, n.d. [1969], Wasserman I, Box 29, Folder 971.

of "the hopes of what Yale can do for women and women can do for Yale." He failed, however, to avoid the all-too-common trap of using familiar but outmoded gender references when he declared, "Yale is a place where a man is honored for his humanity."[38]

The dean of Yale College, Georges May, told the women students that they would demonstrate through their choice of courses whether a student's sex mattered in such selections, thus answering "the hackneyed question whether or not the education of women should be the same as that of men." They would demonstrate, too, how the enrollment of women would affect "Yale's various undergraduate subcultures." In short, although Yale intended to treat women and men students similarly in terms of opportunities and regulations, it knew full well that "not differentiating between men and women was not the same thing as treating women like men."[39] The basic approach to coeducation, as the headmistress of the girls' boarding school Milton Academy observed, was "to begin by treating [the girls] like the boys and see what happens."[40]

In short, women students arrived on a campus that was deeply, unmistakably male. As recently as the year before, as had been the case for many years, the freshman handbook had read: "Treat Yale as you would a good woman; take advantage of her many gifts, nourish yourself with the fruit of her wisdom, curse her if you will, but congratulate yourself in your possession of her."[41] As one male student put it, Yale was "steeped in male tradition."[42] The campus iconography was male; male portraits and statues adorned the campus. Some special spaces, like the Linonia and Brothers Reading Room in the main library, were off limits to women. It was hard for a woman student to avoid "[feeling] like a guest."[43]

38 Kingman Brewster, Jr., Freshman Assembly Address, Sept. 15, 1969, Brewster II, Box 258, Folder 5.

39 Georges May to the Women of the Yale College Classes of 1973, 1972, and 1971, Aug. 1969, Wasserman I, Box 29, Folder 971.

40 Margaret A. Johnson to Kingman Brewster, Jr., Dec. 15, 1969, Wasserman II, Box 1.

41 Quoted by Elga Wasserman, in DVD "40th Anniversary of Coeducation Celebration."

42 Quoted in John Kennedy, "Co-education: The Year They Liberated Yale," 1970, Film Study Center, Yale University.

43 Margaret Homans '74, in DVD "40th Anniversary of Coeducation Celebration."

Besides, the faculty was overwhelmingly male. In the first year of coeducation, there were two women professors: Mary C. Wright, the historian of modern China, the first woman tenured at Yale in arts and sciences (1959) and the first woman full professor (1964), and the poet Marie Borroff, a member of the faculty in the English department since 1959, who had become the second woman full professor (1965). Wright died of cancer in June 1970. The next tenured woman faculty member, Ingeborg Glier, in Germanic languages and literatures, was appointed in 1972.[44] The total number of women on the Yale College faculty inched up slowly between the fall of 1970 and the fall of 1973: among full professors, from 0.7 percent to 1.6 percent; among associate professors, from zero to 3.1 percent; among assistant professors, from 6.0 to 17.3 percent.[45]

It was not only the overwhelmingly male character of the institution that shaped the experiences of the first women students. It was also that there were so few of them that made the process of integrating them into the life of the institution so difficult. All told, in the fall of 1969, the undergraduate student body included 576 women (12.5 percent of the total enrollment) and 4,027 men. In the freshman class of 1973, there were 230 women (18 percent of the class) and 1,025 men.[46] There was nothing easy or comfortable about a 4.5-to-1 ratio in the freshman class or an 8-to-1 ratio in the undergraduate student body.

Women students commented repeatedly on the challenges of having so few women in the first coeducational class. One freshman asked, "In what way are we and everyone else supposed to look at us—is there such a thing as being a human being in class

44 Kirsten E. Lodal, "Engendering an Intellectual Space: The Development of Women's Studies at Yale University, 1969–2001" (unpublished senior essay, History Department, Yale University, 2001), http://wgss.yale.edu/sites/default/files/files/LodalEssayEngendering %20and%20IntellectualSapce.pdf, accessed Jan. 1, 2016.

45 Mary B. Arnstein, Coeducation Report, 1972–73, July 1973, Table 6, Brewster II, Box 258, Folder 11.

46 Yale University news release, Fact Sheet on Yale Co-eds, Sept. 10, 1969, Wasserman II, Box 1; Elga Wasserman, Coeducation 1969–70, Brewster I, Box 60, Folder 12; Yale College Registrar / IPEDS Fall Headcount Surveys, Yale University Office of Institutional Research.

and not 'a woman'?" A second added, "When you're one of two girls in a class, if you're not there, everybody knows it . . . along with the usual pressures of being a college freshman, it can add up to too much." A third observed, poignantly, that she felt "experimented upon."[47] Another woman said, "When we faltered, we felt twice the burden men felt."[48] Students told and retold the anecdote about the male faculty member who was graceless enough to remind undergraduate women that they were responsible for the fact that men could no longer walk naked in Payne Whitney gymnasium.[49]

An upperclass male student, approaching a woman studying in his college library, told her that her "presence was too distracting for him to concentrate on his reading."[50] "I haven't eaten with one of you yet," a senior male student told a female sophomore whom he had invited to sit with him in the dining hall. "This is the first opportunity I've had to meet a coed," remarked a faculty member to another woman sophomore at a fellows' dinner in her residential college.[51] The most distinctive feature of the first year, a woman student commented years later, was "the experience of being watched."[52]

A woman in the class of 1973 wrote in the second year of coeducation:

> Men are angry at the women for being not only tight-assed but apparently tight-spirited: they study too fervently and they refuse to become sufficiently involved in their colleges. Conversely, some men are nervous about having sexual

47 The quotes come from Summary, Freshman Women's Advisory Council meeting, Jan. 29, 1970, Wasserman I, Box 35, Folder 1032.

48 Quoted by Elga Wasserman, in DVD "Coeducating the Male-Only Ivies: A Retrospective."

49 Tamar Lehrich, "Three Sisters," *New Journal* 17 (Mar. 1, 1985): 22.

50 Barbara Wagner '73, "Living through Coeducation," Steering Committee on the 40th Anniversary of Coeducation, *Reflections on Coeducation: A Critical History of Women at Yale* (Yale College, 2010), p. 22.

51 Quoted in Janet Lever and Pepper Schwartz, *Women at Yale: Liberating a College Campus* (Indianapolis, IN: Bobbs-Merrill, 1971), p. 47.

52 Quoted in Nan Robertson, "Women at Yale: Looking Back at a Decade of Change," *New York Times*, Oct. 29, 1979, p. D9, clipping in Wasserman II, Box 5.

relations with women in their colleges, because the tense intimacy of the community precludes privacy. . . . Women find no natural mechanisms for becoming close to one another. Perhaps the most important women's complaint is that they spend so much time sorting out their activities with men that they lose a sense of their own directions; and further, when they do begin to move toward their own goals in some independent way, men feel abandoned and threatened. Grievances and irritations abound.[53]

Challenges in the Classroom

In addition to challenges in their social lives and relationships, undergraduate women faced challenges in the classroom. Being the only woman in a small class invited awkwardness. One woman said that when she answered a question in class, she drew stares from her male classmates: It was "as if the furniture had begun to speak."[54] A junior transfer from Wisconsin said, "I was very conscious of being a girl in my history seminar. I was the only one in twelve. The first day was really funny. I made a point and the professor nearly jumped out of his skin. 'It talks!' He felt attacked. After a couple of days it went a lot easier."[55]

Being invited to give the women's point of view was a common event. Sometimes it was amusing, sometimes burdensome. Sometimes the questions followed logically from the assignment, but sometimes they were far afield. A junior transfer from Sarah Lawrence, who was majoring in philosophy, observed that she was asked repeatedly about gendered themes: "I was asked questions like what did you think when Kierkegaard says such and such about women? Or didn't you think Hegel's view of marriage was a little silly?"[56] A junior transfer from another women's college

---

53 Julia Preston '73, "What Is a Coeducation?," *The New Journal*, Dec. 1970, reprinted in Rachel Donadio, ed., *Different Voices: A Journal Commemorating 25 Years of Coeducation at Yale College* (Yale University, 1995), p. 13, Manuscripts and Archives, Yale University Library.

54 Quoted in Geismar, Rice, and Winant, eds., *Fresh Women*, p. 71.

55 Quoted in Lever and Schwartz, *Women at Yale*, p. 190.

56 Donna Patterson '71, in "Coeducation, Inside and Out: A Collection of Views and an Informal Discussion," *Yale Alumni Magazine* 33 (Apr. 1970): 35.

said, "We were discussing Lolita's character in English class, and they asked me as a woman how it is possible that there would be such a woman at age twelve. And that kind of thing isn't fair. It's obviously intellectually unfair."

Many faculty members did not know how to handle themselves. A junior transfer from Brandeis wrote, in an exercise in a statistics class, that "intuitively it should be one way, but actually it was another. The teacher asked if that was 'woman's intuition.'"[57] In a math class, a woman student was asked for her opinion on the chain rule. Why did the instructor single her out, she asked? To make sure to include the female point of view, he said. "It's a math class, there is no female perspective," she responded.[58] In a psychology course, a woman student often got papers back with comments such as "Not bad for a woman."[59] In directed studies, where the students were reading Plato's *Republic*, the instructor asked the two women students, "Girls, Plato says women are as intelligent as men. Do you think that is true?" One of the students recalled, "We looked at each other in amazement, and said yes." The instructor "grinned and pounced, 'Then why are there no great women philosophers?'" The incident made a lasting impression: "I forget exactly what answer was made," the student said, "but of course it was followed by 'no great women artists, no great women composers, etc. etc.' I left the room shaking, and have never really forgiven Yale or [my instructor]."[60]

Sometimes the insults were stinging in a different way. Jennifer Kemeny, the daughter of the president of Dartmouth, matriculated at Yale in 1971, intent on studying science. On the first day of organic chemistry class, the professor walked around the room, placing course materials on the desks of every man in the class. He pointedly skipped the women students, leaving their copies on his desk in front of the room to pick up after class.[61]

---

57 Quoted in Lever and Schwartz, *Women at Yale*, p. 190.
58 Laurie Stevens '75, in DVD "40th Anniversary of Coeducation Celebration."
59 Judy Berkan '71, in "Coeducation, Inside and Out," 36.
60 Quoted in Geismar, Rice, and Winant, eds., *Fresh Women*, p. 61.
61 Jennifer Kemeny told the story to her parents, who gave slightly different, though basically consistent, accounts (her father said that the materials were lab manuals, her mother, course syllabi). See John Kemeny oral history, p. 95; Jean Kemeny oral history, p. 30.

More painful still was the experience of students who had the temerity to suggest that they were interested in studying women. Wasserman told the story years later of a woman student who came to her office "absolutely dissolved in tears." What was the matter? Wasserman asked. "I talked to the chair of the department about giving a course in women's history," the student said, "and he said, 'That would be like teaching the history of dogs.'"[62]

Men and Women: Learning to Relate to Each Other

Women had constantly to engage the very issue of coeducation: Why were they at Yale? Did they deserve to be there? As a woman in the class of 1974 remarked, "I find myself constantly involved in discussions, debates and even full-fledged arguments . . . around the topic of coeducation. Most of the time I feel trapped in defending a woman's right to even be at Yale. But it bothers me that when I speak on the subject, I feel as if I must defend and speak for the entire female population at Yale, when in actuality I can only speak for myself."[63]

The novelty proved challenging in ways both anticipated and unforeseen. One of the pioneering women students described it this way:

> We were an anomaly, laboratory specimens closely watched for our reactions under the stress of tokenism. Generalization about our psyches was rampant—the girls are too serious, the girls are always in the library, the girls are prima donnas. . . . We were so sought after that we simply had neither the time nor energy left to explore our own insides. We were comfort suppliers and ego boosters receiving no reassurance in return except in terms of our subjective desirability as mere females. We increasingly felt that we had been brought to Yale for the edification of the male students; that we [were] . . . merely appendages to make the traditions more decorative.

---

62 Wasserman oral history I, p. 44.

63 Quoted in Applicants to Elga Wasserman Seminar on Educated Women: Facts, Myths and Possibilities, Spring 1972, Wasserman II, Box 1.

In the end, she concluded, "we became tourist attractions to our male classmates."[64] Another student put the challenge more simply: She had wanted to go to a coeducational college, but she quickly learned that she had enrolled at an all-male school that had let in a few women.[65]

For Yale men, the challenges were different. It was too difficult to meet women students, interact with them in class, and mix informally with them in the residential colleges. Surely there was no benefit to turning out a thousand male leaders, one man in Pierson College observed, "if their capacity for 'leadership' (in that broad sense which includes a capacity for humaneness and sensitivity) is impaired by so lopsided a ratio of men to women as we now endure."[66]

The relationships between Yale men and Yale women were complicated in predictable ways. Some men complained that the women were not attractive enough. When Wasserman visited some residential colleges in the course of planning for coeducation, she heard: "You've got to admit a good looking bunch of women." Her response: Then we'll admit men on the basis of their looks and the size of their biceps.[67] When the first women arrived, they were greeted by a banner hanging on the old campus: "If you must admit women, why this ugly bunch?"[68]

Although women were regarded by their male peers as "a curiosity" and thus subject to constant attention, Yale men were not ready to give up on the time-honored social practice of bringing women from other colleges to campus for weekends.[69] In the words of one Yale freshman woman, that left too many Yale women "sitting around 'in their dungarees' . . . watching the 'imports' come in."[70] The "weekend women," the imports were

64 Lisa Getman, "From Conestoga to Career," remarks prepared for delivery at the annual meeting of the American Council on Education, Miami Beach, FL, Oct. 6, 1972, Wasserman I, Box 23, Folder 921.

65 Diane Polan '73, in Pimsleur, "Boola Boola."

66 Comments from housing questionnaire, attached to Elga Wasserman to Kingman Brewster et al., Jan. 27, 1970, Brewster III, Box 433, Folder 7.

67 Elga Wasserman, in DVD "40th Anniversary of Coeducation Celebration."

68 Laurie Stevens '75, in DVD "40th Anniversary of Coeducation Celebration."

69 Comments Taken from Transfer Questionnaires, Nov. 1969, Wasserman II, Box 1.

70 Minutes, Freshman Women's Advisory Council meeting, Nov. 13, 1969, Wasserman I, Box 35, Folder 1032.

called. Another woman said: "We called them the aliens. It was
a problem when someone you liked showed up on a weekend
with a girl from Smith."[71] Banners hung from some women's windows declared "Happiness is not Importable."[72] It was difficult
for women students to experience the persistent phenomenon
of their male classmates getting "dressed up" in anticipation of
the "weekend arrivals" and "not speaking to us until Monday
morning." Saturday nights were especially challenging; as one
woman wrote, "I feel out of place in my own dining hall without
a date."[73]

The Pressures of Claustrophobic Housing

All of these challenges unfolded in the context of desperately
overcrowded housing. A male student in Silliman College wrote:
"The conditions we are living under severely detract from our academic success and our personal happiness. I, like many others,
came to Yale specifically to avoid depersonalized, overcrowded
education." From a male student in Morse College: "Coeducation
has so far been, to my way of thinking, a pain. . . . It's one thing
to enjoy having girls around and another to have to make continuing concessions to their welfare and comfort." "Please, please,
please reconsider before adding more people to each college," a
woman in Timothy Dwight pleaded. "I feel claustrophobic; we
all do. . . . Crowding conditions induce unhappiness, frustration,
desperation—everything from physical discomfort to nervous
breakdowns."[74] Another woman said, "The toll in tension this
takes is inestimable"; it "affects relationships with roommates,
with men, study habits, and personal happiness. We need space. . . .
We need someplace to go to be alone."[75]

71 Susanne Wofford '73, quoted in *Yale Daily News*, Oct. 15, 1976. "Weekend
women" is the formulation of Darial Sneed '73, in Pimsleur, "Boola Boola."

72 Reese, "When Yale Needed 'Girls,'" 16.

73 Comments Taken from Transfer Questionnaires, Nov. 1969, Wasserman II, Box 1.

74 Comments from housing questionnaire attached to Elga Wasserman to Kingman
Brewster et al., Jan. 27, 1970, Brewster III, Box 433, Folder 7.

75 Comments Taken from Transfer Questionnaires, Nov. 1969.

The entryway system, with a small number of suites accessed from landings in the stairwells on each floor, was not conducive to easy friendships. Each suite was shut off from the others, there were no hallways with a series of open doors, and there were no lounge spaces for relaxed conversation. With women generally confined to one all-female entryway in each college, there was also no way to accomplish easy interaction with men.[76] Dividing the women into twelve colleges made their numbers feel even smaller; it was difficult to find like-minded friends with whom to eat and socialize, friends who might be roommates in a future year.

The practical corollary of the concerns about overcrowding and small numbers was how to make room for the larger female population in year two of coeducation. There would be no transfer students because there was no room for them, but the 230 freshmen in the class of 1973 would be moving into the already crowded residential colleges to make room for 230 new freshman women in Vanderbilt Hall. The most practical solution, it appeared, would be to annex buildings or apartments in the vicinity to each of the colleges. Then there was the question of how to distribute rooms for women spatially within the colleges—by entryway, by floor, or simply at random? And what physical improvements needed to be made in Vanderbilt for the second year of coeducation?[77]

These were the most pressing questions before the various advisory committees empanelled in the first years of coeducation. With the advent of coeducation, the planning committee on coeducation became the university committee on coeducation under the leadership of Wasserman, who also assumed the position of special assistant to the president on the education of women. An

76 Ibid. Wasserman also received thoughtful reports from residential college masters about what they were learning about the experience and concerns of their new women students. See, e.g., Seymour L. Lustman to Elga Wasserman, Nov. 17, 1969, Brewster II, Box 258, Folder 7.

77 In Brewster III, Box 433, Folder 7, see Elga Wasserman to Masters, Oct. 28, 1969, and Wasserman to Yale College Students, Dec. 1969, with attached housing questionnaire. In Brewster I, Box 60, Folder 16, see minutes, University Committee on Coeducation, Nov. 21, 1969. With respect to Vanderbilt, students' desires were practical: It would be helpful to have bathtubs, bathroom shelves, and towel racks, they said; they also asked for access to sewing machines and to spaces for arts and crafts. Summary, Freshman Women's Advisory Council meeting, Feb. 26, 1970, Wasserman I, Box 35, Folder 1032.

undergraduate advisory council met with her and others to address the needs of women students. And an external advisory committee served as "a sounding board" and helped to "lend credibility to Yale's commitment to coeducation."[78]

Wasserman also gathered information about the implementation of coeducation at peer institutions. In a note to Halcy Bohen, assistant dean of students at Princeton, for example, she remarked on how interesting it was "to see that we are taking more or less parallel paths in our two ventures on coeducation."[79] What she did not say in writing, but what the two certainly discussed when they met, was how big an advantage Bohen had in the common work they were doing. With 170 undergraduate women in the first year of coeducation at Princeton, Bohen could know them all personally and respond promptly to issues as they arose. With 576 women at Yale, Wasserman could not begin to do that. Bohen later described Wasserman as "floundering," encountering "a lot of pushback" on a number of fronts, and eager for Bohen's counsel on how Princeton was handling many of the issues shared by the two institutions.[80]

The various committees needed to attend to many other issues as well. In the immediate term, there were problems with security and lighting, thievery, obscene phone calls, and peeping toms, especially in the bathrooms.[81] Longer term, there were questions about counseling and support in the colleges for women undergraduates, gynecological services, and the structure of career advising and mental health services. What should Yale women expect for their futures? What kinds of careers would be available to them? How could they integrate graduate school, jobs, and marriage?

78 Elga Wasserman to Kingman Brewster, Jr., July 11, 1969, Wasserman II, Box 1 (source of the quote); Wasserman to Brewster, Oct. 6, 1969, Brewster II, Box 258, Folder 3. On the work of the committee, see Wasserman to Kingman Brewster, Jr., July 11, 1969; Brewster to Margaret Johnson, Sept. 2, 1969; Wasserman to Susan Hilles, Feb. 20, 1970; Robert D. Cross to Wasserman, Apr. 8, 1970; and Rosemary Park to Wasserman, Apr. 29, 1970, all in Wasserman II, Box 1; Cross to Brewster, Sept. 5, 1969, Brewster II, Box 258, Folder 3.

79 Elga Wasserman to Halcy Bohen, Nov. 7, 1969, Wasserman I, Box 38, Folder 1067.

80 Telephone interview with Halcyone H. Bohen, Jan. 30, 2015.

81 Minutes, Women's Advisory Council Meeting, Oct. 8 and 16 and Nov. 6, 1969, Wasserman I, Box 35, Folder 1032.

The women responded favorably to Wasserman's initiation of programming to address the challenges of combining career, marriage, and family in a variety of fields.[82] Asked for advice about the qualities they would seek in the incoming class, women students focused on "aggressiveness" and exposure "to environments different from their own (such as AFS students)"—that is, students who had lived abroad during their high school years on American Field Service educational and cultural exchanges.[83]

Women Undergraduates: The "Right Number"

The most important issue was how many undergraduate women would be admitted in subsequent years. The *Yale Daily News* regularly pointed out the serious defects in "token" or "partial" coeducation. "The University simply cannot afford to maintain the present social environment in which men outnumber women by an intolerable margin," the paper editorialized. Student groups organized to demand, through petitions and meetings with faculty and corporation committees, that the size of the entering classes be held constant or reduced and that applicants be admitted without regard to sex.[84]

The flashpoint came in February 1970, when a group of forty undergraduate women, calling themselves "Women for a Better Yale," invaded the alumni day luncheon on campus "with clenched fists and placards" to protest "the ratio of women to men in the student body." The *New York Times* relished the story. One freshman, Margaret Coon, it said, "strode to the dais, seized a microphone and lectured the 1,000 stunned guests for three minutes on the plight of women at Yale." Coon said, "There are not enough of us. We are scattered in tiny groups and the only solution is to

82 Wasserman oral history II, p. 22; Comments Taken from Transfer Questionnaires, Nov. 1969.

83 Draft minutes, Upperclass Women's Advisory Council meeting, Jan. 22, 1970; summary, Upperclass Women's Advisory Council meeting, Mar. 5 (source of the quotes) and May 7, 1970, all in Wasserman I, Box 35, Folder 1032.

84 *Yale Daily News*, Feb. 9 ("token," "partial"), 20 ("simply cannot afford"), 23, and 27, 1970.

admit more women at the first possible opportunity." As Coon spoke, "other coeds in the obviously well-planned demonstration marched among the tables of alumni . . . carrying signs reading, 'End Women's Oppression' and 'Women Up From Under.'" The alumni and their wives, the *Times* said, "gaped in amazement at the protesters."[85] A self-described "hard-core male supremacist" in the class of 1943 who attended the luncheon told a reporter, "These ladies should feel privileged to come to Yale and not use this opportunity to tell Yale how to run the place."[86] A member of the class of 1926, acknowledging that the students' presentation was "well-expressed," told the *Yale Daily News* that the luncheon was "neither the time nor the place to express it." He declared, "You invite them here, and now they want to take over the place."[87]

Brewster, acknowledging that the complaints of overcrowding were valid, said that fuller coeducation would be accomplished only "on an incremental basis," a position later reaffirmed by the Yale corporation. For the foreseeable future, Yale would be enrolling freshman classes of 1,000 men and 250 women. Those numbers were part and parcel of fulfilling Yale's "national educational responsibility" and remaining accountable to Yale's alumni.[88]

Brewster's affirmation of Yale's intention to turn out "1,000 male leaders" became a rallying cry in the debate over the future of coeducation. As traditionalists saw it, Brewster was exactly right. It was Yale's role to produce leaders for the public and private spheres, and "leader" was synonymous with "male." The students' alumni day protest was "disgraceful" in the view of one alumnus, proof that women should never have been admitted to Yale.[89] Even some women regarded the behavior of the women protesters as "brazen"

85 *New York Times*, Feb. 22, 1970, clippings in Brewster I, Box 60, Folder 15 (p. 1), and Heller, Box 1, Folder 4 (p. 40).

86 Howard Brown, quoted in *Providence Journal*, Mar. 2, 1970, clipping in Brewster I, Box 60, Folder 15.

87 Quoted in *Yale Daily News*, Feb. 23, 1970.

88 Brewster, quoted in *Yale Daily News*, Feb. 23, 1970. On the corporation's reaffirmation, see *Yale Daily News*, Mar. 9, 1970.

89 John A. Thompson to Kingman Brewster, Jr., Feb. 23, 1970 (source of the quote), and letter to Brewster received Feb. 26, 1970 [signature undecipherable], both in Brewster I, Box 60, Folder 15.

and "incredibly un̲feminine."[90] An alumnus who had frequently counseled Brewster that it would take Yale "25 years to recover from the Co-ed decision" broached a simple solution to the women's protest: "Get rid of them all immediately."[91] An alumnus in the class of 1923 wrote: "Come on President, throw these damn girls out of Yale . . . and fire all students caught taking drugs, so I won't have to be ashamed of being a Yale man any more!"[92] An alumnus of the law school class of 1933 echoed, "Chickens are coming home to roost . . . for the 'limosine [*sic*] liberals' and the 'supercilious sophisticates' who solicited blacks and more recently coeds into what was theretofore a respected, elite institution of learning. You can't very well get rid of those already admitted but for God's sake don't admit any more blacks or coeds in the future."[93]

But others had a different view. "Huzzahs to the young ladies for finally rising on their hind legs, turning on their tormentors, and demanding the fair and equal treatment they have so far been denied," a father of a woman transfer student declared.[94] An alumna of Connecticut College with a daughter at Wellesley wrote, with respect to Yale producing 1,000 male leaders, "Where does this leave your female undergraduates? Don't you believe they should be leaders, too?"[95] A Skidmore graduate wrote: "The obvious implication" of Yale's stated commitment to educating 1,000 male leaders was that Yale was "still primarily committed to educating men" instead of people, and "that women are being exploited and used by Yale University. To not recognize this obvious fact and expect that today's women would be happy and able to live with such discrimination, is absolutely incredible!"[96]

90 *Yale Daily News*, Feb. 23, 1970 ("brazen"); Sara Anne Corrigan to Kingman Brewster, Jr., Feb. 23, 1970, Brewster I, Box 60, Folder 15 ("unfeminine").

91 Richard F. Lawler to Kingman Brewster, Mar. 4, 1970, Brewster I, Box 60, Folder 15.

92 Donald Whitcomb to Kingman Brewster, Mar. 2, 1970, Brewster I, Box 60, Folder 15.

93 John A. Thompson to Kingman Brewster, Jr., Feb. 23, 1970, Brewster I, Box 60, Folder 15.

94 Lloyd Schwartz to Kingman Brewster, Jr., Feb. 24, 1970, Brewster I, Box 60, Folder 15.

95 Anahid Constantian to Kingman Brewster, Jr., Feb. 22, 1970, Brewster I, Box 60, Folder 15.

96 Ann F. Cedarholm to Kingman Brewster, Jr., Feb. 22, 1970, Brewster I, Box 60, Folder 15.

The Costs of Proceeding Too Quickly

The underlying theme of the student protest was the cost of hurrying to institute coeducation without sufficient funding, advance planning, and attention to detail. The lack of planning affected male students as well as females, but the burden for women was particularly acute. In the first year of coeducation, women were add-ons, squeezed into existing facilities, without gender-specific programming or staffing. The first generation of women students had to make do as the price of enrolling at Yale, and many of them felt underappreciated and insufficiently attended to by their university.

The costs of proceeding quickly were illustrated in other areas as well. The women's athletic program is a case in point. By 1972, only three women's sports had achieved varsity status: field hockey, squash, and tennis. The field hockey team was assigned to a parking lot at the Yale Bowl as its practice field. The tennis team got court time, but their coach was a local gym teacher. In 1973–74, five more women's teams—basketball, crew, fencing, gymnastics, and swimming—reached varsity status, while volleyball and lacrosse continued to operate at the club level. But women still needed to fit their practices and contests in around the men's schedules. The women's coaches, save for one, were part-time; the male coaches were full-time. Women's teams had to contend with inadequate dressing and toilet facilities.[97]

As late as the winter of 1975–76, the women's crew team still had no shower facilities at the university boathouse, despite repeated requests. Gender integration was more complicated for crew than for many other sports. Rowing was thought to be unfeminine. The male camaraderie of the boathouse mattered to the success of the team; having women around threatened to disrupt the seriousness of the enterprise. At Princeton, the heavyweight men's coach made

---

97 Deborah L. Rhode, "The 'Woman Question,'" in Yale University Women Faculty Forum, *Gender Matters: Women and Yale in Its Third Century* (Yale University, [2002?]), pp. 158–59; *Yale Daily News*, Oct. 25, 1979; Lawrie Mifflin '73 (captain of field hockey team), in Pimsleur, "Boola Boola"; minutes, University Committee on Coeducation, Apr. 22, 1974, Wasserman I, Box 34, Folder 1022.

plain that "women would row out of the boathouse over his dead body," a view that some male rowers initially echoed.[98]

The issue at Yale had to do not with resistance from the men's team but with resources the university would or would not make available. The Yale boathouse was located on the Housatonic River in Derby, Connecticut, half an hour's bus ride from the campus. Following their practices, male rowers showered there and dressed in dry clothes. Women, wet and sweaty, had to wait to return to campus to clean up. The promised renovation of the boathouse had been delayed repeatedly for financial reasons. Finally the students lost patience. In a protest on March 3, 1976, twenty women rowers entered the office of the director of physical education, Joni Barnett, took off their shirts in the presence of invited guests, including a *Yale Daily News* photographer who also worked for the *New York Times*, and displayed a message emblazoned in blue magic marker across their chests and on their backs: "Title IX." The students said in a prepared statement, "On a day like today, the ice freezes on this skin. Then we sit . . . on the bus as the ice melts and soaks through our suits to meet the sweat that's soaking us from the inside. We sit for half an hour with the chills. . . . Half a dozen of us are sick now." One of the rowers said, "If this were the football team, there would be showers." National newspaper coverage followed, along with mentions on television, on radio, and in *Sports Illustrated*. Embarrassed, the university brought in a fifty-foot trailer to provide a temporary changing room and shower facilities in Derby. That fall, construction began on a new wing of the boathouse to include showers for women.[99]

The concerns of women students were not at odds with the views of university officials charged with seeing to their well-being. As Wasserman wrote in reviewing the first year of coeducation, the two greatest challenges were "the severe imbalance in the ratio of men and women . . . and the increase in undergraduate enrollment

---

98 Ella Van Cleve, "Women's Rowing at Princeton," paper written for Freshman Seminar 131, Jan. 11, 2016, Princeton University, in the possession of Nancy Weiss Malkiel.

99 *Yale Daily News*, Mar. 4 (source of the quotes) and 23 and Dec. 1, 1976; Joyce Banerjee, "A Different Ballgame," *New Journal* 17 (Mar. 1, 1985): 53; Rhode, "The 'Woman Question,'" p. 159.

without a corresponding increase in available housing." By the next year, some of the physical deprivations were remedied, and 320 additional beds became available in newly created annex housing. More encouraging for the longer run was news of the establishment by the senior fellow of the Yale corporation, John Hay Whitney, of a $15 million trust that would permit construction of two new colleges with six hundred beds. Although it would take years for the colleges to come on line, they held the promise of alleviating overcrowding and increasing the number of women undergraduates.[100]

But the new colleges were never built. The plan was to locate them on Whitney Avenue, a main thoroughfare on the eastern edge of the campus, with retail establishments included at street level. Hearings before the city plan commission raised many objections. There were too few retail operations compared with the space currently used for commercial purposes; insufficient parking had been planned; a historic house on the site would be taken down. These objections might have been overcome in different circumstances. But in the context of deteriorating relations between the university and the city of New Haven, a dispute over the university's tax liability blocked the planned construction. William Horowitz, a banker and corporation member who was chairman of the Connecticut State Board of Education and had been long active in Democratic politics in New Haven, thought that the situation could have been resolved if Brewster had been prepared to make a political deal with the mayor. Brewster, Horowitz said, should have talked to the mayor "like a ward politician"—Yale needed the colleges; what could the university do to get the necessary approvals? But acting like a ward politician was not Brewster's style. Despite efforts to resolve the problem in protracted discussions between city officials and university representatives, including negotiations between the mayor and a prominent member of the corporation,

---

100 Elga Wasserman, Coeducation 1969–70 [Aug. 1970], Brewster I, Box 60, Folder 12; Whitney obituary, *New York Times*, Feb. 9, 1982, http://www.nytimes.com/1982/02 /09/obituaries/john-hay-whitney-dies-at-77-publisher-led-in-many-fields.html, accessed Jan. 1, 2015.

Cyrus Vance, the dispute ended with the board of aldermen twice voting to deny zoning changes.[101]

Dramatic escalation of building costs over the next four years, Brewster explained in his annual president's report, meant that "even if the City were to relent in its opposition" (a scenario that did not occur), construction of new colleges "would now be prohibitive." The Whitney gift was redirected, with substantial funds dedicated to rehabilitating and modernizing freshman dormitories. That might make room for more students on the old campus, Brewster said, but it would permit neither "the expansion [nor] the relief from crowding which the new Colleges would have offered."[102] In the end, the growth in enrollment was handled not by constructing new dormitories but by continuing to crowd students in existing facilities and, to a lesser extent, by an increasing numbers of students choosing to live off campus.[103]

The costs of the early months of coeducation were reckoned in more personal terms than the realities of physical overcrowding. As Wasserman wrote in her report on the first year, "When women represent a real minority on campus, they are easily regarded as different, often as superior intellects, but as inferior females. . . . Women at Yale need an unusual sense of self in order to maintain their self-respect in the predominantly male setting. Most have numerous male friends, but miss the opportunity for close friendships with fellow women students. . . . For many women, the current environment does not provide an ideal setting in which to grow and develop as a person." The current environment was "not ideal for the men either," most of whom "continue[d] to turn elsewhere for their social life." Many men "adopt[ed] the attitude . . . that they are not interested in the Yale women anyhow."[104]

101 *Yale Daily News*, Dec. 6 and 8, 1972, and Jan. 31, Feb. 1 and 7, and June 29, 1973; Mary B. Arnstein, The Admission of Women to Yale College, July 1974, pp. 8–9, Brewster II, Box 270, Folder 6; Horowitz oral history, pp. 30–31.

102 Kingman Brewster, Jr., *Report of the President, Yale University: 1974–75* (July 1975), p. 5.

103 On the increasing numbers living off campus, see, e.g., *Yale Daily News*, May 3, 1977. Two new colleges were under construction in 2015, with plans to open them in 2017 to accommodate a planned increase in undergraduate enrollment.

104 Elga Wasserman, Coeducation 1969–70 [Aug. 1970], Brewster I, Box 60, Folder 12.

Women Students: Gaining a Foothold

There is no denying how tough it was for women to be pioneers at Yale. Some of the difficulty was inherent in coeducating any all-male school—in so many situations, male administrators, faculty, and students did not know what to do or how to handle themselves. At Yale the difficulty was compounded by the lack of process and planning that might have eased the women's arrival and by the university's inability to provide living spaces sufficient to avoid the acute pressures of overcrowding. The experience of the earliest years of coeducation is still imprinted on the attitudes toward Yale of some of those first generations of women graduates.

Over time, however, Yale adjusted to the women, and the women adjusted to Yale. Yale women settled into the university in ways that confirmed that coeducation was quickly becoming the norm. Academically, women more than held their own. In terms of standardized testing, as table 6.1 shows, their credentials upon entrance closely mirrored those of their male classmates, with predictable differences by gender, with women outscoring men on the SAT verbal tests but lagging behind men on the SAT math tests.[105]

In the earliest years of coeducation, academic credentials alone were the basis on which women had been admitted to Yale. Unlike men, for whom "personal promise" figured in admission decisions, women in the first four undergraduate cohorts were evaluated principally on the basis of grades, rank in class, and test scores (that changed by 1973, when the admission office figured out how to apply the criterion of "personal promise" to women). That may have had some influence on the fact that in the first half-dozen years of coeducation, women earned higher grades than men, a differential eliminated by the late 1970s. The earliest cohorts of women may also have worked harder in their courses, perhaps perpetuating patterns learned in high school or perhaps deliberately seeking to demonstrate that they fully belonged at Yale.[106]

105 An Analysis of the Impact of Coeducation at Yale College, Jan. 1972, Exhibit 9, Brewster I, Box 257, Folder 7.

106 On admission policy with respect to women, see Joseph A. Soares, *The Power of Privilege: Yale and America's Elite Colleges* (Stanford, CA: Stanford University Press, 2007), p. 111. On women's grades, see Mary B. Arnstein, Coeducation Report 1972–73,

TABLE 6.1. MEAN SAT SCORES OF MATRICULANTS, BY GENDER
YALE COLLEGE CLASSES OF 1973–75

Class Year	Verbal		Math	
	Men	Women	Men	Women
1973	670	690	700	670
1974	680	710	700	680
1975	675	700	700	680

In extracurricular activities, women students began to assume leadership roles in formerly all-male student organizations such as the political union, the debate team, the *Yale Daily News*, Dwight Hall, student agencies, film societies, and music and theater groups. Where all-male groups persisted, as in the case of the venerable a cappella singing group the Whiffenpoofs and the Russian chorus, women formed parallel all-female organizations. By 1975, all nine women's varsity athletic teams (lacrosse now having been elevated to a varsity sport) had winning records, and teams in other sports—soccer, ice hockey, polo, and sailing—were contending for varsity status. Mory's, the fabled private eating and drinking club adjacent to the campus that had added the word "male" to its membership requirements in the wake of coeducation, and had resolutely refused to allow women faculty members and administrators even to attend meetings there of committees on which they served, opened membership to women in 1974 after a lawsuit and years of picketing in front of the club. Some senior secret societies began admitting women early on, but the three most prominent ones, Skull and Bones, Scroll and Key, and Wolf's Head, held out, with Skull and Bones and Wolf's Head continuing to hold out until the spring of 1992.[107]

July 1973, Table 5, and Arnstein, Report to the President from the University Committee on the Education of Women, 1973–74, July 1, 1974, Table 5, both in Brewster II, Box 258, Folder 11; *Yale Daily News*, Feb. 21, 1979.

107 *Yale Daily News*, Oct. 2, 1973, July 1, 1976, Sept. 17 and 25, Oct. 25 and 28, Nov. 6 and 13, and Dec. 18, 1991, and Feb. 11 and Apr. 15, 1992; "Mory's: One Step Closer to Going Dry, or, God Forbid, Female?," *Yale Alumni Magazine* 35 (Mar. 1972):

Particularly in retrospect, many women made plain how much they appreciated the opportunities available to them. Not surprisingly, alumni daughters were especially willing to give Yale the benefit of the doubt. A woman in the class of 1971, who transferred as a junior from Penn, said: "I had a great time. It was a very rich experience."[108] A woman in the class of 1973, "at least fourth generation Yale," said, "I never wished I had gone anywhere else. I don't think anyone . . . had illusions that Yale would be completely prepared, facilities built, and all adjustments made. We arrived with a spirit of adventure. . . . In general . . . most of us were much more interested in becoming part of Yale . . . than in thinking about the newness of what we were doing."[109] An alumni daughter in the class of 1974 added, "I went into my freshman year with a lot of faith in 'Mother Yale,' and this positive attitude lasted throughout my 4 years." There were so many opportunities for personal and intellectual growth. And the benefits were enduring: "For the rest of my life, having been to Yale puts me at an advantage."[110]

But it did not take Yale roots to appreciate a Yale education. A student in the class of 1973, writing in the spring of her freshman year, doubtless spoke for many of her classmates when she said of being at Yale, "I . . . love it. I don't love Yale the institution . . . I love the Yale that practically everyone remembers best, the Yale that is a group of dynamic and almost electric people, who . . . create the experiences that are so exciting, so important, and so unique to Yale. I came expecting a great deal, and I have found a great deal. I enjoy being here."[111]

33; Anne Coffin Hanson, in Pimsleur, "Boola Boola"; *Women at Yale: A Tour*, n.d., p. 4. In Rachel Donadio, ed., *Different Voices: A Journal Commemorating 25 Years of Coeducation at Yale College* (Yale University, 1995), pp. 32, 46–47, 53, Manuscripts and Archives, Yale University Library, see Jessica Moss '95 and Shira Weinert '95, "The Women's Center: Still Crazy After All These Years"; Rachel Nevins '95, "Old Blue for Girls: Women's Singing Groups"; and Tisha Neufville '97, "Claiming the Field: Women's Athletics."

108 Frances Beinecke, quoted in "'On the Advisability and Feasibility of Women at Yale': The Coeducation Debate at Yale College," *Yale Alumni Magazine* 73 (Sept.–Oct. 2009): 51.

109 "New Old Blue," in Geismar, Rice, and Winant, eds., *Fresh Women*, p. 110.

110 Lauren Virshup '74, Alumnae Questionnaire and interview, Jan. 1988, Heller, Box 3, Folder 11. On the theme "the credentials . . . don't hurt," see also, in the same folder, Anne Chafer '73, Alumnae Questionnaire, Jan. 1988.

111 Lucy L. Eddy, "In the Blue," *Yale Alumni Magazine* 33 (Apr. 1970): 24.

A woman in the class of 1972, who had transferred as a sophomore from Berkeley, said later that she had been attracted to Yale by the "challenge of coeducation . . . finding out that I could survive (just barely) in such a competitive, high powered setting during the first year" was a real benefit. She gained so many things from her experiences in and beyond the classroom, and she found that Yale was terrific for confidence-building.[112] A woman in the class of 1973 said that women students had "a feeling of pride in being pioneers."[113] Another woman in the class of 1973 wrote, "I believed it to be my duty to show that women could do anything academically. I coded it to mean that I, that we, had this mission to prove to the world 'that sex [gender] was irrelevant.'" She continued, "Most of us . . . went to Yale because it was a wonderful opportunity for a superb education, not because we wanted to change Yale or be pioneers. . . . Sexism was something we were fighting just by being at Yale and doing well there."[114] And things got better over time as women became "more of an accepted part of things," as "a critical mass of women" made "coeducation more reality than novelty."[115]

---

112 Jennifer Lyman '72, Alumnae Questionnaire and interview, Jan. 1988, Heller, Box 3, Folder 11.

113 Susanne Wofford '73, quoted in *Yale Daily News*, Oct. 15, 1976.

114 "Scholar of the House," in Geismar, Rice, and Winant, eds., *Fresh Women*, pp. 32–33.

115 Stacey Keen '75, Alumnae Questionnaire, Jan. 1988 ("more of an accepted part of things"), and Judith Fabricant-Homer '76, Alumnae Questionnaire and interview, Jan. 1988 ("critical mass," "more reality"), both in Heller, Box 3, Folder 11.

7

Princeton: "The Admission of Women Will Make Princeton a Better University"

Princeton's Patterson report had broad influence beyond the university. A dean at Holy Cross said that it was "by far the most thorough, comprehensive report on this topic that I have ever seen"—"a study of great value not only to Princeton but to everyone in higher education who is concerned about the education of women."[1] An Amherst committee investigating coeducation praised it as "the classic study of the issues, the model consulted by all other colleges."[2] As we have seen, the report weighed importantly in Yale's decision for coeducation; later it would influence deliberations as far afield as Cambridge and Oxford.

The impact of the report on the educational community notwithstanding, Princeton's challenge was local: selling the report to Princeton alumni. From October through early December 1968, the administration held thirty-three meetings with alumni to talk

---

1 John E. Shay, Jr., to Gardner Patterson, Oct. 21, 1968, Patterson, Box 1, Folder 19. For other testimony to the influence of the Patterson report, see, e.g., Robert W. Fuller (Trinity College) to William G. Bowen, Nov. 14, 1968, Bowen provost, Box 19, Folder 3; unidentified historian of higher education at Williams College, quoted in memorandum, J. P. Moran to W. D. Lippincott, Dec. 10, 1968, Goheen, Box 94, Folder 8; Keith Spalding (Franklin and Marshall College) to Patterson, Jan. 28, 1969, Patterson, Box 1, Folder 22; Spalding to Robert F. Goheen, Jan. 28, 1969, Goheen, Box 95, Folder 3.

2 Report of the Amherst Visiting Committee on Coeducation, June 1974, attached to Neil L. Rudenstine to Theodore P. Greene, July 8, 1974, Bowen president, Series 2.4, Box 104, Folder 14. A Princeton faculty member visiting Mt. Holyoke reported the broad consensus there "that Princeton has handled the problem of coeducation very much better than anyone else." Memorandum, L[awrence] Stone to President Bowen, May 10, 1973, Bowen president, Series 2.4, Box 104, Folder 14.

"Princeton, did you say? How interesting.
I'm a Yale man myself."

HARVARD

In 1882 **Elizabeth Cary Agassiz** became president of the new "Harvard Annex," known formally as the Society for the Collegiate Instruction of Women. Designed to offer women students instruction by Harvard faculty members, the Annex took the name Radcliffe College in 1893 and was chartered as a degree-granting institution in 1894. Agassiz's purpose was not to create a free-standing women's college but to have women "accepted by the old and beloved University" and to take every possible advantage of the intellectual resources of Harvard for the benefit of the education of Radcliffe women.

Nathan Marsh Pusey, president of Harvard University from 1953 to 1971, looked favorably on the closer integration of Harvard and Radcliffe Colleges and left a legacy of substantial accomplishment wherein undergraduates at Harvard and Radcliffe increasingly studied together in the same classes, had the option of living in the same dormitories, participated in the same extracurricular activities, graduated in the same commencement ceremonies, and earned the same degrees. But he was unable to effect a merger, due in significant part to the turmoil that followed his decision to call in the police to end the April 1969 antiwar student occupation of University Hall.

Mary Ingraham Bunting, known as Polly, became president of Radcliffe College in 1960, determined to make the education of Radcliffe women equivalent to that of Harvard men. By the time she stepped down in 1972, she had seen to the renovation and expansion of Radcliffe's residential facilities, the creation of a house system, the construction of a new library, and fuller integration of the college into the larger university. She was unable to effect a merger because of turmoil at Harvard and opposition by Radcliffe trustees and alumnae. But in July 1971 she signed an agreement with Derek Bok instituting new administrative and financial arrangements between the two institutions that became known as the "non-merger merger."

In 1972, **Matina Souretis Horner**, an assistant professor of psychology at Harvard, succeeded Polly Bunting as president of Radcliffe. Horner believed that Bunting had gone too far in the 1971 agreement in folding Radcliffe into Harvard, that the financial relationship between the two institutions needed to be rethought, and that there was substantial work still to be done to create equal opportunity for women at Harvard.

Derek Bok, dean of the Harvard Law School, became president of Harvard in 1971. Bok believed that merger was inevitable, but he recognized that Harvard could not pressure Radcliffe to achieve it. Rather, the two colleges could behave as a coeducational institution until Radcliffe was ready to merge. In the meantime, he took a series of interim steps to improve the ratio between men and women undergraduates and to move toward closer cooperation. In 1977 Bok and Horner signed a new agreement stipulating Radcliffe's continued independence of Harvard, asserting that the two institutions would function in a coordinate relationship, and returning to Radcliffe control over its fiscal operations.

In 1989 **Linda S. Wilson**, then vice president for research at the University of Michigan, succeeded Horner as president of Radcliffe. A decade later, after two years of secret negotiations, she and Neil Rudenstine, president of Harvard, signed an agreement finally merging Harvard and Radcliffe. In place of Radcliffe College, the agreement established a new Radcliffe Institute for Advanced Study.

Harvard and Radcliffe announced the merger on April 20, 1999. This photograph, taken on the day of the announcement, shows, from right to left, **Neil Rudenstine**, **Linda Wilson**, **Nancy-Beth Gordon Sheerr**, chairman of the Radcliffe board of trustees, and **Mary Maples Dunn**, who would serve as dean of the new Radcliffe Institute until January 2001, when she was succeeded by Drew Gilpin Faust, later president of Harvard.

YALE

The possibility of undergraduate coeducation at Yale was first raised during the presidency of **A. Whitney Griswold** (1951–63). The dean of admission, Arthur Howe, Jr., told the Yale faculty in September 1956 that all-male schools were "outmoded"—"harmful, academically and socially." Yale was losing some of "the brightest and best" secondary school students "because it was single-sex." When the story got out, and the *New York Times* reported that Yale was considering coeducation, Griswold responded, "There is not the remotest possibility of its taking place at Yale within the foreseeable future."

When **Kingman Brewster, Jr.**, succeeded Griswold as president in 1963, it was clear, as he later noted, that Yale's single-sex status was becoming an increasingly important "handicap in getting the best men" to apply and enroll. Brewster first explored bringing Vassar College to New Haven in a coordinate relationship with Yale. That effort failed, and he turned next to the possibility of Yale's establishing its own coordinate college for women. When Brewster learned in the fall of 1968 that Princeton was seriously considering coeducation, he moved immediately to embrace coeducation for Yale.

Hanna Holborn Gray, daughter of a Yale historian, was a professor of history at the University of Chicago when she was elected to the Yale corporation in 1971, one of the first two women to serve on that body. From 1972 to 1974, she served as dean of the college of arts and sciences at Northwestern University. In 1974 she joined the Yale administration as provost. When Brewster left the university in 1977 to become U.S. ambassador to the Court of St. James's, Gray was named acting president. Brewster had hoped that she might succeed him, but the corporation was unwilling to take the risk. Gray left Yale in 1978 to begin a long and highly successful presidency at the University of Chicago.

When the Yale faculty voted in November 1968 to admit women undergraduates for September 1969, Brewster assigned responsibility for coeducation planning to two colleagues. He asked **Elga R. Wasserman**, a chemist serving as an assistant dean of the graduate school, to head a new planning committee on coeducation. And he named the assistant to the president, **Henry "Sam" Chauncey, Jr.**, a member of the Yale class of 1957, to lead administrative planning. Wasserman focused on matters relating to the education of women, including admissions and residential policies, and Chauncey concentrated on facilities and financial planning, but the two worked closely together.

After the women students arrived, Wasserman's planning committee became the university committee on coeducation, which she chaired, but she had no formal administrative position. Without a seat at the table when important decisions were made, she had limited influence; passed over for administrative appointments, she left Yale in 1973 to enroll in law school. Chauncey, a respected and trusted counselor who had the president's ear, remained an influential administrator at the university for years to come.

While Yale had been educating women in the graduate school of arts and sciences and the professional schools since the late nineteenth century, the arrival of the first women undergraduates in September 1969 caused a huge splash. Reporters and photographers from national newspapers and magazines descended on the campus. "The fuss over coeds," the *Washington Post* said, was "higher education's big freak show." As one freshman woman told a television reporter, "It feels like we're in a goldfish bowl." The campus police festooned the old campus, where the freshman men and women were housed, with banners saying, **"Welcome to the Guys and Dolls of '73."**

PRINCETON

Initially skeptical that coeducation was a priority for Princeton, **Robert F. Goheen**, president of the university from 1957 to 1972, came to realize that the world was changing. Many of the ablest male students in high schools that had long been Princeton's biggest feeders were choosing not to come because the university was not coeducational. Moreover, women were beginning to assume new roles in American society. In 1967 Goheen asked the trustees to authorize a study of the desirability and feasibility of coeducation; in 1968 he strongly endorsed the conclusions of the resulting report; and in 1969 he led the board of trustees to embrace coeducation.

William G. Bowen, professor of economics and public affairs, became Princeton's first full-time provost in July 1967. He understood clearly that Princeton needed to admit women undergraduates to remain a great university, and he helped to influence Goheen to support coeducation and, subsequently, to convince skeptical alumni to accept it as well. Bowen participated actively in the work of the Patterson committee and in planning for and implementing coeducation. When he succeeded Goheen as president of the university in 1972, he led the trustees to adopt a policy of equal access for men and women undergraduates.

Gardner Patterson, an economist on the faculty of the Woodrow Wilson School of Public and International Affairs, was asked by Goheen to undertake the study of the desirability and feasibility of coeducation at Princeton. Beginning work in September 1967, he produced a major report, published a year later, that argued forcefully for the admission of undergraduate women. Highly analytical, heavily grounded in extensive data, the Patterson report weighed importantly in decisions for coeducation at other American colleges and universities and influenced deliberations as far afield as Cambridge and Oxford.

Arthur J. "Jerry" Horton, director of development at Princeton, was the sole dissenter on the Patterson committee. He believed that bringing women to Princeton would spoil the uniqueness, the special ambiance that made the university so successful and would divert resources from other pressing priorities. Horton became the intake point for alumni concerned about coeducation, and he collected many hundreds of letters, cards, and notes from disgruntled graduates. He advised alumni correspondents on strategies for communicating their objections, collected data to support his point of view, and rallied his staff in opposition.

Halcyone Harger "Halcy" Bohen was appointed assistant dean of students at Princeton in 1969 to aid in the implementation of coeducation. Bohen knew the women students individually, followed what was happening to them, and responded quickly to their needs and concerns. She offered access, understanding, and personal support that played a critical role in their adjustment to the university. Bohen instituted programs and activities designed with women in mind—such as modern dance, resident advisers, and sex education and counseling—that proved important for men as well.

Suzanne Keller, a sociologist, was appointed the first female professor at Princeton in 1968. "To be the first of anything is not easy," she said later. "You can't make a mistake; you're on display <u>all the time</u>. Your failings become attributed not to <u>you</u> but to all <u>women</u>." Keller taught Princeton's first courses on gender. Initially, she thought, women students had to "<u>adapt</u>, and <u>bend themselves to fit</u> ... the [masculine] culture already in place" at Princeton. Later, however, she observed that under their influence, there was a noticeable change in "the style of the university": "a freer spirit," with "more wit, humor, less pretentiousness ... more innovation, more insouciance."

DARTMOUTH

John Sloan Dickey, president of Dartmouth from 1945 to 1970, declared in April 1958, "There is no possibility of coeducation at the College in the foreseeable future." Nevertheless, in February 1969 he set in motion a formal study of the possibility of educating women at Dartmouth. As Dickey told the trustee study committee, Dartmouth had many priorities and commitments and limited resources and energy. "The decisive question is whether a 'policy commitment' now to coeducation would significantly increase or limit Dartmouth's total institutional capacity to be a top-quality enterprise of higher education in the foreseeable future."

    John G. Kemeny, professor of mathematics at Dartmouth, succeeded Dickey as president in March 1970. He had been a member of the trustee study committee, and he inherited responsibility for bringing its deliberations to a conclusion. With opposition to coeducation from alumni and significant reservations on the part of some trustees, that proved to be complicated. The intensity of the opposition is illustrated in the title of this book, which comes from a letter written by a Dartmouth alumnus arguing against coeducation. In November 1971, Kemeny won a trustee vote for coeducation, along with an innovative plan for year-round operation to accommodate the increase in the number of students.

    Among colleges and universities that coeducated, Dartmouth was distinctive for the hostile reaction to women students on the part of male students, as well as some faculty members and administrators. So much of the Dartmouth campus culture was assertively, even exclusively, male, and men were strongly invested in sustaining it. Male students were not shy about telling women that they did not belong at Dartmouth. The banners hung from one dormitory—**"No Coeds"** and **"Keep Sage All Male"**—were among the more benign manifestations of the profound difficulty of reshaping the culture to accept and value women.

about the report and address the multitude of questions alumni wanted answered.[3]

Princeton Reaches Out to Alumni

Making this systematic effort to reach out to alumni was another important strategic decision on the part of Robert Goheen, William Bowen, and Gardner Patterson. Alumni had a strong sense of ownership and entitlement, and, they believed, a unique perspective on Princeton. They needed the opportunity to engage directly with the people advocating coeducation. The time and expense involved in months of regional meetings were worth the investment.

One category of issues on the minds of alumni concerned Princeton's strengths. Why think about change when Princeton had been so strong the way it was for such a long time? What was wrong with the applicant pool Princeton attracted? What would be the effects of growth in the size of the undergraduate student body? And if the case for growth were accepted, why add women rather than men? Could the university afford coeducation? What would be the effect of enrolling women on alumni giving? What would enrolling women mean for the quality of education? Why should alumni believe that a coeducational Princeton could meet, or even exceed, the educational standard they had known? The other principal category of issues had to do with process. Why not poll alumni? Had the administration and the trustees already made up their minds? Why should trustees make the decision instead of putting the case to the alumni?[4]

The administrative team fanned out across the country. In Kansas City and Denver, the dean of the college, Edward D. Sullivan, reported, "by far the majority of alumni" present "were enthusiastic about co-education or at least prepared to accept it quite

3 Confirmed Schedule of Meetings on Education of Women, Fall 1968, rev. Nov. 5, 1968, Goheen, Box 94, Folder 6.

4 For a detailed account of one alumni gathering where all of these issues were raised, see W. G. Bowen to R. F. Goheen, Nov. 13, 1968, Goheen, Box 94, Folder 6.

gracefully."[5] The dean of students, Neil Rudenstine, summarized the sentiment of alumni assembled in Buffalo as "generally one of good humored if half reluctant acceptance of the possibility of women at Princeton."[6] In Cleveland the financial vice president, Ricardo Mestres, encountered a much more skeptical crowd, with a number of strongly emotional expressions of opposition and a large number of alumni still on the fence.[7]

In San Francisco, Bowen spoke at an "open, candid and dispassionate" meeting, with the reaction of the assembled alumni and spouses ranging from "mild disapproval to whole-hearted support."[8] Goheen and William D'O. Lippincott, executive director of the alumni council, addressed a large gathering in Chicago, where, after robust discussion, an informal vote showed that a substantial majority believed coeducation to be in the long-run interest of the university.[9] By contrast, "The Battle of Philadelphia" pitted Sullivan, Mestres, and the president of the senior class, Marc Miller, against an "unquestionably hostile" Princeton Club of Philadelphia, where it proved impossible to gain any traction.[10] The next day, however, when Bowen addressed a second luncheon meeting in Philadelphia, along with Richard Darby of the undergraduate assembly, the atmosphere was much more positive, and important issues profited from a thoughtful airing. While the group split in the informal show of hands at the end of the meeting, the open-mindedness of "a large number" of the alumni was what most impressed Bowen about the whole event.[11] In St. Louis, on the other hand, there was nothing but opposition;

5　E. D. Sullivan to Robert F. Goheen, Oct. 14, 1968, Goheen, Box 94, Folder 7.

6　Neil L. Rudenstine to Robert F. Goheen et al., Oct. 28, 1968, Goheen, Box 94, Folder 7.

7　R. A. Mestres to Robert F. Goheen, Oct. 31, 1968, Goheen, Box 94, Folder 6.

8　Denis T. Rice to David G. Rahr, Nov. 5, 1968, Goheen, Box 94, Folder 6; William G. Bowen to Robert F. Goheen, Oct. 28, 1968, Goheen, Box 94, Folder 7.

9　William D'O. Lippincott to Robert F. Goheen, Nov. 4, 1968; John F. Angst to Harold H. Helm, Nov. 15, 1968, both in Goheen, Box 94, Folder 6.

10　Marc E. Miller, "Report on the Battle of Philadelphia, Oct. 30, 1968," Nov. 1, 1968 (source of the quote); E. D. Sullivan to Ricardo Mestres, Nov. 7, 1968; and Mestres to William D'O. Lippincott, Nov. 12, 1968, all in Goheen, Box 94, Folder 6.

11　William G. Bowen to Robert F. Goheen, Nov. 4, 1968; Henderson Supplee, Jr., to Bowen, Nov. 12, 1968, both in Goheen, Box 94, Folder 6.

the same was true in Baltimore, where Bowen found the alumni to be "unquestionably the most hostile to coeducation" of any group he had addressed.[12]

Sometimes it was clear that university spokesmen made little dent with their presentations; alumni came skeptical or opposed and left with the same views. In other cases, however, especially when the principal presenter was Goheen, the audience appeared to be more open-minded. In Washington, D.C., for instance, thoughtful presentations by Goheen and Lippincott and patient responses by Goheen to a large number of challenging questions clearly "changed a great number of Alumni opinions."[13] At a polite but hostile gathering in Pittsburgh, Goheen said, "a number [of alumni] came up to say that I had shaken their disbelief and made them think again about the whole matter."[14] Goheen's persuasiveness and influence were a function of his position. But they also stemmed from his willingness to take seriously the objections raised by alumni and to respond in detail to their concerns. And his courage in staking his presidency on coeducation was in itself persuasive to many alumni.[15]

So was his eloquence. Goheen wrote to an alumnus in Minneapolis who opposed coeducation, "What is Princeton? Many things to many men, of course: the beautiful campus, the hallowed traditions, the love and loyalty of her alumni, your 'vivid memories' of a unique atmosphere. But fundamentally, the University is, and has been, above all, its students and teachers, together fostering a heritage of excellence in education." Going forward, sustaining that excellence would require change: "If Princeton is to remain

12 Lansden McCandless, Jr., to Harold H. Helm, Nov. 29, 1968, Goheen, Box 94, Folder 6; Jeremiah S. Finch and Scott McVay to Robert F. Goheen, Nov. 26, 1968; W. G. Bowen to Goheen, Dec. 4, 1968; George G. Finney, Jr., to Bowen, Dec. 10, 1968, all in Goheen, Box 94, Folder 8.

13 Robert A. J. Bordley to Harold H. Helm, Dec. 3, 1968, and William D'O. Lippincott to Robert F. Goheen, Dec. 2, 1968, both in Goheen, Box 94, Folder 8.

14 Robert F. Goheen, Aide Memoire, Dec. 2, 1968, Goheen, Box 94, Folder 8.

15 See, e.g., Robert F. Goheen to John C. Leslie, Nov. 5, 1968, and Leslie to Goheen, Nov. 18, 1968, both in Goheen, Box 95, Folder 5; John Coleman, Jr., '40, in Letters on Coeducation: Selected Excerpts, Sept. 15–Dec. 6, 1968, p. 3, Goheen, Box 93, Folder 6.

in the first rank of American universities, education of women in some form must come."[16]

Or, as Goheen wrote to an alumnus in Philadelphia who had penned a "careful and thoughtful" critique of the Patterson report,

> Princeton is today one of the leaders among institutions of higher education in America because for more than two centuries it has been able to adapt itself to the needs of its time. The Princeton known and loved by the Class of 1969 is not the same Princeton that was known and loved by the Class of 1940; nor was its Princeton just the same as that of the Class of 1926. And this is how it should be. What is common to today's Princeton and the Princeton that we knew as undergraduates is . . . a continuing dedication to excellence in education and an effective striving on the part of the University . . . to ensure that [its] work . . . is relevant to the times, in central not simply superficial ways.

With women "playing an ever greater role in the affairs of this country," Goheen said, if Princeton failed to coeducate, it would "inevitably become a second-rate institution."[17]

"Can Princeton Do Justice to Women Students?"

What is striking is how little of the discussion of the Patterson report focused on the education of women. It was not that women were absent from the conversation—far from it, because the issue at hand was what would happen if women undergraduates were permitted to enroll at Princeton. Still, most of the conversation was about Princeton as an institution and about Princeton men. Put differently, there were three main actors in this drama: Princeton University, Princeton men, and, potentially, Princeton women. To the extent that women figured in the conversation, it was mainly

---

16 Robert F. Goheen to Frank P. Leslie, Nov. 16, 1967, and Leslie to Goheen, Oct. 4, 1967, both in Goheen, Box 95, Folder 5.

17 Robert F. Goheen to Orvel Sebring, Dec. 26, 1968, Goheen, Box 96, Folder 1.

in terms of how their presence would be good, or less good, for Princeton University and Princeton men. As was the case in so many all-male institutions considering coeducation, women and their needs were largely left out of the equation.

Early on, Patterson had written to a woman who opposed co-education at Princeton, "Our approach has not been 'Do women need Princeton?' but rather, 'Does the Princeton of the future need women?' Will Princeton be a better place if there are women in the undergraduate body?" The committee's primary concern, he said, was "whether the presence of women would heighten the value of the educational experience of the students."[18]

The Patterson report took a similar tack. Patterson made plain that women were fully able "to participate in the intellectual life of the University"; that they enrolled in college with excellent academic records (indeed, stronger records than those of men, on average); that they brought to college "superior cultural achievements and interests"; and that, at Harvard-Radcliffe and Stanford, the schools most comparable to Princeton, their "average academic records" often surpassed those of men. And women typically graduated at slightly higher rates than men.[19]

Going beyond the qualifications of women students, Patterson raised a tantalizing question: "Can Princeton Do Justice to Women Students?" That section of the report—two-thirds of a page in length—began with a promising paragraph:

> It would be a disgrace to Princeton if it were to admit women only because it believed this would serve the interests, however broadly defined, of its male students. Unless the University, its trustees, its faculty and its students are ready to give continuous and serious concern and effort to what it can offer women for their intellectual growth and development; unless we are willing to accept as desirable that women will demand a quality of education in no way inferior to that offered men;

18 Gardner Patterson to Katherine Finney Baetjer, Mar. 25, 1968, Patterson, Box 2, Folder 1.

19 "'The Education of Women at Princeton': A Special Report," *Princeton Alumni Weekly* 69 (Sept. 24, 1968): 10.

unless we are prepared to acknowledge that the restricted roles of women in the past are outmoded, and the intellectual talents of women are "an important personal and public resource to be developed and used with care and courage"; unless we can embrace all of these things, Princeton should abandon all thought of admitting women. *In our opinion, this point cannot be stressed too much.*[20]

But then the text meandered in puzzling ways. After asserting that Princeton could meet the charge, the report said, among other things, that there would be no need for massive curricular changes. Additional facilities would be needed for the creative arts, but those would benefit men as well as women. Women, who were less likely than men to be on a clear pre-professional track, might "profit from greater freedom in the choice of majors and distribution requirements." It might be a good idea to permit "a certain amount of upperclass work taken at other institutions" to count toward requirements for a Princeton degree. It might be desirable to introduce some new introductory courses "with somewhat different content and approaches from those we have now," whose pre-professional emphases were either "greater or lesser" than would be "appropriate for many women students." It might "be necessary, in certain disciplines, for the faculty to make a special effort to encourage women students to generalize and to speculate." And—perhaps the most arresting observation of all—"Princeton would have to avoid graduating a group of 'little men.'"[21] All told, "Can Princeton Do Justice to Women Students?" was the least focused, most poorly reasoned part of the Patterson report.

Princeton was working out its destiny at a moment when American society was in the early stages of a major debate about the role of women, and thus at a watershed moment for the higher education of women in the United States. Some parties to the discussion could see what was at stake. At the Princeton club gathering in Denver, for example, "the best question," Edward D. Sullivan

20 Ibid., 19.
21 Ibid.

later recorded, "was from a wife, a Smith graduate, who in a very thoughtful and articulate fashion wanted to know if Princeton was really prepared to undertake the education of women, if we had learned well enough how to take on a whole new set of emotional and other problems, and were we prepared to accept the really changed image of Princeton when a number of women alumnae joined the ranks." She wondered, too, whether Jerry Horton's view "that women would damage Princeton was widespread and might in itself be damaging to the women who were admitted." She favored coeducation but wanted to be sure that Princeton understood what was at stake.[22]

In a five-page letter written to Sullivan after the meeting, a Princeton wife who had spoken at the gathering wrote to elaborate on her concerns. (It was likely the same woman Sullivan had written about, though, as she said, she was a Wellesley alumna.) Although it was clear that it would be good for Princeton men to admit women, it was not at all clear whether it would be good for women. "Princeton would have to do as well by its women as by its men. But Princeton's accomplishments and sensibilities lie with men." How much thought had Princeton given to the needs of undergraduate women? "Is it feasible," she asked, "for women to receive a personally meaningful and valuable educational experience in an institution so deeply and traditionally male?" "My concern," she said, "is that Princeton is as responsible in doing this, as it is bold; that it recognizes the subtlety, extent and depth of its male tradition and has the institutional courage to become as effective a coeducational institution as it was a men's college."[23]

How much did issues of this sort—admittedly subtle and complex—figure in the Patterson committee discussions? How much were they on Patterson's mind as he wrote? It is not easy to tell from Patterson's text. Patterson acknowledged women's increasing participation in the labor force, presenting data showing that women would use their education by entering into employment

22 Edward D. Sullivan to Robert F. Goheen, Oct. 14, 1968, Goheen, Box 94, Folder 7.
23 Estill Henlein Buchanan to Edward D. Sullivan, Oct. 16, 1968, Patterson, Box 2, Folder 1.

outside the home, especially in professional and technical fields, and arguing that Princeton therefore had the opportunity to help to meet the growing "demand for highly-educated women," thus "responding to national needs and opportunities."[24] He gave reason to believe that he understood that the university was facing a sea change in American society in terms of roles and expectations for women—for their education, as well as for their later lives. But that was about as far as he went.

Harold Helm Addresses the Board

The Princeton trustees had been fully apprised of the discussion of the Patterson report, both by means of reports and letters sent to Harold Helm from local alumni leaders and through updates at the October board and November executive committee meetings.[25] Later in November came the review by the Ford Foundation of the financial projections in the Patterson report. The reviewers opined that the projections were grounded in "exhaustive care and preparation" and pronounced the cost estimates to be "solidly based," with "a reasonable margin for error."[26] In mid-December, Helm reported to the executive committee that the special trustee committee expected to bring a recommendation to the board at the January meeting.[27]

The board convened on January 11, 1969, with thirty-two of thirty-six trustees present, along with eight emeritus trustees.[28]

24 "'The Education of Women at Princeton': A Special Report," 14–15.

25 Minutes of Meeting of the Board of Trustees, Princeton University, Oct. 18, 1968, pp. 7–9, and Princeton University, Minutes of a Stated Meeting of the Executive Committee, Nov. 15, 1968, pp. 2–5, both in Princeton trustees, Series 1, Vol. 67.

26 Marshall A. Robinson to Harold H. Helm, Nov. 4, 1968, attached to Helm to Board of Trustees, Nov. 22, 1968, Goheen, Box 93, Folder 6.

27 Princeton University, Minutes of a Stated Meeting of the Executive Committee, Dec. 13, 1968, p. 5, Princeton trustees, Series 3, Box 4, Folder 6. For an account by another member of the Special Trustee Committee of the committee's work and deliberations, see W. H. Rea to Norman McClave, Jr., Jan. 14, 1969, attached to Rea to Messrs. Goheen, Oates, and Helm, Jan. 14, 1969, Goheen, Box 95, Folder 5.

28 James F. Oates and Harold H. Helm to All Princeton Alumni, Jan. 11, 1969, Bowen provost, Box 18, Folder 6. As mentioned earlier, emeritus trustees received notice of all meetings and were invited to attend but had no vote.

Helm had prepared a report reviewing the work of his committee. He had one version to present to the committee on January 10, asking approval for a recommendation to the board, and another version to present to the board on the 11th, asking for trustee action. Helm concluded his presentation to the committee this way: "Gentlemen, despite the impressive negative arguments brought out by our alumni (including a majority of my best friends), I urge you to adopt the position that the desirability of the education of women at Princeton is essentially an educational question. Looking down the road, Princeton—if it is to continue to be a leader in the field of education—must participate in the education of women at the undergraduate level."

Helm had not started there in terms of his own thinking. In coming to embrace coeducation as central to Princeton's future, he said, he had been "largely influenced by the clear voice of our faculty, administrative leaders, and alumni who are themselves educators."[29] James Oates, chairman of the trustee executive committee, later said essentially the same thing: "A man who was not an expert in education had no choice but to follow his educational experts."[30] Asked what accounted for Helm's change of mind, when Helm's brother, also a Princeton alumnus, also from Louisville, and so much like Harold in so many ways, had remained a fierce opponent of coeducation, Helm's widow, Mary, said that it was really very simple: "Harold studied the question."[31]

The written record is silent on the committee's discussion of Helm's presentation. We know that Helm presented the same report, again orally, to the board the next day. "Your Committee has reached the conclusion," Helm said, "and voted—though not unanimously—that the desirability of Princeton's participating in the education of women is fundamentally an educational question and that the Princeton Trustees should look largely to the faculty, to our administrative leaders, and to the alumni identified with

29 Report of the Chairman of the Special Trustees' Committee on the Education of Women at Princeton, Jan. 10, 1969, Goheen, Box 94, Folder 2.

30 Quoted in Luther Munford, "Coeducation at Princeton: The Struggle of an Idea at a University in Transition," *Daily Princetonian*, Oct. 21, 1969, p. 12.

31 Quoted in Bowen oral history, June 9, 2009, p. 24.

education to guide us in this area." The advice of those groups—
"almost unanimous"—was that "the admission of women will
make Princeton a better University in the years ahead, and that
Princeton, one of the conspicuous leaders in education, has a responsibility to offer its undergraduate as well as its graduate facilities to women." The committee recommended "approval in
principle" of coeducation.[32]

S. Barksdale Penick, Jr., '25, a pharmaceutical executive in New
York, moved that the board adopt the recommendation. The board
voted by a show of hands, with twenty-four in favor and eight
opposed. It was understood that the exact vote would be made
public, though no formal record was made of the identities of the
yeas and nays.[33] Goheen and Helm had decided "not to press the
board for unanimity," Bowen later explained. "And the eight no
votes were important because what they demonstrated was that
this was a discussion and a debate and it wasn't anything forced
on anybody; if you thought 'no,' then you voted no. And to their
credit all eight dissenters stayed on the board."[34] Some years later,
one of the eight said to Bowen, "Every trustee should have the
right to change one of his votes, and if I were given that opportunity, I would today vote in favor of coeducation."[35]

Following the board meeting, Oates and Helm issued a statement to alumni transmitting the report that the special committee
had made to the board. "It is characteristic of all highly important
issues that they are complex and consequently promote strong differences of opinion," they wrote. "We are confident that the deep
opposition to the education of women at Princeton held by a number of alumni is, in large measure, a clear reflection of their equally
deep devotion to Princeton. Princeton will remain, and it is the

32 Report of the Chairman of the Special Trustees' Committee on the Education of
Women at Princeton, Jan. 10, 1969.

33 Minutes of Meeting of the Board of Trustees, Princeton University, Jan. 11, 1969,
pp. 4–5, Princeton trustees, Series 1, Vol. 67.

34 Bowen oral history, June 9, 2009, p. 23.

35 I am indebted to William G. Bowen for this story, which he also recounts in *Lessons
Learned: Reflections of a University President* (Princeton, NJ, and Oxford: Princeton University Press, 2011), p. 70.

hope that much of this devotion will find a basis for renewed dedication to it."[36]

Planning Begins for the "Very Complicated Problem Now Before Us"

In the wake of the trustees' action, planning for coeducation began in earnest. Unlike the case at Yale, this planning would entail careful deliberation, and it would be undertaken before seeking final approval of coeducation. Financial projections had to be refined. Options for housing women students had to be identified, along with needs with respect to social facilities. Admission policy needed to be reviewed, preliminary plans for the admission of women developed, and a recommendation made in terms of timing for the initial enrollment of women students. Academic aspects of the education of women students needed to be explored. Decisions had to be made about staffing, especially where women administrators would have to be hired. And some fundamental decisions remained to be thrashed out—in particular, how to assess the relative merits of coordinate and coeducational arrangements. Toward those ends, immediately following the January board meeting, Goheen established an ad hoc committee of administrators, faculty members, and students, which he chaired. The committee would "oversee and make final recommendations for all aspects of the very complicated problem now before us," with an eye toward bringing plans for implementation to the board in either April or June.[37]

Other internal committees and outside consultants were to work on specific aspects of the planning.[38] To help the university decide

36 James F. Oates and Harold H. Helm to All Princeton Alumni, Jan. 11, 1969, Bowen provost, Box 18, Folder 6. The report of the Special Committee was published as "Trustees' Statement on Coeducation," *Princeton Alumni Weekly* 69 (Jan. 12, 1969): 11–12.

37 Robert F. Goheen to Neil L. Rudenstine, Jan. 17, 1969, Goheen, Box 94, Folder 4 (source of the quote); Princeton University, The President's Report, 1968–69, pp. 6–9, Goheen, Box 119, Folder 10; J. A. Farrington to Messrs. Craig et al., Jan. 23, 1969, Goheen, Box 96, Folder 4.

38 In Goheen, Box 96, Folder 4, see Neil Rudenstine to Robert F. Goheen, Jan. 7, 1969, and J. P. Moran to Goheen, Jan. 31, 1969. In Goheen, Box 94, Folder 4, see Goheen to

between coordinate and coeducational arrangements, a group of "distinguished educators with experience in coeducation" was invited for two days of meetings with the Goheen committee to discuss the matter, along with the many other practical issues Princeton needed to consider. The consultants included the president of Radcliffe, Polly Bunting; the dean of Sarah Lawrence, Jacquelyn Mattfeld; the vice chancellor for educational plans and programs at UCLA, Rosemary Park; an associate professor of political science at the University of Chicago, Susanne Hoeber Rudolph; and an associate dean of students at Stanford, Sally Mahoney.[39] On the central issue of coordinate versus coeducation, Rudolph and Bunting argued unambiguously in favor of coeducation; it would do Princeton no good to start out where Radcliffe had been years ago, especially in seeking to replicate the kinds of single-sex living arrangements Radcliffe was "trying to escape from." Although Park made a case for the advantages of coordinate arrangements "at the moment," she made clear that coeducation would be the preferred mode in the future.[40] The meetings with these experts, a member of Goheen's implementation committee said later, "marked a distinct change in Goheen's thinking. Before he was an objective investigator intellectually convinced. Afterwards, he had a sense of urgency."[41]

Rudenstine, Jan. 17, 1969. In Princeton trustees, Series 5, Box 58, Folder 23, see Interim Report of the Committee on Social Facilities, Mar. 17, 1969. In ODUS, Box 7, Folder 4, see Moran to Goheen, Jan. 24, 1969; [Moran,] Draft, The Evolution of Physical Plans for the Education of Women at Princeton, Jan. 28, 1969; Moran, Draft, A Summary of the Decisions and Open Questions Relating to the Education of Women at Princeton, Jan. 28, 1969; Moran to Goheen, Jan. 30, 1969; and Rudenstine to Members of the Social Facilities Committee, Feb. 5, 1969. In Patterson, Box 4, Folder 9, see Rudenstine to Goheen et al., Feb. 7, 1969.

39 In Goheen, Box 94, Folder 4, see Princeton University news release, Feb. 9, 1969, and Coeducation at Princeton: Notes on the meeting of Feb. 9–10 with Mmes. Park, Mattfeld, and Rudolph, with some additions from Dean Sullivan's interview with Miss Mahoney on Feb. 11 and Feb. 14, 1969. In ODUS, Box 7, Folder 4, see Neil Rudenstine notes, Policy Meeting with Women Administrators, on typescript, Academic Planning and Related Matters, Feb. 9–10, 1969.

40 Susanne Hoeber Rudolph to Robert F. Goheen, Feb. 14, 1969; Goheen to Rudolph, Feb. 26, 1969; Mary Ingraham Bunting to Goheen, Feb. 16, 1969 (source of the quote); Rosemary Park to Goheen, Feb. 13, 1969, all in Goheen, Box 94, Folder 4.

41 Quoted in Munford, "Coeducation at Princeton," p. 12.

In late February 1969, Goheen made a preliminary report to the trustees. His committee had reached a number of conclusions. First, there was no reason to anticipate that coeducation would bring any "significant changes" in the academic program. Second, hiring women faculty members and administrators would be "extremely important." Third, there was every reason to expect that Princeton would attract outstanding women applicants. Fourth, the consultants had recommended that Princeton plan for coeducational living and dining arrangements.

As for the schedule for the admission of women and the projected growth in enrollment in the near term, the committee thought that it would be "highly desirable" for the first women students to matriculate in 1969–70. The university could begin with perhaps 130 women students in 1969–70, housing them in Pyne Hall, and "move ahead in a steady, though gradual way to a population of 650 women in 1973–74," assuming the acquisition of the Princeton Inn for dormitory use beginning in 1970–71. And 650 women was simply a stopping point along the way; Princeton should "move as promptly as possible . . . to at least 1000 women undergraduates" to achieve the "'critical mass' of women" necessary to make coeducation work. Goheen gave the trustees detailed tables specifying year-by-year enrollment projections, housing and dining arrangements, institutional space needs for academic instruction and administration, requirements for athletic plant and programs, and capital and operating costs.[42]

In March the Goheen committee published a comprehensive report, *The Education of Undergraduate Women at Princeton: An Examination of Coordinate versus Coeducational Patterns*, which was distributed to faculty, students, and alumni.[43] The report explored the advantages and disadvantages of five models of coordinate education and coeducation in place at colleges and universities around the country. The arrangements ranged from separate institutions that shared, through explicit agreement, faculty and facilities, like those

42 Robert F. Goheen to Special Trustee Committee on Coeducation, Feb. 20, 1969, Goheen, Box 94, Folder 4.

43 *The Education of Undergraduate Women at Princeton: An Examination of Coordinate versus Coeducational Patterns*, Mar. 1969, preface, Goheen, Box 94, Folder 1.

at Barnard-Columbia and Douglass-Rutgers, to a single institution with no set ratio of men to women, like those at many of the major state and city universities.[44] The report also presented the Goheen committee's appraisal of the model that would be "best for Princeton": a single, fully coeducational institution "with an established ratio of women to men students, but with no separate residential college" for women. This model would provide the most favorable conditions for the highest-quality educational experience for men and women, who would "benefit significantly from the continued exchange of ideas, attitudes, and perspectives that comes from a shared educational experience." The "integrated environment" in and beyond the classroom would give students the best chance of "com[ing] to know and respect one another as individuals"—to know each other "as people and friends" rather than simply "as 'dates' for special occasions." And with an array of dining and social facilities, students could expect "considerable choice" of "arrangements best suited to their own interests and needs." That model would also be the least expensive in operating and capital costs.[45]

Coed Week Shows That "It's Good to Have Girls Around"

While the Goheen committee engaged in planning for implementation, Princeton undergraduates took their own initiative to illustrate what would be entailed in bringing women to Princeton. Coeducation week brought more than eight hundred women (selected by a student committee from more than twenty-five hundred applicants) from thirty eastern colleges and universities to campus for the second week in February for classes, concerts, plays, films, parties, athletic events, and discussions of planning for coeducation. To make room for the women, men voluntarily gave up their dormitory rooms for the week.[46] At least, they were supposed to. Two Smith students reported that the eight male "owners" of their suite "never really abandoned their rooms. Amidst popcorn

44 Ibid., preface and p. 1.

45 Ibid., preface and pp. 15–19.

46 *Daily Princetonian*, Jan. 17 and Feb. 11, 12, 14, and 22, 1969; "Princeton Coed Week: Calendar of Events," and "Backstage at Coed Week," *Nassau Review*, Feb. 7, 1969, pp. 5, 6; *New York Times*, Feb. 13, 1969, clippings in Horton, Box 2, Folder 7.

parties, discussion groups, pleasant chats, and studying, the guys managed to come early and stay late."[47] The venture was copied from the initiative at Yale the previous November. Its objective— like that at Yale—was to hasten the arrival of real coeducation.

Some students made fun of the plan as "little more than a glori- fied college weekend." Some warned that it was important to "prove to the skeptics" that there was more to the week than the obvious pleasure of having women on campus.[48] But there was also convinc- ing testimony on the other side. The chief organizer, Meir J. Riba- low, a junior English major, told the *New York Times*, "It's good intellectually and every other way to have girls around, and does the fact that it's also fun mean that there's anything wrong with it?" One Princeton senior said, "Maybe it was just the novelty of the thing, but I felt much more alert and turned-on intellectually with the chicks around." Some faculty echoed his view: "I enjoyed lectur- ing much more with girls in my class," said an assistant professor of sociology, Stephen L. Klineberg. "Girls are stimulating creatures to have around."[49] The Smith students made a similar point: "The per- vasive intellectual climate, which is stimulating not bookish, stands out in our minds." It was not clear, however, that women's intellects were uppermost on men's minds; "some girls had the suspicion that the guys were more interested in their legs than in their ideas."[50]

In the judgment of the *Daily Princetonian*, coed week had real- ized its purposes: "It proved that girls are not necessarily disrup- tive in classes and showed the skeptics that a girl can indeed make cogent remarks in precept. Even more important was the change in atmosphere that took place during the week. For one week Prince- ton was a more humane place to go to school. . . . The whole cam- pus seemed more natural."[51]

---

47 Gainor Davis and Alicia Campi, "Princeton Coeds Sacrifice Privacy for Intellect," *Sophian*, Feb. 20, 1969, Box 17, Smith College Archives. The theme of coed week as a party—"totally a party"—was confirmed in an interview with Carol Mann, Nov. 7, 2014, New York City. Mann, then a sophomore at Smith, went to Princeton for the week as "a way to have a break" from her routine in Northampton.

48 *Daily Princetonian*, Feb. 10 and 11, 1969.

49 Quoted in *New York Times*, Feb. 13, 1969, clipping in Horton, Box 2, Folder 7.

50 Davis and Campi, "Princeton Coeds Sacrifice Privacy for Intellect."

51 Editorial, *Daily Princetonian*, Feb. 17, 1969.

For the administration, coed week provided useful insights, including an unscientific preview of the courses women students might favor and an early introduction to the social impact of women on campus. And there were smaller discoveries: Women needed full-length mirrors. They took long showers. Parts of the campus had inadequate lighting. As the dean of students, Neil Rudenstine, told the *Washington Post*, "We're learning quite a bit, thanks to the students. . . . The closer we come to the day when women will be living here on a full-time basis, the more things that don't normally occur to the male mind must be worked out if they are to be happy here. We can hardly be said to have the woman's point of view."[52]

Addressing the Question of Admissions

As the remainder of the winter unfolded, there were signs that coeducation would be coming to Princeton. One pressing question had to do with admissions. In the fall of 1968, with the publication of the Patterson report and the news that Princeton was considering coeducation, women high school students had begun to inquire about the possibility of applying, and admission officers had begun to notice "prettier faces at traditionally all-male question-and-answer sessions in high schools around the country."[53] Princeton's director of admission, John T. Osander, had a standard reply to letters of interest from women students. Whether or not Princeton would embrace coeducation "would not be resolved for some time," and it was not known yet "when the first undergraduate women could be admitted in the event that the decision is affirmative." The admission office would keep an inquiring female student's name on file and send application materials in the event that it became possible to consider women's applications.[54]

<hr>

52 *Washington Post*, Feb. 16, 1969, clipping in Horton, Box 2, Folder 7.

53 Princeton University, Office of Admission, Annual Report, 1968–69, p. 3, Admission Office, Box 10.

54 Admission Office form letter from John T. Osander to women who wrote expressing interest in Princeton, n.d. but Fall 1968, Admission Office, Box 4, Folder 6.

With the board's decision in January to approve coeducation in principle, inquiries from women high school students accelerated. With his sights set at that point on a decision by the board in April to admit freshman women to the class of 1974, Osander told interested women that if such an action were taken, the admission office would forward application forms and a Princeton catalogue to each of them in the fall of 1969.[55] In late January, Osander told a friend with a daughter interested in Princeton that "they haven't told me yet what we're up to" but that he thought it "very unlikely that we will be accepting applications from freshman women for next fall."[56]

At the same time, however, Osander engaged the faculty committee on admission in discussion of "the ramification" of the trustee decision. A subcommittee on female students was already at work considering "long-range details concerning the admission of women," but Osander wanted the full committee's advice on the feasibility of admitting freshmen and/or transfer students for September 1969. Given the tightness of the available time, the need to develop a carefully-thought-out admission policy for women, the difficulty of recruiting excellent candidates on limited notice, the imagined limitations on scholarship funds for women, and other practical considerations, the committee recommended against admitting women freshmen in the fall of 1969 but said that transfer students would be more manageable.[57]

The administration was in a different place. The right course, in terms of competitiveness and community expectations, was to allow a small number of freshman women to matriculate for 1969–70. The admission office had to be ready in the event that the administration could persuade the trustees to act affirmatively in April. Although there would be no effort to solicit applications from women, Goheen authorized the office in mid-February to distribute application forms for 1969–70 to potential women

55 Admission Office form letter from John T. Osander, n.d. but after Jan. 11, 1969, Admission Office, Box 11.

56 John T. Osander to Robert E. Goudreau, Jan. 20, 1969, Admission Office, Box 11.

57 Faculty Committee on Admission to President Goheen, Jan. 15, 1969, attached to Minutes of Faculty Committee on Admission Meeting, Jan. 14, 1969, ODUS, Box 7, Folder 4.

freshmen as well as to transfer students who were inquiring about the possibility of applying. And—at Goheen's instigation—Osander hired Carol J. Thompson, a former Radcliffe admission interviewer and the wife of an assistant professor of politics, Dennis Thompson, as assistant to the director to respond to questions from women high school students and their families and to process and evaluate applications from women.[58]

Some of Osander's counterparts at other institutions thanked him for the information he sent about what was happening at Princeton and wished him good luck. "I have a sneaking suspicion that we may be faced with the same situation at a not too distant date," wrote the director of admission at Johns Hopkins.[59] The dean at Radcliffe sent advice that Princeton's expectation of four years of high school mathematics "might be intimidating" to female applicants. Radcliffe had some "star performers" who entered "with only three years." Osander responded, "I confess that we quickly adapted our male information leaflet to women and it is only through comments such as yours that we can learn the points that need modification."[60]

But Osander's mail also included gentle taunts from his professional colleagues for Princeton's continuing uncertainty. From the director of admission at Chatham College, the women's college in Pittsburgh: "Wish you well? Yes, but only when Princeton is ready for women and when they are truly welcome." From the director of admission at the all-male Hobart College in upstate New York: "At least your office will be brightened by the

---

58 In Admission Office, Box 10, see Princeton University, Office of Admission, Annual Report, 1968–69, pp. 4–5. In Admission Office, Box 4, Folder 6, see John T. Osander, Information to Women, Admission Office leaflet, Feb. 1969; Information for Female Applicants for Admission as Freshmen, Feb. 1969; Osander, form letter to Director of Admission, Feb. 7, 1969; and Osander, form letter to Guidance Counselor, Feb. 12, 1969. In Bowen provost, Box 18, Folder 9, see Carol J. Thompson to W. G. Bowen, Oct. 7 and 14, 1968, and Bowen to R. F. Goheen, Jan. 20, 1969. See also interview with Thompson, Apr. 24, 2012, Cambridge, MA; *Daily Princetonian*, Feb. 12, 1969; and Robert K. Durkee, "On the Campus," *Princeton Alumni Weekly*, 69 (Mar. 4, 1969): 4.

59 W. L. Brinkley to John T. Osander, Feb. 27, 1969, Admission Office, Box 11.

60 Margaret W. Stimpson to John T. Osander, Feb. 21, 1969, and Osander to Stimpson, Mar. 17, 1969, both in Admission Office, Box 11.

sweet young things and their shorty skirts."[61] From the director of admission at Brown University: "I have heard of confusion and screwed-up arrangements, but who in heaven's name suggested that you go out and solicit applications from women when you may not be able to even consider the applications?" And from the University of North Carolina, where freshman women had only recently been admitted: "I can only offer my condolences to you. We find that females are much harder to deal with than their male counterparts."[62]

Now Osander's letter to prospective women applicants changed again. "We invite you to submit an application to us <u>provided you realize that we may be unable to give you an admission decision</u> should the Trustees decide freshmen women cannot be admitted in 1969." There would be a deadline for applications from women students of March 15; if the trustees took an affirmative decision in April, notices of action on those applications would be mailed immediately, and students would be expected to adhere to the normal reply date of May 1.[63] For transfer applicants the deadline was May 1, and decisions were promised "sometime between late May and the end of June."[64]

At alumni day on February 22, President Goheen told the thousand Princetonians assembled that the admission of women would make the university "a better educational experience—better intellectually and better in human terms." Goheen predicted that women would be increasingly involved in responsible positions in the United States and abroad. All in all, he said, "the wise direction of human affairs will call . . . for women and men who can work together and who are used to working together. . . . A Princeton

---

61 Peggy Donaldson (Chatham) to John T. Osander, Feb. 18, 1969, and John S. Witte (Hobart) to Osander, Feb. 18, 1969, both in Admission Office, Box 11.

62 Charles H. Doebler (Brown) to John T. Osander, Feb. 27, 1969; Osander to Doebler, Mar. 17, 1969; and Richard Cashwell (North Carolina) to Osander, Feb. 26, 1969, all in Admission Office, Box 11.

63 Admission Office, letter from John T. Osander to women applicants, n.d., Admission Office, Box 4, Folder 6.

64 Admission Office, letter from John T. Osander to women transfer applicants, n.d., Admission Office, Box 11.

which had assumed no part in educating both women and men . . .
would in retrospect have been shortsighted in the extreme."[65]

At the same time, students kept up the pressure for coeducation.
The alumni day issue of the *Daily Princetonian* was full of stories about planning for coeducation, which the paper pronounced
to be "inevitable."[66] The momentum on campus was strong and
compelling. Coeducation was coming to Princeton, and it would
be coming sooner rather than later.[67]

At the April 7 university faculty meeting, the provost reported
on the work of the Goheen committee and reviewed, in confidence,
the many details of planning that had already been shared with the
special trustee committee. A decision on the recommendation for
coeducation and on steps toward implementing it, he said, might
be made at the April 19 board meeting.[68]

As the meeting approached, the admission office worked to
complete its review of the 505 applications that it had received
from women students and made plans to produce two sets of letters ready to be mailed on April 20. One set expressed thanks for
the applications but said that the trustees had not authorized the
admission of women for the fall of 1969. The other set, prepared
in the event of favorable action by the board, informed applicants
whether or not they had been admitted to the university's first
coeducational freshman class. Preliminary review of the applications had been handled by Carol Thompson and two other faculty
wives: Peggy Klineberg, wife of an assistant professor of sociology,
Stephen Klineberg, and Susan Jones, wife of an assistant professor
of chemistry, Maitland Jones. Review by the male admission staff
followed.[69]

Part of the challenge of integrating women into the admission
office was cultural. Unlike at Yale, where Inky Clark had made

65 Goheen, quoted in Princeton University news release, Feb. 22, 1969, Subject Files
Princeton, Coeducation, Box 376, Folder 3.

66 Editorial, *Daily Princetonian*, Feb. 22, 1969.

67 *Daily Princetonian*, Feb. 22, 1969.

68 William G. Bowen, Notes for presentation at faculty meeting of Apr. 7, 1969, on
implementing education of women decision, and Abstract and Summary of Actions Taken,
University Faculty Meeting, Apr. 7, 1969, both in Patterson, Box 4, Folder 9.

69 *Daily Princetonian*, Apr. 2 and 18, 1969.

a deliberate effort to diversify his staff, the Princeton office was still made up primarily of Princeton graduates. It was a tight-knit group, given to playing sports or working out together at lunchtime and to talking in sports metaphors—for example, "batting up" candidates for discussion—and the men in the office were accustomed to looking for applicants rather like themselves, that is, "regular" Princetonians. Carol Thompson, by contrast, came out of the Radcliffe admission office, where the primary emphasis had been on the intellectual qualities of applicants. Accordingly, she focused on the intellectual strengths of the women in Princeton's pool, on their academic interests, on evidence of their effectiveness in leadership roles, on their adaptability to challenging situations.[70]

The men and women often agreed in their appraisal of applicants but sometimes had different perspectives based on gender. "All of the girls were exceptionally bright and talented young women," Thompson commented later. "But we tried to avoid the superficial types by finding the ones who not only had interests, but had the will to do something about their interests." Of the women reviewers, Osander said, "They did a remarkably sound job for people not experienced in admission. But sometimes we had some dandy arguments. All the men would look at a girl's academic record and her SAT's and decide not to take her. Then Carol would say that she 'felt' something about the girl on the basis of her writing sample. She and the other gals put a lot of emphasis on qualities of heart in addition to sheer intelligence. Sometimes they won the fight, sometimes we did."[71]

Princeton Prepares for the Arrival of Women Undergraduates

As Goheen prepared to go to the board, he had in hand a financial commitment that would make possible the action he was recommending. Trustee Laurance S. Rockefeller had already pledged an anonymous gift of $4 million.[72] And Goheen had begun

---

70 Thompson interview.

71 "Plans for Coeducation," *Princeton Alumni Weekly* 69 (May 6, 1969): 10.

72 Robert F. Goheen, Aide-Mémoire re Laurance Rockefeller and the Education of Women, Feb. 27, 1969, Goheen, Box 94, Folder 4; "Plans for Coeducation," 8.

conversations with Charles S. Robertson that would bear fruit in early May with an anonymous gift from Charles and Marie Robertson of $300,000 "to help us get started with the education of women."[73]

The special trustee committee had been hard at work since the January meeting of the board. It had met three times, most recently on April 18. Helm reported to the board the next morning that his committee agreed with the recommendation of the Goheen committee for full coeducation with an established ratio of women to men students. Helm said, further, that his committee had studied and strongly endorsed the plan of implementation developed by the administration. He noted especially the proposed conversion of the Princeton Inn to an undergraduate residential facility. The committee had been surprised at first by the proposal but had become convinced that it was the right thing to do. The inn could not be available until 1970–71, however, and Pyne Hall would be used for women students in 1969–70. All told, the capital requirements for the plan totaled about $8 million, a figure lower than originally imagined. It would be a good thing to get started right away; it would allow the university "to gain experience as soon as possible with women's education."[74]

Helm then turned to the president and provost to speak about the administration's plan for implementation. Goheen emphasized the fact that the costs would be less than the Patterson report had contemplated due to the relatively low cost of acquiring the Princeton Inn and the more limited need for other new facilities than had originally been imagined. Bowen spoke about women applicants to the freshman class. Fears that, in the absence of active recruitment and with limited notice, there might be an insufficient pool had proven to be groundless. The 505 completed applications included "an exceptionally large number of very well qualified women." Pending approval by the board, the admission

73 Robert F. Goheen to Charles S. Robertson, Mar. 17, 1969, Goheen, Box 94, Folder 5; Robertson to Goheen, Mar. 23 and Apr. 23, 1969, Goheen, Box 95, Folder 6; Goheen, Aide-Mémoire re Charles S. Robertson ('26), May 9, 1969, Goheen, Box 94, Folder 1.

74 Report of the Chairman of the Special Trustees' Committee on the Education of Women, Apr. 18, 1969, Princeton trustees, Series 5, Box 58, Folder 23.

office hoped to extend offers to 130 students, including 22 alumni daughters (a slightly higher percentage of admitted students than was the case with alumni sons), with the expectation of yielding a freshman class that included about 90 women. All of the women ranked "in the upper range of male applicants."

The financial vice president, Ricardo Mestres, told the trustees about the Princeton Inn. The inn was a gracious, Dutch colonial–style stone and brick hotel on Alexander Street on the western edge of the campus. In the rear, it looked out over a golf course, with the Graduate College, marked by its Gothic Cleveland Tower, visible in the distance. The university had built the inn in 1924; it owned 85 percent of the shares, with current equity of about $1.4 million. Most of the inn's business was group business from outside the university; it was little used by alumni save for football weekends, alumni days, reunions, and trustee meetings. Operating costs were high, and the inn yielded little income to the university (in the previous year, the sum had been $9,000). Costs for acquisition and conversion of the inn were estimated at $1.5 million. Although it would cost about $21,000 per student to construct new dormitory space, the cost per student of converting the inn would be approximately $5,000.

Mestres told the trustees, too, that although he had not participated in the work of the Patterson committee, he had reviewed the final report's figures carefully and had requested that a 10 percent contingency be added. He said that he was confident of the reliability of the projections in the recommendation before the board. He noted that Princeton had a reserve of $30 million that could be drawn upon if circumstances required and that it was "equally important . . . to make an educational investment as to make a financial investment." Coeducation would not be the only financial risk that Princeton had ever taken. Mestres said, too, that he had originally been opposed to coeducation but that, after much conversation with colleagues in education and careful consideration of the Patterson report, he had become "convinced that coeducation was the proper decision, and that the longer the delay, the more disaffection" there would be. He said that Princeton alumni would rally behind a decision of the board, as they had in the past, and he noted that, concern over the Patterson report notwithstanding, the annual giving campaign "had brought in a record total."[75]

By June 30, when the final tally of alumni giving could be made, Mestres's assurances were amply justified. Although *participation* in annual giving declined from the previous year's 66.1 percent to 61.6 percent, the *total dollars* given—$3,509,932—exceeded by a half-million dollars the total contributed in 1967–68 and constituted by far the largest amount ever given to the university in the nearly three-decades-long history of annual giving.[76]

And there was good news from Goheen about pledges in hand to support coeducation. "With this tremendous support at the outset," he said, he was confident that "the remainder of the financial needs could be met." Helm observed that there was more risk in delay than in action; delay might accentuate divisions in the larger university community. Oates invited a motion, and Helm read his committee's recommendations: "the adoption of a coeducational plan," starting modestly in terms of the number of women and increasing gradually "subject to experience and available financing," and "the adoption of the specific implementation plan developed by the administration." Further discussion ensued. Even Dean Mathey, the longtime chairman of the trustee finance committee, who had been so fiercely skeptical of the financial projections in the Patterson report, said that he "had been impressed by the presentation and the saving of $5 million by the use of the Inn" and that "he would cast one phantom vote [as a non-voting emeritus trustee] in favor of the proposal."

Oates noted that he and Helm had "received a great deal of negative mail," and that "many devoted and respected alumni" were "seriously concerned." It seemed clear to him, he said, "that those

75 Minutes of Meeting of the Board of Trustees, Princeton University, Apr. 19, 1969, pp. 10–15, Princeton trustees, Series 1, Vol. 67. On the inn, see also Robert F. Goheen to Special Trustee Committee on Coeducation, Feb. 20, 1969, rev. Apr. 8, 1969, Table 2, p. 2, ftn.; Princeton University news release, "The Princeton Inn," Apr. 20, 1969, attached to Docket, Stated Meeting of the Trustees of Princeton University, Apr. 19, 1969, both in Princeton trustees, Series 5, Box 58, Folder 23.

76 Princeton University Annual Giving Dollar and Participation Totals by Campaign Year, http://giving.princeton.edu/agstats/AG_Dollars_Participation_by_Year.pdf, courtesy of William M. Hardt.

wishing to delay" a decision by the board "wished to defeat coed-ucation." Helm again read his committee's two recommendations, and Oates called for a vote on each one separately. The first mo-tion—to approve coeducation—was carried by a vote of 28 to 3; the second—to approve the proposed implementation plan—won 22 ayes against 9 nays.[77]

"We Won't Be Upstaged by Yale"

Unspoken at the time, but clearly on everyone's minds, was the effect of Yale's decision in favor of coeducation on Princeton's tim-ing. The Princeton trustees might well have announced in April 1969 that Princeton would admit women as of September 1970, a timetable that would have been consistent with the orderly process and careful planning so characteristic of the university's decision-making. But women were coming to Yale in September 1969, and Princeton could not imagine allowing Yale to take the lead. As Go-heen reflected years later, enrolling undergraduate women degree candidates in September 1969 "prevented Yale from upstaging us with its move to coeducation at the same time."[78]

The university issued three news releases. The first announced the decision for coeducation, beginning in the fall of 1969.[79] A second release elaborated on the decision to acquire the Princeton Inn.[80] The third release announced that Princeton was mailing letters of accep-tance to 130 female high school seniors, inviting them to join the class of 1973.[81] The admitted group had outstanding qualifications,

77 Minutes of Meeting of the Board of Trustees, Princeton University, Apr. 19, 1969, pp. 15–16, Princeton trustees, Series 1, Vol. 67.

78 Robert F. Goheen, "Reminiscence on the Coeducating of Princeton," 20th Anniver-sary Keynote Event, Mar. 31, 1989, typescript in the possession of Nancy Weiss Malkiel.

79 Princeton University news release, "Coeducation at Princeton," Apr. 20, 1969, attached to Docket, Stated Meeting of the Trustees of Princeton University, Apr. 19, 1969, Princeton trustees, Series 5, Box 58, Folder 23.

80 Princeton University news release, "The Princeton Inn," Apr. 20, 1969, attached to Docket, Stated Meeting of the Trustees of Princeton University, Apr. 19, 1969, Princeton trustees, Series 5, Box 58, Folder 23.

81 Princeton University news release, "Women at Princeton," Apr. 20, 1969, attached to Docket, Stated Meeting of the Trustees of Princeton University, Apr. 19, 1969, Prince-ton trustees, Series 5, Box 58, Folder 23. The letters to male applicants had been sent on

according to the director of admission, who offered some examples of the exceptional young women the university hoped to enroll.[82] ("The boys are in for a shock," an admission officer commented. "Some of these girls are going to knock them on their ears."[83])

Later, taking care not to draw too heavily on applicants from any single women's college, the admission office extended offers of admission to 60 transfer students. These students were chosen from among 279 applicants in the hope of yielding 50 matriculants.[84]

Nationally, the press hailed Princeton's move. It was front-page news in the *New York Times*—though the *Times* was more interested in the trustees' decision at the same meeting to allow the election of one graduating senior each year as a young alumni trustee.[85] *Newsweek* devoted a full page to the remarkable nonviolent transformation of two "male sanctuaries," Princeton and Yale, into coed schools.[86] The campus response to the trustees' decision was overwhelmingly favorable. As Oates and Goheen announced the news at a press conference on Sunday, the radio station WPRB interrupted its coverage of the event to play Handel's *Hallelujah Chorus*. The *Daily Princetonian*, so often critical of the president and the board for their slowness to act and their unresponsiveness to student wishes, changed its tune in an editorial on Monday: "The trustees finally chose to side with progressive forces in the administration and student body to make coeducation a reality this fall. . . . The decision shows courage and responsiveness to student needs."[87]

April 19. Princeton University news release, "Admission at Princeton," Apr. 18, 1969, Admission Office, Box 1, Folder 7.

82 Princeton University news release, "Women at Princeton," Apr. 20, 1969.

83 "Plans for Coeducation," 9.

84 In Goheen, Box 96, Folder 4, see Admission by Transfer, Feb. 1969. In Admission Office, Box 10, see Princeton University, Office of Admission, Annual Report, 1968–1969, pp. 6–7. In Goheen, Box 94, Folder 1, see Ruth M. Adams to Robert F. Goheen, May 1, 1969; Goheen to Adams, May 9, 1969; and Goheen to John T. Osander, May 9, 1969. Adams had asked Goheen for help in limiting the number of transfer students accepted from any single institution, because Wellesley had "just suffered a demoralizing raid by Yale."

85 *New York Times*, Apr. 21, 1969, p. 1.

86 "Girls Among the Ivy," *Newsweek*, May 12, 1969, p. 71, clipping in Subject Files Princeton, Coeducation, Box 376, Folder 3.

87 Munford, "Coeducation at Princeton," p. 13; editorial, *Daily Princetonian*, Apr. 21, 1969.

Writing to Oates on behalf of the faculty, Harold W. Kuhn, a professor of economics who had brought the resolution of support for the Patterson report to the faculty for action the previous November, praised the board for "new evidence of Princeton's vigor and forward movement."[88] And administrative staff members, including members of the development office who had been outspoken in their opposition to coeducation, rallied around the decision, whether enthusiastically or of necessity, prompted at least in part by a meeting with Mestres, who called them together to convey a simple message: "The trustees have made a decision. Those of you who can support it strongly should come back to work"—and those who could not support it, Mestres implied but did not need to say explicitly, should be considering other employment.[89]

To be sure, complaints from alumni continued, along with threats to withhold funds. But these were the exceptions; alumni generally accepted the decision of the board, "due in no small measure," in Bowen's words, "to the leadership of high-profile alumni who had been opposed to coeducation but who rallied to the university's cause once the decision was made."[90]

Alumni with daughters and granddaughters had a special incentive to change their minds. An old friend and classmate of Goheen's from Newark—by his own description, "the biggest Tiger in the tank"—had written previously to express his distress about the "biased" Patterson report and to associate himself with Horton's dissent. He now wrote to Goheen about his pleasure at his daughter's acceptance to Princeton as a transfer student. "Thought you might be interested in the enclosed shot of the old curmudgeon and daughter snapped at the moment of receipt of a telegram from one J. Osander relative to the action taken on a certain application for transfer from Wellesley," he wrote. "I surrender—unequivocally; and the strangest part of it is that I feel no pain at all." Thanking his classmate, Goheen expressed his pleasure that "as far as

---

88 Harold W. Kuhn to James F. Oates, Jr., Apr. 21, 1969, Goheen, Box 95, Folder 4.

89 Quoted in Bowen, *Lessons Learned*, p. 72, n. 3. For the development office engagement going forward, see, e.g., Arthur J. Horton, RFG-Ho Meeting: Notes for Topic A (Coeducation), May 1, 1969, Goheen, Box 94, Folder 1.

90 Bowen, *Lessons Learned*, pp. 72–73.

coeducation is concerned," his old friend had "come over to the side of the godly."[91]

It was Goheen, after all, who had provided the vision, leadership, and sheer courage to bring coeducation to Princeton. "Having a hand" in that enterprise, he said later, with characteristic modesty, meant "being in on the single most gratifying accomplishment of the university during my presidency."[92] But knowledgeable observers understood that "having a hand in" and "being in on" fell well short of describing Goheen's critical agency in making coeducation a reality. As Charles Robertson wrote to Goheen following the trustees' decision, "When the Class of 1973 returns for its twenty fifth reunion—among them not a few grandmothers—there is bound to be some reminiscing concerning the birth of coeducation at Princeton way back when. The voices of your detractors will long since have been stilled and girls on campus will occasion as much eyebrow raising as the Nassau Hall tiger." And President Emeritus Goheen will be "widely acclaimed for his foresight, courage, will and ever present common sense. . . . My firm prediction is that the outstanding senior Class of '98 will nominate as the Man Who Has Done the Most for Princeton one Robert F. Goheen."[93]

91 Robert P. Hazlehurst, Jr., to James F. Oates, Jr., Dec. 2, 1968; Hazlehurst to Robert F. Goheen, Jan. 7 and June 13, 1969; and Goheen to Hazlehurst, Dec. 20, 1968, and June 24, 1969, all in Goheen, Box 95, Folder 4.

92 Robert F. Goheen, "A President Recalls Coeducation," *Daily Princetonian*, Apr. 13, 1989.

93 Charles S. Robertson to Robert F. Goheen, Apr. 23, 1969, Goheen, Box 95, Folder 6.

8

Harvard-Radcliffe:
Negotiating the "Non-Merger Merger"

As Princeton was making its decision about coeducation, Harvard was embarking on serious consideration of merger with Radcliffe. On March 3, 1969, when the Harvard corporation took up the request of the Radcliffe council to begin discussion of merger, the general disposition of the group was favorable. "We can say at once," Harvard president Nathan Pusey wrote to Radcliffe president Polly Bunting, that "in principle, we welcome the prospect of a merger. . . . We shall be happy to join with you in discussion of when and how a merger might be effected." Consideration of the many aspects of merger had to start with the faculty of arts and sciences, because the corporation "would want to be sure of that Faculty's readiness to assume full responsibility for the collegiate life of Radcliffe." Pusey promised Bunting that Harvard would get to work "to identify as early as possible the questions needing answers" and expressed the hope that those questions could be "resolved and the merger accomplished by the fall of 1970."[1]

Merger Talks Begin, and Radcliffe Alumnae React

At the Harvard faculty meeting on April 8, on a motion from Bunting, the faculty voted to ask Pusey to appoint committees "to consider the feasibility of the proposed merger" and to make recommendations by the next fall about the range of issues—admissions,

1 Nathan M. Pusey to Mary I. Bunting, Mar. 3, 1969, Bunting, Box 41, Folder 646.

financial aid, discipline, housing, and others—that would need to be addressed if such a change were to occur.[2]

As the discussions unfolded, Radcliffe kept its alumnae informed about the state of affairs, sending regular communications and leading discussions at alumnae gatherings that elicited the predictable range of responses for and against merger.[3] "I am very enthusiastic about this merger and . . . very annoyed at these alumnae of ours who can't face progress," an alumna in New York wrote to Bunting. "This is an educational decision to be made by <u>educators</u> not amateurs."[4] A member of the class of 1937 from Virginia Beach concurred: The issue was "the best interests of the higher education of . . . women," and "decisions should be taken in light of the future and not the past."[5] A member of the class of 1950 from Nutley, New Jersey, convinced that "closer social, extra-curricular, and dormitory ties will only enhance the scope of both schools," called the proposal for merger "an example of the kind of intelligent flexibility and willingness to change administrative structure which . . . will make possible a more meaningful and relevant education for our young people."[6]

But not everyone saw it that way. There were so many reasons not to trust Harvard. A Radcliffe alumna in the class of 1953 from New York City pronounced that "turn[ing] over to Harvard the job of providing for the special needs of women" would be "a big mistake."[7] By agreeing to merger, a member of the class of 1920 wrote from Spain, Radcliffe women would be "plac[ing] themselves"—admittedly "inadvertently"—"into the

2 Docket, Faculty of Arts and Sciences, Special Meeting, Apr. 8, 1969, and Votes Passed, Faculty of Arts and Sciences, Apr. 8, 1969, both in Bunting, Box 42a, Folder 655.

3 Mary I. Bunting and Helen H. Gilbert, Memorandum No. 1 to Radcliffe Alumnae, Mar. 25, 1969, Bunting, Box 40, Folder 625; Dorothea M. Hanna to Fellow Alumnae, Apr. 1, 1969, Bunting, Box 40, Folder 624; Excerpts from Mrs. Bunting's Remarks at the Alumnae Luncheon, June 14, 1969, Bunting, Box 40, Folder 618. For a long, very detailed set of alumnae responses, see Questions and Comments about Radcliffe-Harvard Merger, Radcliffe Club of Boston, June 7, 1969, Bunting, Box 42a, Folder 655.

4 Maurine Rothschild to Mary I. Bunting, Mar. 15, 1969, Bunting, Box 42a, Folder 656.

5 Evelyn W. Bradshaw to Mary I. Bunting, Mar. 31, 1969, Bunting, Box 42a, Folder 656.

6 Ann Kubie Rabinowitz to Mary I. Bunting, Mar. 4, 1969, Bunting, Box 42a, Folder 656.

7 Eleanor Levin Zuckerman, letter to the editor, *Radcliffe Quarterly* 54 (Mar. 1970): 28.

lion's mouth."[8] A member of the class of 1951 from Concord, Massachusetts, thought that merger would constitute "a clear admission on Radcliffe's part of failure to develop an educational plan uniquely appropriate to women." If what students had in mind in terms of coeducational housing was "unlimited opportunity for sexual relations with Harvard men," Radcliffe had no "obligation to provide such facilities." And if students wanted the physical and educational attributes of the Harvard house system, Radcliffe could develop those arrangements on its own.[9] "Shocked" that merger had been decided "without any real consultation with the alumnae" and believing that the plan had been "railroaded through because of pressure from the undergraduates," a member of the 50th reunion class from Maine wrote "in alarm and sorrow" that she felt "not only let down but betrayed by my alma mater."[10]

The appointment of committees to study aspects of merger, recommended by the Harvard faculty on April 8, was delayed significantly by developments that had nothing to do with coeducation. On April 9, Harvard students who were members of SDS occupied the main administration building, University Hall, to protest Harvard's complicity in the Vietnam War and to demand that the university sever its ties with ROTC. The protesters had other objectives as well, including the creation of a black studies program on campus and an end to evictions of low-income residents from property the university planned to develop in Boston and Cambridge. The next morning, Pusey called in the police to clear University Hall. Watching their fellow students clubbed by the police radicalized the student body; students declared a strike and engaged in an eleven-day boycott of classes that paralyzed the campus. In the months that followed, the Harvard faculty and administration focused on the aftermath of the occupation: disciplining protesters, addressing issues at stake in the strike, and rethinking some aspects

---

8 Suzanne d'Orssaud, letter to the editor, *Radcliffe Quarterly* 54 (June 1970): 46.

9 Lydia Hurd Smith to Mary I. Bunting, Apr. 1, 1969, Bunting, Box 42a, Folder 656.

10 Mary Peabody Hotson to Mary I. Bunting, May 27, 1969, Bunting, Box 42a, Folder 656.

of university organization to include student participation in some faculty and administrative committees.[11]

In the summer of 1969, Pusey finally appointed committees to study aspects of merger. One was to address admissions and financial aid; a second, budget and personnel; a third, extracurricular activities and student services; and a fourth, residential living. We cannot know what might have happened if the committees had begun their work the previous spring, when there was clear momentum toward merger. By fall, however, there had been ample opportunity for opponents to mobilize their forces, and the road ahead proved to be more complicated than either Pusey or Bunting might have imagined.[12]

In December, the Harvard faculty of arts and sciences voted to authorize an experimental housing exchange for the spring semester of fifty students between each of three pairs of Harvard and Radcliffe houses, the terms having been negotiated between the faculty masters of the respective houses. The next week, the Harvard corporation endorsed the plan.[13] At the same time, the corporation agreed to permit the Radcliffe senior class to take part in Harvard's commencement exercises, effective in June 1970, a request that had originated with Radcliffe seniors.[14] (As it happened, in a conversation in 1960 with McGeorge Bundy, dean of the Harvard faculty of arts and sciences, Bunting had proposed a merged commencement, provided that the initiative would come from Harvard, but Pusey had counseled that the time was not yet

11 Jennifer J. Stetzer, "From Sympathizers to Organizers," in Laurel Thatcher Ulrich, ed., *Yards and Gates: Gender in Harvard and Radcliffe History* (New York: Palgrave Macmillan, 2004), pp. 271–79; Anne de Saint Phalle, "On Campus," *Radcliffe Quarterly* 53 (June 1969): 16–17.

12 Morton Keller and Phyllis Keller, in *Making Harvard Modern: The Rise of America's University*, updated ed. (New York: Oxford University Press, 2007), p. 283, make a persuasive case for the effects of delay in fueling opposition to the merger.

13 Minutes, Harvard Faculty of Arts and Sciences, Dec. 9, 1969, Bunting, Box 44, Folder 714; Meeting of the President and Fellows of Harvard College, Dec. 15, 1969, Bunting, Box 43, Folder 687. For a longer account of how the exchange was intended to work, see Mary I. Bunting to Radcliffe Parents, Jan. 28, 1970, Bunting, Box 43, Folder 687.

14 Meeting of the President and Fellows of Harvard College, Dec. 15, 1969; Nathan M. Pusey to Karen M. Nelson, Nov. 18, 1969; Mary I. Bunting to Pusey, Dec. 3, 1969; and Pusey to Bunting, Dec. 18, 1969, all in Bunting, Box 43, Folder 688.

right for that.[15] "We welcome," Pusey now told Bunting, "this additional sign of 'growing together.'"[16]

In January 1970, Bunting and the chairman of the Radcliffe board, Helen Homans Gilbert, updated Radcliffe alumnae about developments relevant to the proposed merger. "We continue to look on merger . . . as a major advance with many benefits for our students, for the University, and for the education of women," they wrote. "Thanks to the temper of the times and to Radcliffe's strength, there is an opportunity now at Harvard to create a great university in which there will be equal pride in the opportunities offered to women and to men. This is the fulfillment that we both envision and are working to secure."[17]

Securing that fulfillment proved to be complicated. There was serious resistance to merger at Radcliffe, and it was not simply a function of institutional chauvinism. Skepticism of Harvard was well grounded in the reality of Harvard's history. Since 1948 Harvard had had one tenured position for a woman faculty member, who held the Zemurray Stone Radcliffe professorship, created specifically for a distinguished woman scholar (the incumbents had been distinguished indeed: the medieval historian Helen Maud Cam in 1948–54, the anthropologist Cora DuBois in 1954–70, and the classicist Emily Vermeule in 1970–94). Although there were a handful of women assistant professors, faculty members who were not tenured held little influence in the university, and there was no path to tenure from the assistant professor rank. Harvard had no women administrators. And the number of male undergraduates at Harvard was four times the number of Radcliffe women. There was reasonable cause to worry about submerging Radcliffe into a less-than-hospitable male university.

The Radcliffe alumnae association's merger committee tried to envision a restructured relationship between Radcliffe and Harvard that would be consistent with their desire "to preserve

15 David W. Bailey to Nathan M. Pusey, Aug. 4, 1960, with handwritten note on Pusey's reaction, Pusey, Box 217, Folder Radcliffe College, 1960–61.

16 Nathan M. Pusey to Mary I. Bunting, Dec. 18, 1969, Bunting, Box 43, Folder 688.

17 Mary I. Bunting and Helen H. Gilbert, Memorandum No. 2 to Radcliffe Alumnae, Jan. 23, 1970, Bunting, Box 44, Folder 714.

a Radcliffe entity which can focus on the interests and contributions of women, and to provide a richer educational experience for undergraduate women." But becoming part of Harvard "without losing [Radcliffe's] identity" was a difficult proposition. The committee believed that the full incorporation of women "into the mainstream" at Harvard would have to precede any further consideration of "the dissolution of Radcliffe College." That was not going to happen any time soon, and in the meantime, Radcliffe ought to be doing what it could to implement provisions to "aid women in completing and in making full use of their education." A closer relationship between Harvard and a strengthened Radcliffe was one thing; a merger, which would effectively eliminate Radcliffe, should be off the table in the near term.[18]

Harvard's Committee on Admissions and Financial Aid Says No

At Harvard, the faculty of arts and sciences next took up the question of merger in February 1970, when it addressed the report of the committee that had been working on admissions and financial aid. In a long report presented in late January, that committee recommended against merger. The committee said that although improvements could be made in the relationship of the two institutions and in the educational experience of Harvard and Radcliffe students, "action toward a legal merger of Harvard and Radcliffe, without full consideration of all foreseeable consequences, could eventually produce profound damage to the quality of education at Harvard."

Merger, it said, "would unnecessarily and irreversibly dissolve an important institutional voice for women's interests." Although there was "value to women of fuller integration into the social and intellectual activities of Harvard," women needed to retain "an organizational locus, a forum, of their own." Moreover, merger "would inevitably result in an undesirable increase in the size of the undergraduate [student] body." Harvard's approach to education was "to do something special with a small number of people,

18 "Report of the 'Merger' Committee," *Radcliffe Quarterly* 54 (Mar. 1970): 21.

rather than something less excellent with a large number." Merger posed an impossible "trilemma" for admissions: "<u>We cannot have our present size and our present male enrollment and an equal sex admission ratio</u>." Taking a decision to merge without confronting in advance issues like these would be a serious mistake.[19]

The committee on admissions and financial aid was the first of the four committees working on aspects of merger to submit a report. Figuring out how to proceed in response to such a negative recommendation was a tricky proposition. The presidents of both Harvard and Radcliffe were in favor of merger; three committees had yet to be heard from. Closing down any consideration of merger was surely premature. How would the faculty best deal with the strongly negative resolution submitted by the committee?

The original plan had been for two resolutions to be on the docket for the faculty meeting: the resolution from the committee on admissions and financial aid and a positive resolution looking forward to gradual merger. For whatever reason, the pro-merger motion did not appear, and it was the negative resolution that framed the faculty's discussion.[20]

It was not that the admissions and financial aid committee meant to postpone indefinitely giving the faculty's opinion on the Harvard-Radcliffe relationship. Rather, the committee sought "to prevent a premature decision arrived at without full and careful discussion." Bunting told the faculty "why some modification of the present relationship between Harvard and Radcliffe was needed" and asked that "all options be kept open" until all the committees working on aspects of the relationship had the chance to report, which would lead to better-informed deliberations.[21]

In the end, after extensive discussion, the faculty approved a four-part resolution:

19 "The Harvard-Radcliffe Relationship: Admission and Financial Aid," report of the Committee on Admissions and Scholarships, Jan. 30, 1970, Bunting, Box 48, Folder 776.

20 The account of the pro-merger resolution came from Caroline W. Bynum, assistant professor of history, in minutes, Radcliffe Alumnae Association Study Committee on Merger, Feb. 23, 1970, Bunting, Box 44, Folder 714.

21 Minutes, Faculty Meeting, Feb. 10, 1970, Bunting, Box 44, Folder 714.

It is the sense of this Faculty: <u>That</u> we reaffirm our commitment to the full and equal participation of Radcliffe students in the intellectual and social life of the University community; <u>That</u> we have not sufficiently considered the various and serious potential consequences of the complete and irrevocable merger of Harvard and Radcliffe colleges; <u>That</u> an alternate adjustment in the relationship would in no way inhibit such changes as the current experiment in coeducational living, or impede new and vigorous efforts to improve the education and status of women in our community; <u>That</u> a [new] committee should be established . . . to study the reports of the four . . . committees when they are presented and to consider fully other aspects of the question of the future relationship between the two institutions; and that the report of this committee and those of the existing committees should be presented to the Faculty . . . in order that it might discuss and vote upon the issues before action is taken by the governing boards.

The first three clauses had been presented in the original resolution from the committee. Gone altogether was the committee's clause that read, "<u>That</u> the dissolution of Radcliffe College would be an enormous cost for its members past and present to bear, and that the presumed advantages have not yet been made clear." And the new final clause, a constructive, forward-looking statement proposed by Giles Constable, professor of history and a Radcliffe house master, replaced the much more negative wording that had been proposed by the committee: "<u>That</u> . . . decision on the question of merger or other changes in the relationships between the colleges be deferred until all considerations, pro and con, and all voices within the two communities have been heard."[22] That wording, Caroline W. Bynum, an assistant professor of history,

22 In Bunting, Box 44, Folder 714, see Docket, Faculty of Arts and Sciences, Feb. 10, 1970; minutes, Faculty Meeting, Feb. 10, 1970; and memorandum, Mary I. Bunting to the Board of Trustees, Feb. 13, 1970. In Bunting, Box 44, Folder 704, see Constable amendment, Faculty Meeting, Feb. 10, 1970.

later pointed out, "contained no action clause, and might well have buried merger."[23]

Coresidential Living Will Foster Enhanced Personal Growth

The next report to come to the Harvard faculty was from the committee on coresidential living, chaired by Jerome Kagan, a developmental psychologist in the department of social relations. The committee, formally the committee on residential life at Harvard and Radcliffe colleges, had been appointed by Pusey in July 1969. It included faculty members (some of them house masters), administrators, and Harvard and Radcliffe students. The committee's charge was to "examine the issues surrounding coresidential living" and, if it favored such a move, "to suggest an implementation plan." The committee did favor it, largely because of the overwhelming support of students. A poll showed that 91 percent of respondents wanted coresidential living, mainly because it would allow men and women to get to know each other in informal settings unrelated to romantic relationships and "the dating ritual." It would also address the sense of isolation of many Radcliffe students, who felt like second-class citizens in the larger university.

The committee recommended that coresidential living begin in the fall of 1970, with the option available in three or four Harvard houses and all three Radcliffe houses. Harvard freshmen would continue to live in all-male dormitories in the yard. Radcliffe freshmen would have the choice of coresidential or all-female accommodations in the Radcliffe quadrangle.[24] On March 3, the faculty approved coresidential living, effective in the fall of 1970.[25] A member of the Harvard class of 1933 declared that Harvard had

23 Minutes, Radcliffe Alumnae Association Study Committee on Merger, Feb. 23, 1970, Bunting, Box 44, Folder 714.

24 Committee on Residential Life at Harvard and Radcliffe Colleges, Report to the President, n.d., Bunting, Box 43, Folder 687.

25 Faculty Docket, Mar. 3, 1970, and votes passed, meeting of the Faculty of Arts and Sciences, Mar. 3, 1970, both in Bunting, Box 43, Folder 687.

thereby torn "down the scheme set up by the civilized to govern the relations between the sexes. . . . Civilization is dead."[26]

Radcliffe's Frustrations with the Joint Committee

Also in early March, the Harvard dean of the faculty of arts and sciences, economist John T. Dunlop, constituted the new committee voted for by the faculty in February. Chaired by the dean of the college, historian Ernest R. May, the committee included four other faculty members and two undergraduates. The committee's first charge, Dunlop said, was to recommend near-term actions to fulfill the expressed commitment of the faculty "to the full and equal participation of Radcliffe students in the intellectual and social life of the community." The committee's second assignment was more complicated: "to make recommendations in order to clarify plans regarding the direction of the longer term relationships involved in the education of men and women at Radcliffe and Harvard." For that part of the work the committee would need to await the reports of the various committees engaged in studying aspects of merger. And when the May committee completed its work, it would be reporting to a new committee composed of representatives of the Harvard corporation and the Radcliffe council.[27]

The Radcliffe members of the joint committee were Helen Gilbert, chairman of the Radcliffe board and a trustee of the college for twenty years, and Frances Donovan, a trustee and former president of the Radcliffe alumnae association who was chairing the Radcliffe trustees' committee on merger.[28] The two representatives from the Harvard corporation were Francis H. Burr, senior fellow of the corporation, a member of the Radcliffe council, a member of the class of 1935, a graduate of the Harvard Law School, and a partner in the Boston law firm Ropes and Gray, and Hugh Calkins, a member of the class of 1945, also a graduate of the Harvard Law

---

26 Quoted in Drew Gilpin Faust, "Mingling Promiscuously: A History of Women and Men at Harvard," in Ulrich, ed., *Yards and Gates*, p. 323.

27 John T. Dunlop to Ernest R. May, Mar. 3, 1970, Bunting, Box 44, Folder 714.

28 Mary I. Bunting to Nathan M. Pusey, Mar. 5, 1970, Bunting, Box 44, Folder 707.

School, and a partner in the Cleveland law firm Jones, Day, Cockley, and Reavis. Calkins's wife was a member of the Radcliffe class of 1948. Pusey and Bunting served ex officio. Gilbert and Calkins were designated co-chairmen of the committee.[29]

As the joint committee began its work, it was not clear where the members stood on merger. Pusey and Bunting had already made their commitments clear. There was no evidence of the positions likely to be taken by Burr and Calkins, although Burr said later that he was "skeptical" about the idea—"there were too many differences, and too much strong feeling left over from the past" to merge the two institutions at that point.[30]

In an uncirculated draft in July 1969, Helen Gilbert had raised a number of questions about merger. What did Harvard really have in mind in terms of women's education? "In the baldest terms," she said, "Harvard appears to want to stay ahead of Yale and Princeton and merely absorb Radcliffe." Before embarking on merger, Radcliffe needed to have a clearer sense of Harvard's commitments to women. How would Radcliffe's "spirit," its "identity," be preserved? In a merged institution, who would see to the "protection of . . . present and future women students"?[31] As for Frances Donovan's concerns, the hesitations of the Radcliffe trustees' study committee on merger would be made known before the joint committee got down to work.[32]

The establishment of the corporation-council committee took the question of merger out of the hands of the faculty. But the joint committee proceeded at what Radcliffe members considered to be an excessively slow pace. As Gilbert wrote to Calkins in August 1970, "I am at the end of my patience and I think I speak for a collective Radcliffe patience." Radcliffe, she said, had had "the decency to agree to discuss 'merger'" and had been willing to wait, at Pusey's request, "until the Faculty agreed to equality for

29 Nathan M. Pusey to Mary I. Bunting, Mar. 9, 1970, Bunting, Box 44, Folder 707.
30 Burr oral history, p. 1.
31 Helen Homans Gilbert, untitled typescript, July 26, 1969, Bunting, Box 45a, Folder 715.
32 Preliminary Report of the Trustee Committee to Study "Merger," Mar. 12, 1970, rev. May 11, 1970, Bunting, Box 46, Folder 733.

women at Harvard." Radcliffe had been assured "that the summer of 1970 would see a top committee of Harvard Corporation
members and Radcliffe Trustees get to the details and work out a
new Harvard-Radcliffe agreement." But Gilbert and Calkins had
had only "one very brief and unsatisfactory breakfast meeting," at
Gilbert's "prodding," with "no other communications, two meetings cancelled, and no further word—and it is now mid-August."
If the Harvard committee members were unwilling to meet, they
should allow the Radcliffe representatives to "tell our constituency
the true situation."[33]

Polly Bunting Takes a Stand

During that same summer, Bunting worked out her own thinking
about merger in a long typescript. Two questions were "of paramount importance." One was immediate: What would be the best
"organizational structure" to accomplish "presently accepted educational objectives" for Harvard and Radcliffe students? The second
was longer-range: What structures would be "best suited to advance
the higher education of women at all levels throughout the University?" If Harvard were to be "the one major university in the
country that did not take direct and full responsibility" for educating women, it could be a "serious mistake." Bunting continued,
"Radcliffe's ultimate goal should be to see that Harvard becomes
a university in which the educational objectives and potentialities
of individual women are valued and met as fully as are those of
men. . . . I do not think this goal can be achieved unless Harvard is
given and assumes full responsibility for the education of women.
The trick is to transfer Radcliffe's remaining responsibilities at a time
and in a manner that will assure women's future in the University."

Further, "Radcliffe and Harvard undergraduates act as members of a single group," Bunting said. It was time to create a corporate structure consistent with that reality. "The duplication
caused by our two-headed structure," she wrote, with separate administrations and separate governing boards, "results in needless

---

33 Helen Homans Gilbert to Hugh Calkins, Aug. 14, 1970, Bunting, Box 48, Folder 776.

inefficiencies and complicates planning. At best, it requires the expenditure of a great deal of time to coordinate policies. At worst, it encourages divisiveness within the University community." Consolidation would yield savings, which could be invested in improved programs and services for students and improved salaries and benefits for staff.

And what did Radcliffe students most need? In Bunting's judgment, two things were "most important." The first was more women on the Harvard faculty, the second, "greater acceptance and respect" by male faculty members for the students' "intellectual interests and aspirations." Both of those were more likely to be accomplished, she said, "by giving Harvard full and clear responsibility for [women's] education than by continuing to divide the responsibility between Radcliffe and Harvard."

In sum, Bunting concluded, "some form of merger . . . seems now the only realistic alternative." Objectives for undergraduate education could be accomplished "more economically . . . and more effectively" if the colleges were merged. And merger would make it more likely that the Radcliffe Institute, which Bunting had created to assist "able and motivated women in furthering their careers," would continue to thrive.[34]

Other Committees Weigh In

The joint corporation-council committee heard from other committees addressing aspects of merger.[35] A committee of Harvard overseers pointed to factors that had lessened "the pressure for immediate and complete merger," including the advent of coresidential living, the establishment of a joint Harvard-Radcliffe administrative board, and the decision to hold a joint commencement, which meant that many aspects of merger had been functionally achieved. The committee also noted the difficulty of working out the details of merger before Pusey's planned retirement in June

34 Mary I. Bunting, Reflections on Merger, July, 1970, Bunting, Box 48, Folder 776.
35 See, e.g., Chase N. Peterson to Mrs. Gilbert and Members of the Harvard-Radcliffe Committee, July 28, 1970, Bunting, Box 48, Folder 776.

1971 and observed that the incoming Harvard president would have his own ideas on the Harvard-Radcliffe relationship. And the committee commented that the growth of the women's liberation movement had worked against merger: "The thought is that the preservation of Radcliffe College as an entity will serve the cause of womankind."[36]

The Radcliffe committees were opposed to the whole idea. The more Radcliffe alumnae leaders thought about merger, the less they liked it. Merger would mean that Radcliffe would "be lost by default," "chipped away by the erosion caused by a series of decisions, urged by the president and acquiesced in by all of us." With "society generally . . . at last recognizing the necessity of reducing inequities to women and . . . beginning to understand the role that women potentially could play," it was essential that Radcliffe "remain even stronger." A separate Radcliffe would continue to make "useful contributions to the education of women"; a merged Radcliffe would silence "an eloquent champion of educational opportunities for women."[37]

The Radcliffe trustee committee studying merger reported that merger at that time would be "premature." Instead, Radcliffe should "work for a closer relationship with Harvard." It "should cooperate actively in bringing the two institutions together step by step." A "gradual approach" would permit important initiatives, like coresidential living, to go forward without taking the "irrevocable step" of dismantling the college. With Radcliffe playing its role as "spokesman for the interests of women," there was a better chance of "creat[ing] a better understanding at Harvard on matters of special interest to women."[38]

---

36 Robert L. Hoguet, interim report of the "Overseer group on the Harvard-Radcliffe matter," attached to Hoguet to Helen Homans Gilbert, June 24, 1970, Gilbert, Box 1, Folder 7. On the establishment of the joint administrative board, see Mary I. Bunting to Sargent Kennedy, June 4, 1970, Bunting, Box 44, Folder 706.

37 Miriam Green Hurley, Ruth Grover Wright, Alice Blackmer Skinner, and Maryel Finney Hartung, Statement to the Governing Boards of Radcliffe College, June 10, 1970, Bunting, Box 44, Folder 714. See also Wright to Hugh Calkins, Nov. 1, 1970, Bunting, Box 48, Folder 776.

38 Preliminary Report of the Trustee Committee to Study "Merger," Mar. 12, 1970, rev. May 11, 1970, Bunting, Box 46, Folder 733. On the Radcliffe reservations, see also Barbara Voss, "Merger: A View from Radcliffe's Side," *Harvard Bulletin*, Mar. 23, 1970,

As a member of the Radcliffe board, Carol Pforzheimer, put it later, describing a meeting where the trustees were discussing merger, "We went around the table giving our impressions of how we felt about it and I, somehow, pulled myself up and thought to myself 'Who am I to be sitting here at the demise of Radcliffe College?' And I said 'No' when they came to me. And everybody had the same uncomfortable feeling. That the colleges were moving too fast."[39]

Besides, many committee members believed, the president of Radcliffe was also moving too fast. Helen Gilbert, Bunting's first board chair and generally an admirer of the president, had spoken of Bunting "plung[ing]" ahead, with Gilbert "hanging on her by the coattail."[40] Gilbert's successor as chairman, Susan Storey Lyman, who took over when Matina Horner became president, was less admiring. Bunting, she thought, was not always fully forthcoming with the board; on some critical issues she was "way ahead of the [trustee] executive committee," to the point that she "overstepped" what Lyman considered her role.[41]

As merger was under discussion, four alumnae leaders had spoken directly to the issue of Bunting's leadership in a statement in June 1970: "In fact, we are witnessing the curious and, we believe, unprecedented phenomenon of seeing a president of one of the most prestigious women's colleges in the world seek to dissolve the college to which she was so honorably inducted in 1960."[42] A new member of the alumnae association board opined, "If there be truth in the accusation . . . that the President is delivering Radcliffe to Harvard, it may also be true that the officers charged with representing the Alumnae are delivering that body, without its full assent, into the hands of those who oppose the President."[43]

---

pp. 19–20, Wasserman I, Box 20, Folder 901; typescript, Questions for the March, 1970, Quarterly, Bunting, Box 48, Folder 775.

39 Pforzheimer oral history, p. 2.

40 Gilbert oral history, interview no. 2, May 12, 1982, pp. 38 ("coattail") and 39 ("she just plunged"), Gilbert, Box 1, Folder 1.

41 Lyman oral history, pp. 12, 15, 16, 18, 20, 21.

42 Hurley, Wright, Skinner, and Hartung, Statement to the Governing Boards of Radcliffe College, June 10, 1970.

43 Joan Braverman Pinck to Barbara Voss, Nov. 19, 1970, Gilbert, Box 1, Folder 7.

Finally, in December 1970, after at least a half-dozen drafts, the joint corporation-council committee issued its report. Total corporate merger, the committee believed, was "not desirable at this time." There were other ways of accomplishing the advantages of merger. The committee echoed the commitment of the faculty "to the full and equal participation of Radcliffe students in the intellectual and social life of the University." It urged Harvard to add "a similar commitment" with respect to women "as faculty members, as alumnae, and as members of the Governing Boards." Radcliffe should "stand as a guarantor of progress towards these goals."

In terms of specific arrangements, the committee proposed, first, that Harvard operate the Radcliffe houses and other dormitories as part of the Harvard house system. The process of upgrading Radcliffe's residential facilities to create a house system comparable to Harvard's should continue apace, with Harvard sharing responsibility for fund-raising.

The committee's second proposal concerned administrative arrangements at Radcliffe. Instead of a president, there should be a dean, appointed jointly by the governing boards of Harvard and Radcliffe, who would be a member of the faculty of arts and sciences and a member of the Harvard council of deans. Women should be appropriately represented on the faculty and among house masters, college deans, and senior tutors. The Radcliffe dean's office should be replaced by the house master–senior tutor system long in place at Harvard.

Third, the committee proposed that certain entities relating particularly to women remain under the administration of the dean of Radcliffe College: career counseling, the Radcliffe Institute, the Schlesinger Library, and the alumnae office. For the moment, Radcliffe should continue to take responsibility for admissions and financial aid for women students.

Fourth, the committee addressed financial matters. The Radcliffe operating budget was in deficit; closing the gap should be a joint Harvard-Radcliffe responsibility. Radcliffe should turn over to Harvard its unrestricted endowment income, current gifts (unless designated for specific purposes), and the small percentage of tuition income that it had retained under the 1943 agreement.

Harvard should use the income to pay Radcliffe's expenses. Harvard and Radcliffe should engage to the extent practicable in joint fund-raising. Business operations of the two colleges—buildings and grounds, dining halls, the comptroller's office—should be brought together. Radcliffe would continue to own its own property and to manage its own endowment.

Finally, the committee recommended that the Harvard and Radcliffe governing boards work in tandem to the extent possible. These new arrangements, the committee said, should be instantiated in a revised contract between Harvard and Radcliffe, to be effective at the end of June 1971, a contract that would be subject to review—and, at the extreme, to termination—in the academic year 1974–75.[44]

The president of the Radcliffe alumnae association reported mixed reaction to the report. A common thread in alumnae opinion was that the report did not really address the underlying problems with respect to the status of women in the university. Nor was it especially imaginative. Other colleges and universities were experimenting with educational patterns more diverse and more interesting than the "rigid coeducation" toward which Harvard seemed to be moving. It would have been desirable to have the committee think more broadly about possibilities for the future of the two institutions.[45]

Important changes were coming to Harvard and Radcliffe that bore on the reception of the joint corporation-council committee report. Pusey was set to retire in June 1971 and Bunting in June 1972.[46] The two most vigorous proponents of merger, then, would be unable to exert the kind of leadership required to move the committee's recommendations forward. Some people favored waiting for Pusey's successor, Derek Bok, dean of the Harvard Law School, to take office before taking any action on the report. Pusey

44 Report of Committee on Harvard-Radcliffe Relationships, Dec. 8, 1970, Bunting, Box 48, Folder 775.

45 Barbara Fischer Voss to the Radcliffe Board of Trustees, Jan. 21, 1971, Bunting, Box 48, Folder 774.

46 Statement Issued by the Radcliffe College News Office, Jan. 29, 1971, and Mary I. Bunting to Radcliffe Alumna, Feb. 10, 1971, both in Bunting, Box 46, Folder 742.

thought otherwise, and so did Bok. The work had been going on for nearly two years; it was "unlikely," Bok said, that he could "contribute any significant new insights in the next few months."[47]

The "Non-Merger Merger" Is Approved

In late January 1971, the joint committee issued a revised version of its report reflecting the many comments it had received after the report had been made public seven weeks earlier. Some of the revisions were simply semantic. The most notable substantive change was a clause permitting the Radcliffe trustees to designate the dean as president of Radcliffe College.[48] The new arrangements came to be known popularly as the "non-merger merger."[49]

On January 28, the Radcliffe trustees approved and the Radcliffe council "accepted in principle" the revised report of the committee on Harvard-Radcliffe relationships. On February 1, the Harvard corporation followed suit, and the Harvard board of overseers provided the final approval on March 8. The agreement was clearly in Radcliffe's interest, Bunting and Gilbert wrote to Radcliffe alumnae. Radcliffe would retain "its corporate identity and title to all of its properties and endowments." The plan would relieve "pressing financial and administrative problems." The agreement provided two notable features bearing on the future of women's education in Harvard University. First, Harvard would be taking "responsibility for the environment in which Radcliffe students live and learn as well as for their formal instruction." Not only that, but in assuming management of Radcliffe's operations— houses, dining services, buildings and grounds, and others— Harvard was also taking "responsibility for our mounting deficit." Harvard's willingness "to enlarge its sphere of responsibility" in

47 Derek Bok to Helen H. Gilbert, Jan. 20, 1971, Bunting, Box 48, Folder 775.

48 Revised Report of Committee on Harvard-Radcliffe Relationships, Jan. 25, 1971, Bunting, Box 48, Folder 775.

49 See, e.g., The Harvard-Radcliffe Relationship, Nov. 1, 1973, Horner, Series 5, Box 8, Folder 5; Robin Freedberg, "Merger Non-Merger Merger Sub-Merger Merger Re-Merger," *Harvard Crimson*, Commencement 1974, clipping in Subject Files Radcliffe, Series 5, Box 16, Folder 8.

this way "gives unmistakable evidence, which we did not have in the past, of her commitment to the education of women." Second, there was to be an "enlargement of [the] sphere of influence" of the Radcliffe president, who would now be expected to "take a special interest in initiating and extending educational opportunities for women under the Faculty of Arts and Sciences." Bunting and Gilbert were optimistic about the "new relationship," they said; "by working together [Harvard and Radcliffe] can provide richer intellectual opportunities for undergraduates in both Colleges and advance the status of women at Harvard as well as effect significant economies."[50]

Gilbert, who, like Bunting, would have preferred full merger, recognized that most Radcliffe alumnae and even the Radcliffe trustees were simply not ready to relinquish Radcliffe's corporate identity. Despite the fact that Harvard and Radcliffe were de facto coeducational, there was a fierce attachment to Radcliffe as its own institution. It was more a matter of emotional sentiment than it was of rational logic. Radcliffe had long been understood to be preeminent among the Seven Sisters colleges, the most elite of an elite group of institutions. Going to Radcliffe, being a Radcliffe alumna, conveyed a status, symbolic or real, that mattered hugely to Radcliffe graduates.[51] Although Gilbert was not "surprised at the opposition," she was surprised at how extensive it was. Under those circumstances, she said, the non-merger merger was "probably . . . the best bargain" they could get. Gilbert counted on the fact that the agreement "would evolve" and would "be under constant review."[52]

In short, with undergraduate coeducation at Yale and Princeton well into its second year, Harvard and Radcliffe were finally working out terms for functional coeducation between two still-independent institutions.

50 Mary I. Bunting and Helen H. Gilbert, Memorandum No. 3 to Radcliffe Alumnae, Feb. 10, 1971, Bunting, Box 48, Folder 775. See also Harvard University news release, Feb. 1, 1971, Bunting, Box 48, Folder 776, and Bunting to Radcliffe Parents and Friends, Feb. 16, 1971, Bunting, Box 46, Folder 742.

51 Interview with Caroline W. Bynum '62, Jan. 13, 2015, Princeton, NJ. See also ML Bundy oral history, July 12, 2005, p. 20.

52 Gilbert oral history, interview no. 3, May 17, 1982, pp. 52 ("best bargain," "evolve"), 54 ("constant review"), 55 ("surprised").

9

Princeton: "I Felt I Was in a Foreign Country"

While Harvard and Radcliffe had begun to work through structural changes in their relationship, Princeton's challenge was more practical: Robert Goheen and his colleagues had five months to prepare for the arrival of Princeton's first undergraduate women.

The First Appointments of Women Administrators

One of their first tasks was to hire women administrators to help with the planning and implementation of coeducation. The most important appointment would be a woman dean, a "very capable woman," to "coordinate the integration of women undergraduates in the whole range of activities, services, etc. at Princeton."[1] William Bowen found the candidate: Halcyone ("Halcy") Harger Bohen, a cum laude graduate of Smith College with a master of arts in teaching from Radcliffe. She had experience as a high school teacher and a writer, but at that point she was at home, raising three small daughters. Her then-husband, Frederick M. Bohen, had been a graduate student and an assistant dean at the Woodrow Wilson School, and Halcy Bohen was well known to William Bowen, who described her as "an extremely engaging individual" with "the outlook, the temperament, and the personal qualities which would make her extremely effective in dealing with

---

1 A. J. Maruca to President Goheen, Provost Bowen, and Dean Sullivan, Apr. 28, 1969, Bowen provost, Box 18, Folder 9.

the young ladies whom we shall have with us." The fact that she was married and a mother, Bohen said later, meant that she was "conventional enough not to rock the boat." Intrigued by "the 'lady deaning' position," Bohen responded that she was "surprised and bemused by, and grateful for" Bowen's interest and willing to take on the work.[2]

With Bohen signed up as an assistant dean of students, two other women were added to the staff. Patricia Albjerg Graham, a history professor at Barnard, came to Princeton for the year as an American Council on Education fellow to work with the dean of the faculty, economist Richard A. Lester, on revising policies (for example, on nepotism) and creating new ones (such as on maternity leave) to facilitate the integration of women into the faculty.[3] In the provost's office, Bowen hired Mary E. Proctor, an M.P.A. student at the Woodrow Wilson School, as an assistant to help implement coeducation. Proctor was a Radcliffe alumna who had worked for three years for the U.S. Information Agency in Brazil before she entered graduate school.[4]

Proctor had addressed the alumni council in April 1969 on "the possible pitfalls for women at Princeton," a talk expanded into an article, "Why a (Princeton) Woman Can't Be More Like a Man," in the *Princeton Alumni Weekly*. Her account of her Princeton experience spoke to the challenges that would confront the first women undergraduates: "We had not kidded ourselves that it would be easy to adjust to an all-male college, but most of us have found the experience more uncomfortable than we had anticipated." Proctor warned, "The ten girls from the Woodrow Wilson School

2 In Bowen provost, Box 18, Folder 9, see Halcyone H. Bohen resume, June 10, 1969; W. G. Bowen to E. D. Sullivan and N. Rudenstine, June 12, 1969; and Bohen to Bowen, June 10, 1969. See also telephone interview with Bohen, Jan. 30, 2015 ("conventional enough").

3 Kirsten Bibbins, Anne Chiang, and Heather Stephenson, eds., *Women Reflect about Princeton* (Princeton University, 1989), p. 26; Marcia Synnott, "A Friendly Rivalry: Yale and Princeton Pursue Parallel Paths to Coeducation," in Leslie Miller-Bernal and Susan L. Poulson, eds., *Going Coed: Women's Experiences in Formerly Men's Colleges and Universities, 1950–2000* (Nashville, TN: Vanderbilt University Press, 2004), pp. 118–19.

4 A. J. Maruca to President Goheen, Provost Bowen, and Dean Sullivan, Apr. 28, 1969, and Bowen to Mary E. Proctor, May 2 and July 8, 1969, all in Bowen provost, Box 18, Folder 9.

are worldly wise compared to next year's incoming freshmen. . . . Unless Princeton is willing to undergo the changes that will make it a truly heterosexual university, admitting girls might do more harm than good."[5]

Proctor's warning hinted at the challenges that lay ahead. The next academic year would open with 101 women freshmen and 48 transfer students, along with 21 women visiting as critical languages students. That meant 170 undergraduate women on a campus with 3,251 undergraduate men.[6] The ratio—about 19 to 1—was dramatically different from the 3-to-1 ratio the Patterson report had described as optimal for coeducation at Princeton.

In short, Princeton embarked on a plan for the first year of coeducation that ran directly into the minefields Patterson had warned against. As Patterson said, "Very small numbers make it most difficult for women to do things privately or anonymously—to experiment, to make mistakes, to ask a question that turns out to be a silly one, without being noticed and without having these mistakes follow them." Moreover, "very small numbers would probably also discourage all but the most confident, strong-willed and determined women."[7] Patterson's forecast proved prescient in many ways.

The Arrival of Freshman Women at Pyne Hall: "A Hassle and a Half"

The plan was to house all the women in Pyne Hall, a fifty-seven-year-old traditional stone Collegiate Gothic dormitory. The building was refurbished over the summer, with new lounges, a kitchen, a laundry room, and additional bathrooms.[8] There were curtains on the windows and locks on the doors. "Quite frankly, it's a hassle and a half," Mary Azoy, a junior transfer student from Bradford

---

5 Mary E. Proctor, "Why a (Princeton) Woman Can't Be More Like a Man," *Princeton Alumni Weekly* 69 (May 13, 1969): 10–12.

6 Princeton data from Princeton University Registrar's Office.

7 "'The Education of Women at Princeton': A Special Report," *Princeton Alumni Weekly* 69 (Sept. 24, 1968): 22–23.

8 Luther Munford, "Coeducation at Princeton: The Struggle of an Idea at a University in Transition," *Daily Princetonian*, Oct. 21, 1969, p. 13.

Junior College, said later of the installation of locks on the entry-way doors. "Most of the girls in my own entry are as irritated as I am, simply because it's not fun to feel like a bloody gold brick stuffed away in a corner of Ft. Knox."[9]

Bohen wrote to the incoming women students about their liv-ing arrangements—the layout of Pyne Hall, the entryway system, assignment of roommates, furnishings in the rooms, and ameni-ties, from lounges and laundry facilities to sewing machines. She told them about the graduate students in Pyne, who would "plan informal social events and programs" and see to the "individual welfare" of the undergraduates in their charge. Seniors who had been critical languages students the year before would live in Pyne to help with the adjustment of the new students.[10] Bohen said, in closing, "I look forward to an interesting year together."[11]

The women arrived on Saturday, September 6. Hordes of men invaded Pyne courtyard. So did reporters for local and national newspapers and television networks. The *New York Times* told the story this way: "The first coeds moved into 223-year-old Princeton College this weekend, trailing behind them gaggles of helpful male students loaded down with their trunks and books and tennis rackets." June Fletcher, a freshman from Elberon, New Jersey, who had been named "Miss Bikini, U.S.A." in a contest the summer before her admission, said, "I've met so many boys today they're all just one big blur." Fletcher's roommate, Lisa Derota of Kinnelon, New Jersey, said, "'My father says he's going to put iron bars on the windows tomorrow.'"[12] (Fletcher was the most highly publicized freshman woman. Writing about her SAT scores and extracurricular achievements, the *Princeton Alumni Weekly* chose, chauvinistically, also to publish "her non-academic statistics"—"35–25–35."[13])

9 Mary L. Azoy '71, "Notes on Coeducation: A Princeton Woman's Impressions," *Princeton Alumni Weekly* 70 (Oct. 14, 1969): 13.

10 Halcyone H. Bohen to All Incoming Women Students, Aug. 20, 1969, ODUS, Box 7, Folder 9. For an update, see Bohen to All Women Students, Sept. 19, 1969, ODUS, Box 27, Folder 21.

11 Halcyone H. Bohen to All Incoming Women Students, Aug. 20, 1969.

12 *New York Times*, Sept. 8, 1969, clipping in Horton, Box 2, Folder 6.

13 Editor's note, in "Letters," *Princeton Alumni Weekly* 70 (Sept. 23, 1969): 3.

Pioneering Women: Ambition, Opportunity, Adventure, Challenge

The arrival of the women, the *New York Times* said, would bring a major change to the traditional mode of social life at Princeton—"frantic weekends in search of girls at far-away places like Vassar or Smith and equally frantic party weekends with imported dates on the campus." A senior, Robert Henrikson, predicted, "It will put an end to the weekend syndrome where you work like hell at studying half the week, then leave town and go beserk [*sic*] for the other half." A friend of Henrikson added, "Yeah, now we'll go beserk all the time."[14]

A reporter for *Women's Wear Daily* asked why women had chosen Princeton. "I came for academic reasons," Fletcher responded. "I just applied for kicks," said Maureen Flanagan, adding, "It was a good opportunity and also Princeton has the best academics in the country." Anita Fefer said, "It's exciting. There aren't too many opportunities to be first at anything anymore." Dalia Howarth said, "I wanted to invade the male stronghold. It's a challenge."[15]

The opportunity to be a pioneer exerted a strong pull. Robin Herman's father had heard that Princeton was accepting women and told her she had to apply. "I thought," she said, "if I could get an Ivy League education and participate in a historical social change at the same time then it was worth much more to me than just four years of college."[16] Carol Obertubbesing read that Princeton might admit women: "I like to do things that are a little different, and I like to be the first to do something, and so I thought, 'Well, why not apply?'"[17] Marion Freeman, a fifth-generation Princetonian, had been headed for Radcliffe. "It wasn't that I necessarily had a drive to go to Princeton," she said later. "But if it was going coed, sure, I gave it a try."[18]

14 *New York Times*, Sept. 8, 1969.

15 *Women's Wear Daily*, Sept. 9, 1969, clipping in Subject Files Princeton, Coeducation, Box 376, Folder 3.

16 Quoted in Lisa Outar, "On the Vanguard," *Daily Princetonian*, Mar. 10, 1993, pp. 1–2.

17 Obertubbesing oral history, p. 2.

18 Quoted in Wendy Plump, "O Pioneers," *Princeton Living*, Sept. 1994, clipping in Subject Files Princeton, Coeducation, Box 376, Folder 6.

Ambition, opportunity, adventure, and challenge: These were among the chief attractions Princeton had to offer. Mara Minerva said she had come to Princeton because she was looking for "a university with a lot of diversity, and a university that isn't afraid to change." The Woodrow Wilson School attracted her. "Plus, it's very exciting,'" she said, "being in the first class of girls." Deborah Leff said that "a Princeton diploma is an important ticket for whatever you want to do after college," which in her case included law school and a job on Capitol Hill in a U.S. senator's office. Asked if she thought her fellow women students "were as ambitious as she," she responded, "As a matter of fact, almost every girl I've met here is interested in a career. There aren't many husband hunters." Two cases in point: Among the women interviewed for a feature about the new freshmen in the *Princeton Alumni Weekly,* Laurie Watson said that she was looking forward to a career in medicine. Stephanie Fowler told the interviewer that she had always wanted to be a writer for *Sports Illustrated.*[19]

Helen Zia said later that the new Princeton women were "an intimidating bunch, eager to make history," bent on being "pioneers in the uncharted world of the male bastion."[20] But not everyone thought in terms of being a pioneer. Interviewed for a retrospective on the coming of coeducation, Sally Fields put it this way: "Were we trailblazers? To a degree. Independent? Sure. Risk-takers? Maybe. . . . But I didn't think of myself that way then. I just thought of myself as somebody who had gotten into a great school."[21]

The *Daily Princetonian* told the story of orientation week this way: "Pyne Hall had become a perpetual party." One woman transfer student said later, "It was a zoo. Drunks came knocking on doors at all hours soliciting for their parties; the noise was incredible. I don't think I slept for two or three days." Another

19 "The Multifarious Freshwomen," interviews by Andrew Kesler '71, *Princeton Alumni Weekly* 70 (Oct. 7, 1969): 10–12.

20 Quoted in Bibbins, Chiang, and Stephenson, eds., *Women Reflect About Princeton,* p. 27.

21 Quoted in Plump, "O Pioneers."

woman said the men were "like flies."[22] Christine Stansell, a junior transfer from Rice, observed that each woman student was "her own kind of magnet"—"like a planet with guy satellites [orbiting] around her."[23]

The First Year of Coeducation: A Complicated Proposition

For male students, having women students on campus was a complicated proposition. The novelty was compelling; so were the opportunities for informal personal interactions. But every male student in the classes of 1970–73 had applied to Princeton (and, in the cases of 1970–72, come to Princeton) expecting an all-male school. Not surprisingly, the arrival of women brought difficulties and adjustments, and even some hostility.[24]

With so few women, it was difficult to imagine a normal campus experience. "There's still a lot of pressure on the girls," said Celeste Brickler. "We have to be charming all the time. When more girls are admitted, it will be easier for everybody—boys and girls."[25] And when more girls were admitted, the national press would not be following their every move. There would not be a journalist sitting on the sink in the women's bathroom in Pyne, interviewing students. Barbara Walters would not be filming on campus for a segment on coeducation at Princeton for the *Today Show*.[26] Nor would there be gestures like that of Duncan Van Norden '35, a strong opponent of coeducation who, in an about-face, sent each of the new female freshmen a large yellow chrysanthemum.[27]

It was the critical languages students, back at Princeton for a second year as members of the class of 1970, who had the best perspective on the newly coed scene. "Boys are braver now that we have coeducation," Sue Jean Lee told the *Daily Princetonian*.

---

22 Munford, "Coeducation at Princeton," p. 13.

23 Interview with M. Christine Stansell '71, Jan. 20, 2015, New York City.

24 Telephone interview with Robin Herman '73, Mar. 10, 2015.

25 "The Multifarious Freshwomen," 12.

26 Telephone interview with Marsha Levy-Warren '73, Mar. 9, 2015; Princeton University news release, Oct. 21, 1969 (Barbara Walters), Goheen, Box 94, Folder 1.

27 *Women's Wear Daily*, Sept. 9, 1969.

"Last year they just avoided us." Mae Wong said that coeducation made her "feel more comfortable." She said, "Last year, I was the only girl in one of my seminars; whenever I said anything all the boys turned around and stared at me with their mouths open."[28]

It would be some time before a woman student would not be the only woman in her class, and that was difficult. Emily Trenholm Fisher said, "There were times when if I was the only woman in a precept, if I spoke I felt as if I was speaking for everyone. You know, The Women Are Speaking!"—that "really wasn't comfortable."[29] "Members of the class tend to feel that the girl has to be knocked down at all costs," Karen Hodges said. "The Women's Liberation Front would hate me because I'm afraid to state opinions."[30]

Such discomfort was not universal. Sally Fields, who would major in statistics and take courses in math, statistics, and engineering, was often the only woman in her classes. "It didn't bother me a bit, though," she said. "I felt like if I had something to say, I raised my hand. . . . I never didn't raise my hand because I was the only woman."[31]

In addition to how women felt about being the only woman in a class, there were issues about how they were treated. Laurie Watson told the story of showing up—late, as usual—for her astrophysics class. The professor asked her to come up to look through the telescope at the front of the room. At first the image was blurry. The men in the room began to laugh. Watson looked again and "discovered that the telescope was pointed to a pin-up poster of a nude female tacked to the back wall of the room."[32] Ann Hibner told the *Trenton Sunday Times Advertiser*, "Girls are treated very differently in classes than boys. In my literature class I'm very much teased."[33] Maureen Ferguson told the *New York Times*, "I find that

28 Quoted in *Daily Princetonian*, Sept. 19, 1969.
29 Quoted in Plump, "O Pioneers."
30 Quoted in *Trenton Sunday Times Advertiser*, Jan. 11, 1970, clipping in ODUS, Box 7, Folder 9.
31 Quoted in Plump, "O Pioneers."
32 Carlo H. Balestri, "25 Years of Coeducation: Breaking Down Barriers; The First Four Years," *Daily Princetonian*, Oct. 11, 1994, p. 1.
33 Quoted in *Trenton Sunday Times Advertiser*, Jan. 11, 1970.

I'm usually the only girl in most of my classes. At the beginning of the year, I couldn't help thinking whenever I said something that I was representing all coeds, or even all women." One professor "insists on calling me Mr. Ferguson," she said. "When we're being informal, he calls me 'sir.'"[34]

With at most a small handful of women in any class, the women stood out. Part of the experience was "the circles of empty seats left around lone girls in lecture."[35] The issue was not discrimination; most women "felt that they were treated as an aberration or as something new that had to be studied and quantified." Whenever a woman did anything, as Anne Smagorinsky noted, it was "the first time a woman had done it. It was thrust upon us constantly."[36]

"The issue of being female always came up," Marsha Levy said. "I think we almost all were asked at one point or another, 'So what is the female point of view on this? What does the other side think?'" She added, "I think my experience (as an exchange student in India) did me good, because I felt I was in a foreign country."[37] In her first two years, she said later, she never had another woman student in any of her precepts: "I had never before felt so alone as a girl."[38]

For some women, being asked for the woman's point of view was annoying. For others, it was intimidating. "You lost the sense of being a person, of being yourself," Levy said.[39] "Being the center of attention . . . as the only girl" was extremely difficult, Alison Amonette said. "Faculty were always asking for the girl's opinion, which immediately dried up any thought that might have flowed out of me."[40] Asked so often for "the 'women's opinion,'"

34 Quoted in *New York Times*, Apr. 14, 1970, clipping in Horton, Box 2, Folder 6. On the same theme, see Zaharko oral history, p. 23.

35 Jane Leifer '73, "Trials of the Coed 100: The Coeducation of Princeton; Four Years After," *Princeton Alumni Weekly* 73 (May 29, 1973): 9.

36 Balestri, "25 Years of Coeducation," p. 6.

37 Quoted in ibid. See also Obertubbesing oral history, pp. 6, 10; Zaharko oral history, pp. 38–39; Kemper oral history, p. 13.

38 Levy-Warren interview.

39 Ibid.

40 Alison Amonette, interview by Halcy Bohen, June 4, 1973, ODUS, Box 27, Folder 21.

June Fletcher said, "I felt I had to prove to men that women were intellectual equals."[41]

Patricia Kuntz '74, the first woman to receive a B.S.E. degree after four years in engineering, recalled walking into the first meeting for engineering students and having everyone rise and shout, "a girl, a girl, a girl." She, too, was often asked for the "woman's point of view," subject matter notwithstanding (she concentrated in aerospace and mechanical sciences, a department in which gendered perspectives were hard to imagine), and she was "often apologized to in engineering classes when a derivation went wrong and the professor said something 'not meant for feminine ears.'"[42] Alicia Campi, a critical languages student from Smith at Princeton for the year, remarked, "I feel I am a trial experiment in what is still a male institution."[43]

These experiences eased after the first year as faculty members became more accustomed to teaching women students and male students became more accustomed to having women in their classes. Fewer faculty and students made comments that made it obvious that women were not welcome. But some faculty members who had been outwardly antagonistic remained recalcitrant. In a course in Roman law, the professor made no bones about his views. "Hello, gentlemen," he said at the beginning of each class. He told dirty jokes and recited limericks in Latin, the translation of which was "very insulting to women." When he passed out blue books for the midterm exam, he declared, "One blue book a man!" But when he learned that a woman student in the course had been doing particularly well, he changed his tune. Handing out blue books for the final exam, he announced, "One blue book a man and woman!" That was the woman's "great triumph": his acknowledgment "by the end of the class that I was there!"[44]

---

41 Quoted in *Town Topics* (Princeton, NJ), June 11, 1973, Subject Files Princeton, Coeducation, Box 376, Folder 4.

42 Quoted in Yvonne Ng and Jennifer Rexford, eds., *She's an Engineer? Princeton Alumnae Reflect* (Princeton University, 1993), p. 61.

43 Alicia Campi, "Princeton Co-ed Notes Ambivalent Male Reaction," *Sophian*, Oct. 16, 1969, Box 18, Smith College Archives.

44 Taylor oral history, pp. 19–20 (Roman law); Nelson oral history, p. 3 (limericks, translation); Levy-Warren interview (antagonism).

Women in Men's Spaces

For women, showing up in previously all-male spaces challenged prevailing norms. The feeling that men dominated the campus was inescapable. It was not that anyone ever said explicitly, "This place belongs to men." But there was a pervasive sense that the campus was marked with signs that said, "No women here." As Christine Stansell recalled, the combination of Princeton's history and the small number of women students made it "so uncomfortable to be female in those spaces." Stansell told the story of venturing into a large study room in the library, the only woman among some forty men. "A giggle started around the room," she said. "My face was burning. I never went back." Princeton, she said, "was the first place I was ever treated as an 'other' whose feelings and experiences didn't matter."[45]

Outside the classroom, it was hard for Princeton women to make friends with other women and even harder to get dates with Princeton men. The structure of Pyne, with two suites on each of four floors in each entryway, no long hallways, and no easy access from one entryway to another, made it difficult to enjoy informal interactions with other women. And men took the view that with so few women on campus, it was inevitable that each of them already had many other suitors. Why risk getting shot down by asking for a date with someone who was bound to have one already? As a result, many women were dateless on Saturday nights.[46]

Even when Princeton came closer to the targeted 3-to-1 male-female ratio, the challenges remained. A man in the class of 1976 described the problem this way: "Male students claim the . . . ratio insures the impossibility of normal relationships, while women counter that the men let themselves be scared off too easily, that if they would just make the attempt to get to know the female students [it would improve the situation]."[47] Another male student said of the ratio: "I call it the 'Princeton dilemma.' If a girl's

45 Stansell interview.
46 *Trenton Sunday Times Advertiser*, Jan. 11, 1970.
47 Brad Swanson, "On the Campus," *Princeton Alumni Weekly* 74 (Feb. 19, 1974): 5.

good-looking, she's probably surrounded by a buffoon squad, and you don't want to wade through all those guys to get to her. And if she's ugly, who wants to bother with her?"[48]

It was hard for men to give up customary social patterns. In Princeton tradition, "women were for the weekends" and "social and intellectual life didn't mix." With a 19-to-1 ratio, it was easier for most men to continue to find dates at women's colleges. A critical languages student, Holly Hoffmeister, had predicted the previous spring: "The stereotype will be 'that Princeton girls are dogs. By January the myth will have arisen that you still have to go to a girl's school to get a good date.'"[49] Hoffmeister's prediction was on the mark. "Are you a girl or a coed?" Ronnie-Gail Emden remembered being asked.[50] As Deborah Leff told the *New York Times* in April 1970, "Having so few girls here now puts pressure on the guys to bring in imports for the weekend, and coeds only get asked out when a guy can't get an import."[51] The continued importing of dates made life awkward for Princeton women. As Robin Herman reflected later, "You'd be great friends with some fellow during the week, and on weekends he'd date someone else."[52] Mary Proctor said, "Boys at Princeton are used to girls who play dumb. The men have been taught to view the world in competitive terms . . . they get tired of competition and go after bits of fluff on the weekends."[53]

Princeton's First Women Faculty

Along with the challenge of learning to go to school with women, male undergraduates had to adjust to having women teachers. In the fall of 1969, there were three women in the professorial ranks: Suzanne Keller, a professor of sociology tenured a year earlier after

48 Quoted in Susan Williams '74, "On the Campus," *Princeton Alumni Weekly* 73 (Mar. 20, 1973): 7.

49 Munford, "Coeducation at Princeton," p. 14. See also Zaharko oral history, p. 25.

50 Emden oral history, p. 16.

51 Quoted in *New York Times*, Apr. 14, 1970, clipping in Horton, Box 2, Folder 6.

52 Quoted in Leslie Aldridge Westoff, "Newspaper Sports Reporter," *Princeton Alumni Weekly* 78 (June 5, 1978): 36.

53 Quoted in Munford, "Coeducation at Princeton," p. 14.

having spent three years at Princeton as a visiting lecturer, and two new assistant professors, Karen Woodard Brazell in East Asian studies, and Nancy J. Weiss in history.

Karen Brazell, a 1961 graduate of the University of Michigan, joined the faculty in East Asian studies after earning her Ph.D. at Columbia in 1969. Her first book, *The Confessions of Lady Nijo* (1973), won a National Book Award for translation in 1974. An accomplished scholar of Japanese literature and theater, she asked her department for an early tenure review when she received an offer of a tenured associate professorship from Cornell. The department declined to recommend tenure, and Brazell left Princeton in 1974 for Cornell, where she was later promoted to full professor and awarded a named chair.[54]

In the fall of 1968, Nancy Weiss was a teaching assistant in Harvard's first black history course, a team-taught course led by her adviser, the biographer of Franklin D. Roosevelt, Frank Freidel. One day Freidel came to class and told Weiss that he had recommended her for a job at Princeton. He had received a call from his friend Wesley Frank Craven, the historian of colonial America who was leading the Princeton search. That was the way junior faculty were hired: no ads, no job talk, just calls seeking candidates from the chairman of a search to his friends at other institutions. Freidel and Weiss both laughed at the idea. There were, of course, no women at Princeton, but Freidel said he thought it would be good for Princeton to have to consider the possibility. When Weiss was invited for an interview, the history department chairman, Lawrence Stone, a world-famous scholar of early modern England, told her that the department did not have a policy against hiring women. It was just that no one had ever suggested it before.

Weiss was offered the job, and she joined the faculty in the fall of 1969. At twenty-five, she was nearly a contemporary of the juniors and seniors she was teaching, and in that first year she was clearly a novelty. Invited to dinner at an eating club by a group of her

54 "Professor Emerita Karen Brazell Dies at Age 73," *Cornell Chronicle*, Jan. 23, 2012, http://news.cornell.edu/stories/2012/01/professor-emerita-karen-brazell-dies-age-73, and "Karen Woodard Brazell," http://prabook.org/web/person-view.html?profileId=434677, both accessed Aug. 27, 2015. See also *Daily Princetonian*, Mar. 15 and May 6, 1974.

students, she engaged in conversation with other students who assumed, until well into the meal, that she was someone's date—and were greatly embarrassed to discover that they had been talking so casually with a member of the faculty. A junior in one of Weiss's courses confided that she was his first woman teacher since sixth grade. One of her junior independent work advisees brought an apple to her during office hours. When she entered her classroom, the young men stood. At semester's end, in their course evaluations, the students took note of Weiss's gender and tried to make some sense of its effect on the classroom. "There is less idle joking in your class," one wrote, apparently approvingly. "You teach from a feminine point of view," another said.

As the number of women appointed to the faculty started to grow, some male students began to comment unguardedly on the new appointments. "I could never take a course with a woman" was a typical remark. "There was an interesting discussion," Weiss told a reporter, of the question "How could we listen to a lecture while being distracted by a woman's voice and form?"[55]

Suzanne Keller, a native of Vienna, had earned her B.A. at Hunter College in 1948 and her Ph.D. at Columbia in 1955. Before joining the Princeton faculty as a visiting lecturer in 1966, she had taught at a half-dozen other institutions. Her first book, *Beyond the Ruling Class*, was published in 1963, her second, *The Urban Neighborhood*, in 1968.[56]

Keller's appointment as the first female professor at Princeton was announced on May 5, 1968.[57] Her previous letters of appointment had followed the format for male faculty appointments: "Dear Sir," the engraved letterhead began. Even the appointment to tenure was insufficient to break the pattern: "Dear Sir," the secretary of the university, Jeremiah S. Finch, wrote, "I have the honor to inform you that at a meeting of the Trustees of Princeton

55 Giselle Price, "Women Faculty: Reshaping Princeton with Fresh Energies," *Thursday Magazine, Daily Princetonian*, Feb. 20, 1986.

56 Suzanne Keller curriculum vitae, Keller; *Town Topics* (Princeton, NJ), May 9, 1968, clipping in Keller.

57 Princeton University news release, May 6, 1968, Keller.

University held today you were appointed Professor . . . effective July 1, 1968."[58]

Keller later described the phenomenon of integrating the Princeton faculty:

> When I alighted in Princeton in the late 1960s, I was stunned. Princeton was so beautiful. . . . It was steeped in tradition and history and it had an aura of confidence and great possibilities. But . . . it was imbalanced in important respects. . . . Women were missing from the public Princeton. To be sure, women served as staff . . . but they were publicly invisible. So when I was admitted into the pantheon, it created something of an upheaval. . . . My tenure appointment challenged what had been assumed to be a timeless male fraternity. And the result . . . was nothing short of pandemonium.[59]

"The publicity generated by Princeton's decision to break through the gender barrier was stupefying," Keller wrote later. "I was hounded by photographers and by the ringing of the telephone at all hours for interviews."[60] One enterprising reporter phoned at 4 a.m. "Do you know what time it is?" Keller asked him. "Forget the time, lady, you're news," the reporter shot back.[61] "I often felt," she observed later, "that I had moved from being a person to becoming a CURIOSITY."[62] Local newspapers had some fun with the news. "Lady Professor Moves into Tigers' Den," one headline read. "Tiger's Growl Adds a Feminine Note," said another. "There's a Lady in the Tiger's Smile," a third declared.[63] The national press

58 Jeremiah S. Finch to Suzanne Keller, Apr. 15, 1967, Apr. 20, 1968, Keller.

59 Suzanne Keller, "Reflections on My 'Graduation' from Princeton," May 6, 2004, Keller.

60 Suzanne Keller, "Bridging Worlds: A Sociologist's Memoir," in Ann Goetting and Sarah Fenstermaker, eds., *Individual Voices, Collective Visions: Fifty Years of Women in Sociology* (Philadelphia: Temple University Press, 1995), p. 165, Keller.

61 Typescript, "Bridging Worlds: A Sociologist's Memoir," last revision, Oct. 12, 1992, Keller.

62 Suzanne Keller, Notes for Panel on Women at Princeton, W.I.L.D. Conference, Apr. 7, 1990, Keller.

63 *Star-Ledger* (Newark, NJ), May 6, 1969; unidentified clipping [May 1968]; and *Trenton Evening Times*, May 16, 1968, all clippings in Keller.

was more straightforward about it: The UPI account, published in the *Daily News* in New York, was headlined "Lady Prof for Princeton." The *San Francisco Chronicle* carried the news under the heading "Historical First for Princeton," and the *New York Times* said, simply, "First Woman Gets Princeton Tenure."[64]

Keller recognized the distance between one precedent-making faculty appointment and any regularization of gender relationships at Princeton. "To be the first of anything is not easy," she said. "You can't make a mistake; you're on display all the time. Your failings become attributed not to you but to all women." She said that she was "put on countless committees—and asked to represent woman WRIT LARGE." She was asked repeatedly, "Give us the woman's point of view." At such a moment, she said, "it's hard to argue gender theory."[65]

It was not that colleagues treated her badly. They "were very polite and many were very supportive."[66] But Princeton was "an institution run by men for men," where "women appeared in two main guises: (1) as weekend dates and (2) as subordinates—gofers, secretaries, librarians, lab assistants, cooks, and servers in the school cafeteria—all essential, even indispensable . . . but all showing women as second-class and therefore as secondary. If you saw only this anonymous army of assistants and servers you would probably conclude—without having to be told or being very prejudiced—that women cannot be too important and certainly cannot run things."

"Such beliefs were not unique to Princeton," Keller continued, "but until recently were quite typical of the society at large. . . . Despite prejudice and discrimination in the big world, women and men did live and work together day by day and cooperate in a myriad [of] ways. But at Princeton, women were invisible or discounted during the week and hysterically in evidence on weekends."[67]

64 *Daily News* (New York), May 6, 1968; *San Francisco Chronicle*, May 6, 1968; and *New York Times*, May 6, 1968, all clippings in Keller.

65 Keller, notes for Panel on Women at Princeton.

66 Ibid.

67 Suzanne Keller, "Of Times and Change: Happenings on the Way to Gender Equality," speech to Gilman School, Baltimore, MD, Apr. 21, 1982, Keller.

Keller taught the first courses on gender in Princeton's history: The Family and, later, Sex and Society. She said, "It was a hard struggle . . . the hardest thing I have ever done." Some students were simply not ready to think in terms of gender equity for Princeton, and they were not shy about saying so. Keller recalled that one student came to class during the second week of one course with "a list of 'conclusions' about genetic male superiority and female inferiority. . . . His mind was totally made up <u>before</u> he looked at the evidence!"[68]

But things changed quickly. Describing her first class in the second year of coeducation, Keller told a reporter for the *Daily Princetonian*, "It was like a breath of fresh air. There was questioning everywhere, questions of gender. Questions asking, 'Is this a revolution?' Of course there were still lots of letters protesting women, but there was a new ferment, fever and intellectual excitement."[69] There was a "heady climate" at Princeton in those early days, Keller said, remarking on "the sense of exhilaration . . . and the challenge of the new. One felt swept up in one of those grand assaults on the conventional wisdom <u>that transforms</u> everyone's life—forever. I think it added a vitality to this university—a scope and breadth it did not have before."[70]

Despite all the excitement, all the headiness, fundamentally changing Princeton would take much more than adding some number of women faculty and students. As Keller observed,

> Gender integration is not in the main a matter of <u>admission or entry</u> for the <u>individual</u> only. . . . It is a matter of a change in the culture of a place—the beliefs, assumptions, standards, and patterns of being and doing that have prevailed heretofore. . . . This is why the women students at first did not feel at home here—without knowing exactly why, and especially after having been told how <u>fortunate</u> they are. In the main, they had but <u>one</u> choice in an institution deeply imprinted

68 Keller, notes for Panel on Women at Princeton.
69 Quoted in Balestri, "25 Years of Coeducation," p. 6.
70 Keller, notes for Panel on Women at Princeton.

with a <u>masculine</u> culture, <u>masculine</u> standards of performance and ambition: Namely <u>adapt</u>, and <u>bend themselves to fit</u>, as well as possible, to the culture already in place. They were actors in an <u>androcentric play</u>.[71]

As administrators planned for the second year of coeducation, they surely were not thinking about the large, complex, subtle themes that Keller laid out. Rather, they focused on practical matters: the number of women who could be admitted, the balance between freshmen and transfer students, and the configuration of housing, dining, and social facilities for the near as well as the longer term.[72] They focused on remedying deficits of the first year, from the inadequate supply of restrooms to the absence of special health services for women to the lack of facilities and staffing to support varsity athletics, intramural sports, and physical education for women students.[73] They focused, too, on decisions taken in the first year that needed to be tweaked or completely rethought. Everyone knew that the experience of the first year needed improvement. As Neil Rudenstine, dean of students, said, "There were so many things we could not have anticipated," and there had been "inevitable missteps." Princeton had not been "ready to take a large number of women and make them feel at home."[74]

Halcy Bohen: "A Godsend"

Many of Princeton's plans had, of necessity, been made hastily. Many choices that had appeared to be sensible turned out to be at odds with what the women preferred. Women students gave Princeton administrators a lot of slack and credit. They understood that their situation was better than that of their counterparts at Yale, who told them that they "had to 'agitate' for everything they

71 Ibid.
72 W. G. Bowen, Planning for Coeducation: Issues to Be Decided, Oct. 2, 1969, attached to Bowen to All Concerned, Oct. 2, 1969, and Bowen to E. D. Sullivan et al., Dec. 1, 1969, both in Goheen, Box 94, Folder 1.
73 Levy-Warren interview; Herman interview.
74 Interview with Neil Rudenstine, Feb. 9, 2015, Princeton, NJ.

gained on that campus, from decent living quarters to good sports programs to equality in the classroom." At Princeton, by contrast, they found the atmosphere to be "welcoming and supportive," and "they never had to be militant to be heard."[75]

Emily Trenholm Fisher reflected later, "I think Princeton did a better job than Yale of adjusting and listening to us." Marion Freeman added, "Princeton was actually quite generous with us, a much more sophisticated and trusting attitude than one might have expected. The university recognized that they had not studied how they were going to go coed in a very detailed manner. They just sort of did it and acknowledged that there was much to be worked out."[76]

Halcy Bohen was a large part of the reason that Princeton listened so well. The small number of women admitted in the first year of coeducation had a significant upside in that Bohen could know all of the students personally, be on top of what was happening to them on a day-to-day basis, and respond quickly to their needs and concerns. As a result, Rudenstine observed, she "won the trust" of the women students.[77]

As Bohen noted later, women students "got a lot of attention and time. . . . By starting small, we learned a lot." It also helped that Bohen had the ear of Rudenstine and Bowen. They lived near one another, and they saw each other frequently as neighbors as well as colleagues. They built the kind of trust that helped them do their jobs. Rudenstine gave Bohen room to do what she thought necessary to make the women students feel welcome and supported by the university. She "kept pushing the envelope," he said, suggesting new initiatives that would never have occurred to him. The administration "knew that the first classes of women would feel displaced," Rudenstine said, but they did not know precisely what the issues would be. Bohen both identified the issues and offered proposals for improvement. Given the confidence she

75 Plump, "O Pioneers" ("agitate"); Robin Herman, "In the Wink of an Eyelash, Swish of a Skirt, Traditions Fall and Women Conquer Princeton," *Daily Princetonian,* June 20, 1970, p. 48 ("militant").

76 Fisher and Freeman, quoted in Plump, "O Pioneers."

77 Bohen interview; Rudenstine interview.

enjoyed from Rudenstine and Bowen, Bohen said that she "felt great support around her," which made the job of attending to Princeton's women students much easier to do.[78]

To women students, she was a godsend. Deedee Eisenberg '71 recalled later that Bohen "made a point of inviting me into her office and asking me how things were going and making sure I would come back regularly so that she could listen to any concerns I had. That was probably the best thing the University did."[79] Women students knew they could go to Bohen at any time. She hosted events at her home that brought students together with members of the faculty. She invited students in small groups for Sunday brunches. She queried them about their experiences and took seriously what they reported. Sitting around the dining room table, with Bohen's small children in evidence, Princeton's women undergraduates felt as though they were at home. The atmosphere made students comfortable voicing experiences and concerns they had no other way to express and they bonded with Bohen and with one another. The brunches "made us feel less lonely, more welcome," Marsha Levy recalled. They "really contributed to breaking down some of the barriers" that kept women so isolated from one another.[80]

Coeducation: The Second Year, 1970–1971

In February 1970, Goheen reconstituted his ad hoc committee on coeducation planning. An early result of the committee's work was that the university raised the hoped-for number of incoming women freshmen to 175 from the originally planned 160 and increased the final target for women undergraduates from 1,000 to 1,200.[81]

---

78 Ibid.

79 Merrell Noden, "Going Back: After 35 Years, the Pioneering Women of '71 Reconnect with Each Other," *Princeton Alumni Weekly* 106 (July 19, 2006): 38.

80 Levy-Warren interview. On Bohen's importance to the students, see also Herman interview. On the events hosted at Bohen's home, see Changes at Princeton since Coeducation, 1969–73, memorandum, Halcy Bohen to All Women in the Class of '73, June 8, 1973, Bowen president, Series 18.2, Box 397, Folder 4.

81 Meeting of Ad Hoc Group Concerned with Planning for Coeducation, William G. Bowen to Persons Listed Below, Feb. 17, 1970, Bowen provost, Box 18, Folder 2; Bowen, handwritten notes, Planning for Coeducation, Mar. 18, 1970, Bowen provost, Box 18, Folder 7; Minutes of Meeting of Ad Hoc Committee on Coeducation, Mar. 18, 1970,

Coeducation brought a spike in applications for the class of 1974. The number from women quadrupled over the previous year, and the number from men rose by 13 percent, "a steeper increase," director of admission John T. Osander reported later, "than in any of the baby boom years of the early 1960's." It was "Princeton's first significant increase in male applications in five years"—providing strong confirmation for the argument that co-education would make a real difference in the university's attrac-tiveness to secondary school students, as the Patterson report had argued. Moreover, the number of the candidates for admission considered outstanding, both academically and non-academically, a group that had remained constant at about 400 to 500 students from 1965 to 1969, doubled in 1970.[82]

For the second year of coeducation, in addition to the 175 new freshman women, there would be 85 women transfer students and critical languages students, for a total of over 400 undergraduate women on campus—a number not large in itself but very large in comparison with the 170 women undergraduates in 1969–70.[83] The women would be housed in a half-dozen dormitories. A section of the Princeton Inn, with bathrooms located within bedroom suites, would allow for experimentation with mixing of male and female rooms to learn "whether such a pattern [could] be satisfactory."[84] The diversity of living options would "respond to the preferences of different kinds of students at different stages of their careers."[85]

ODUS, Box 31, Folder 3; *Daily Princetonian*, Apr. 10 (editorial) and 14, 1970; A Status Report on Planning for Coeducation at Princeton: Report of a Special Committee at the End of the First Year of Coeducation, Sept. 1970, Goheen Box 97, Folder 1.

82 Princeton University, Office of Admission, Annual Report, 1969–1970, pp. 1, 3, Admission Office, Box 10.

83 Ibid., pp. 6, B-1. For the 1970–71 enrollment, see Princeton data from Princeton University Registrar's Office. The total number of critical languages students in 1970–71 was eighteen; registrar data do not show the breakdown by gender. In any event, the num-ber of women critical languages students would have been quite small.

84 Princeton University, Minutes of a Stated Meeting of the Executive Committee, Feb. 20, 1970, pp. 4–5, Princeton trustees, Series 1, Vol. 68 (source of the quote); Coedu-cational Dormitory Arrangements, 1970–71, Deans Bohen and Rudenstine to Undergrad-uate Life Committee, Feb. 27, 1970, ODUS, Box 31, Folder 2.

85 A Status Report on Planning for Coeducation at Princeton: Report of a Special Committee at the End of the First Year of Coeducation, Sept. 1970, p. 5, Goheen Box 97,

Departing from the practice of segregating women in separate residential facilities required some explanation to the trustees. Rudenstine assured them that experience at other schools demonstrated that housing men and women together "does not intensify social and sexual pressures on students, but rather seems to foster the kind of friendship relations that actually discourage romantic activities."[86]

As the new academic year began, the ad hoc committee on coeducation planning announced a plan to further accelerate the growth in the number of women students. Instead of the initial target of 650 women by 1973–74, the committee said that it should be possible to enroll more than 800, an increase made possible by a new plan to build 150 bed spaces south of the Princeton Inn, which had both the physical space for new construction and the capacity to feed additional students. That, together with some rescheduling of classes at the lunch hour to enable a larger number of students to be fed in commons and the student center, as well as re-rating of existing dormitory space, would make the extra growth feasible.[87]

In February 1971, the new chairman of the trustee executive committee, R. Manning Brown '36, chairman and chief executive officer of the New York Life Insurance Company, announced that the $10 million initial funding objective for coeducation had been met. With a $5 million bequest from the estate of Cyrus H. McCormick 1879, the university had been able to match the pledge of $4 million that Laurance Rockefeller had made as a memorial to

---

Folder 1; Women's Dormitory Residences for 1970–71, Neil L. Rudenstine memorandum to Trustee Committee on Student Life, Jan. 12, 1970, ODUS, Box 31, Folder 2 ("respond to the preferences").

86 Robert F. Goheen to William G. Bowen, Jan. 9, 1970; Women's Dormitory Residences for 1970–71, Neil L. Rudenstine memorandum to Trustee Committee on Student Life, Jan. 12, 1970, both in ODUS, Box 31, Folder 2; Princeton University, Minutes of a Stated Meeting of the Executive Committee, Feb. 20, 1970, p. 5.

87 A Status Report on Planning for Coeducation at Princeton: Report of a Special Committee at the End of the First Year of Coeducation, Sept. 1970, pp. 20ff., Goheen, Box 97, Folder 1; John M. Fenton, "Coeducation: An Interim Report," *Princeton Alumni Weekly* 71 (Nov. 24, 1970): 6–7.

his grandmother, Laura Spelman Rockefeller. Other gifts totaling $1 million completed the total.[88]

With the funding in hand, the administration took every opportunity to find ways to accommodate larger numbers of women students. The proposed target for enrollment for freshman women in 1971–72 increased from 200 to 300 and the target for transfer women from 80 to 90.[89] With the opening of the school year, there were 327 freshman women and a total of 751 regularly enrolled women in all four classes, for a male-female ratio of 4.2 to 1. And there were a handful of critical languages students on campus for the final year of that program.[90]

The increase in numbers, together with the dispersal of women among different dormitories, made their lives much better. Robin Herman, writing in the *Daily Princetonian*'s freshman issue, said, "The second year of coeducation was decidedly easier on the girls than the first year. The most important feature was the restoration of the girls' anonymity."[91] With more women on campus, the simple fact of what women saw when they walked around changed significantly. There were "so many more girls," Deborah Leff said. "You're not all alone. . . . The guys don't hang around the dorm to pick up women like they used to do at Pyne Hall last year." And with the increase in numbers, "the social pressure has eased tremendously." Halcy Bohen reported, "The novelty is over this year, and people are feeling less tension. I've had a number of girls come up to me and say: 'I'm so much more comfortable this

88 Princeton University news release, Feb. 21, 1971, Subject Files Princeton, Coeducation, Box 376, Folder 4.

89 Minutes of Meeting of the Board of Trustees, Apr. 17, 1971, pp. 4–7, and Revised Recommendations on Coeducational Enrollments, Robert F. Goheen to The Trustees, Apr. 13, 1971, Appendix A, Princeton trustees, Series 1, Vol. 69.

90 Princeton data from Princeton University Registrar's Office; Recommendations for Women and Married Student Housing, 1971–72, Halcy H. Bohen to Members of the Undergraduate Life Committee, Feb. 10, 1971, ODUS, Box 31, Folder 2; *Daily Princetonian*, Nov. 24, 1971. The total number of critical languages students in 1971–72 was ten; again, registrar data do not show the breakdown by gender. In any event, the number of women critical languages students would have been extremely small.

91 Robin Herman, "Women Still Find Way Difficult as Coeducation Grows," *Daily Princetonian*, June 19, 1971, p. 33. For other testimony to the same effect, see Fields oral history, passim; Emden oral history, passim.

year—I feel like I belong here.' Or they say . . . 'I can't imagine myself anyplace else.'"[92]

That said, there was still more work to do to normalize women's experiences at Princeton. Robin Herman explained in the *Daily Princetonian*,

> If a Princeton coed is not a distinctive individual when she comes here, she is forced to be by her situation. She cannot fade into the woodwork, for she goes to a school that . . . is not truly "coeducational" yet. The process of evolving into such a coeducational institution demands a commitment from her that will make her four years at Princeton a bit more strenuous than four years at a school where the birth pains of coeducation are over. . . . There are still many "firsts" that must be made before a female student can feel at home at Princeton University. She is still waiting to be able to share an equal claim on the place with her male peers.[93]

But important steps were being taken toward that goal. Women were participating in a range of extracurricular activities. They became reporters for the *Princetonian*; members of the glee club, Triangle club, and band; Orange Key tour guides; broadcasters for radio station WPRB; and officers of student government. The first female a capella singing group, the Tigerlilies, was established in 1971, and the first coed group, the Katzenjammers, in 1973.

A women's locker room was opened in the gym. Free gynecological services were provided, and, later, a sex education, counseling, and health clinic (SECH) was set up. A big sister program was established for entering freshmen, and a resident adviser (RA) program matched individual juniors or seniors with small groups of freshmen to provide advice and support as the new students became acculturated to the university. Some of these programs, initiated with women in mind, turned out to be important for men as well. That was true of SECH and the RA program; it was also

---

92 Quoted in Fenton, "Coeducation: An Interim Report," 7–8.
93 Herman, "Women Still Find Way Difficult as Coeducation Grows," p. 33.

true of modern dance, where the first course, instituted on the assumption that it would be especially attractive to women, enrolled a majority of men. As Bohen reflected, "What men thought women needed turned out to be what men needed too."[94]

Two Princeton women, Marjory Gengler '73 and Helena Novakova '72, won first and third places, respectively, in the eastern intercollegiate tennis tournament for women in the fall of 1970.[95] Gengler later recalled an afternoon in 1971 when the men's and women's tennis teams were playing at home, the men on four courts in the front, the women on four courts in the back. When Gengler's match began, the men's coach, John Conroy, "stopped one of the men's matches and moved Gengler onto a front court—a symbolic gesture not lost on the crowd."[96]

In terms of residential life, intermingling men's and women's rooms at the Princeton Inn appeared to be working well. Maureen Ferguson '73 said that the inn had a "marvelous, relaxed, family kind of atmosphere. . . . Everybody leaves his door open. In the evening, we take a break from studying and meet in one guy's room for coffee." Stephen Isaacs '72 said, "There are girls on the same floor as guys, and you just walk across the hall and rap with a girl about your class reading. You don't get hung up about girls being a separate species."[97]

For the first time, upperclass women had opportunities to join the Prospect Street eating clubs. In the spring of 1970, a handful of women had been accepted at three clubs, Campus, Charter, and Colonial. Now every club debated whether to admit women to their membership, and eight of them—Campus, Cap and Gown, Charter, Cloister, Colonial, Dial Lodge, Quadrangle,

---

94 Changes at Princeton since Coeducation, 1969–73; Debbie Goldstein, "Traditional Male Bastions Fall as Women Infiltrate Activities," *Daily Princetonian*, June 19, 1971, p. 34; "Orange Key," *Bric-a-Brac*, 1970, p. 78; Kemper oral history, passim; Emden oral history, pp. 11–12; Bohen, quoted in "Celebration of Coeducation at Princeton," *Princeton Weekly Bulletin* 78 (Apr. 10, 1989): 2.

95 Fenton, "Coeducation: An Interim Report," 8.

96 David Williamson, "Narrowing the Gap in Women's Athletics," *Princeton Alumni Weekly*, Jan. 11 and 25, 1989, quoted in Catherine Keyser, *Transforming the Tiger: A Celebration of Undergraduate Women at Princeton University* (Princeton University, 2001), p. 66.

97 Quoted in Fenton, "Coeducation: An Interim Report," 8.

and Tower—did so during the selection process, known locally as "bicker," in 1971. Cannon Club remained all-male until it closed for lack of membership in 1975, leaving three clubs—Cottage, Ivy, and Tiger Inn—as single-sex hold-outs.[98]

Continuing Challenges and Further Progress

For all of the improvements that resulted from larger numbers of women, their residential dispersal around the campus, and their participation in a growing array of activities, Princeton women and Princeton men still had learning to do about living together in relative harmony. Occasional flashpoints illustrated the complexities of gender relationships on a college campus still in the process of becoming fully coeducational. In March 1971, two seniors, Christine Stansell and Susan Petty, entered the room of a classmate, Gary Oleson, in Wilson College, and slashed the *Playboy* pin-ups on his wall. Petty said that they were following "a tradition of political disobedience that goes back to Thoreau and Gandhi."[99] The two women had been "incredibly grossed out" by the pin-ups and had decided to take matters into their own hands.[100]

At a meeting of the discipline committee, Stansell and Petty pasted forty *Playboy* images on the wall, along with an obscene sign they said they had found on the door of one of their rooms. The committee decided that slashing Oleson's pin-ups was "a serious infringement of important personal rights," and the two women were placed on disciplinary probation until the end of the term.[101] They were, the humor magazine *The Princeton Tiger* joked, "the first martyrs of the women's liberation movement at Princeton."[102]

98 *Daily Princetonian*, Dec. 4 and 11, 1970; Luther T. Munford '71, "On the Campus," *Princeton Alumni Weekly* 71 (Jan. 26, 1971): 8; Robert Earle '72, "On the Campus," *Princeton Alumni Weekly* 72 (Dec. 7, 1971): 5; Joel Achenbach, "Traditions Fall as Women Join the Clubs," *Daily Princetonian* supplement, "Women at Princeton: The First Ten Years," Nov. 1979, p. S-6.

99 Quoted in *Daily Princetonian*, Apr. 8, 1971.

100 Quoted in Andrew Wilson '72, "On the Campus," *Princeton Alumni Weekly* 71 (Apr. 13, 1971): 7.

101 *Daily Princetonian*, Apr. 8, 1971.

102 "Paradise Ripped-Off," *Princeton Tiger*, May 1971, p. 20, Princeton publications, Series 3, Box 9.

Over time, Bohen tried to create an environment in which women students could talk about the experience of being women at Princeton, their hopes for the future, and the challenges of balancing family and career. The idea was to have conversations that mixed women undergraduates, graduate students, faculty and staff members, and some women from the town. Bohen hoped to encourage undergraduates "to think ahead beyond their time here, and thereby to make use of their student years in a way that would stand them in good stead over a lifetime." For the adult women, the conversations were stimulating, and they enjoyed meeting women they had not known. But Bohen's hopes and expectations did not always match the more immediate concerns of Princeton's women undergraduates. A forum planned for orientation week in 1970, for example, drew an enthusiastic group of adults but a small number of students. "I think the main lesson learned from my point of view," Bohen later reflected, "was that for freshmen discussion stressing the whole of their lives beyond college is premature; they are much more concerned about immediate problems of functioning in this environment and have little inclination to think beyond first classes and tests and dates and roommates." In contrast, bringing women seniors together with women faculty and administrators worked well, given students' readiness at the end of their college years "to evaluate their experience here at Princeton, to examine their own life-views at the moment and to think ahead about their next steps."[103]

Whether or not women students were ready to confront the issues Bohen was trying to raise, it was an important effort. As Bohen explained, "'Conflicting signals,' summoning young women to full-time careers and at the same time to domestic responsibilities, make this a confusing time to be a young woman in America. . . . American girls are not only taught to achieve and compete in school using the same skills and measures that boys use, they now—by the coeducation of places like Princeton—are encouraged . . . to aspire to the same . . . achievements as the best

103 Women Students, Halcy H. Bohen to Neil Rudenstine, Jan. 6, 1971, ODUS, Box 31, Folder 2 (source of the quotes); Changes at Princeton since Coeducation, 1969–73.

young males in America." But they were still expected to become wives and mothers, and it was hard for them to know how to balance roles and set priorities.[104]

Some women students were focused on such questions. In the fall of 1971, a small group of women created a women's center, located on the second floor of Green Hall Annex on Nassau Street at the corner of Washington Road. The point, said Marsha A. Rosenthal '74, one of the founders, was to "[make] women aware of themselves and of the new ideas being brought out concerning the changing sex roles in society."[105] The center sponsored speakers, consciousness-raising groups, reading and discussion groups, movies, self-defense training, and meetings about issues of concern to women on campus. It embraced political activism in such areas as affirmative action, sexual harassment, and women's studies. The center received university funding in 1974, the same year it moved into more commodious space when the annex was renovated and renamed Aaron Burr Hall. In 1978, the dean of students' office took oversight responsibility for the center and hired a full-time director.[106]

Recognizing that undergraduate women needed access to successful older women who could serve as role models, the university had begun to increase the number of adult women in the community. By 1971–72, almost three dozen women were on the faculty, nearly half of them in the professorial ranks.[107] That October, the board of trustees seated its first two women members: Mary St. John Douglas, a Bennington alumna working as a research chemist at the American Red Cross Blood Research Laboratory

104 Princeton University news release, Jan. 30, 1972, Subject Files Princeton, Coeducation, Box 376, Folder 4.

105 Bob Musen, "Coed Views New Female Roles," *Daily Princetonian*, Feb. 23, 1972, p. 1.

106 Aida Rodriguez, Report on the Activities of the Princeton Women's Center, Apr. 26, 1973, PUWO, Box 1, Folder Undergraduate Women's Task Force; Lynn Chancer, "Feminist Activities: Why the Lack of Involvement?," *Daily Princetonian*, Feb. 28, 1975, pp. 1, 4, 5, 8; Martha Kramer, "Women's Center Coordinator Sheets Seeks Less Political Image for Group," *Daily Princetonian*, Sept. 15, 1977, p. 8; Keyser, *Transforming the Tiger*, p. 58.

107 *Daily Princetonian*, Apr. 23, 1971; Dean of the Faculty records, Princeton University, courtesy of Toni Turano.

in Bethesda, Maryland; and Susan Savage Speers, a Bryn Mawr graduate working as an English and Latin teacher at New Canaan Country School in Connecticut. Both women were wives, daughters, and sisters of Princeton alumni.[108]

The next year, with the changing of the guard in the Princeton presidency as William Bowen succeeded Robert Goheen, Sheldon Hackney, a historian of the American South, took Bowen's place as provost and Neil Rudenstine replaced Edward Sullivan as dean of the college. And there was now a woman in the senior administrative ranks. Adele Smith Simmons, a Radcliffe graduate with a Ph.D. from Oxford, dean of students at Jackson College (the women's college of Tufts University), had been appointed dean of student affairs. That fall, the fourth coeducational undergraduate class matriculated at Princeton, with 788 men and 299 women, bringing the total number of undergraduate women on campus to 975, or 24 percent of the undergraduate student body.[109]

Revisiting the "Multifarious Freshwomen"

With the approaching graduation of the class of 1973, the media paid considerable attention to the women, what they had experienced, and what they had accomplished. The *Princeton Alumni Weekly* went back to interview the "multifarious freshwomen," seven women it had profiled in October 1969. Margery Hite would graduate a year behind her classmates; she had taken a year off to attend college near her home in Washington State. An anthropology major and a member of the new Princeton University Women's Organization (PUWO), she said, "I guess my interest in women's issues originated in my experiences freshman year. . . . I found the whole Princeton tradition so chauvinistic—the custom of spooning [men banging spoons on tables when women entered the eating commons], for example, and being yelled at from windows as we walked by. It was so medieval!"

---

108 Princeton University news release, Oct. 19, 1971, Subject Files Princeton, Coeducation, Box 376, Folder 4; *Daily Princetonian*, Sept. 14, 1971.
109 Princeton data from Princeton University Registrar's Office.

Laurie Watson, an independent concentrator in comparative political socialization, still headed for medical school, said, "Coeducation at Princeton has become a success, mainly due to the attitude and type of girls coming in now. They're much more well-rounded than we were—they're sports-minded or musically talented, for example, as well as academic." Stephanie Fowler, an art history major, said, "Ever since I was little I've wanted to be the first woman to do something. I was one of the first women to go to a male college, but I'm not satisfied with that. I guess I'll have to be the first woman to do something else." Celeste Brickler, one of twelve black women in the class, said, as Hite and Watson had, "Princeton is a more relaxed place now. The first year it was a male institution with a few women tacked on; now it tends more to fit the image of a coed institution. . . . I feel free here to be a person. I have a lot more confidence in myself now, derived mostly from social situations I've dealt with." Deborah Leff, a Woodrow Wilson School concentrator, said, "Princeton's attitude toward women has changed drastically. . . . The first year we were not an integral part of campus life. We were a curiosity then, not a changing influence. The more women there are at Princeton, the better it gets."[110]

At graduation, the women of the class of 1973 could take considerable satisfaction in their accomplishments. They had outperformed their male counterparts academically. Women accounted for 18 percent of the class but 32 percent of elections to Phi Beta Kappa.[111] Princeton's sole Marshall Scholarship in 1973 had been awarded to a woman, Annalyn Swan, and of three Fulbright recipients, one was a woman. Marsha Levy had won the M. Taylor Pyne Honor Prize and had been elected the first woman young alumni trustee. Women had given Princeton athletics a huge shot in the

---

110 "The Multifarious Seniors," interviews by Ellen Foley James, *Princeton Alumni Weekly* 73 (Jan. 23, 1973): 12–17.

111 On outperformance, see William G. Bowen's account of the annual report of the dean of the college for 1971–72, where Dean Edward Sullivan "conclude[d] that women consistently outperform men in terms of academic performance." Coeducation, memorandum, WGB to Speech File, n.d., Bowen president, Series 18.2, Box 397, Folder 4. On Phi Beta Kappa, see James Axtell, *The Making of Princeton University: From Woodrow Wilson to the Present* (Princeton, NJ, and Oxford: Princeton University Press, 2006), p. 163, n. 118.

arm. They fielded undefeated teams in tennis, squash, and swimming; the women's sailing team had become "a national power"; and the women's crew won the eastern championship. The *Princeton Alumni Weekly* featured Marjory Gengler '73, captain of the tennis team. The legend on the cover: "Princeton's Best Athlete."[112]

"Next September," Jane Leifer '73 wrote in the *Princeton Alumni Weekly*, "all the males at this university will have applied here knowing that it is a coeducational campus. . . . It means that no one will really talk about coeducation and bad times, and the scars which have amazed and obsessed so many of us. It means that I would love to be a freshman, even again, even at Princeton."[113]

---

112 "Pioneering Women in '73 Look Back on Era of Major Changes Here," *Town Topics* (Princeton, NJ), June 11, 1973, clipping in Subject Files Princeton, Coeducation, Box 376, Folder 4; "Women at Princeton Outdo the Men," *New York Times*, June 10, 1973, clipping in Bowen president, Series 2.4, Box 104, Folder 14.

113 Leifer, "Trials of the Coed 100," 11.

10

Harvard-Radcliffe: Playing in the "Big Yard" with the Boys

While men and women were learning to go to school together at Princeton, Harvard and Radcliffe were trying out new forms of cooperation. The Harvard and Radcliffe presidents stood side by side in delivering welcoming speeches to entering freshmen and baccalaureate addresses to graduating seniors. Women began to live in Harvard houses and in freshman dorms in Harvard Yard. Parents of Radcliffe and Harvard freshmen joined in the same parents' weekend. Women students became eligible to compete for prizes and traveling and other postgraduate fellowships reserved previously for men. Women and men had equal claim on tickets to major football games. The athletic departments were merged. Women began, very, very slowly, to be appointed to the Harvard faculty. Radcliffe alumnae gained the right to vote in elections for the Harvard board of overseers, and the first two women took their seats on that governing body.[1]

---

1 Telephone interview with Derek Bok, Jan. 21, 2015. In Subject Files Radcliffe, Series 5, Box 14, Folder 22, see Harvard and Radcliffe Colleges, excerpt from Report of the President of Harvard College and Reports of Departments, 1972–73, and Harvard and Radcliffe Colleges, report of John B. Fox, Jr., to the Dean of the Faculty of Arts and Sciences, for the academic year 1978–79. In Bunting, Box 52, Folder 840, see Mary I. Bunting to Parents of Radcliffe Class of 1975, Sept. 14, 1971. In Bunting, Box 51, Folder 822, see minutes, meeting of the President and Fellows of Harvard College, Oct. 4, 1971, and Feb. 28, 1972, and Harvard University news release, Nov. 22, 1971. In Bunting, Box 47, Folder 743, see Faculty of Arts and Sciences, Harvard University, Report of the Committee on the Status of Women in the Faculty of Arts and Sciences, Apr. 1971, and minutes, meeting of the Faculty of Arts and Sciences, May 25, 1971. See also Ruth Glushien, "On Campus," *Radcliffe Quarterly* 56 (Mar. 1972): 19.

Radcliffe student views of the evolving relationship between the two institutions were mixed. The student government established a committee on the preservation of Radcliffe College to find ways to maintain the integrity of the college.[2] But as the undergraduate correspondent for the *Radcliffe Quarterly* reported, there was "no Jonah complex" at Radcliffe. Students did not "feel swallowed in Harvard's administrative belly." Instead, she said, "life at Radcliffe has undergone a real renaissance, with an increased interest in quadrangle activities and a sense of long-delayed acceptance into the university community."[3]

The Question of the Ratio

One of Derek Bok's first initiatives as president of Harvard had to do with the numbers of men and women undergraduates. He knew that the 4-to-1 male-female ratio was "a big problem"; he knew, too, that it had not been fixed as a matter of policy but rather had grown out of Radcliffe's history. Radcliffe had neither space nor resources to accommodate more students. With the experiment in coresidential living underway, however, the ratio was increasingly difficult to sustain, "especially in an era when the rights of women had suddenly become a very prominent issue."

Bok understood that declaring equal access was "too radical a step." Different constituencies had irreconcilable positions on the subject. Harvard alumni were determined that there be no decrease in the number of men admitted; students wanted equal access without increasing the size of the college. As well, Harvard alumni supported annual giving at a per capita rate over four times that of Radcliffe alumnae. Doing anything to disrupt that loyalty could be expensive for a university—like all universities—whose financial future was uncertain.[4]

2 Barbara Fischer Voss, "These Last Two Complicated Years," *Radcliffe Quarterly* 55 (Aug. 1971): 10.

3 Glushien, "On Campus," 19.

4 Admission of Undergraduates: A Statement by President Derek C. Bok, Oct. 5, 1971, Bunting, Box 51, Folder 818; Bok oral history, pp. 2–3 (source of the quotes).

And what Bok surely knew, but did not remark on, was that Harvard's closest competitors, Princeton and Yale, were threatening to overtake Harvard in terms of reducing the ratio of men to women. Princeton, where the ratio had been 19 to 1 in 1969–70, had closed the gap to 8 to 1 in 1970–71. Yale, which had started with a ratio of 7 men to 1 woman in 1969–70, had reached just under 5 to 1 the next year. By the third year of coeducation, Princeton's ratio was slightly higher than 4 to 1, and Yale's 4.5 to 1.[5] With these institutions competing for the best students, Harvard could not afford to wait to address the ratio.

Taking advantage of the "honeymoon" period of his new presidency, Bok chose to "make a halfway step" to get started, declaring an interim ratio of 2.5 to 1 by presidential "fiat" while a committee worked to determine a sustainable arrangement for the long run. Bok's fiat meant that the number of women in each entering class would increase from slightly more than 300 to approximately 450 (numbers still small in the context of Princeton and Yale) during the first four years of the new Harvard-Radcliffe agreement, with a modest decrease in the number of men and a modest overall increase in the size of the undergraduate student body.[6] The Radcliffe and Harvard admission offices moved into renovated quarters in Byerly Hall in the Radcliffe yard, permitting easy cross-office communication and increased sharing of certain activities and initiatives, a prelude to a later time when the two offices would be merged.[7] (Straightforward as such a merger may sound, it was fraught with complexity. The salary of the highest-paid person on the Radcliffe side matched the salary of the lowest-paid person on the Harvard staff. And when very

5 Princeton data from Princeton University Registrar's Office; Yale data from Yale College Registrar / IPEDS Fall Headcount Surveys, Yale University Office of Institutional Research.

6 Admission of Undergraduates: A Statement by President Derek C. Bok, Oct. 5, 1971, Bunting, Box 51, Folder 818; Bok oral history, pp. 2–3 ("halfway step"); Bok interview ("honeymoon," "fiat"). See also, on the subject of future admission policy, especially with respect to gender, memorandum, Derek Bok to Henry Rosovsky, Matina Horner, and Robert Kiely, Aug. 1973, Horner, Box 6, Folder 18.

7 Matina Horner remarks, meeting of the Board of Overseers of Harvard College, Mar. 12, 1973, attached to Robert Shenton to Horner, Apr. 27, 1973, Horner, Box 7, Folder 1; Bunting oral history, interview no. 9, Oct. 25, 1978, pp. 255–56.

experienced women from the Radcliffe staff were assigned to cover geographical areas for the combined office, some Harvard alumni objected—"We don't want a woman, she doesn't know anything about Harvard."[8])

A Legacy of Success—but a Remaining Anomaly

Nathan Pusey retired from the presidency of Harvard having accomplished closer integration of Harvard and Radcliffe. He had succeeded in admitting to the Harvard graduate school of arts and sciences women who would otherwise have matriculated for graduate study at Radcliffe. On his watch, Harvard had begun awarding degrees to all Radcliffe students, Radcliffe undergraduates had begun taking part in Harvard's commencement, the separate administrative boards had been dissolved and a joint Harvard-Radcliffe administrative board established, and Harvard and Radcliffe had embarked on the early stages of coresidential living. In short, undergraduates at Harvard and Radcliffe studied together in the same classes, had the option of living in the same dormitories, participated in the same extracurricular activities, graduated in the same commencement ceremonies, and earned the same bachelor's degrees.

The same accomplishments could also be credited to Polly Bunting, who had seen to the creation of a Radcliffe house system, the renovation of existing dormitories and the building of a new set of residential facilities at Currier House, the integration of faculty and tutors into Radcliffe houses, and the building of Hilles library, which served Radcliffe women and also attracted Harvard men to the Radcliffe quad. Moreover, she had created the Radcliffe Institute, a pioneering vehicle through which talented adult women had the time, opportunity, and support to engage fully in intellectual pursuits or creative work that would shape their lives and careers.

But the remaining anomaly at Harvard and Radcliffe—two separate corporate structures, with separate governing boards, endowments, budgets, and administrative arrangements—had not

8 Mary Anne Schwalbe, in ML Bundy oral history, July 12, 2005, pp. 19–20, 23.

been addressed before Pusey left office. Both Pusey and Bunting wanted to effect a merger, but they were unable to accomplish it. Pusey's freedom of action was limited in significant part by the Vietnam War–related turmoil that rocked the Harvard campus from November 1966 through April 1969. Calling in the police to clear University Hall in the wake of the student takeover had been hugely controversial, with damage to Pusey's credibility in the corporation as well as the faculty. It also resulted in the foreshortening of Pusey's term as president, which was originally intended to run until he reached retirement age in 1973. In March 1970, however, he announced that he would step down in June 1971. Buffeted by forces largely external to Harvard, unable smoothly to manage the university amidst the turmoil those forces caused on campus, Pusey lost the authority and the maneuvering room to lean on the Harvard faculty to embrace the internal rearrangements required for merger. And Bunting, who had no faculty of her own and no independent authority over the Harvard faculty, could not herself have led them to a different conclusion. With the reluctance of many Radcliffe trustees to relinquish what they considered to be fundamental aspects of Radcliffe's identity, it is clear why something so seemingly straightforward as merger could be so difficult to achieve.[9]

Matina Horner: *The New President of Radcliffe*

On July 1, 1971, the first day of Bok's term as president, Bunting and Bok signed the new amendment to the 1943 agreement, which effected the administrative and financial arrangements proposed in the report of the joint committee.[10] Paul Buck, the historian who had been dean of the faculty of arts and sciences at Harvard

9 On the anger directed at Pusey and his early departure from the presidency, see Morton Keller and Phyllis Keller, *Making Harvard Modern: The Rise of America's University*, updated ed. (New York: Oxford University Press, 2007), pp. 320ff., 327, 336.

10 1971 Amendment to Agreement Between President and Fellows of Harvard College and Trustees of Radcliffe College, executed July 1, 1971, Subject Files Radcliffe, Series 5, Box 15, Folder 21. See also Radcliffe College news release, July 4, 1971, Bunting, Box 48, Folder 776, where Bunting and Bok comment on the revised agreement.

when the 1943 agreement was concluded, wrote to Bunting, "You leave to your successor a Radcliffe fully developed and prepared to share actively in whatever Harvard University has in store for it in the years ahead. You brought to the job just the right traits—(too long of a list to cite as a whole)—among which wisdom, vision, complete understanding [of] the University's role, courage, humor when the going was rough, vigor and persistent consistency were outstanding. You leave office with the admiration and affection of the academic world."[11]

Coeducation, then, had been functionally achieved at Harvard and Radcliffe when Bunting left office in 1972; merger was yet to come. The summer of 1972 brought the arrival of a new president for Radcliffe, the psychologist Matina Souretis Horner, an assistant professor of clinical psychology best known for her scholarship on women's fear of success. Bok made plain at the time of Horner's inauguration that "the future of Radcliffe is ultimately for Radcliffe to decide." He said, "To merge or not to merge is clearly *not* the question. . . . The critical problem is to identify the special needs of Radcliffe women within the University and to seek creative forms of organization that will insure that these needs are adequately protected and imaginatively served." These needs, Bok said, might involve living arrangements for women, health services, counseling and career guidance, material in the curriculum, research on problems of special concern to women, and educational opportunities for women at different life stages.[12]

Horner could comfortably embrace Bok's agenda. In anticipation of the review that was scheduled for 1974–75, Bok and Horner charged a committee of faculty, administrators, alumni/ae, students, Harvard overseers, and Radcliffe trustees, chaired by physics professor Karl Strauch, to begin working in the spring of 1974 to assess the appropriateness of current admission policies (should there continue to be a "fixed ratio" of men to women, should there be "some form of sex-blind admissions," or should

11 Paul Buck to Mary I. Bunting, Apr. 25, 1971, Bunting, Box 46, Folder 742.
12 "Bok: 'The Future of Radcliffe Is Ultimately for Radcliffe to Decide,'" *Harvard University Gazette* 68 (Nov. 24, 1972): 1–2, clipping in Subject Files Radcliffe, Series 5, Box 24, Folder 34.

there be, in the extreme case, "a one-to-one ratio"?); the adequacy and appropriateness of financial aid programs; the effectiveness of current administrative arrangements (some offices and services had been combined as a result of the 1971 agreement, whereas some—like admissions—had been left separate); and "the educational needs of women" (what were the "distinctive curricular, counseling, housing and other needs of women undergraduates," and "what institutional arrangements and programs" should be put in place to meet those needs?).[13]

At the annual meeting of the Harvard alumni association in June 1974, Bok spoke about "pressing issues affecting the role of women" at Harvard and Radcliffe. When the class of 1974 arrived at Harvard, he said, "Only 20% were women, and no effort was made to explain why women alone were subject to a seemingly arbitrary limit on the number admitted. Only one of the four hundred tenured faculty in the College was a woman, and even she was appointed to a chair restricted to members of her sex. Outside of the Radcliffe administration, no women occupied a high administrative post in the Faculty of Arts & Sciences."

These issues, Bok continued, needed to be confronted, and the Strauch committee would be making proposals that the university would be debating in the months to come. As for governance, it would be a mistake to "devote too much attention to the symbolic importance of the prerogatives of Governing Boards or the ownership of endowments." What was at stake, instead, was the fact that Radcliffe and Harvard were "united in a common enterprise of overriding importance: how to provide the best possible education to our undergraduates—men and women alike. With this aim in mind, our common task must be to devise a system of governance that will produce the soundest educational decisions, the least amount of bureaucracy and red tape, and the most appropriate safeguards to insure equality for our women students."[14]

13 Derek C. Bok and Matina Horner to Karl Strauch, Dec. 18, 1973, Horner, Box 8, Folder 5.

14 Harvard University news release, Text of remarks prepared for delivery by President Derek C. Bok at the Annual Meeting of the Associated Harvard Alumni in Tercentenary Theatre, Harvard Yard, on June 12, 1974, Horner, Box 24, Folder 3.

For all of Horner's concurrence with the agenda Bok laid out, she was uncomfortable with the current state of the corporate arrangements between Radcliffe and Harvard. The 1971 agreement had given Harvard control of Radcliffe's day-to-day operations along with all of Radcliffe's endowment and tuition income. But the financial arrangements were not fully clear, and Horner was not persuaded that the policies or the numbers were right. It was not easy to determine which expenses belonged to Radcliffe and which "should be covered by Harvard." Harvard seemed to be making all the decisions about what to put on the Radcliffe budget, how to credit Radcliffe income against Radcliffe expenses, and the amount of the deficit for which Radcliffe was said to be responsible. And male students at Harvard still had access to facilities and services that were not yet available to women. Horner believed that Radcliffe was actually "covering much more than the marginal cost of educating the women." She set about the painstaking work of understanding Radcliffe's endowment and budgets in order to make a case to right the financial relationship between the two institutions.[15]

Horner believed that Bunting had gone too far in folding Radcliffe into Harvard. The mission, Horner said, was to achieve equal opportunity for women at Harvard. But it was hard for people to understand what *equal* really meant. In many respects it meant opening to women opportunities that were available to men. But there were ways in which women's needs differed from men's, which meant that offering identical opportunities was not sufficient. The challenge went beyond affording opportunity—should women simply be invited to participate in a historically male activity, or should the whole enterprise be rethought to respect everyone's voices and bring to bear the best of both worlds? The mission, Horner thought, included providing equal access in admissions, encouraging the hiring of women faculty, introducing women's studies into the curriculum, and making certain that

---

15 Radcliffe College, *Report of the President, 1972–1977*, p. 6 ("covered by Harvard"); Horner oral history, unpaginated ("marginal cost"); telephone interview with Matina Horner, Feb. 9, 2015. See also ML Bundy oral history, July 12, 2005, p. 16.

women undergraduates had access to the extracurricular opportunities, mentoring, and career advising that would enable them to take full advantage of the educational opportunities the university offered. "The time had not yet come," Horner thought, "for merging the undergraduate activity."[16]

In the context of the growing force of the women's movement in the early 1970s, Horner, by raising the flag for Radcliffe, was articulating a feminist stance that would be well received by Radcliffe alumnae.[17] The same was true of her board. As Giles Constable, professor of history at Harvard who was by then a Radcliffe trustee, put it, Radcliffe "had the responsibility to stand up for the interests of women," and it was essential to ask whether the current arrangements between the two institutions were "really in the best interests of women." Constable said that "Harvard needed Radcliffe as much as Radcliffe needed Harvard." The possibility of close integration with Radcliffe provided "a magnificent opportunity for Harvard to get in ahead of its rivals" on coeducation. Radcliffe, "too deferential to Harvard," long accustomed to being "grateful for any crumb it could get from Harvard's table," needed to seek a better bargain than the "very hard" one Harvard had struck. And that, Constable said, was what Horner was trying to do—"to get as good a bargain as she could."[18]

The principle of independence mattered hugely to Radcliffe alumnae.[19] As the then-chairman of the Radcliffe board, Susan Storey Lyman, said, "When you fold your corporation into another corporation, it's over—you eliminate any power you have."[20] Supported by Radcliffe trustees who worried about losing their college's corporate identity, Horner backed away from the path toward merger that Bunting had pursued.

16 Horner oral history, unpaginated (source of the quote); Horner interview.
17 Solomon oral history, p. 48.
18 Interview with Giles Constable, Jan. 16, 2015, Princeton, NJ.
19 Ibid.
20 Lyman, quoted in Rosalind S. Helderman and Adam A. Sofen, "Radcliffe Enters Historic Merger with Harvard," *Harvard Crimson*, Apr. 21, 1999, clipping in Subject Files Radcliffe, Series 5, Box 17, Folder 11.

Recommendations of the Strauch Committee

The Strauch committee reported at the end of February 1975. Its work was grounded in two premises: Men and women should have the same opportunities at Harvard, and Harvard should be educating more women. The largest part of the report concerned admissions. The committee recommended abolition of the quota system determining the number of men and women in each entering class in favor of a policy of equal access for men and women in admissions and equality in financial aid. They recommended, as well, the unification of the admission offices. The merged office should engage in vigorous recruitment of women applicants, who lagged well behind the number of men in the applicant pool. Along with the move to equal access should come only a modest increase in numbers of students. The committee anticipated that the male-female ratio of 2.5 to 1 mandated in 1971 (down from 4 to 1 in 1970) and set to be achieved in 1975–76 would likely reach 1.5 to 1 "within a reasonable period."[21] (The Harvard ratio actually reached 1.5 to 1 in 1980; Princeton and Yale would reach 1.5 to 1 only as the decade of the 1980s drew to a close.[22])

The Strauch committee also recommended a grab-bag of other measures: accelerated progress toward more significant representation of women in the faculty and administration, the provision of counseling for men and women students about the challenges of combining family and career, the elimination of restrictions by gender on prizes and fellowships, improvements in athletic facilities for women, and physical improvements to make the social, recreational, and living facilities in the Radcliffe houses more comparable to those at Harvard.[23]

---

21 Report of the Committee to Consider Aspects of the Harvard-Radcliffe Relationship that Affect Administrative Arrangements, Admissions, Financial Aid and Educational Policy, Feb. 26, 1975, Subject Files Radcliffe, Series 5, Box 15, Folder 22.

22 Princeton data from Princeton University Registrar's Office; Yale data from Yale College Registrar / IPEDS Fall Headcount Surveys, Yale University Office of Institutional Research; Harvard data from "Gender Distribution at Time of First Enrollment, Harvard College," Harvard College Institutional Research Office.

23 Report of the Committee to Consider Aspects of the Harvard-Radcliffe Relationship.

Although equal access might have been an explosive proposal, the fact that Bok had already decreed a change in the male-female ratio from 4 to 1 to 2.5 to 1 without eliciting significant opposition, and the fact that it would take time to equalize the number of men and women in the applicant pool, meant that the committee report would be more easily received. "So it was possible," Bok reflected, "to do what always works best at Harvard, not some huge, drastic, immediate change that shakes people up, but fairly gradual, steady progress from one state to the next."[24]

With the approval of the governing boards of Harvard and Radcliffe, the combined admission office began operating on July 1, 1975. The ratio of men to women reached 2.5 to 1 with the admission of the class of 1979. Further progress was made toward equalization of the ratio of men to women in the house system, though the physical differences between the houses in the Radcliffe quad and the traditional Harvard houses remained pronounced.[25]

The Joint Policy Committee

Also in 1975, a new paragraph was added to the 1971 agreement providing for the appointment of a joint policy committee, composed of senior administrators and members of the governing boards of each institution, "to discuss matters of mutual concern to Harvard and Radcliffe," to resolve any problems that might arise in implementing the agreement, to provide final approval of the annual budget for the programs retained by Radcliffe and of capital improvements or alterations to buildings in the Radcliffe quadrangle, and to decide how the costs of such construction and renovation should be divided between the two institutions.[26]

---

24 Bok oral history, p. 3.

25 Harvard and Radcliffe Colleges, Charles P. Whitlock, Dean of Harvard College, to the Dean of the Faculty of Arts and Sciences, preprint from the Report of the President of Harvard College and Reports of Departments, 1974–75, in Subject Files Radcliffe, Series 5, Box 14, Folder 22.

26 1971 Amendment to Agreement between President and Fellows of Harvard College and Trustees of Radcliffe College, as amended Mar. 3, 1975, Subject Files Radcliffe, Series 5, Box 15, Folder 21.

The Radcliffe members of the joint policy committee were the chairman and vice chairman of the Radcliffe board, Susan Storey Lyman and Mary Bundy; the president of the college, Matina Horner; and the vice president and dean of the Radcliffe Institute, Patricia Albjerg Graham. The Harvard representatives were the senior member of the corporation, Francis H. Burr; a second member of the corporation; the president of the university, Derek Bok; the dean of the faculty of arts and sciences, Henry Rosovsky; and the financial vice president, Hale Champion.

Horner felt especially confident of the goodwill of Bok and Burr. She was sure that Bok "wanted to do the right thing for and by women." When he was dean of the law school, he had invited her to address his faculty about her research and to do a study of the experiences of the school's female graduates. Bok's "willingness to confront his own faculty on gender issues" had struck Horner as "a very good sign." As for Burr, holding the position of senior fellow of the corporation meant that he served simultaneously as a Radcliffe trustee. On the Radcliffe board, Horner said, Burr made plain that "his responsibility was to Radcliffe," and he focused on "how to do the right thing" for the college. It was not a matter of Harvard versus Radcliffe; Burr was "very helpful," Horner said, "in showing how with integrity to wear both hats."[27]

Horner thought that the joint policy committee would enable people of goodwill from both institutions to find common ground. Where lower-level administrators obstructed cooperation, the joint committee would enable the achievement of consensus among high-ranking officials.[28] But at least one member of the committee had a more skeptical view. The Harvard position, Patricia Graham said later, was "that Harvard would simply absorb Radcliffe and take over its endowment." The committee "wanted

27 Horner interview. Mary Lothrop Bundy, vice chairman of the Radcliffe board and, simultaneously, a member of the Harvard board of overseers, made a similar point. Burr, she said, "had a genius for being able . . . to wear two different hats, his Harvard hat and his Radcliffe hat, and to be able to think constructively from the point of view of Radcliffe's benefit as well and do that wholeheartedly, as well as be able to consider the joint questions that Harvard and Radcliffe needed to address together." ML Bundy oral history, June 15, 2005, p. 9.

28 Horner interview.

to get Radcliffe out of the undergraduate business and take all of Radcliffe's money."[29]

The seemingly inexorable progress toward merger came to an abrupt halt with the Radcliffe trustees' decision in November 1976 that Radcliffe would remain an independent entity. Although the details were to be worked out by the joint policy committee, it was clear that Radcliffe would continue to administer programs to promote women's education, notably the Radcliffe Institute and the Schlesinger Library. As Horner explained, "Radcliffe's charge to promote the higher education of women goes above and beyond our responsibility to them as undergraduates. The big danger down the road is that people will sit back and relax and assume that all is well for women. Radcliffe can't afford to let that happen—there are too many missions ahead. . . . It is a great tribute to the character and commitment of Radcliffe's trustees and alumnae that despite the fog and enormous pressures, they were not swept away in a tide."[30]

Not everyone saw it that way. Henry Rosovsky had argued that institutional separateness was detrimental to the well-being of women undergraduates. "In 1974," he wrote later, perhaps only partly tongue-in-cheek, "I suggested that the two colleges be merged and proposed a new name for the united entity: Harcliffe. Very few were amused, least of all the ruling circles at Radcliffe. . . . Instead, we developed an *entente cordiale*—the degree of cordiality was subject to distinct cyclical variations—that I construed as mandating co-education and that Radcliffe interpreted as allocating to itself the role of women's champion in the Harvard community."[31]

1977: Radcliffe's "Declaration of Independence"

In 1977, a new agreement signed by Horner and Bok, intended to replace the 1943 agreement, stipulated that Radcliffe would "continue as an independent institution to carry out programs to promote the

29 Graham oral history, p. 5.

30 "Coeducation: A Harrowing Experiment," *Harvard Independent*, Dec. 2–8, 1976, Subject Files Radcliffe, Series 5, Box 16, Folder 7.

31 Henry Rosovsky, *The University: An Owner's Manual* (New York: W. W. Norton, 1990), pp. 39–40.

higher education of women." Harvard and Radcliffe, the agreement said, had "concluded that a coordinate relationship between the two institutions is the most appropriate way at this time to achieve their shared educational objectives in an effective and economical manner." Radcliffe would remain legally independent of Harvard, and it would take back at least symbolic control over fiscal matters that had been ceded to Harvard in 1971. Radcliffe would still turn tuition monies over to Harvard, along with a specified contribution from endowment income and unrestricted funds to financial aid for women undergraduates. Radcliffe would retain ownership of its property and continue to manage its own endowment.

The agreement made plain that Harvard had full control over undergraduate education. Radcliffe was delegating to Harvard "all responsibility for undergraduate instruction and for the administration and management of undergraduate affairs and for the establishment of policies affecting undergraduates." The Harvard faculty would provide the same instruction for Radcliffe as for Harvard undergraduates, and admissions would adhere to a policy of equal access, with a joint Harvard-Radcliffe admission office. Harvard would manage the Radcliffe library, operate a unified house system, and issue degrees to women undergraduates. In short, Radcliffe students would have the same rights and privileges as Harvard students.

And yet, giving mixed messages, Radcliffe asserted its continuing responsibility for women undergraduates. Despite the establishment of a joint admission office, women students would be admitted to and enrolled in Radcliffe College. By virtue of that fact, they would also be enrolled at Harvard. And while Harvard would issue degrees to Radcliffe students, their diplomas would also bear the seal and the signature of the president of Radcliffe College. The president of Radcliffe would "participate in the establishment of policy affecting undergraduates" through service on all manner of councils, committees, and boards and would be consulted on appointments of deans whose portfolios focused on undergraduates. A new Harvard-Radcliffe committee would make "annual visitations to examine and review the status and role of women undergraduates," about which it would report to the Harvard overseers and Radcliffe trustees. And the joint policy committee would continue to function as a vehicle for dialogue between the two institutions.[32]

Just what the 1977 agreement meant depended on one's perspective. To Francis Burr, senior fellow of the Harvard corporation and a trustee of Radcliffe, circumstances had changed greatly since the non-merger merger agreement in 1971. Even though older alumnae held fast to their association with Radcliffe, younger women had come to identify with Harvard. The university "had loosened up quite a lot on its attitudes" with respect to women and their access to facilities and opportunities—athletic facilities, libraries, laboratories—attitudes that had previously been "just terrible," "very antediluvian." It was time to move toward merger.[33]

Burr's Radcliffe trustee colleague Carol Pforzheimer had a different take on the agreement: "We took back the administration of the College with control financially and administratively. To the benefit of Radcliffe."[34] Patricia Graham made a related point: "The '77 Agreement prevented Harvard from taking over Radcliffe's money."[35] The *Radcliffe Quarterly* put it this way: Radcliffe had "declared her independence."[36] What Pforzheimer and the *Quarterly* saw as so positive could also be interpreted negatively. The way the *Harvard Crimson* portrayed it, the agreement signaled that Radcliffe was "retiring into its own corner."[37]

32 Derek C. Bok and Matina S. Horner, Agreement between President and Fellows of Harvard College and Radcliffe College, May 11, 1977, and Harvard University news release of the same date, both in Subject Files Radcliffe, Series 5, Box 15, Folder 23. See also Susan S. Lyman to Alumnae, Former Trustees, and Friends of Radcliffe, May 10, 1977, Subject Files Radcliffe, Series 5, Box 16, Folder 7; Dorothy Elia Howells, *A Century to Celebrate: Radcliffe College, 1879–1979* (Radcliffe College, 1979), pp. 37–38. For examples of reports of the new Harvard-Radcliffe Committee to Examine and Review the Status and Role of Women Undergraduates, see 1981 Report, Horner, Box 46, Folder 6; 1984 Report, Horner, Box 70, Folder 10; 1993 Report, Wilson, Box 81, Folder 679; 1996 Report, Wilson, Box 103, Folder 936; 1998 Report, Wilson, Box 121, Folder 1192.

33 Burr oral history, p. 1.

34 Pforzheimer oral history, p. 3.

35 Graham oral history, p. 14.

36 Aida K. Press, "Radcliffe Declares Her Independence," *Radcliffe Quarterly* 63 (Sept. 1977): 1.

37 Laurie Hays, "Retiring into Its Own Corner," *Harvard Crimson*, June 16, 1977, clipping in Subject Files Radcliffe, Series 5, Box 16, Folder 8.

To Horner, the 1977 agreement was a feminist statement. She later described the years 1972 to 1977 as a "funny period" in her presidency, one in which "the Radcliffe woman undergraduate thought she should be 'a Harvard (wo)man.'" Women were "beginning to decide," Horner observed, "that this is in fact not all they want, or have to settle for."[38]

Helen Homans Gilbert's Resignation from the Board

The new agreement was the last straw for Helen Homans Gilbert. After more than a quarter century as a Radcliffe trustee, she decided to resign from the board. She had already said publicly that she feared that Radcliffe was "missing the boat" in "calling a halt" to the progress toward merger.[39] In October 1977, Gilbert wrote to Susan Storey Lyman, "I have struggled long and hard to live with the new agreement with Harvard. I voted for it in the hopes that I could. However I have found I cannot." The terms of the new agreement, she thought, constituted "a threat to the close and friendly relationship with all segments of Harvard, without which, in my opinion, Radcliffe cannot exist." So many people were interpreting the new agreement "as a desire for us to go it alone."[40] Gilbert had tried very hard to avoid that position. She had "finally decided that Radcliffe should merge—if that is the right word—with Harvard. I wanted the Institute to be the center for women within the University—and the Schlesinger [Library] to be there too. I think we could have struck a good bargain for those endeavors we cared about."[41]

Given Gilbert's long and devoted leadership at Radcliffe, her decision came as a shock to her fellow board members. Lyman

---

38 "Peaceful Coexistence," *Harvard Independent*, Apr. 26–May 2, 1979, clipping in Subject Files Radcliffe, Series 5, Box 15, Folder 23.

39 Gilbert, quoted in "Radcliffe Trustees Nix Corporate Merger," *Harvard Independent*, Dec. 2–8, 1976, Subject Files Radcliffe, Series 5, Box 16, Folder 7.

40 Helen Homans Gilbert to Susan Storey Lyman, Oct. 19, 1977, Horner, Box 26, Folder 13. See also Gilbert to Lou ?, Nov. 11, 1977, in the same folder.

41 Helen Homans Gilbert to Carol [Pforzheimer?], Nov. 29, 1977, Horner, Box 26, Folder 13.

tried to talk Gilbert into reconsidering, but to no avail.[42] Gilbert's public posture, if it was necessary to have one, would be that she "would have wished Radcliffe to move otherwise."[43] But to her fellow Radcliffe trustees, she was significantly blunter. "I just can't be a fund raiser for this Radcliffe," Gilbert told Lyman, and "if I can't do that I best get off."[44] To another friend, she was more direct: "I should have long since gotten the hell out as I want the exact opposite of the present arrangement."[45]

Commenting retrospectively, Bok had perhaps the most measured view of what was happening. When he took office, he said later, Harvard and Radcliffe had been "part-way down a path that could only lead in one direction." He said, "It made no sense to go on indefinitely pretending you had two separate administrations and so forth; there was one college and it needed to be administered in a uniform manner, but with complete equity among men and women." He believed that the legacy of Radcliffe "would be best perpetuated by having it become the best center in the world on issues relating to women, building on the advantages of the Schlesinger Library and the Bunting Institute, and so forth." But Bok understood that the path forward would not be linear:

> I always felt that the whole history of women at Harvard was such that Harvard had no right to try to push and accelerate that process. There was a great deal of suspicion, particularly among older alumnae, and for very good reason. I felt we just had to be patient. . . . Eventually the logic of this would play out and we would all merge together, but if Harvard was in the position of pushing and demanding and putting pressure and so forth, that would not achieve the end result in the

42 Susan Storey Lyman to Helen Homans Gilbert, Oct. 31, 1977, and n.d. ("Sunday"), both in Horner, Box 26, Folder 13.

43 Helen Homans Gilbert to Susan Storey Lyman, Nov. 29, 1977, Horner, Box 26, Folder 13.

44 Helen Homans Gilbert to Susan Storey Lyman, Veterans Day, 1977, Horner, Box 26, Folder 13. On the same theme, in the same folder, see Gilbert to Carol [Pforzheimer?], Nov. 29, 1977.

45 Helen Homans Gilbert to Bob ?, Nov. 11, 1977, Horner, Box 26, Folder 13.

right way. The defects of our past, I think, precluded us from playing that role. We had to be patient, helpful, understanding, but never with the feeling that the arrangements during my time should be permanent.[46]

It was "functionally possible," Bok said, for Harvard and Radcliffe to behave as a coeducational institution. There was "nothing to be served," he thought, by "forcing the matter," by "pressing for the formalities of creating a single institution." Harvard did not have "the moral standing" to try to "throw its weight around," and "trying to battle it out" would have "left everybody diminished." There was nothing to be lost by waiting. The Radcliffe president could "share the stage"; the two institutions could maintain some formal independence. Over time, "history would take its course," and the two institutions would merge.[47]

Bok tried to set a tone for positive cooperation, but the process was not always easy. On the Harvard side, necessary adjustments involved changes in past practice and challenges to longstanding privilege, as in the case of providing equal time for women's athletics. On the Radcliffe side, there was both a genuine concern about adequate attention to women's needs and a heightened sensitivity to perceived slights of various sorts. Where the stakes were high, as in equal access in undergraduate admissions, the record was positive. Where they were smaller and more symbolic, the situation tended to be fraught. "Harvard would do things that seemed to us to be simply sensible and realistic," Bok said, "and to Radcliffe they symbolically would mean a lack of respect, an assault on the role that Radcliffe claimed to play." Accordingly, the relationship between the two institutions was complicated by "repeated disagreements," "little disagreements about Radcliffe being taken for granted, Radcliffe's legitimate interests being overlooked, and these things grated."[48]

46 Bok oral history, pp. 3–4.
47 Bok interview.
48 Bok oral history, p. 6.

1999: *The Harvard-Radcliffe Merger*

It was only at the close of the 1990s, with Bok and Horner's successors long in place, that the merger Nathan Pusey and Polly Bunting had envisioned, and Derek Bok had anticipated, finally took place. The process had been slower than Bok had imagined. He had thought that Horner's retirement from the presidency in 1989 might have been the "occasion for final merger," and it surprised him that Radcliffe decided instead to search for another president. "I thought," he said later, "that was prolonging things beyond where they ought to be prolonged." He had the sense, he explained, "that to some extent, the whole business was being perpetuated by the feeling that financially the only way Radcliffe could maintain itself was by claiming that it still had a vigorous role in undergraduate education, because that's the tie that mattered to so many of the alumnae."[49]

In April 1999, after two years of secret negotiations, Neil Rudenstine, now president of Harvard, and Linda S. Wilson, now president of Radcliffe, signed an agreement that recognized what had long been reality. Full coeducation had long since been realized in Cambridge, and Harvard and Radcliffe were functionally one institution. Radcliffe had been struggling to define its role; it had not been easy to find ways to attach undergraduate women at Harvard to Radcliffe College, nor had it been possible for Wilson to raise funds to support the midcareer programs she imagined Radcliffe would offer to alumnae. The situation had an *Alice in Wonderland* aspect to it, Rudenstine observed: "There was no longer a Radcliffe College, but there was a Radcliffe College." Many Radcliffe board members, as well as younger alumnae, favored eliminating the fiction that Radcliffe was still a college.[50]

The new agreement, characterized as a merger, effectively put Radcliffe College out of business. In its place, the two institutions planned a new Radcliffe Institute for Advanced Study, which was to be "an integral part of Harvard." The institute would be "an

---

49 Ibid., p. 5.
50 Interview with Neil Rudenstine, Feb. 9, 2015, Princeton, NJ.

interdisciplinary center where leading scholars can promote learning and scholarship across a broad array of academic and professional fields within the setting of a major university." One of the
emphases of the institute, reflecting its historic roots, would be
"a continuing commitment to the study of women, gender, and
society." Scholars and artists in many fields would be invited to the
institute for a year of independent study. The institute would also
offer symposia, colloquia, workshops, and conferences for the university community. The Bunting Institute, as the Radcliffe Institute
had been renamed, would be subsumed in the new Institute for
Advanced Study, which would build on but significantly enlarge
its work. The Schlesinger Library would operate under the aegis of
the new institute. Radcliffe would transfer its endowment and real
estate to Harvard. Radcliffe would no longer have a president. The
institute would be led by a dean who would function as the tenth
peer of the deans of Harvard's nine faculties.

"Our new design will make the Radcliffe of the future a larger
and more significant institution squarely within Harvard and
offer stellar new opportunities to explore issues of deep concern
to women," said the chairman of the Radcliffe board of trustees,
Nancy-Beth Gordon Sheerr.[51] Bok called the merger "the realization of Polly Bunting's vision, recognizing that there were a whole
set of new issues other than undergraduate education that were
terribly important to the society that were not being addressed
adequately and thus created an opportunity for Radcliffe."[52] Linda
Wilson, who would step down from the Radcliffe presidency in
July 1999 after ten years of service, described the institute as "a
new incarnation of Radcliffe College that will bring substantial
growth in its role and scope, and greater clarity in its mission."[53]

51 Radcliffe and Harvard Announce Historic Agreement, Radcliffe College news
release, Apr. 20, 1999, attached to Linda S. Wilson to Alumnae and Friends, Apr. 19, 1999,
Subject Files Radcliffe, Series 5, Box 17, Folder 11. For more detail, see "Radcliffe: A New
Incarnation," *Harvard Gazette*, Apr. 20, 1999, clipping in Subject Files Radcliffe, Series 5,
Box 17, Folder 13, and "Radcliffe and Harvard Announce Proposed Merger," *Radcliffe
Quarterly* 85 (Summer 1999): 2–9.
52 Bok oral history, p. 4.
53 Statement of President Linda S. Wilson, Apr. 20, 1999, Wilson, Box 126, Folder
1243.

That new incarnation, Wilson said, "will make the commitment to women [at Harvard] much more obvious." She added that "moving inside"—that is, "symbolically becoming part of the university"—"will give Radcliffe greater stature."[54] Rudenstine remarked both on the significance of the establishment of a new, well-resourced center for advanced interdisciplinary scholarship, of which there were few in the world, and on what the merger meant for men and women at Harvard. "This places the responsibility on Harvard," he said "for making sure undergraduate education is excellent both for women and men."[55]

Indeed, there had been little clarity of mission since Harvard had become fully coeducational in the 1970s. Despite the firm determination of Matina Horner and the Radcliffe trustees to hold onto a role for Radcliffe in undergraduate education, it had been difficult to figure out what that role really entailed. Horner's Radcliffe had insisted on accepting applications from and admitting women students who would otherwise be fully enrolled at Harvard. They had continued, too, to put the Radcliffe seal alongside the Harvard seal on the diplomas of women graduates. And Radcliffe had offered some programs of significance to women students, like mentorships and internships. But the combination of these policies and practices had not added up to something that could be described as a college.

Reactions to the Merger

Unless observers were fully versed in the twists and turns of Harvard-Radcliffe history, it was easy to misunderstand what was going on. To the *Boston Globe*, the announcement meant that Radcliffe was "ced[ing] the education of undergraduate women to its longtime male partner"—a move that was in fact more than

---

54 Wilson, quoted in "Radcliffe to Become a Harvard Institute," *Boston Globe*, Apr. 21, 1999, clipping in Subject Files Radcliffe, Series 5, Box 17, Folder 13.

55 Rudenstine, quoted in "Radcliffe to Become a Harvard Institute"; "Radcliffe Packing Up and Going to Harvard," *New York Times*, Apr. 21, 1999, clipping in Subject Files Radcliffe, Series 5, Box 17, Folder 13.

twenty years in the past.[56] The *Los Angeles Times* had a better grasp of the chronology, though no one associated with Radcliffe would have liked the paper's framing of the agreement as "a burial that took place twenty years after the funeral."[57] The *New York Times* headline was more accurate: "Radcliffe Packing Up and Going to Harvard."[58] The *Harvard Crimson* was closest to the mark: "Radcliffe's 'College' Days End."[59]

Alumnae reactions ran the gamut, from exuberant ("It's finally happened!") to saddened ("A portion of my life has just disappeared") to mistrustful ("I do not trust that Harvard has a commitment to women in academia. One needs only look at its track record in terms of promotions and tenure for women") to downright angry: "I thought I had more time—time to develop a cogent, concise, persuasive argument for why we should have a Radcliffe College, not just so that I would not be a[n] alumna of a 'disappeared' institution, but so that undergraduate women at Harvard would always have a place, if not a room, of their own. . . . So, goodby[e] Radcliffe—I loved you while you lived, even as a vestige of what you once were. I mourn your loss: to me, to Harvard, to my fellow alumnae."[60]

Amidst the anger and disappointment, there was real thoughtfulness in communications from alumnae that captured both what was being given up as a result of the merger and what might be achieved through the new arrangements. In terms of what was being given up, even recent graduates who had participated fully in life at Harvard could articulate what Radcliffe had meant to them. An alumna in the class of 1978, who had lived in Harvard Yard as a freshman and then in a Harvard house, said that she

---

56 "Radcliffe to Become a Harvard Institute."

57 Quoted in Keller and Keller, *Making Harvard Modern*, p. 352.

58 *New York Times*, Apr. 21, 1999.

59 *Harvard Crimson*, Apr. 21, 1999, clipping in Subject Files Radcliffe, Series 5, Box 17, Folder 11.

60 Frances M. Fuller to Linda S. Wilson, received Apr. 28, 1999, Wilson, Box 126, Folder 1244 ("finally happened"); Abby Cheever, quoted in Diane Mercer, Alumnae responses during telephone conversations re Harvard/Radcliffe merger, Apr. 1999, Wilson, Box 127, Folder 1246 ("disappeared"); Joanne M. Pearson to Wilson, May 6, 1999, Wilson, Box 126, Folder 1245 ("I do not trust"); Nancy Milczanowski to Wilson, Apr. 27, 1999, Wilson, Box 126, Folder 1244 ("I thought I had more time").

and her roommates had "always identified strongly as Radcliffe women, and always felt we had a home at Radcliffe. With Radcliffe on our side, we always knew we had available to us mentors, special seminars, career services sensitive to our goals and needs, a President and staff who would serve as much-needed role models, advisors, and advocates for women undergraduates, and simply a haven from the male-dominated hurly-burly of life at Harvard." Where would Harvard women now find that kind of support and those kinds of resources?[61]

As for the gains the new arrangements might bring, many alumnae looked optimistically toward a promising future. One wrote to Wilson and Sheerr, "For Radcliffe to become a true and full part of Harvard, to me, is the best of outcomes. . . . It will always be remembered that the two of you provided the women of Radcliffe with the well-deserved opportunity to play in the 'big yard' with the boys."[62]

In July 1999 Mary Maples Dunn, director of the Schlesinger Library since her retirement from the presidency of Smith College in 1995, took up the deanship of the Radcliffe Institute as the search was conducted for a permanent dean. In January 2001, Drew Gilpin Faust, an American historian on the faculty of the University of Pennsylvania, succeeded Dunn as dean. In February 2007 Faust was elected president of Harvard University. In a move that was likely beyond the imagining of even the staunchest defenders of Radcliffe, the dean of the Radcliffe Institute took her place at Harvard's very center.

---

61 Renee R. Matalon to President Wilson and Members of the Radcliffe Administration, Apr. 23, 1999, Wilson, Box 127, Folder 1246.

62 Nina Segre to Linda Wilson and Nancy-Beth Sheerr, May 17, 1999, Wilson, Box 127, Folder 1246.

11

Yale: Yale Is "Not Yet Coeducational"

Coeducation was the biggest step, but by no means the most controversial, taken at Yale by Kingman Brewster's administration as the tumultuous 1960s drew to a close. The diversification of the undergraduate student body had been a big red flag to Old Blues.[1] But what set alumni off more than anything else was what they perceived as Brewster's embrace of radicalism. "The choice in those times," Brewster later reflected, "was between the risk of liberty—called 'permissiveness' by its detractors—and risks of order at any price—called 'repression' by its critics." Under his leadership, he said, "Yale tended to choose the former risk."[2]

"Radicalism" and Its Effects on Coeducation

The first evidence of what many alumni saw as Brewster's embrace of radicalism was his unwillingness to muzzle or dismiss Yale's highly controversial chaplain, William Sloane Coffin, an antiwar activist who advocated civil disobedience, draft resistance, and other actions that were anathema to many Yale alumni.[3] As Brewster later explained, the university "stood fast in its indulgence of the freedom of its Chaplain to preach his conscience and to practice what he preached. When he seemed strident and overreaching he was chastised. When he invited a judicial test of conscientious

---

1 See, e.g., Beinecke oral history, p. 18.

2 Kingman Brewster, Jr., *Report of the President: The Decade 1963–1973*, p. 1. This is Brewster's annual report for 1972–73.

3 Geoffrey Kabaservice, *The Guardians: Kingman Brewster, His Circle, and the Rise of the Liberal Establishment* (New York: Henry Holt, 2004), pp. 318–21.

nonviolent civil disobedience he was supported. The line was not always easy to draw. The University was a better place because, thanks in part to the Chaplain, moral issues were confronted in moral terms."[4]

The next incendiary action, as many disgruntled alumni saw it, was Brewster's decision to declare his opposition to the war "in a personal capacity" in remarks at the large Vietnam moratorium rally on the New Haven green in October 1969.[5] After that came the April 1970 trial in the New Haven superior court of the national leader of the Black Panthers, Bobby Seale, along with a dozen other Black Panthers, for the torture-murder of an alleged police informant. Yale students demonstrated to protest the Panthers' imprisonment, and local black leaders urged students to go on strike to force the university to demand that the Panthers be released from jail. At a rally in Boston on April 15, Abbie Hoffman, spokesman for the Youth International Party, known as Yippies, said that in two weeks radicals would "go to New Haven to burn Yale down."[6]

On Friday, May 1, many thousands of demonstrators from around the country massed on the green to protest Seale's trial and show support for the Panthers. Controversially, Brewster chose to keep the campus open and to welcome the demonstrators, even offering food and housing, despite the mayhem caused by the banner-waving, drum-banging, rock-hurling, obscenity-shouting protesters. With local and national media crews jostling for position, tear gas wafted across the green as police and national guardsmen massed in front of city hall and the courthouse, bayonets and rifles at the ready. Responding to FBI predictions of a massive bloodbath, President Richard M. Nixon ordered four thousand marines and paratroopers to be ready at a moment's notice to restore order. That night three bombs detonated in the Yale ice hockey rink, where a rock concert and dance were underway. Miraculously, there were no casualties; most people had left the

4 Brewster, *Report of the President: The Decade 1963–1973*, p. 1.
5 May oral history, p. 5.
6 Kabaservice, *The Guardians*, pp. 402–9 (the quote is from p. 405).

building for the green only moments before the explosion.[7] "We adopted the strategy of trust, in contrast to the strategy of mass arrest," Brewster said later. "It worked. Not only was Yale spared, but the country, too, was given heart by the University's refusal to assume that all protesters were maliciously motivated."[8]

But many alumni did not share Brewster's optimistic view that "it worked." Black Panthers, antiwar radicalism, massive demonstrations around and on the campus, the university president's apparent embrace of the demonstrators—all of that was deeply offensive to many Yale alumni. Even worse, perhaps, was Brewster's statement at the April 23 faculty meeting that he was skeptical about whether a black revolutionary could get a fair trial anywhere in the United States.[9] In response, the vice president of the United States, Spiro T. Agnew, urged Yale alumni to remove Brewster from office. "I do not feel," Agnew said, "that students of Yale University can get a fair impression of their country under the tutelage of Kingman Brewster."[10]

Brewster had made a deliberate choice, he said: "I took the considered risk of speaking my mind on issues such as the war and the draft and the legal harassment of black revolutionaries. These were matters which racked the entire university community. My decision . . . was the result of a deliberate balance of judgment about what degree of speaking out was best for the University under the circumstances: how to avoid excessive exploitation of the presidential office, and how to avoid being a moral eunuch on a morally anguished campus."[11]

Coffin said that in "allow[ing] for controversy" on campus, Brewster "made Yale safe for its differences."[12] Members of the corporation stood shoulder to shoulder with Brewster; showing up to support the president, as at a campus meeting at the Yale rink

---

7 Ibid., pp. 1–4, 9, 405–11.

8 Brewster, *Report of the President: The Decade 1963–1973*, p. 2.

9 Kingman Brewster, Jr., Statement at the Yale College Faculty Meeting, Apr. 23, 1970, quoted in Kabaservice, *The Guardians*, p. 3.

10 Kabaservice, *The Guardians*, p. 3; Agnew, quoted in *Yale Daily News*, Oct. 12, 1973.

11 Brewster, *Report of the President: The Decade 1963–1973*, p. 3.

12 Coffin, quoted in "From Friends and Colleagues," in *Kingman Brewster: Remembrances* (Yale University, 1997), p. 40.

in May 1970 about whether to retain ROTC, made an important symbolic statement to the university community.[13]

But whether Brewster had in fact struck the right balance in his public positions was a matter of intense debate in alumni circles. A staunch Brewster supporter who joined the corporation in 1971, William S. Beinecke, president and chairman of the Sperry and Hutchinson Company (which offered S&H Green Stamps), noted years later, in a significant understatement, that Brewster's statement at the April 23 faculty meeting led to "a division among the alumni respecting the President of the University."[14] William Bundy noted that although he himself was not ready to criticize Brewster for making the statement, "the Bobby Seale thing hurt [Brewster] with a lot of alumni."[15] Another member of the corporation, Caryl P. Haskins, a biophysicist who was president of the Carnegie Institution of Washington, said that he considered Brewster's statement to be "a big mistake." More conservative alumni, especially in the older classes, he said, saw Brewster "as an out-and-out radical and even as a traitor to his class."[16]

The uproar over the Vietnam War, the Black Panthers, the demonstrations on and around the campus, may seem on the surface to have been unrelated to coeducation. In fact, however, the events of late spring 1970 bore directly on coeducation in two ways. The first was positive. As students worked together for causes larger than their own parochial interests, the barriers dividing men and women became more porous and less consequential. Elga Wasserman, who had played an important role in instituting coeducation at Yale, reflected later that "the threat from the outside" had the effect of "mak[ing] coeducation jell."[17] External crises unified the campus; students "forgot they were men and women; they were suddenly people," classmates, part of a larger

13 See, e.g., WP Bundy oral history, Apr. 24, 1992, p. 24; Lindsay oral history, pp. 20–21.

14 Beinecke oral history, p. 11.

15 WP Bundy oral history, Apr. 24, 1992, p. 36. On the same point, see Dilworth oral history, p. 33.

16 Haskins oral history, pp. 33, 45.

17 Elga Wasserman, in DVD "Coeducating the Male-Only Ivies: A Retrospective," Wesleyan University, Oct. 12, 2013.

community.[18] A woman in the class of 1973 said that with so much else going on, the "social barriers" between men and women broke down.[19] Two other alumnae—one in the class of 1973, the other in that of 1998—put it this way: As the student community became more radicalized and more united, "some of the pickier issues of coeducation," along with "issues of dating and gender," came to be seen as "of little importance."[20] The negative effect had to do with the ways in which rising alumni anger at Brewster limited his degrees of freedom. It was hard to fight several battles at once, and more fully implementing coeducation was one of the short-term casualties.

A Rebellion Fomented by LUX ET VERITAS

As Brewster admitted to John William Ward, the president of Amherst, he and his colleagues had been "very apprehensive about what the coeducating of Yale's undergraduate mission would do to alumni feelings and tangible support." One-sixth of the alumni body, he estimated—mainly older alumni—were "outraged. . . . Often the outrage was couched in terms of failure of consultation or the precipitate style of the decision, but fundamentally they were against the desecration of their Yale by females."[21]

By August 1970 a group of conservative alumni had organized an oppositional alumni group, LUX ET VERITAS, with the name (meaning "light and truth") taken from the university's motto. By establishing an "independent channel of communication" with alumni who felt that their views were not being heard and taken seriously by the administration, the LUX founders hoped "to

---

18 Elga Wasserman, in Julie Pimsleur, "Boola Boola . . . Yale Goes Coed," 1990, Film Study Center, Yale University. See also Wasserman oral history II, p. 89.

19 Lawrie Mifflin '73, in Pimsleur, "Boola Boola."

20 Nina Glickson '73 ("pickier issues"), quoted in Sherrie Selwyn '98, "The Social Scene in 1969," in Rachel Donadio, ed., *Different Voices: A Journal Commemorating 25 Years of Coeducation at Yale College* (Yale University, 1995), p. 17, Manuscripts and Archives, Yale University Library.

21 Kingman Brewster, Jr., to John William Ward, Nov. 17, 1972, Brewster II, Box 258, Folder 1.

establish a dialogue" that could be useful to Brewster as well as the alumni.[22]

But that was only a small part of the story. Increasing numbers of undergraduate alumni were disaffected, as evidenced by the decline in dollars and participation in the alumni fund for 1969–70. As the organizers of LUX ET VERITAS explained in a statement to the *Yale Daily News*, there were many reasons for the "growing discontent," including "the increasing politicization of the campus; the growing acceptance by segments of the University community [of the view] that the American democratic system, including its judicial system, is oppressive; and the apparent growth of an intolerance toward opposing views"—in other words, everything to do with Brewster, Vietnam, and the Black Panther trial. In addition, there had been "substantive changes" in the university—by which they meant diversification of the student body and coeducation— that had been undertaken without adequate consultation or explanation to alumni. Better communication would allow disaffected alumni to "make their views heard" and to have some influence on university policy going forward.[23]

The founders of LUX ET VERITAS reached out to the alumni body to solicit opinions, participation, and financial support. They asked: Are you concerned about the tremendous changes at Yale in recent years? Do you care about encouraging Yale "to remain an open unpolarized university"? Do you agree that the balance is shifting from education to political activism, so that Yale "is in danger of being politicized; that it risks becoming a place where all shades of opinion are not examined freely and on their own merits"?[24]

In January 1971 LUX ET VERITAS sent Brewster the first results of the replies to a questionnaire they had mailed to thirty-eight thousand alumni. Of the four thousand respondents, 72 percent saw a need for more effective communication of alumni opinion

22 Louis M. Loeb, John D. Garrison, J. William Stack, Jr., and John W. Castles 3rd to Kingman Brewster, Nov. 5, 1970, Brewster II, Box 292, Folder 15.

23 LUX ET VERITAS Statement for the *Yale Daily News*, attached to Loeb et al. to Kingman Brewster.

24 J. William Stack, Jr., and John W. Castles 3rd to Fellow Yale Alumnus, Nov. 27, 1970, Brewster II, Box 292, Folder 15.

to the university administration; only 27 percent said that alumni opinion was fairly and reasonably considered by the administration. Only 25 percent felt well informed about faculty and student opinions and about university policy on admissions, faculty appointments and tenure, and freedom of expression.[25]

LUX ET VERITAS broadened its efforts over the next several years, publishing a periodic newsletter, the LUX ET VERITAS JOURNAL, which called the attention of alumni to developments on campus that LUX considered especially egregious.[26] Coeducation was a particular point of controversy. It had been accomplished "too hastily and . . . in the wrong manner"—that is, by integrating women into the residential colleges. Tampering with Yale's long history of "all-male camaraderie" threatened the university's time-honored success in "training men in leadership and character." Coeducation should be reconfigured as coordinate education, with women either in their own residential colleges or, even better, in a separate women's college to be established by the university.[27]

Coeducation Loses Some Steam

Brewster and his colleagues in the corporation understood the extent of alumni discontent, but LUX's efforts to rally opposition did not change the fundamental directions of the university. Whether Brewster might have pushed more aggressively on certain fronts

25 Summary of First Survey Report, attached to John Bolton to Kingman Brewster, Jan. 27, 1971, and Report on the Results of the LUX ET VERITAS, Inc., First Survey, Jan. 19, 1971, both in Brewster II, Box 292, Folder 15.

26 In Brewster II, Box 292, Folder 16, see J. William Stack, Jr., and John W. Castles 3rd to Fellow Yale Alumnus, Nov. 1971; Summary of Second Survey Report, attached to John R. Bolton to Kingman Brewster, June 7, 1971; LUX ET VERITAS, INC., JOURNAL, Number 1, n.d., received Sept. 16, 1971; Edward Young to Yale Student, n.d., received Oct. 15, 1971; and LUX ET VERITAS, INC., JOURNAL, Number 2, n.d., received Dec. 6, 1971. In Brewster II, Box 259, Folder 1, see Castles to Henry Chauncey, Jr., Aug. 14, 1972, and Chauncey to Castles, Aug. 30, 1972. In Brewster II, Box 292, Folder 18, see Stack and Castles to Fellow Yale Alumnus, n.d., received Dec. 5, 1972, transmitting Lux et Veritas, A Report on Yale Admissions, 1950–72. In AYA Box 28, Folder 45, see LUX ET VERITAS, INC., JOURNAL, Number 3, n.d. [Spring 1972]. See also "Coeducation at Yale Criticized as 'Hasty,'" *New Haven Register*, Sept. 19, 1972, clipping in Wasserman II, Box 1.

27 LUX ET VERITAS, "Coeducation at Yale," n.d. [1972], Brewster II, Box 258, Folder 1. See also "Coeducation at Yale Criticized as 'Hasty.'"

had organized opposition not existed is impossible to know. What is clear is that he, together with the corporation, tempered the extent of the changes that might have come if Yale had been prepared to embrace equal access for men and women.

The university committee on coeducation pressed repeatedly for the earliest possible achievement of "a more equal ratio of men to women."[28] Elga Wasserman urged Brewster to address the relationship of coeducation to the university's long-range goals. What was the optimum size of the undergraduate college and of the residential colleges? How could the goal of enrolling fifteen hundred undergraduate women best be accomplished?[29] Taken on their own merits, those were complicated questions. But the Brewster administration overcomplicated them by placing them in a much larger context. The dean of the college, Georges May, told Brewster that the ratio of men to women "could not be intelligently determined without an examination of the basic assumptions lying behind our entire undergraduate educational approach." To take one example, what variations in housing patterns might be imagined for the future? If more students were to live off campus, it would be possible to admit more women more quickly. If Yale remained committed to residence in the colleges, the increase would likely happen more slowly.[30]

Still, the pressure for action on the ratio continued. Students flooded the corporation with petitions requesting "an immediate end to discriminatory admissions policies towards women."[31] Brewster held fast to the gradual, incremental approach that had undergirded his willingness to embark on coeducation. Although no one believed that "either the overcrowding or the present lopsided ratio of men to women" was "conducive to an effective educational and social situation," there were overriding considerations

28 Elga Wasserman, Coeducation 1969–70 [Aug. 1970], Brewster I, Box 60, Folder 12.

29 In Brewster II, Box 259, Folder 1, see Elga Wasserman to Kingman Brewster, Jr., Oct. 14, 1970, and Wasserman to Members of the Faculty and Administration, n.d. [Oct. 1970]. In Wasserman I, Box 21, Folder 907, see Wasserman to Georges May, Oct. 28, 1970.

30 Georges May to Kingman Brewster, Dec. 3, 1970, May, Box 10, Folder 155.

31 See the variously titled copies of Petition to the Corporation of Yale University, and Coeducation Petition, Brewster I, Box 60, Folder 13, 1970.

that prevented him from acting to address the problem.[32] He tried out his reasoning in a document he drafted (but apparently never disseminated) in November 1972. Yale was committed to coeducation, but "equal concern for the education of both women and men" did not "dictate arithmetical equilibrium." Although it was important to pay attention to the "consequences of an excessive imbalance," it was also necessary to be mindful of the dangers of diminishing the "traditional educational opportunity" that Yale offered men. Admitting more women should be accomplished with no "greater reduction in the number of men than proves necessary."[33]

Brewster also drafted a response to the report of the university committee on coeducation: "I would not have recommended in the fall of 1968 the move to immediate coeducation on a limited basis if I had not been able to assure anyone who asked that we did not intend to reduce the number of men in Yale College." The university decided to proceed, aware of the likely costs: "We knew that this move would result in overcrowding," he said. "We also knew that we could not admit a sufficient number of women to achieve a desirable balance until new facilities were built." The overriding constraint was that "coeducation would not be acceptable to many of our most loyal alumni if it meant a cut-back in the size of the male population in Yale College. Therefore the assurance that the precipitate move to coeducation on a pilot basis would not cause us to reduce the number of men was explicit and unambiguous."

Retreating from that assurance was not an option. "A private University," Brewster explained, "depends upon two things": "the willingness of the alumni to support us without expecting to agree with us about everything we do" and "their confidence that even though they don't agree with us they can count on the credibility of our motivation, our integrity and the reliability of any assurances or promises we make." That meant not "back-tracking on

32 Kingman Brewster, Jr., draft memorandum in response to the report of Mrs. Wasserman's Committee on Coeducation, Dec. 4, 1970, Brewster II, Box 259, Folder 1.

33 Kingman Brewster, Jr., untitled typescript, Nov. 10, 1972, Brewster II, Box 258, Folder 1.

assurances given unambiguously," on "explicit promises" to maintain the number of male students at Yale.[34]

The response Brewster finally sent to Wasserman was terse and to the point: "The Corporation," he wrote, "is mindful of two very clear commitments. The first was the unambiguous statement that the decision to move ahead with a pilot effort with coeducation before building additional facilities would not lead us to reduce the admissions of men to Yale College. The second was to give top priority to achieving a minimum enrollment of fifteen hundred undergraduate women as soon as possible." With funds in hand (or so it was still believed) for the construction of two new residential colleges, the next challenge was to achieve the goal of enrolling fifteen hundred women, or some equivalent ratio of women to men. Whether that would require still more new residential facilities, or whether it would be facilitated by other developments—changes in student preferences with respect to on- and off-campus living, changes in length of the undergraduate degree program, decisions about the size of Yale College—would be considered once May's successor as dean had been designated.[35]

Elga Wasserman Lobbies Unsuccessfully to Be Heard

Inherent in Elga Wasserman's efforts to get Brewster's attention was a structural challenge. The committees Wasserman led were deliberative and advisory. At best they could lobby politely, but neither they nor Wasserman had the authority to implement their desires.[36] Wasserman held no formal administrative portfolio, and, as she pointed out repeatedly to Brewster, she was not at the table in the administrative circles and standing committee meetings where important decisions were made.[37] In short, she had none of

34 Kingman Brewster, Jr., draft memorandum in response to the report of Mrs. Wasserman's Committee on Coeducation, Dec. 4, 1970.

35 Kingman Brewster, Jr., to Elga Wasserman, Dec. 14, 1970, Wasserman II, Box 3.

36 Minutes, University Committee on Coeducation, Nov. 14, 1969, Brewster I, Box 60, Folder 16.

37 See, e.g., Elga Wasserman to Kingman Brewster, Jr., Sept. 26, 1969, Brewster I, Box 60, Folder 16; May 21, 1970, Wasserman II, Box 3; and May 11, 1970, Brewster I, Box 60, Folder 13.

the advantages of status and close relationships with senior colleagues that facilitated Halcy Bohen's work at Princeton.[38] Nor was Wasserman generally appreciated (as Bohen so clearly was) as a constructive, collegial player, the sort of colleague one wanted at the table. Instead, she was often perceived as difficult. Georges May, who had "great respect" for Wasserman, expressed privately to the provost, Charles Taylor, his concern that Wasserman was underutilized and undervalued. She was, he said, "a much more able and imaginative person than seems to be called for by the present mission of her office." Henry Chauncey confirmed years later that Wasserman's sense of being left out of policy discussions and decisions was well founded.[39]

Wasserman continued trying to get Brewster's attention. She wanted to be "in a more central position and thereby more effective," she told him in February 1971.[40] "I am asking for stronger support from you in carrying out my . . . responsibilities," she wrote in March. "Without participation at the policymaking level I cannot be effective in improving coeducation at Yale."[41] And in May she said, "I continue to feel a lack of day to day contact with individuals involved in policy making and implementation, as well as a need for more clearcut agreement concerning my specific responsibilities. Can we discuss these issues soon?"[42]

At the same time, Wasserman lobbied senior officers on matters related to women. To Brewster she complained that a meeting of the university council had been scheduled at Mory's: "I think it entirely inappropriate to schedule university meetings at Mory's as long as Mory's remains a segregated facility."[43] To Chauncey, upon hearing news of a departure from the admission office, she wrote about the importance of filling the vacancy with a woman:

38 Telephone interview with Halcyone H. Bohen, Jan. 30, 2015.

39 Georges May to Charles H. Taylor, Nov. 10, 1970, May, Box 10, Folder 155; interview with Henry S. Chauncey, Jr., Apr. 13, 2012, New Haven, CT.

40 Elga Wasserman to Kingman Brewster, Jr., Feb. 15, 1971, Brewster I, Box 257, Folder 7.

41 Elga Wasserman to Kingman Brewster, Jr., Mar. 12, 1971, Wasserman II, Box 3.

42 Elga Wasserman to Kingman Brewster, Jr., May 21, 1971, Brewster II, Box 259, Folder 1.

43 Elga Wasserman to Kingman Brewster, Jr., May 6, 1971, Brewster I, Box 220, Folder 1.

"We certainly will not project an image of equal treatment for women if our senior administrative staff remains predominantly male."[44] To the new dean of Yale College, Horace Taft, she wrote about women candidates for faculty appointments in the sociology department.[45] Although the substance of her communications was unimpeachable, the tone—in which a woman without formal administrative portfolio lectured senior colleagues about how to do business—is unlikely to have contributed to effective working relationships with those men.

In the end, Wasserman's status was never addressed. When her husband took a sabbatical in 1972–73, she took a leave of absence to travel with him in Europe and to work with Yale psychiatry professor Kenneth Keniston on a research project for the Carnegie Council on Children. As her leave came to a close in September 1973, Wasserman, having been passed over for appointments in the dean's and the provost's offices for which she believed herself to be well qualified, left the university's employ to enroll at Yale Law School. She had worked for change, she told Brewster, in what she believed to be "a constructive and effective manner." She knew that the "pressures for change" would inevitably challenge "established Yale traditions," but her job required confronting "staunch defenders of the status quo." Wasserman concluded that the termination of her Yale appointment had to have been "the result of differences of opinion which arose as an inevitable consequence of the nature of the job with which I had been entrusted."[46]

Fall 1972: "Plausible Options" and the 60–40 Ratio

Although the university committee on coeducation continued to meet in 1972–73 under the chairmanship of Mary Arnstein, wife

---

44 Elga Wasserman to Henry Chauncey, Jr., July 22, 1971, Brewster I, Box 220, Folder 1.

45 Elga Wasserman to Horace Taft, Dec. 17, 1971, Brewster I, Box 220, Folder 1.

46 Elga Wasserman to Kingman Brewster, Jr., Feb. 13, 1973, Wasserman II, Box 3 (source of the quotes); Wasserman oral history II, pp. 59–60, 73–74. The Yale Faculty and Professional Women's Forum said that she was being let go because of "her outspokenness in the fight for quality education for women and equality for women in hiring practices." Yale Faculty and Professional Women's Forum, letter to the editor, *Yale Daily News*, Feb. 23, 1973, Brewster II, Box 333, Folder 2.

of Robert L. Arnstein, psychiatrist-in-chief at university health services, it never had the authority to accomplish anything of consequence, and Arnstein had no better seat at the table than Wasserman had had. The following year, programs that had been initiated in the coeducation office were transferred to other offices around the university. Arnstein's committee took on a new name, the university committee on the education of women, with the charge to oversee programs transferred to other offices, to serve as an advisory group to the president, and to take up "issues relating to the needs of all women within the University community."[47] But decentralization meant dissipation of effort, a loss redressed in 1977 with the appointment of Judith Berman Brandenburg, a psychologist at Queen's College in New York, to a new position, associate dean of Yale College with special responsibility for the education of women. Working closely with women faculty members, Brandenburg spearheaded efforts to establish a women's studies program and chaired a committee that developed grievance procedures for sexual harassment complaints.[48]

A faculty study group on Yale College, appointed by Brewster in April 1971 under the leadership of political science professor Robert Dahl, finally brought Yale's undergraduate admission policy before the corporation for action.[49] The group was charged with broad responsibility for making recommendations about the future of Yale College. Reporting in April 1972, it recommended, among other things, that admission should be granted "without regard to sex." The study group anticipated a student body of

47 Kingman Brewster, Jr., draft letter, reappointments for membership of University Committee on the Education of Women, 1973–74, n.d., Brewster II, Box 270, Folder 6 (source of the quote); minutes, University Committee on the Education of Women, Sept. 17, 1973, Wasserman I, Box 34, Folder 1024; Mary B. Arnstein, Report to the President from the University Committee on the Education of Women, 1973–74, July 1, 1974, Brewster II, Box 258, Folder 11.

48 "Former Dean Judith Brandenburg, Launched Women's Studies," *Yale Bulletin & Calendar*, Mar. 21, 2003, http://www.yale.edu/opa/arc-ybc/v31.n22/story27.html, accessed Jan. 1, 2016.

49 Minutes, University Committee on Coeducation, Nov. 23, 1971, Wasserman I, Box 21, Folder 904; minutes, Women's Advisory Council, Apr. 12, 1972, Wasserman I, Box 35, Folder 1035; Kingman Brewster, Jr., Appendix "A," Feb. 14, 1972, addendum to Brewster to Members of the Yale Corporation, Oct. 4, 1972, Brewster II, Box 259, Folder 3.

about 60 percent men, 40 percent women. Should either sex constitute more than 60 percent of an entering class, the imbalance should be corrected through "active recruitment" of "the underrepresented sex."[50]

In October, Brewster sent the corporation a long memo laying out the "plausible options" with respect to admissions, with comments on the pros and cons of each. The memo offered three choices: a 50–50 balance of men to women; sex-blind admissions, which would likely yield something like a 60–40 split; or a quota limiting the proportion of women to a lower threshold. Brewster hoped that his memo would stimulate widespread discussion on campus.[51]

Indeed, lively discussion followed. The Calhoun college council reported that "Calhoun students want more coeducation and they want it now."[52] Students throughout the colleges made plain their desire "for immediate implementation of a 50–50 arrangement or sex-blind admissions."[53] Echoing the Dahl report, the Yale college council—the federation of the twelve college councils—resolved that "Yale should admit students without regard to sex and with a 40% minimum proportion of either sex," a position endorsed by three thousand students, just over 60 percent of the undergraduate student body.[54] An advisory council of undergraduate women recommended immediate adoption of "a 'sex blind' admissions policy

50 *Report of the Study Group on Yale College*, 1972, p. 49, quoted in Mary B. Arnstein, The Admission of Women to Yale College, July 1974, Brewster II, Box 270, Folder 6; minutes, University Committee on Coeducation, Oct. 30, 1972, Wasserman I, Box 21, Folder 906; University Committee on Coeducation to Kingman Brewster, Jr., Oct. 30, 1972, Brewster I, Box 257, Folder 7.

51 Kingman Brewster, Jr., to Members of the Yale Corporation, Oct. 4, 1972, Brewster II, Box 259, Folder 3 (source of the quote); Brewster, Background Memorandum on Coeducation Admissions Policy, Oct. 18, 1972, Brewster II, Box 258, Folder 1; minutes, University Committee on Coeducation, Oct. 16, 1972, Brewster II, Box 259, Folder 1; Oct. 30, 1972, Wasserman I, Box 21, Folder 906.

52 Calhoun Council Referendum on Coeducation, Oct. 30, 1972, Brewster II, Box 258, Folder 1. In the same folder, see also Ezra Stiles College Council Resolution, Oct. 30, 1972.

53 Minutes, University Committee on Coeducation, Nov. 6, 1972, Wasserman I, Box 21, Folder 906.

54 Resolution, Yale College Council, Nov. 1, 1972 (source of the quote); Gilbert R. Oberfield, Chairman of the Yale College Council, to the President and Fellows of the Yale Corporation, Nov. 10, 1972, both in Brewster II, Box 258, Folder 1.

with an understanding that the ratio should fall within an approximate 60–40 percentage range."[55]

The issue was not simply one of regularizing a ratio but one of
accepting the strongest applicants to the college. The numbers of
women admitted to the freshman class had changed very little in
the first years of coeducation. There had been 230 women in the
entering class of 1973 (18 percent), 258 in 1974, and 249 in 1975.
That number had grown to 311 in the class of 1976 (23 percent),
but there were many highly qualified women for whom there was
no room.[56]

The dean of admission, Worth David, wrote Brewster conveying
his office's recommendation that "the University adopt a policy of
admission on the basis of qualifications, without regard to sex," with
recruiting by the admission office "to correct imbalance in the event
that an entering class is comprised of more than 60% of one sex."
With the policy currently in place, the admission committee had
been forced to reject women "in favor of less well-qualified male applicants." And the quota was affecting the pool. Some students were
declining to apply because of Yale's discriminatory policy; some
well-qualified women appeared unwilling to subject themselves to
"a selection process which a quota has rendered unduly rigorous."[57]

At the request of the newly established Association of Yale
Alumni (AYA), which wanted time to sound out alumni opinion,
Brewster waited an extra month to take his recommendation to
the corporation.[58] For the first time, the corporation would be acting on matters related to coeducation with two women among its
members, both elected in 1971: Hanna Holborn Gray, professor of
history at the University of Chicago, with a B.A. from Bryn Mawr
and a Ph.D. from Harvard, the daughter of Hajo Holborn, the distinguished historian of modern Germany who had taught at Yale
for thirty-five years, and Marian Wright Edelman, a civil rights

55 Women's Advisory Council on Coeducation to the Members of the Yale Corporation, Nov. 2, 1972, Brewster II, Box 258, Folder 1.

56 Mary B. Arnstein, Coeducation Report 1972–73, July 1973, Table 7, Brewster II,
Box 258, Folder 11.

57 Worth David to Kingman Brewster, Jr., Nov. 8, 1972, Brewster II, Box 258, Folder 4.

58 *Yale Daily News*, Nov. 17, 1972; "Trustees Vote to Increase the Number of
Women," *Yale Alumni Magazine* 36 (Jan. 1973): 30.

activist and public-interest lawyer, with a B.A. from Spelman College and an L.L.B from Yale (1963), who would shortly found the Children's Defense Fund.

Following the president's guidance, the corporation opted not for equal access but rather for increased numbers of women and a modest decrease in the number of men, with a ratio of 60 percent men to 40 percent women imagined as the outer limit of what could be sustained in light of Yale's historic commitment to educating male leaders. On December 9, 1972, the corporation voted to increase significantly the number of women admitted to the class of 1977—admitting somewhere between 100 and 130 more students, depending on the overall size of the class—and stated as university policy the admission of students "on their merits without setting numerical quotas for the number of men and women." Like other "special objectives sought by admissions policy," the corporation said, "the objective of achieving and maintaining a satisfactory balance in the number of men and women in residence" might best be achieved "by special recruiting efforts rather than by rigid quotas imposed on the selection process."[59]

In supplementary notes, members of the corporation elaborated on their thinking. "Merit and potential" should be the criteria for admission to Yale College. Gender "should not be the deciding factor in a candidate's chance of admission." They believed strongly "that there must be a far closer balance" between the numbers of men and women in the college and that it was "very important to increase as soon as practicable the total number of women in all classes in Yale College so that there are at least half as many women in the college as there are men." That might mean as much as a 10 to 15 percent reduction in the number of men admitted to the entering class, a decrease they were prepared to accept. The majority of corporation members thought that a 60–40 male-female ratio was about right, so long as it was achieved by special recruiting efforts rather than rigid quotas, minimums, or ceilings.[60]

59 Minutes of Meeting of Yale Corporation, Dec. 9, 1972, Brewster II, Box 258, Folder 8.

60 Yale Corporation, Supplementary Notes, Dec. 9, 1972, Brewster II, Box 258, Folder 8.

As forward-looking as many members of the corporation were, they were also deeply committed to the Yale they had known. Embracing the 60–40 ratio allowed the corporation to make some modest progress on enrolling women without threatening the commitment to alumni to produce a thousand male leaders. It also enabled a consensus among corporation members with varying views about how quickly change should occur.[61]

Although the AYA leadership had taken a position consistent with the corporation's action, by no means all alumni were on board.[62] The president of the alumni group in Mobile, Alabama, registered strong objections to "demands for 'equalization.'" If there were to be a specified ratio based on sex, untold mischief would follow, with campaigns for "more 'equality' for brunettes," redheads, and blondes. One might even anticipate a campaign "for bald students to receive their pro rata share of openings at Yale." Furthermore, "Yale was created as a university for men, designed for men," and it was a mistake to imagine bending to make "concessions" to the "whims" and "passing passions" of the young in order "to satisfy the growing demands of the feminists."[63] A lawyer in Chicago put his concerns starkly: "I have always believed that Yale was a college to train men, and I mean men not women, for positions of leadership in this country." Admitting fewer men would mean producing fewer leaders.[64]

Kingman Brewster's Legacy

Neither Brewster nor the corporation sought to reshape the historic commitments of the university. Rather, they were trying to balance objectives that were in clear tension with one another: on the one hand, the educational imperative to bring more undergraduate women into the college, recognizing that the housing stock

61 Interview with Hanna Holborn Gray, Nov. 18, 2014, New York City.

62 AYA Board of Governors Report on Coeducation, Dec. 2, 1972, Brewster II, Box 258, Folder 1. The AYA had recommended that a 60–40 admission policy be implemented over a period of five years and that the number of men not be reduced by more than 10 percent.

63 Sidney J. Gerhardt to Jonathan Fanton, Dec. 5, 1972, Brewster II, Box 258, Folder 1.

64 Gardner Brown to Kingman Brewster, Jr., Dec. 27, 1972, Brewster II, Box 259, Folder 4.

precluded any significant increase in enrollment, and, on the other, the practical desire not to upset the applecart by disrespecting the fact that Yale had been, and still was in many ways, fundamentally a male institution. It was one thing to make progress toward real coeducation, but it was another to go too far. For Brewster and the corporation in 1972, equal access would have crossed the outer limit of acceptability.

When President Jimmy Carter named Brewster ambassador to the Court of St. James's in 1977, it afforded the opportunity for a highly controversial university president's graceful departure. And it left behind the still-uncompleted business of making Yale fully coeducational. The decision of the corporation in 1972 to increase the number of women admitted to the class of 1977 led to an enrolled freshman class with 848 men and 440 women, or 34 percent.[65] As table 11.1 shows, the balance of men and women in the undergraduate student body had changed significantly under Brewster's leadership.

In 1979, for the first time, the undergraduate student body reached the planned threshold of 40 percent women.[66] Nonetheless, there were still innocent slips that reminded women students of Yale's firmly entrenched all-male history. Brewster himself unwittingly offended women students in an off-the-cuff newspaper interview by describing himself as a "60–40 man" and by speaking of the ratio between the sexes in terms of what would work best in terms of "dancing partners." As he explained to students who objected to the reference, "I've come from a generation where we had a lot of dinner dances and they were always better if there were more men than women. I am a survivor from another social era and didn't intend my metaphor to have tremendous significance. I am not likely to use it again if it is going to cause so many echoes."[67]

---

65 Mary B. Arnstein, Report to the President from the University Committee on the Education of Women, 1973–74, July 1, 1974, Table 1, Brewster II, Box 258, Folder 11.

66 Yale College Registrar / IPEDS Fall Headcount Surveys, Yale University Office of Institutional Research.

67 *Honolulu Advertiser* interview, reprinted in *Yale Daily News*, Apr. 25, 1973 ("60–40 man," "dancing partners"); Notes on Kingman Brewster, Jr., meeting with the Sisterhood, May 16, 1973, Brewster II, Box 258, Folder 2.

TABLE 11.1. ENROLLMENT BY GENDER, YALE COLLEGE, 1969–77

Fall of	Men	Women	Total	Percent Women
1969	4,027	576	4,603	12.5
1970	3,934	803	4,737	17.0
1971	3,874	858	4,732	18.1
1972	3,859	1,037	4,896	21.2
1973	3,681	1,262	4,943	25.5
1974	3,345	1,378	4,723	29.2
1975	3,421	1,724	5,145	33.5
1976	3,283	1,948	5,231	37.2
1977	3,242	1,972	5,214	37.8

The "Title IX" protest in 1976 to gain showers for the women's crew team is another example of the inequities that continued at Yale. That same year, in a booklet for incoming freshman women, the Yale undergraduate women's caucus wrote, "Women at Yale are treated differently than men on both an institutional and personal level." Although there was no longer active discrimination against women, there were many ways in which Yale was still falling short of helping women students to deal with more "subtle and more pervasive discriminations." As one of the pioneering women students put it, "There is still the feeling deep inside that at Yale, in graduate school, in a challenging job, we are there on sufferance and we must prove ourselves worthy of the benevolence that puts us there."[68] A woman who transferred to Yale from Pembroke as a junior in 1969 explained it this way: "Institutions that admit women on a quota system while rejecting many with higher qualifications than those offered by some of the men accepted,

68 Lisa Getman, "From Conestoga to Career," remarks prepared for delivery at the annual meeting of the American Council on Education, Miami Beach, FL, Oct. 6, 1972, Wasserman I, Box 23, Folder 921.

institutions whose tenured faculty is 99 percent male, institutions in which the majority of administrative positions are filled by men, are not yet coeducational."[69]

Ironically, Yale had a unique chance to lead its peer institutions by naming a woman as president in the late 1970s. Hanna Holborn Gray had joined the Yale administration as provost in 1974. Dean of the college of arts and sciences at Northwestern University since 1972, she had served on the corporation since 1971. When Brewster left New Haven for London after commencement in May 1977, Gray was named acting president of the university. Brewster had hoped that she might succeed him, but, anticipating an uproar from alumni, the corporation was unwilling to take the risk. After a difficult year as acting president, Gray left New Haven to begin a long and highly successful presidency at the University of Chicago.[70]

69 Katherine L. Jelly, "Coeducation: One Student's View," remarks prepared for delivery at the annual meeting of the American Council on Education, Miami Beach, FL, Oct. 6, 1972, Wasserman I, Box 23, Folder 921.

70 Kabaservice, *The Guardians*, pp. 454–55.

12

Princeton: "We're All Coeds Now"

Like Yale, Princeton had to deal with pressure for equal access in admissions. The issue came to a head with the April 1973 release of the report of the commission on the future of the college. Appointed by President Robert Goheen in the late winter of 1970 and chaired by sociology professor Marvin Bressler, the nineteen-member commission had been working since early 1971 on "a major review of undergraduate education at Princeton."[1]

The Case for Equal Access

The commission recommended that the university abandon quotas based on sex and adopt a policy of equal access for men and women. The case for equal access was made on three grounds: equality of opportunity, the likely illegality of discrimination on the basis of sex, and the inimical effects of a quota system on efforts to persuade the most qualified women to apply to and matriculate at Princeton.[2]

The moral and educational arguments were compelling. So were the legal considerations. In 1971 U.S. Representative Edith Green (D-Oregon) had offered an amendment to Title IX of the 1972 Higher Education Act to make federal funding of private institutions contingent on cessation of discrimination by sex in the admission of undergraduate students. Senator Birch E. Bayh,

---

1 *The Report of the Commission on the Future of the College, Princeton University,* April 1973. The quote is from p. 3.
2 Ibid., pp. 71–125; *Daily Princetonian,* Mar. 30, 1973.

Democrat of Indiana, had introduced a similar measure in the U.S. Senate. The Green amendment had been narrowly defeated in the House. Although Princeton's trustees had initially resisted the idea of modifying institutional policy as a condition of accepting federal funding, there were no guarantees that the federal government was going to let the issue drop. Indeed, Green resubmitted her bill, with hearings likely to be held early in 1973.[3]

With the Bressler commission's recommendation, equal access had to be taken seriously. The faculty voted for it unanimously; the undergraduate assembly favored it by a vote of 36 to 1.[4] A subcommittee of the trustee curriculum committee, led by John B. Coburn, began work on it in September 1973. In October the full committee engaged the subject: Would equal access improve the quality of undergraduate education? What had the trustees promised in terms of the number of male students going forward? What were the legal implications of equal access?[5]

Goheen, now retired from the presidency, testified to the intent of the trustees. They had authorized the Patterson study "with the 'understanding' that the number of male students in the entering class would not be reduced." It was taken as a "given," "a point of departure for the study." But although it was a "clear understanding," Goheen said, it was not "a formal commitment." He told his successor, William Bowen, that "no one believed that the Board could be bound indefinitely by such a statement."[6] Still, some trustees and other influential alumni believed that a pledge had been made and that "the integrity of the Board and its word" were

---

3 Minutes of Meeting of the Board of Trustees, Princeton University, Apr. 17, 1971, p. 6, Princeton trustees, Series 1, Vol. 69; *Daily Princetonian*, Oct. 14, 1971, and Nov. 21, 1973.

4 Faculty Committee on Undergraduate Admission and Financial Aid and Faculty Committee on the Course of Study to the Faculty, Dec. 3, 1973; R. Manning Brown, Jr., and William G. Bowen to Dear Princetonian, Jan. 24, 1974, both in Subject Files Princeton, Coeducation, Box 377, Folder 7; *Daily Princetonian*, Nov. 20 and 21, 1973.

5 Report of the Sub-Committee on Equal Access of the Curriculum Committee, John B. Coburn to Members of the Board of Trustees, Jan. 1974, Subject Files Princeton, Coeducation, Box 377, Folder 7.

6 History of Coeducation, memorandum, William G. Bowen to W. H. Weathersby, July 16, 1973, Bowen president, Series 2.4, Box 104, Folder 15. On the same theme, in the same series, see memorandum, J[eremiah] S. F[inch] to B[owen], Sept. 7, 1973, Box 105, Folder 1.

at stake. Coburn worried "about the new administration seeming to repudiate a commitment of the previous administration after so short a lapse of time."[7]

At the curriculum committee meeting, the secretary of the university, Jeremiah S. Finch, reviewed the history of the deliberations in 1969, and the new general counsel, Thomas H. Wright, reported on the legal considerations. Wright judged that equal access would "eventually be legally required of the University." A Newark law firm, hired to give an advisory opinion on New Jersey law, agreed. On December 7, the curriculum committee voted unanimously to approve the recommendation for equal access.[8] The next day, the alumni council executive committee endorsed it on a vote of 24 to 3.[9]

The board convened to address the matter on January 19, 1974. They had before them a detailed memorandum from Coburn providing the reasons for the curriculum committee's vote. Equal access, the committee believed, would "enable Princeton to improve the quality of her undergraduate student body, and thus of her education, as she admits the persons best qualified by ability and character to take advantage of her educational resources." As well, "the principle" of equal access was "consistent with the University's fundamental concern for fairness." And legal changes would soon compel equal access. It would be better for Princeton "to take the initiative rather than be forced to such a policy by the public law or legal challenges."[10]

Harold Helm, now a trustee emeritus, who had chaired the committee that recommended adoption of coeducation, emphasized to the board "that any such understanding has to be reviewed in

7 The words "integrity of the Board" are those of H. Chapman Rose, as reported in memorandum, Paul B. Firstenberg to William G. Bowen, Oct. 3, 1973, Bowen president, Series 2.4, Box 105, Folder 1. Coburn's concerns are reported in memorandum, N. L. Rudenstine to Bowen, Nov. 14, 1973, in the same folder.

8 Report of the Sub-Committee on Equal Access of the Curriculum Committee. See also memorandum, Jeremiah S. Finch to John B. Coburn, Sept. 22, 1973, Bowen president, Series 2.4, Box 105, Folder 1.

9 Memorandum, David G. Rahr to William G. Bowen, Dec. 28, 1973, Bowen president, Series 2.4, Box 105, Folder 1.

10 Recommendations on Equal Access, memorandum, Chairman of the Curriculum Committee to the Board of Trustees, Jan. 11, 1974, Bowen president, Series 2.2, Box 59, Folder 8.

the light of changing circumstances, that each successive Board of Trustees has to decide what it believes to be right for Princeton, and that, in his judgment, the Board of Trustees acting in 1969 did not intend to bind all future Boards, even if that were possible."[11] By a vote of 28 to 3, the board adopted a policy of equal access, to take effect for the class of 1978.[12]

1974: "We're All Coeds Now"

After the trustees' announcement of equal access, as a male student later told the story in the Princeton yearbook, the *Bric-a-Brac*, a morning precept began with "a brief discussion of the impact true coeducation might have at Princeton. The preceptor then turned to the lone woman seated at the long walnut table and asked, inevitably, for 'the coed's point of view.' Without a pause or a smile, she responded, 'Why look at me? We're all coeds now.'"[13]

The implicit commitment to maintain male enrollment at 800 in each class was highly sensitive. Alumni had been agitated enough by the decision for coeducation. Agitating them once again on the premise of a broken promise would be destructive for the university. President Bowen and R. Manning Brown, chairman of the trustee executive committee, sent a five-page letter about the decision to alumni leaders. They reported on Helm's statement at the board meeting, reviewed the discussion that followed, and reported the judgment of the trustees that "a policy of equal access accompanied by a decision to limit the growth of the college will best serve the long-term interests of the University." They also reminded their audience of the variation over time in the number of men at Princeton, from classes of about 600 to 650 in the 1920s to the 1940s, to about 750 in the 1950s, to about 800 in the 1960s before the decision for coeducation.[14]

---

11 Brown and Bowen to Dear Princetonian.

12 Princeton University news release, Jan. 19, 1974, Subject Files Princeton, Coeducation, Box 376, Folder 4.

13 Jim Lytle, "Enlivening the Classroom," in "Coeducation: '69–'74," *Bric-a-Brac*, 1974, p. 18.

14 Brown and Bowen to Dear Princetonian.

As Bowen reflected years later, the key was "the proper framing of the real question"; with quotas certain to become illegal, "the choice was simple: (1) stick to the implied promise of maintaining a fixed number of men students and allow the total size of the college to grow . . . or (2) decide on the size of the college and allow the number of men to diminish . . . to accommodate well-qualified women applicants. Put this way, the overwhelming number of people opted to keep the size of Princeton under control and allow the number of men to vary."[15]

Challenges to Full Coeducation

For all the early successes of coeducation, for all the smoothness of the trustee decision for equal access, various counterforces illustrated the complexities of coeducating Princeton in the 1970s. These included the reactions of very conservative alumni, the effort to bring women's studies into the Princeton curriculum, and women's place in the eating clubs.

THE RISE OF THE CONCERNED ALUMNI OF PRINCETON

The prospect of coeducation had enraged conservative alumni. One group, organized in the spring of 1969 under the label A.C.T.I.O.N. (Alumni Committee to Involve Ourselves Now), tried to intervene in the areas they found most offensive, from coeducation to the recruitment of African American students, to loose morals on campus, to what they considered to be coddling of student protesters. The group hoped to mobilize an insurgent slate of alumni trustees to help restore what its members considered the right values for Princeton. President Goheen called A.C.T.I.O.N. a "group of self-appointed critics" whose "deliberate effort to divide the alumni body and set part of it against the administration and trustees is quite reprehensible."[16]

15 I am indebted to William G. Bowen for these observations.

16 *New York Times*, Mar. 13, 1969, clipping in Subject Files Princeton, Box 376, Folder 3; *Daily Princetonian*, Mar. 13 and June 6, 1969; A.C.T.I.O.N. letter, *Princeton Alumni Weekly* 69 (Apr. 22, 1969): 5, 18; Goheen, quoted in Luther Munford, "View from Old Nassau," *Daily Princetonian*, Nov. 25, 1969.

That coeducation was only one among many perceived problems with Princeton was an important point. As one alumnus in the class of 1949 put it, "You want coeducation—you want to kill the eating clubs—you want to turn Princeton into an institution designed to meet the requirements of the average—please feel free to do so—but do not ask me to support it."[17] An alumnus in the class of 1958 from Louisville put it this way: "When the girls, hippies, etc. come in I go out."[18] An alumnus in the class of 1944 from Bronxville, New York, had a longer list of objections: coeducation; the "reverse discrimination" implicit in the effort to attract black students; "the spineless, supine attitude with which the administration confronts S.D.S. and A.B.C. groups on campus [Students for a Democratic Society and the Association of Black Collegians], both of which are known to be Communist-affiliated on a national scale"; the administration's active encouragement of "the eventual abolition of the club system"; and—as was true on so many other campuses—the "general 'out of step' attitude of the Princeton faculty and administration."[19] A member of the class of 1918 in Englewood, Florida, declared: "For my money, Princeton should be—and forever remain—an institution for White, Male, Christians (preferably Scotch Presbyterians)."[20]

These were the themes that motivated the establishment in 1972 of a new organization of extremely conservative alumni, Concerned Alumni of Princeton (CAP), Princeton's equivalent of LUX ET VERITAS at Yale. Everything about the "new" Princeton was troubling: not only coeducation and the admission of significant numbers of black students but also the increasing emphasis on drawing students from more modest socioeconomic backgrounds and from public schools, the downplaying of the admission of alumni sons, campus protests over the Vietnam War, the retreat from ROTC, and a philosophical imbalance that tilted toward

17 Henry D. Prickett to Dear Sirs, [Feb. or Mar.] 1969, Horton, Box 4, Folder 3.

18 James E. Kaiser, handwritten note to Jacob Barlow II, Mar. 1969, Horton, Box 4, Folder 4.

19 William F. Mathieson, Jr., to Douglas D. Donald, Feb. 19, 1969, Horton, Box 4, Folder 3.

20 David Ross Winans to John F. Maloney, Jan. 31, 1969, Horton, Box 4, Folder 1.

leftists and "liberal-radical[s]" among the faculty.[21] What unified supporters of CAP, a member of the advisory board explained, was "love of the University and concern for the (mis-)direction it appears to have taken over the past decade."[22]

CAP was established under the leadership of Shelby Cullom Davis '30 and Asa S. Bushnell '21. Davis, who had made his fortune in investment banking, was then serving as U.S. ambassador to Switzerland. Bushnell, by then retired, had served for decades as the first commissioner of the Eastern College Athletic Conference and as a board member of the U.S. Olympic Committee. Their stated purpose for the new organization sounded innocent enough: CAP "hopes to provide a moderating influence with Princeton's best interests and its future in mind."[23] CAP planned to publish a new magazine, *Prospect*, "to **inform** alumni fully and accurately, to encourage expression of alumni **views**, to foster greater alumni **influence** in decision making, and to achieve a Better and Stronger Princeton."[24] Bailey Brower, Jr., '49 wrote to Bushnell after the first issue of *Prospect* was distributed, "If Alumni only knew what is actually happening at the University they would pull their hair out in disgust."[25]

Equal access was "the latest program being espoused by those out to destroy Princeton," a member of the CAP advisory board wrote to members of the board of trustees: "From a fine university, proud of its traditions, we can now see Princeton taking its place as a 'me too' copy of a second rate state university. . . . For Princeton's sake, no more girls, no more expansion!"[26]

---

21 See, e.g., in CAP, Box 1, Folder 1, Robert H. E. Hein to Ben L. Spinelli, Jan. 7, 1970, and Jere Patterson to Hein, Jan. 12, 1972. In CAP, Box 1, Folder 3, see Shelby Cullom Davis to Lawrence A. Tisch, Feb. 6, 1974 ("liberal-radical"). See also Les Gapay, "Disgruntled Old Grads Form Militant Groups, Cut Gifts to Colleges," *Wall Street Journal*, June 1, 1971, clipping in CAP, Box 1, Folder 7.

22 Robert H. E. Hein, letter to the editor, *Princeton Alumni Weekly*, Oct. 27, 1972, CAP, Box 1, Folder 1.

23 Shelby Cullom Davis and Asa S. Bushnell to Robert H. E. Hein, Sept. 14, 1972, CAP, Box 1, Folder 1.

24 Asa S. Bushnell and Shelby Cullom Davis to Fellow Princetonian, *Prospect*, Oct. 9, 1972, Princeton publications, Series I, Box 15.

25 Bailey Brower, Jr., to Asa S. Bushnell, Oct. 24, 1972, CAP, Box 1, Folder 1.

26 Robert H. E. Hein to Donald Kipp, Jan. 14, 1974, and Hein to Michael Blumenthal, Jan. 15, 1974 ("'me too' copy," "no more expansion"), both in CAP, Box 1, Folder 3.

CAP had a group of undergraduate sympathizers who styled themselves as Undergraduates for a Stable America. They kept watch to ferret out leftist views in faculty lectures. They also made no bones about the fact that they favored rolling back coeducation. To women students, the attitude of CAP sympathizers was "absolutely infuriating." Robin Herman recalled the message she heard from some male students: "I have nothing against you, Robin—I just don't think girls should be at Princeton." At the tenth reunion of the class of 1973, some of the men sported buttons declaring "Bring Back the Old Princeton." In response, the women of '73 designed a banner, "Coeducation Begins," which they carried at all subsequent reunions.[27]

CAP was more of an annoyance, a distraction, than it was a truly powerful disruptive force. From the point of view of the administration, however, it stepped over the line when it started manipulating survey data to advance its political agenda and when it disseminated patently false allegations about Princeton to alumni and parents. In November 1975, a report prepared by a new committee on alumni affairs of the board of trustees sought explicitly to discredit CAP. The report said, "We think CAP's methods are unworthy of its ends and that its opposition has been carping, not constructive. We . . . are confident that [CAP] has hurt the university far more than it has helped." The report was mailed to all alumni "in an effort to 'take the wind out of CAP's sails.'"[28]

Bowen observed years later, "I think, in retrospect, that we paid too much attention to CAP—inadvertently giving too much credence to their views. We finally adopted the policy that we would set our own agenda, not be the prisoner of CAP's agenda. That approach worked very well and CAP eventually just went away."[29]

27 Telephone interview with Robin Herman '73, Mar. 10, 2015.
28 "Princeton Starts Campaign to Discredit Alumni Group," *Trenton Evening Times*, Nov. 14, 1975, clipping in CAP, Box 1, Folder 7.
29 I am indebted to William G. Bowen for these reflections.

RESISTANCE TO WOMEN'S STUDIES

Another challenge to the relatively smooth instantiation of co-education at Princeton concerned the effort to make the study of women and gender part of the curriculum. The decade of the 1970s saw the emergence of women's studies as a field of scholarly study in American colleges and universities. By December 1970, more than 100 courses had been created; by 1980 there were at least 20,000 courses and 350 programs.[30] Cornell established a women's studies program in 1972; Dartmouth's program was instituted in 1978, Yale's in 1979, Harvard's—the last in the Ivy League—in 1986. Princeton's experience illustrates the complexity of venturing into this intellectually exhilarating but politically contested terrain.

It was difficult to persuade male faculty members that gender was an appropriate area for study. Just as Yale had a history professor who compared women's history to the history of dogs, so Princeton had an English professor who declared, to a woman student expressing an interest in writing her junior independent paper on women writers, "I'm interested in auto mechanics, but I don't try to bring that into the curriculum." When Harvard polled department chairs about including women's studies in their offerings, one male faculty member responded that "his department did not offer any relevant courses—but also had no classes dedicated to the study of 'cannibals, children, or veterans of foreign wars.'"[31] Many male professors regarded women's studies with skepticism or outright hostility. Women's studies was often thought to be frivolous, faddish, political, a movement based on women's desire for representation rather than on a commitment to serious intellectual inquiry.[32]

---

30 Catharine R. Stimpson with Nina Kressner Cobb, *Women's Studies in the United States: A Report to the Ford Foundation* (New York: Ford Foundation, 1986), p. 4.

31 Drew Gilpin Faust, "Mingling Promiscuously: A History of Women and Men at Harvard," in Laurel Thatcher Ulrich, ed., *Yards and Gates: Gender in Harvard and Radcliffe History* (New York: Palgrave Macmillan, 2004), p. 324.

32 See, e.g., "Founding the Committee for Women's Studies," in Ulrich, ed., *Yards and Gates*, pp. 299–302.

The initial strategy of the small group of women faculty at Princeton who were interested in the study of gender was to encourage students to approach department chairs to ask that they offer courses relating to gender. Such courses were offered occasionally in departments including sociology, politics, history, psychology, and English. But making a commitment to regular course offerings about gender meant hiring scholars who studied gender, and most departments had other hiring priorities. Moreover, some assistant professors whose research was related to gender failed to win reappointment or promotion to tenure—evidence, it was claimed, that specializing in the study of gender would be toxic to a woman's academic career. Under the imprimatur of the dean of the faculty, physicist Aaron Lemonick, some of the tenured women faculty members met with selected department chairs to suggest how the university might make better progress in appointing women faculty and offering courses related to gender, but their efforts met with relatively little enthusiasm.

At the same time, students made it clear that they wanted to study gender. From 1975 to 1980, more than two hundred senior theses were written on topics that would fall under the rubric of women's studies.[33] In 1979 a new group called WHEN—Women's Studies Hiring, Education Network—was organized at the women's center to press for the establishment of an undergraduate certificate program in women's studies and for the promotion to tenure of more female faculty members.[34] Impatient with the very slow progress on women's studies, women students affiliated with the women's center threatened a march on Nassau Hall.

Lemonick and the dean of the college, psychologist Joan S. Girgus, responded in the winter of 1979–80 by appointing an ad hoc

---

33 Margaret M. Keenan, "The Controversy over Women's Studies: And the Related Issue of Whether Princeton Is Hiring and Tenuring Enough Women Faculty Members Come to the Fore as the University Marks the 10th Anniversary of Coeducation," *Princeton Alumni Weekly*, Apr. 21, 1980, p. 13, cited in Catherine Keyser, *Transforming the Tiger: A Celebration of Undergraduate Women at Princeton University* (Princeton University, 2001), p. 47.

34 Elena Kagan, "The Women's Center: Gaining a New Identity amidst Controversy," and Kagan, "Karp Leads Women's Center with Chutzpah, Aggressiveness," both in *Daily Princetonian* supplement, "Women at Princeton: The First Ten Years," Nov. 1979, pp. S-1, S-7.

committee of senior faculty members to advise on whether women's studies belonged in the Princeton curriculum. The committee was made up of four senior women faculty members who studied gender (it was considered too risky for junior women faculty, many of whom had scholarly interests in gender, to be identified publicly with the effort) and four prominent male faculty members who, if they were persuaded in committee of the importance of studying gender, could help make a case for the establishment of an undergraduate certificate program. The undergraduate student government selected seven women students to serve on the committee. History professor Nancy Weiss, though not herself a scholar who studied gender, was appointed chair.

The committee read widely in the field, consulted outside experts, studied course syllabi and program descriptions from other institutions, and solicited the views of undergraduates, graduate students, and faculty members. It made an inventory of women's studies courses that had been offered at Princeton and considered the proposal for a program prepared by WHEN.

In the end, the group agreed unanimously that the study of gender was an important new intellectual venture, fundamentally interdisciplinary, that raised questions that were recasting the basic assumptions of many of the disciplines. As the report of the ad hoc committee on the future of women's studies put it:

> The Ad Hoc Committee is convinced that women's studies is an area of great intellectual vitality and excitement. It has both a subject matter—the political, economic, social, and cultural activity of women, and the function of gender roles in societies and cultures, past and present—and a critical thrust. Adding women to the population studied and asking questions that posit gender as a cultural construct instead of accepting gender categories as natural, fundamentally alters the assumptions and modes of analysis of some aspects of some traditional academic disciplines. Ideally, women's studies should pervade, inform, and invigorate a wide variety of established disciplines by raising new questions and suggesting new, sometimes interdisciplinary approaches. We believe

that women's studies should be an integral part of a Princeton education in the 1980's.[35]

The ad hoc committee report was completed in May 1980. On January 5, 1981, at an unusually well-attended faculty meeting, the proposal for an interdisciplinary undergraduate certificate program in women's studies was approved overwhelmingly, with only two dissenting votes. The program began in 1981–82 under Weiss's temporary leadership. The first appointed director, anthropologist Kay Barbara Warren, took office in 1982–83.

EATING CLUBS: THE LAST BASTION OF MALE PRIVILEGE

The third challenge to achieving full coeducation at Princeton concerned the admission of women to the all-male eating clubs. The clubs were private—they owned their own buildings, were funded by student dues, and were run by undergraduate officers accountable to governing boards made up of alumni. But the clubs were bound up inextricably with the university. Their membership was made up exclusively of Princeton students. They had fed the large majority of juniors and seniors at Princeton since the late nineteenth century. And the university provided the clubs with a variety of services, among them access to alumni records and mailing services, garbage collection and snow plowing, and, later, access to the university's computer network.

Women students began in the late 1970s to challenge their exclusion from Cottage, Ivy, and Tiger Inn. In February 1977, two women in the class of 1979 tried to bicker (the colloquial term for seeking admission to the selective eating clubs) at the three clubs, but their failed effort did not cause any stir. In February 1978, five women, including Sally Frank '80, tried to bicker at the all-male clubs, but they encountered many obstacles, including some clubs' refusal to grant them interviews. When Frank tried again to bicker at Cottage in the fall of 1978, the reaction was much

35 Report of the Ad Hoc Committee on the Future of Women's Studies, Princeton University, May 1980, in the possession of Nancy Weiss Malkiel.

stronger. Members poured beer over her head, threw several more beers at her, and shouted, "Let's throw Sally Frank into the fountain." Frank responded by filing a complaint with the New Jersey Civil Rights Division against the university, Cottage, Ivy, and Tiger on the grounds that they discriminated against women. As Frank went public with her charges of sex discrimination, she continued to be harassed, now verbally, "through anonymous phone calls, drunken screams of mockery, and insulting comments."

The New Jersey Civil Rights Division ruled in June 1979 that the clubs were "distinctly private" and that the division had no jurisdiction. Frank then filed a complaint with the U.S. Department of Health, Education, and Welfare, but HEW dismissed it on the grounds that the clubs were private. Frank recognized that private clubs had the right to discriminate against women. In her view, however, the eating clubs did not meet that test; they were so closely affiliated with the university as to be the equivalent of public accommodations, and excluding women from membership deprived women of advantages and opportunities available to Princeton men. But Frank's concerns were grounded in more than a legal argument; they were "based on the moral conviction that the discrimination [was] wrong." Discrimination in the clubs "create[d] an atmosphere on campus in which sexism [was] more accepted"—an atmosphere at odds with the imperative that Princeton men should learn "to accept women as equals."[36] That conviction led Frank to resubmit her complaint to the New Jersey Civil Rights Division in November 1979. Two years later, the division came to the same conclusion that it had earlier: The clubs were private, and state anti-discrimination laws did not pertain to them.

Frank appealed the decision to the Appellate Division of the New Jersey Superior Court. In August 1983, the court sent the complaint back to the New Jersey Civil Rights Division for

---

36 "Sally Frank: The Morality of Discrimination," *Princeton Forerunner*, May 1, 1979, clipping in Princeton publications, Series 3, Box 35; Colleen Baker, "Coeducation at Princeton: Sally Frank's Legal Battle against the Eating Clubs and the Social Reaction of Princeton's Campus," paper written for Freshman Seminar 149, Jan. 15, 2013, Princeton University, in the possession of Nancy Weiss Malkiel. On the earlier attempt, see Bob Cooper and Seth Chandler, "1976–77: Year of Resignations, Labor Problems, Admissions Controversies," *Daily Princetonian*, July 25, 1977, p. 11.

reconsideration. In May 1985, the division reached a different conclusion: The eating clubs were public accommodations, there was ample evidence of sex discrimination in their admission practices, and the university—inextricably linked as it was with the clubs—had aided and abetted that discrimination.

Cottage Club decided in 1986 to admit women and reached a settlement with Frank. The university also settled with her. That left Ivy and Tiger as the targets of Frank's legal battle. In May 1987, the New Jersey Civil Rights Division issued a final decision ordering the two clubs to admit women in the next round of bicker and awarding Frank compensatory damages. The clubs responded with an appeal to the Appellate Division of the New Jersey Superior Court. In October 1988, the case was sent back to the Civil Rights Division on grounds of procedural errors in the previous investigation. Frank appealed again, this time to the New Jersey Supreme Court, which heard the case beginning in January 1990. While the case made its way through the court, both clubs took their first votes to admit women—decisions that, by their rules, would need to be confirmed by second votes the following year. In July 1990, the New Jersey Supreme Court ruled that Ivy and Tiger could no longer refuse to admit women to membership on grounds of gender. Efforts to appeal the court ruling came to naught, and Ivy and Tiger began extending bids to women in bicker in 1991 and settled with Frank in 1992.[37]

In 1990, at Bowen's urging, the alumni council gave Frank one of its awards for distinguished service to Princeton. The citation referred to her as a "loving critic" who had "committed herself to coeducation and an increased role for women in the life of the University. She campaigned for a Women's Studies program, for more tenured women faculty, and for the Women's Center." She had become, the citation said, "a symbol to student and alumni activists who look to her for inspiration and encouragement."[38] There was no mention of Frank's legal campaign against the all-male clubs, but everyone knew what Frank stood for. As Bowen recalled, the

37 Baker, "Coeducation at Princeton."
38 "The Alumni Council Award for Service to Princeton: Sally B. Frank '80," text courtesy of Margaret Miller.

decision to honor Frank "enraged" some alumni leaders. But he knew it was the right move. "Honoring her in this way was an important statement of the University's values."[39]

An "Infinitely Richer, More Intellectually Interesting, More Warmly Human" Princeton

As the first decade of coeducation at Princeton came to a close, faculty members noted the many positive qualities women students had brought to the university. Suzanne Keller remarked on the change in "the style of the university": There was "a freer spirit," with "more wit, humor, less pretentiousness . . . more innovation, more insouciance."[40] Edward D. Sullivan, professor of Romance languages and literatures, dean of the college from 1966 to 1972 and later chairman of the humanities council, said, "This university is, in my view, infinitely richer, more varied, more intellectually interesting, more warmly human than it ever was before 1969, however much I enjoyed the Princeton that I first knew in 1946." Charles C. Gillispie, professor of history and director of the program in history and philosophy of science, said, "I have no doubt that [coeducation] is the best thing that has happened to Princeton since 1746."[41]

Hitherto skeptical alumni had been won over as well. It was one thing to be opposed to coeducation in the abstract; it was a different situation when daughters and granddaughters eagerly seized the opportunity to enroll. And the women students themselves, with their credentials and accomplishments, easily made the case for the wisdom of Princeton's new direction. "It seemed to me," Bowen told John William Ward, the president of Amherst, who had asked about alumni reactions to coeducation at Princeton, "that many people who were against coeducation 'in principle' would not be against real live women students when they saw them—and when they saw

39 I am indebted to William G. Bowen for this story.

40 Quoted in William McCleery, *Conversations on the Character of Princeton* (Princeton University, 1986), p. 58.

41 Quoted in William G. Bowen, "Coeducation at Princeton," *Princeton University, Report of the President*, April 1980, p. 18.

how impressive they were."[42] To that point, after hearing Laurie Watson speak on a panel in the early months of coeducation, an alumnus told Bowen, "It was easy for me to be against coeducation; it is impossible for me to be against Laurie Watson!"[43]

By the close of the 1970s, Princeton had seen its first woman valedictorian as well as its first woman Latin salutatorian—as it happened, in the same year, 1975, when the faculty chose Cynthia Chase and Lisa Siegman to speak for the graduating class at commencement. In 1977, the first year that women were eligible for the competition, Suzanne Perles '75 was named a Rhodes Scholar. Like Marsha Levy, Nancy Peretsman '76 had been elected to serve as a young alumni trustee. Three more women—Jo R. Backer '75, Sonia Sotomayor '76, and Nancy J. Newman '78—had followed Levy in winning the M. Taylor Pyne Honor Prize. Five women had been elected class presidents. Anne Mackay-Smith '80 had been elected the first woman chairman of the *Daily Princetonian*. Robin Herman '73 had become the first sports editor of the *Princetonian*, and Elena Kagan '81 regularly handled football reporting for the paper. Both of them had gone on to positions of broader responsibility at the paper: Herman as managing editor, Kagan as editorial chairman. Tower Club became the first eating club to elect a woman president. Quadrangle followed suit, and in 1979–80, two of thirteen clubs were headed by women.[44]

And coeducation had accomplished what its proponents had hoped for in terms of encouraging larger numbers of qualified applicants to apply to Princeton. In March 1974, Princeton's new director of admission, Timothy C. Callard '63, announced that completed applications for the class of 1978 were up by 13 percent, "an increase sharply countering the national trend." The number of applications from women grew by more than 18 percent over

42 William G. Bowen to John William Ward, Nov. 10, 1972, Bowen president, Series 2.4, Box 104, Folder 14.

43 I am indebted to William G. Bowen for this story.

44 Emily Buchanan '81, "On the Campus: Coeducation's Tenth," *Princeton Alumni Weekly* 80 (Dec. 3, 1979): 17; Keyser, *Transforming the Tiger*, p. 76; *Report of the Steering Committee on Undergraduate Women's Leadership* (Princeton University, Mar. 2011), pp. 25–28; "New Trustee Peretsman '76 Targets Academic Pressure," *Daily Princetonian*, June 4, 1976, p. 1.

the previous year—not unexpected, given the new policy of equal access. That the number of applications from men grew by 10 percent came as a surprise. "The overall jump," Callard said, was "the largest single-year increase this year among Ivy League schools . . . and, this is at a time when many colleges in the country are actually experiencing declining enrollments."[45]

All told, from 1968–69 (for the class of 1973) to 1978–79 (for the class of 1983), the total number of applications rose from 6,088 to 11,106, an increase of 82 percent. Moreover, there was a marked increase in the quality of the pool. The number of applicants with verbal SAT scores over 700 increased 72 percent, and the number with math SAT scores over 700 increased 59 percent— and that at a time when the number of graduating seniors with those credentials was declining significantly. Beyond SAT scores, there were other indices of quality: The number of student council presidents applying to Princeton increased 87 percent; the number of editors-in-chief, 109 percent; and the number of athletic team captains, 102 percent.[46]

Significant progress had also been made in appointing women to the Princeton faculty. In 1969–70 Princeton had one tenured woman faculty member, two women assistant professors, and 17 women teaching as lecturers and instructors (for example, in foreign languages). In 1979–80, Princeton had 10 tenured women, 40 women assistant professors, and 35 women teaching as lecturers and instructors—that out of a total faculty of 371 tenured professors, 196 assistant professors, and 122 lecturers and instructors. Women had also been appointed to the senior administrative ranks. Bowen had worked hard to identify women who would be strong candidates for appointment, and at various points during the 1970s women had held three of the senior deanships at Princeton—dean of student affairs, Africanist Adele Smith Simmons (1972–77); dean of the graduate school, Byzantinist Nina G. Garsoian (1977–79); and dean of the college, psychologist Joan S. Girgus (1977–87).[47]

45 Princeton University news release, Mar. 20, 1974, Admission Office, Box 1, Folder 7.

46 Bowen, "Coeducation at Princeton," pp. 6, 8–9.

47 Ibid., pp. 20–21. On Bowen's efforts to identify candidates, see, e.g., William G. Bowen to Patricia Graham, Jan. 26, 1972, and Bowen to Elga R. Wasserman, Jan. 26, 1972, both in Bowen president, Series 2.1, Box 48, Folder 2.

After her retirement from the presidency of Radcliffe in 1972, Polly Bunting had accepted Bowen's invitation to come to Princeton for three years as "assistant to the president for special projects." Bunting set up a program in continuing education, advised Bowen about a range of educational issues (whether Princeton should establish additional professional schools and how it might strengthen work in the life sciences), gave moral and practical support to women faculty and staff, and provided counsel and wisdom on a host of other issues. By bringing someone of Bunting's stature to the university, Bowen conveyed a powerful message: Princeton had to move forward, and change—orderly, constructive change—was coming. The director of personnel, Will Reed, remembered Bunting this way: "She was reasoned and skillful. She was such a lady but with such a powerful mind and with such a reputation . . . when she spoke, people listened." Bowen "could have brought in someone who was a radical and was going to scare everybody. But instead he brought in somebody who was so reasonable and of such substance that she won the day over and over again."[48]

Equal access may have been a red flag for some disgruntled alumni, but it was not nearly as disruptive as critics had feared in terms of changing the ratio of undergraduate men to women. As table 12.1 shows, the number of women crept up slowly, and equal access proved to be more important in the near term as a statement of institutional policy than as an instrument for genuine change in the composition of the student body. Indeed—and ironically—Princeton, which in some of the early years of coeducation had matched or outdistanced Yale in the percentage of women in the undergraduate student body and where the board had stepped forward decisively to approve equal access, ended up making progress more slowly than Yale, where the corporation declined to embrace equal access in favor of a 60–40 male-female ratio.[49]

48 Elaine Yaffe, *Mary Ingraham Bunting: Her Two Lives* (Savannah, GA: Frederic C. Beil, 2005), pp. 273–80 ("assistant to the president for special projects" is on p. 274; the Reed quote is on p. 279).

49 As William G. Bowen has pointed out, "This was due in part to the greater numerical importance of engineering at Princeton than at Yale, and to the fact that in those years women were less interested than men in engineering."

TABLE 12.1. UNDERGRADUATE ENROLLMENT BY GENDER,
YALE AND PRINCETON, 1969–80

Fall of	Percent Women, Yale	Percent Women, Princeton
1969	12.5	4.4
1970	17.0	10.7
1971	18.1	19.0
1972	21.2	24.0
1973	25.5	26.7
1974	29.2	29.2
1975	33.5	30.5
1976	37.2	32.0
1977	37.8	33.0
1978	38.8	34.6
1979	40.7	35.8
1980	41.8	36.9

Princeton reached the threshold of 40 percent women in 1990 and, in 2010, finally approached a 50–50 male-female ratio, a ratio Yale had approximated since 1997.[50] One of the factors in Princeton's slowness was a stubborn imbalance of men and women in the applicant pool, possibly due to the comparatively large proportion of the student body made up of engineers, possibly due to the continuing perception of Princeton as socially conservative, given the influence of the eating clubs. Given Princeton's history and traditions, what is remarkable is not that gender balance took so long but that coeducation was as effective as it was.

50 Yale data from Yale College Registrar / IPEDS Fall Headcount Surveys, Yale University Office of Institutional Research; Princeton data from Princeton University Registrar's Office.

Part II

The Seven Sisters:
Vassar, Smith, and Wellesley

13

Vassar: "Separate Education for Women Has No Future"

We turn next to coeducation in the elite women's colleges. The Seven Sisters were highly prestigious, and they were closely connected to the men's colleges and universities. As we have already seen, the history of coeducation at Harvard was inextricably linked to the evolving status of its coordinate partner, Radcliffe; with the impulse for coeducation, Vassar and Wellesley emerged for a time as potential partners, respectively, of Yale and Dartmouth. As we shall see, Vassar went coed at the same time as the men's schools and for many of the same reasons; Smith and Wellesley seriously entertained coeducation but chose to back away.

"The Problems with Vassar": Alan Simpson's Analysis

Like Yale and Princeton, Vassar embarked on coeducation in large part because application patterns revealed that single-sex education was no longer as attractive to the college's traditional student constituency as it had been historically. The issue was not solely the appeal of single-sex education but also the appeal of single-sex education *at Vassar* in comparison with its Seven Sisters peers. Vassar was different from Yale and Princeton in two important ways. First, the reduction in the quality and numbers of applications that Vassar had experienced over the course of the 1960s was more dramatic than it was at the men's colleges. Second, no one doubted that if Yale and Princeton coeducated, excellent women students would want to enroll. No one was sure that talented men would want to go to Vassar.

In the fall of 1966, the president of Vassar, Alan Simpson, began to explore alternate arrangements for Vassar's future. Simpson had come to Vassar confident about its mission as a liberal arts college devoted to educating talented women.[1] But he soon found that the realities of collegiate life in Poughkeepsie were more complicated than Vassar's reputation suggested.

A wealthy brewer, Matthew Vassar, had founded Vassar in 1865 to provide collegiate education for women equal to the education for men at Harvard and Yale. It was the second of the group of women's colleges that became known as the Seven Sisters. Mt. Holyoke began as a seminary in 1837; Smith and Wellesley opened as colleges in 1875, Bryn Mawr in 1885, Barnard in 1889, and Radcliffe in 1894.

With a large building to fill and a limited constituency of students in 1865 who were ready to tackle a college curriculum, Vassar was obliged to open with a preparatory division, which accounted for two-thirds of Vassar's earliest cohorts of students.[2] Over time, the preparatory division was closed, and Vassar became one of the most famous and prestigious of the women's colleges. The first person appointed to the faculty in 1865 had been Maria Mitchell, the first American woman to work as a professional astronomer, famed for her discovery in 1847 of a comet that would be named in her honor. The college boasted distinguished alumnae, like the poet Edna St. Vincent Millay, a member of the class of 1917, and the author Mary McCarthy, a member of the class of 1933. Thanks to McCarthy's novel *The Group*, collegiate life at Vassar became a staple of the popular culture of the 1960s. A semiautobiographical, fictionalized account of the work experience, family lives, and sexual relationships of eight young women who had graduated from Vassar in 1933, *The Group* was on the best-seller list for two years after its publication in 1963 and was

1 See, e.g., Alan Simpson, "Inaugural Address," *Vassar Alumnae Magazine* 50 (Dec. 1964): 13–15, Vassar College Library.

2 Elizabeth A. Daniels and Clyde Griffen, *"Full Steam Ahead in Poughkeepsie": The Story of Coeducation at Vassar, 1966–1974* (Vassar College, 2000), foreword and p. 77.

made into a film by United Artists in 1966. As late as the fall of 1968, having internalized Vassar's self-image of prestige and distinction, the Vassar chaplain could stand up in a faculty meeting and claim, in all sincerity, "Vassar College is the Woman's College in the mind of God."[3]

But neither fame nor notoriety nor the deity's apparent blessing bore on the reality of collegiate life at Vassar in the latter half of the 1960s. In September 1964, in Simpson's first meeting with his trustee executive committee, he reported on his "tentative impressions about the strengths and weaknesses of the college." For all the strengths, Vassar had two especially worrisome weaknesses: the quality of the student body and the quality of the faculty. Simpson expressed the hope that Vassar would be able to "attract a greater number of students of first rate quality," and he expressed regret that "the faculty did not include more truly distinguished teachers and scholars." On both counts, he emphasized "the necessity of working towards increasing the ferment of intellectual excitement on the campus." In December, Simpson raised another red flag when he told the executive committee that at Vassar (as was probably true of the other Seven Sisters), standards for the promotion and tenure of faculty members were "softer" than at first-rate universities and that the Vassar faculty tended to "underestimate the importance of scholarship in making recommendations for promotion."[4]

As Simpson quickly came to understand, Vassar's principal problem was its geographical setting. Each of the other Seven Sisters benefited from locations close to men's colleges and universities. Radcliffe had Harvard down the street. Smith and Mt. Holyoke had Amherst and the University of Massachusetts a bus ride away. Wellesley, on the outskirts of Boston, offered access to both Harvard and MIT. Barnard was across the street from Columbia, Bryn Mawr a little over two miles up the road from Haverford.

---

3 Ibid., pp. 11, 89 (source of the quote).

4 Vassar trustees (E), Sept. 15, 1964, pp. 11–12, and Dec. 8, 1964, p. 7. At the March 1965 meeting of the executive committee, Simpson elaborated in some detail his views about the appropriate balance between teaching and scholarship at a college like Vassar; see ibid., Mar. 9, 1965, pp. 7–8.

By contrast, Poughkeepsie was off the beaten track. Except for West Point, a half-hour away on the Hudson River, no colleges were nearby. Vassar had a reputation as a "suitcase school" where students packed their bags on Thursday afternoon and unpacked on Monday. The college's dean of residence estimated that more than 75 percent of students were away from campus every week-end. New students at Vassar learned quickly how to budget their time for social purposes. The train to New York City took about two hours (it would have taken roughly the same amount of time to drive). With a car, it was possible to get to Yale in an hour and three quarters to two hours; to Princeton, in two and a half to three hours.[5]

For most of the previous century, Vassar's isolation had not been of significant consequence, but by the mid-1960s it was clearly becoming a problem. It affected recruitment of faculty members. It also affected recruitment of students. Vassar women, who came increasingly from public secondary schools, were growing more dissatisfied with their geographical distance from men's colleges. Real concerns developed about Vassar's competitiveness in admissions in relation to several other Seven Sisters schools.

A questionnaire sent after the admission season in 1966 to students admitted to the class of 1970 who had chosen to go elsewhere put the problem in sharp relief. Vassar had experienced unusual difficulty filling its incoming class, and the college wanted to know why. The findings were troubling. Many of the students Vassar admitted were being rejected by the colleges it considered to be its closest peers, like Radcliffe, Wellesley, Smith, and Bryn Mawr. And where students were admitted to Vassar and one or more of those institutions, the college was not drawing what it thought to be its fair share of acceptances. At the same time, Vassar

5 Vassar College, *A Self-Study Report*, Feb. 1979, p. 75 ("suitcase school"), Middle States; Colton Johnson, "Conversations about Vassar History with Historian Elizabeth A. Daniels," Conversation 2: "The Simpson Years, 1964–1977," 1995, *Vassar Encyclopedia*, http://vcencyclopedia.vassar.edu/interviews-reflections/daniels/conversation-two.html, accessed May 23, 2014; Elizabeth Daniels, "Interview with Elizabeth Moffatt Drouilhet" (college warden or dean of residence), Part 4: June 1982, http://vcencyclopedia.vassar.edu /interviews-reflections/elizabeth-moffatt-drouilhet.html, accessed May 23, 2014; Laura Jones, "As the Students See It," *Vassar Alumnae Magazine* 54 (Feb. 1969): 2.

won more of the cross-admits from the less competitive Seven Sisters, Barnard and Mt. Holyoke, as well as from the next tier of women's colleges, like Goucher, Connecticut, Jackson, and Elmira. Among the reasons students gave for not accepting Vassar's offer, the most important were location—nearness to a metropolitan center—and proximity to men.[6]

John Wilkie's Proposal of New Directions

As early as the spring of 1966, the question of how Vassar would best address these challenges had become a topic of lively discussion for Simpson and the trustees. Vassar's board chair, John Wilkie, a utilities executive who served as president and chairman of Central Hudson Gas and Electric Corporation, took an active role in shaping the agenda. Although Wilkie believed that Vassar should continue to be a women's college, he told Simpson privately that the college faced real risks: losing existing faculty and "increasing difficulty in attracting new faculty of requisite quality"; losing "its traditional share" of able, motivated students; and, perhaps most worrying, "becoming known as good but self-satisfied, possibly retrospective as a force in our society, defensive rather than aggressive, with a great tradition but an uncertain future."

What could be done to counter these risks? Wilkie imagined a number of initiatives: establishing a coordinate men's college (unlikely to work; at best, it would probably be of "lesser standing" than Vassar); developing "some form of coordination with an existing men's college or university of equivalent standing" (hard to do, given geography and the desirability of maintaining control of "a solution to our possible future problems"); developing studies in some promising new fields; pursuing adult education; and moving into graduate education.[7] Wilkie thought that

6 Clyde Griffen, Report on Questionnaires about Choice of College, n.d. [1966], Dean of College/Faculty, Box 42; memorandum, Griffen to Alan Simpson, Sept. 11, 1966, Dean of Students, Box 5.

7 John Wilkie to Alan Simpson, Memorandum of Apr. 9, 1966, with respect to Vassar's future, Wilkie, Box 12.

the trustees needed to grapple with fundamental questions about Vassar's future.[8]

Consistent with Wilkie's focus on new options for the future, in September 1966 Simpson convened and chaired a committee on new dimensions composed of trustees, administrators, and faculty members. The committee's mission was to imagine a range of possibilities for the college's future, including coeducation, graduate education, new interdisciplinary majors, and new degree programs combining off-campus experiences with academic study on campus.[9] The committee was mindful of the balancing act between preparing Vassar women for their traditional roles in their families and their communities and the "increasing demand on the part of young women for greater relevance in their academic experience to life away from the campus and to their future careers." Undergirding the committee's deliberations was the desire to find "ways of revitalizing the undergraduate experience to make it more relevant to modern woman's need to get involved with society while still an undergraduate and to prepare herself for life after college."[10]

As we have seen, the new dimensions work was temporarily sidelined by Kingman Brewster's invitation to Simpson to investigate the potential for what Simpson called a "royal marriage" between Vassar and Yale.[11] The Vassar-Yale study, authorized by the Vassar board in December 1966, quickly occupied a disproportionate share of staff time, high-level deliberations, and public discussion at the college. New dimensions soon receded into the background.

Nonetheless, the Vassar trustees made it clear that the new dimensions work was to proceed while Vassar-Yale was underway, with "alternative studies" carried out "with the same care and intensity as the Vassar-Yale study." The trustees were genuinely divided on the question of moving to New Haven, and they wanted to get as clear an understanding as possible of the

---

8 John Wilkie, Vassar Trusteeship, 1940–1975, draft, Nov. 1975, pp. 37–38, Wilkie, Box 12.

9 Vassar trustees (E), Sept. 13, 1966, p. 9; Vassar trustees, Oct. 22, 1966, p. 2.

10 Vassar trustees, May 13, 1967, p. 15.

11 Quoted in Daniels and Griffen, *"Full Steam Ahead in Poughkeepsie,"* p. 36.

college's options. The emphasis on alternative studies was also motivated by the strength of alumnae opposition to Vassar-Yale, which made it necessary to pursue a good-faith effort to look at other options, a responsibility Simpson delegated to the dean of studies, Elizabeth Daniels, who was given release time and a modest budget to investigate alternatives.[12]

Another reason to continue investigating alternatives was to preserve the Vassar board's freedom of action. If relocation to New Haven proved feasible, the board would have a real choice between moving to Yale and pursuing other carefully researched alternatives. If relocation proved infeasible, the college would be that much further along in identifying other possible directions.[13] Underlying both Vassar-Yale and new dimensions were two assumptions—that "some form of coeducation and some form of graduate school affiliation are essential"—and an overriding purpose to identify "imaginative educational ideas for the education of women in the light of the present-day and future needs of the nation."[14]

"For God, for Country, for Yale and Vassar"—or Not

Vassar planned to proceed with care and deliberation, making good use of data and exploring options in detail. But accomplishing that goal calmly and dispassionately was virtually impossible as students and alumnae weighed in with strong, highly passionate views. When Simpson announced on December 17, 1966, that the Vassar and Yale boards had agreed to study the possibilities for cooperation between the two institutions, a crowd of four hundred Vassar students assembled, cheering enthusiastically, unfurling banners welcoming the proposed marriage, and singing staples of the Yale musical repertory, like "Boola Boola" and the "Whiffenpoof" song—giving every indication that they were ready to pack for the move. The next issue of the student newspaper, the *Miscellany News*, captured the mood in a headline amending Yale's

12 Wilkie, Vassar Trusteeship, p. 38; Vassar trustees, Feb. 11, 1967, pp. 4–5 (source of the quote); Daniels and Griffen, *"Full Steam Ahead in Poughkeepsie,"* p. 31.

13 Vassar trustees, Feb. 11, 1967, p. 4.

14 Ibid., May 13, 1967, pp. 14–15.

familiar motto: "For God, for Country, for Yale and Vassar."[15] In the spring of 1967, nearly half the student body (696 students) signed a letter to the *Vassar Alumnae Magazine* conveying their support for the Vassar-Yale study and their provisional interest in relocation.[16]

Alumnae reacted differently. The fact that the news had come through newspapers rather than communication from the college rankled. As an alumna in the class of 1914 wrote from La Jolla, California, it was "a shabby and sneaky way to treat the alumnae."[17] A member of the class of 1922 from Cambridge, Massachusetts, who had found the news "splashed across [the] front page" in the *Boston Globe*, noted how difficult it had been for alumnae to have the story "bruited . . . about" in the press without hearing anything from the college.[18] An alumna of the class of 1911 from Wellesley echoed, "Why on earth was this sprung on us as it was!"[19]

Even accepting the possibility that the news slipped out before the college could control the rollout, alumnae could not understand why it then took two months to hear from their president. Simpson published an open letter to alumnae in the February 1967 issue of the *Vassar Alumnae Magazine*. It was not reassuring. "I am writing to you about the academic bombshell of December 16," Simpson began. "If there had been any way of alerting the Vassar family, you can be sure we would have taken it." But speaking about the study "before the trustees had approved it" would have produced instantaneous press coverage, and "hold[ing] the press at bay, once the approval had been given, was impossible. We tried! Telephone teams were armed with long lists of alumnae workers and benefactors. But the time shrank as the news leaked. We are just too famous to be allowed a private life."[20]

15 Ron Minkoff, "Should Vassar Marry Yale?," *Vassar Miscellany News*, May 6, 1977, p. 10; Daniels and Griffen, *"Full Steam Ahead in Poughkeepsie,"* pp. 24–25.

16 Letter from 696 Vassar students to the editor, *Vassar Alumnae Magazine* 52 (June 1967): 40. See also, in the same issue, on the same page, a letter from five students making the opposite case.

17 Margaret Addington Curry to Mrs. [Seth] Taft, Jan. 3, 1967, Vassar-Yale (V), Box 2.

18 Caroline A. Albright to Frances Prindle Taft, Feb. 17, 1967, Vassar-Yale (V), Box 2.

19 Sophia L. Morrill to Mrs. Seth C. Taft, Feb. 6, 1967, Vassar-Yale (V), Box 2.

20 Alan Simpson, "An Open Letter to the Alumnae," *Vassar Alumnae Magazine* 52 (Feb. 1967): 2.

Simpson's letter did not sit well with alumnae. Writing from Chicago, a member of the class of 1961 spoke for many of her counterparts when she called it "insultingly preemptive and uninformative."[21] But even if alumnae accepted Simpson's explanation for the leak, the question remained: Why such a long silence from the college? A member of the class of 1938 opined from Hamden, Connecticut, that "the 'leak' which gave us the news left us feeling we had been ignored as if we had no vital interest."[22] Writing from Washington, D.C., a member of the class of 1918 thanked the president of the alumnae association, Frances Prindle Taft, for the letter *she* wrote to alumnae and said that she could not understand why the president of the college had been unable to follow suit. "President Simpson did not have to wait for the magazine, he could have done just what you have done, write a letter and turn it over to the alumnae office to be processed and sent out."[23] Either Simpson did not want alumnae to know what was going on or he did not care about their views.

And alumnae certainly had strong views. On the whole, they were vehemently opposed to the prospect of joining up with Yale in New Haven. Vassar had a beautiful campus, a dedicated faculty, a long tradition of commitment to women's education. What on earth would be accomplished, a member of the class of 1905 in Shrewsbury, Massachusetts, wondered, by tying Vassar "to the tail of Yale's kite"?[24] A member of the class of 1922 from Cambridge, Massachusetts, declared herself "shocked and dismayed at the possibility of moving Vassar to New Haven."[25] A member of the class of 1909 in Leonia, New Jersey, called it "the height of idiocy."[26] An alumna of the class of 1907 from New York City

21 Jane Elizabeth Sutter to Mrs. Seth C. Taft, Mar. 6, 1967, Vassar-Yale (V), Box 2.

22 Alice W. Phillips to John Wilkie, Sept. 23, 1967, Wilkie, Box 12.

23 Julia F. Fiebeger to Mrs. [Seth] Taft, Mar. 5, 1967, Vassar-Yale (V), Box 2. On the same theme, see, in the same collection, Louise T. Erskine to Taft, Mar. 11, 1967, and Maria Leiper to Mrs. Taft, May 26, 1967. See also Margaret Smith to Doris Evans Bard, Sept. 19, 1967, Wilkie, Box 12.

24 Katharine French Rockwell to John Wilkie, Sept. 5, 1967, Wilkie, Box 12. For a similar view—"tail of a comet"—see, in the same collection, Mary Frances B. Gray to Wilkie, Sept. 12, [1967].

25 Caroline A. Albright to Frances Prindle Taft, Feb. 17, 1967, Vassar-Yale (V), Box 2.

26 Ruth Blankenhorn to Mrs. Frances Taft, May 6, 1967, Vassar-Yale (V), Box 2. On the same theme, see, in the same collection, Eleanor S. Dickson to Taft, Oct. 13, 1967

characterized it as "insane."[27] When a member of the class of 1918 in Grosse Pointe, Michigan, talked to fellow alumnae in her region about the possible move, "they just shrug[ged] their shoulders and refuse[d] to be concerned because the idea is just too preposterous."[28]

From a member of the class of 1959 in Philadelphia came this outburst: "I am sending this letter to add fuel to what is undoubtedly already a conflagration of protest." She had no objection to cooperation with Yale, nor to Vassar going coed. But going to New Haven? "Should the college be forced to move from its present location, it would be the same, in my mind, as its having ceased to exist."[29] A member of the class of 1923 in Washington, Connecticut, wrote: "Is Vassar so sick morally and spiritually; physically and financially; intellectually and emotionally, that euthanasia must be practiced? This is what the proposed move amounts to."[30]

Predictably, alumnae tied their opposition to withholding financial support. An alumna in the class of 1910 in New Haven spoke for many of them: "Not another cent to Vassar from me while there is a possibility that the college may be moving to New Haven. Also, I shall change my will and leave nothing—like a parent with a wayward daughter."[31] Declaring herself "inalterably opposed" to the proposed relocation, an alumna of the class of 1924 from New York City noted that she had "named Vassar as heir to 35%

("this idiot scheme"), and Ida Dunstan Williams to Taft, Oct. 30, 1967 ("fool-hardy, if not downright idiotic to pull up stakes").

27 Laura Benet to Mrs. Seth V. Taft, Jan. 23, 1967, Vassar-Yale (V), Box 2. In the same box, see also Grace E. McGuire to Taft, Mar. 19, [1967].

28 Katharine Ogden to Frances Prindle Taft, Feb. 25, 1967, Vassar-Yale (V), Box 2.

29 Ellen Knox Roston to Alan Simpson, Dec. 17, 1966, Vassar-Yale (V) Box 2. The same formulation—"will have ceased to exist"—appears, in the same collection, in Ruth Chandler Moore to the Trustees of Vassar College, Sept. 29, 1967. See also Iva A. Appleyard to John Wilkie, Sept. 6, 1967, Wilkie, Box 12.

30 Eleanor Vallandigham Salter to Mrs. Seth Taft, Apr. 2, 1967, Vassar-Yale (V), Box 2.

31 Louise Chamberlain Prentice to Mrs. [Seth] Taft, Mar. 16, 1967, Vassar-Yale (V), Box 2. On changing wills, see, in the same collection, Isabel R. Mann to Ruth W. Brainard, Mar. 31, 1967; Clara Snydacker Steeholm to Taft, Apr. 24, 1967; and Ruth Chandler Moore to the Trustees of Vassar College, Sept. 29, 1967. See also Mary Quarles to Alan Simpson, June 2, 1967; Julia A. Parker to [John] Wilkie, July 20, 1967; and Martha McChesney Wilkinson to Wilkie, Nov. 18, 1967, all in Wilkie, Box 12.

of my residuary estate." She added, "Needless to say, I am writing a new will!"[32]

But some Vassar graduates appreciated the "advantages to joining up with Yale" and thought "the whole idea . . . exciting."[33] From a member of the class of 1945 in Winchester, Massachusetts, came a strong affirmation: "The fact that Vassar, in order to further its goal of excellence in education, is willing to consider such a major change—is to me—thrilling."[34] Writing from New York City, a member of the class of 1960 favored the move as a way of preventing "the possibility of the college slowly becoming an intellectual backwater, unable to provide any more the absolutely first-rate education that its students deserve."[35]

Some alumnae underscored the importance of distinguishing between the physical setting and the essence of the college. "I am well aware of the wonders of the [Vassar] campus itself, of the beauty and space of the physical surroundings," wrote a member of the class of 1948 from Washington, D.C. "But that is not what makes Vassar, or any institution. It is who is teaching, the books and other resources available, the interaction between students, mediated and also given direction by the quality of the faculty."[36] And some alumnae saw virtues in physical relocation. As a member of the class of 1929 from Bethesda, Maryland, representing the views of "many V.C. friends," stated, "We know that the isolation of our campus hindered our growth as persons and our education

---

32 Claudia Lyon to Mrs. [Seth] Taft, Jan. 4, 1967, Vassar-Yale (V), Box 2. On the theme of "breach of faith with the many generous alumnae and other benefactors of the college," see, in the same collection, Eleanor Prendergast to Taft, Jan. 7, 1967 (source of the quote); M. Louise Strachan to Taft, Feb. 7, 1967; Caroline A. Albright to Taft, Feb. 17, 1967; and Ella Keats Whiting to Taft, May 12, 1967.

33 Barbara Levy to Franny [Taft], Dec. 27, [1966] ("advantages"), and Edith Cruikshank to [Taft], Feb. 4, 1967 ("exciting"), both in Vassar-Yale (V), Box 2. In the same collection, see also Barbara Currier to Alan Simpson, Jan. 3, 1967; Marjorie B. Creelman to [Taft], Feb. 23, 1967; Elizabeth McCarthy Badlian to [Taft], Mar 7, 1967; Ingrid Stadler to Simpson, Mar. 18, 1967; Priscilla Lee Campbell to Simpson, May 19, 1967; and Avery Taylor Vincent to Simpson, May 25, 1967.

34 Constance W. Rendall to Mrs. [Seth] Taft, Feb. 28, 1967, Vassar-Yale (V), Box 2.

35 Margaret Dauler Wilson, letter to the editor, *Vassar Alumnae Magazine* 52 (June 1967): 39.

36 Molly Geiger Schuchat to Mrs. Seth C. Taft and Alan Simpson, Feb. 23, 1967, Vassar-Yale (V), Box 2.

for life in a changing world. Today's students need to know men
& cities, not spend 4 years in a rural nunnery."[37] Another member
of the class of 1929, writing from New London, Connecticut, declared emphatically, "Teen age girls should not be two-and-a-half
hours travel distant from high-grade men. The integration of Yale
and Vassar is ideal, educationally and socially. DO IT."[38]

Simpson was convinced that Vassar had to take seriously the
prospect of an alternative future in order to sustain its status as a
leading liberal arts college. In February 1967 he wrote to the president of the Vassar alumnae association, "I am not worrying about
Vassar's capacity to survive but about what we must do now to
guarantee that she stays at the top." Simpson's chief concern was
"in making Vassar the best imaginable college," and he thought
that required change.[39] As he told the Vassar trustees in May 1967,
he had "become increasingly convinced that separate education
for women [had] no future at [Vassar's] level," a conclusion borne
out by the results of a recent poll of undergraduates, in which
more than 80 percent of respondents favored "sharing their Vassar
education with male students."[40] From the point of view of Vassar students, Simpson explained later, it was clear that "the *world*
is coeducational." With all the taboos separating the sexes "van-
ished or . . . vanishing," students believed that educating men and
women separately was "very *unnatural.*"[41]

Faculty Recruitment, Admissions, and Alumnae Distrust

The second imperative toward an alternative future for Vassar involved faculty recruitment. Simpson told the board about
his "frustrating experiences . . . in trying to bring distinguished
faculty to Vassar." Alumnae told Simpson repeatedly about the

---

37 Hannah M. Biemiller to [John] Wilkie, Aug. 23, 1967, Wilkie, Box 12.

38 Ruby Turner Morris to John Wilkie, Aug. 24, 1967, Wilkie, Box 12.

39 Alan Simpson to Franny Taft, Jan. 11, 1967, Vassar-Yale (V), Box 2.

40 Vassar trustees, May 13, 1967, p. 12 ("separate education for women"), July 11,
1968, p. 7 ("sharing their Vassar education").

41 Alan Simpson, "On Vassar," *College Board Review* 82 (Winter 1971–72): 22,
clipping in Subject Files Vassar 8.32.

pride they took in Vassar's "illustrious faculty," but in Simpson's judgment, the faculty was "not as illustrious as it was before the war when many of these alumnae were in college." As for admissions, Vassar's "competitive appeal" was in jeopardy. For the class of 1971, "Vassar had three applicants for every candidate accepted, Wellesley had five, and Radcliffe eight." A large number of Vassar's applicants "were totally unrealistic in terms of acceptability."[42]

The admissions picture would only grow more worrisome. With so much uncertainty about what Vassar would be like and where it would be located, 1,180 candidates applied for admission as entering freshmen in the fall of 1968—a drop of 200 from the previous year and the smallest applicant group the college had seen since 1953.[43] The following year, the number of applicants was even smaller: 1,132—a decline of 18 percent in just three years.[44] The number of early-decision candidates—students who applied only to Vassar, with the promise to enroll if they were admitted—dropped by 25 percent over the same period.[45]

Clearly, Simpson's concerns about Vassar's future were justified. But he had not yet mastered the challenge of communicating effectively with his alumnae. Adding to alumnae concern that Simpson had failed to inform them about the Yale study in a direct and timely fashion was the impression that he had made up his mind and was selling too aggressively. At the annual meeting of the Vassar alumnae association in June 1967, Simpson's speech struck many of his listeners as "a completely slanted, intellectually dishonest report," a brief for the move to New Haven instead of a balanced account. Alumnae alleged that the views of the faculty were being misrepresented and that Simpson had canceled reports at the meeting from other senior administrators who might have

42 Vassar trustees, May 13, 1967, p. 12.

43 Jean L. Harry, Annual Report of the Committee on Admission, 1967–68, Dec. 11, 1968, Simpson, Box 41.

44 Statistical Report on Candidates for Admission, 1969, Dean of Students, Box 5; The New Vassar, 1964–1970: Report of the President, Dec. 1970, p. 10, Vassar-Yale (V), Box 2.

45 Vassar trustees, Feb. 8, 1969, p. 2.

presented a more complicated picture of campus sentiment.[46] The result was a widespread impression "that deliberate manoeuvrings [*sic*] are going on to negate the alternatives."[47] It was also alleged that Simpson had stacked the joint Vassar-Yale trustee study committee with supporters of the move to New Haven. Further, it was reported that after a tour of Vassar clubs to make the case for the Yale study, Simpson had declared that he was "tired" of what he described as the "Weeping Winnies and Moaning Minnies" he encountered at every stop.[48] In short, bringing the alumnae along was neither Simpson's principal preoccupation nor his greatest strength as a leader.[49]

To make matters worse, Simpson had to contend with two developments that further inflamed alumnae distress. The first was the opposition of a venerable predecessor, Henry Noble Mac-Cracken, the fifth president of the college, who had served from 1915 to 1946. "Prexy," as he was known by legions of admirers, had been hugely popular and influential, not only at Vassar but more broadly. It was at his initiative, for example, that the Seven Sisters had been constituted as a group of women's colleges that operated with common interests.

Paying no attention to the unspoken principle of refraining from intervening in the business conducted by a successor, MacCracken proposed in a January 1967 interview with the *Poughkeepsie Journal* that, instead of contemplating a move to New Haven, Vassar join the mid-Hudson community to explore the establishment of a university for advanced study, which might be located on the Vassar farm. Merging Vassar with Yale, he said, "would be an ethical breach of trust in the more than 1000 individual endowments to Vassar College dating back 106 years."[50] So that alumnae would

46 Alicia Craig Faxon to [John] Wilkie, June 12, 1967, Vassar-Yale (V), Box 2. In the same box, see also Roxanne W. Beardsley to Mrs. Robert L. Foote, Aug. 8, 1967.

47 Roxanne W. Beardsley to Ralph Connor, Aug. 9, 1967, Vassar-Yale (V), Box 2.

48 Ruth Chandler Moore to the Trustees of Vassar College, Sept. 29, 1967, Vassar-Yale (V), Box 2.

49 On alumnae distrust of Simpson, see, e.g., Millicent B. Yater to John Wilkie, Oct. 22, 1967, Wilkie, Box 12; Joanie Sadler to Franny [Taft], n.d. [1967], and Margaret Ayers Erskine to Taft, n.d. [1967], both in Vassar-Yale (V), Box 2.

50 MacCracken, quoted in Ruth Andrus, letter to the editor, *Vassar Alumnae Magazine* 52 (Apr. 1967): 33.

not miss hearing his views, he published a letter in the April 1967 *Vassar Alumnae Magazine* touting the virtues of a new state university center that could grow up around the nucleus of the existing college.[51] The publicity attendant on MacCracken's declaration provided a rallying point for alumnae upset about the direction Simpson was taking.

The second unanticipated development was the publication in October 1967 in *Life* of a pair of highly inflammatory articles against merger by a Vassar alumna on the magazine's staff, Dorothy Seiberling Steinberg of the class of 1943. Seiberling had been a writer and editor at *Life* for many years and currently held the position of senior editor. The self-appointed leader of Alumnae for Vassar's Future, Seiberling had already made plain in the alumnae magazine that she was strongly opposed to the proposed Yale merger.[52] Taking her opposition to the pages of a national magazine to stir the pot more publicly was the next step.

Seiberling published a two-part account, "The Vassar-Yale Union," that took up five pages in the October 13 issue. The first article, "Can Vassar Find Happiness in New Haven?," was richly illustrated with color photographs of the Vassar campus, contrasted with a black-and-white photograph of the probable site in New Haven, said to consist of forty acres overlooking factories and slums. Vassar, Seiberling wrote, "is caught in her greatest crisis. She faces exile, marriage, sellout, reincarnation, submergence or sublimation—depending on the point of view."[53] In the second article, "How Dare They Do It?," Seiberling wrote, "How can they consider plunging into a congested city at a time when colleges—and the human soul—crave space? How can they contemplate trading an intimate personal environment for the mounting depersonalization of the multiversity? Most of all, how can they abandon and destroy an institution of long and great distinction whose

51 Henry Noble MacCracken, letter to the editor, *Vassar Alumnae Magazine* 52 (Apr. 1967): 35.

52 See, e.g., Dorothy Seiberling Steinberg, letter to the editor, *Vassar Alumnae Magazine* 52 (Apr. 1967): 34.

53 Dorothy Seiberling, "Can Vassar Find Happiness in New Haven?," *Life* 63 (Oct. 13, 1967): 119, http://books.google.com/books?id=OUkEAAAAMBAJ&printsec=f, accessed June 20, 2014.

potential for valuable service and leadership is still strong? For destroyed it would be if the move should take place. Vassar is inseparable from its century-old home."[54]

Studying the Alternatives to Vassar-Yale

Although the Vassar-Yale study drew most of the public attention and elicited the strongest reactions, the study of alternatives by the committee on new dimensions was also proceeding. Perhaps taking a cue from MacCracken, the committee envisioned that Vassar might become "an educational complex," cooperating with other institutions in the mid-Hudson region to create an educational program based on the college's traditional strengths in the liberal arts but giving "a new shape to . . . liberal arts education."[55]

The committee foresaw two undergraduate colleges—Vassar, with a revised curriculum "adapted to new needs," and a new men's college, "free-standing, coordinate, or coeducational with Vassar." The curriculum would be more flexible, experimental, and interdisciplinary, less bounded by requirements, more open to independent work and to extended work off campus involving practical application of ideas explored in the classroom.[56] As for the men's college, the committee was clear that "Vassar should introduce some form of coeducation." Coeducation would do more than "solve a few of Vassar's current problems and improve its 'image.'" It would "enable Vassar to fit more sensibly into the overall pattern of American education" and would "help keep Vassar in the forefront of quality education where it wants to be."[57]

At the graduate level, two institutes plus selected graduate programs would represent "a new, interdisciplinary approach to advanced work in untraditional fields," namely "the study of man and his environment" and "the study of teaching." The institutes

54 Dorothy Seiberling, "How Dare They Do It?," *Life* 63 (Oct. 13, 1967): 123, http://books.google.com/books?id=OUkEAAAAMBAJ&printsec=f, accessed June 20, 2014.

55 Committee on New Dimensions, A Preliminary Report on Alternatives, Sept. 1, 1967, pp. 4–5, Subject Files Vassar 8.29.

56 Ibid., pp. 6, 8–19.

57 Ibid., pp. 20, 26–41.

would offer master's degrees, sponsor research, and engage under-graduates in courses and fieldwork.[58]

The committee imagined that the new Vassar complex would involve linkages with other institutions in the region. The State University of New York, it appeared, might have some interest in establishing an educational center—a cluster of colleges—in the vicinity of Poughkeepsie. Union College, based in Schenectady, some 95 miles to the north, was said to be exploring the possibility of creating a graduate center in science and engineering in the mid-Hudson area in partnership with Vassar and the IBM Corporation, which was headquartered in Armonk but had research laboratories in Poughkeepsie. It was possible, too, that Rensselaer Polytechnic Institute, located almost 90 miles upstate in Troy, and Syracuse University, 225 miles to the northwest, might have some interest in such a venture. There was some talk that the Brooklyn Polytechnic Institute might be interested in moving 80 miles north and joining in.[59]

All of these proposals matched the desires of local businesses in Poughkeepsie, which saw Vassar as the centerpiece of the development of graduate educational facilities in the mid-Hudson region.[60] Members of the New York State Assembly made a similar case: Higher education was a major industry in New York, and Governor Nelson Rockefeller, who had presidential ambitions, would not "sit idly while the jewel of our higher education resources leaves the State." There would be state funds for scholarships at private college and universities, as well as for the establishment of a university center "awarding graduate degrees, with Vassar College at its nucleus."[61]

The new dimensions proposal was imaginative, far-reaching, and highly complex, with many moving parts. It took Vassar into the yet-unexplored territory of graduate education, and it depended

58 Ibid., pp. 6, 47–76.

59 Ibid., pp. 6, 78–86; Vassar trustees, Nov. 8, 1967, p. 5, Feb. 8, 1969, p. 7, and May 10, 1969, pp. 9–10; Daniels and Griffen, *"Full Steam Ahead in Poughkeepsie,"* pp. 94–95.

60 "Business Firms Press Vassar College to Stay," *Poughkeepsie Journal,* Oct. 20, 1967, clipping in Vassar-Yale (V), Box 2.

61 Bertram L. Podell to Mrs. Seth Taft, Oct. 9, 1967, Vassar-Yale (V), Box 2.

on cooperation with many other institutions whose willingness to work with the college had yet to be tested. In contrast, Vassar-Yale had the virtue of being simple and straightforward. Although the details had yet to be worked out, the basic concept—that Vassar would move to New Haven and enter upon a "royal marriage" with Yale—could not have been clearer. Vassar-Yale could be easily captured and comprehended. Making sense of new dimensions was a lot harder.

The plan was for the two study committees to submit near-final drafts of their reports to the trustees in early September 1967. The trustees would then consider them over a period of weeks. Once the trustees decided on their preferred "concept of Vassar's best future course," *their* proposal would be disseminated more broadly—referred to the faculty for consideration and discussed with the alumnae association board and with representatives of the student body.[62] That plan did not sit well with faculty members, who would have liked to have the full texts of both reports, but the trustees preferred to go public with only a "consolidated single proposal."[63]

It was not only the faculty who wanted in on the discussions before a final direction had been determined. Eager to repair frayed communications between the college and alumnae, alumnae leaders hoped also to be part of the deliberations before a final decision was made. But with uncertainty about when the trustees would reach a consensus on Vassar's direction, it was hard to plan for the desired joint discussion between the trustees and the directors of the alumnae association.[64] When the alumnae council met in late October, the trustees still had made no public statement about where they were heading. Although it was clear that the trustees were "hard at work," alumnae got little sense of the specific "progress of their labors."[65]

62 Alan Simpson and John Wilkie to Dear Alumnae, Oct. 2, 1967, Wilkie, Box 12.

63 Minutes, Meeting of the Executive Committee of the Vassar College Board of Trustees with the Faculty Committee on Conference, Sept. 10, 1967, Vassar trustees (E).

64 John Wilkie to Franny Taft, Aug. 23, 1967, Vassar-Yale (V), Box 2.

65 Winnie Castle Millikin to John Wilkie, Oct. 26, 1967, Wilkie, Box 12.

At the beginning of November, the assistant to the president and secretary to the board of trustees, Florence C. Wislocki, wrote in confidence to the president of the alumnae association, Frances Taft, about the deeply dispiriting lack of action in Poughkeepsie: "There is nothing of note to report here, which in itself is bad, and allows tension to mount and morale to decline. The general thought is that we are not going to move (which I have been sure of since the beginning) but every effort is being made to allow Alan to save his face. It may be too late for that and he continues to make stupid mistakes."[66]

In the judgment of Alison Bernstein, a member of the class of 1969 who had been president of student government and who was the first young alumna to be elected to the board of trustees, the problem was partly one of leadership and partly one of instincts. Simpson, she said, came across as an Oxford don—charming, erudite, a father figure to many students. But he never understood feminism, "never really got women's education," and "never quite got what made Vassar special." Simpson's limitations made charting Vassar's future directions particularly challenging.[67]

---

66 Fliss Wislocki to Franny Taft, Nov. 6, 1967, Vassar-Yale (V), Box 2.
67 Telephone interview with Alison Bernstein '69, Feb. 9, 2015.

14

Vassar: "Vassar for <u>Men</u>?"

On November 16, 1967, the Vassar board announced its decision
that "the College should remain in its birthplace" and build its
own future without reference to Yale. Informing the community of
the decision at a special convocation in the chapel, Alan Simpson
was jeered by the assembled students. In a statement read at a special meeting of the faculty on November 20, the board said, "This
decision has been influenced by loyalty to a place as spacious and
beautiful as ours, by confidence in the future of our region, by the
desire to be mistress in our own house, by our commitment to the
education of women, and by faith in the originality of the Vassar
spirit in the discovery of new paths to excellence."[1] As the board
chair, John Wilkie, said later, the grounds for the decision "were
primarily the maintenance of Vassar's undergraduate educational
traditions and objectives, and its continuing identity."[2]

After the Yale-Vassar Decision: Proposals for Coeducation

On November 20 the trustees sent to the faculty a set of proposals, which had grown out of the work of the committee on new
dimensions, for Vassar to take up the education of men, as well as
for curricular reform, graduate institutes, and cooperative educational ventures in the region. At the same time, the board approved
a large-scale building program that would be funded by a capital

---

1 A Statement by the Trustees of Vassar Cõllege, Vassar faculty, vol. 18, Nov. 20,
1967. On the convocation in the chapel, see Ron Minkoff, "Should Vassar Marry Yale?,"
Vassar Miscellany News, May 6, 1977, p. 10.
2 John Wilkie, Vassar Trusteeship, 1940–1975, draft, Nov. 1975, p. 39, Wilkie, Box 12.

campaign. (The college needed, among other new facilities, dining and social spaces, student residences, a theater, and a biological sciences building.[3]) At a special faculty meeting on November 29, Wilkie explained the rationale for the trustee decisions.[4]

Of all of the proposals, the most transformative was the presumption that Vassar would embark on the education of men. Although the trustees had framed their discussion in terms of coordinate education, it quickly became clear that the most compelling option for Vassar was full coeducation.[5] As Simpson explained later, Vassar chose coeducation over coordinate education "because we thought it would be simpler and quicker and happier and cheaper."[6]

Two faculty members were charged with investigating how best to accomplish coeducation. They were Clyde Griffen and George Langdon, Jr., historians who had been deeply involved in the Vassar-Yale study.[7] Their report, issued on May 27, 1968, outlined four possible approaches: establishing an independent college for men, creating a semiautonomous men's institution with a common faculty and board of trustees, implementing an experimental program of study for men at Vassar, and embarking on full coeducation.[8]

On May 30, 1968, by a vote of 102 to 3, the Vassar faculty approved a resolution favoring coeducation.[9] In committee meetings

3 A Statement by the Trustees of Vassar College, Vassar faculty, vol. 18, Nov. 20, 1967. The trustees' proposals were disseminated to the alumnae in Board of Trustees, "A Proposal Presented to the Faculty of Vassar College," *Vassar Alumnae Magazine* 53 (Dec. 1967): 9–12, Vassar College Library.

4 Vassar faculty, vol. 18, Nov. 29, 1967. Wilkie's statement to the faculty was disseminated to the alumnae in John Wilkie, "Remarks to the Faculty," *Vassar Alumnae Magazine* 53 (Feb. 1968): 4–6.

5 Models for implementing men's education, attached to Alan Simpson to Forward Planning Committee, May 15, 1968; minutes, Forward Planning Committee meeting, May 22, 1968, Simpson, Box 4, FPC folder, n.d.

6 Alan Simpson, "On Vassar," *College Board Review* 82 (Winter 1971–72): 18, clipping in Subject Files Vassar 8.32.

7 Vassar trustees (E), Jan. 18, 1968.

8 Summary Statement: Possible Approaches for Implementing Men's Education, May 27, 1968, Subject Files Vassar 8.30; "The Great Experiment," *Vassar Miscellany News*, Oct. 15, 1976.

9 Vassar faculty, vol. 18, May 30, 1968.

of faculty, administrators, and trustees, the options were reviewed, the choices considered, and the determination to focus on full co-education confirmed.[10] On July 11 the trustees voted in principle for coeducation, with instructions to the faculty and administration to return with specific proposals for implementation.[11]

Looking back some years later, Wilkie enumerated the factors pointing toward coeducation: "the increasing proportion of Vassar students coming from co-educational high schools, the increasing competition and allure of men's colleges which admitted women . . . the greater freedom of association between young women and men, [and] the relative remoteness of the Vassar campus from sources of congenial male companionship." The trustee decision, Wilkie said, was "natural and inevitable."[12]

The *Miscellany News* called the decision to pursue coeducation "wise and in the tradition of innovation at Vassar." Coeducation would bring the hoped-for benefits of interaction between men and women in the classroom and would result in the "normal" social life students desired.[13]

The decision was taken almost without comment from alumnae. In other circumstances, and certainly in cases in which men's colleges decided to coeducate, such decisions evoked strong expressions of opinion from alumni, many of them highly critical. In Vassar's case, the alumnae had had their say with regard to the possibility of moving the college to New Haven, and the intensity of their opposition had weighed heavily in the trustees' decision not to make the move. With that option off the table, alumnae could breathe a collective sigh of relief. They could keep their beautiful,

10 See, e.g., Summary Statement: Possible Approaches for Implementing Men's Education; Minutes, Meeting of the Forward Planning Committee with the Faculty Committee on Conference, June 29, 1968, Simpson, Box 4, FPC folder, n.d.

11 "A Recommendation of Coeducation as the Method of Introducing Men's Education at Vassar College and a Consideration of Issues Involved in Implementation," July 3, 1968, attached to Alan Simpson to Board of Trustees, July 3, 1968, Simpson, Box 4, FPC folder, n.d.; Vassar trustees, July 11, 1968, p. 7. On implementation, see, e.g., Issues Involved in the Implementation of Men's Education at Vassar College, Sept. 1, 1968, as well as Dwight W. Chapman, Probable Changes in Course Enrollments at Vassar Consequent upon the Admission of Men, Dec. 1968, both in Dean of College/Faculty, Box 67.

12 Wilkie, Vassar Trusteeship, pp. 39–40.

13 Editorial, "Coeducation—A Bold Challenge," *Vassar Miscellany News*, Oct. 4, 1968.

serene, spacious, pastoral campus, with its historic buildings and extraordinary plantings. They had dodged the feared relocation to a crowded quarter of a busy city. They had kept their independence as a fine liberal arts college with a distinguished history instead of losing their identity and becoming an appendage to a large university. The proposed merger had put coeducation in perspective. Having feared much worse, alumnae could accept as the lesser of two evils the much less disruptive prospect of sharing their college with men.[14]

The implementation plan approved by the trustees in late October called for the college to grow from its current enrollment of sixteen hundred to an eventual target of twenty-four hundred, with a 1-to-1 ratio (or as much parity as could reasonably be achieved) of women and men. Upperclass male transfer students would be permitted to matriculate in the fall of 1969; male freshmen would be admitted for the fall of 1970. Exchange programs with men's colleges in the spring of 1969 and in the academic year 1969–70 would further increase the initial presence of men on campus.[15]

Moving Ahead with Coeducation
(and Keeping Alumnae Apprised)

Keeping alumnae apprised of the board's plans for coeducation was extremely important. Admitting men was not a simple matter, and it needed to be explained carefully. In a letter to alumnae in October 1968, Simpson wrote, "Hardly a week passes without reading of some private university or college or secondary school which is reconsidering its commitment to separate education. Whatever nostalgias some of us may feel, we should be proud of the fact that we are leading, not following, this movement." Simpson spelled out plans for implementing coeducation and underscored the

14 Telephone interview with Alison Bernstein '69, Feb. 9, 2015. Bernstein joined the Vassar board in the fall of 1969.

15 Vassar trustees, July 11, 1968, pp. 7–8, and Oct. 19, 1968, pp. 2, 6; *Vassar Miscellany News*, Oct. 4, 1968. On the male exchange students who came to Vassar from Colgate, Trinity, and Williams in the spring of 1969, see Vassar College news release, Dec. 10, 1968, Subject Files Vassar 8.31.

enthusiasm on campus for the college's new direction. And he rallied alumnae to come on board. "Morale on the campus has never been higher. We are all enjoying the sensation—rare today—of working together for common ends."[16]

As for the other proposals made by the committee on new dimensions, the Vassar faculty overhauled the undergraduate curriculum along the lines the committee had recommended. The new plan, implemented in 1969–70, eliminated distribution requirements, expanded opportunities for study and work off campus, gave students the option of constructing their own majors, and loosened the time schedule for earning degrees.[17]

The other academic initiatives proposed by the committee—the two institutes and the educational center—never bore fruit. The State University of New York pulled back on tentative plans to establish a graduate center in the mid-Hudson region, and graduate studies proved to be beyond Vassar's reach. When Simpson approached major foundations for funding for the institutes, they demurred on the grounds that such initiatives were the responsibility of research universities. And the graduate center in science and technology, imagined as a collaborative venture with IBM, foundered as a result of faculty resistance and student animus toward IBM.[18]

In March 1969, the New York State Board of Regents amended Vassar's charter to allow admission of men as regular degree candidates.[19] The great experiment was set to go forward.

Whether Vassar could attract male applicants in sufficient number and of sufficient quality was a worrisome question. There were no precedents. The benign version of the worry, easy to discuss publicly, focused on credentials—would the men measure up to Vassar's women? The more complicated version concerned "the kind of men" who would be attracted to a women's

16 Alan Simpson to Dear Alumna, Oct. 22, 1968, Subject Files Vassar 8.30.

17 Nell Eurich, "The New Vassar: The Comprehensive Plan," Sept. 1969, Subject Files Vassar 8.31; Vassar faculty, vol. 19, Oct. 9, 1968.

18 Mary Knox and John Kalish, "President and His Wife: Interview with the Simpsons," *Vassar Chronicle*, Mar. 31, 1977; Vassar College, *A Self-Study Report*, Feb. 1979, p. 3, Middle States.

19 Vassar College news release, Mar. 17, 1969, and Robert D. Stone to Carroll L. Wainwright, Jr., Mar. 3, 1969, both in Simpson, Box 58, Amendment of Charter folder.

college—that is, the fear that the college would appeal only to men who were gay.[20]

Seventy-seven undergraduate men enrolled at Vassar in the spring of 1968–69 as exchange students from Williams, Trinity, Colgate, and Haverford.[21] The next year, 1969–70, Vassar enrolled 1,620 students—1,529 women and 91 male transfer students. Men and women lived in the same dormitories. At the initiative of the student senate and with the approval of the cognizant faculty committee, student regulations were relaxed. Curfews were eliminated, students were no longer required to sign out when they left campus, and parietals were abolished on weekends. Later the student government won the right to eliminate parietals altogether.[22]

In the immediate term, coeducation accomplished what its proponents had hoped for by reinvigorating interest in Vassar among talented high school seniors. With the college so prominently in the news as the pioneer in admitting men to a leading women's institution, Vassar saw a significant spike in applications: more than 1,400 applications from women for the class of 1974, an increase of almost 30 percent over the previous year and the largest number in five years. In addition, Vassar received 475 applications from men who aspired to become Vassar's first male freshmen.[23] It was anticipated that the new freshman class would number 337 women and 192 men. Data provided by the new director of admission, Richard Stephenson, showed that the women students outranked the men academically; two-thirds of women freshmen, but only two-fifths of men, had ranked in the top 10 percent of their high school classes.[24]

---

20 Bernstein interview.

21 Vassar trustees (E), Jan. 21, 1969.

22 Memorandum, Elizabeth M. Drouilhet to Faculty Committee on Student Affairs, Dec. 16, 1968; Report of the Dean of Residence to the President and the Board of Trustees, n.d. [1969]; and Alison Bernstein and Marty Beyer, Open Letter to President Simpson, Feb. 24, 1969, all in Dean of Students, Box 2; Vassar trustees (E), Mar. 11, 1969; "Vassar in Transition," *Vassar Alumnae Magazine* 54 (Apr. 1969): 4.

23 Simpson, "On Vassar," p. 18; Richard D. Stephenson, "The New Vassar: Admission," Aug. 1970, pp. 3, 5–6, Subject Files Vassar 8.31; George Kannar, "Can Men Save Women's Colleges?," *Parade*, Jan. 17, 1971, p. 9, clipping in Subject Files Vassar 8.29.

24 Annual Report on Admission, 1969–70, Richard D. Stephenson to J. M. Duggan, Vassar faculty, vol. 20, May 20, 1970.

Public Stress, Private Worries

Although the public report on the first round of coeducational admissions was upbeat, privately Stephenson flagged two areas of
potential concern. One had to do with male applicants: "Whether
or not the surprisingly strong interest among men can be increased
or even maintained after this 'charter' year is uncertain." The other
had to do with women who were admitted but declined to enroll:
"The continued weakening of our hold on women admitted is not
only ominous but of unknown origin."[25] As he later elaborated,
"Whatever the source of the rumor, women . . . believe Vassar to
have slipped in recent years and appear to allow their sense of our
academic inferiority to carry greater weight in their decisions than
their knowledge of our other attractions." Vassar's "attractiveness
to women" remained "badly in need of repair."[26]

Publicly, Stephenson gave alumnae a realistic sense of Vassar's
relative standing among selective colleges and universities. He
pointed out that despite Vassar's historic distinction, "fewer students sought admission to [the college] in 1968 than in 1958," that
Vassar's "share of the best [high school] graduates [had] not increased," and that Vassar's overall yield was in decline. The college
had to work very hard to attract significant numbers of talented
applicants and to enroll those who were admitted.[27]

In the academic year 1970–71, the first for freshman men at
Vassar, enrollment grew to 1,779 (1,448 women and 331 men). In
1971–72, enrollment grew to 1,994 (1,446 women and 548 men).
Among entering freshmen, 400 were women, 244 men.[28]

A report in the popular press on the first year of full coeducation
indicated that most classes included "a sprinkling of males" and
that male students were organizing teams to compete in basketball

25 Ibid.

26 Memorandum, Richard D. Stephenson to John M. Duggan, Aug. 7, 1970, Dean of
Students, Box 5.

27 Richard D. Stephenson, "Some Preliminary Observations on Admission to Vassar,"
Vassar Alumnae Magazine 55 (Feb. 1970): 14–16.

28 Simpson, "On Vassar," p. 19; Vassar trustees (E), Sept. 15, 1970; Vassar College
news release, n.d. [likely Sept. 17, 1970], Subject Files Vassar 8.31; memorandum, Richard
D. Stephenson to J. M. Duggan, June 18, 1971, Dean of Students, Box 5.

and touch football. By all accounts, there was a positive spirit on campus. Simpson said, "Coeducation adds to the variety of the whole educational experience. It is a lift to morale and everyone's spirits." Faculty members attested to coeducation's effect in enlivening the intellectual atmosphere on campus; Vassar had become "a less pastoral and more demanding place to teach." The president of student government, a woman, agreed that "the place is more alive now. Maybe that's a sign of the changing times, but coeducation is involved there, too."[29]

Why Men Enrolled at Vassar

Stephenson claimed that Vassar's first freshman men came because "they were looking for the best education they could get, and our reputation for rigorous scholarship was what really mattered to them."[30] In the fall of 1973, a woman student interviewed a number of Vassar men for a feature in the *Vassar Quarterly*. Rob Stoddard '72, who had transferred from Duke, said that he came to Vassar because "I wanted to explore more academically, the Vassar curriculum was much more flexible. I had a very negative reaction to Duke; the social life was very much a 'dating' set-up and there was no opportunity to live off-campus." Sam Beal '74 said that he "chose Vassar over Harvard because I wanted to come to a small school—personal contact among students and between students and faculty is important to me." Mark Schneider '73 acknowledged that he had applied "almost as a joke," but that he had been "pleasantly surprised by Vassar's familiarity, warmth and friendliness." Academic reasons were paramount in the decisions of many of the men who were interviewed: "I'm here to get an education—anything else is secondary," said John Lawrence '75. "I came for the history department," said Neil Masters '75. Academically, he said, Vassar had proven to be "everything I wanted it to be."[31]

29 Kannar, "Can Men Save Women's Colleges?," pp. 9, 11.

30 Quoted in Vassar College news release, n.d. [likely Sept. 17, 1970].

31 Students quoted in Marian Lindberg, "The Student View: Men at Vassar: A Collage," *Vassar Quarterly* 70 (Fall 1973): 6–8.

But there was also a different story about the motivations of Vassar's first male students. What they wanted, according to a report by a retired psychology professor who surveyed and interviewed them, was "to experience coeducation at first hand." They took the view that "the segregated college [was] a somewhat defective preparation for the sexual integration of the rest of life."[32] Rob Stoddard confirmed the point in the *Vassar Quarterly* interview: "The major plus was meeting people in a natural situation, getting to know someone in a relaxed atmosphere and not having to rely on 'dating' to make friends with women."[33]

In the public press, some male students were less reflective—and more candid. "I came for the girls" was a typical explanation. "But now it's more than that," one student elaborated. "The situation at Vassar gives you a chance to develop parts of your personality that you wouldn't develop elsewhere. I don't mean that you feel like Casanova, but you do feel like a fuller person because you're a man at Vassar." As for the balance of factors leading to men's interest in the college, one student probably spoke for many of his peers when he said: "Any boy who says he transferred here for academic reasons is lying. The social situation is too good to be true." Male students found women students to be friendly and welcoming. As one man put it, "I've never had so many girlfriends—girls who are friends—in all my life."[34] Years later, a male student asked what it was like to be a man at Vassar made the same point: "Fantasy Island," he said with a sigh. "There's no reason for a man to commit himself."[35]

James Mundy, an alumnus of the class of 1974 who returned to Vassar as director of the college's art center, characterized the first male students as "'individual thinkers' who could stand up to the ribbing of being a man at a woman's school." The students, he recalled, included "pranksters and eccentrics," like the president of the class of 1974, a transvestite who had been born a male, who dressed up in hot pants, wig, high heels, and a heavily padded

32 Dwight W. Chapman, "Men Who Chose Vassar," *Vassar Quarterly* 57 (Winter 1971): 1–2.

33 Quoted in Lindberg, "The Student View," 10.

34 Quoted in Kannar, "Can Men Save Women's Colleges?," p. 11.

35 Quoted in Nan Robertson, "Campus Dating: What Going Coed Has Done," *New York Times*, June 1, 1981, clipping in Subject Files Vassar 8.32.

body stocking for the last campus mixer with West Point cadets. Even thirty years later, "to be a male Vassar student," Mundy observed, "you still have to be comfortable with yourself as a boy and interested in a feminine and feminist environment."[36]

"An Unqualified Success, an Unqualified Source of Satisfaction"

Vassar worked hard to put the most positive face on a situation without precedent in higher education. Simpson had asserted that coeducation at Vassar would be distinguished by "equality of the sexes." There was no reason to worry that his women students would "become 'softly supine ladies'" or that they would be "pushed around by the men": "Vassar is going to have 'coeducation with a difference.' Vassar is not going to have male-dominated coeducation. Vassar is certainly not going to have male-dominated coeducation of the type that a Yale or Princeton or Harvard has." Among other things, Vassar was aiming for a balance between the sexes—ideally, a 1 to 1 ratio by 1975. By the winter of 1971–72, Simpson felt confident enough about what Vassar had accomplished to declare coeducation "an unqualified success, an unqualified source of satisfaction to us."[37]

Simpson's assertions undoubtedly reflected his convictions, but they were also designed for public consumption. So was the upbeat message of Stephenson, the director of admission, who told the *New York Times* in the fall of 1974, "I'm convinced that whatever our problems are now, Vassar would be in a hell of a lot more trouble if it weren't coed. We couldn't continue in isolation, we had to be more like the real world. Smith, Bryn Mawr and all the others could stay women['s colleges] only because they're close to men's colleges. But not Vassar."[38]

Privately, Stephenson took a more measured—and probably more realistic—view. Attracting men to Vassar, he acknowledged

36 James Mundy, quoted in Rebecca Paley, "Goodbye, Girls Only," *Poughkeepsie Journal*, Nov. 21, 1999, clipping in Subject Files Vassar 8.32.

37 Vassar trustees, Feb. 8, 1969, p. 2 ("equality of the sexes," "softly supine ladies"); Simpson, "On Vassar," pp. 19, 23.

38 Quoted in "Coed Status Pleases Vassar Despite Problems," *New York Times*, Nov. 19, 1974, p. 45.

in 1972, was very hard to do. The problem lay in part with the competition, of course, but it also emanated from so many aspects of the college's identity and behavior. As for competition, once the novelty of applying to Vassar wore off, men considering Vassar also had the option of the many men's colleges that had recently coeducated, colleges that were "far, far safer in their changeless maleness than Vassar."

Stephenson observed that "unless Vassar's essential character changes, I doubt that we will ever have great appeal to the upper middle-class, 'all-around guy' typified in my mind by the stereotype of the Dartmouth, Amherst, or Williams man." Vassar's orientation was "almost totally intellectual." Those other schools offered men academic excellence but much more. Indeed, academic excellence was "virtually the only reason for a man to choose Vassar." As a result, Vassar's male student body was "'intellectual' rather than 'all-around,' a little off-beat, arty or esthetic, not [made up of] the sort of guy who is 'one of the boys.'" Fraternities, athletic teams, and other "trappings of maleness" were not part of the Vassar culture.

The problem was that Vassar appeared "to some degree inhospitable to men." It was not that the atmosphere was "hostile" but that it was suffused with a strong "aura of feminism" suggesting that men might not be fully welcome. "Our preoccupation with the status of women and their encouragement," Stephenson believed, "has led us to neglect our men and has obscured from us the fact that men are not women and neither behave in the same ways nor necessarily desire the same things. . . . We have done everything possible to preserve the ascendancy of women, but have made no countervailing effort whatever in behalf of our men."

Among other problems, some Vassar faculty exhibited a troubling "antipathy" toward male students. The college provided an inadequate sports program for men, and it paid insufficient attention to encouraging all-male extracurricular activities. Nor had it done anything to organize men into interest groups that might establish an "esprit de corps" among them (for example, an all-male dormitory). The admission office failed to differentiate in any way between men and women in many aspects of recruitment, from school visits to interviews to campus tours. By maintaining strictly academic criteria for admission, with the same standard of secondary school performance expected for men and for women, it missed the opportunity to take account of the strengths of all-around male applicants. It was a mistake to fixate on whether male candidates for admission measured up to female candidates on the traditional quantitative measures; men's strengths could be better appreciated by considering a broader set of criteria. Vassar needed to address these issues to make headway in attracting and enrolling a broad cross-section of men.[39]

Proponents of women's education had feared that bringing male students into a women's college would mean that men would dominate classroom discussions and take over the leadership roles in which women had traditionally flourished. Vassar's vice president for student affairs, John M. Duggan, denied that such displacement was happening in Poughkeepsie. "Men and women at Vassar are not terribly hung up on playing sex roles, the men always running everything," he said during the first year of full coeducation. "Women's Liberation stands to gain now that Vassar is coed because men are being sensitized to the idea of intelligent women doing intelligent jobs. Men with experience at a predominantly women's college will be more sensitive to what women can do in business and other public affairs."[40]

In the first years of coeducation, women retained major leadership positions such as president of student government and editor-in-chief of the *Miscellany News*.[41] In 1973, however, both positions were held by men.[42] The first male president of student government, Steve Heuglin, struck the right note in his address at convocation in the fall of 1973 when he said, "Vassar went co-educational to

39 Reflections on Coeducation from an Admission Point of View for the Little Compton Conference, memorandum, Richard D. Stephenson to J. M. Duggan, June 2, 1972, Dean of Students, Box 5. In the same box, see also The Improvement of Coeducation, memorandum, Stephenson to Duggan, Aug. 28, 1974, and a 35-page, untitled report from Stephenson, Oct. 7, 1974.

40 Quoted in Kannar, "Can Men Save Women's Colleges?," pp. 9, 11.

41 Simpson, "On Vassar," p. 19.

42 "Shakeup Leaves Male on Top," *Vassar Miscellany News*, Feb. 9, 1973; Vickie Ong, "The New Vassar: Coed 'Partnership,'" *Honolulu Advertiser*, Jan. 15, 1974, Subject Files Vassar 8.32.

share its tradition and extend its mission to men, not to yield it to them."[43] But there were moments, the *Misc* lamented, when it looked as though Vassar was becoming "just like any other co-ed school with the guys running the show. Let's not kid ourselves. It's happening already. Most of the positions in this year's all-college, class, and dormitory elections were captured by men. Not surprising, because most of the candidates were men."[44] As one man told a reporter, "That kind of stuff looks good on law-school applications."[45]

It was a sensitive point. Simpson told a different reporter that campus leadership roles had "certainly . . . not been turned over lock, stock and barrel to the men. If I found my girls submitting to second place, I'd have something to say to them."[46] Over time, leadership positions rotated back and forth among men and women, a more benign pattern than the feared specter of men replacing women at the helm of every important campus organization.[47] Some examples: In 1974 and 1975, women held the positions of president of student government, editor of the newspaper, and president of the senior class, while a man served in 1975 as editor of the yearbook. In 1979 a man was president of student government; in 1980, the position was held by a woman, while a man served as editor of the yearbook.[48]

Differing Opinions on the Evolving Vassar

For some faculty and students, the forward progress in making Vassar comfortably coeducational was palpable; the glitches along the way would be resolved by achieving parity between men and women in undergraduate enrollment. But others worried that in

43 Heuglin, quoted in Nancy O. Ruggles to Mary Jane Checchi, Nov. 8, 1973, Dean of Students, Box 5.

44 Editorial, "The Evolving Vassar," *Vassar Miscellany News*, May 11, 1973.

45 Quoted in Susan Lydon, "The Case against Coeducation, or I Guess, Vassar Wasn't So Bad After All," *Ms.*, Sept. 1973, clipping in Dean of Students, Box 5.

46 Simpson quoted in Ong, "The New Vassar."

47 William H. Honan, "Three Decades of Men at Vassar," *New York Times*, May 14, 2000, Section 14, p. 5, clipping in Subject Files Vassar 8.32.

48 Natalie J. Marshall to Theresia Sauter, Oct. 16, 1975, Dean of Students, Box 5; *Vassarion*, 1975, 1980, 2000, Vassar College Library; Lucinda Franks, "Whatever Happened to Vassar?," *New York Times Magazine*, Sept. 9, 1979, p. 124.

the drive toward parity, the college might be jettisoning elements of its fundamental identity.

One of the skeptics was Christine Havelock, a professor of art history, who made the case that parity should be abandoned: "Let's, for heaven's sake, relax and accept and seek only qualified men and women, and let the ratio come out as it will. And let us not throw away the one strength we have: our long tradition of educating women." Vassar, after all, was "an educational institution, not Noah's Ark; we do not need to have a one to one ratio."[49] Another skeptic was Alison Bernstein. "No other women's college," she said, "has gone into attracting men with the zeal that Vassar has. It's hard to tell how much coeducation was really due to economic necessity and how much to educational philosophy. A school cannot reverse a whole history of image-making, and I don't see why we can't find men who are interested in Vassar as it was. Let's forget parity, this Noah's Ark notion."[50]

The then-chairman of the board, Elizabeth Runkle Purcell of the class of 1931, took a different view. Addressing graduating seniors at Vassar's commencement in June 1973, Purcell posed this question: "Isn't a famous woman's college denying its historic mission" in becoming coeducational? Purcell's answer: "No." Vassar was developing a distinctive kind of coeducation, where women would be central to the enterprise as full participating members, subject neither to marginalization nor to discrimination: "Vassar's commitment in this second century is every bit as new and exciting as it was in its original commitment in 1861."[51]

But simply asserting the point was not enough to quell the debate on and beyond the campus about whether the determination to achieve "coequal coeducation"—parity in the numbers of men

49 Christine M. Havelock, Speech at the Faculty Meeting, Apr. 25, 1973, attachment 6, Vassar faculty, vol. 21, Apr. 25, 1973. Also see Jason Isaacson, "Christine Havelock: Coeducation and Vassar's Commitment to Women," *Vassar Quarterly* 70 (Fall 1973): 18–19.

50 Bernstein, quoted in Ann Marie Cunningham, "Do Women's Colleges Need Men? Second Thoughts," *Mademoiselle*, Feb. 1974, p. 182, clipping in Subject Files Vassar 8.32. See also Alison R. Bernstein, "The Greening of a Young Trustee," *Vassar Quarterly* 70 (Fall 1973): 30–31.

51 Purcell, quoted in "A History of Coeducation," *Vassar College Encyclopedia*, http://vcencyclopedia.vassar.edu/coeducation/a-history-of-coeducation.html, accessed July 16, 2013. Purcell's full statement is presented in Elizabeth Runkle Purcell, "Clarifying Goals," *Vassar Quarterly* 70 (Fall 1973): 11–12.

and women—conflicted with the college's historic commitment to women's education. Seeking a more definitive resolution, the board of trustees established a committee to take stock of what Vassar had accomplished. The committee worked during two academic years, 1973–75. Its mandate was to review the progress of coeducation, with particular attention to "the college's goals, its standards of admission, and its programs for the recruitment of male and female students of the highest quality." The committee would also examine the quality of life on campus, curricular offerings and academic performance, and job and scholarship opportunities.[52]

In a brief statement in December 1974, the committee reiterated emphatically the college's commitment to coeducation and reaffirmed the goal of enrolling a student body of "approximately the same number of women and men of the highest quality." And it repeated the now often-stated mantra about Vassar's distinctive mission with respect to coeducation: "to pioneer in the kind of education which will achieve true equality between the sexes."[53]

In a final report in May 1975, the committee gave a clear endorsement of the growing success of coeducation at Vassar: "Six years of experience have produced an intellectual and social partnership between the sexes which seemed almost impossible a short time ago. Women and men accept one another's presence naturally today and the scare theories of 'male dominance' and 'diminished commitment to the education of women' have not come to pass. Although the students, faculty and administration appreciate the reality of this harmony between the sexes on the Vassar campus, unhappily the world outside is still insufficiently aware of it."

Although "coeducation at Vassar [was] off to a good start," however, "much remain[ed] to be done." The committee noted that Vassar needed to make "a special effort . . . to recruit qualified men," and it provided specific suggestions with respect to more aggressive recruitment by the admission office, a more robust athletic program for men, and a comprehensive public relations effort

---

52 Charge to the Coeducation Committee, n.d., and Report of the Trustee Committee on Coeducation, Dec. 11, 1974 (source of the quote), both attached to Board of Trustees minutes, Dec. 11, 1974, Subject Files Vassar 8.30.

53 Report of the Trustee Committee on Coeducation, Dec. 11, 1974.

to highlight the successes of men at Vassar. As Vassar succeeded in enrolling more male students of high quality, the result would be "a unique institution where women help to educate men and men help to educate women."[54]

The committee's work underscored the obvious difference between coeducating colleges for women and coeducating colleges for men. There was no difficulty at all in getting women to apply to Princeton and Yale—the widely recognized prestige of those universities, the allure of finally being allowed to breach the barriers at a venerable, highly selective, heretofore all-male institution, made it easy to attract women applicants. But it was not at all easy to persuade men to apply to a college that had, until very recently, been exclusively for women.

Marketing to Male Students and Persistent Yield Problems

In the wake of the trustee committee report, Vassar redoubled its efforts to market itself to male students. With a new director of admission, Richard Moll, taking over in 1975, the college developed new promotional literature and actively recruited male applicants—so much so, in fact, that some student critics suggested that the college was creating inaccurate, stereotypic images of Vassar men and, more generally, going overboard in refashioning its traditional image and message in a way that detracted from its commitment to educating women.[55]

"Vassar for Men?," an admission pamphlet published in 1976, began, "Surprise! There are 750 men at Vassar. The freshman class is 41% male." The pamphlet was intended, in Moll's words, "to reassure counselors and parents as well as college candidates." Moll wrote, "We at Vassar understand that for a man to seriously consider a college with a fine, famous female tradition is 'different,' more different perhaps than a woman's considering Yale." Taking a cue from the recommendations of the trustee committee, the

54 Final Report of the Trustee Committee on Coeducation, May 10, 1975, Subject Files Vassar 8.30.

55 *Vassar Miscellany News*, Sept. 17, 1976.

pamphlet touted the academic credentials and accomplishments as well as the extracurricular achievements of Vassar men.[56]

"Vassar for <u>Men</u>?" became a lightning rod on campus. It drew a heated response from the student government and the campus press for lack of student input into its drafting and for its one-sided portrayal of male students as "both predominantly athletic and aggressive to the point of domination," a charge that Moll and Simpson denied.[57] Moll had other problems beyond this controversy. Although he succeeded in increasing the pool of male applicants, thus making Vassar look more selective, there were real questions about the quality of many of those applicants.[58]

For all the emphasis on measuring Vassar's success in attracting men, the less public question, really at the heart of any assessment of the effectiveness of coeducation, was how well the college was doing in attracting women. Vassar had undertaken coeducation because it had been having trouble drawing a robust pool of highly qualified female applicants and persuading women who were admitted that they should enroll. If coeducation was successful, there should have been an increase in applications from able women and a higher yield.

Although not talked about publicly, the record on these counts was mixed. The challenge laid out in 1970 by Stephenson when he had declared that Vassar's "attractiveness to women . . . remains badly in need of repair" had been only partially addressed.[59] The problem lay less in the number of applicants (which stayed relatively constant in the years 1970–74 and then grew) than in the yield and the quality of the enrolling students. With competition for admitted students coming not just from women's colleges but also from newly coeducational men's colleges and universities, the yield became more challenging to sustain. Among women students

56 "Vassar for <u>Men</u>?," Subject Files Vassar 8.31; Moll, quoted in *Vassar Miscellany News*, Sept. 17, 1976.

57 "Vassar for Men: An Alternative View," *Vassar Miscellany News*, Oct. 15, 1976 ("athletic and aggressive"); editorial, "The Administration and the Referendum," and "The Administration's Answers," *Vassar Chronicle*, Oct. 7, 1976.

58 Bernstein interview.

59 Memorandum, Richard D. Stephenson to John M. Duggan, Aug. 7, 1970, Dean of Students, Box 5.

admitted to the classes of 1974, 1975, and 1976, the average yield was 45 percent. Among women admitted to the classes of 1977 and 1978, it was 33 percent.[60]

It was also challenging to sustain the quality of the women students who enrolled. In terms of median SAT scores, the classes of the 1960s were as strong as any Vassar had seen. But as a wider range of college choices became available to the ablest high school women, there was a notable decline in median SAT scores among women who matriculated at Vassar, as shown in table 14.1.

A second measure of the changing quality of Vassar's women students comes from their high school rank in class. Roughly two-thirds of Vassar women in the classes of 1967 through 1974 had been in the top decile of their high school graduating class. That was true of just under half of the women entering in the class of 1980 and just over two-fifths of the women entering in the class of 1982, as shown in table 14.2.

A separate issue concerned the qualifications of Vassar men. Measured by median SAT scores, the record was positive—perhaps more positive than contemporaries would have imagined. Male students not only held their own on SAT scores in comparison with Vassar women; they sometimes presented superior credentials, as shown in table 14.3.

60 These data, along with those in the following tables, are drawn from these sources: In Middle States, Vassar College, Report on the Faculty, Students, and Educational Resources, Middle States Association Case Study, Feb. 23–26, 1969, and Profile, Vassar's Class of 1980, in Vassar College, *A Self-Study Report*, Feb. 1979, p. 45. In Vassar faculty, vol. 18, Nov. 8, 1967, Jean L. Harry, Report of the Committee on Admission for the Academic Year 1966–67. In Vassar faculty, vol. 19, Dec. 11, 1968, Harry, Report of the Committee on Admission for the Academic Year 1967–68. In Vassar faculty, vol. 20, May 20, 1970, Annual Report on Admission, 1969–70, Richard D. Stephenson to J. M. Duggan. In Dean of Students, Box 5, Statistical Report on Candidates for Admission, 1968; Statistical Report on Candidates for Admission, 1969; Total Candidates Acted on by the Office of Admission, [1974]; Freshman Admission Statistics, 1964–71; Statistics on New Students Entering Vassar in the Fall of 1976, Sept. 1976; Class of 1982: Highlights, May 11, 1978, attached to Preliminary Admissions Profile, May 12, 1978; Vassar College Profile—Class of 1983; and Class of 1984, May 15, 1980. See also Vassar College Class of 1979, internal annual report from the Office of Admission, provided by the Office of Institutional Research, Vassar College. It is important to note the limitations in the data: some years are missing; some data are reported as medians, some as means.

TABLE 14.1. MEDIAN SAT SCORES: VASSAR WOMEN,
1964–74, 1978–79, 1982

Class Year	Verbal Median	Math Median
1964	656	640
1965	660	642
1966	650	626
1967	659	629
1968	656	640
1969	660	642
1970	650	626
1971	659	629
1972	658	627
1973	637	618
1974	654	613
1978[a]	579	578
1979[a]	558	555
1982	570	560

[a]Mean, not median.

On rank in class, however, as table 14.2 illustrates, entering women students significantly outdistanced entering men—
evidence, most likely, that high school women simply worked
harder than high school men of similar abilities.

Ten Years Later: Evaluating Success

The study of coeducation undertaken by the trustee committee in
1973–75 would be replicated in somewhat different form a decade
later, when Simpson's successor as president, Virginia B. Smith, appointed an advisory group of administrators, faculty, and students
"to explore new ways to achieve a more general awareness about
the success of Vassar's coeducational program." Smith claimed that

TABLE 14.2. RANK IN CLASS: VASSAR WOMEN AND MEN,
1967–68, 1971–74, 1980, 1982–83

Percentage in First Decile of High School Graduating Class

Class Year	Women	Men
1967	62.8	NA
1968	66.1	NA
1971	64.4	NA
1972	66.1	NA
1973	66.2	NA
1974	66.2	40.8
1980	49.1	33.2
1982	43.5	20.5
1983	46.5	19.6

Note: NA = not available.

TABLE 14.3. MEDIAN SAT SCORES: VASSAR WOMEN AND MEN,
1974, 1978, 1982, 1984

Class Year	Verbal, Women	Math, Women	Verbal, Men	Math, Men
1974	654	613	652	664
1978[a]	579	578	597	625
1982	570	560	580	600
1984[a]	605	584	584	607

[a]Mean, not median.

Vassar had been "the most successful" of the women's colleges that had coeducated—a group that by then included Bennington, Connecticut, Elmira, Manhattanville, Pitzer, Sarah Lawrence, and Skidmore (Goucher would follow in 1986 and Wheaton in 1988). But Smith also "acknowledged that a broad cross-section of the public still [did] not think of [Vassar] as a coeducational institution." Her charge to the advisory group was to figure out what to do about that.[61]

The advisory group found "substantial objective evidence" of the success of coeducation at Vassar. The number of enrolled men had almost tripled over the fifteen-year history of coeducation, from 323 in 1970 to 919 in 1984. Male students had been well qualified academically on entrance, with credentials comparable to, and perhaps slightly better than, those of their female counterparts. Men had performed well academically; they had won academic prizes and been elected to Phi Beta Kappa in rough proportion to their share of the student body. They had been fully engaged in the extracurricular life of the college and had held a slightly larger proportion of leadership positions than would have been dictated by their representation in the student body. The group also found "substantial subjective evidence" of the success of coeducation in testimony from students, faculty, and administrators.

Off campus, the situation was perceived differently. Especially among some alumnae, guidance counselors, and parents of prospective applicants, there was "a deep unwillingness to believe that a man can receive as good an education at a college which served only women as he can at a college which served only men." What could be done to "eliminate the difference" between the way those on campus perceived the college and the views of outsiders? The advisory group urged a redoubled effort "to convey three basic aspects of Vassar as it exists today." The first aspect was that of being "a first-rate, independent college of the liberal arts with high academic standards and a commitment to serious intellectual work," a college that offered "rare and, in some cases, unique educational opportunities." The second aspect was the "health and high quality of student life at Vassar." The third was the idea that a liberal

---

61 "Report on Coeducation," Advisory Group on Coeducation to Virginia B. Smith, Apr. 26, 1984, Subject Files Vassar 8.30.

arts education at Vassar "can—and does—lead to stimulating and rewarding jobs."[62]

By the close of the 1970s, the male-female ratio at Vassar had settled at 40–60, a level that would be maintained for many years. It was not the 50–50 that Simpson and the trustees had aspired to, but it was a ratio reflective of patterns at other liberal arts colleges, including the historically coeducational Oberlin and Swarthmore, where the absence of engineering programs and the relative de-emphasis of intercollegiate athletics acted as disincentives to male applicants. In addition, as the new century approached, men accounted for less than 45 percent of undergraduates nationally, another trend that worked against gender parity at Vassar.

But it was not clear that achieving gender parity really mattered in terms of day-to-day life on campus. Male students learned to build good relationships with their female peers and came to pride themselves on being what one alumnus called "brothers in a special sisterhood."[63] In the words of another alumnus, "No one except those annoying admissions folks obsessed about [the sex ratio] on a daily basis. . . . What we did obsess about was the notion that, as a group, we were unique."[64] The college claimed that "the Vassar male became a 'type' unto himself—socially aware, sensitive, and humble." Over the years, even with the 40–60 ratio, "gender imbalance" appeared not to be a significant factor in shaping the spirit of the campus.[65]

Where the ratio may still have mattered was in public perceptions about the college's identity. Ironically, Vassar's prominence as a women's college, its historical success in projecting itself as a women's college of the first rank that educated exceptional women, may have made it more difficult to recruit and enroll male

---

62 Ibid.

63 Jeff Silverman '72, quoted in Elizabeth A. Daniels and Clyde Griffen, *"Full Steam Ahead in Poughkeepsie": The Story of Coeducation at Vassar, 1966–1974* (Vassar College, 2000), p. 124.

64 Unidentified alumnus in the class of 1978, quoted in ibid., pp. 119–20.

65 "A History of Coeducation," *Vassar College Encyclopedia*, http://vcencyclopedia .vassar.edu/coeducation/a-history-of-coeducation.html, accessed July 16, 2013.

applicants. As the dean of the faculty at Vassar put it thirty years after the advent of coeducation, "It's like merchandising. If you have the most famous product, it's that much more difficult to reposition yourself. Even some high school guidance counselors still haven't figured out that Vassar accepts men." The dean of admission and financial aid echoed, "I can travel the world and the people I meet recognize the name Vassar, but many still think Vassar is a women's college."[66]

66 Cunningham, "Do Women's Colleges Need Men?," p. 123; Honan, "Three Decades of Men at Vassar," p. 5 (source of the quotes).

15

Smith: "A Looming Problem Which Is Going to Have to Be Faced"

As the cascade of decisions for coeducation escalated, other leading women's colleges needed to decide where they stood. Despite challenges of geography, resources, and competitiveness in admissions, Mt. Holyoke, in South Hadley, Massachusetts, affirmed that it would remain single-sex. Bryn Mawr, just over two miles up the road from the all-male Haverford College on the Main Line outside Philadelphia, was able to take good advantage of opportunities for collaboration—cross-registration for courses, residential exchanges, shared extracurricular activities—without compromising its identity as an independent women's college. The collaboration continued even after Haverford admitted women in 1980. Barnard, across Broadway from Columbia University in the Morningside Heights neighborhood of New York City, had functioned from the time of its founding in 1889 as a coordinate college, benefiting from many of Columbia's resources but maintaining its own faculty, endowment, and board of trustees. Efforts by Columbia in the 1970s to effect a merger met fierce resistance at Barnard, which reaffirmed its status as an autonomous women's college in a coordinate relationship with the university, even as Columbia College admitted women in 1983.[1]

---

1 *Yale Daily News*, Nov. 16, 1971; Norma Rosen, "Mt. Holyoke Forever Will Be for Women Only," *New York Times Magazine*, Apr. 9, 1972, pp. 36–37, 56ff.; "A Brief History of Bryn Mawr College," https://www.brynmawr.edu/about/history, accessed July 8, 2015; Andrea Walton, "Rekindling a Legacy: Barnard College Remains a Women's College," in

For the two most prestigious freestanding women's colleges in Massachusetts, Smith and Wellesley, the question of how to proceed proved to be more complicated. Both schools entertained formal recommendations for coeducation but rejected them to embrace their histories as single-sex institutions. Looking at the stories of their respective deliberations helps us understand some of the imperatives that drove decision-making in this complex terrain.

Situating Smith in Its Historical and Geographical Context

Founded in 1875 in Northampton, Smith College was dedicated to realizing the goal set forth by its founder, Sophia Smith, "to furnish for my own sex means and facilities for education equal to those which are offered now in our Colleges to young men."[2] By the 1960s, with twenty-three hundred students, Smith was the largest private women's college in the United States. The college took pride in its rigorous academic program. Even a century later, Smith liked to point out that it had been the first women's college to open exclusively with a collegiate curriculum. (Others, which had built large structures before opening that needed to be filled, had begun with secondary school divisions to bring many of the early incoming students up to college grade. Smith, with a cottage system, was able to open with a smaller student population.) And, unlike some of its peers, Smith did not offer instruction in home economics.[3] Smith's students presented academic credentials on entrance that closely mirrored those at Princeton and Yale.[4]

Leslie Miller-Bernal and Susan L. Poulson, eds., *Challenged by Coeducation: Women's Colleges Since the 1960s* (Nashville, TN: Vanderbilt University Press, 2006), pp. 289–327.

2 Sophia Smith will, Mar. 1870, in "Smith History," http://www.smith.edu/about-smith/smith-history, accessed Aug. 12, 2014.

3 Thomas C. Mendenhall, Some Reflections of an Alleged Male Chauvinist, Apr. 1974, Mendenhall, Series 9, Box 1.

4 Institutions tended not to report scores in the same way, but one can deduce comparability even so. In 1968, e.g., the *median* SAT verbal score for the freshman class at Smith was 670, the median math score 660, the median score on the English achievement test 680; at Princeton, the *mean* scores were 641 verbal, 684 math, and 657 for achievements. See Coeducation at Smith College: A Report to the President and the College Planning Committee, Dec. 1969, Table 3, Rose, Box 1; Princeton University admission records, in the possession of Nancy Weiss Malkiel.

Smith also benefited from its location in the Connecticut River Valley in relatively close proximity to Mt. Holyoke as well as Amherst, a liberal arts college for men, and the University of Massachusetts, a major public university whose flagship campus was also located in Amherst. By the 1960s the four institutions had considerable experience with basic forms of cooperation—students' ability to take courses on other campuses was the principal example—that would lead to the establishment of an institutionalized cooperative structure, Four Colleges, Inc., in 1965. The four joined forces to plan for a fifth institution, Hampshire, an experimental liberal arts college with a non-traditional curriculum, which opened in 1970 on a tract of farmland on the outskirts of Amherst. In 1966 Four Colleges became Five Colleges, Inc.; over time, forms of cooperation became more varied, including faculty appointed jointly among the institutions, joint academic departments and interdisciplinary programs, shared library services, and shared administrative positions.[5]

The reality of geography, however, was the limiting case in determining to what extent students at any of the schools could avail themselves of the human and intellectual resources of a large, diverse, coeducational university community. At best, it was a twenty-five-minute drive from Smith to Amherst and twenty minutes from Smith to the University of Massachusetts, from Mt. Holyoke to Amherst, and from Hampshire to Smith.[6] The colleges ran buses that made the circuit, but, no matter how much service was improved over the years, it still took a long time to get from one campus to another, and enrolling in a course on another campus involved a commitment of a significant part of a student's day. Academic calendars at the five institutions did not match; nor did weekly course schedules. If a student took a course at another school, the chance for easy, informal socialization before or after

5 Highlights of Five Colleges, Incorporated, update, Jan. 15, 2013, courtesy of Neal Abraham, executive director, Five Colleges, Incorporated. For an account of the student experience with cooperation among the colleges, see Nancy Weiss, "Academic Cooperation in the Valley," *Smith Alumnae Quarterly* 60 (Apr. 1969): 8–11.

6 Elapsed times courtesy of Neal Abraham, communicated by e-mail from Carol Aleman to Nancy Weiss Malkiel, Apr. 1, 2013.

class was less available than it was for students living and studying on the same campus. Geography similarly limited shared extracurricular pursuits.

As late as the 1960s, Smith was unusual among women's colleges in having a majority of men on its faculty, a fact that the college regularly touted in its recruiting literature—presumably on the assumption that it added some element of gravity and distinction to the academic enterprise. Like many of the women's colleges, it also had a long tradition of male leadership. From the founding president, L. Clark Seelye, to the sixth incumbent in the position, Thomas Corwin Mendenhall, inaugurated in 1959, Smith's presidents had been men. Mendenhall came to Smith from Yale, where he had been a professor of history and master of Berkeley College. He had been a Yale undergraduate in the class of 1932 and a Rhodes Scholar at Balliol College, Oxford. Mendenhall's mother, Dorothy Reed Mendenhall, a member of the class of 1895 at Smith, had been one of the first women to graduate from the Johns Hopkins University Medical School, and she had made a significant discovery in medical science, identifying the cell that was a primary characteristic of Hodgkin's disease. An early feminist, she had had a huge influence on her son, impressing upon him through her example the benefits for women of single-sex education. Mendenhall's wife, Cornelia Baker Mendenhall, was a 1935 graduate of Vassar. The Mendenhalls had three daughters: Bethany and Mary followed their mother to Vassar, and Cornelia was a member of the class of 1966 at Smith.[7]

"Good Wife, Mother, or Citizen"

Mendenhall was schooled in the tradition whereby the ablest young women aspired to attend one of the most prestigious women's colleges. His views about women's education were both conventional and forward-looking. He grappled regularly with questions

---

7 On the importance of Dorothy Reed Mendenhall's influence on Thomas Corwin Mendenhall, I am indebted to Thomas Mendenhall's daughter, Cornelia Mendenhall Small. Telephone interview, Nov. 12, 2014.

regarding the changing roles of women in American society and the ways in which their education at Smith would prepare them for their futures. A college like Smith, he said in his inaugural address, would enable young women both "to prepare broadly for later specialization in a profession" and "to perfect those qualities of mind, heart, and judgment so essential to life and leadership at home and in the community."[8] Mendenhall knew that some Smith women would go on to graduate or professional schools, but he also knew that for most Smith graduates, four years in Northampton would mark the end of formal education. Ideally, he said, that education would have equipped such a Smith woman "to understand, evaluate, and solve, with learning, humility, and discrimination whatever problems she may encounter on the way to the good life as the good wife, mother, or citizen."[9]

"Good wife, mother, or citizen"—that phrase encapsulated so much of what Mendenhall believed about the likely futures of the women Smith was educating in the 1960s. He was "absolutely awed" by the leadership ability of Smith women, and he knew that they would assume roles in their communities through which they would do great good in the world. But he also knew about societal expectations for women: The women Smith was educating were supposed to become good wives and good mothers. It is not clear whether he took those realities as givens or whether he wrestled with the difficulty of reconciling them.[10]

As Mendenhall put it in his inaugural address, women needed to appreciate that "the liberal arts offer the best possible training to work through and triumph over their lives as wives, mothers, citizens, and convincing human beings. With the rising tempo and complexity of our society these roles will become increasingly important to the well-being of that society. Their dignity, dimension and significance must be understood as offering just as worthwhile

8 Inauguration of Thomas Corwin Mendenhall, President of Smith College, Oct. 15, 1959, Mendenhall, Series 16, Box 1.

9 "Higher Education for Women—For Better or For Worse," Address by President Thomas C. Mendenhall, Smith College, n.d., Mendenhall, Series 16, Box 5. In terms of a likely date for the talk, Mendenhall identifies himself in it as "a rookie president."

10 Small interview.

a career for a young woman as any of the traditional professions where a half-century ago women first fought for equality of opportunity."[11] It was "supremely important," he believed, to understand that the "primary purpose" of a liberal education was "to make one's mind a pleasant place in which to spend one's leisure."[12]

The difference in life paths between women and men was a recurring theme for Mendenhall, and he elaborated his views in many talks on and beyond the campus. Marriage and motherhood would be "full-time jobs" for women for extended periods; marriage and fatherhood would never be more than part-time commitments for men. Combining "marriage, family, and work" was possible for women, but it would not be easy, and it would require "adjustments" and "sacrifices," "patience and perspective," and "resources of character and judgment, humanity and understanding, self-sufficiency and service to others" that would be developed and nurtured through a rigorous liberal arts education.[13] Although Mendenhall surely knew about other models—women who pursued careers and remained unmarried, women who partnered with other women in companionate and lesbian relationships—he did not speak publicly about them.

For all of his emphasis on the relative roles of wives and husbands, Mendenhall recognized that for women college students, falling in love and finding a mate ranked significantly higher in importance than it did for their male counterparts.[14] But he told students that there was more to be accomplished in college than finding a husband, and he repeatedly lamented their appetite for early marriages. The propensity for students to drop out of college to get married was a particular source of concern to him: "I don't

11 Inauguration of Thomas Corwin Mendenhall.
12 Thomas C. Mendenhall, Last Chapel—1963, Mendenhall, Series 16, Box 2.
13 Thomas C. Mendenhall, Medal Assembly, Nov. 4, 1965 ("adjustments," "sacrifices"); Mendenhall, "The Education of Women and the Progress of the Race," Pierce College, n.d. ("marriage, family, and work," "resources of character and judgment"); and transcript, Mendenhall, "Thought, Word, and Deed," Wells College, 1965 ("full-time jobs," "patience and perspective"), all in Mendenhall, Series 16, Box 3. On the same theme, see also Mendenhall notes, "Women in Modern Society," n.d., Mendenhall, Series 16, Box 5.
14 Thomas C. Mendenhall, First Chapel, Sept. 17, 1968, Mendenhall, Series 16, Box 4.

think marriage is a good thing or has much chance for success when it is embarked upon before either party has matured enough to discover himself as a human being."[15] The preoccupation with finding a husband made women less likely to take intellectual risks, forge their own paths in creative scholarship, and make the decisions and take the responsibilities for which their education equipped them.[16] Attending a women's college allowed women students to gain "a little distance and objectivity on [their] relations to the opposite sex."[17]

Mendenhall's views about the future prospects of Smith students existed in some tension with each other. On the one hand, he was fully supportive of the importance of meeting the challenge of realizing "the proper and full use of the educated woman."[18] On the other hand, he cautioned, in one of his Wednesday morning addresses to the college, that "the increasing concern among you for a vocation after college produces its own kind of dilemma and leads to an ignoring, or a denial, of the creativity and importance of making a home."[19]

Mendenhall's Views on Coeducation

As for coeducation, Mendenhall brought certain assumptions to his presidency, doubtless the product of his experience at Yale and his family's tradition of educating young women in women's colleges. Early in his tenure at Smith, he remarked that he was "inclined to agree with the high school senior who . . . said to a friend: 'first you have to decide whether you want to go to a coeducational school or an educational one.'"[20] But he knew that Smith would need to justify its continued existence as a single-sex

---

15 Thomas C. Mendenhall to Mrs. George V. Bobrinskoy, Jr. [Betsey Shaw Bobrinskoy '48], July 10, 1964, Mendenhall, Series 6, Box 2.

16 Inauguration of Thomas Corwin Mendenhall. See also a number of Mendenhall's addresses to Smith students—e.g., First Chapel—1962, Mendenhall, Series 16, Box 2.

17 Mendenhall, First Chapel, Sept. 17, 1968.

18 Mendenhall, Last Chapel—1963.

19 Thomas C. Mendenhall, Assembly Talk, Mar. 10, 1965, Mendenhall, Series 16, Box 3.

20 "Higher Education for Women—For Better or For Worse."

institution, and he took the issue much more seriously than this remark might suggest.

In a long typescript in 1964, he laid out the arguments, pro and con. Coeducation would mean significant growth in the size of the student body. Adding male students would require "physical changes or additions to the plant" that would be "considerably more expensive" than additions for a larger population of women students. And there was a real question about whether Smith—or any women's college—could find enough men of the same ability as their women students who would have an interest in matriculating.

Would there be reasons—"want of faculty, money, or students"— that would force the college to adopt coeducation, no matter what course it might prefer? As for faculty and money, he thought not. With respect to students, "the most serious threat" would be "the coming of coeducation to Dartmouth, Williams, Amherst, Princeton, and Yale." Even if that were to happen, he thought that "there would still be some qualified applicants left for Smith."

Should Smith choose voluntarily to coeducate? On the one hand, Mendenhall cited the views in some quarters that "the woman's college is an unnatural, anachronistic survival, doomed to disappear" and that "the environment for learning is greatly improved by the addition of men." On the other side he noted two compelling arguments. First, if the quality of a women's college were to be maintained and the case for it "put vigorously before its potential public," then "Smith and its sisters" would be likely to "manage to survive and keep attracting promising students." Second, "the educationally-segregated campus" had "positive advantages" given "the romantic intemperance of the coeducational campus and the widespread confusion over the purpose of a college education."

Where did the balance of the arguments lie? "If one were founding de novo a college," Mendenhall concluded, "one would probably opt for at least [a] coordinate plan. . . . But if one must start with Smith College, its particular location, size, and traditions, the debate does come down, for the writer at least, to a draw!"[21]

---

21 Typescript, Thomas C. Mendenhall, "Some Thoughts on Coeducation and the Future of Smith College," Aug. 11, 1964, Mendenhall, Series 9, Box 1.

VASSAR

By the mid-1960s, Vassar College's geographical isolation was becoming a serious problem. It affected recruitment of faculty members as well as students. With the growing dissatisfaction of Vassar women about their distance from men's colleges, there were real concerns about Vassar's competitiveness in admissions in relation to other leading women's colleges. **Alan Simpson,** president of Vassar from 1964 to 1977, responded enthusiastically to Kingman Brewster's invitation in December 1966 to investigate the potential for a "royal marriage" between Vassar and Yale. Strong opposition from alumnae to relocating the college to New Haven led the Vassar board to call off the proposed plan in November 1967.

Simpson convened a committee on new dimensions to explore options for Vassar's future. He assigned the dean of studies, **Elizabeth "Betty" Daniels**, to investigate alternatives to relocating to New Haven. The committee envisioned Vassar as "an educational complex" cooperating with other institutions in the mid-Hudson region. There would be two undergraduate colleges—Vassar, with a revised, more experimental curriculum, and a new men's college, coordinate or coeducational with Vassar. Two graduate institutes plus selected graduate programs would take "a new, interdisciplinary approach to advanced work in untraditional fields." Few of these proposals came to fruition.

The Vassar faculty voted in May 1968 to admit men to the college. Vassar enrolled male transfer students in 1969–70 and male freshmen the following year. Simpson insisted that Vassar would have "coeducation with a difference," distinguished by "equality of the sexes," not male-dominated coeducation. As this photograph of **dining in the dorms in the 1970s** suggests, male students built good relationships with their female peers and prided themselves on being "brothers in a special sisterhood." Still, the challenge of attracting male applicants in sufficient numbers and of sufficient quality remained a persistent issue. By the close of the 1970s, the male-female ratio at Vassar settled at 40–60, a level maintained for many years.

SMITH

Thomas Corwin Mendenhall, president of Smith College from 1959 to 1975, knew that the college had to think seriously about coeducation. It was not that he favored it, but developments elsewhere—first the Yale-Vassar study, then the consideration of coeducation at so many men's colleges and universities—meant that he could not avoid engaging the issue. Coeducation would mean significant growth in the size of the student body, with major costs that the college could not easily afford. And there was a real question whether Smith—or any women's college—could find enough male students of the same ability as their female students who would have an interest in matriculating.

Mendenhall asked sociology professor **Ely Chinoy** to undertake a serious study of the issue. In a report made public in the spring of 1970, Chinoy argued that coeducation would be desirable and feasible for Smith. Mendenhall called the Chinoy report "one man's analysis" and charged a committee of trustees, administrators, faculty, and students to draw up a recommendation as to how Smith should proceed. A dramatic reversal of student sentiment about coeducation, influenced significantly by the emerging women's movement, provided cover for the committee to recommend against coeducation in April 1971. The Smith board affirmed that view in February 1972.

WELLESLEY

Coeducation was not on the agenda of **Ruth Adams**, president of Wellesley College from 1966 to 1972. But the highly publicized attention to coeducation at such institutions as Yale, Princeton, Vassar, and Smith made it impossible to avoid raising the subject. Adams said, "If we refuse to do any thinking about coeducation, we would be the greatest female ostrich in the educational zoo." In consultation with her executive vice president, political science professor **Philip Phibbs**, Adams proposed to the trustees the appointment of a commission on the future of the college. The commission, made up of trustees, administrators, faculty, and students, began work in the spring of 1969.

By design, the commission had a very broad agenda, of which the education of men was only a small part. In its report, issued in March 1971, the commission recommended that the college acquire the legal capacity to grant degrees to men and that it consider for admission men who applied as transfer students. Those recommendations led Adams, who had been a member of the commission, to append a letter of dissent to the published commission report. Like Adams, Phibbs believed that Wellesley should build on its historic strengths to remain a college for women. In April 1971, the Wellesley trustees reaffirmed "the primary commitment of Wellesley College to the education of women."

BRITISH REPORTS

The 1960s brought scrutiny of the British university system. The first of two major reports—the Report of the Committee on Higher Education (1963), chaired by **Lord Robbins**, professor of economics at the London School of Economics—made the case for expansion of British universities, with a proposed tripling of capacity, so that anyone who qualified would find a place.

Focusing on Oxford, the second report—the Report of the Commission of Inquiry (1966), chaired by **Oliver Franks**, provost of Worcester College, Oxford—argued for broader recruitment of students, growth in the size of the student population, and increasing the number of women undergraduates.

The Cambridge version of the Franks Commission was the Bridges Syndicate, chaired by **Lord Bridges**, former head of the civil service. Its main focus was to provide fellowships for the growing population of university teaching officers who had no college affiliations, as well as affiliations for university staff and postgraduate students. In response to the Bridges report (1962), the colleges expanded their fellowships and collaborated in founding three colleges expressly for graduate students, which also increased opportunities for the election of fellows.

CHURCHILL

In the 1960s, the University of Cambridge lagged other British universities in the percentage of women among its students. The women's colleges lacked resources to admit more women; any progress would have to come from men's colleges deciding to go mixed. Enrolling its first students in 1960, Churchill College was the newest Cambridge college, with the briefest history, the fewest traditions, the most recently assembled fellowship, and the least consequential ties to alumni. All of that enabled it to take the lead on coeducation.

Starting in 1965, Churchill began the process of amending its statutes to permit the admission of women. A committee appointed to consider the issue deliberated but delayed reporting. The senior tutor, **R. H. Tizard** (top), stepped in to drive the process. With the unexpected death of the master in 1967, further consideration of the matter remained on hold. Taking office in 1968, the new master, **Sir William Hawthorne** (middle), head of the department of engineering at Cambridge, opposed coeducation. But the college fellowship had taken hold of the idea, and Tizard brought the deliberations to a successful conclusion. In March 1969 the governing body voted to admit women for the fall of 1972.

KING'S

King's College, much older and more traditional than Churchill, was a less obvious leader in the move to coeducation. As recently as March 1966, the governing body had reaffirmed that women would not be members of the college. The turnaround came with the election later that year of a new provost, **Edmund Leach**, a social anthropologist with a reputation as a "radical intellectual" and an agent of change. Under his leadership, King's upended many of its formal traditions and recruited students from a broader range of schools. Admitting women was part of these moves. A committee report issued in May 1969 laid out the case. Later that month, the governing body voted to join the colleges going mixed in the fall of 1972.

CLARE

At Clare, the second-oldest college of the University of Cambridge, the master, **Sir Eric Ashby**, a botanist who had been vice-chancellor of Queen's University, Belfast, made the critical difference in the decision for coeducation. Ashby led Clare to broaden recruitment of students and liberalize many traditions, and he pressed for coeducation. In April 1969 the governing body voted for it. But the college statute prohibiting the admission of women still needed to be repealed. At a meeting in May 1969, the motion for repeal failed to get the two-thirds majority needed. Drawing on his political savvy and management skills, Ashby staged a process of reconsideration that resulted in an affirmative decision a year later.

JESUS COLLEGE

Jesus College, Oxford, was "a liberal college," "socially unpretentious," with low "snob value" and high-powered academic achievement. The impediments to coeducation in a more conservative, more socially prestigious college were less consequential there. The principal, **Hrothgar John Habakkuk**, a Welshman who held the Chichele chair of economic history at Oxford, led his college to embrace coeducation. Beginning in the winter of 1971–72, he also chaired the Jesus group, the committee of Oxford men's and women's colleges that set conditions to admit women to five men's colleges in the fall of 1974.

WADHAM

Students helped to press Oxford colleges to embrace coeducation. Beginning in 1968, with Wadham in the lead, junior common rooms passed resolutions favoring it. The Wadham resolution came late in the long tenure of the warden, **Sir Maurice Bowra**, a scholar of ancient Greek literature. Bowra, who would retire in 1970, established a committee at Wadham to investigate coeducation and initiated discussions on the subject with the Oxford women's colleges. Men's colleges inclined toward coresidence had either a fellowship with a longstanding sympathy for liberal causes or significant turnover of fellows in the 1960s, with a new, much younger generation who regarded coresidence as a desirable norm. Wadham had both.

In March 1970, the Wadham committee reported in favor of coeducation. Consideration of the report was deferred until the installation of the new warden that fall. In the search for Bowra's successor, the fellows applied an explicit test of each candidate's views on coresidence. The successful candidate was a philosopher of mind and logic, **Stuart Hampshire**, who came from the newly coeducational Princeton University and strongly favored coresidence for Wadham. Hampshire played an important role in organizing other Oxford colleges for joint deliberations about coresidence, an effort that culminated in the decisive work of the Jesus group.

ST. CATHERINE'S

St. Catherine's originated in the nineteenth century as St. Catherine's Society, which allowed non-collegiate students who could not afford the cost of three or four years at college to study at Oxford and earn a degree. In 1962, a decade-long effort by the historian **A.L.C. Bullock**, censor of the society, made St. Catherine's—known familiarly as St. Catz—the newest college at Oxford. Like Wadham, St. Catz had a reputation as "a left-wing, progressive place." Bullock, now master of the new college, led St. Catz to embrace coeducation on the grounds of what he called "the desirability of making an Oxford education available on equal terms to women as well as to men."

BRASENOSE

The principal of Brasenose College, the economist **Sir Noel Hall**, had no personal interest in coeducation, and he was nervous about what he presumed would be the negative reaction from old members of the college if the subject was even raised. But Hall had a group of young fellows, newly elected in the late 1960s, who were very interested in it. These men pushed the Brasenose governing body to address the issue. In June 1971, the governing body voted to amend the college statutes to allow women to become members. "Brasenose," *The Times* wrote, "thus becomes Oxford's new front-runner in what is proving a marathon run-up to coeducation in Oxford colleges."

HERTFORD

Pressure for coeducation at Hertford came from the fellows, many of them younger men appointed in the 1960s. They wanted to increase the pool of good candidates for admission to what had been a middling college; admitting women was both the right thing to do and a way to attract better students. By the time the philosopher **Geoffrey Warnock** became principal in January 1972, the fellows were ready to act. Despite what they interpreted as Warnock's reluctance, the governing body voted in February to change Hertford's statutes to enable women to become members of the college. With Brasenose, Jesus, St. Catz, and Wadham, Hertford admitted women students in 1974.

Although spelling out the arguments in the 1964 typescript may have functioned mainly to help Mendenhall clarify his own thinking, he soon began talking about the subject with the college community. In a Wednesday morning assembly address in the spring of 1965, he said, "Smith is a woman's college, at least for the moment. This is not to deny that we must seriously weigh the pros and cons of coeducation, but in the meantime try to realize the very considerable advantages that accrue to a woman's college. In short, as we come to understand the nature of our institution we must work to maximize its advantages, identify and build on its strength, attempt to remedy its weaknesses or compensate for or become reconciled to them."[22]

Smith's Response to Vassar-Yale

That summer, some faculty began paying attention to the subject of coeducation for Smith. A newly established faculty planning committee charged with considering matters bearing on long-range planning had on its agenda a variety of matters referred by the faculty, including the feasibility of coeducation. The issue was deferred in light of the forthcoming capital campaign. Changing course at such a sensitive time would likely have complicated fund-raising among alumnae. In addition, the prospect of the opening in 1970 of Hampshire College meant that there would likely be more male students taking courses at Smith, with "possibilities of experience and experiment that might be relevant in any future determination concerning co-education."[23]

When the chairman of the faculty planning committee, professor of sociology Ely Chinoy, presented the committee's report at a faculty meeting in April 1966, questions were raised about whether there would ever be a way to consider coeducation without worrying about the effect on fund-raising, because development efforts would always be ongoing. Chinoy explained that the question was

22 Mendenhall, Assembly Talk, Mar. 10, 1965.
23 Report from Faculty Planning Committee, Apr. 27, 1966, Exhibit D, attached to Smith faculty, vol. 13, Apr. 27, 1966.

being deferred only until the new campaign began, not until it ended. Mendenhall interjected that "anyone in the Administration, or on the Faculty or Board of Trustees, should have the coeducation question continuously on his mind, for it is a continuing and critical problem." He concluded by raising one of the considerations he had spelled out in expressing his thoughts on coeducation in the summer of 1964: Was Smith losing faculty or students because it was not coeducational? At the moment, he said, that was not the case.[24]

But developments beyond Smith's control kept coeducation on the college's agenda. The decision of Yale and Vassar to undertake a serious study of the viability of moving Vassar to New Haven clearly rattled Mendenhall. He characterized it as "perhaps the single most powerful stimulus on all separate institutions in the direction of coordinate or coeducational operations one can imagine." He continued, "This dramatic prod may accelerate the process into a rout, particularly at the two most vulnerable points for all of us separates, our attractive and holding power for first-rate faculty and undergraduates of quality."[25] Writing to Franklin Patterson, who had been designated president of the still-nascent Hampshire College, Mendenhall wondered whether Hampshire should open as a men's college, thus improving the ratio of men to women in the valley. Writing to Calvin Plimpton, president of Amherst College, he wondered whether Amherst and Smith (as well as Amherst and Mt. Holyoke) might explore further coordinate arrangements, such as joint academic departments, to bring more men and women into classes together. Were that not to happen, Mendenhall feared, Smith and Holyoke might have to face all too soon "the unhappy choice of an expensive move or the equally expensive creation of a coordinate men's college on our own campuses."[26]

At a meeting of the Smith trustee executive committee in January 1967, Mendenhall observed that "the rapprochement of Vassar and

24 Smith faculty, vol. 13, Apr. 27, 1966, p. 219.

25 Memorandum, Thomas C. Mendenhall to Frank Patterson, Dec. 27, 1966, Mendenhall, Series 8, Box 1.

26 Ibid.; memorandum, Thomas C. Mendenhall to Calvin Plimpton, Dec. 28, 1966, Mendenhall, Series 9, Box 2.

Yale is obliging every separate college to review its own situation." Both the administration and the faculty planning committee were taking up the question of coeducation, he said. Mendenhall outlined some of the alternatives the college could consider: moving elsewhere "to join up with a men's university," inviting Hampshire "to combine and form a co-educational college," admitting male undergraduates to a coeducational Smith, and remaining a separate college for women while working "more actively to increase the cooperation in the Valley." The executive committee thought that the first option was unrealistic—Smith was simply too big to be an attractive partner for another university. The second option seemed unlikely as well—it would preclude Hampshire from becoming an experimental college, as had originally been intended. The executive committee took the view that remaining all-female and pressing for further cooperation in the valley was the right course to pursue, acknowledging that future events might require serious consideration of coeducation.[27]

Reporting to the faculty at their January meeting, Mendenhall recounted the discussions that had taken place at the board meeting and recommended further development of relationships among the four colleges. He encouraged the faculty to get to know their counterparts at the other institutions and to consider ways in which further cooperative arrangements could be developed. The valley offered the opportunity, he said, "to build . . . a quite unique form of coordinate education—predominantly undergraduate, yet enjoying many of the resources of a university, separate but not isolated."[28]

Mendenhall's basic approach was to undertake broad public discussion of coeducation so that any decisions the college took would come in the context of full understanding of the options at hand. In February 1967, in a newly inaugurated column, "A Voice from College Hall," in the *Smith Alumnae Quarterly*, Mendenhall addressed the Yale-Vassar discussions and explained his thinking about the advantages and disadvantages of coeducation for the benefit of the Smith alumnae body. He contrasted "the very

27 Minutes, Executive Committee, Jan. 16, 1967, Smith trustees, vol. 10, pp. 265–66.
28 Smith faculty, vol. 13, Jan. 25, 1967, p. 33.

fashionable belief" in the educational advantages of mixed classes with the conviction of many educators that there were "distinct advantages in teaching the sexes separately" at "certain points in their intellectual and emotional development" and that the opportunity to pursue formal education "without the distracting crosscurrents of the mixed classroom" might be preferable for many young women. He pointed out that experience suggested that "separate schooling" gave "graduates of women's colleges . . . an all-important self-confidence as well as a good education." As for the belief that "opportunities for the two sexes to mingle outside the classroom must be made easy and frequent," he observed that meeting members of the opposite sex was not the primary purpose of a college education and that there were advantages for women in living and working with other women.[29]

In April 1967, the faculty planning committee made an initial report on coeducation. The committee framed its deliberations in terms of the likely outcome twenty years hence if Smith remained a college for women. The potential for "erosion of the quality of the faculty" was one serious concern. The second concern was student recruitment. In the face of competition from a raft of newly coeducational colleges and universities, how would Smith fare in seeking "to draw the kind of student body it would like to have"? The committee came to the view that "maintenance of Smith as a high quality college providing the best possible education for women may well be jeopardized if some efforts are not made to move in the direction of co-education."

What might those efforts be? The committee ruled out full coeducation, which would entail men enrolling at Smith as candidates for the bachelor's degree. The "difficulties and disadvantages" of such a move were thought to be "so great as to render that suggestion undesirable and unrealistic." As for establishing a coordinate college for men "with a separate identity but with substantially shared faculty and resources," the committee said that such a proposal should be "set aside" for the present.

---

29 Thomas C. Mendenhall, "A Voice from College Hall," *Smith Alumnae Quarterly* 58 (Feb. 1967): 15.

A third option, "a greater measure of cooperation" in the valley, "notably with Amherst," seemed to the committee to be the most realistic course, provided that complicated practical issues, such as transportation and coordination of academic calendars, could be worked out. At the graduate level, further cooperation with the University of Massachusetts might provide opportunities for faculty interested especially in graduate teaching and research.

The committee acknowledged that achieving greater cooperation in the valley might not work to bring about the desired ends. It proposed to continue to explore the possibility of a coordinate college for men in Northampton while keeping close watch on the development of further cooperative efforts and to make a final report on the subject in June 1970.[30] In May 1967, the trustees voted to accept the committee's report and to urge "vigorous pursuit" of cooperation in the valley, "but not to reject the possibility of coeducation in the future."[31]

If Cooperation Fails: The Fort Hill Proposal

Mendenhall forwarded the report to Calvin Plimpton and Prosser Gifford, respectively the president and the dean of the faculty at Amherst. The report, he said, represented a widely held conviction among Smith faculty, students, and trustees that "Smith must do all it can to effect more coordination and cooperation specifically with Amherst and generally with the colleges in the Valley." Mendenhall worried, however, that Amherst was "rather uninterested" in further cooperation, and he implored Plimpton and Gifford to join him in serious consideration of "the spectrum of possible coordinate activities, transportation, calendar, joint departments, shared offerings, etc." He wanted to begin by seeing what could be done in terms of two-way cooperation between Amherst and Smith because he believed that starting with two institutions was

---

30 Report of the Faculty Planning Committee on Co-Education at Smith College, Apr. 1967, Mendenhall, Series 9, Box 1.

31 Smith faculty, vol. 13, Apr. 26, 1967, p. 48; minutes, Board of Trustees, June 6, 1967, Smith trustees, vol. 10, p. 286.

easier and likelier to be productive, with the possibility of expansion to the others in the future.[32]

The unlikelihood of a real breakthrough in bringing about workable new collaborative arrangements notwithstanding, Mendenhall and the dean of the faculty at Smith, the classical archaeologist Phyllis Williams Lehmann, nevertheless embarked on a series of meetings with Plimpton and Gifford, talks that Mendenhall told the trustees were "proving pleasant and should prove ultimately profitable."[33] Not counting on a constructive response from Amherst, however, Mendenhall quietly pursued a different path: Smith should take steps to establish a coordinate college for junior and senior men at an eight-acre site in Northampton known as Fort Hill, located just a few minutes' walk from the edge of the Smith campus. The college should announce that objective in advance of the forthcoming capital campaign, with the understanding that funds would be sought for the new venture only after the successful completion of the $45 million campaign in 1973. Enrollment of women undergraduates at Smith would be scaled back modestly to two thousand; Fort Hill would enroll eight hundred male juniors and seniors.

Mendenhall thought that the proposed plan had many advantages. Smith would remain "predominantly female," with "much of its original separate character." Men could be recruited "at a point (junior year) when coeducation seems to have the most to recommend it." With their majors known, men could be selected in such a way as to "balance up the present distribution of majors." Announcing the proposal at the outset of the campaign would put to rest "the inescapable, inevitable question"—"What is Smith doing about coeducation?"—that would otherwise dog fund-raising. And near-term efforts to strengthen cooperation in the valley "would be fundamentally consistent with this ultimate goal of a two-year college for men."[34]

32 Memorandum, Thomas C. Mendenhall to Calvin Plimpton and Prosser Gifford, May 4, 1967, Mendenhall, Series 8, Box 1.

33 Minutes, Executive Committee, Dec. 7, 1967, Smith trustees, vol. 10, p. 334.

34 T[homas] C. Mendenhall, A Proposal (Confidential) to My Fellow Trustees, June 13, 1967, Appendix C, Minutes, Executive Committee, June 20, 1967, Smith trustees, vol. 10.

In presenting the proposal to the trustees, Mendenhall said that he had "always been willing to admit that some form of coeducation might prove inevitable and necessary at Smith in order to maintain faculty and students of quality." Up to that point, he had not "seen any practicable way around the dilemma of Smith's present size," which meant that enrolling 2,300 men would result in a college of 4,600 students, whereas keeping the present numbers would "deprive 1000 or more women of a Smith education in order to accept 1000 or more men." Fort Hill, he said, was "the first solution to the problem for which he [could] develop a genuine enthusiasm."

The executive committee engaged Mendenhall's proposal without reaching any conclusions. Three aspects of the plan drew the most attention: Would Smith succeed in attracting male students of comparable ability to women students? Was it realistic to contemplate a large financial commitment, albeit at some unspecified point in the future? And what would faculty, students, and alumnae make of Fort Hill? There was general agreement that "no answer to any of these questions could be much more than an educated guess."[35]

By the time the 1967–68 academic year opened, it was clear that the Fort Hill proposal was dead. Mendenhall had discussed the idea with individual trustees and members of the administration, as well as with the faculty planning committee, now with a majority of new members. The previous committee had "rather strongly supported" the idea, but the new committee was more cautious. It was willing for Mendenhall to announce that Smith was "investigating the feasibility of establishing a coordinate college of from 800 to 1,000 men, possibly limited to members of the junior and senior classes," but it did not want to do anything to "deter the College from intensifying its present efforts at cooperation with the other institutions in the Valley." Nor did it believe that any fundraising for the coordinate college should be undertaken until the goals of the capital campaign had been achieved.

---

35 Minutes, Executive Committee, June 20, 1967, Smith trustees, vol. 10, p. 310.

The committee felt that it could not go any further without doing "more 'research' into the whole matter."

Although there was some interest in the Fort Hill proposal among trustees and members of the faculty planning committee, there was also "great concern [about] whether the time was ripe or whether the situation in fact required it." Mendenhall presented a lengthy account of his further thinking about the pros and cons of the Fort Hill proposal to the board's executive committee in September 1967. In the end, he said, he had come to the conclusion that "on balance," it would be unwise to advocate the Fort Hill proposal "at the present time." Mendenhall said that Fort Hill still "seemed to him and many others the most financially practicable and educationally desirable alternative for some kind of coeducation at Smith," and that it would remain one of the options under consideration by the faculty and college planning committees, but that the public response to anyone who asked about coeducation at Smith would "stress both the possibilities which were being actively sought in better cooperation in the Valley and the studies of the question which were continuing at Smith." Mendenhall apologized to the trustees for the "distraction" caused by the Fort Hill proposal but said that he thought that "on balance," the discussions had been "beneficial."[36]

Coeducation at Smith: Continuing Investigation

The faculty planning committee, now led by a classicist, Charles Henderson, Jr., resumed deliberations on the options for Smith. By the Christmas holidays, it had "reached a consensus, though by no means yet an enthusiastic one, that an expansion of the 'male presence' at Smith [would be] desirable, provided the present academic standards can be maintained." But there was so much opinion and data to be collected and digested before a "sound judgment" could be made about how best to proceed, and the committee believed that it would be more productive for a single faculty member to be relieved of his teaching and assigned to the task on a full-time basis

36 Minutes, Executive Committee, Sept. 29, 1967, Smith trustees, vol. 10, pp. 318–22.

instead of counting on the part-time efforts of the committee's six members.[37]

That recommendation notwithstanding, the responsibility for collection and analysis of data remained for the moment with the planning committee. It had a wealth of data. One set came from a questionnaire aimed at secondary school students, worked out in collaboration with Princeton University and distributed anonymously to selected secondary schools.[38] Another came from a survey of Smith students conducted by the social science research center at the college, which focused on attitudes with respect to the future of women's colleges.[39] A third came from a survey of the Smith faculty focusing on issues related to coeducation, distributed by the faculty planning committee.[40]

In May 1968 the committee presented a report to the faculty on the work it had done thus far in terms of assembling and analyzing data. There was little evidence to support the view that "the way for Smith to maintain its excellence and improve its competitive position is simply to continue on its present course of single-sex education."[41] All of the studies pointed toward the desirability of some form of coeducation at Smith. The high school questionnaire made plain that coeducation would make a college more appealing to prospective students, male as well as female. Only 5 percent of 5,000 respondents preferred a single-sex liberal arts college.[42] The survey of Smith students revealed that a large majority of 661 respondents favored coeducation, development of a neighboring

37 Charles Henderson, Jr., to Thomas C. Mendenhall, Dec. 19, 1967, Mendenhall, Series 9, Box 1.

38 Special Questionnaire on Seniors' Attitudes toward College, n.d. [1967], and Coding System—Questionnaire to Secondary School Seniors, n.d. [1967], Chinoy, Box 706.

39 In Jahnige, Box 1, see Peter I. Rose (director, Social Science Research Center) to Dear Student, Nov. 27, 1967, and A Study of the College Experience, n.d. In Mendenhall, Series 9, Box 2, see Social Science Research Center, Student Questionnaire, Fall 1967, Marginal Tabulations, n.d.

40 Faculty Planning Committee, survey pretest, Feb. 12, 1968, Rose, Box 1; Faculty Attitudes toward Coeducation, n.d., Mendenhall, Series 9, Box 1.

41 Report of the Faculty Planning Committee, Co-Education at Smith College, May 1968, Mendenhall, Series 9, Box 1.

42 Selective Summary of the High School Questionnaire, n.d., Mendenhall, Series 9, Box 2.

coordinate college, or merger with a men's college.[43] And the survey of Smith faculty showed that two-thirds of the respondents felt that coeducation was "fundamental to the improvement of the undergraduate life and program of Smith College."[44]

The committee recommended that the college redouble its efforts toward cooperation with institutions in and outside the valley—making the most of five-college cooperation and instituting semester- and year-long student exchanges with other colleges and universities. Calling coeducation at Smith "essential in whatever forms seem desirable," the committee recommended that the faculty, administration, and trustees "proceed to active consideration of ways, means, and alternatives" for accomplishing it.[45]

Speaking to the Smith trustees in early May of 1968, Mendenhall called coeducation "a looming problem which is going to have to be faced."[46] At last chapel in late May, he noted that a majority of the Smith faculty saw "some form of coeducation" as "inevitable" and that students "increasingly" saw coeducation as a "welcome, necessary, inevitable development at Smith." He pointed out, however, that the gains that coeducation would bring would be "accompanied by genuine losses." He said, "There are certain very real advantages for many young women and young men in having the opportunity to receive part of their formal education free from the constant presence and distractions of the opposite sex."[47]

The more Mendenhall spoke about coeducation, the more specific he became in pointing out the advantages of single-sex

43 Selective Summary of the Student Questionnaire, n.d., Mendenhall, Series 9, Box 2. The results of the student survey were reported in "Student Coeducation Survey Released," *Sophian*, Feb. 6, 1969, Box 17, Smith College Archives. See also the much more detailed analysis in Peter I. Rose, Smith College and the Issue of Coeducation: Report No. 1: The Pulse of the Campus (Preliminary Draft), Apr. 1968, Chinoy, Box 706.

44 Selective Summary of the Faculty Questionnaire, n.d., Mendenhall, Series 9, Box 2. See also "Results of Faculty Survey on Coeducation," *Sophian*, Feb. 27, 1969, Box 17. For more detailed analyses, see Peter I. Rose, Smith College and the Issue of Coeducation: Report No. 2: The Views of the Faculty (Preliminary Draft), May 1968, Chinoy, Box 706; Faculty Attitudes toward Coeducation, n.d. [stamped Feb. 26, 1969], Mendenhall, Series 9, Box 1.

45 Report of the Faculty Planning Committee, Co-Education at Smith College, May 1968.

46 Minutes, Board of Trustees, May 4, 1968, Smith trustees, vol. 10, p. 361.

47 Thomas C. Mendenhall, Last Chapel, May 31, 1968, Mendenhall, Series 16, Box 4.

education. Smith afforded students the opportunity to be first-class citizens, to have all the resources of the college focused on their "needs, interests, and the full development of [their] capabilities as . . . independent human being[s]." As he said at first chapel in September 1968, "You can and do major in a science or economics, for instance, without any hesitation because you might find yourself in competition with men. In a college for women you can develop and exercise your talents and interests in a host of ways, run your own affairs, in short learn to live and work with other women, a rare chance in our excessively heterosexual society."[48]

At the same time, Mendenhall moved to take action on the proposals made by the faculty planning committee. In September 1968, together with John Sawyer, the president of Williams College, he invited the presidents of five men's and five women's colleges—Amherst, Bowdoin, Dartmouth, Wesleyan, Williams, Connecticut, Mt. Holyoke, Smith, Vassar, and Wheaton—to consider a group exchange wherein a specified number of students from one of the men's colleges could enroll for a semester or a year at one of the women's colleges, and vice versa.[49] The plan was announced in October, and the resulting Ten-College Exchange, expanded first to include Trinity College and further expanded to a Twelve-College Exchange as Wellesley joined the group, began in 1969–70.[50] "**AMEN!**" declared the Smith student newspaper, the *Sophian*, celebrating the fact that a "male presence" would be "felt on campus next year."[51]

Meanwhile, Mendenhall continued to focus on coeducation at Smith. As he told the faculty in September 1968, he was asking the faculty planning committee both to "work on various aspects of Five-College Cooperation" and to "consider the problem of ways

48 Thomas C. Mendenhall, First Chapel, Sept. 17, 1968, Mendenhall, Series 16, Box 4.

49 Memorandum, Thomas C. Mendenhall to College Planning Committee, Aug. 21, 1968, Mendenhall, Series 14, Box 6; Mendenhall and John E. Sawyer to Our Eight Fellow Presidents, Sept. 10, 1968; Mendenhall and Sawyer, Suggested Ground Rules for an Experimental Exchange of Students, Sept. 11, 1968, Minutes, Executive Committee, Appendixes B and C, Oct. 7, 1968, Smith trustees, vol. 10, pp. 393–95.

50 Smith faculty, vol. 13, Oct. 23, 1968, p. 128. On Wellesley's decision to join the exchange as of 1970–71, see Ruth M. Adams to Philip Driscoll, Mar. 10, 1970, Mendenhall, Series 14, Box 6.

51 *Sophian*, Oct. 24, 1968, Box 17.

and means and alternatives for admitting men as candidates for undergraduate degrees at Smith." Noting Princeton's estimate that implementing coeducation there might cost $24 million, Mendenhall pointed out that Smith had a campaign underway to raise $45 million "just to keep the College in operation as it is now in kind and quality." Mendenhall told the faculty, "We are on the horns of a dilemma. We may not be able to afford co-education, and we may not be able to afford not to be co-educational."[52]

With the endorsement of the faculty planning committee and the college planning committee and the approval of the trustees, Mendenhall told the faculty in October that plans were being made for a study of "the feasibility of coeducation at Smith: that is, a study of what in fact we can afford, and of what, in fact, we most desire."[53] Following the suggestion the previous winter from the faculty planning committee, he asked Ely Chinoy, the sociologist who had chaired the planning committee for three years, to take up the project, with the understanding that he would be relieved of his teaching responsibilities during the spring semester of 1969.[54]

In October, too, when presidents, deans of faculty, deans of students, and faculty representatives of the Seven Sisters convened for their annual conference, the report of the meeting noted that "Smith urgently feels the pressure to become coeducational" and would have to make a decision in the next few years.[55]

---

52 Smith faculty, vol. 13, Sept. 18, 1968, p. 117. On the growth in participation in academic exchanges among the colleges in the valley, see Nancy Weiss, "Academic Cooperation in the Valley," *Smith Alumnae Quarterly* 60 (April 1969): 8–11; Statistics on the Extent to Which Some Coeducation Already Exists for Smith Undergraduates, Nov. 8, 1968, Mendenhall, Series 9, Box 1.

53 Smith faculty, vol. 13, Oct. 23, 1968, p. 128.

54 Minutes, Executive Committee, Dec. 11, 1968, Smith trustees, vol. 10, p. 406.

55 Report on the Seven College Conference Held at Bryn Mawr, Oct. 25–26, 1968, Mendenhall, Series 14, Box 5.

16

Smith: "Recommitting to Its Original, Pioneering Purpose"

As Ely Chinoy embarked on his study of the feasibility of coeducation at Smith, Thomas Mendenhall continued to wrestle privately with his own thinking on the subject, working out his ideas, as was his custom, in a long essay he wrote in January 1969. He asked: Would coeducation "preserve and strengthen quality education for young women at Smith?" And "If it were decided that coeducation was desirable, in what form would it be practicable and feasible?" There followed a thoughtful account of the history of the college, the advantages to women students of a single-sex environment, and the current pressures toward coeducation. The center of the piece was a lengthy analysis of the proposal to build a coordinate college for eight hundred men at Fort Hill, which Mendenhall still considered the best option for Smith. He said that he was "convinced" that Smith should "venture into coeducation . . . if she can," and that the new campus at Fort Hill was the way to accomplish that objective.[1]

Chinoy Studies the Question

Mendenhall's essay appears to have had a purpose beyond clarifying his thinking. It was prepared as a fund-raising document for the Clark family, who had previously funded the college's new

---

1 Thomas C. Mendenhall, "Coeducation and the Future of Smith College," Jan. 21, 1969, Mendenhall, Series 9, Box 1.

science center and might be in a position to give the college the "$12 million of expendable capital" necessary to set Smith on this important new course. Mendenhall described them in the essay as "the only friends of Smith I know who could even contemplate such a second founding fund" (the first having been Sophia Smith's founding gift of $350,000).[2] There is no evidence, however, of discussions or negotiations over the proposal.

Whether Chinoy was aware of Mendenhall's thinking is also not known. In March 1969, Chinoy called an open meeting of the faculty to describe the work he was doing and to gather faculty opinions about coeducation.[3] In April the *Smith Alumnae Quarterly* devoted part of the magazine to articles on coeducation.[4] In April, too, Chinoy surveyed Smith students and found enthusiasm for coeducation comparable to the results of the survey conducted two years earlier. He also considered the alumnae survey, which showed divided views about Smith and coeducation. He studied surveys done previously for the faculty planning committee and analyzed the data that had been collected. He gathered information from institutions that had already implemented coeducation or were debating it. And he explored in some detail the question of feasibility.[5]

Two questions animated Chinoy's investigation. If Smith remained a women's college, what would be the effect on recruitment

2 Ibid.; Thomas C. Mendenhall to the Clark Family, Jan. 21, 1969, Mendenhall, Series 5, Box 4, cited in Mary Frances Donley Forcier, "Transforming Institutional Gender Identity: The Challenge of Coeducation at Dartmouth, Lehigh, Smith and Vassar, 1945–1971" (Ph.D. dissertation, Carnegie Mellon University, 2005), p. 263, n. 10.

3 "Faculty Ponder Costs, Benefits of Coeducation," *Sophian*, Mar. 13, 1969, Box 17, Smith College Archives.

4 *Smith Alumnae Quarterly* 60 (Apr. 1969): "Coeducation," p. 12; Lawrence A. Fink, "It's Good But Is It Necessary?," p. 13; "Let's Discuss Coeducation Without the Faculty, the Alumnae or the Administration," pp. 14–17; "Alumnae Comments on Coeducation for Smith," p. 18.

5 *Coeducation at Smith College: A Report to the President and the College Planning Committee*, Dec. 1969, Rose, Box 1. The data from the alumnae survey are presented in Alumnae Questionnaire 1968: Sample of Respondents and Non-Respondents, stamped Nov. 13, 1968, Mendenhall, Series 9, Box 2. The data from the second student survey are presented in two studies by the College Planning Committee, the first, Attitudes toward Coeducation, Marginals, and the second, Cross Tabulation: Class by Various Other Variables, both Apr. 1969, Chinoy, Box 706.

and retention of students and faculty? And which environment—coeducation or single-sex education—would be better for women students?[6]

By many measures Smith was doing better than it had previously in recruiting high-quality students. Median board scores had improved from 1960 to 1965 and appeared to be holding steady. Median verbal scores for classes entering in 1956, 1958, 1961, 1966, and 1968 were 612, 615, 645, 679, and 670, respectively; median math scores were 542, 564, 605, 666, and 660. Comparing the class entering in 1958 and the class entering in 1968, there had been a dramatic improvement in such indices as freshmen presenting 18 or more academic units (with a unit defined as a subject studied for one year in high school), freshmen presenting 20 or more academic units, the number of freshmen entering with three or more units in science and four or more units in mathematics, the number taking Advanced Placement examinations, the number of Advanced Placement examinations taken, and the number of scores of 4 or 5 on those exams.[7]

The record with respect to the number of applicants and the proportion who accepted offers of admission was more problematic, however, and it was too soon to tell what would happen when women students had the opportunity to apply to formerly male institutions. Applications had reached a high of 2,580 in 1965 but had dropped steadily in 1966, 1967, and 1968 to a low of 2,222, with an increase to 2,406 in 1969. Was 1969 an aberration, with the decline from 1965 to 1968 more indicative of future patterns? It was too soon to tell.

There was another warning signal as well: Since 1965, an increasing number of applicants had had to be admitted—1,001 in 1965, 1,345 in 1969—to secure an entering class of the desired size. The proportion of students who accepted offers of admission had been declining steadily, from 61.5 percent in 1965 and 1966 to what looked to be 57.6 percent in 1969. Moreover, there had

6 *Coeducation at Smith College: A Report to the President and the College Planning Committee*, p. 2.

7 "News from Northampton," *Smith Alumnae Quarterly* 58 (Nov. 1966): 21; Jane Sehmann, "College Hall," *Smith Alumnae Quarterly* 60 (Nov. 1968): 44.

been a shift in terms of Smith's principal competition. In 1961, 54 percent of admitted students who turned down Smith's offers went to other Seven Sisters schools and 20 percent to coeducational institutions. In 1965, the numbers were 47 percent to the Seven Sisters and 28 percent to coeducational schools. In 1969, 34 percent chose the Seven Sisters and 39 percent coeducational colleges and universities.[8]

It was not yet clear what was going to happen over time to Smith's competitive position. In the short run, Chinoy thought, Smith would likely fare well in recruiting "a substantial number of excellent students." Longer term, however, the college would "probably experience increasing difficulty in maintaining the quality of the student body." Would it be possible to maintain the college's "present high standards" for the size of the population the college enrolled each year? What kinds of students would be coming to a women's college when "virtually all other colleges of comparable quality are coeducational?" Neither of those questions could be answered definitively. In the end, Chinoy judged that more and more of the strongest women applicants were going to opt for coeducational institutions and that the quality of the student body would not be "as readily maintained" if Smith remained a college for women.[9]

As for faculty recruitment and retention, the interest in coeducation was correlated with age and length of service, with the oldest, longest-serving faculty members least invested in coeducation and the youngest, newest faculty more focused on its benefits. Even so, although a majority of the faculty preferred coeducation, when faculty members were asked to rank their priorities, higher faculty salaries, increased scholarships for students, and additional funds for library acquisitions far outranked coeducation. Only 27 percent of faculty members ranked coeducation among their top three priorities; just 7 percent designated it the most important step for the college to take.[10]

---

8 *Coeducation at Smith College: A Report to the President and the College Planning Committee*, pp. 8–12, 15.

9 Ibid., pp. 16, 45.

10 Ibid., pp. 6–7.

Would coeducation provide a better educational experience for women students? Chinoy thought that the answer was yes. Indeed, the main reasons for considering coeducation were educational: the prospect of "greater liveliness" in the intellectual interchanges in a coeducational classroom, with the "expression of more varied points of view," and the likelihood of "richer, more varied, and more relaxed relationships between men and women" than were possible when male-female interactions were confined to social life on weekends. Moreover, given the ever-increasing participation of women in "the workaday world of business, the professions, politics, and community affairs," the "discontinuity between life in a women's college and the society into which its graduates go" seemed increasingly difficult to sustain.[11]

"On balance," Chinoy concluded, "coeducation is desirable." He had carefully analyzed likely enrollment patterns, the need for additional faculty members and administrative staff, classroom utilization, library capacity, and requirements for new facilities, and he believed that if "the necessary capital funds" could be raised, coeducation would also be "feasible."[12]

Considering the Chinoy Report—and Other Possibilities

Chinoy conveyed his report to the president and the college planning committee in an initial typescript in October 1969. After review, it was finalized in December and transmitted to faculty, students, trustees, and alumnae leaders in January 1970. In April 1970, it was printed in summary form in *A Letter from Smith College* for dissemination to alumnae, parents, and friends of the college.[13] The Chinoy report was the Smith equivalent of Princeton's Patterson report, and it resembled that report in its balance,

11 Ibid., p. 45.
12 Letter of transmittal, Chinoy to Mendenhall, in ibid.
13 Coeducation at Smith College: A Report to the President and the College Planning Committee, Oct. 1969, Mendenhall, Series 9, Box 2; minutes, Board of Trustees, Nov. 1, 1969, Smith trustees, vol. 10, pp. 466–67; *Coeducation at Smith College: A Report to the President and the College Planning Committee*, summarized in *A Letter from Smith College*, Apr. 1970, pp. 3–8, Smith College Archives.

thoroughness, grounding in data, and judicious examination of arguments for and against coeducation. What was different was the degree to which the report was embraced by the administration. At Princeton the president had clearly accepted the analysis in the Patterson report, and the provost had been deeply involved in developing that analysis; what was at issue was a matter of process before a decision could be reached on how to proceed. At Smith the embrace was more tentative. The Chinoy report, Mendenhall said in disseminating it, was an important step in Smith's review of "the alternative of coeducation," a review that had "become a necessity for every separate college for men or for women" in the United States. But the report was a step along the way in that review, not a decision or a conclusion; it was "one man's analysis of the desirability and feasibility of coeducation at Smith College." There was still much work to be done, with further inquiry into some of the subjects Chinoy addressed and careful consideration by college committees and leaders of the right course for Smith.[14]

Moreover, as Mendenhall's comment to the *New York Times* upon release of the report suggested, the president remained hesitant. "I believe that coeducation is a much more serious step for a women's college than a men's," he said, "because there are women for whom Smith is the opportunity to have a first-rate education slightly apart from competition. We must decide to what extent we have the obligation to maintain that option."[15]

The Chinoy report was not the only radical document on the table for Mendenhall's consideration in the fall of 1969. There were also some far-reaching ideas for more cooperation among the colleges in the valley, ideas conveyed privately among institutional leaders rather than in any public report or forum. In a memo to Chinoy in October 1969, the coordinator of Five Colleges, Inc., North Burn, spelled out some options that could be considered in

14 Letter of transmittal, Thomas C. Mendenhall to Faculty, Students, Trustees, Counselors, and Officers of the Alumnae Association, Jan. 1970, in *Coeducation at Smith College: A Report to the President and the College Planning Committee.*

15 Quoted in "Study at Smith Calls for Coeducation," *New York Times*, Feb. 22, 1970, p. 69.

lieu of making a major capital investment in coeducation. Amherst might recruit all the men for the three colleges, thus avoiding the problem of whether a women's college could attract male students of sufficiently high caliber. Some number of men from Amherst, along with male honors students from the university, might take up residence at Smith and Mt. Holyoke, with women students living at Amherst and UMass. The colleges and the university could set up Five-College recreational facilities. A major increase in the investment in the Five-College bus system would enable more trips among the institutions, which would greatly facilitate the interchange of students. Why not declare a five-year moratorium on decisions about coeducation and try instead to develop some imaginative alternatives taking better advantage of the resources of the valley?[16]

In a long memo to Amherst's president, Calvin Plimpton, in November 1969, Amherst's dean, Prosser Gifford, mused about other radical possibilities. Amherst, Smith, Mt. Holyoke, and Hampshire might decide jointly to increase their enrollments and become coeducational institutions, with male-female ratios ranging from 2 to 1 at Amherst to 1.5 to 1 at Smith and 1 to 1 at Mt. Holyoke and Hampshire. With "parity among the four institutions," there would be a good chance that the women's colleges, and even Hampshire, might succeed in "attracting high quality men candidates." Alternatively, Amherst might increase modestly in size but remain all-male while the other three institutions became coeducational, with "Amherst south at [Mt.] Holyoke and Amherst west at Smith, each with about 1000 students." Gifford's third option, like the first, had all four colleges becoming coeducational but without the significant increase in enrollment, which would mean a decrease of 1,000 women students in the colleges.[17]

A second plan, spelled out by the president of Mt. Holyoke, David B. Truman, in response to Gifford's memo, would have kept each of the three single-sex colleges at their current sizes—Amherst

16 North Burn to Eli [*sic*] Chinoy, Oct. 3, 1969, Mendenhall, Series 9, Box 1.
17 Memorandum, Prosser Gifford to Calvin Plimpton, Nov. 3, 1969, attached to memorandum, T. C. Mendenhall to the Planning-Plus Committee, Oct. 21, 1970, Mendenhall, Series 9, Box 1.

at 1,200, Mt. Holyoke at 1,700, and Smith at 2,300—thus avoiding "the almost hopeless task [for the women's colleges] of recruiting men," but would have instituted significant residential coeducation. Each college would have put a number of bed spaces in a pool—perhaps 400 for Amherst and 200 each for Smith and Mt. Holyoke; that number of students would be assigned residentially for a year or more to a campus other than their own.[18]

But these ideas were for private consumption, and there was no reason to believe that any of the five institutions would be prepared to accept them. In the meantime, Mendenhall had to deal with the recommendation on the table, for coeducation at Smith. He did not intend to move hastily. Following the release of the report, Mendenhall told an all-college meeting that a decision might be made within two years. Among other things, Smith would need to consult intensively with the other four institutions in the valley.[19] Calling for action on the basis of the report, the *Sophian* declared that "the decision to be made is not whether coeducation itself is good or bad but whether it is good or bad for Smith."[20] The newspaper did its part subsequently to illuminate the range of faculty and student views on the subject. In the end, the paper presented both sides of the argument. One editorial declared against coeducation. Smith, it said, was a place where "we as women can come to know ourselves and each other thoroughly, and feel how we can be a political force." There continued to be a national need for "a female college of Smith's calibre."[21] A second editorial declared that "the existence of a women's college can no longer be justified" and that Smith should embark on "'creeping coeducation,' whereby the number of males accepted would be solely

18 David B. Truman to Calvin H. Plimpton, Dec. 5, 1969, attached to memorandum, T. C. Mendenhall to the Planning-Plus Committee.

19 "Chinoy's Report Terms Coeducation Desirable, Possible," *Sophian*, Feb. 12, 1970, Box 18.

20 Editorial, "Coeducation," *Sophian*, Feb. 12, 1970, Box 18.

21 "Coeducation Reactions Run from Fear of 'Little Brothers' to 'Necessary,'" *Sophian*, Feb. 19, 1970, Box 18; editorial, "No Coeducation," *Sophian*, Nov. 12, 1970, Box 19. In Box 19, see also two accounts of the Women's Liberation view of coeducation, "Student Pans 'Lib' View" and "Women's Lib Questions Value of Coeducation for Smith," both in *Sophian*, Oct. 22, 1970.

dependent upon the number of qualified males who appl[ied]." Coeducation, it said, would best facilitate "the long-range goal" of integrating women into the larger society.[22]

Meanwhile, Mendenhall was continuing to work out his own views, as evidenced in a series of letters to alumnae. To an alumna in the class of 1964 in Toledo, he wrote, "Somehow we should try to keep our identity as a predominantly female institution, otherwise we go the way of most other coeducational colleges."[23] To an alumna in the class of 1937 in West Orange, New Jersey, he said, "There is considerable reason to believe that an increasing number of young women and young men prefer coeducation to separate education. . . . I try desperately to discover whether this . . . is a fad or a permanent trend." He hoped that with male exchange students at Smith for the year and men from Amherst and the university taking courses on campus, Smith students would see that "in fact we have something approximating the best of all worlds!"[24]

To an alumna in the class of 1965 in Princeton, New Jersey, Mendenhall wrote that it would be possible to take a very small number of male candidates for the Smith degree when and as they presented themselves. They could live in annexes on campus, as was the case for men who came on the Twelve-College Exchange. They could go about their work, comfortable with an "extreme minority situation" in ways that would not be possible for women at Princeton or Yale. "My concern," he said,

> is not to have us seem obdurately wedded to a single sex institution but ready to admit that men may wish to take advantage of a first-rate education if Smith offers it and, if they come along, we'll accept them. Many might be coming in the upperclass years as transfers. I would not see us doing anything to enlist them, certainly as freshmen, but I think we

22 Editorial, "Coeducation for Smith," *Sophian*, Dec. 10, 1970, Box 19.
23 Thomas C. Mendenhall to Mrs. Frank D. Jacobs [Lynn Balshone Jacobs '64], Mar. 13, 1970, Mendenhall, Series 9, Box 1.
24 Thomas C. Mendenhall to Mrs. G. Seaver Jones [Louise H. Jones '37], Mar. 13, 1970, Mendenhall, Series 9, Box 1. There are similar themes in Mendenhall to Ruth Tomlinson '14, Mar. 19, 1970, Mendenhall, Series 9, Box 1.

would find it increasingly uncomfortable to say to this rather small number of men students who had good reason to come to Smith that we could not give them a degree.[25]

Legal Hurdles and the Rise of Feminism

One matter to be resolved was the college's legal authority to issue bachelor's degrees to men. Smith had been chartered to provide higher education for women, and it needed specific legal authorization to award degrees to men. It proposed to follow the same route—petition to the Supreme Judicial Court of Massachusetts—that had enabled it, in 1964, to award graduate degrees to men.[26] In 1964 it had been clear that the college wanted to follow that course. This time around, however, the college had not yet made a decision about whether it wanted to accept male candidates for the bachelor's degree. And awarding degrees to men could arise in a range of different situations, from active recruitment of male students for full-fledged coeducation to what Mendenhall called "creeping coeducation," where men already at Smith on the Twelve-College Exchange might petition to stay to complete their degrees. Would it be possible to start the court proceedings to determine the college's authority to award degrees to men without implying that the college had made a decision about coeducation? Mendenhall sought legal advice about how best to proceed.[27] The advice from Ropes & Gray, the Boston law firm the college used, was that the trustees should have made the decision to proceed with undergraduate coeducation in the event that the college's petition to the court were to be successful. And there should have been a faculty vote in favor of coeducation, because it was, in essence, an

25 Thomas C. Mendenhall to Nancy Weiss '65, Nov. 2, 1970, Mendenhall, Series 9, Box 1.

26 Commonwealth of Massachusetts Supreme Judicial Court, Final Decree, *The Trustees of the Smith College v. Attorney General*, [Jan. 8, 1964,] attached to William E. Dwyer to Thomas C. Mendenhall, Mar. 12, 1968, Mendenhall, Series 9, Box 1.

27 Minutes, Executive Committee, Feb. 10, 1970, Smith trustees, vol. 10, pp. 474–75; minutes, Board of Trustees, Feb. 28, 1970, Smith trustees, vol. 10, p. 486; Thomas C. Mendenhall to Warren T. Farr, Feb. 16, 1970, Mendenhall, Series 9, Box 1.

academic matter. Without those prerequisites, seeking legal redress would be premature.[28]

Under those circumstances, the trustees were not prepared to pursue legal action. At a meeting on May 2, they did, however, authorize Mendenhall to work out with the presidents of Amherst and Mt. Holyoke "procedures by which the three colleges could coordinate their exploration of the question of coeducation," thus enabling each college to come to a decision based on the fullest possible information "about the thinking of the other institutions" but without in any way taking any college's decision out of its own hands.[29]

By late September, Mendenhall reported to the trustee executive committee that he had met periodically with Plimpton and Truman but that thus far "none of us has come up with a formula for the three colleges which seems very practical."[30] To further clarify his own thinking, he had prepared another paper spelling out what he believed to be the alternatives available to the college. It was time to make a decision. A small group, consisting predominantly of administrators, should weigh the evidence and come to a recommendation.[31] Toward that end, he told the trustees that he had asked an augmented college planning committee made up of trustees, administrators, faculty, and students to draw up a recommendation about how Smith should proceed.[32] He anticipated having the fruits of their deliberations before the end of the 1970–71 academic year.[33]

The augmented planning committee sent yet another questionnaire to Smith students in December 1970. This time there was

28 O. M. Shaw to Thomas C. Mendenhall, Feb. 23, Mar. 13, and Apr. 24, 1970; Mendenhall to Shaw, Mar. 23, 1970; and Mendenhall, Coeducation and Smith: A Report on the Legal Situation and Some Questions for the College Planning Committee, May 1, 1970, all in Mendenhall, Series 9, Box 1.

29 Minutes, Board of Trustees, May 2, 1970, Smith trustees, vol. 10, pp. 499–500 (the quotes come from p. 499).

30 Minutes, Executive Committee, Sept. 25, 1970, Smith trustees, vol. 11, p. 525.

31 Thomas C. Mendenhall, "Coeducation: Where Are We Now?," Sept. 1970, Mendenhall, Series 9, Box 1.

32 Minutes, Executive Committee, Sept. 25, 1970, Smith trustees, vol. 11, p. 525.

33 Minutes, Executive Committee, Dec. 11, 1970, Smith trustees, vol. 11, p. 543, and Feb. 12, 1971, p. 551.

"a marked increase in the levels of satisfaction with Smith" and a dramatic reversal of the sentiments about single-sex education versus coeducation that had been voiced by students when they were polled in April 1969. Almost 60 percent of respondents now favored keeping Smith single-sex; only 36.5 percent favored co-education. In the previous poll, 31 percent of the respondents had said that Smith should remain a women's college; 51 percent had favored full coeducation at Smith, and another 14 percent had indicated a preference for the establishment of a coordinate men's college.[34]

What had happened to effect such a marked change? The academic year 1969–70 had been a time of unusual ferment and tumult on American campuses and in the larger society. Most dramatic had been the U.S. bombing of Cambodia on April 30, followed on May 4 by the fatal shooting of four student antiwar protesters at Kent State University and on May 15 by the killing of two African American students at Jackson State University. Campuses around the country had exploded in protest.

At the same time, public attention was focused increasingly on the new women's movement, in which Smith women were on the front lines. As noted previously, two alumnae had positions of special prominence. One was Betty Friedan '43, whose book *The Feminine Mystique*, published in 1963, had caused a sensation in raising public consciousness about "the problem that has no name"—the toxic, claustrophobic pressures of domesticity crippling women's lives and family dynamics in suburban America. Friedan was writing about the malaise afflicting well-educated, white, middle-class women—the women so many new Smith graduates were likely to become.[35]

The other prominent Smith alumna in the women's movement was Gloria Steinem '56, one of the founders and a contributing editor and political columnist for *New York Magazine*. Her seminal article in the magazine in April 1969, "After Black Power, Women's

34 College Planning Committee, Survey of Attitudes toward Coeducation at Smith, Dec. 1970, Jahnige, Box 1; Student Attitudes toward Coeducation, Dec. 1970 (source of the quote), Mendenhall, Series 9, Box 1.
35 Betty Friedan, *The Feminine Mystique* (New York: W. W. Norton, 1963).

Liberation," one of the first reports on the new wave of feminism, brought Steinem national attention as a feminist leader. Steinem also began to speak publicly about such feminist issues as abortion rights and the Equal Rights Amendment. In appearances around the country, Steinem articulated a new feminist agenda. In 1971 she joined Friedan and other feminists in founding the National Women's Political Caucus to work on behalf of women's issues. That same year she launched a new magazine, *Ms.*, intended as the voice of the new feminist generation.[36]

The senior class at Smith chose Steinem as their graduation speaker in 1971. She had already spoken at Vassar's commencement in 1970.[37] But it was not immediately obvious that the college would accept the students' choice. Mendenhall scanned the list of preferred speakers presented to him by the president of the senior class, Catherine Smith. Steinem was their "first choice by far." She was "hot stuff already," and the students were extremely enthusiastic about having her come.[38] But it was uncommon to have a woman speaker at commencement, and it was certainly uncommon to have a woman speaker who had written about women activists "'rap[ping]' . . . about their essential second-classness" and deciding to "change society from the bottom up by radicalizing . . . the consciousness of women"; a woman speaker who had written about the coven of members of the Women's International Terrorist Conspiracy from Hell (WITCH) who had demonstrated against "that bastion of white supremacy: Wall Street"; a woman speaker who had sponsored a play about abortion followed by "two hours of personal and detailed testimony—in public—by girls who have had abortions and Tell It Like It Is."[39] Catherine Smith remembered that Mendenhall looked over the list of proposed speakers and made plain that he wanted to try some of the

36 Gloria Steinem, *Outrageous Acts and Everyday Rebellions*, 2nd ed. (New York: Henry Holt, 1995), pp. 3–23; Gloria Steinem, "After Black Power, Women's Liberation," *New York Magazine*, Apr. 4, 1969, http://nymag.com/news/politics/46802/, accessed Apr. 3, 2013.

37 For Steinem's address at Vassar, see Gloria Steinem, "Living the Revolution," *Vassar Quarterly* 56 (Fall 1970): 12–15, Vassar College Library.

38 E-mail, Catherine H. Smith to Nancy Weiss Malkiel, Apr. 3, 2013.

39 Steinem, "After Black Power, Women's Liberation."

safer choices, but no one else on the list could come, so "he HAD to ask Gloria."[40]

The women's liberation movement played a significant role in Smith students' changing opinions on the subject of coeducation, a reversal that proved to be highly consequential in the path the college chose to follow. Steinem herself made the point at commencement: "I think that my presence here today is a small part, a very small part of a change in the heads of students." The women's movement, she said, was "a revolution we live every day." If it succeeded in overturning "five thousand years of patriarchy," she concluded, "perhaps . . . historians will look back at this time and say that for the first time the human animal stopped dividing itself up according to visible difference, according to race, according to sex, and started to look for the real, and the human potential inside."[41]

With so much public attention to women's empowerment, there was "a shift in our way of looking at ourselves as a college FOR women," Catherine Smith recalled. Robert Averitt, the economics professor who chaired the augmented planning committee, said that the movement was "a powerful influence on student opinion." According to Peter Rose, the sociology professor who had conducted many of the studies that informed the Chinoy report, the women's movement—particularly in its Smith incarnation, with Friedan and Steinem at the forefront—led students and faculty alike to ask themselves whether Smith was really prepared to "sell [its] birthright" as a leading institution for women.[42]

40 E-mail, Smith to Malkiel. Steinem's biographer tells the story differently, in quite specific but unattributed detail: "Steinem was not the class of 1971's first choice—indeed, she was not even on their original list, which included men ranging from Canadian Prime Minister Pierre Trudeau (their first choice) through psychoanalyst Erik Erikson, who declined because of illness, to Paul Newman, William F. Buckley, Jr., and Edmund Muskie, all of whom either declined or weren't asked. Such a list of prominent and unobtainable persons, as deans and college presidents know to their sorrow, is far from atypical." Carolyn G. Heilbrun, *The Education of a Woman: The Life of Gloria Steinem* (New York: Ballantine Books, 1995), p. 195, n. 1.

41 Gloria Steinem, "The Politics of Women," Smith College Commencement, May 31, 1971, Class of 1971 Records, Smith College Archives. For a briefer version of the speech, see Steinem, "The Commencement Address: The Politics of Women," *Smith Alumnae Quarterly* 62 (Aug. 1971): 13–16.

42 See, e.g., e-mail, Smith to Malkiel; e-mail, Robert Averitt to Malkiel, Apr. 3, 2013; e-mail, Peter Rose to Malkiel, Apr. 3, 2013; telephone interview with Rose, Apr. 4, 2013.

The reversal drew attention in the national press. "Coeducation: The Girls Are Having Second Thoughts," read the *New York Times* headline for a column by their chief education reporter, Fred M. Hechinger. Hechinger noted the change in student sentiment and reported that "Smith College, which a year ago seemed ready to go coeducational, is unofficially reported to be abandoning such plans."[43] *Newsweek* followed suit: "Two years ago . . . the young women of Smith College voted nearly 2–1 in favor of admitting men to their own school. But last December, after they had had time to count their blessings, the Smithies reconsidered and urged by an almost identical margin that Smith remain a women's college."[44]

"To Provide for Women Education of the Highest Quality"

The final report of the augmented planning committee, distributed at the end of April 1971, recommended that Smith remain a college dedicated to the education of women. A small number of men would continue to study on campus as visitors through the Five-College and Twelve-College Exchange programs, and the college should explore ways to take advantage of even closer cooperative arrangements with its sister institutions in the valley. But there was every reason to maintain Smith's historic purpose: to provide for young women an education comparable to the best education available to young men. Although the question of coeducation should remain under review, the best course for Smith was to resist the rush to coeducation and to emphasize instead what it had long done so well: providing women with first-class educational opportunities not necessarily available to women in traditionally coeducational institutions.[45]

43 *New York Times*, Mar. 14, 1971, clipping in Mendenhall, Series 9, Box 1.

44 "Best of Both Worlds," *Newsweek*, Apr. 5, 1971, p. 86, clipping in Mendenhall, Series 9, Box 1.

45 "Smith College and the Question of Coeducation: A Report with Recommendations Submitted to the Faculty and the Board of Trustees by the Augmented College Planning Committee," Apr. 1971, Mendenhall, Series 9, Box 1. The gist of the report was communicated broadly to alumnae in "Coeducation Study Recommends Stay 'Predominantly for Women,'" *A Letter from Smith College*, May 1971, Smith College Archives.

It was late in the year to imagine action on the recommendations by either the faculty or the trustees, but in the absence of
proposals for significant change, there appeared to be no urgency
to the matter.[46] In October 1971, after considerable discussion in
two successive meetings, with some significant sentiment still being
voiced in favor of coeducation, the faculty voted by a substantial
majority to adopt the recommendations.[47] In February 1972 the
board of trustees followed suit, modifying slightly the language
of the principal recommendation to incorporate a specific reference to academic excellence: "The College should confirm that its
leading purpose is to provide for women education of the highest
quality, which it finds to be consistent both with the intention of
its founder and with the needs of the present time."[48]

Given that Smith had seemed so clearly headed for some form of
coeducation, what factors ultimately led to the board's decision?
First, the role of Steinem's commencement address should not be
underestimated. Steinem said that she had imagined that Smith, as
a women's college, would have been "taking the lead" in the "larger
change of consciousness" in American society, wherein it had become clear "that the so-called masculine-feminine differences are
largely societal, not biological at all; that those differences have
application only to reproduction" and that "they have no meaning
for education, job selection, or life style. Indeed, that the myths of
feminine inferiority have been used largely to suppress the talents
and strengths of half the human race." Smith still had work to
do in "turning out whole human beings," examining "repressive
myths" about male and female roles, and coming to terms with the
reality that the "inferior position" of women was not "ordained by
God or by biology, but was and is . . . political"—that is, work to
do in equipping women with "the philosophical and tactical tools"

46 Smith faculty, Apr. 28, 1971, vol. 14, p. 48; minutes, Board of Trustees, May 1,
1971, Smith trustees, vol. 11, p. 577.

47 Smith faculty, Oct. 6 and 27, 1971, and Jan. 26, 1972, vol. 14, pp. 85–86, 89–91, 103.

48 Minutes, Board of Trustees, Feb. 26, 1972, in Smith trustees, vol. 11, pp. 633–34.
The text of the six recommendations presented by the committee, modestly amended by
the faculty and further amended by the board, is presented in these minutes. The recommendations approved by the board were presented to the alumnae in "Smith to Remain a
College for Women," *Smith Alumnae Quarterly* 63 (Apr. 1972): 2.

to go out into the world and realize their full potential. Given that, Steinem said, Smith should remain single-sex:

> I think one of the questions before us now is the integration, the sexual integration of Smith College. I think . . . that we are not ready for it yet. Our heads are not together enough yet as women to be integrated. That this college has to turn into a real college for all women . . . that it has to become, again, a feminist institution, a radicalizing institution, so that when we integrate we will understand that we are not receiving the benefit of the great intellectual male presence which is going to validate our classroom experience, but that we have to offer the elements of the female culture . . . which the males very, very badly need.[49]

Second, other institutions' experiences with coeducation played a role in the board's decision. It had been "widely observed," the augmented planning committee said, that "in many coeducational situations women are not given equal place with men and tend to accept a lesser status." That reality, the committee said, "appears to have been important in slowing down and even reversing the trend of opinion that had been moving in the direction of a complete conversion of women's colleges to full coeducation."[50] Catherine Smith, the president of the senior class and one of two student members of the augmented planning committee, recalled Smith students coming back from their exchange years at coeducational institutions having "missed their friends, the teachers, the class sizes"—"it was some kind of validation of Smith," she said. In addition, Smith students learned that students from women's colleges who had transferred to newly coeducational campuses "were being named secretaries of organizations, not presidents." Catherine Smith recalled, "Those of us left behind [at Smith] found some vindication" in that.[51]

49 Steinem, "The Politics of Women."
50 "Smith College and the Question of Coeducation," p. 4.
51 E-mail, Smith to Malkiel.

Third, the college was committed to diversifying the student body, and allocating scholarship money for minority and other lower-income students competed with allocating money for coeducation. For many faculty members, even supporters of coeducation, the college's investment in student financial aid needed to take precedence.[52]

The fourth factor was Smith's location in the Pioneer Valley. Unlike Vassar, which had no peer institutions in the vicinity of Poughkeepsie and thus had to make the difficult decision about whether it was still possible to go it alone as a college for women, Smith had Amherst nearby. As unrealistic as it was to imagine that fuller collaboration among the institutions in the valley could substitute for coeducation, that was a significant part of the bet the Smith trustees were making. Nancy LeaMond '72, president of student government, the other undergraduate who served on the augmented planning committee, said that it was her impression that the trustees were counting on Amherst as a long-term partner—a hope that proved unrealistic when Amherst decided to admit its own undergraduate women students beginning in 1975.[53]

The fifth factor bearing on Smith's decision not to embark on coeducation—probably the most decisive in the end—was the college's leadership. The institutional change required to implement coeducation would be enormously challenging to accomplish. At colleges and universities that decided for coeducation, the president's clear commitment and active leadership were critical to rallying the trustees, the alumni, and the institution to embark on a major sea change in identity and purpose. Mendenhall could not provide that leadership because he was genuinely ambivalent about the right direction for Smith. "In private and deep down," his daughter Cornelia said, "he did not want Smith to go coed." And yet he felt acutely the responsibility of stewardship of a venerable institution; he needed to give serious consideration to coeducation for Smith if coeducation elsewhere "threatened

---

52 "Smith College and the Question of Coeducation," p. 4. Peter Rose identifies himself as one of the supporters of coeducation who voted in favor of the college's remaining a women's college because of his commitment to diversifying the student body. Rose interview.
53 Telephone interview with Nancy LeaMond, Apr. 26, 2013.

to leave Smith in the dust."[54] He was genuinely torn about what Smith should do, and he explored in good faith the many alternatives that the college might contemplate. Donald Robinson, a professor of government who knew Mendenhall well, described him as open to facts and "waiting to see how things played out." In the end, in the absence of clear conviction on his part, Mendenhall was unprepared to push for a change of such formidable proportions.[55]

Without decisive direction from the president, the augmented planning committee was free to recommend, as it did, that the college not embrace coeducation. The trustee members of the committee reported that alumnae preferred that Smith remain single-sex, but, as the committee's chair, Robert Averitt, recalled, the "primary loyalty" of the trustees "was to Smith," so they were ready to accept whatever the committee recommended "with good spirit." The other administrators on the committee "tended to follow [Mendenhall's] lead," but he "was not leading." The sentiment among the faculty on the committee was split. As for the student representatives, "once the student survey showed strong support for single-sex," they "believed it their job to represent that sentiment." Chinoy, of course, strongly favored coeducation, but Averitt took the opposite view. "The future of the College," he argued, "depend[ed] on three major factors—the quality of students, of faculty, and money." At the time, "Smith was attracting high quality students, quality faculty, and significant funding. Thus the argument for a dramatic change to coed should give reasons why we should expect a turn for the worse if a shift to coed was not made." Chinoy, Averitt said, "could not offer a compelling forecast of decline if we remained what we had always been."[56]

Smith College, as Mendenhall put it at last chapel in the spring of 1973, had "recommitted itself to its original, pioneering purpose."[57]

---

54 Telephone interview with Cornelia Mendenhall Small, Nov. 12, 2014.

55 E-mail, Rose to Malkiel; Rose interview; e-mail, Averitt to Malkiel; telephone interview with Donald Robinson, Apr. 11, 2013; telephone interview with Philip Green, Apr. 20, 2013; e-mail, Smith to Malkiel.

56 E-mail, Averitt to Malkiel.

57 Thomas C. Mendenhall, Last Chapel—May 1973, Mendenhall, Series 16, Box 4.

17

Wellesley: "Should Wellesley Jump on the Bandwagon?"

Although Smith so often seemed to be on the verge of acquiescing to, if not actively embracing, coeducation, Wellesley was much more reserved. To be sure, the college studied coeducation. Such a study was almost obligatory, given what was going on at so many of its peer institutions. But it was difficult to find someone in a position of authority at Wellesley who ever made the compelling educational argument for coeducation or who took up the task of driving the college to admit men. The underlying cause was largely the reticence about coeducation on the part of the college's ninth president, Ruth Marie Adams.

Ruth Adams and the Turbulent 1960s

Elected president in March 1966 to take office in July, Adams had been dean of Douglass College since 1960, the successor to Polly Bunting. A specialist in Victorian literature, she had been a member of the English department at the University of Rochester before taking up the deanship at Douglass.[1]

Adams assumed the presidency of a thriving college. Applications were strong, and the student body was impressive in its credentials and accomplishment. Wellesley students acquitted themselves successfully in prestigious national competitions for

---

1 Minutes, Special Meeting of the Board of Trustees, Mar. 16, 1966, Adams, Box 40, Folder Trustees Minutes, 1963–70.

postgraduate scholarships. Among the Seven Sisters, Wellesley had the largest endowment. All in all, the college had a plausible claim to being the strongest of that distinguished group of peers.

The world in which Adams had signed on to be president of Wellesley turned out to be dramatically different from the world in which she had to lead. Like most colleges and universities, Wellesley in the late 1960s was in important ways very much unlike Wellesley in the middle of the decade. The president had to wrestle with issues she could not have anticipated, some benign (the demand for on-campus parking for seniors), some disruptive (the demand for abolition of parietal rules). And there were other issues of the times: students' desire to participate more actively in college governance, the demand for more regularly enrolled black students and for courses in African American studies, and the intense opposition to the Vietnam War, with pressure from students for the college to stake out a political position.[2]

Some knowledgeable observers have opined that Adams's long-serving predecessor, Margaret Clapp, would likely have handled these challenging matters with the decisiveness, sure-footedness, and tight control that characterized her long and successful presidency (1949–66). Whether or not that would have been true is open for debate; the turmoil of the late 1960s proved to be the undoing of a number of theretofore very successful college and university presidents. What is clear, however, is that Adams did not feel comfortable amid all the turmoil, and decisiveness, sure-footedness, and control are not descriptors that can be applied to her leadership of the college.[3]

In so many ways, Adams found herself at odds with her students. Not with all of them, by any means; some students knew her well, looked up to her, felt empowered by her, and were inspired by

2 These issues are discussed in Adams, Box 40, Folder Trustees Minutes, 1963–70, and Folder Trustees: Executive Committee Minutes, 1964–69.

3 The observations about Clapp's likely performance in this terrain come from telephone interview with Mary Lefkowitz, Aug. 23, 2013, and telephone interview with Philip Phibbs, Sept. 3, 2013. For the caution about how Clapp might have dealt with the challenges of the late 1960s, I am indebted to a subsequent president of Wellesley and a great admirer of Clapp, Nannerl O. Keohane.

her example and encouragement to become leaders.[4] But the campus issues of the day made it difficult for most students to enjoy that kind of relationship with their president and for the president to feel at ease with many of her students. Such issues as relaxing parietal rules in the dormitories and taking an institutional stand on the war in Southeast Asia found Adams in a different position from the majority of the student body. Although she wisely declined to stake out a confrontational stance, it pained her to play the roles she was required to assume. Perhaps because of her discomfort with the issues at hand, and perhaps because she was repeatedly challenged by her students and their commitments, her usual affect was one of stiffness and rigidity. The more she bristled at student demands and criticism and the more she put off dealing with the issues they raised, the more she fueled student unhappiness with her leadership.[5]

Coeducation at Wellesley: A Reluctant Exploration

Coeducation was not on Adams's agenda. But the highly publicized attention to coeducation at such institutions as Yale, Princeton, Vassar, and Smith made it impossible to avoid raising the subject. Adams talked it over with Philip M. Phibbs, the college's new executive vice president. Phibbs had joined the faculty in 1961. He was an associate professor of political science who had, in July 1968, become executive assistant to the president, a new role created at least in part at the suggestion of the trustees, who recognized that Adams would profit from having some administrative support. Phibbs screened the president's correspondence

4 E-mail, Evangeline Morphos '71 to Nancy Weiss Malkiel, Aug. 5, 2014; telephone interview with Morphos, Aug. 15, 2014.

5 Interview with Geneva Overholser '70, Nov. 15, 2013, New York City. On parietals, see minutes, Executive Committee of the Board of Trustees, Dec. 2, 1969, Wellesley trustees, Folder Minutes of the Full Board and Executive Committee, 1969–70 (Nov. 8, 1969–Dec. 2, 1969); Ruth M. Adams to Class Presidents, Class Representatives, Club Presidents, Acquaintanceship Chairmen, and Development Fund Chairmen, Dec. 1, 1969, attached to minutes, Board of Trustees, Jan. 21, 1970, Wellesley trustees, Folder Minutes of the Full Board and Executive Committee, 1969–70 (Jan. 21, 1970–June 6, 1970). On the war in Southeast Asia, see minutes, Executive Committee of the Board of Trustees, May 4, 1970, Wellesley trustees, Folder Minutes of the Full Board and Executive Committee, 1969–70 (Jan. 21, 1970–June 6, 1970).

and drafted responses, and members of the administrative staff reported to Adams through him, an arrangement that did not sit well in administrative circles. In the interest of clarifying Phibbs's responsibilities, in early December 1968 his title was changed to executive vice president. In practice, he was the second-ranking administrative officer of the college.[6]

Neither Adams nor Phibbs favored coeducation. Based on his experience as a faculty member, Phibbs had come to appreciate the many strengths of a women's college. The students he taught and observed "grew and flourished in special ways." Wellesley nurtured their intellectual abilities and fostered the development of their leadership skills. Phibbs was convinced that the single-sex option in American higher education needed to be preserved. Adams held a similar view. At the same time, she was nervous about taking up such a controversial, divisive issue. She and Phibbs agreed that he would sound out other senior administrators to see what they thought.[7]

In December 1968, Phibbs sought the views of the director of admission, the dean of students, and the dean of the college. "Let me emphasize immediately," he said, "that Wellesley has no present plans to move in any particular direction on this matter." But with coeducation emerging as an issue at other institutions, it would be prudent to think the matter through so that Wellesley would be "in a better position to make an appropriate decision."

Phibbs asked for his colleagues' "guesses, insightful and knowledgeable guesses, about the future." He also asked, "What are the implications for Wellesley as Yale, Princeton, Vassar and other institutions go coeducational?" And what did they "think that Wellesley should do?" Suppose Wellesley "does not move toward coeducation in some form while these other institutions do?"[8]

6 Minutes, Executive Committee of the Board of Trustees, Dec. 2, 1968, Adams, Box 40, Folder Trustees: Executive Committee Minutes, 1964–1969; curriculum vitae, Philip Monford Phibbs, Adams, Box 25, Folder Phibbs, Philip, 1971–72; Phibbs interview; "New Executive Assistant to the President," *Wellesley Alumnae Magazine* 53 (Autumn 1968): 21; "Philip M. Phibbs and the Wellesley Scene," *Wellesley Alumnae Magazine* 57 (Winter 1973): 22–25, both in Wellesley College Archives.

7 Phibbs interview.

8 Philip M. Phibbs to Miss [Phyllis] Fleming, Mrs. [Joan B.] Melvin, and Miss [Barbara] Clough, Dec. 12, 1968, Adams, Box 12, Folder Commission on the Future of the College: Coeducation, 1968–1973.

As they looked toward the January 1969 board meeting, Phibbs and Adams agreed that it would be a good idea to discuss setting up "a committee to consider the future orientation of the college." With "all the noise . . . about coeducation, coordinate education, etc.," Phibbs said, "it would be helpful if we could demonstrate that the issue is being actively and seriously considered. It might also enable us eventually to lay the issue to rest in one way or the other."

Phibbs thought that Wellesley's consideration of the issue might begin with a question on which other institutions seemed not to have focused: "Is there a need in American higher education for a first rate institution devoted to women?" Other questions would follow: "Can such an institution really attract outstanding students? What adaptations can be made to make men reasonably accessible to women in such an institution—what is the middle ground between coeducation and isolation? If all the answers to such questions are essentially negative, then in what direction toward coeducation should we move?" The committee, Phibbs thought, would be "a study group rather than a representative body"; it would consist of "thoughtful, concerned but essentially uncommitted individuals" drawn from among trustees, faculty, students, administrators, and alumnae, individuals prepared to "reach their conclusions after rather than before they undertook a thorough and careful study."[9]

Phibbs met with Adams to discuss how to proceed. In a handwritten note to himself, he scribbled, "Consult with Hillary. I think we may want to make announcement of a study of higher education for women and clearly state that Wellesley will dare to be different." By "Hillary" Phibbs was referring to Hillary Rodham, the senior who was president of student government. Phibbs knew her well. As a junior, Rodham had been a student in Phibbs's senior seminar on philosophies of international relations. Phibbs was in charge of the college's internship program in Washington, and he had helped Rodham secure a summer internship. After Phibbs was

9 Memorandum, Phil Phibbs to Miss Adams, Jan. 6, 1969, Adams, Box 12, Folder Commission on the Future of the College: Coeducation, 1968–1973.

named executive assistant to the president, Adams had asked him to take over her role as adviser to the student government. Phibbs and Rodham had worked together to address issues and respond to student concerns. It was only natural, then, that he would think of consulting her about the proposed study. "Miss A said to do," he noted; "talk in confidence and get advice on how to proceed."[10]

A study committee had multiple advantages. The first was straightforward: A real issue needed to be thought through. Co-education was a highly complex matter, and it was important that people appreciate and grapple with that complexity. There was a second advantage, more tactical in nature: Setting up such a committee was a "useful way of delaying immediate action" and "let[ting] events unfold." With people from multiple constituencies working on the question, the result would likely be broader buy-in; and with the "passage of time" and the surfacing of the major issues, it might well become clearer "how Wellesley College could move most successfully" in such complicated terrain.[11] The third advantage was rooted in Wellesley's tradition, in which inclusiveness of multiple constituencies and respect for shared governance had long characterized the way the college did its business.[12]

At the board meeting in mid-January, a small group was constituted to begin quietly to explore the future of women's colleges and "the implications for Wellesley."[13] But keeping consideration of coeducation under wraps was not realistic. In mid-February, Adams wrote to the board about the "increasing discussion at the college about the possibility of coeducation at Wellesley." The trustee subcommittee investigating the question agreed that it was time to announce the trustees' interest in the issue.[14] Adams made a statement to that effect at the February 13 meeting of the academic council. After rehearsing the circumstances that had led to

10 Phibbs interview; undated, unsigned note, "Consult with Hillary," Adams, Box 12, Folder Commission on the Future of the College: Coeducation, 1968–1973.

11 Phibbs interview.

12 I am indebted to Nannerl O. Keohane for this insight.

13 Minutes, Board of Trustees, Jan. 16, 1969, Adams, Box 40, Folder Trustees: Executive Committee Minutes, 1964–69.

14 Ruth M. Adams to Dear Trustee, Feb. 13, 1969, Adams, Box 12, Folder Commission on the Future of the College: Coeducation, 1968–1973.

the establishment of the trustee subcommittee, Adams said that the subcommittee had "proposed that a special college commission be formed to undertake a thorough study of Wellesley's historic role as a college for women."

The commission, Adams said, would "investigate the legal and economic implications and particularly the educational merits of separate education and the various forms of coeducation." In that context, it would examine challenging questions on the agenda for so many colleges and universities:

> Is the learning process for women significantly different from that for men; are some teaching methods and certain curricular elements more appropriate in the education of women; will there be a need in the immediate and in the distant future for a first-rate institution devoted primarily to the education of women; is there a significant body of outstanding students who will want separate education and will enjoy, indeed will flourish intellectually in this environment; how can the horizons of such an institution be broadened to establish close and continuing contact with all aspects of the world around the college?

Adams continued, "If the answers to these and similar questions suggest that Wellesley's historic role is no longer appropriate, the commission should consider the direction in which the college should move. It should investigate the costs, relative merits and implications of coordinate education, coeducation and other possible arrangements. The implications of each in terms of new facilities, additional faculty and staff, the quality of male students which could be attracted—these and many other questions would have to be examined." The commission would include trustees, faculty, students, administrators, and alumnae, who would function not as representatives of their constituencies but rather as "thoughtful, independent individuals devoting their best efforts to a serious evaluation of Wellesley's future."

Adams concluded her remarks to the academic council with a notable peroration:

If the conclusion ultimately is that Wellesley should move toward some form of coeducation, we should respond imaginatively and creatively. We should not allow a great past to endanger a great future. Or, if the conclusion is that there will continue to be a need in the totality of higher education in America for an outstanding women's college fulfilling a desire for separate education on the part of a substantial number of our most highly qualified young women, then Wellesley should continue to plan in its customary spirit of independence.[15]

At the annual alumnae meeting that spring, Adams, eschewing the lofty rhetoric, declared: "If we refuse to do any thinking about coeducation, we would be the greatest female ostrich in the educational zoo."[16]

The Commission's Investigation of Wellesley's Options

Before the commission began its work in the spring of 1969, Wellesley students, taking their cue from their counterparts at Yale and Princeton, organized a local version of coed week, with plans for as many as two hundred to three hundred male students to spend the week of April 7–12 on campus as guests of Wellesley women. The schedule included attendance at classes, special lectures and films, poetry and play readings, song and dance, tennis and touch football, parties, and debates with MIT and Princeton, the latter on the subject, "Should Wellesley Be Co-ed?"[17]

At the first meeting of the commission in early May, a trustee, Mary Ann Dilley Staub, a member of the class of 1937, was elected

---

15 Ruth M. Adams Statement, Academic Council, Feb. 13, 1969, attached to Adams to Dear Trustee, Feb. 13, 1969, Adams, Box 12, Folder Commission on the Future of the College: Coeducation, 1968–73.

16 "Miss Adams Answers Some Questions," *Wellesley Alumnae Magazine* 53 (Summer 1969): 40.

17 Memorandum, Miss Cornwall to Mr. Schneider, Mar. 18, 1969; memorandum, Schneider to Mrs. Marsh, Mar. 19, 1969; memorandum, Joan B. Melvin to Miss Adams, Mar. 21, 1969; memorandum, Schneider to Melvin, Mar. 25, 1969; and memorandum, Melvin to Adams et al., Apr. 3, 1969, all in Adams, Box 12, Folder Commission on the Future of the College: Coeducation, 1968–73.

chairman and a faculty member, Mary Lefkowitz, a member of the class of 1957 and an assistant professor of Greek and Latin, vice chairman. (By the second year of the commission's work, Lefkowitz had been promoted to associate professor and was chairing her department.) The members decided that they would begin their work by casting a wide net: "identifying the strengths and weaknesses of education at Wellesley College today."[18] Looking back, Lefkowitz called the broadening of the agenda "a clever political move." By setting their work in the large context of the future of the college instead of focusing exclusively on coeducation, the commission lowered the temperature of what would otherwise have been a more explosive inquiry.[19]

The commission established subcommittees on admission patterns, learning patterns, and life patterns for women. The subcommittee on admission patterns focused on whether a single-sex Wellesley could continue to attract a sufficient number of students of the quality to which the college was accustomed. The subcommittee on learning patterns sought to understand "the difference in learning patterns of women" and men. Women came to college "at a more advanced social level, possibly a more advanced level of intellectual achievement," than men. But then men appeared to catch up; how should that fact be accounted for? Was there an argument for continuing to "accelerat[e] our young women" so that they might earn both a bachelor's and a master's degree in four years of enrollment? The subcommittee on life patterns, noting that women "go into education, withdraw from it, and return at various times during their lives," focused on the question of how to construct a curriculum to meet women's needs throughout their lives.[20] There would be other subcommittees on the education and

18 Minutes, Wellesley College Commission, May 10, 1969, Adams, Box 13, Folder Commission on the Future of the College: Minutes, 1969–70.

19 Lefkowitz interview.

20 Minutes, Wellesley College Commission, May 10, 1969, Adams, Box 13, Folder Commission on the Future of the College: Minutes, 1969–70; untitled typescript re first Commission meeting, May 12, 1969; Ruth M. Adams to Carolyn Lyon, May 29, 1969 (source of the quotes), both in Adams, Box 13, Folder Commission on the Future of the College: General, 1969–1972.

needs of women, the education and needs of men, summer programs, consortia, and exchange programs.

The full commission began by gathering written materials that might be relevant from other colleges and universities. They visited sixteen other institutions, women's colleges as well as coeducational schools. Later, they invited administrators from other colleges and universities to meet with them to share perspectives and experiences.[21]

As for the options available to Wellesley, the commission initially imagined a range of possibilities. The college could "remain the same," with the probability of attracting different—likely less-qualified—students. As a women's college, it could enhance its potential attractiveness by "chang[ing] the curriculum radically," or it could "(loudly) avow its role in the separate education of women," becoming a "truly feminist" institution with a militant "approach to women's separatism and superiority." Alternatively, Wellesley could "opt for co-education," again, with the probability of attracting less-qualified students, because "the top girls" would choose to attend universities or "established co-ed colleges like Swarthmore and Oberlin," and the male students who would be interested in Wellesley "would not be particularly well-qualified or representative of the 'normal' male college population."

Another option was for Wellesley to expand its coordinate arrangements with MIT, through which Wellesley and MIT students were able to take courses on the other campus—expansion that might extend even to the point of "complete assimilation," wherein Wellesley would "become the liberal arts college of MIT." Yet another possibility was to "solicit a take-over by the state of Massachusetts," becoming "a state-supported, co-ed institution."[22]

These options were elaborated and further complicated by a long, discursive memo that Adams sent to the commission on the

---

21 Dilley Staub to the Members of the Wellesley College Commission, July 9, 1969; Mary Lefkowitz to Nell Eurich, Oct. 10, 1969; and Ruth M. Adams to Deane W. Malott, Oct. 15, 1969, all in Adams, Box 13, Folder Commission on the Future of the College: Minutes, 1969–70.

22 Minutes, Commission on the Future of the College, July 11, 1969, Adams, Box 13, Folder Commission on the Future of the College: Minutes, 1969–70.

eve of their September meeting. Adams remarked, first, that Wellesley students and faculty were torn between "two desires: first, the desire for the resources in curriculum, activities and equipment that can be provided by a large university; and second, the desire for the liveable human scale that exists at a small college." She argued for the human scale: "Wellesley should not grow larger than a two thousand student body."

Adams's second topic was "regional affiliations for higher education," like Wellesley's arrangements with MIT. Partnerships of that sort would only grow more prevalent, she speculated, and Boston "offer[ed] rich opportunities for further extension of such affiliations." Wellesley might, for example, incorporate experience in hospitals or work in medical schools into the undergraduate pre-medical curriculum. The college might develop academic work in the field of suburban studies, using Boston and its environs as a "laboratory for such investigations."

Adams's third topic was "the education of women." Was it true that it was different from the education of men? If so, in what ways did it differ? Should alternative educational paths be available to women? If so, of what might they consist? Her fourth topic addressed the varied purposes of a college education and the varied constituencies a college like Wellesley enrolled. She speculated about more flexible arrangements—a four-year program in which well-qualified students could earn both a bachelor's and a master's degree or an accelerated three-year B.A. She said that the college should also think about how to educate women who could do college work only on a part-time basis and about what Wellesley could do for the woman who wanted "to take only one or two courses for a particular reason of her own identifying."

Adams imagined, too, the possibilities of a community of women of all ages—"undergraduate, and graduate, and teaching faculty, and research staff"—a community that would include "'enough' men to educate women in how to get along with men," that is, to satisfy the requirement that Wellesley women needed men for their own education. How to bring them into the community—by exchanges, visits, or enrollment—remained to be determined. The community would also include "accomplished women as role models," not only academic women but "the political woman, the business woman, the professional woman," married as well as single, with "all ranges of women's accomplishment and potential being illustrated."

Adams remarked on two overriding realities. First, in a coeducational institution "the intellectual independence of women" was "not fully realized"—witness the social pressures that affected students' choices of major areas of study, such that a woman physics major was a rarity in a coeducational institution but perfectly normal at Wellesley. And second, a practical caution: "A man's college can more easily recruit good women as undergraduates than a good women's college can recruit men as undergraduates."[23]

By the November meeting of the commission, the faculty representatives and the dean of the college had interviewed nearly every member of the faculty. "Items of consensus" included these: "Wellesley must change in some way," "Wellesley should remain a small, liberal arts college," and "coeducation, or some form of men on campus, is essential." The students, who had held meetings with some 150 students, said that they were surprised at hearing "more conservative reactions than [they had] anticipated." Students appreciated Wellesley's "size and location" and "the quality of the Wellesley education and degree." They recognized "the problem of remaining a women's college and losing high-quality applicants vs. that of becoming coeducational and attracting men who are less well qualified than the women."[24]

Narrowing the Options, Searching for Consensus

At the December meeting, the commission identified three options that merited further exploration: remaining a women's college, becoming coeducational, or taking some middle ground between the two that involved cooperative arrangements with other institutions. The members met with four students who had been invited

23 Ruth M. Adams, Miscellaneous Topics for Discussion by the Wellesley College Commission, Sept. 10, 1969, Adams, Box 13, Folder Commission on the Future of the College: Minutes, 1969–70.

24 Minutes, Commission on the Future of the College, Nov. 7, 8, and 9, 1969, Cmsn. Future College, Box 1, Folder Commission: Minutes and Publicity Releases, May 1969– Dec. 1970.

to make the case for remaining a women's college.[25] One of them, Evangeline Morphos, a junior, explained later, "One of my basic oppositions to co-education was snobbery. I didn't feel that Wellesley could attract the same level of male applicants as female applicants. . . . It never occurred to me that the caliber of women applying would also drop because of the competition." She also recalled, "The reality was [that] a number of us were active, enjoying leadership roles at Wellesley, and just couldn't see giving them up. We were keenly aware of how our sisters at Radcliffe were treated in both the social and extra-curricular hierarchy of Harvard College."[26]

The four students also wrote a long opinion piece for the *Harvard Crimson*. Coeducation was not a panacea, they asserted; it "can create as many problems as it can solve." Women students clearly profited from "the advantages" offered by a women's college. There was much to be said for a college where "the education of women is of primary importance," where the curriculum would be planned with the "needs of the female student" as the main consideration, and where it was possible for women to excel academically and retain their femininity without worrying about "intense academic competition with men." Wellesley ought not to be left "in the position of taking in boys, like laundry, in order to support itself." Wellesley should be looking for "unique solutions" rather than joining the rush to coeducation. It was possible to have it both ways; "Wellesley could be more like a women's college in the university complex of Boston than an isolated and secluded girls' school" while at the same time meeting its "responsibility to offer a fine education to those girls who do not care for a completely coeducational institution."[27]

25 Minutes, Commission on the Future of the College, Dec. 12, 13, and 14, 1969, Cmsn. Future College, Box 1, Folder Commission: Minutes and Publicity Releases, May 1969–Dec. 1970.

26 E-mail, Morphos to Malkiel.

27 Mary Combs '71, Jenny Meyer '72, Evangeline Morphos '71, and Ruth Reisner '71, "Must Wellesley Go Coed to Survive?," *Harvard Crimson*, Dec. 16, 1969, http:// www.thecrimson.com/article/1969/12/16/must-wellesley-go-coed-to-survive/, accessed Aug. 18, 2014. I am indebted to Evangeline Morphos for bringing this opinion piece to my attention.

At the conclusion of the December meeting the members of the commission agreed to try their hands at writing position papers about the central issues under discussion. In her own paper, written in late January 1970, Ruth Adams revisited themes she had written about in her September 1969 memo, added some points, and sharpened her focus. She articulated premises that she believed to be of paramount importance. A sufficient number of "women of high quality" would choose "to attend an institution that devotes itself to preparing them to lead satisfying lives," and "such an institution must commit itself to educating the whole woman for her lifetime," no matter what direction her life course followed. She might become a professional, a teacher and scholar, a community volunteer, a wife and mother, or some combination of these alternatives; her education would be sufficiently robust, but sufficiently varied and flexible, to lead her down any of these paths.

As for coeducation, Adams characterized it as "a fine but not an essential mode of education." Adams doubted that men would ever be "of higher quality" than the women Wellesley could attract. She did not believe that men would "introduce a different point of view" in classroom discussions or that they would produce "a different <u>and better</u> classroom performance." She did not believe that having men as regular members of the campus community "would create a more normal social atmosphere." She did not think it would be possible "to create a coeducational institution that gives the [necessary] range and quality of attention to women's needs." If Wellesley absolutely had to educate men, she said, it should happen through a coordinate college, not coeducation. "I am wary," she concluded, "of abandoning the commitment of a century because of the pressures of a decade."[28]

At the commission's next meeting in February 1970, two consultants who had been engaged to assist in the commission's work, Scott M. Cunningham and Stephen Greyser, partners in Management Analysis Center, Inc., and faculty members at the Harvard Business School, circulated their written synthesis of the thirteen

---

28 Ruth M. Adams, "Wellesley in the Future," Jan. 29, 1970, Adams, Box 13, Folder Commission on the Future of the College: General, 1969–72.

position papers composed by members of the group. They noted four areas of broad agreement: the basic commitment of the college to women's education; the importance of a flexible, innovative curriculum, including new interdisciplinary institutes involving elements of work study or study in the field; the recognition that although the college's distinctive identity needed to be preserved, change would have to be embraced, of whatever kind and at whatever pace; and the fact that coeducation, in some form, would have to be addressed, whether initially through such mechanisms as exchanges, cross-registration, and "other intermediate programs" or directly through the matriculation of male students. By vote the commission declared commitments to "the education of women" and to "a program that includes men on the campus."[29]

Drawing on the expertise of a professional organization for institutional research, the commission made plans to survey Wellesley faculty members, students, alumnae, and 290 secondary schools whose students had applied to Wellesley over the previous five years. The student questionnaire would be circulated in the spring of 1970, the questionnaire for faculty and administrators at the same time, and an alumnae questionnaire in late spring or early summer. The commission had already collected data about the attitudes of secondary school students, which would be supplemented by selected interviews.[30]

Wellesley Students, Faculty, and Alumnae: Divided Opinion

Wellesley students had mixed views about coeducation. In addition to the interviews conducted by the student members of the commission, in the fall of 1969 interviews had been done by the *Wellesley Alumnae Magazine* of three students described as

29 Minutes, Commission on the Future of the College, Feb. 20–22, 1970, Cmsn. Future College, Box 1, Folder Commission: Minutes and Publicity Releases, May 1969–Dec. 1970. On Cunningham and Greyser, see minutes, Board of Trustees, Jan. 21, 1970, Wellesley trustees, Folder Minutes of the Full Board and Executive Committee, 1969–1970 (Jan. 21, 1970–June 6, 1970).

30 Mary Ann D. Staub, untitled typewritten report on the activities of the Wellesley College Commission, Sept. 15, 1969; Summary Report: Wellesley Commission Meetings, Feb. 20–22, 1970, both in Cmsn. Future College, Box 1, Folder Commission: Minutes and Publicity Releases, May 1969–Dec. 1970.

representative of "those from whom we seldom hear." A junior, Elizabeth Ditmer, said that she was "strongly in favor of coeducation at Wellesley as soon as possible." Having men on campus would make the atmosphere "more natural," and it would "give Wellesley a new perspective." In contrast, a sophomore, Anne Mitchell, called coeducation "a trend and, at this point, a fad." It was probably inevitable that Wellesley would go coed sometime in the future, but coeducation needed "inspired forethought" and careful planning; it would not be to the advantage of the college or of male students "to jump in with both feet" by admitting men in the near term. A senior, Lee Chambers, opined that "the historic reasons for separate women's educational institutions [were] long past." Coeducation, she said, would likely enhance both the intellectual and the political climate on campus and "allow for more realistic male-female relationships."[31]

The student survey confirmed these varied views, showing mixed satisfaction with Wellesley. Although Wellesley had been the first choice of 80 percent of the students, only 48 percent "consider[ed] Wellesley to be 'the best' or 'one of the best' choices they could have made," and 12 percent said that their choice had been "a mistake." Fifty-one percent said that "they would choose Wellesley again." Of those who would go elsewhere, 61 percent would choose "an established coed school," 16 percent "a men's school that recently started admitting women."

As for men at Wellesley, 61 percent of students said that having men on campus should be "a major priority" for the college; 65 percent thought that a male presence would improve Wellesley's educational quality, and 86 percent said that it would improve the college's social quality. About half of the students thought that a student body evenly balanced between men and women would be the best arrangement.[32]

Members of the faculty, too, had already made known their wide range of views. In addition to the interviews done by the

---

31 "What Are the Others Thinking?," *Wellesley Alumnae Magazine* 54 (Autumn 1969): 10–11.

32 Summary of Results of Student Questionnaire, Sept. 1970, Commission on the Future of the College, Report to the Trustees, Mar. 1971, Appendix M-1, pp. 225–28, typescript version, https://archive.org/stream/ReportToTheTrustees, accessed Sept. 19, 2015.

faculty members on the commission, in the fall of 1969 interviews were conducted by the *Wellesley Alumnae Magazine* of three professors, asking what they thought: "Should Wellesley jump on the bandwagon" for coeducation? It was not a simple question. To Dorothea J. Widmayer, associate professor of biological sciences, the imperative was for the college to decide one way or the other and "know why we are doing whatever we choose." Her main concern, she said, was whether Wellesley could attract male students of a sufficiently high caliber to make coeducation viable. A related concern was whether Wellesley could continue to draw first-rate *women* students if the college remained single-sex. Calling coeducation "the biggest red herring around these days," John M. Cooper, Jr., assistant professor of history, noted that the real issue was the challenge of "maintain[ing] the excellence of a small liberal arts college." Cooper worried that the rush toward coeducation would lead the college to "brush aside all its concern with the problems of women." "The one really strong argument . . . for coeducation," he said, was "that it may be the only way . . . that you can continue to attract top-flight female students." Marshall I. Goldman, professor of economics, noted the importance of "product differentiation" in the educational market. If all colleges were to go coed, "there would be no good option for a female student who wants to go to an all-girl's school." Offering that option, at a high level of excellence, might be Wellesley's comparative advantage.[33]

The commission's survey of faculty confirmed the mix of views that the magazine's interviews had suggested. Like students, many faculty members believed that it would be a good thing to have as many as 50 percent men in the student body; 40 percent deemed it "strongly desirable," 18 percent "somewhat desirable," but 23 percent "undesirable." Those who favored coeducation imagined benefits across the board—in classes, campus organizations and activities, and social life. Faculty were especially well disposed to bringing more men to Wellesley through exchange programs (82 percent in favor) but less eager to accept transfer students or enroll

33 "Where Do We Go from Here?," *Wellesley Alumnae Magazine* 54 (Autumn 1969): 13–14.

male freshmen, though each of those options attracted the support of roughly half of the faculty.[34]

Like students and faculty, alumnae had mixed views about co-education, but they were the constituency least in favor of the idea. When the establishment of the commission was announced, they began to declare themselves, some in reasoned analysis, others in colorful prose. Coeducation had supporters: From a member of the class of 1909 in Montreal came the assertion that "the association with male students would be beneficial, and broadening," and a member of the class of 1964 in Cambridge, Massachusetts, insisted that Wellesley should be educating *"people, not women."*[35] But the opponents were more vocal. "It seems to me Wellesley has had no trouble attracting a suitable and talented student body [and] a distinguished and learned faculty," wrote a member of the class of 1958 from Weston, Massachusetts. In the interests of maintaining "a healthy diversity" among educational institutions, she said, "Wellesley [should] remain a distinguished college for women."[36] Other correspondents were more dramatic: From a member of the class of 1927 in New York City: *"Wellesley coeducational?* God forbid!" From a member of the class of 1914 in Baltimore: "When it is made coeducational, my Wellesley will be dead."[37]

In the main, alumnae loved Wellesley. They were highly satisfied with their college experience. As for men on campus, only 30 percent of alumnae surveyed thought that men should make up half of the student body. Sixteen percent said that "'no men' would be the most desirable proportion." All told, 27 percent expressed a "strong

34 Summary of Initial Results of Faculty-Administration Questionnaire, Oct. 1970, Commission on the Future of the College, Report to the Trustees, Mar. 1971, Appendix M-2, pp. 229–32, typescript version.

35 Helen Slack Wickenden and Andrea Leers Manheim in "Letters: Alumnae Respond to Miss Adams' Letter Announcing Establishment of the Wellesley Commission," *Wellesley Alumnae Magazine* 53 (Summer 1969): 24.

36 Sandra Soule Ashley in "Letters: Alumnae Respond to Miss Adams' Letter Announcing Establishment of the Wellesley Commission," *Wellesley Alumnae Magazine* 53 (Summer 1969): 24. In the same issue of the magazine, on the same page, see also the letter from Ann Callaway Polelle.

37 Dorris Clarke and Jean Watson Fowler in "Letters: Alumnae Respond to Miss Adams' Letter Announcing Establishment of the Wellesley Commission," *Wellesley Alumnae Magazine* 53 (Summer 1969): 25.

desire" for Wellesley to remain a women's college—a finding that varied by age, with 39 percent of graduates from classes before 1930, but 9 percent of those from classes of 1965–69, taking this view.[38]

Adams answered many of the letters that came from alumnae. "This particular issue," she wrote in a representative response, "is one on which opinion is sharply divided and based upon intensely held convictions. This is the reason that led us to believe a thorough and careful study was required." Whatever the outcome, Adams assured correspondents that "it will have been decided thoughtfully and not on the basis of emotion or faddishness." Adams knew that the commission's conclusions would not please everyone, but she hoped that everyone would "agree that the commission examined the matter fully and fairly" and that alumnae would be prepared to join those on campus in "continu[ing] to work together effectively for Wellesley's future."[39]

The commission also planned to engage alumnae in person, scheduling nine regional councils of alumnae for the fall of 1970. Commission members as well as a senior administrator from the college would address each of the regional councils; the gatherings would involve progress reports on the work of the commission, reports on the results of the alumnae survey, and small-group discussions so that alumnae would have ample opportunity to air their views.[40] The approach, in its inclusiveness, was characteristic of the way the college did its business.[41]

38 Summary of Results of Alumnae Questionnaire, Sept. 1970, Commission on the Future of the College, Report to the Trustees, Mar. 1971, Appendix M-3, pp. 233–34, typescript version.

39 Ruth M. Adams to Mrs. George H. Ashley, Mar. 18, 1969 ("opinion is sharply divided"), and Adams to Mrs. Norman S. Matthews, Mar. 18, 1969 ("examined the matter fully and fairly," "work together effectively"), both in Adams, Box 13, Folder Commission on the Future of the College: Correspondence, 1969–73; Adams to Wilma A. Buchman, July 1, 1969 ("not on the basis of emotion or faddishness"), Adams, Box 13, Folder Commission on the Future of the College: General, 1969–72.

40 Minutes, Commission on the Future of the College, Feb. 20–22, 1970; minutes, Commission on the Future of the College, Aug. 5–7, 1970, both in Cmsn. Future College, Box 1, Folder Commission: Minutes and Publicity Releases, May 1969–Dec. 1970; Regional Councils 1970: Commission Session Agenda, attached to minutes, Commission on the Future of the College, Sept. 11–13, 1970, Adams, Box 13, Folder Commission on the Future of the College: Minutes, 1969–70; Mary Ann D. Staub, Betty Freyhof Johnson, and Barbara Barnes Hauptfuhrer to Dear Alumna, Fall 1970, Adams, Box 13, Folder Commission on the Future of the College: General, 1969–72.

41 I am indebted to Nannerl O. Keohane for this insight.

The Problem of Admissions: Declining Applications and Yield

The views of current students, faculty, and alumnae were important, but equally important were the behaviors of the high school students who might comprise the Wellesley student body going forward. As early as the fall of 1967, the student newspaper, the *Wellesley News*, was worrying about Wellesley's appeal to high school students. Wellesley, the paper said, was accustomed to "sit[ting] back and select[ing] the 'cream of the intellectual crop'" from "its plethora of outstanding applicants." But "Wellesley's popularity" appeared to be "on the decline." The number of applications had been dropping; so had the yield. "Apparently Wellesley is not only attracting fewer applicants, but an increasing number of those who are accepted prefer to study elsewhere. What has happened to Wellesley's popularity?"[42]

Wellesley normally received the third-largest number of applications among the Seven Sisters, following Radcliffe and Smith. The total number of applicants to Wellesley had been relatively strong—2,197 for entry in 1967, 2,102 for 1968, 2,312 for 1969—but the number had dipped to 1,986 for 1970 and 1,852 for 1971. Analysis of those data revealed two striking findings. One had to do with early decision (ED). Wellesley was drawing well in relation to its Seven Sisters peers—for the class entering in 1968, there had been 361 ED applicants at Wellesley compared with 218 at Smith, 182 at Mt. Holyoke, 101 at Barnard, 91 at Vassar, and 67 at Bryn Mawr. However, Wellesley's ED applicants for entry in 1969 had dropped to 284, considerably narrowing the gap between numbers of applicants to Wellesley and Smith (271 applicants). By 1970 Smith was outperforming Wellesley in this area; Smith had 210 ED applicants, Wellesley 188. In short, Wellesley had experienced a 48 percent drop in ED applications over the three-year period. And the downturn would continue: For the class entering in 1972, Wellesley had 153 ED applicants compared with 211 at Smith.[43]

42 "The Decline and Fall," *Wellesley News*, Sept. 10, 1967, p. 2, Wellesley College Library.

43 In EVP, Box 1, Folder Admission, 1968–70, see Seven College Admission Statistics—1968. In Adams, Box 8, Folder Admission: Statistics, 1969–73, see Seven College Admission Statistics—1969; Seven College Admission Statistics—1970; Seven College

The other troubling finding concerned the college choices of students who had rejected Wellesley's admission offer. The data collected by the commission conveyed a stark message: "The number of top-notch female graduates of secondary schools . . . who enter women's colleges has been declining steadily over-all, and especially in the private-school population." Between 1965 and 1969, at the schools from which top-ranking students had applied to Wellesley, the percentage of students matriculating at women's colleges had declined from 35 to 23 percent.[44]

It had been the case historically that the large majority of admitted students who chose not to go to Wellesley matriculated instead at another women's college, with Radcliffe and Smith taking the largest number of the cross-admits. But that changed for the students admitted for entry in 1969. Compared with the percentages opting for other women's colleges in the previous four years—57.9, 60.1, 55.4, and 52.2 from 1965 through 1968—only 39.9 percent of the 1969 cohort chose another women's college, whereas 47.5 percent chose coeducational or coordinate colleges, a number of which were admitting women for the first time.[45] For the 1970 cohort, 24.4 percent who said no to Wellesley chose another women's college, whereas 69 percent matriculated at coeducational or coordinate colleges.[46]

In an interim report in June 1970, the commission summarized its work thus far and noted also the areas in which it had "acted as a catalyst" for changes already instituted or planned

---

Admission Statistics (Comparison), Nov. 18, 1970; Seven College General Admission Statistics—1971; and Seven College Admission Statistics—1972.

44 *Report of the Commission on the Future of Wellesley College*, Mar. 1971, p. 75, n. 2, Adams, Box 13, Folder Commission on the Future of the College: Report, 1970–71; memorandum, Alan Schechter and Blair McElroy to Members of Wellesley College Commission, Nov. 3, 1969 (source of the quote), Adams, Box 13, Folder Commission on the Future of the College: General, 1969–72.

45 Five-Year Study of Accepted Candidates Who Did Not Choose to Enter Wellesley College, July 3, 1969, EVP, Box 1, Folder Admission, 1968–70. These percentages are based on known decisions; the total number of students declining admission includes a small percentage whose choices are unknown.

46 Admission Statistics and Comments, memorandum, Mary Ellen Ames to Wellesley College Commission, Nov. 13, 1970, Adams, Box 8, Folder Admission: Statistics, 1967–72. Again, these percentages represent known decisions; some 6.5 percent of students declining admission to Wellesley made choices that are unknown.

for implementation in 1970–71: for example, "continued expansion of the MIT exchange and alignment of MIT's and Wellesley's daily class calendars; Wellesley's entry into the Twelve College Exchange; and greater flexibility in [Wellesley's] leave of absence policy."[47] These changes were all well and good, but as we shall see in the next chapter, there were opportunities for bolder initiatives, initiatives seriously explored and then set aside, that might have changed Wellesley more profoundly.

47 Interim Report from the Commission on the Future of the College, June 22, 1970, Cmsn. Future College, Box 1, Folder Commission Minutes and Publicity Releases, May 1969–Dec. 1970.

18

Wellesley: "Having the Courage to Remain a Women's College"

While the commission was doing its work, Ruth Adams and other administrators explored a more innovative way of engaging Wellesley with another institution. The idea, which had originated at Dartmouth, was to see what might come of what the president of Dartmouth, John G. Kemeny, characterized as "a much closer relationship between Wellesley and Dartmouth."[1]

"Significant Cooperation" between Wellesley and Dartmouth

In the spring and summer of 1970, faculty and administrators at Wellesley and Dartmouth investigated opportunities for "significant cooperation."[2] A small delegation from Wellesley visited Hanover at Kemeny's invitation, and representatives of Dartmouth visited Wellesley.[3] By mid-July, each institution had a proposal for an exchange, with two hundred to three hundred students and five or more faculty members switching campuses for a year or

---

1 John G. Kemeny to Ruth M. Adams, Mar. 4, 1970, Adams, Box 19, Folder Commission on the Future of the College: Exchanges, Dartmouth-Wellesley Proposal, 1970–71.

2 Dartmouth-Wellesley Exchange, draft news release, rev. Sept. 17, 1970, attached to Leonard M. Rieser to Members of the Trustee Study Committee, Sept. 15, 1970, Kemeny, Box 8440. The final version, released on Sept. 24, 1970, is attached to Ruth M. Adams and John G. Kemeny to Thomas C. Mendenhall, Sept. 22, 1970, Mendenhall, Series 14, Box 6.

3 Schedule of Wellesley Visit Wednesday, May 27, and Thursday, May 28, [1970,] and Wellesley-Dartmouth Meeting, June 24, 1970, both in Adams, Box 19, Folder Commission on the Future of the College: Exchanges, Dartmouth-Wellesley Proposal, 1970–71.

more, along with some collaboration between academic departments in long-range planning.[4]

The proposal would provide mutual advantage in terms of complementary academic strengths, with the specialized advanced offerings of one institution available to students at the other. Another obvious advantage would be men and women going to school together. Forwarding the two proposals to her board chair, Nelson Darling, Adams explained that "each institution is nervously looking at co-education and trying to find ways in which to avoid this if at all possible. The exchange concept seems to be both educationally valid, socially useful, and a means of being 'co-educational' without consequentially changing the nature of either college."[5]

In August, six Wellesley faculty members spent a day in Hanover meeting with Dartmouth faculty members in the same or similar fields.[6] Most of the Wellesley reactions were positive, though a professor of economics noted "the widespread confusion" in the conversations "of 'educational' (meaning curricular) benefits with 'coeducational benefits.'" A historian called the proposed exchange "a neat way of smoothing the transition to full coeducation (though certainly not a substitute for it)." A Wellesley classicist reported that she and her Dartmouth counterpart agreed that the partnership between the two institutions would be "highly beneficial to our respective foreign language programs." And an English professor said that she came back from Hanover with "a far more lively sense of the possibilities of inter-college cooperation." The advantages of the exchange for small departments would lie in the

4 In Dickey, Box 7200, see minutes, Trustee Study Committee Meeting, June 4, 1970, attached to Leonard M. Rieser to Members of the Trustee Study Committee, June 15, 1970. In Cmsn. Future College, Box 1, Folder Commission: Studies: Dartmouth, see Executive Minutes of the Commission on the Future of the College, June 10, 1970. In Adams, Box 19, Folder Commission on the Future of the College: Exchanges, Dartmouth-Wellesley Proposal, 1970–71, see Proposals (Wellesley's Proposal), June 24, 1970, and Wellesley-Dartmouth Educational Partnership: A Proposal (Dartmouth Draft), July 15, 1970.

5 Ruth M. Adams to Nelson Darling, Jr., July 21, 1970, Adams, Box 19, Folder Commission on the Future of the College: Exchanges, Dartmouth-Wellesley Proposal, 1970–71.

6 Memorandum, Blair McElroy to Mrs. Bell, Mrs. [sic] Cohen, Mrs. Lefkowitz, Mr. London, Mr. Norvig, Mrs. Spacks, July 31, 1970, and Dartmouth-Wellesley Meeting, Participants, Aug. 11, 1970, both in Adams, Box 19, Folder Commission on the Future of the College: Exchanges, Dartmouth-Wellesley Proposal, 1970–71.

expansion of intellectual opportunity and field coverage afforded by combining the resources of the two institutions. For large departments, in which intellectual approaches might differ between the schools, students would benefit from being exposed to both.[7]

In September a group of faculty from Dartmouth paid a return visit to Wellesley, where they met with a broader group of Wellesley faculty to continue the conversation. In the meeting among faculty in English, for example, the consensus was that "the principal value for our students . . . would be in the provision of opportunities for the kind of diversity supplied by a temporary change in locale, by the chance to learn in a different atmosphere with different associates and presumably therefore with somewhat different perspectives and angles of vision." The delegates also saw clear benefits in exchanging faculty members, who would gain professionally by working with different colleagues and different students.[8]

Following the Dartmouth visit, Adams wrote to the academic council at Wellesley to describe the discussions, outline the proposals, and ask for comment. Shortly thereafter, she wrote to the Wellesley community to introduce the idea and, again, invite comment.[9] Adams and Kemeny also shared information about the ongoing discussions with presidents of other institutions participating in the Twelve-College Exchange.[10]

At the same time, at convocation at Dartmouth, Kemeny outlined the concept of the partnership and expressed excitement

7 Reports from Wellesley Faculty Members Who Have Participated in Meetings with Dartmouth Faculty, n.d. [Aug. 1970], Adams, Box 19, Folder Commission on the Future of the College: Exchanges, Dartmouth-Wellesley Proposal, 1970–71.

8 David Ferry to Wellesley College Commission, Sept. 10, 1970, Cmsn. Future College, Box 1, Folder Commission: Studies: Dartmouth. For other reports on the September 9 meeting, see Blair McElroy to Mr. Phibbs, Sept. 10, 1970; Louis Dickstein to McElroy, Sept. 10, 1970; and Grazia Avitabile to McElroy, Sept. 10, 1970, all in Adams, Box 19, Folder Commission on the Future of the College: Exchanges, Dartmouth-Wellesley Proposal, 1970–71. See also Mary Allen to McElroy, Sept. 17, 1970, Cmsn. Future College, Box 1, Folder Commission: Studies: Dartmouth.

9 Ruth M. Adams to Members of Academic Council, Sept. 11, 1970, and Adams to Members of the Wellesley College Community, Sept. 18, 1970, both in Adams, Box 19, Folder Commission on the Future of the College: Exchanges, Dartmouth-Wellesley Proposal, 1970–71.

10 Wellesley College news release, Sept. 24, 1970, Adams, Box 19, Folder Commission on the Future of the College: Exchanges, Dartmouth-Wellesley Proposal, 1970–71.

about the opportunities that it could bring. "It seems to me," he said, "to open up a number of new avenues, to give more flexibility, to give more freedom, without in any way encroaching on any one's particular plans. If you don't like it, you don't have to participate in it—it is as simple as that!" The plan "might set an example for many national experiments," as well as being "very important for the future of Dartmouth."[11]

In October, at Wellesley, a committee of faculty members and students was formed to learn as much as possible about attitudes of faculty and students about the proposed "special relationship."[12] On the Dartmouth side, department and program chairs contacted their counterparts at Wellesley to initiate conversations about possible cooperation, and several groups of students made visits to Wellesley.[13] The responses from faculty members were varied: "considerable mild approval of the exchange as an idea," along with "considerable skepticism about its workability." As for students, there was "very substantial support" for the proposal.[14]

As Wellesley departments reported their views, only a few were strongly opposed, but, with a couple of exceptions, there was also no "wild enthusiasm."[15] The philosophy department was not supportive; the proposed exchange felt "like a substitute for real substantive action on the question of coeducation" and threatened to "jeopardize . . . the highly valuable exchange with M.I.T." Mathematics was divided; "the reactions have ranged from 'great' to 'it is for the birds.'" Biological sciences was among the small

11 John G. Kemeny, Convocation Address, Sept. 24, 1970, Kemeny personal, Box 14, Folder 13.

12 David Ferry to Members of Academic Council, Oct. 20, 1970, Adams, Box 19, Folder Commission on the Future of the College: Exchanges, Dartmouth-Wellesley Proposal, 1970–71.

13 Leonard M. Rieser to Phillip [*sic*] Phibbs, Oct. 27, 1970, Adams, Box 19, Folder Commission on the Future of the College: Exchanges, Dartmouth-Wellesley Proposal, 1970–71.

14 General Summary of Assessment by Committee Assessing Faculty Opinion about Wellesley-Dartmouth Exchange, Nov. 1970, and Recommendations of the Student Members of the Dartmouth Study Committee, Nov. 1970, both in Cmsn. Future College, Box 1, Folder Commission: Studies: Dartmouth.

15 Mary Allen, Paul Cohen, and David Ferry to Commission [on the Future of the College], stamped Nov. 18, 1970, Adams, Box 19, Folder Commission on the Future of the College: Exchanges, Dartmouth-Wellesley Proposal, 1970–71.

number of departments that saw advantages in the broader range of course offerings.[16] As the faculty members soliciting departmental views summed up, "It is clear that no <u>negative</u> conclusion need be reached on the basis of this report, and equally clear that there is no really impressive <u>positive</u> mandate either."[17]

The Commission's Continuing Deliberations

At the same time that Wellesley explored possibilities for an exchange with Dartmouth, the commission continued its work, focusing during the summer and early fall of 1970 on issues ancillary to coeducation. At the November meeting, however, the key question would be addressed: What would the commission recommend with respect to coeducation at Wellesley?

Senior administrators who were not part of the commission's deliberations began to weigh in with their opposition to coeducation. The vice president for resources, Albert E. Holland, opined that a decision for coeducation would have "a very adverse effect" on alumnae giving, an effect that would be "as permanent as the decision will be irrevocable."[18] Philip Phibbs, the executive vice president, wrote privately to the president and then also to the commission. To Adams he emphasized the importance of "the historic role" of the college, the "preservation of diversity in higher education," and the opportunities Wellesley provided "for growth and development for women intellectually and . . . in leadership." He noted "the limited places already available for women at quality institutions" and said that "Wellesley should not reduce this

16 Ingrid Stadler to Paul Cohen, Nov. 10, 1970 (philosophy); Torsten Norvig to Commission on the Future of the College, Nov. 16, 1970 (mathematics); and Delaphine G. R. Wyckoff to Dartmouth Exchange Committee, Nov. 16, 1970 (biological sciences), all in Cmsn. Future College, Box 1, Folder Commission: Studies: Dartmouth. There are many other lengthy responses in this folder representing the views of other academic departments at Wellesley.

17 Mary Allen, Paul Cohen, and David Ferry to Commission [on the Future of the College], stamped Nov. 18, 1970.

18 There are two versions of this memorandum in Adams, Box 12, Folder Commission on the Future of the College: Coeducation, 1968–1973: A. E. Holland to Miss Adams, Mr. Phibbs, Mrs. Johnson, Mrs. Staub, Nov. 20, 1970, and Holland to Adams, Phibbs, Johnson, Staub, carrying the dates of Nov. 19 and Nov. 20, 1970.

number by cutting back to admit men." And he urged attention to "the special needs of women."[19] Phibbs made similar points in his letter to the commission. He noted that a decision for coeducation would "effectively eliminate one option in higher education." And he made the case for endorsing the formulation that Mary Ann Dilley Staub, the chairman of the commission, had used recently in addressing an all-college meeting when she spoke of envisioning Wellesley as "a coeducational women's college"—an institution where women were at "the center of concern and attention," an institution that "emphasized the importance of quality education for women while welcoming the presence of male students as guests at the institution."[20]

At its November and December meetings, the commission wrestled with challenging issues of substance and priority. They also began to confront the reality that their many imaginative proposals significantly exceeded available funds.[21] With respect to the education of men, the commission debated a substantial list of still-controversial questions. Should the trustees be asked now to acquire the legal authority to grant degrees to men so that the desire to grant such degrees, should it arise in the near term, would not be blocked by the absence of such authority? Or would even asking the question presume a decision that had not yet been made? And could the authority, once secured, be held in check, or would it launch the college on a course that would lead inevitably to granting degrees to men?

What would be the right way to bring men to the Wellesley campus? As visitors who would come to study at Wellesley on exchange programs? As visitors on exchange programs who might be permitted to stay on to qualify for a Wellesley degree? As fully

19 Memorandum, Philip M. Phibbs to Miss Adams, Nov. 18, 1970, Adams, Box 12, Folder Commission on the Future of the College: Coeducation, 1968–73. Phibbs elaborated his views in a much longer memorandum in the same folder, Phibbs to Adams, Nov. 20, 1970.

20 Memorandum, Philip M. Phibbs to Wellesley College Commission, Nov. 20, 1970, Adams, Box 12, Folder Commission on the Future of the College: Coeducation, 1968–73.

21 Minutes, Commission on the Future of the College, Nov. 20–22 and Dec. 11–13, 1970, both in Cmsn. Future College, Box 1, Folder Commission: Minutes and Publicity Releases, May 1969–Dec. 1970.

matriculated students, limited to the upperclass years? Or as fully matriculated students, including freshmen? And what would be the right balance of women and men? One option, often discussed, called for 1,750 women and 250 men. A variant put the numbers at 1,500 and 500. Should Wellesley declare an intention to aim eventually for an even balance of men and women?

The commission was a highly diverse group, grappling with challenging issues. As one of the student members, Geneva Overholser, recalled, the conversations were "broad-ranging" and "collegial," a model of thoughtfulness and rational analysis. That the members maintained so much civility and mutual respect was particularly impressive. The person most obviously uncomfortable with the proceedings was Adams. Overholser recalled that Adams "had trouble interacting with the group. . . . Her manner was rather cold anyway. She was probably shy and nervous. And she was frightened about the future of the college," which "was being challenged on so many fronts." Had she been more "open and flexible," she would have strengthened her authority within the group. In Overholser's assessment, Adams's "fearful and uncertain" demeanor was "of a piece with her leadership generally."[22]

For all the collegiality within the commission, it was clear that even as late as December 1970, it was deeply divided. A draft report circulated in early January 1971 was "not satisfactory to all members." The commission met in mid-January and "found that there were still consequential but not unresolvable differences of opinion about the phrasing of a number of recommendations." As a result, the original plan—to have a final report ready to transmit to the board of trustees in January 1971—was revised, with the expectation that the report would be sent to the trustees in advance of their April meeting.[23]

22 Interview with Geneva Overholser '70, Nov. 15, 2013, New York City.

23 In Wellesley trustees, Folder Minutes of the Full Board and Executive Committee, 1970–71 (Jan. 21, 1971–Apr. 15, 1971), see minutes, Executive Committee of the Board of Trustees, Jan. 20, 1971, and minutes, Board of Trustees, Jan. 21, 1971. In Adams, Box 13, Folder Commission on the Future of the College: Report, 1970–71, see Nelson Darling to All Members of the Wellesley College Community, Jan. 25, 1971, and memorandum, Commission on the Future of the College to the College Community, Jan. 26, 1971 (source of the quotes).

The commission hoped, nevertheless, that while it was working to bring the report to completion, the trustees would act to get the Wellesley-Dartmouth exchange started for 1971–72. Members of the commission had met informally with the president and provost of Dartmouth in November 1970, and the committee on educational policy at Dartmouth and the executive committee of the Dartmouth faculty had approved the exchange. The Dartmouth trustees had taken note of the proposal in January 1971.[24]

Forward movement was now up to Wellesley. Time was of the essence because students would need to enroll in the exchange by February 5 under the terms of the Twelve-College Exchange, which would be the vehicle for the exchange in its first year. But the Wellesley trustees were unwilling to act on the exchange, not because it lacked merit but because "they did not wish to take any final action on any one proposal until the report of the Commission [was] completed and [could] be considered in its entirety."[25] What that meant (though the board did not realize it) was that the proposal for the Dartmouth exchange was effectively mooted.

By early February it was clear that unanimity among members of the commission on every issue would be impossible to achieve, and Dilley Staub asked the members to initial copies of the draft report to indicate which sections or paragraphs they could and could not support. After opinions were tabulated, the report might stand as it was, and "divergences [might be] reported to the Trustees in numbers of those who support and those who do not."[26]

A Wide-Ranging "Philosophy for Wellesley's Future"

By the end of February 1971 the report had been completed, and it was transmitted to the board for consideration at a special meeting

24 Philip M. Phibbs to Dilley Staub, Oct. 19, 1970, Adams, Box 19, Folder Commission on the Future of the College: Exchanges, Dartmouth-Wellesley Proposal, 1970–71; Agenda, Commission on the Future of the College, [Nov. 20–22, 1970,] Adams, Box 13, Folder Commission on the Future of the College: Report, 1970–71; *The Dartmouth*, Nov. 5, 1970, Women at Dartmouth, Box 6593.

25 Minutes, Board of Trustees, Jan. 21, 1971, Wellesley trustees, Folder Minutes of the Full Board and Executive Committee, 1970–71 (Jan. 21, 1971–Apr. 15, 1971).

26 Memorandum, Dilley Staub to Commission Members, Feb. 4, 1971, Adams, Box 13, Folder Commission on the Future of the College: Report, 1970–71.

on March 22.[27] The report began by articulating "a philosophy for
Wellesley's future":

- "Wellesley should go forward as a strong liberal arts college, with enduring concern for the education of women in
  order to continue to prepare young women realistically for
  life and active service in a society that looks and calls for
  leadership."
- There would be a "continuing need for an educational program that adapts with imagination and flexibility to the
  present and anticipates the future, in terms both of students' current interests and the potential value of their education in later years."
- The college would have "a stronger educational program
  if it educates both men and women, but . . . in a way dif-
  fering from what is commonly viewed as traditional coeducation." Men and women should be "educated together
  in such a way that each will come to respect the other's
  distinctive and individual capabilities, that women's capacities for competence and leadership can be recognized, and
  that students can be prepared to live in a society in which
  there is equality of opportunity for women and men."[28]

The commission offered recommendations about the educational program, the education of women, minorities, counseling,
and the composition of the student body. By design, they produced
"a hodge-podge of unrelated ideas," as Phibbs characterized their
work. They recommended that research be undertaken on new educational patterns for freshmen and sophomores; that a program
be developed in suburban-regional studies; that opportunities for
foreign study be expanded; that the cognizant faculty committee
investigate giving academic credit for independent field work; that

27 Minutes, Executive Committee of the Board of Trustees, Mar. 3, 1971, Wellesley
trustees, Folder Minutes of the Full Board and Executive Committee, 1970–71 (Jan. 21,
1971–Apr. 15, 1971).

28 *Report of the Commission on the Future of Wellesley College*, Mar. 1971, p. 5,
Adams, Box 13, Folder Commission on the Future of the College: Report, 1970–71.

programs of advanced study be explored; that additional courses be developed on women and on race; that the normal time to the B.A. degree be revised, with options ranging from three to five years; that the college redouble its efforts to recruit minority students and diversify the faculty; that the college work toward enhanced academic and personal counseling for the increasingly diverse campus community; and that the college pursue educational research with a new office and a faculty committee. The commission recommended, too, that the high ratio of women to men on the faculty be maintained and that women continue to be represented prominently in "the most important policy-making positions and offices."[29]

The most controversial part of the report had to do with coeducation. "In our opinion," the commission said, the "ideal of equal educational opportunities for women" articulated by Henry Fowle Durant in his founding gift to the college "today requires reinterpretation. Dedication to his ideal in the 1970's implies the introduction of men onto the campus, where they will work together with women in the classroom and in related activities." Although the commission recommended that "Wellesley should include men as students," it said that Wellesley "should not, however, become a coeducational college in the traditional sense, where activities and leadership roles are oriented primarily to men and where the great majority of faculty and administrators are men." It would be essential to preserve the opportunities that had accrued historically to women at Wellesley. In addition, it would be a good thing for men to have "some of their undergraduate education in an environment where women—students, faculty, and administrators—are in positions of leadership and responsibility."[30]

The report struck a middle ground between the views of commission members who favored full coeducation and those who argued that Wellesley should remain a college that granted degrees only to women. It recommended "that every effort be made" to

---

29 Telephone interview with Philip Phibbs, Sept. 3, 2013; *Report of the Commission on the Future of Wellesley College*, pp. 6–7.

30 *Report of the Commission on the Future of Wellesley College*, p. 75.

maintain the number of women educated by Wellesley at 1,750, with 1,500 women and 500 men on campus and another 250 women away on exchange programs or leaves of absence. And it recommended approval of the proposed Dartmouth-Wellesley exchange and continuation of the MIT exchange.

By a split vote (9 to 4) the commission recommended "that immediate steps be taken for the College to acquire the legal capacity to grant degrees to men." And it said that men should be "considered for admission to Wellesley as degree candidates (a) after having been exchange students who then apply for transfer to Wellesley, or (b) as transfer students who have completed two years at another institution." These actions were to be undertaken as an experiment, with the understanding that every step would be evaluated along the way and that no step precluded partial or even complete rethinking of the enterprise.[31]

In Phibbs's assessment, everything about the commission pointed toward its lack of influence. It was "not a distinguished committee." It did not include the strongest trustees or faculty members. The report was all over the map. It did not present a single vision or a composite view of a new future. But it was never intended to. The report was largely ignored; it neither galvanized the college nor offered a blueprint for action.[32]

The commission's recommendations were nevertheless covered widely in the local and national press, with a range of headlines over what were essentially identical stories. The *New York Times* gave the clearest indication of what was actually happening: "Wellesley Panel Asks Limited Admission of Men." Using the United Press International account, the Hyannis, Massachusetts, *Standard Times* said, "Wellesley Mulls Men." The Portland, Maine, *Express* told its readers, "Wellesley Wary on Male Coeds." Printing the same Associated Press account, the Newport, Rhode Island *News* headlined, "Wellesley Taking Men."[33]

31 Ibid., pp. 8, 78.
32 Phibbs interview.
33 *New York Times*; Hyannis, MA, *Standard Times*; Portland, ME, *Express*; and Newport, RI, *News*, all Mar. 23, 1971, clippings in Adams, Box 12, Folder Commission on the Future of the College: Coeducation, 1968–73.

The bigger story, however, was the dissent of two key members of the commission and the way the board handled the receipt of a controversial, contested report.

The Dissent of Adams and Lefkowitz

Both Ruth Adams and Mary Lefkowitz appended personal letters to the published commission report. Adams had long felt herself to be in a difficult spot. As she told the executive committee, it had been a mistake for the president to be a member of a commission that was going to make recommendations to the board. She had already made her views clear in a series of votes that had been taken in the commission; that made it awkward for her to take an independent position later as president and as a member of the board.[34] But it was also awkward for her to be identified publicly with a report with which she had a fundamental disagreement, and she felt that she had no choice but to make her views known in a letter of dissent.

Adams wrote that she parted company with other members of the commission over the issue of Wellesley "grant[ing] degrees to men and accept[ing] them as transfer students." Wellesley, she said, had "an historical commitment to the education of women, a commitment that, in these times of heightened consciousness on the part of women, is perhaps more consequential than for many prior years. Creative thinking about the education of women is a national and international need, and one which Wellesley should undertake to fill. While such education should include social and classroom experiences with men, it does not require the granting of degrees to men."

Adams said that she could not agree with the assertion that "Wellesley does not and will not receive applications from young women of superior quality, in sufficient numbers to maintain the college at its customary size and standards." Instead of diverting

---

34 Minutes, Executive Committee of the Board of Trustees, Jan. 20, 1971, Wellesley trustees, Folder Minutes of the Full Board and Executive Committee, 1970–71 (Jan. 21, 1971–Apr. 15, 1971).

resources to the expensive venture of coeducation, Adams said, Wellesley should be investing in the college's distinctive strengths. "We should devote our energies and our resources to building from within, to keeping Wellesley the best of the women's colleges in America, indeed in the world."[35]

Adams was more expansive in summarizing her reasoning at a meeting of the trustee executive committee. Beyond the arguments in her letter, there was an additional argument reminiscent of what had happened at Smith: the "changing attitude toward coeducation in the past year, coming from women's lib and self-evaluations."[36]

Lefkowitz, vice chairman of the commission, argued in her dissenting letter that the commission lacked the expertise, research, and documentation to support the recommendations for coeducation, as well as some of its other proposals. The commission was, after all, a politically constituted group, and it did not have the capacity to "set forth in precise detail the methods by which true coeducation could be achieved at Wellesley," which meant that important policy decisions had been left "to be executed on an *ad hoc* basis" by others. Lefkowitz said that she had changed her views about coeducation over the course of the twenty-two months of the commission's work. Initially she had thought that "Wellesley's problems could be solved most effectively by instituting coeducation" along the lines described in the report. Now, with Wellesley in a situation of constrained financial resources, she would give priority to other recommendations, especially those having to do with the education of women. Regarding coeducation, she said, "I am convinced that we need more time and information to determine whether or not the proposed program for admitting men as degree candidates would in fact achieve the desired goal of an ideal environment for educating both men and women." More evidence—admission statistics, experience with exchanges, and study by professionals capable of conducting well-grounded,

35 Ruth M. Adams to the Board of Trustees, Mar. 3, 1971, in *Report of the Commission on the Future of Wellesley College*, p. 80.

36 Minutes, Executive Committee of the Board of Trustees, Mar. 3, 1971, Wellesley trustees, Folder Minutes of the Full Board and Executive Committee, 1970–71 (Jan. 21, 1971–Apr. 15, 1971).

intensive evaluations—would permit more effective judgment about these questions in the years to come.[37]

For the board, responding to the commission report was no simple matter. A clear recommendation for coeducation would have been complicated enough to handle. In this case, with the sensitivity of the proposals regarding education for men and degrees for men, the clear divisions within the commission, the dissent of the president and the vice chairman of the commission, and the president obviously at odds with the trustee chairman of the commission, the situation was unusually fraught.

The Vice President for Resources Plots Strategy

In advance of the report's release, the vice president for resources, Albert Holland, wrote a memo advising Adams and Phibbs on strategy for the senior administration and the board. He had talked over the matter with Betty Freyhof Johnson, the trustee who chaired Wellesley's national development effort, and the advice reflected both of their views. Holland saw the tension between Adams and Staub as the heart of the matter. "Dilley Staub," he said, "seems to be very upset that Miss Adams does not believe that an immediate acceptance of all the Commission's recommendations is desirable, but that the recommendation on CE [coeducation] or DFM [degrees for men] should be given long and thoughtful study by the Trustees before any decision is made." He worried about the "distinct possibility that the Board members may be pressured into approving the Commission's recommendations in toto."

Holland said that he and Johnson agreed that coeducation "would be very injurious to the College at this time." There was no need "to take such drastic action." Moreover, time was on Wellesley's side; there was evidence that "recent experiments in coeducation [had] not been a stunning success." Given that it had taken the commission nearly two years "to come up with this recommendation" and that the commission was split, "the Trustees

37 Mary R. Lefkowitz to the Board of Trustees, Mar. 3, 1971, in *Report of the Commission on the Future of Wellesley College*, pp. 80–81.

ought to take a good long time to think things through." Adams, he emphasized, "IS IN AN UNASSAILABLE POSITION WHEN AS PRES- IDENT OF THE MOST FEMALE OF WOMEN'S COLLEGES, SHE SAYS THAT A DECISION TO CHANGE THE FUNDAMENTAL NATURE OF THE COLLEGE SHOULD BE MADE ONLY AFTER LONG, THOUGHTFUL AND PRAYERFUL CONSIDERATION BY THE TRUSTEES."

But it would not be easy to accomplish that goal, Holland reasoned:

> We have determined opponents. First of all, the proponents of coeducation who tell us that Degrees for Men does not mean coeducation and that the decision can be reversed (they are wrong on both counts) took their stand long ago and now have wrapped themselves in it. They will be out lobbying. Then there is Dilley, who looks upon this disastrous compro- mise as a tremendous personal triumph and as an example of unexampled leadership. She has a stake in her creation and she feels that having brought about this compromise, she must, and as we all know, she will, fight to the death for it.

How, then, should Adams and the board proceed? "The basic position," Holland advised, should be "to thank the Commission members for all their hard work, approve every recommendation we can approve, and then say 'we are not rejecting the recom- mendation on coeducation (DFM, etc.) but it represents such a fundamental change in the nature of the College that we will re- serve decision on this particular recommendation until we have as Trustees thoroughly explored the options open to the College.'" Alternatively, the board could vote to reject the recommendation for the time being and agree to consider it again in two years.

Adams's statement of dissent, Holland advised, should be in- cluded in the summary account of the report in the college bulletin as well as in the full report that would be printed in the alumnae magazine. Adams should send it, as well, to each member of the commission, explaining in some detail her reasons "for believing more time is necessary" and including a copy of a recent article in the *Boston Globe*, "Women's Colleges Turning Off from the Rush to 'Coeducation,'" which noted the shift in student sentiment at Smith and the "mounting evidence that the women's colleges at least are looking at coeducation with a more jaundiced eye and are discovering a new appreciation for the virtues of temporary separation from the male-dominated society." The *Globe* article, Holland said, should also be sent to the trustees, with a note from Adams explaining "what she is planning to do" and inviting their comments. In the case of trustees who did not agree with her position, Adams "should have a personal talk with them, maybe with another Trustee going along."

It should also be made clear "on every possible occasion" that the function of the commission was "to recommend," but the function "of deciding rests with the Board." Although faculty and students would doubtless want to discuss the commission report, Holland advised that the point be made clearly "that the operative decisions rest with the Trustees" and that there was no hurry to make any immediate decisions. At the special meeting of the trustees on March 22, 1971, Holland said, the board should "receive the Commission Report, listen to any verbal addenda any Commission members wish to make, then thank the Commission warmly for its efforts and discharge it." If, as Holland hoped, "a strong majority on the Board comes to favor reserving decision," it would be up to the board chair, Nelson Darling, "to handle Dilley."

"It is extremely important," Holland counseled, "that those of us who favor reserving the decision on CE or DFM be sunny, assured, and filled with praise for the Commission and its Chairman." If "Commission members who favor CE or DFM become sulky or enraged," the appropriate response would be "amaze[ment] that this would happen when after all we are only recommending that the Trustees give this all-important matter thoughtful, prayerful and deliberate consideration."[38]

---

38 Memorandum, Bert [Albert] Holland to Miss Adams and Mr. Phibbs, Mar. 5, 1971, Adams, Box 13, Folder Commission on the Future of the College: Report, 1970–71; Nina McCain, "Women's Colleges Turning Off from the Rush to 'Coeducation,'" *Boston Globe*, Feb. 27, 1971, clipping in Adams, Box 12, Folder Commission on the Future of the College: Coeducation, 1968–73.

Action on and Reactions to the Commission's Report

Holland's memo tracked closely with what Adams and the board chose to do. At the suggestion of Betty Johnson, the *Globe* article was sent to the trustees from the national development fund office under Johnson's initials. "The idea here," Adams told Holland after talking with Johnson, "is not to involve the President in the actual fighting on the battlefield but to keep a general's position on the hillside overlooking the maneuvers of the troops."[39]

The board's statement on receipt of the report sounded very much like Holland. At the meeting on March 22, the board voted to receive "with enthusiastic appreciation the report of the Commission, commending the Commission for the precision with which it has identified major areas of development and concern." The enthusiasm applied to much of the report: "The Board is impressed by the consistent emphasis on excellence of education and particularly the education of women. It is excited by the suggestion for change in curriculum and teaching methods. It commends the priority placed on an improved program of counseling. It notes with approval the reaffirmation of the College's commitment to minority groups on campus."

But when it came to coeducation, the tone of the board's response changed: "The Commission's recommendations concerning men as undergraduates at Wellesley have been thoughtfully evolved and must be given an equally thoughtful consideration by the Board of Trustees. . . . The Board commits itself to instigate orderly and expedient procedures for consideration of and action upon all of the Commission's recommendations by both its own members and other appropriate elements of the College community."[40]

39 Memorandum, Ruth M. Adams to Mr. Holland, Mar. 9, 1971, Adams, Box 13, Folder Commission on the Future of the College: Report, 1970–71.

40 Minutes, Special Meeting of the Board of Trustees, Mar. 22, 1971, Wellesley trustees, Folder Minutes of the Full Board and Executive Committee, 1970–71 (Jan. 21, 1971–Apr. 15, 1971). The board's action was reported in a memorandum from Ruth M. Adams to Members of the Wellesley College Community, Mar. 23, 1971, as well as in the preface to the published *Report of the Commission on the Future of Wellesley College*, p. 1, both in Adams, Box 13, Folder Commission on the Future of the College: Report, 1970–71.

Among alumnae, Adams's dissent drew strong support. "I . . . congratulate you with all my heart on your 'appended statement,'" wrote an alumna in the class of 1926 from Needham, Massachusetts. "I shout my admiration of your wisdom and your leadership."[41] A graduate of the class of 1913 in Hamden, Connecticut, echoed, "I heartily endorse your statement as to the wisdom of granting Wellesley degrees to men."[42] From a member of the class of 1960 in New York City: "I am proud that you had the courage to reassert Wellesley's commitment to women."[43] A member of the class of 1939 sent a succinct telegram from Washington, D.C.: "Hurrah for your defense . . . for New England tradition of feminine independence."[44] Adams wrote, in response, "It is nice to know that one is not too solitary in holding such a position."[45]

The board of trustees convened on April 14–15 to act on the report. The trustees met with interested students and faculty to hear their views. They talked at length with members of the commission. And they talked among themselves, in a thoughtful exploration of the key issues, including the pros and cons of educating women in all-female and coeducational environments and the possible mechanisms for increasing the interaction between Wellesley students and their male counterparts.[46] On April 15 the board "affirm[ed] as general college policy the basic commitments outlined" in the report; referred to the appropriate campus policy-making groups the recommendations with respect to the educational program, the

41 Elizabeth R. Payne to Ruth Adams, Mar. 24, 1971, Adams, Box 13, Folder Commission on the Future of the College: Correspondence, 1969–1973.

42 Marian Corliss Spencer to Ruth Adams, Mar. 26, 1971, Adams, Box 13, Folder Commission on the Future of the College: Correspondence, 1969–1973. In the same folder, on the same theme, see also Anne Paulsen Scheibner to Adams, Apr. 6, 1971.

43 Peggy Powell to Ruth Adams, n.d. [Apr. 1971], Adams, Box 13, Folder Commission on the Future of the College: Correspondence, 1969–1973.

44 Telegram, Marjorie Ashcroft Wilson to Ruth Adams, Mar. 30, 1971, Adams, Box 13, Folder Commission on the Future of the College: Correspondence, 1969–1973.

45 See, e.g., Ruth M. Adams to Mrs. Will Wilson, Jr. [Marjorie Ashcroft Wilson], Apr. 1, 1971, Adams, Box 13, Folder Commission on the Future of the College: Correspondence, 1969–73.

46 Notes Taken at Meeting of the Board of Trustees, Apr. 14, 1971, and Trustee Comments, Apr. 15, 1971, attached to Minutes, Board of Trustees Meeting, Apr. 15, 1971, both in Wellesley trustees, Folder Minutes of the Full Board and Executive Committee, 1970–71 (Jan. 21, 1971–Apr. 15, 1971).

education of women, counseling, and minorities; and asked the president to report regularly to the board on action taken on those recommendations.

As for the critical issue of coeducation, "After a lengthy and very thoughtful series of discussions about the appropriate role for the College in American higher education, the Board voted unanimously to reaffirm the primary commitment of Wellesley College to the education of women and to indicate the Board's support for exchange programs which would bring male students to the campus." A motion to approve the recommendation of the commission that degrees be granted to men was defeated.[47]

The board's decision drew appreciative comments from alumnae. A member of the class of 1944 from Brunswick, Maine, spoke for many of her fellow graduates: "I am so proud of Wellesley for having the courage to remain a women's college," she wrote. "It's not that I disapprove of coeducation—it's just that I value more the College's willingness to stand for something, and not be just another follower."[48]

On campus, however, the board's decision caused a furor. In a blistering editorial, the *Wellesley News* called it "Noeducation." The paper asked, "What made us come this close and then shy away? . . . Certainly part of the problem was the students' failure to confront the Board of Trustees. Perhaps the trustees felt that the college was maintaining academic excellence as a single sex school, and since there seemed to be no objection to this state, there was no reason to alter it." The result would be "the creation of an alternative shelter for women who cannot face the competition for admission to coeducational schools, or for women who need four years of confidence-boosting." The editorial raised further questions: "Are we really this frightened that men will take over? Do we have this little faith in Wellesley's commitment to women?" If Wellesley declined to change, the paper said, continuing to run "at

47 Memorandum, Nelson J. Darling, Jr., to Members of the Wellesley College Community, Apr. 16, 1971, Adams, Box 12, Folder Commission on the Future of the College: Coeducation, 1968–73.

48 Margaret Dunlop to Ruth Adams, May 3, 1971, Adams, Box 13, Folder Commission on the Future of the College: Correspondence, 1969–73.

the same rate while every other college is running faster," it was sure to "lose out in the end."[49]

The following week, a columnist for the *Wellesley News* wrote a long account criticizing the inadequacy of the board's consultation with faculty and students. Why, when so many of the commission's other recommendations had been referred to the academic council for action, had coeducation been treated differently? Surely it, too, was an educational issue that ought to be in the purview of that group.[50] In a long letter published in the same issue of the newspaper, three student members of the commission called on the board to hold formal discussions with faculty and students and reconsider their decision after such discussions had taken place.[51]

The Faculty Backlash

The faculty made plain their dismay that the board had acted before the academic council had had the opportunity for formal discussion of the report. As a faculty petition put it, no matter where they stood on degrees for men, numerous faculty members were "deeply disturbed" that the board had acted "without an adequate representation of faculty opinion." The signatories to the petition—some 70 percent of the faculty, including members who had served on the commission—asked the president to call a special meeting of the council for April 29 for a formal discussion of the commission report.[52]

At that meeting the faculty approved, by a vote of 85 in favor to 7 opposed, with 8 abstentions, a resolution "respectfully request[ing] that the Board of Trustees refer questions relating to fundamental aspects of educational policy to the Academic Council for formal debate before making its decisions on these matters."

49 "Noeducation," *Wellesley News*, Apr. 22, 1971, p. 2, Wellesley College Library.

50 *Wellesley News*, Apr. 29, 1971, p. 2.

51 Letter from Joan Lister, Page Talbott, and Louisa Kasdon, in *Wellesley News*, Apr. 29, 1971, p. 3.

52 The undated, untitled petitions, signed in Apr. 1971 by 124 members of the faculty, are in Adams, Box 12, Folder Commission on the Future of the College: Coeducation, 1968–1973.

There was discussion about the board's decision. The point was made that "few members of the faculty [had] availed themselves of the opportunity [that had been offered] to meet with groups from the Board of Trustees," a comment countered by the observation that those meetings were scheduled on Wednesday afternoon, when many faculty members had classes and labs, and by the insistence that even full attendance at those meetings "would not in any way have been a substitute for the kind of debate which ought to take place in Academic Council." The president observed that the trustees had the authority to take the action they took and followed appropriate procedure.

A faculty member moved that "immediate steps should be taken for the College to acquire the legal capacity to grant degrees to men" and that the board should be asked to reconsider their position. Spirited discussion followed. The motion passed by a vote of 67 in favor to 27 opposed, with 9 abstentions. Another motion, asking the board to send the council an account of the reasons for their vote against granting degrees to men, failed to gain a second. The president agreed that no matter how the reconsideration came out, she would ask the trustees for a statement of the reasons for their decision.[53]

A subsequent memo to the trustees signed by 48 faculty members opposed to granting degrees to men said that the vote in the April 29 meeting "was not representative of the opinion of faculty (who number approximately 175) not only because of unavoidable absences but because it was taken in an open meeting of Academic Council."[54]

In May ten faculty members circulated a survey to their colleagues to seek information about where they stood on coeducation at Wellesley. It might have been assumed that such information

53 Minutes, Special Meeting of Academic Council, Apr. 29, 1971, Adams, Box 12, Folder Commission on the Future of the College: Coeducation, 1968–73. For Adams's report to the trustees, see minutes, Executive Committee of the Board of Trustees, May 13, 1971, Wellesley trustees, Folder Minutes of the Full Board and Executive Committee, 1970–71 (May 13, 1971–June 5, 1971).

54 Memo to the Trustees, n.d., but May 1971, attached to Elizabeth S. Blake to Ruth Adams, May 17, 1971, Adams, Box 12, Folder Commission on the Future of the College: Coeducation, 1968–73.

had already been gathered in the course of the commission's work, but this group felt that faculty discussion of coeducation was just beginning.[55] When the returns came in, with a 92 percent response rate, the consensus was that Wellesley should "define a clear set of programs and policies embodying a commitment to women and in that context . . . grant degrees to a limited number of men." Making this "new commitment to women" was seen as the sensible middle ground between "stand[ing] still" (as the position of the trustees was interpreted) and "becom[ing] coeducational in the traditional manner."[56]

At the same time, a different group of a dozen faculty members sent the faculty a set of proposals about "a plan of action which aims toward an eventual mixed-sex college but without abandoning Wellesley's commitment to women." They called their ideal "the new coeducation"—"the education of men and women together in a context of genuine equality." Wellesley would work over the next four years to develop "women's full sense of their individual worth" through intellectual challenge and efforts to combat the social conditioning that relegated women to the status of the "second sex." Wellesley would become "a living laboratory for women's education into full social and psychological, as well as intellectual, equality with men." Once those goals had been accomplished and the college's centennial celebration concluded, it would be time to ask the trustees to reconsider their stance on gaining legal authority to grant degrees to men. Within a decade after that, the college would "attain . . . a fully mixed student body" with "a new form of coeducation" emphasizing "the fullest possible development of each individual," with none of the old social conditioning of men and women about relative sex roles.[57] As a faculty member who participated in both groups explained to Adams, the point was to

55 Lilian Anderson et al. to Faculty Member, May 11, 1971, Adams, Box 13, Folder Commission on the Future of the College: Correspondence, 1969–73. There are detailed handwritten tallies of the responses to the many questions in the survey.

56 Lilian Anderson et al. to Dear Faculty Member, May 28, 1971, Adams, Box 12, Folder Commission on the Future of the College: Coeducation, 1968–73.

57 Memo to Dear Colleague, May 1971, attached to Elizabeth S. Blake to Ruth Adams, May 17, 1971, Adams, Box 12, Folder Commission on the Future of the College: Coeducation, 1968–1973.

do something about the "stand-off position into which the faculty and the Trustees seem to have gotten themselves" by "seek[ing] a positive stance for the College, some kind of rallying ideal."[58]

The Board's Response to Faculty Proposals

In June, after considering the motions approved by the academic council on April 29, the board approved a statement that Adams was asked to transmit to the council. The statement began: "The Board of Trustees wishes to record its regret that its decision not to grant degrees to men was viewed by many members of Academic Council as a failure to observe the proper and reinforcing roles of the Academic Council and the Board of Trustees." The board went on to make a number of specific observations. It had "sought to elicit opinions and reactions from all concerned individuals and groups," and it intended to continue "to seek to obtain the views of members of the college community" before it acted on any major issues. Recognizing that there could be a time in the future when "changed circumstances" might "dictate reexamination of the matter of granting degrees to men," the board felt strongly "the need for certainty, for a clear-cut, unequivocal position" that could guide planning in the years immediately ahead. Thus it judged that "it would be a grave mistake to reopen the question at this time."

Along with the statement came a detailed account of the board's deliberations in April, explaining the rationale for their decision that "Wellesley should remain a college granting degrees only to women." The board had raised the many concerns, questions, and contentions that had been discussed at length in the commission and the academic council. They had noted the absence of hard data or any body of research to support the case for or against coeducation. Focusing on "educational rather than social justifications for a change in the constitution of the student body," they had come

---

58 Elizabeth S. Blake to Ruth Adams, May 17, 1971, Adams, Box 12, Folder Commission on the Future of the College: Coeducation, 1968–73.

to the view that "the belief that coeducation was superior to single sex education remained not proven."[59]

Ironically, given the strong opposition of the *Wellesley News* to the board's decision, the paper later came around to support it. The intensification of the women's liberation movement doubtless played a role. In March 1973, in a front-page editorial, the paper said, "NEWS is convinced that until women are fully accepted as equals to men—not by law, but by custom—and until women receive the same job opportunities, wages and prestige as men, there is a vital role for women's colleges. As long as women are kept off Boards of trustees, out of jobs and in hot pants, the world needs a Wellesley College." Wellesley was not a "cloister" for sheltered women; nor was it "'copping out' on coeducation." Rather, "Wellesley ha[d] recognized the **educational advantages** of an education without men." Women at schools like Wellesley were taken seriously as students and were trained to be leaders. "Women are not an afterthought at Wellesley," the editorial concluded. "Women belong here."[60]

The President's Departure from Wellesley for Dartmouth

In August 1971, Ruth Adams announced her intention to retire from the presidency of Wellesley in June 1972.[61] It had been a difficult presidency, and Adams had seemed singularly uncomfortable and ill equipped to be a truly effective leader. Unlike Margaret Clapp, who had fully inhabited the role, Adams had long since delegated all financial matters to her executive vice president, and she had been notably ill at ease in her dealings with students. She had been subject to withering criticism from some of Clapp's staunch alumnae supporters, who had found Adams's administrative style wanting by comparison.

59 Statement by the Board of Trustees, June 5, 1971, attached to Nelson J. Darling, Jr., to Ruth Adams, June 7, 1971, Adams, Box 12, Folder Commission on the Future of the College: Coeducation, 1968–1973.

60 "an editorial . . . ," *Wellesley News*, Mar. 15, 1973, p. 1.

61 Ruth M. Adams to Erwin D. Canham [member of the Wellesley board of trustees], Aug. 4, 1971; Adams to Members of the Wellesley College Community, Aug. 13, 1971, both in Adams, Box 26, Folder Adams, Ruth: Resignation, 1971–72.

Some of the most experienced, influential faculty members also had real questions about Adams's leadership—her investment in the role, the amount of time she was spending in the office, her vision, her ability to move the college forward. It appeared to many people that Philip Phibbs and the dean of the college, professor of physics Phyllis Fleming, were doing much of the work that the president would normally do.[62] In addition, with disputes over civil rights and Vietnam roiling the Wellesley campus, like so many others in the late 1960s, Adams, who personified the institution, inevitably absorbed a lot of the anger that the tumultuous times generated. All of these factors contributed to Adams's sense of insecurity about her position, her growing conviction that she was an outsider who was not fully embraced by the Wellesley community. Personal reasons added to her stress. Her father had died, and she had had two bouts of heart trouble, one of which took her to the hospital. With all of that, as Phibbs told the story, Adams was simply "physically and emotionally exhausted."[63]

In this context, the invitation that Dartmouth made to Adams provided a welcome transition out of a job that she had come to find deeply uncomfortable. In January 1972, Adams told the Wellesley trustees that she would be moving to Hanover that summer to take up a new vice presidential position, where—ironically—she would help Dartmouth with the implementation of coeducation.[64] "I do not identify myself as getting out of education for women," she told the *Wellesley News*. "Dartmouth is serious about going coed in a sophisticated way. The college is committed not just for social reasons, but wants really to offer superior education to women. If I can be of help, I'll help to realize their desire to do an excellent job."[65]

In April 1972, the trustees elected Barbara W. Newell, a Vassar alumna who was associate provost for graduate study and research

62 Phibbs interview; telephone interview with Mary Lefkowitz, Aug. 23, 2013; e-mail, Dorothea Widmayer to Nancy Weiss Malkiel, Sept. 2, 2013.

63 Phibbs interview.

64 Minutes, Board of Trustees, Jan. 20, 1972, Wellesley trustees, Folder Minutes of the Full Board and Executive Committee, 1971–72 (Sept. 8, 1971–Jan. 20, 1972).

65 Adams, quoted in "Adams as Dartmouth VP to Work on Coeducation," *Wellesley News*, Feb. 10, 1972, p. 3.

and professor of economics at the University of Pittsburgh, as the tenth president of Wellesley College, effective September 1, 1972. In the interim between Adams's departure for Dartmouth on July 1 and Newell's arrival, Phibbs served as acting president of the college.[66] As Wellesley legend has it, during Phibbs's tenure— "the only two months" that a man has ever been president of the college—lightning struck the tower of the principal administration building, Green Hall, "the main [architectural] feature of the Wellesley landscape."[67]

For her part, Newell—benefiting importantly from the influence of the women's movement—made a very public point of reaffirming the college's determination to remain all-female, a commitment renewed by the board of trustees in January 1973. "Coeducation has failed," she asserted in announcing the board's decision. "Women coeds receive conflicting signals on the 'femininity' of intellectual vigor and do not take full advantage of college. The current trend toward coeducation has increased, rather than lessened, male domination of American higher education, I fear." She continued, "It is naïve to believe that any movement for educational equity for women can come out of such colleges and universities. This leadership will have to be sustained by colleges like Wellesley which not only resist the trend toward coeducation but affirm the need for equal education for women."[68]

66 Minutes, Board of Trustees, Apr. 20, 1972, Wellesley trustees, Folder Minutes of the Full Board and Executive Committee, 1971–72 (Feb. 11, 1972–June 3, 1972). In the summer of 1972, Phibbs left Wellesley to become president of the University of Puget Sound in Tacoma, Washington. See University of Puget Sound news release, June 24, 1972, Adams, Box 25, Folder Phibbs, Philip, 1971–72; "Phibbs to Leave to Become Univ. Pres.," *Wellesley News*, Sept. 14, 1972, p. 1.

67 I am indebted for this observation to Nannerl O. Keohane, Barbara Newell's successor as president of Wellesley.

68 Quoted in "Wellesley Says It Won't Go Coed," *New York Times*, Mar. 9, 1973, p. 43. On the effect of the women's movement, see "Coed Status Pleases Vassar Despite Problems," *New York Times*, Nov. 19, 1974, p. 45.

Part III

Revisiting the Ivies: Dartmouth

19

Dartmouth: "For God's Sake, for Everyone's Sake, Keep the Damned Women Out"

When Princeton and Yale admitted women, Dartmouth became the only Ivy League school without a coordinate women's college or plans to coeducate. As the competitive landscape changed, the numbers of applications to Dartmouth declined. The pressures that made coeducation the logical outcome at other institutions operated at Dartmouth as well. At the same time, the virtues of an all-male community were celebrated more assertively at Dartmouth than anywhere else. Compared with its peer institutions, Dartmouth took longer and followed a more torturous path to a conclusion about the right steps to take with respect to the education of women. And it did so without the forceful leadership of a decisive president in strong partnership with a willing board that had served Princeton and Yale so well.

When Dartmouth finally came to a decision, it combined the by-then-conventional move to coeducation with an unexpected twist: expanding enrollment by using a summer term and rethinking the normal sequence of eight consecutive terms in residence—an educational innovation not imagined or attempted by any of its peers.

The Dartmouth *Stirs the Pot*

As at its peer institutions, the possibility of coeducation at Dartmouth was first broached by the student newspaper, which played the multiple roles of looking for news to report, creating news, and agitating, even if quietly, for institutional change. In the fall of 1959, *The Dartmouth* sponsored a panel discussion on the subject among administrators, faculty, and students. It was well understood that coeducation was not on Dartmouth's agenda. The president, John Sloan Dickey, had made that plain in April 1958 when he declared, "There is no possibility of coeducation at the College in the foreseeable future."[1] But *The Dartmouth*, like any student newspaper, liked to stir the pot, and sponsoring the panel discussion served that purpose nicely. The principal themes of that discussion were then presented in a series of articles in the paper in early January 1960. The panelists, who were divided on the merits of the case, addressed the academic and social benefits of coeducation, the likely effects of coeducation on various aspects of life at Dartmouth, and the feasibility of instituting coeducation.[2] Interviewing other students and faculty members in the wake of the series, the newspaper again found divided opinions about whether coeducation would be good for the college.[3]

The Dartmouth next addressed the issue of coeducation in 1965. In the winter, it printed letters from students on both sides of the debate.[4] In the spring, the paper reported on a poll of undergraduates that revealed a 50–50 split on the desirability of bringing women students to Hanover. Opponents of coeducation claimed that it would be at odds with the camaraderie and spirit, the cherished traditions, of the all-male college—in short, that it would destroy the very characteristics that made Dartmouth distinctive. Supporters said that the all-male environment was "unnatural and harmful." As one student put it, "This place isn't real."[5] *The*

---

1 *The Dartmouth*, Apr. 7, 1958, quoted in Siobhan Gorman, "Perfume in the Paper: *The Dartmouth*'s Coverage of the College's Decision to Coeducate," p. 2, paper written for History 13, Mar. 14, 1997, Dartmouth College, Dartmouth College Library.

2 *The Dartmouth*, Jan. 6–9, 1960, Women at Dartmouth, Box 6593.

3 Ibid., Jan. 12, 13, 15, and 16, 1960.

4 Joanna Henderson Sternick, "'Lest the Old Traditions Fail': A Chronicle of the Coming of Women to Dartmouth," ch. 6, pp. 11–14, independent study project, Nov. 1973, Higher Education Center, University of Massachusetts, Amherst, Rauner Special Collections Library, Dartmouth College.

5 *The Dartmouth*, Apr. 7, 1965, Women at Dartmouth, Box 6593.

Dartmouth's survey of alumni and faculty found, not surprisingly, that alumni were generally opposed to coeducation, whereas members of the faculty were for it.[6] A series of interviews with administrators followed, again with arguments offered pro and con.[7]

Women Come to Hanover: Early Experiences

Dartmouth first began to get some practical experience with undergraduate women in the summer of 1963, when the college initiated a credit-bearing summer academic term for students, including women, from Dartmouth and other colleges and universities. With a temperate climate and easy access to mountains and lakes, New Hampshire was a particularly appealing summer destination. Running a summer term was a good way to use the college's facilities for productive purposes—and to make some money in the process.[8]

At the same time, Dartmouth students began to devise programs to bring women students to campus during the academic year. In March 1967, nearly four hundred women from Colby Junior College, Mt. Holyoke, Smith, and Wellesley came for what the Dartmouth student organizers called "The Great Day" of coeducational book discussions and social activities.[9] In May 1967, a student committee for coeducation organized to press for the introduction of some form of coeducation. The students imagined a range of possibilities, from an exchange program with a women's college to the establishment of an autonomous women's college nearby to the establishment of a coordinate women's college where students would take courses at Dartmouth and, finally, to the admission of women to Dartmouth.[10] That same month, the

6 Ibid., Apr. 8, 1965.

7 Ibid., Apr. 9, 12, and 15, 1965.

8 Ibid., Sept. 24, Oct. 11, and Nov. 20, 1962, and May 22, 1963, and "The Feminine Touch . . . ," *Dartmouth Alumni Magazine*, Oct. 1965, all in Women at Dartmouth, Box 6593.

9 *The Dartmouth*, Mar. 3, 1967, Women at Dartmouth, Box 6592; "Great Day," *Dartmouth Alumni Magazine*, Apr. 1967, Women at Dartmouth, Box 6593.

10 *The Dartmouth*, May 22, 1967, Women at Dartmouth, Box 6593.

graduating class established a fund for the promotion of coeducation at the college.[11]

In January 1968, the student committee for coeducation brought two hundred women students from Mt. Holyoke for Dartmouth's version of coed week—five days of attending classes and special lectures, participating in extracurricular and social activities, and engaging in discussions about coeducation.[12] At the closing forum, the dean of the college, Thaddeus Seymour, said, "The question is no longer whether Dartmouth should go coeducational, but when and how."[13] In April 1968, the committee issued a report calling for experimentation with forms of coeducation, to include the admission of up to thirty students from women's colleges as "special transfer students" to a more structured program in which women students could come to the college for a term to fill beds vacant because of increasing numbers of men taking time off to study elsewhere for a limited period.[14] The following September, seven women, on leave from their own colleges, matriculated at Dartmouth as special students in drama, a step thought likely to alleviate the problem of finding women to participate in theater productions staged by the drama department and the Dartmouth Players.[15]

In January 1969, a second coed week brought nearly a thousand women students to campus, this time from eighteen colleges and universities, including Mt. Holyoke, Smith, Vassar, and Wellesley.[16] In the words of one Smith student, "This wasn't co-education at all! This was a super-mixer." Another student remarked, "It was really fun. . . . The whole week was great—but the intellectual

11 Ibid., May 26, 1967.

12 Ibid., Jan. 24, 1968, Women at Dartmouth, Box 6592; ibid., Jan. 26, 29, and 31, 1968, Women at Dartmouth, Box 6593.

13 Quoted in Charles E. Widmayer, *John Sloan Dickey: A Chronicle of His Presidency of Dartmouth College* (Dartmouth College, 1991; distributed by University Press of New England, Hanover, NH, and London), p. 244.

14 *The Dartmouth*, Apr. 15 and 18, 1968, Women at Dartmouth, Box 6593.

15 Trustee Study Committee, Report to the Alumni Council, Jan. 15, 1971, Dickey, Box 8432; Sternick, "'Lest the Old Traditions Fail,'" ch. 6, p. 30.

16 *The Dartmouth*, Dec. 3, 1968, Jan. 21, 27, and Feb. 19, 1969, Women at Dartmouth, Box 6593; ibid., Jan. 10 and 23, 1969; and "COED WEEK: A Taste of the Future?," *Dartmouth Alumni Magazine*, Mar. 1969, all in Women at Dartmouth, Box 6592.

plane wasn't too high." Students held parties in their rooms, and fraternities held socials. Each day a Dartmouth student drew the name of a visiting student out of a barrel and escorted her to dinner. In an introductory psychology class, the instructor lectured on the topic "After Orgasm, What?" Dartmouth Indians, dressed in full regalia, invaded the lecture hall and took some female visitors captive.[17] "It has become evident," *The Dartmouth* declared, "that Dartmouth must become coeducational. It is our opinion that the sooner the better."[18]

John Sloan Dickey Establishes an Exploratory Committee

The principal engine for consideration of coeducation at Dartmouth turned out to be the Dartmouth campus conference, a multipartite group of trustees, administrators, faculty, and students convened by Dickey in September 1968 "to discuss matters of common interest about the College." With no functional student government at Dartmouth and with protests roiling campuses around the country, Dickey decided to establish a forum where students could have "more of a voice in the conduct of College affairs" and where concerns of all sorts could be aired in a calm, non-confrontational setting. Topics ranged broadly, from college governance and budget and financial matters to residential life. Not surprisingly, given the temper of the times, the campus conference also began discussing the prospect of coeducation for Dartmouth. In January 1969, the campus conference adopted a resolution calling coeducation "a subject of top priority" and asking the trustees to appoint a special committee to study it.[19]

It was in this context that in February 1969 Dartmouth's trustee executive committee announced a formal study of the possibility of educating women at Dartmouth. The study committee, led by the chairman of the executive committee, Dudley W. Orr '39, in partnership with the provost and dean of the faculty

---

17 *Sophian*, Feb. 13, 1969, Box 17, Smith College Archives.
18 Quoted in Widmayer, *John Sloan Dickey*, p. 263.
19 Ibid., pp. 258, 261–62.

of arts and sciences, professor of physics Leonard M. Rieser '44, included other trustees, members of the faculty, undergraduates, administrators, and alumni.[20] Its charge was to examine the full range of Dartmouth's commitments for the 1970s "with particular attention to . . . the question of the education of women in the college."[21]

As background for the study, Dickey prepared a memo to help the trustees "see the matter in a full-bodied way." It was the first document about coeducation at Dartmouth, he said, that took the matter "as something meriting and requiring analysis and study rather than a campaign of polemical avowals."[22] Dickey himself would not be seeing the coeducation study through to its conclusion. Now in his twenty-fourth year in office, he had announced that he would retire from the Dartmouth presidency sometime during the college's bicentennial year, 1969–70. The wisdom he shared with the trustees was simply that, wisdom born of a long and successful presidency.[23]

"The decisive question," Dickey began, "is whether a 'policy commitment' now to coeducation would significantly increase or limit Dartmouth's total institutional capacity to be a top-quality enterprise of higher education during the foreseeable future." The studies made at other institutions would provide helpful background, but Dartmouth was distinctive, and it was essential to identify and give full weight to "singular factors of time and circumstance in the Dartmouth situation" and to engage in the closest possible examination of "all the concrete plusses and minuses" in order to arrive at a sustainable recommendation. The college's other plans and aspirations needed to be taken into account. So did the importance of maintaining a male student population of sufficient size to enable Dartmouth to continue to compete athletically in the Ivy League.[24]

20 Dartmouth College news release, Feb. 19, 1969, Dickey, Box 7195.

21 Trustee Study Committee, Report to the Alumni Council, Jan. 15, 1971.

22 John Sloan Dickey, "The Coeducation Study," Feb. 4, 1969; Dickey to Dudley W. Orr, Feb. 4, 1969 (source of the quotes), both in Dickey, Box 7195.

23 Widmayer, *John Sloan Dickey*, p. 256.

24 Dickey, "The Coeducation Study."

Responding to a question about coeducation in an interview in *YANKEE* magazine, Dickey said, "I don't believe that co-education here is inevitable, nor is it necessarily wrong. I do urge that it should be examined in relation to all other commitments Dartmouth sees ahead for the next decade. I think we must have concrete answers as to whether Dartmouth's limited resources and limited energies if directed towards the education of women would create a stronger institution than if they were directed to other new programs."[25]

As the work of the study committee went forward, there was much discussion on campus about the desirability of bringing women to Dartmouth. And, for the first time, there were significant numbers of women on campus, thanks to the inauguration in the fall of 1969 of the Ten- (expanded in 1970 to Twelve-) College Exchange, the venture described earlier that enabled students from a group of women's colleges and a group of men's colleges to spend a semester or a year at one of the other colleges. The participating institutions were all relatively small and, in the main, geographically relatively remote. There was typically more interest among women in going to men's colleges than among men in going to women's colleges. In the first year of the exchange, 70 women students came to Dartmouth for the year, with 15 Dartmouth men leaving to study at some of the women's colleges.[26] The number of women coming to Dartmouth increased to 75 in 1970, and the number of men leaving grew to 45.[27] In 1971, 150 women came to Dartmouth.[28]

One of the women students who came on the Twelve-College Exchange, who would later graduate from Dartmouth and be elected to the board of trustees, called the exchange students "a Trojan horse in [the] midst" of Dartmouth's opponents of coeducation:

25 Statement by President Dickey, n.d., Dickey, Box 8432; Dickey quoted in A. Alexander Fanelli to Mayo Johnson, Nov. 7, 1969, Dickey, Box 7200.

26 *The Dartmouth*, Sept. 25, 1969, Women at Dartmouth, Box 6592; ibid., Feb. 21, 1969; "Coed Exchange," *Dartmouth Alumni Magazine*, Nov. 1969, both in Women at Dartmouth, Box 6593.

27 Trustee Study Committee, Report to the Alumni Council, Jan. 15, 1971.

28 John G. Kemeny to Donald E. Wilbur, July 21, 1971, Kemeny, Box 8449; Dartmouth College news release, Nov. 22, 1971, Coed III.

"Full time undergraduates, dormed on Massachusetts Row, women taking the final exams in math, raising their hands in economics and philosophy classes, playing basketball in the gym, hosting talk shows on WDCR. Truth be told, the women had arrived. . . . And we were not going to leave without a fight."[29]

The work of the study committee unfolded over a period of years, much longer than Dickey had anticipated. In an interim report to the board of trustees and the Dartmouth alumni council in December 1969, Dudley Orr, Leonard Rieser, and one of the faculty members serving on the committee, professor of mathematics John G. Kemeny, explained how they were proceeding. They had three reasons to be studying coeducation, Orr said. "First, it is part of the tradition of Dartmouth College to respond to the aspirations and values of the society of which it is a part." By 1969, "19 out of 20 college-age men and women in America [were] in coeducational institutions." Orr continued, "Coeducation is the rule . . . we are the exception." In order to "maintain its eminence," Dartmouth had to "consider the possibility of coeducation as part of its formal educational program."

The second reason for studying coeducation was student and faculty support for it. The third reason was that Dartmouth's principal competitors had "gone into the business."[30] As Orr told the alumni council, "If you're in the milk business and all of your competitors start making ice cream, perhaps you ought to look into the ice cream business, as well."[31] With Princeton and Yale having embraced coeducation, Dartmouth was compelled to see what might be in it for them—and what the consequences might be one way or the other for Dartmouth's ability to attract the best students to the college. That did not mean, as Rieser pointed out, that Dartmouth had to go coeducational, but it did mean that they could not ignore the competition.[32]

29 Kate Stith-Cabranes '73, quoted in *Claiming Their Rightful Place: Coeducation at Dartmouth, 1972–1997* (Dartmouth College, 1997), p. 7, Dartmouth College Library.

30 "The Pros and Cons of Coeducation," *Dartmouth Alumni Magazine*, Feb. 1970, p. 33, Women at Dartmouth, Box 6592.

31 Orr, quoted in Dartmouth Alumni Council Bulletin, Dec. 30, 1969, typescript, Jan. 26, 1970, Cmsn. Future College, Box 1, Folder Commission: Studies: Dartmouth.

32 "The Pros and Cons of Coeducation," p. 33.

Kemeny, too, stressed what he called the "extremely tight and highly competitive market" in which Dartmouth was operating. Dartmouth was now unique among Ivy League schools as the only all-male institution. Was that an advantage or a disadvantage? The study committee would be gathering information to speak to the question. Kemeny pointed to a survey done the previous January, which showed that 84 percent of undergraduate respondents favored coeducation and that 53 percent would not advise a younger brother to go to an all-male Dartmouth. Students, Kemeny said, longed for more normal, less strained relationships with women than could be achieved during hectic weekend visits. Faculty members testified about the benefits to classroom discussion when men and women studied together. Alumni, on the other hand, argued that spending four years in an all-male environment contributed to Dartmouth's great success in training leaders. Then there was the question of cost: Could Dartmouth afford coeducation? The committee needed to take all these issues into account, and subcommittees were at work on detailed analyses on which a recommendation might be based.[33]

1970: John Kemeny Becomes President of Dartmouth

In January 1970, Kemeny, a member of the Dartmouth faculty since 1953, was named to succeed Dickey as president, effective March 1, 1970.[34] He had seen himself as an unlikely choice for the post because he was both a Hungarian immigrant who still had a pronounced foreign accent and a Jew, and no Ivy League institution had ever appointed a president who was either foreign-born or Jewish. A Princeton-educated mathematician, Kemeny had chaired the mathematics department at Dartmouth, but his principal scholarly contributions had come in the new field of computer science, where he was best known as the co-inventor in 1964 of the programming language BASIC.

Kemeny did not start out as a proponent of coeducation at Dartmouth. He said later that he "had never sat down to think

33 Ibid., pp. 35ff.
34 *The Dartmouth*, Jan. 27 and Feb. 2, 1970, Women at Dartmouth, Box 6593.

through whether it was good for young men to spend the ages 18–22 in an all-male environment." Although he "certainly believed in equal opportunities for women," he was "still prepared to accept the argument that if we wanted to train leaders, they had to learn how to succeed in a 'Man's world.'"[35]

All of that changed, he said, in the 1960s, as "women were assuming an increasing number of leadership positions in many fields" and as male students came to Dartmouth "not because it was all-male, but in spite of it." Complaining that they saw women students only in the context of "high-pressure weekend dating relations," male students said that they yearned for informal interactions that would permit "a long conversation" during the week "over a soft drink."[36] Moreover, alumni whom Kemeny had gotten to know well often told him privately that "while in many ways they loved Dartmouth, Dartmouth had had a very negative impact on them as far as relations with women are concerned." By that they meant "never having learned how to have easy, friendly relations with women and being shy with them, or over-aggressive"—a lack of experience that had had "a strongly distorting effect on their lives."[37] Kemeny worried that in sustaining an all-male institution "there was a strong danger that we'd be turning out a generation of male chauvinist pigs who would not be able to work with women as equals in the professions."[38] By 1969 he "was convinced that coeducation was essential for Dartmouth."[39]

Although Kemeny favored coeducation, he was savvy enough, in light of his appointment to the presidency, not to be heavy-handed in pushing his own views. What he said, in committee and publicly, was that if one were setting out to found a college like Dartmouth in the latter part of the twentieth century, it would surely be coeducational, but that in coming to any decision one

---

35 Typescript, John G. Kemeny, "A Mathematician's Journey," n.d., "1969," pp. 5–6, Kemeny personal, Box 20, Folder 3.

36 Ibid., p. 6.

37 John Kemeny oral history, p. 92.

38 Ibid.

39 Kemeny, "A Mathematician's Journey," "1969," p. 6.

needed to take account of two hundred years of Dartmouth's all-male history and traditions.[40]

The Committee Surveys Its Constituents

In April 1970, the study committee announced plans for a survey of Dartmouth undergraduates, alumni, faculty, and administrators.[41] The poll offered multiple options: the status quo, with about thirty-two hundred male undergraduates and a small number of visiting women exchange students each year; identifying a sister school, an existing women's college not within commuting distance of Hanover, and setting up "massive exchanges" wherein students would spend at least three semesters at the other institution; expansion, keeping the same number of men and adding a thousand women students, with concomitant increases in faculty and facilities; more fully using existing capacity to allow the admission of a significant number of women without reducing the number of men or expanding staff and physical plant; and coeducation within the size of the existing student body, which would mean reducing the number of men to allow for a desirable ratio of men to women.[42]

The opinion survey of a selected sample of Dartmouth alumni was undertaken by the polling expert Oliver Quayle '42, whose firm conducted lengthy interviews with 1,005 alumni in May 1970. Alumni were asked about coeducation as well as a range of other issues relating to the college. Alumni preferred having women going to school nearby, without any direct link to the college, over having Dartmouth take any responsibility for the education of women. If Dartmouth were to take some responsibility, some form of coordinate education was clearly preferred to having women actually enroll at the college. Alumni were most receptive to the idea that a free-standing women's college might be established within a few miles of Dartmouth. The next-best

40 Minutes, Trustee Study Committee, Mar. 2, 1970, Kemeny, Box 8436; *The Dartmouth*, Feb. 2, 1970, Women at Dartmouth, Box 6593.
41 *The Dartmouth*, Apr. 13, 1970, Women at Dartmouth, Box 6593.
42 Ibid., Apr. 23, 1970.

idea was that an existing women's college might relocate to the Hanover area.

The alternative that Dartmouth would be directly involved in women's education, either by establishing its own women's college nearby or by allowing women students to matriculate directly at Dartmouth, generated significantly more reservations. Kemeny later summed up the results this way: Some 60 percent of the respondents were willing to entertain "the education of women at Dartmouth *in some form*," but "no specific plan could come close to mustering majority support." Moreover, "Of the 40 percent of the alumni who were opposed to any form of coeducation, more than half had extremely strong feelings on the subject." Older alumni were most strongly opposed to coeducation; younger graduates were more receptive.[43]

As Kemeny later observed, there was "an interesting sidelight" to the views of alumni. When coeducation was discussed at alumni gatherings, wives of alumni were "more opposed to coeducation" than their husbands were. "The most plausible explanation," he said, came from his wife, Jean Alexander Kemeny, who hypothesized that "the wives may have felt that, had Dartmouth been coed, they might never have met their husbands."[44] (Jean Kemeny later told the same story, substituting one word: "If it [Dartmouth] were coeducational, maybe they wouldn't have been able to get their husbands."[45])

The survey of the student body, conducted in the spring of 1970, showed that 83 percent of respondents favored some form of coeducation. A majority said that they would not recommend an all-male Dartmouth to a qualified younger brother. In a poll of faculty and administrators conducted in late May 1970, 91 percent of

43 John G. Kemeny, "The First Five Years: A Report by the 13th President," *Dartmouth Alumni Magazine*, Apr. 1975, p. 11, Kemeny, Box 8474. For a detailed report on the survey and the findings, see Surveys of Dartmouth Opinion: A Special Supplement of the *Dartmouth Alumni Magazine*, Sept. 1970, Coed II. For a statistical summary that compares the results of this survey with the one conducted in December 1970 with alumni leaders, see Coeducation at Dartmouth: Opinions of Alumni and Alumni Officers, Jan. 1971, Coed II.

44 Kemeny, "A Mathematician's Journey," "Coeducation," p. 1.

45 Jean Kemeny oral history, p. 24.

faculty and 62 percent of administrators responding favored co-education.[46] Of the options with respect to coeducation, the two that garnered the most support were the establishment of a coordinate college for women in or near Hanover and the admission of women as degree candidates with a plan for off-campus or summer study so that the number of men would remain more or less constant and the total number of students on campus would not be increased.[47]

In a preliminary report to the board in June 1970, the study committee recommended that Dartmouth embark on the education of a significant number of women. American society was changing; young men and women had grown up going to school together, interacting socially, and learning to respect each other's rights and talents. Segregated education at the college level was out of sync with their experiences, expectations, and ambitions. What made Dartmouth attractive to students was its academic excellence, not that it was all-male. How long would young men continue to tolerate segregated education when they had other good choices?

"The demand for coeducation," the committee said, "stems from the fact that men and women from birth live together: as brothers and sisters, as schoolmates, as husbands and wives. . . . It becomes increasingly difficult to justify that at Dartmouth we choose as a matter of policy to isolate young men and women during their college years."[48]

In addition, the external environment was changing in ways that bore significantly on Dartmouth's capacity to attract the students it wanted. Dartmouth was the one Ivy League institution where applications had decreased for the classes of 1969 through 1974, and the yield on admitted students was declining. Some of the principal boarding schools that had traditionally sent students

---

46 Trustee Study Committee, Report to the Alumni Council, Jan. 15, 1971. Again, for a detailed report on the surveys and the findings, see Surveys of Dartmouth Opinion: A Special Supplement of the *Dartmouth Alumni Magazine*, Sept. 1970, Coed II.

47 Trustee Study Committee, Report to the Alumni Council, Jan. 15, 1971.

48 Trustee Study Committee, Introductory Statement, revised June 10, 1970, attached to Leonard M. Rieser to Members of the Trustee Study Committee, June 15, 1970, Dickey, Box 7200.

to Dartmouth—Andover, Exeter, Choate, St. Paul's—were themselves moving toward coeducation. "The likelihood," the trustee study committee observed, "that secondary school students who have been outstanding candidates for admission to Dartmouth will continue to enroll in an all male institution is now seriously open to question."[49]

The Investigation Continues

The mechanisms for accomplishing coeducation at Dartmouth were not fully worked out when the trustee study committee reported to the board in June 1970, but the committee's tentative recommendations included fuller use of the summer term and of exchanges, study abroad, and internships and other projects away from Hanover. The committee looked forward to a ratio of men to women of 3 to 1, to be achieved within the decade. The board asked the committee to return in the fall with more detailed plans, including studies by a newly constituted task force on the financial feasibility of models for realizing these recommendations.[50] Following the October board meeting, the further study became more focused as the task force on financial feasibility was directed to examine closely a model whereby the number of undergraduates on campus would stay constant at thirty-two hundred and the total number of matriculants would increase to thirty-six hundred, with the additional four hundred enrollments accommodated through more robust use of a summer term or expanded participation in off-campus education.[51]

In December 1970, when Kemeny sent a questionnaire to students asking their views on a variety of issues, 88 percent of the respondents said that they favored coeducation. Sixty-two percent said that they would be prepared to spend one summer in Hanover in order to make coeducation work financially; 81 percent

49 Trustee Study Committee, Report to the Alumni Council, Jan. 15, 1971.

50 Recommendations to the Board of Trustees from the Trustee Study Committee, attached to Leonard M. Rieser to Members of the Trustee Study Committee, June 15, 1970, Dickey, Box 7200.

51 Trustee Study Committee, Report to the Alumni Council, Jan. 15, 1971.

responded favorably to the notion of requiring a term of off-campus study.[52]

Another survey sent in December asked for opinions on coeducation from alumni leaders. The questions matched those posed in the Quayle survey in May. The results, based on 639 completed questionnaires, showed the political challenges of summoning support for the admission of women to Dartmouth. Although only 14 percent of the respondents said that a decision to make Dartmouth fully coeducational would have a negative effect on their financial support for the college, three-quarters said that they preferred the establishment of a new women's college with its own endowment, the move to Hanover of an established women's college, or the creation of an exchange with an established women's college—this despite the fact that efforts of this kind had been suggested elsewhere and were widely known not to have worked. Only one quarter of the respondents preferred admitting women to the college. And 62 percent said that increasing the number of women students in the Hanover area would result in the loss of "important advantages of an all-male environment."[53]

By mid-January 1971, when the study committee made a preliminary report to the alumni council, the answer was clear to the original question animating the committee's deliberations—"Can a first-rate education in the liberal arts in the 1970s be offered in a community essentially limited to men?" Now, the committee said, there were two overarching questions still to be addressed: What approach to educating women at Dartmouth would be "most likely to promote continuity in those values and characteristics which have made Dartmouth a much sought after College?" And what arrangements for bringing undergraduate women to Dartmouth would "best guarantee that the perception they have of themselves and which others have of them will be as Dartmouth students, not simply coeds at Dartmouth"?[54]

---

52 John G. Kemeny, Analysis of a Questionnaire, Jan. 5, 1971, Kemeny, Box 8442.

53 Coeducation at Dartmouth: Opinions of Alumni and Alumni Officers, Jan. 1971, Coed II.

54 Trustee Study Committee, Report to the Alumni Council, Jan. 15, 1971.

Like Princeton and Yale before it, Dartmouth tried to find ways to bring undergraduate women to Hanover without embarking on full-fledged coeducation.[55] Some plan other than coeducation would be cheaper and easier to accomplish; it would permit the preservation of the historic strengths and traditions so valued by graduates of the all-male institution; and—most important—it would provide a way to overcome the deficits of monastic education without inflaming alumni opposition. As Rieser had told the Dartmouth alumni council, the trustee study committee had posed "a simple question": "Would Dartmouth be stronger if Smith were within walking distance?"[56] It did not take much imagination to know that the answer was yes.

Kemeny personally explored a variety of arrangements that might be made for the education of women at Dartmouth. Following on Princeton's pursuit of Sarah Lawrence and Yale's courtship of Vassar, he investigated the possibility of moving Wheaton or Skidmore to Hanover.[57] Another idea was to find a donor interested in supporting the establishment of a new coordinate college for women in close proximity to the Dartmouth campus. But nothing came of those ideas.[58]

More serious was the aspiration for a robust exchange of students and faculty with Wellesley. As we have seen, the idea was fully explored by administrators and faculty members at both colleges but ultimately failed to come to fruition. Complications at Wellesley centered around tepid faculty support and, more important, the impossibility of gaining trustee approval before the completion of the report of the Commission on the Future of the College, a schedule that mooted the possibility of starting even a pilot exchange in 1971–72.[59] On the Dartmouth side, complications arose due to the

55 See, e.g., Leonard M. Rieser to John G. Kemeny, Mar. 5, 1970, Kemeny, Box 8436, which spells out several alternate approaches.

56 Dartmouth Alumni Council Bulletin, Dec. 30, 1969, typescript, Jan. 26, 1970, Cmsn. Future College, Box 1, Folder Commission: Studies: Dartmouth.

57 On Wheaton, see John F. Meck to John G. Kemeny, Apr. 3, 1970, Kemeny, Box 8436, and May 27, 1970, Dickey, Box 7200. On Skidmore, see Meck to Kemeny, Dudley W. Orr, and Leonard M. Rieser, May 6, 1970, Dickey, Box 7200.

58 Alexander L. Winship II to Oliver A. Quayle III, June 3, 1970, Dickey, Box 7200.

59 Minutes, Board of Trustees, Jan. 21, 1971, Wellesley trustees, Folder Minutes of the Full Board and Executive Committee, 1970–71 (Jan. 21, 1971–Apr. 15, 1971).

torturous unfolding of deliberations with respect to coeducation. Kemeny tried to reassure Ruth Adams, the president of Wellesley, that the possibility of coeducation at Dartmouth would not "prejudice any of the plans we have discussed."[60] But that turned out to be incorrect. By the next year, Adams had announced her retirement and Kemeny was working hard to bring the Dartmouth deliberations about coeducation to a conclusion. Although desultory efforts were made toward planning an exchange for 1972–73, there was little appetite to move forward with it. In November 1971, Kemeny acknowledged to the Dartmouth radio station that a large-scale exchange was not realistic.[61]

In early April of 1971, the trustee study committee recommended to the board that Dartmouth begin to admit women for the fall of 1972, with the goal of realizing a total enrollment of 800 women undergraduates "as soon as feasible." The women students might be fully matriculated undergraduates, undergraduates in an associated school, or undergraduates in a coordinate college. The number of students on campus should not increase beyond 3,150 at any given time, nor should the total male undergraduate enrollment drop below 3,000. Additional undergraduate degree candidates would be accommodated through increased use of the summer term and off-campus study.[62]

In mid-April the faculty voted overwhelmingly to recommend to the trustees the full matriculation of undergraduate women by September 1972. They, too, recommended that the resulting increase in the size of the undergraduate student body be accommodated through a summer term academically equivalent to the other three terms. If it proved necessary, the faculty would mandate participation in off-campus or summer terms to keep the on-campus

60 John Kemeny to Ruth Adams, Apr. 12, 1971, Adams, Box 19, Folder Commission on the Future of the College: Exchanges, Dartmouth-Wellesley Proposal, 1970–71.

61 On the continued efforts to plan for an exchange, see Helen J. Falkson to Philip Phibbs, Oct. 4, 1971; Procedures for Wellesley-Dartmouth Student Exchange, Oct. 6, 1971; and Ruth M. Adams to John Kemeny, Oct. 6, 1971, all in Adams, Box 19, Folder Commission on the Future of the College: Exchanges, Dartmouth-Wellesley Proposal, 1970–71. On the Kemeny interview, see typed excerpt reported in *The Dartmouth*, Nov. 22, 1971, Adams, Box 19, Folder Commission on the Future of the College: Exchanges, Dartmouth-Wellesley Proposal, 1970–71.

62 Recommendations of the Trustee Study Committee, Unanimously Approved Apr. 3, 1971, Kemeny, Box 8440.

enrollment at roughly 3,000 students. The faculty thought that the matter was settled, and they reacted with disbelief to the news that the trustees had slowed the process down by mandating study of an associated school for women, with a report to be brought to the October board meeting.

The Trustees Consider an "Associated School"

Just what the trustees had in mind in authorizing study of an associated school was by no means clear. An associated school might have separate trustees; its students might take all or almost all of their courses at Dartmouth; it could even grant a Dartmouth degree. It might present the opportunity to seek a major naming gift, which would solve the problem of the financial challenges of embarking on coeducation. Nor was it clear what the difference was between an associated school and a coordinate institution. But it was very clear that authorizing study of an associated school was essential to holding together a board that otherwise threatened to divide in counterproductive ways. At a special faculty meeting held in May 1971, convened by petition, the faculty—doubtless unaware of the complicated politics of the board—voted to reaffirm its support for full coeducation and asked the board to rethink the study of an associated school.[63]

Kemeny acknowledged later that he had been wrong in seriously entertaining options for bringing women to Dartmouth that fell short of outright coeducation. He had been "prepared to compromise," he wrote in 1975, "because I felt that an associated school would provide almost all of the educational advantages of coeducation and would gain much wider acceptance from the alumni." But, he continued, "The faculty voted overwhelmingly against that

---

63 *The Dartmouth*, Apr. 13, 15, 22, 23, 26, and 27 and May 3, 1971, and "Trustees Vote to Consider Associated School for Women," *Dartmouth Alumni Magazine*, May 1971, p. 21, all in Women at Dartmouth, Box 6593. In Kemeny, Box 8440, see Leonard Rieser to Members of the Trustee Study Committee, Apr. 21, 1971. In Kemeny, Box 8442, see Charles J. Zimmerman to John G. Kemeny, May 26, 1971, and Kemeny to the Board of Trustees, May 19, 1971, with the attached account in *The Dartmouth*, May 18, 1971.

plan. In view of our experience in the past three years, it is clear that the faculty was right."[64]

In 1971, however, Kemeny saw things differently. Making plain that he was not happy with the action of the faculty, he told the student press that it "could mean serious delays" in bringing women students to Dartmouth and that it put the board "in a difficult position," between the faculty and the alumni. At the same time, Kemeny announced the appointment of a faculty committee to make recommendations about implementing year-round operations.[65]

The trustees agreed to discuss the matter of the associated school once again at their June meeting, where the decision was made to set up a conference committee of faculty, trustees, and administrators to try to reach consensus on how to proceed.[66] In October the board unanimously approved five principles, recommended by the conference committee, under which coeducation would be administered: All prospective undergraduates would apply to and be evaluated by the same admission office. Financial aid and student employment would be administered equally for all undergraduates. A single faculty would be responsible for undergraduate education. All undergraduates would be subject to the same regulations with respect to housing and dining, medical care, counseling, and other services. Finally, all undergraduates who fulfilled degree requirements would be awarded Dartmouth degrees. Approval of the principles did not mean that the trustees would approve coeducation when they met in November. Rather, it meant that if coeducation were to be instituted, the principles would be honored.[67]

If members of the faculty were concerned that the trustees were not focused on outright coeducation, members of the alumni body were concerned about the opposite. Dartmouth, many alumni believed, was moving precipitately to embrace coeducation, which

64 Kemeny, "The First Five Years," p. 12.

65 Kemeny, quoted in *The Dartmouth*, May 8, 1971, Women at Dartmouth, Box 6592. On the Committee on Year-Round Operation, see *The Dartmouth*, May 21, Sept. 28, Oct. 20, and Nov. 4, 5, and 10, 1971, Women at Dartmouth, Box 6593.

66 *The Dartmouth*, May 19 and Oct. 14, 1971, Women at Dartmouth, Box 6593.

67 Ibid., Oct. 14, 1971.

would destroy much of what they treasured about their undergraduate experiences at the college. The ferocity of the opposition
was plain from the first airing of the idea. An alumnus in the class
of 1918 wrote, "I am opposed to the proposition! There should be
at least one liberal arts college for men only." An all-male Dartmouth would continue to attract serious students; the college had
built an excellent "reputation for leadership and the training of
leaders," and the trustees should do nothing to endanger it. "Let
Yale and Princeton have the men who are attracted by coeducation. Let Dartmouth continue to compete for those who want the
'best' liberal arts education which Dartmouth is now supplying to
the market!"[68]

To an alumnus in the class of 1922, coeducation was a "muddle-
headed" idea.[69] An alumnus in the class of 1968 lamented that
it would threaten "the strong and unique fellowship" that made
Dartmouth so distinctive.[70] A member of the class of 1935 expressed the view that "man-to-man competitiveness and companionship" were key elements of Dartmouth's ability to mold men of
"rare qualities" and its record in producing leaders. Dartmouth,
he said, is "a man's college that builds MEN!" If women were to be
admitted, Dartmouth would lose "its uniqueness, its vitality, and
its greatness."[71]

A member of the class of 1920 told the trustees, "I am absolutely
against Co-education at Dartmouth College in any form, shape or
manner. If Eleazar Wheelock or John Wentworth or Daniel Webster
had wanted it that way, they would have changed it long ago."[72]

---

68 Richard P. White '18 to Lloyd D. Brace, Jan. 19, 1970, Dickey, Box 7200.

69 Donald J. Tobin '22, letter to the editor, *Dartmouth Alumni Magazine*, June 1969,
p. 6, Women at Dartmouth, Box 6593.

70 Noel Augustyn '68, letter to the editor, *Dartmouth Alumni Magazine*, May 1969,
pp. 5–6, Women at Dartmouth, Box 6593. On the same theme, see P. Evan Lasky '63,
letter to the editor, *Dartmouth Alumni Magazine*, May 1970, p. 2, Women at Dartmouth,
Box 6593.

71 Richard K. Montgomery '35, letter to the editor, *Dartmouth Alumni Magazine*, Feb.
1971, pp. 5 and 6, Women at Dartmouth, Box 6592. On a similar theme, see Henry O.
Lowell '14, letter to the editor, *Dartmouth Alumni Magazine*, July 1971, p. 5, Women at
Dartmouth, Box 6593.

72 Albert H. Steinbrecher '20 to the Board of Trustees, Dec. 10, 1969, Dickey, Box
7200.

Should Dartmouth admit women, another alumnus suggested, it would need to be renamed: "As the castrated bull must be renamed steer, so, too, must a coeducational Dartmouth find a new identity, for its character is fundamentally altered."[73] One correspondent summed up the case: "For God's sake, for Dartmouth's sake, and for everyone's sake, keep the damned women out."[74]

And, of course, the expected warnings materialized: If coeducation were to be instituted, alumni would withdraw from volunteer efforts on behalf of the college, such as recruiting and interviewing prospective students, and would also withdraw their financial support.[75]

Not every alumnus was opposed to coeducation. Calling on the trustees to institute coeducation "as soon as possible," a member of the class of 1947 opined, "A co-educational experience is a much more realistic one and will better prepare students for all phases of life than a strictly male education."[76] A member of the class of 1964 said, "If coeducation does not begin immediately, coming generations will find Dartmouth an irrelevant institution" that "only the reactionary or the perverted would want to attend."[77] A member of the class of 1967 put it this way: "Gentlemen, men were not made to be sent off scores of miles from women, especially at so critical a time in life as the age of college students. It . . . is just plain *wrong*; monosexual schools are more than a reflection of a horrifying ignorance of human beings, they are dangerous. That men manage to come through four years at Dartmouth relatively unscathed is a

73 Richard W. Stanley '53 to Leonard M. Rieser, Feb. 24, 1970, Dickey, Box 7200. On the fundamental alteration in character, see also Warren F. Upham '16 to John G. Kemeny, Jan. 25, 1971, Kemeny, Box 8442.

74 William O. Keyes '29 to Dudley W. Orr, Jan. 2, 1970, Dickey, Box 7200. On the same theme, see, e.g., Hartley M. Caldwell, ex '23, to the Board of Trustees, Mar. 19, 1971, Kemeny, Box 8442.

75 See, e.g., Richard W. Stanley '53 to Leonard M. Rieser, Feb. 24, 1970, and W. M. Bollenbach, Jr., '49 to John G. Kemeny, May 11, 1970, both in Dickey, Box 7200. See also Donald E. Wilbur '24 to Kemeny, July 12, 1971, Kemeny, Box 8449.

76 Robert B. Kirsch '47 to President, Board of Trustees, Nov. 25, 1969, Dickey, Box 7200.

77 Roger L. Simon '64, letter to the editor, *Dartmouth Alumni Magazine*, Oct. 1969, p. 8, Women at Dartmouth, Box 6592. On a similar theme, see Roy S. Pfeil '55, letter to the editor, *Dartmouth Alumni Magazine*, Oct. 1971, p. 2, Women at Dartmouth, Box 6593, and J. Moreau Brown '39 to John G. Kemeny, June 16, 1971, Kemeny, Box 8442.

tribute to their flexibility, but it is no excuse for keeping the system as is."[78]

In October of 1971, the board of trustees, knowing already that the faculty strongly favored coeducation, asked for a faculty vote on the year-round operation of the college. That vote triggered an article in the *New York Times* on October 27. Based on an interview with Kemeny, the article described accurately the proposal for year-round operation, together with coeducation, that would be presented to the board at its late-November meeting. Dartmouth would have four terms of about ten weeks each. Students would normally complete their degree requirements in eleven rather than twelve terms: a traditional freshman year of three terms on campus, followed by eight out of twelve possible terms for sophomore, junior, and senior years, one of which would be a summer term, normally before or after the junior year. Students would be able to create personalized academic calendars, taking account of the seasons (Was spending the winter in Hanover appealing or not? Were there special educational programs—ecology, for example—that could best be accomplished at certain times of year?) and having the chance to make room for significant job experiences or foreign study. "The plan has generated enormous excitement at the college," Kemeny told the *Times*. "What all started out as a means of expanding economically for coeducation has now emerged as a new pattern for higher education."[79]

What was not accurate was the article's headline: "Dartmouth Acts to Admit Coeds."[80] The headline was "disastrous," the board chair, Charles J. Zimmerman '23, told his colleagues. The *Times* story "created an outburst of indignation on the part of many alumni," who "have felt that the ground has been cut out from under the Board of Trustees to the extent where a fair, objective, and independent decision by the Board has become an impossibility."

78 Lance M. Dodes '67, letter to the editor, *Dartmouth Alumni Magazine*, July 1969, p. 5, Women at Dartmouth, Box 6593.

79 *New York Times*, Oct. 27, 1971, attached to Interim Information Bulletin, Charles J. Zimmerman to the Board of Trustees of Dartmouth College, Nov. 8, 1971, Kemeny, Box 8446.

80 Ibid.

That was not true, Zimmerman assured angry correspondents: "The Board will not be pressured into making a decision either pro or con. Each member of the Board, I am confident, will vote his own conscience and vote for what he considers to be in the best interests of keeping Dartmouth as a̲ and, hopefully, t̲h̲e̲ pre-eminent undergraduate college in the United States."[81]

How that would unfold, however, was far from clear as the board prepared to make a decision in November.

81 Zimmerman, Interim Information Bulletin ("disastrous," "ground has been cut out"), with attachment, Charles J. Zimmerman to Lawrence Marx, Jr., Nov. 5, 1971 ("outburst," "Board will not be pressured"), Kemeny, Box 8446.

20

Dartmouth: "Our Cohogs"

Charles Zimmerman's assurances were well founded. The Dartmouth board was not about to be pressured into any decisions. But there was more work to be done before the late-November 1971 meeting, when the board would be ready to show its hand.

The Board Solicits Expert Opinion

The board asked for a vote of the student body to provide up-to-date information about student sentiment. With 87 percent of students voting, the results favored coeducation by a margin of 72 to 27 percent and year-round operation with coeducation by 57 to 42 percent.[1] The board also reviewed two reports by the consulting firm Cresap, McCormick and Paget, one about coeducation at Yale and Princeton, the other assessing Dartmouth's estimates of the costs of admitting women. Alumni opposed to coeducation had argued that Dartmouth should wait to see how things were going at Yale and Princeton. Although their motive—to slow down the prospect of coeducation at Dartmouth—may have been suspect, there was real usefulness in Cresap, McCormick and Paget's analysis of finances, academics, and social life at Yale and Princeton

---

1 John G. Kemeny, Results of the Student Poll, Nov. 19, 1971, and Charles J. Zimmerman, Report on the Dartmouth Trustee Meeting of November 20–21, 1971, in "The Decision on Year Round Operation and Coeducation," *The Bulletin*, Nov. 23, 1971, both in Kemeny, Box 8446.

and in their conclusion that the effect of coeducation had been "overwhelmingly positive."[2]

The board was briefed as well by a Washington attorney about the political and legal environment with respect to equal rights legislation. The college had been following closely the effort by U.S. Representative Edith Green (D-Oregon) to prohibit discrimination on the basis of sex in educational programs or activities at institutions receiving federal aid. The concern was how Green's initiative would affect Dartmouth should it choose to embark on coeducation, because equal access was never part of the conversation in Hanover. With the presumed quota on the number of women to be admitted, some women applicants would surely be denied admission in favor of men with lesser credentials, clear evidence of discrimination. Whether establishing an associated school or coordinate college would be legally permissible was not yet known. In the end, the Senate did not include a sex discrimination amendment in the Higher Education Act, and the House of Representatives struck the Green amendment when it approved the bill in early November.[3] The decision gave Dartmouth the flexibility it desired to proceed according to plan.

The board met all day Saturday, November 20, to consider the reports and discuss the many issues involved in year-round operation and coeducation. The vote would be taken on Sunday.[4] For all of John Kemeny's personal conviction about the desirability

---

2 Zimmerman, Report on the Dartmouth Trustee Meeting of November 20–21, 1971; text of John G. Kemeny statement on coeducation and year-round operation, *The Dartmouth*, Nov. 22, 1971, Coed III ("overwhelmingly positive"); [Cresap, McCormick, and Paget,] "An Analysis of the Impact of Coeducation at Princeton and Yale Universities," Nov. 1971, Dartmouth College Library.

3 Amendment to Section 601 of Civil Rights Act—Rep. Edith Green's Proposal, Apr. 7, 1971, Coed III; John Meck to President Kemeny and Provost Rieser, Apr. 12, 1971, Kemeny, Box 8442; *The Dartmouth*, Apr. 27, Oct. 5, and Nov. 8, 1971, Women at Dartmouth, Box 6593; Green to Alfred B. Fitt, June 7, 1971, Kemeny, Box 8449; Charles J. Zimmerman to Harry C. McPherson, Jr., Nov. 5, 1971, attached to Interim Information Bulletin, Zimmerman to the Board of Trustees of Dartmouth College, Nov. 8, 1971, Kemeny, Box 8446.

4 Typescript, John G. Kemeny, "A Mathematician's Journey," n.d., "Coeducation," p. 3, Kemeny personal, Box 20, Folder 3.

of coeducation, he had not (or not yet) been able to build the sure command over his board that characterized Robert Goheen's leadership at Princeton or to equal the strong influence that Kingman Brewster wielded at Yale. Kemeny had been president for only twenty-one months, and he had a modest reservoir of shared experience with his trustee colleagues. He had inherited a study launched by his predecessor, and even though he had come to the presidency as a member of the study committee, it was not the sort of scenario for accomplishing major institutional change that a governance expert would ever have scripted. As the Dartmouth board approached the moment of decision, then, Kemeny was not certain that he would be able to win a vote for coeducation.

The Board Votes for Coeducation and the Dartmouth Plan

Kemeny went home after the board meeting on Saturday "very tired and worried." Jean Kemeny recalled later that he was, uncharacteristically, "quite depressed." He told her, "I don't have the votes." She told him to make a list of how he thought each trustee would vote. He made three columns—"Yes," "Maybe," and "No." "The first was the shortest and the last the longest," he recalled. "It looked like I needed all the people listed as 'Maybe' just to get a bare majority."

Jean studied the list and focused immediately on one man John had listed as a "No"—Lloyd Brace '25, chairman of the First National Bank of Boston, Zimmerman's immediate predecessor as chairman of the Dartmouth board, the man who had led the search committee that selected Kemeny as president. Jean recalled the story Brace had told them about the discrimination his daughter encountered in medical school and in training to be a surgeon. That experience, she thought, would lead Brace to vote "Yes." As John Kemeny recorded later, Brace "took the floor" in the Sunday meeting and explained, calmly and eloquently, "why he felt it was *essential* for Dartmouth to admit women. The world was changing . . . the traditional reasons for all-male colleges were disappearing. Our students needed to learn to work with both men and women. And we did not want to eliminate half the leadership talent in admitting students." Given Brace's standing and influence, he swayed a number of votes.[5]

On November 21, the board voted unanimously to adopt the Dartmouth Plan for year-round operation and, by a "substantial majority," to admit the first women candidates for the Dartmouth degree, effective in September 1972. Projected enrollment would be three thousand males, a thousand females. The total number of undergraduates on campus would be limited to about thirty-four hundred.[6]

To the last, board members who were uneasy about coeducation did what they could to slow it down. Zimmerman suggested, for example, that they might announce a decision for coeducation but postpone implementation for two years, a prospect that appealed to a number of reluctant trustees. The governor of New Hampshire, Walter Peterson, a Dartmouth alumnus serving on the board by virtue of office, spoke up forcefully to oppose that proposal. His political experience, he said, told him that unpopular moves ought to be made quickly and decisively. Postponing implementation would give the opposition time to rally to get the decision reversed. Peterson was "so persuasive," Kemeny recalled, that "he single-handedly changed the board's mind on that one issue."

The margin in favor of coeducation was 12 to 4. One of the opponents suggested that if coeducation had to happen, it would be better to have a unanimous vote. But only two of the dissenters were willing to switch their votes, so the public announcement followed the board's normal practice of not disclosing the actual vote count.[7] This action stood in contrast to Princeton's handling of its trustee vote, wherein a decision was made to be candid about differences of opinion—indeed, as William G. Bowen reflected, "to

5 Ibid., p. 4 (source of the quotes, except "quite depressed," which comes from Jean Kemeny); John Kemeny oral history, p. 77; Jean Kemeny oral history, p. 23. The Kemenys told the same story, but Jean Kemeny identified the trustee as Charles Zimmerman instead of Lloyd Brace.

6 Dartmouth College news release, Nov. 22, 1971; text of John G. Kemeny statement on coeducation and year-round operation, *The Dartmouth*, Nov. 22, 1971, both in Coed III.

7 John Kemeny oral history, pp. 78 (source of the quote), 79.

celebrate them as evidence that real thought, and not pressure, had led to the affirmative vote."[8]

In a statement following the meeting, the trustees explained their decision:

> The historic purpose of Dartmouth College has been to train leaders for society. It is clear that women now will be playing an increasing role of leadership in our society and that Dartmouth can, and should, contribute to their education, making it possible for them to become, as Dartmouth men have through two centuries, outstanding doctors, lawyers, business leaders, scientists, and leaders in government. In endorsing both coeducation and the Dartmouth Plan for year-round operation we are acting to assure that Dartmouth will continue to serve as a leader in innovation in undergraduate education.[9]

Although Dartmouth lagged behind Princeton and Yale in making the decision for coeducation, it trumped them in making an affirmative case for why the college should be in the business of educating women and in the way it accommodated the planned increase in numbers through year-round operation. Zimmerman said that the plan for year-round operation constituted "a breakthrough in making higher education more effective and more economical."[10] Kemeny called it "a new venture in American higher education," a "creative design for expanding student enrollment without overcrowding and without major capital expenses for the expansion of the physical plant." "It is our firm conviction," Kemeny said, "that this new plan will make Dartmouth even more attractive to young men and women who prize freedom of choice."[11]

8 I am indebted to William G. Bowen for this observation.

9 Dartmouth College news release, Nov. 22, 1971, Coed III.

10 Zimmerman, Report on the Dartmouth Trustee Meeting of November 20–21, 1971.

11 Statement by President John G. Kemeny, THE DARTMOUTH PLAN, in "The Decision on Year Round Operation and Coeducation," *The Bulletin*, Nov. 23, 1971, Kemeny, Box 8446.

Alumni and Students Respond

The responses from alumni, predictably, were divided. Plenty of enthusiasts waxed eloquent about their delight. A member of the class of 1918 declared, "Dartmouth in the future is sure to be a greater College with coeds than it could possibly be without them."[12] A member of the class of 1947 wrote, "I am delighted with the enlightened decision of dear old Dartmouth to go co-educational at last. Now I can contemplate in good conscience sending my son—repeat son—to Dartmouth, should he be admissible and wish to go."[13] But there were also plenty of outspoken opponents. A member of the class of 1940 wrote, "The Board of Trustees choked on the gutless decision of Dartmouth coeds."[14] A member of the class of 1922 put it this way: "By vote of the Trustees this revered college has, in effect, been destroyed. . . . The Dartmouth we knew will be gone forever."[15]

Although most undergraduates enthusiastically supported the decision to admit women, a small, highly vocal minority did not hesitate to voice dissenting views. In a dormitory meeting in advance of the decision, in the presence of assistant provost Marilyn Austin Baldwin, at that time the highest-ranking woman administrator at Dartmouth, one student said, "I just want you to know I don't consider women to be my equal. I don't want them in the classroom with me, and the woman I marry had better know her place or I'll knock her down into it." Another student told Baldwin, "I have a friend at Williams, and Williams has 165 women. One hundred sixty-three of them are pigs." Another student, speaking after Baldwin had left the dormitory, declared that "the only reason for having coeducation is sex." On the evening of November 21, after Kemeny announced the trustees' decision, a male

---

12 Robert Fish '18, quoted in Jean Alexander Kemeny, *It's Different at Dartmouth: A Memoir* (Brattleboro, VT: Stephen Greene Press, 1979), p. 161.

13 Russell A. Fraser '47, letter to the editor, *Dartmouth Alumni Magazine*, Feb. 1972, p. 2, Coed III.

14 Ted Ellsworth '40, letter to the editor, *Dartmouth Alumni Magazine*, Feb. 1972, p. 2, Coed III.

15 F. Anthony Hanlon '22, letter to the editor, *Dartmouth Alumni Magazine*, Jan. 1972, pp. 2, 4, Coed III.

undergraduate burst into the room of a woman exchange student who was writing a paper for one of her courses. Ripping a piece of paper out of the woman's typewriter, the man told her, "I can't get back at Kemeny, but I can get at you."[16]

Women Arrive at Dartmouth

Dartmouth did what it could to prepare for the new world coming in the fall of 1972. Kemeny knew that the college needed to make additional appointments of women administrators. His boldest move was to bring Ruth Adams to Dartmouth as vice president, with the goal of working to smooth the way for the integration of women into the student body. The two presidents had struck up a close relationship over the course of discussions about the proposed Dartmouth-Wellesley exchange, and with Adams leaving the Wellesley presidency under some duress at the end of the academic year 1971–72, Kemeny saw an opportunity to provide a graceful exit for his friend and a boon to his college. Adams later described her portfolio at Dartmouth as seeing to "the comfort and ease of the undergraduates." As well, she worked to increase employment opportunities for women in faculty and administrative posts.[17]

With the arrival of the first undergraduate women in September 1972, Dartmouth embarked on the fraught process of having male students learn to relate to women. That fall, 177 freshmen and 74 transfer students became the first fully matriculated women undergraduates in Dartmouth's history. With 100 women studying at Dartmouth on the Twelve-College Exchange, there were about 350 women on campus, for a male-female ratio of 9 to 1.[18]

16 Richard M. Zuckerman '72, "The Undergraduate Chair," *Dartmouth Alumni Magazine*, Jan. 1972, p. 22, Women at Dartmouth, Box 6592.

17 "Ruth Adams to Be Vice President," *Dartmouth Alumni Magazine*, Feb. 1972, p. 13, Women at Dartmouth, Box 6592; Adams oral history, p. 2 (source of the quote). As evidence of the closeness of the relationship between the two presidents, see John Kemeny to Adams, Apr. 12, 1971, a letter signed "Love, John," and Adams to Kemeny, Apr. 21, 1971, a letter sent in an envelope marked "personal," and signed "Yours affectionately." Both letters are in Adams, Box 19, Folder Commission on the Future of the College: Exchanges, Dartmouth-Wellesley Proposal, 1970–71.

18 *Claiming Their Rightful Place: Coeducation at Dartmouth, 1972–1997* (Dartmouth College, 1997), p. 12, Dartmouth College Library.

The new women freshmen looked very much like their male counterparts in terms of geography, ethnicity, socioeconomic status, public-private school background (a 70–30 ratio), and legacy status (more than a quarter were daughters of alumni). The women of the class of 1976 were greeted by the class of 1926, which presented each of them with a scroll of welcome and a corsage. Women students were housed in dormitories across the campus, with the choice of all-female or mixed residences. Alterations were made to bathrooms, better lighting was installed in remote areas of the campus, and new dressing-room and locker facilities were added to the gymnasium. Physical education classes were coeducational except for field hockey for women and handball and soccer for men. Dance, a new offering, was open to students of both sexes. Even intramural touch football was to be coeducational.[19]

The tone for the year was set at the opening convocation, when the president addressed the entering class: "Welcome Men and *Women* of Dartmouth." As one woman recalled, "Everybody just got up . . . and cheered . . . the place just went crazy, that was incredibly moving." She described "the great sense of camaraderie," "the shared spirit" among men and women in the class of 1976. "We were all proud to be a part of that pioneering class."[20]

In the classroom, the experiences of the new Dartmouth women were as mixed as they had been for the first cohorts of women at Yale and Princeton. Some faculty members believed that there was no difference between women and men in terms of class participation. Others said that men were "the talkers," while women remained relatively quiet, but that women were usually better prepared and on paper outperformed their male classmates.[21]

A woman in the class of 1976 recalled a wholly positive experience in the classroom: "Fall of my freshman year, I was lucky enough to have fabulously inclusive professors who were as excited

19 Mary Ross, "Coeducation Becomes a Reality," *Dartmouth Alumni Magazine*, Oct. 1972, pp. 20–21, 107, Women at Dartmouth, Box 6592.

20 Martha Beatie '76 oral history interview, in Jacqueline Sievert, "Blazing the Trail: The Early Days of Coeducation at Dartmouth," paper written for Master of Arts in Liberal Studies 191, May 29, 2008, Dartmouth College, Dartmouth College Library.

21 Bruce Kimball and Andrew Newman, "The First Coed Year," *Dartmouth Alumni Magazine*, June 1973, p. 22, Women at Dartmouth, Box 6592.

about coeducation as I was."[22] A woman in the class of 1973 who had transferred to Dartmouth from Smith recalled taking a large lecture course with a professor who told her later that "he had spent the entire night up studying for the first day of class to be sure he got Ms. Shaffer down properly as he went through Mr. So and So, Mr. So and So, as he went through the class roll call . . . because he wanted to be so sure he didn't offend me."[23] A woman in the class of 1975 who had transferred from Barnard observed later that "the professors seemed to welcome the civilizing presence of women in the classroom." Some of her fellow transfer students, she said, "reported that they did far better at Dartmouth than they had from their former institutions, that their comments in class were regarded as brilliant and profound."[24]

At the same time, there were many classes with only one woman student, who so often felt the need "to prove [her]self," and who was so often asked to present "the women's point of view."[25] Even when there were more women in the room, some male faculty members made a regular practice of posing the gendered question, "Miss so-and-so, *as a woman*, what is your reading of this text?"[26] Some faculty members went to the opposite extreme and made no adjustments for women students. In a literature class the professor—in the words of a woman in the class of 1979, "bulky, middle-aged, heavy-set, tweedy, standard-issue type," "straight out of central casting"—announced on the first day of class, "My name is MANN. I am teaching a book about a sperm whale named Moby Dick. Anybody who has a *problem* with that can leave right now. I have been teaching here for thirty years and I am not about to change my ways because there might *suddenly* be in my classroom a *delicate flower* whose *feminine sensibilities* I

22 Sara Hunter '76 oral history interview, in Sievert paper.

23 Marie Shaffer '73 oral history interview, in Sievert paper.

24 Caroline Preston '75, "Woodward Hall, October, 1972," typescript submission for *Claiming Their Rightful Place*, Aug. 5, 1997, Women at Dartmouth, Box 6592, Folder 8.

25 Hilary Smith '78, in script for the video project "Breaking Tradition," Oct. 6, 1987, p. 12, Women's Studies Program, Dartmouth College, Dartmouth College Library.

26 Gina Barreca, *Babes in Boyland: A Personal History of Co-Education in the Ivy League* (Hanover, NH, and London: University Press of New England, 2005), p. 47. I am indebted to Marilyn Austin-Nelson for calling this book to my attention.

might *offend*."[27] More troubling were the explicit insults, like that from the professor in an art history course who posted slides of nudes, "pretend[ing] that he couldn't tell what he was doing and run[ning] his hands up and down the thigh of the nude . . . on the screen" or from the professor in an oceanography course who showed "pictures of sea creatures, shrimp and lobster, naked women, squid."[28]

In interviews with *The Dartmouth*, male students expressed surprise and relief at how well the integration of the campus seemed to be going. "I was quite pleasantly surprised at the choices the college made in co-eds," one man said. "They're not all superbrains, but they are intelligent. They're not all pseudo-beauties, but, rather, a well-rounded group." Other men said that they found it "easier to study" and that there was more "action on campus than before." Students who had been opposed to coeducation on the grounds that it would threaten the spirit of male fellowship now admitted that "the new feminine element had not disturbed this traditional spirit of comradeship." Some men who imagined that women would be coming to Hanover for other than "scholastic reasons" now acknowledged that they were simply "coming to go to school."[29]

Women Receive Mixed Signals

There were plenty of signs that women were welcome at Dartmouth. In the first year of coeducation, Dartmouth's storied winter carnival abandoned its forty-three-year-old "Queen of the Snows" beauty pageant.[30] Six of twenty-one fraternities decided to admit women to full membership.[31] Women's athletics got off to a strong start, with teams competing in field hockey, squash, basketball, tennis, and lacrosse. The outing club offered a women's skiing

27 Barreca, *Babes in Boyland*, pp. 41–42.
28 ? Kricorian, in the script for the video project "Breaking Tradition," p. 12.
29 *The Dartmouth*, Oct. 3, 1972, Women at Dartmouth, Box 6592.
30 Ibid., Jan. 15, 1973.
31 Ibid., Jan. 29, 1973.

program.[32] It was not that the athletic department had favored coeducation—far from it. But "once they had lost the battle," reflected Agnes Bixler Kurtz, a Smith alumna who was hired in 1972 to start up women's athletics at Dartmouth, "they wanted to do it right."[33] "Doing it right" turned out to be a work in progress, as Kurtz struggled constantly for funding, facilities, coaching staff, and practice time for women commensurate with what was accorded to men.[34] However, by the end of the 1970s there were twelve varsity and five junior varsity teams for women, and the fencing and sailing teams were coed.[35]

At the same time, however, women saw many indications that Dartmouth was still very much a men's institution. Following a review, the trustees reaffirmed that "Men of Dartmouth" would remain the college's alma mater. An anthem to the virtues of Dartmouth's male fellowship, the song "capture[d]," in the words of the *Dartmouth Alumni Magazine*, "the independent spirit of derring-do that has characterized the Dartmouth man for more than 200 years." The closing stanza—"They have the still North in their hearts, the hill winds in their veins, and the granite of New Hampshire in their muscles and their brains"—led some women students to poke fun at Dartmouth men. As one of them wrote, "If men want to sing about rocks in their heads, it's fine with me."[36]

A woman in the class of 1984 recalled, "In September of 1980 I stood with my arms around my new classmates, singing Men of Dartmouth, excited and proud to be a Dartmouth student and to share in the Dartmouth traditions. Some of us, women especially, laughed at the lyrics, not only the words about the granite of New Hampshire in our muscles and our brains, but also the stuff about the sturdy sons, the brother standing by brother, the old chivalric

32 Ibid., May 17, 1973.

33 Kurtz oral history, p. 5.

34 Philippa M. Guthrie, "The Implementation of Coeducation at Dartmouth College, 1972–1982," paper written for History Independent Study, June 4, 1982, Dartmouth College, Rauner Special Collections Library, Dartmouth College.

35 *Many Sighs and Many Cheers: Women at Dartmouth*, Dartmouth College Admissions Office, n.d. (but likely 1977), Coed III; Kurtz oral history, p. 18.

36 "It's Still 'Men of Dartmouth,'" *Dartmouth Alumni Magazine*, Nov. 1972, p. 21, Women at Dartmouth, Box 6592.

faith." But she came to change her mind. "It didn't take long, though, before the words stopped making me laugh and started to rankle. 'Whose school is this?' I began to wonder. After a while, I refused to stand up and sing during the song." She reflected, "Tradition and loyalty and responsibility are admirable values, but they can also be used to promote discrimination, exclusion, and oppression. I stopped singing 'Men of Dartmouth' because to me it represented a past where women were systematically denied economic, political and social freedoms simply because they were women."[37]

In 1988 Dartmouth introduced a new alma mater, "Alma Mater," later known as "Dear Old Dartmouth," with modest changes to reflect coeducation:[38]

Old version: "Men of Dartmouth"

Men of Dartmouth, give a rouse
For the college on the hill
For the Lone Pine above her,
And the loyal sons who love her.
Give a rouse, give a rouse, with a will!
For the sons of old Dartmouth
The sturdy sons of Dartmouth,
Though 'round the girdled earth they roam,
Her spell on them remains;
They have the still North in their hearts,
The hill winds in their veins,
And the granite of New Hampshire
In their muscles and their brains.

Men of Dartmouth set a watch
Lest the old traditions fail!
Stand as brother stands by brother!
Dare a deed for thee old Mother!

37 Julie Roberts '84, quoted in *Claiming Their Rightful Place*, p. 13.
38 "Dartmouth Herstory," Timeline for Baker Exhibit, 25th Anniversary of Coeducation, Fall 1997, Women at Dartmouth, Box 6592. Princeton's alma mater was revised at the same time.

Greet the world, from the hills with a hail!
For the sons of old Dartmouth,
The loyal sons of Dartmouth,
Around the world they keep for her
Their old chivalric faith;
They have the still North in their soul,
The hill winds in their breath,
And the granite of New Hampshire
Is made part of them 'til death.[39]

New version: "Dear Old Dartmouth"
(excerpts; changes in bold type):

Dear old Dartmouth, give a rouse
For the College on the hill,
For the Lone Pine above her,
And the loyal **ones** who love her.
Give a rouse, give a rouse, with a will!
For the sons of old Dartmouth,
For the daughters of Dartmouth.

Dear old Dartmouth, set a watch,
Lest the old traditions fail.
Stand as **sister** stands by brother.
Dare a deed for thee old mother.
Greet the world from the hills with a hail!
For the sons of old Dartmouth,
For the daughters of Dartmouth.[40]

"I can remember standing on the Green," a woman in the class of 1984 said later, "trying to sing the new verse to the alma mater that incorporated women and feeling the sudden loss of the basses

---

39 Lyrics found at All Poetry website, http://allpoetry.com/poem/8550995-Men-Of
-Dartmouth-by-Richard_Hovey, accessed Sept. 30, 2013.
40 Lyrics found at The Dartmouth College Mandrake Band! website, http://dcmb
.dartmouth.edu/music/alma-mater, accessed Sept. 30, 2013.

and tenors. I felt self-conscious, wondering if I sounded defiant or ridiculous. But I sang it just the same, because I knew that our presence had changed the college forever."[41]

Women Encounter the Dominant, Aggressive Male Culture

The change in the alma mater came only in 1988. In the early years of coeducation, much of the Dartmouth campus culture was assertively, even exclusively, male, and men were strongly invested in sustaining it. Men were not shy about telling women students that they did not belong at Dartmouth. A woman in the class of 1975 recalled her experiences in the first few months of coeducation as reminiscent of a Fellini movie—"an innocent wandering through a surreal landscape filled with grotesques and bizarre incidents. . . . It sometimes felt as if I were wearing a sandwich board that announced, 'Hello, I'm a Dartmouth Coed. Please share your views on Dartmouth coeducation with me.'" As she remembered, "In the library, in classrooms, in restaurants, male students and alums sidled up and explained—politely, earnestly—that women didn't belong here . . . and that we should consider going back to where we came from. . . . I wasn't enlightened enough to realize how sexist and offensive these 'discussions' were. Instead I, earnestly and politely, apologized for having the temerity to encroach on their male bastion."[42]

But women with enough self-confidence and bravado mustered more pointed rejoinders. A woman in the class of 1979 recalled her retort to the male student who told her that Dartmouth "never should have admitted women. When my grandfather went here, there were no women." Her response: "Hey, when your grandfather went here there were also no indoor lights. Sometimes things get better."[43]

The campus culture was deeply rooted in Dartmouth's setting. With the college's isolation in a rural environment, social life

41 Susan Schoenberger '84, quoted in *Claiming Their Rightful Place*, p. 13.
42 Caroline D. Preston '75, quoted in *Claiming Their Rightful Place*, p. 10.
43 Barreca, *Babes in Boyland*, pp. 5–6.

revolved around fraternities, and fraternity life was often synonymous with boorishness, drunkenness, degrading and sometimes
dangerous initiation activities, physical intimidation, aggressive
sexual encounters, and crude, offensive behavior toward women.
Buying into that behavior was a way for Dartmouth men to fit
in, to be part of the culture. For those who were uncomfortable
with the behavior, the choices were limited. Men could separate
themselves from it, but standing up to the behavior was simply too
difficult. Anyone who challenged the dominant culture would have
paid "a tremendous social price."[44]

A woman in the class of 1979 described the Dartmouth social
scene:

> I'd meet a cute guy at a party and talk for a while. We would
> then be interrupted by some buddy of his who would drag
> him off to another room to watch a friend of theirs "power-
> boot" (the local vernacular for "projectile vomiting"). . . . If
> a guy said he wanted to spend the weekend with his girl-
> friend . . . he'd be taunted by his pals who would yell in beery
> bass voices, "Whatsa matter with you, Skip? We're gonna get
> plowed, absolutely blind this weekend, then we're *all* gonna
> power-boot. And you wanna see that broad again? Whad-
> dayou, a fag or something?"[45]

Offering a different perspective on the same culture, a man in
the class of 1975 recalled his fraternity's practice of awarding a
plaque bearing two halves of a ping-pong ball, with red dots in
the middle of each half, to the brother who had spent the weekend
with the woman with the smallest breasts.[46]

Even as late as the mid-1980s, a freshman woman wrote to *The
Dartmouth* recounting the frightening story of walking past fraternity row at night with her roommate, on the way back to their

44 See, e.g., Andy Merton, "Hanging on (by a Jockstrap) to Tradition at Dartmouth,"
Esquire, June 19, 1979, pp. 57–58, 60, Women at Dartmouth, Box 6592; telephone interview with Daniel M. Nelson '75, Feb. 4, 2015 ("social price").

45 Barreca, *Babes in Boyland*, p. 47.

46 Nelson interview.

dormitory, and having "verbal assaults hurled at us," along with pumpkins and large chunks of snow and ice. "We expect to be safe here. These are not crazed lunatics throwing things at us or verbally threatening us, these are our classmates, members of the 'Dartmouth family.' The most upsetting part is that there is nothing we can do to protect ourselves. There is no defense against cowards who get their kicks out of throwing things at women from darkened windows."[47]

Women protested against deeply offensive fraternity behavior. One example: T-shirts for an Alpha Chi Alpha fraternity party featuring images of a woman's bikini-clad torso with Alpha on her breasts, Chi on her vagina, and "rules" of conduct spelled out for the party ("All beached whales will be harpooned," "Excess clothing will be removed," "Everyone must be balmed and baked," "Everyone gets lei'd").[48] A second example: the Zeta Psi newsletter, "Eleven Men in Search of Spread Legs," which, following earlier disciplinary action against the fraternity, resulted in a year's suspension of Zeta Psi's recognition by the college.[49]

But it did not take overt sexist behavior and obscene insults to remind women that they were not fully part of the college. Even the administrators handling the most straightforward institutional functions were occasionally tripped up by the fact that women were part of the student body, and some students interpreted administrative sloppiness as evidence of sexism. "One more small slap in the face," a woman in the class of 1973 observed in response to a letter about graduation mailed to seniors by the dean of the college, Carroll Brewster. Even though more than thirty women would be graduating, Brewster's communication read:

47 Megan McDonald '90, letter to the editor, *The Dartmouth*, Nov. 13, 1986, in handwritten journal recorded in the mid-1980s by radical women of the group "Womyn's Issues League," or W.I.L., kept in the Women's Studies Office at Dartmouth in the early 1990s, Women at Dartmouth, Box 6591. On women's feeling unsafe on campus as a result of graffiti, obscene phone calls and messages, and offensive actions on the part of men, see also *The Dartmouth*, Feb. 9, 1987, clipping in the same journal.

48 Women's Issues League to Dean of the College Edward J. Shanahan, Apr. 4, 1987, in W.I.L. handwritten journal.

49 "Eleven Men in Search of Spread Legs"; handwritten notes, Apr. 20, 1987; and *The Dartmouth*, Apr. 23, 1987, all in W.I.L. handwritten journal.

"Cap and gown are worn with shirt and tie, dark trousers and dark shoes." An "unintentioned mistake, perhaps," the student remarked, "but it seems to me that someone could have caught it if he wanted to."[50]

Some campus institutions were slow to embrace change. At the outset of the second year of coeducation, the glee club, recruiting freshmen, said that it would remain all-male for the foreseeable future. Only after the president and the dean of freshmen sent letters of complaint did the director of the glee club (a faculty member who was also chairman of the music department) agree to begin admitting women. First there would be two groups—a men's glee club and a women's glee club—that would perform separately and, sometimes, together as a mixed chorus. After some years, the director would merge them into "one solid chorale."[51]

Other indications of the challenges of embracing coeducation were more troubling and more explosive. In the spring of 1973, in the context of fraternity initiations, a letter slipped during the night under the doors of student rooms in an all-female dormitory, Woodward Hall, listed a series of "demands" that would have to be met for women to "become . . . viable member[s] of our community." One demand stated, "The upper part of your body must remain naked before our eyes when you eat in Thayer. Perhaps you consider this unreasonable. Well, f— you. Your services must be made available at all times." Another demand read, "The girls' softball team must also play naked on the Green." Women students were admonished to comply with the demands. "These are not idle threats. Our movement is large. Things must change."[52]

The executive committee of the Dartmouth faculty responded to this and other "violations of the rights of women students" with a resolution condemning "all actions contrary to the aim and spirit of coeducation." Women students belonged on campus, "on an equal status with men." The resolution continued: "No woman student is an intruder. Any student who believes otherwise

50 Letter to the editor, *The Dartmouth*, May 2, 1973, Women at Dartmouth, Box 6593.
51 Letter to the editor, *The Dartmouth*, Oct. 2, 1973, Women at Dartmouth, Box 6593.
52 Quoted in *The Dartmouth*, Apr. 11, 1973, Women at Dartmouth, Box 6592.

is mistaken. Any action that implies otherwise is inappropriate and not to be tolerated. The person, privacy, and property of every student on campus must be held inviolate. Obscene insults, warnings, threats, and destructive acts aimed at women students cannot be passively ignored. Nor can they be excused as pranks, harmless jokes, or sick aberrations."[53]

"The most frightening aspect of this affair," said the vice president for student affairs, Donald Kreider, "is that many students thought it was funny or even the deserved punishment to a group on campus who had brought it upon themselves." Ruth Adams added: "Attitudes are what must be changed before Dartmouth can be a truly coeducational school—that is a place where the two sexes take each other calmly maybe even for granted."[54]

The Woodward Hall letter was not the only flashpoint in the first years of coeducation. Members of Beta Theta Pi fraternity rampaged through the women's floor in another dormitory, Butterfield Hall, earning a penalty of social probation and eviction from their fraternity house.[55] Less aggressive assaults reinforced the theme articulated so offensively in the Woodward Hall letter. Men sitting on the roof of Massachusetts Hall shouted numbers from one to ten as women students walked by—with the numbers meant as ratings of the women's attractiveness. The same happened in the dining hall, where men held up signs bearing numerical ratings "as if you had just completed a dive." One woman reflected, "No matter how cool you were, no matter how self-possessed you were as a woman and mind you a lot of us were 18 at the time it was devastating."[56] Men serenaded women's dormitories with obscenities. Fraternities put snow sculptures on their front lawns in the form of women's breasts. Banners hanging from fraternities or all-male dormitories declared, "No Coeds" and "Better Dead

53 Text of faculty resolution in *The Dartmouth*, May 3, 1973, Women at Dartmouth, Box 6593.

54 Quoted in *The Dartmouth*, Apr. 24, 1973, Women at Dartmouth, Box 6593.

55 Kimball and Newman, "The First Coed Year," p. 24; Joanna H. Sternick, letter to the editor, *The Dartmouth*, May 14, 1973, Women at Dartmouth, Box 6593.

56 Hilary Smith '78, in script for the video project "Breaking Tradition," Oct. 6, 1987, p. 10. See also Barreca, *Babes in Boyland*, p. 5.

Than Coed." Campus graffiti conveyed the same message: "Coeds go home."[57] Even as late as the mid-1980s, a woman student noted that on the door to the bathroom on her hallway, under the word WOMEN, handwritten in black letters, were the words GO HOME.[58]

Dartmouth Confronts the Challenges of Cultural Change

Male students liked to refer to their female counterparts as "co-hogs," a phonetic spelling of *quahog*, a thick-shelled clam, a nickname meant as a derogatory reference to female genitalia.[59] It was customary to see and hear the term in regular use. Bed sheets hung from an all-male dormitory put the case in the simplest imperative form: "Cohogs go home." But vicious use of the word did not end there. In the spring of 1975—the third year of coeducation—it reached a new level of notoriety after the annual Hums competition, which involved the rendition of original songs by each of the fraternities. The entry from Theta Delta, sung to the tune of "This Old Man," consisted of ten verses, five of which went as follows:

> Our cohogs, they play one,
> They're all here to spoil our fun.
>
> *Chorus:*
> With a knick-knack, paddywhack,
> Send the bitches home,
> Our cohogs go to bed alone.
>
> Our cohogs, they play three,
> They all have to squat to pee.
> [*chorus*]
>
> Our cohogs, they play four,
> They are all a bunch of whores.
> [*chorus*]

57 *The Dartmouth*, May 14, 1973, Women at Dartmouth, Box 6593; Adams oral history, p. 9; Barreca, *Babes in Boyland*, p. 4.

58 "Women Go Home," in W.I.L. handwritten journal.

59 Merton, "Hanging On," p. 58.

Our cohogs, they play six,
They all love those Tri Kapp dicks.
[*chorus*]

Our cohogs, they play seven,
They have ruined our masculine heaven.
[*chorus*][60]

The three Hums judges included the college's dean, Carroll Brewster, a known opponent of coeducation who, Kemeny learned later, enjoyed spending time at rowdy fraternity parties and participated actively "in some of the anti-women songs and remarks that were made there." (As Kemeny noted, "When the chief student affairs officer lets it go by in his presence, he's sending a signal to the student body.") Brewster had already made clear his opinions of women's treatment by fraternities. In one incident, when a fraternity raided a women's dormitory in the middle of the night and engaged in "all kinds of outrageous acts," Brewster had been out of town, and Kemeny had asked the dean of freshmen, Ralph Manuel, to handle the discipline. Manuel put the fraternity on social probation for the rest of the academic year. When Brewster returned, he reversed the action. In the Hums competition, Brewster took obvious delight in awarding first prize to "Our Cohogs"—and in joining members of the fraternity in an exuberant public rendition of the song.[61] Ironically, Brewster would leave Dartmouth later that year to take up the presidency of Hollins College, a women's college in Roanoke, Virginia.

Brewster's behavior helps to explain why it was so hard for administrators and faculty to change the campus culture. Dartmouth had administrators and faculty who were not enthusiastic about coeducation; some of them expressed themselves openly, and some kept their views to themselves, but it was no secret that a rump faction wanted to keep Dartmouth as it had always been, and they

60 Ibid., p. 60; Mary Kelley, "Looking Back, Looking Forward: Coeducation as Process," Oct. 17, 1997, in *Claiming Their Rightful Place*, pp. 25–26; Guthrie, "The Implementation of Coeducation at Dartmouth College, 1972–1982," p. 33.
61 Merton, "Hanging On," p. 60; John Kemeny oral history, pp. 82 (source of the quotes), 83.

found support among sympathetic trustees. Some adults in the community took the view that although student behavior could sometimes get out of hand, it was just one more expression of the way college boys had always behaved. But even if administrators and faculty had presented a unified stance against the most offensive student behavior, the campus culture would have been extremely difficult to reshape according to less obnoxiously sexist norms.[62]

In the late winter of 1979, in the context of an intense campus discussion of sexism, racism, and other problems at the college, the *New York Times* reported on a day of speeches and workshops on campus, referencing the speech given by an undergraduate woman who "urged more vigorous recruiting of minority women, expansion of the women's studies program, free day care facilities, equal financing for women's and men's athletics and a review of all tenure decisions for the last two years at Dartmouth." Three weeks later, the student received an envelope containing a copy of the *Times* story, with the word "Why?" scrawled next to the paragraph reporting on her remarks. Typed below the story was a note that read: "Hope you are happy with this, you ungrateful bitch. You have done a terrible disservice to Dartmouth. . . . If you don't like the place, get out." The noted was signed, "A loyal alumnus."[63]

But some loyal alumni who had been strongly opposed to coeducation changed their minds as they came to know individual women students and as their daughters and granddaughters began to matriculate at Dartmouth. A woman in the class of 1977, who sang with the a cappella group Dartmouth Distractions, recounted her experience at a dinner in Boston at the outset of coeducation. Each of the Distractions was seated with a group of alumni. Her table consisted of men she estimated to be close to celebrating their fiftieth reunion. As she sat down, one of the men said, "Oops! We were going to be the anti-coeducation table!" After the Distractions sang, she recalled, "the distinguished looking fellow sitting

---

62 Nelson interview; telephone interview with Marilyn Austin-Nelson, Jan. 29, 2015.
63 Merton, "Hanging On," p. 65.

next to me put his arm around me and said, 'If they are all like you, I'm going to have to change my mind about coeducation!' Pretty soon most of the gentlemen were discussing how to get their granddaughters interested in applying to the College."[64]

The conversion experience was widely shared. John Kemeny recalled "a very difficult evening at a 50th reunion banquet" soon after he became president. The speaker had given "an eloquent speech against change, particularly against coeducation." As Kemeny told the story, "Ten years later, that distinguished alumnus sent an 'emissary.' If he admitted via the emissary that he had been wrong on coeducation, would I receive him and please not mention the issue?" Kemeny agreed, and the two men had what he later characterized as "a very pleasant visit." The common ground that enabled the good conversation: the alumnus's granddaughter, "who was having a wonderful time at Dartmouth."[65]

Jean Kemeny recalled a lunch John Kemeny had with an alumnus in the South. "My two sons and I went to Dartmouth," the man told Kemeny. "For years, the three of us have worked hard for her. But when the Trustees voted to make the College coed, we decided to have nothing more to do with Dartmouth!" After a long pause, the alumnus continued, "On the other hand, my daughter—a sophomore at Dartmouth—has shown us the error of our ways!"[66]

Applications Increase, and the Quota System Goes

Coeducation served to increase the total number of applications to Dartmouth, and the combination of coeducation and year-round operation served also to make the college "more attractive to male students." The numbers of applications grew as shown in table 20.1:[67]

---

64 Martha Hennessey '77, in *Claiming Their Rightful Place*, p. 8.
65 Kemeny, "A Mathematician's Journey," n.d., "Coeducation," pp. 8–9.
66 Jean Alexander Kemeny, *It's Different at Dartmouth*, p. 93.
67 John G. Kemeny, "The First Five Years: A Report by the Thirteenth President," *Dartmouth Alumni Magazine*, Apr. 1975, p. 15, Kemeny, Box 8474.

TABLE 20.1. APPLICATIONS TO DARTMOUTH CLASSES
BY GENDER, 1975–78

Gender	1975	1976	1977	1978
Male	4,464	4,819	5,383	5,706
Female		956	1,790	2,090
Total	4,464	5,775	7,173	7,796

Like other institutions that began coeducation in this period, Dartmouth came to reconsider its initial quota regulating the number of men (three thousand) and women (one thousand) in the undergraduate student body. Faculty and students protested that the quota was discriminatory; as the number of highly qualified women applicants began to rise, the admission office was compelled to turn down excellent female candidates in favor of less impressive males. The board responded by abandoning the quota and embarking on a new admission policy whereby decisions would be based on the "potential" of candidates "for making a significant, positive impact on society." That policy left the door open to continuing to tilt admission decisions toward men. As Kemeny explained to the *New York Times*, "I have no doubt that women have just as much ability as men. But the fact is that they do not have as many opportunities open to them as men, and not as many women choose to have fulltime careers."[68]

The trustees decided that the best way to determine how to implement the new policy was to have the trustee committee on student affairs engage in a year of conversation on the matter with students, faculty, and alumni. In January 1977, the board took stock of what had been learned and "voted to establish guidelines to permit an additional 25 women in the class of 1981 and up to 15 additional women in succeeding classes, depending on the quality of applicants in the pool." The board hoped that such

---

68 "Coeducation Widens in Ivy League Colleges," *New York Times*, May 12, 1976, p. 47 ("just as much ability"); "Dartmouth Struggles with Coeducation as Students Press for More Women," *New York Times*, May 28, 1977, p. 46 ("significant, positive impact").

incremental progress would keep the decision off the radar screen and thereby blunt or "delay alumni opposition," which generally centered on fears of decreasing the number of men in the under-graduate student body. But pressures continued "for a less discriminatory policy," and members of the board began to believe that any kind of quota system was "sending the wrong signal." Finally, in April 1979, the board voted to adopt a sex-blind admission policy, beginning with the class of 1984.[69]

In fact, the male student population had fallen below 3,000 well before the decision for equal access, and after a slightly slower start, Dartmouth compared favorably with its peers in achieving reasonable gender balance in the undergraduate student body. By the fall of 1980, the ratio of men to women at Dartmouth was 2 to 1, compared with 1.4 to 1 at Yale and 1.7 to 1 at Princeton. By 1990 Dartmouth had essentially caught up, with a ratio of 1.3 to 1, as at Yale, compared with 1.4 to 1 at Princeton. And by 1995 all three schools had settled at 1.1 to 1. Although the Dartmouth student population grew by more than 18 percent—more than 650 students—over the three decades from 1980 to 2010, as shown in table 20.2, the number of women students increased by more than 76 percent—more than 900 students—a function of a modest decrease in the number of men. And all of this happened without protest—indeed, without attracting much attention—and certainly without damaging Dartmouth's Ivy League athletic standing.[70]

In the spring of 1979, a woman in the senior class wrote to Kemeny, almost on the spur of the moment, in the wake of a discussion in her feminist philosophy course. "We were talking about givens in the use of language—Adam and Eve, men and women, boys and girls—how men always came first," she said later. "President Kemeny," she wrote at the time, "during my four

69 "Dartmouth Struggles with Coeducation as Students Press for More Women"; John Kemeny oral history, pp. 102–4 (source of the quotes); David McLaughlin, "An Education for Women," *The Dartmouth*, Feb. 10, 1987, clipping in W.I.L. handwritten journal.

70 Dartmouth data from IPEDS Fall Enrollment Survey, Dartmouth College Office of Institutional Research; Yale data from Yale College Registrar / IPEDS Fall Headcount Surveys, Yale University Office of Institutional Research; Princeton data from Princeton University Registrar's Office.

TABLE 20.2. DARTMOUTH UNDERGRADUATE ENROLLMENT BY GENDER,
FIVE-YEAR INTERVALS, 1980–2010

Fall of	Men	Women	Total	Male-Female Ratio
1980	2,395	1,194	3,589	2 to 1
1985	2,027	1,458	3,485	1.4 to 1
1990	2,150	1,623	3,773	1.3 to 1
1995	2,043	1,836	3,879	1.1 to 1
2000	2,105	1,952	4,057	1.1 to 1
2005	2,064	2,046	4,110	1.1 to 1
2010	2,143	2,105	4,248	1.1 to 1

years at Dartmouth you have always addressed student audiences as 'Men and Women of Dartmouth.' When you are addressing my graduating class, would you please say 'Women and Men of Dartmouth'?"[71] When Kemeny did that at commencement, the audience erupted in wild applause. A woman in the class of 1980 recalled: "'Women and men of Dartmouth'—it reverberated through the audience. . . . The symbolism was not lost on any of us. It was a dramatically different statement from 'Men and women of Dartmouth.' Tears came to our eyes, shivers went down our spines, and cheers (mostly female) resounded through the audience. We knew we had made it, that we belonged, and that people who mattered wanted it that way."[72]

Dartmouth had moved a step closer to real coeducation.

71 Elizabeth P. Roberts '79, in *Claiming Their Rightful Place*, p. 12.
72 Elizabeth Pickar Gray '80, in *Claiming Their Rightful Place*, p. 12.

Part IV

The United Kingdom:
Cambridge and Oxford

<h1 style="text-align:center">21</h1>

Cambridge: "Like Dropping a Hydrogen Bomb in the Middle of the University"

The advent of coeducation—also called coresidence—at Cambridge and Oxford was grounded in local circumstances specific to the United Kingdom, but it was also influenced by many of the same developments that affected decisions for coeducation in the United States.

Setting the Context

The 1960s brought focused scrutiny of the British university system. The first of two major reports—the Report of the Committee on Higher Education, chaired by Lord (Lionel) Robbins, professor of economics at the London School of Economics, in 1963—made the case for expansion of British universities, with a proposed tripling of capacity, such that anyone who qualified would find a place. The number of eighteen-year-olds in Britain was expected to grow exponentially, with the number of students expected to double once between 1961–62 and 1967–68 and again by 1975–76.[1] To accommodate all qualified students, the number of universities would need to increase significantly, with new ones built and existing colleges of technology elevated to university status. At the time that the Robbins committee reported, less than 5 percent of British

1 "1963—The Government intrudes with the Robbins report on the future of Higher Education," in *1972: Cambridge: Churchill, Clare, King's, Lucy Cavendish: A Celebration of the Admission of Female Undergraduates*, slides exhibited for the 40th anniversary celebratory dinner at Churchill College, Apr. 20, 2013, Churchill, CCRF/112/5/10.

youth enrolled in universities, and of those, less than a quarter were women. Lord Robbins argued that a large pool of talent was being denied entry to universities. For the future strength of the United Kingdom, that situation needed to change.[2]

The second report—the Report of the Commission of Inquiry, chaired by Oliver Franks, provost of Worcester College, Oxford— focused on Oxford. The commission was constituted to consider the implications of the Robbins report for Oxford—to focus on "the part which Oxford plays now and should play in the future in the system of higher education in the United Kingdom." It collected data, conducted surveys, invited written comment, and held public hearings. It began meeting in April 1964 and issued its report in March 1966.[3]

The Franks Commission addressed matters relating to university governance and administrative reform, as well as topics including effectiveness of teaching methods, structure of examinations, methods of selecting undergraduates, and balance of undergraduates and graduate students. Notably, the commission argued for broader recruitment of students, reaching beyond traditional independent boarding schools to more diverse, less elite state schools in order to accomplish "the social representation of the nation in Oxford's student body." It argued, too, for growth in the size of the student population. It noted the importance of increasing the number of women undergraduates, but because the heads of women's colleges who were part of the commission were opposed to coeducation, it did not address the prospect of mixed colleges.[4]

The Cambridge version of the Franks Commission was the Bridges Syndicate. The syndicate was chaired by Lord (Edward E.) Bridges, former head of the civil service. Sir Eric Ashby, master of

2 *Higher Education: Report of the Committee Appointed by the Prime Minister under the Chairmanship of Lord Robbins* (London: Her Majesty's Stationery Office, 1963), http://www.educationengland.org.uk/documents/robbins/robbins1963.html, accessed Nov. 11, 2013.

3 University of Oxford, *Report of Commission of Inquiry*, vol.1: *Report, Recommendations, and Statutory Appendix* (Oxford: Clarendon Press, 1966). The quote is from p. 11.

4 Ibid. The quote is from p. 35.

Clare College, served as deputy to Lord Bridges. Its main focus was the relationship between the colleges and the burgeoning population of academic and non-academic staff, visiting scholars, and postgraduate students. The collegiate structure at Cambridge accommodated undergraduates and small groups of fellows, who taught and tutored the students. But it was not hospitable to members of the academic staff who were not fellows, a population that comprised 45 percent of the university's academic staff by 1961–62. A huge divide separated the university and the colleges. The purpose of the Bridges Syndicate was to propose measures "to close the gap" by providing fellowships for university teaching officers who had no college affiliations, as well as a home base for university staff and postgraduate students.

Although proposals in the Bridges report (1962) for new institutional relationships between the university and the colleges were not accepted, the colleges did address many of the issues on which the report focused. They expanded their fellowships and collaborated in founding three colleges for graduate students, which also meant increased opportunities for election of fellows. One of the new graduate colleges, University College (later renamed Wolfson), was founded by the university. The second, Darwin College, was the joint creation of Trinity, St. John's, and Gonville and Caius Colleges. The third, Clare Hall, which served also as a center for visiting scholars, was founded by Clare College, a project in which Ashby took the lead. The proportion of university teaching officers who had college fellowships rose from 50 percent in 1960 to 84 percent in 1989. The work of the syndicate also stimulated the creation of new physical facilities, notably the University Centre, with places to eat, drink, and meet.[5]

The Bridges report, Ashby noted, "stirred the Cambridge conscience to do something about issues on which the Colleges or

5 Christopher N. L. Brooke, *A History of the University of Cambridge*, vol. 4: *1870–1990* (Cambridge: Cambridge University Press, 1993), pp. 573–75; Eric Ashby, Biographical Notes, p. 65, typescript, n.d., Clare, CCPP/1/ASH; Alan Burges and Richard J. Eden, "Eric Ashby (1904–1992)," *Oxford Dictionary of National Biography* (Oxford: Oxford University Press, 2004), http://www.oxforddnb.com/view/article/50791, accessed May 17, 2013; typescript, Eric Ashby, "The Founding of Clare Hall," n.d., Clare, CCPP/ASH/3.

the University were vulnerable. One of these . . . was the need to increase the intake of women undergraduates."[6] The Bridges Syndicate enabled Ashby to cut his teeth on Cambridge university politics. "This couldn't have come at a better time for me," Ashby said. "I learned an enormous lot about the whole University system."[7]

Beyond the ferment generated by the three reports, there was a clear desire to expand opportunities for women to study at Cambridge and Oxford. In British provincial universities, many of them founded in the modern era, coeducation was taken for granted. But Oxford dated to the eleventh century and Cambridge to the fourteenth—long before there was any possibility of higher education for women. Beginning in the late nineteenth century, women's colleges were founded at Cambridge—Girton (1873), Newnham (1875), and New Hall (1954)—and at Oxford—Lady Margaret Hall (1878), St. Anne's (1879), Somerville (1879), St. Hugh's (1886), and St. Hilda's (1893). It took an inordinately long time for the universities to grant these institutions full collegiate status. Oxford first awarded degrees to women in 1920, Cambridge in 1948.

Although the women's colleges had ample measures of prestige and distinction, they lacked capacity and resources to educate large numbers of students. As a result, the number of women students at Cambridge and Oxford was very small. In 1963–64, women accounted for 16 percent of Oxford students, compared with 28 percent of students in British universities as a whole. An even greater disparity operated at Cambridge, where only 9.65 percent of undergraduates in 1964–65 were women, the lowest percentage of any university in the country.[8] At a time when the women's colleges could not afford to expand, the question of how best to increase the number of places available to women students was front and center on the two universities' agendas.

6 Eric Ashby, "How Ever Did Women Get into Clare?," *Clare Association Annual*, 1986–87, p. 8, Clare, CCCS/4/5.

7 Ashby oral history, p. 13.

8 Joseph A. Soares, *The Decline of Privilege: The Modernization of Oxford University* (Stanford, CA: Stanford University Press, 1999), p. 96; R. H. Tizard, Admission of Women: Report to the College Council, Oct. 23, 1967, Churchill, CCGB/111; "1962—Cambridge University takes a critical look at itself," in *1972: Cambridge: Churchill, Clare, King's, Lucy Cavendish.*

In the United States, as we have seen, the prime movers in adopting coeducation were motivated by what they perceived to be strategic necessity: Applications were beginning to decline, and the "best boys" were beginning to make clear that they did not want to go to all-male institutions. In the United Kingdom, the overwhelming power and prestige of Cambridge and Oxford made it less likely that the "best boys" would opt for other, already coeducational institutions. And yet there was new competition for students with the founding between 1961 and 1965 of "new universities" at East Anglia, Essex, Kent, Lancaster, Sussex, Warwick, and York. The new universities offered broader, more flexible, more interdisciplinary, more innovative curricula. Committed to avoiding excessive specialization, they also sought to provide opportunities for students to pursue studies in multiple fields rather than having to choose a single academic focus as in the older, more traditional universities. And they emphasized new styles of learning—inquiry-based learning, enterprise-related learning, learning based in interdisciplinary schools rather than departments. Unlike the red-brick universities, the new universities were built as compact campuses located on the periphery of cities, and they offered students highly prized opportunities to build community. They also offered coeducation. With "no tradition of gender segregation or discrimination," they proved to be particularly attractive to women students. By 1966–67, women accounted for 35 to 38 percent of the students at Essex, Lancaster, Sussex, and Warwick and 41 to 43 percent at East Anglia, Kent, and York.[9]

The popularity of the new universities among women students helped to prompt Oxford and Cambridge to consider mixed colleges. Strategic advantage for Oxford and Cambridge meant not "losing out" in the competition for "highly able girls."[10] But additional issues of strategic advantage were involved in particular

9 "The Utopian Universities: A Fifty Year Retrospective," conference at the Institute of Historical Research, University of London, Oct. 23–24, 2014; Carol Dyhouse, *Students: A Gendered History* (London and New York: Routledge, 2006), pp. 100–102 (the quote is on p. 100).

10 Carol Dyhouse remarks, "The Utopian Universities: A Fifty Year Retrospective"; Dyhouse, *Students: A Gendered History*, p. 103 (source of the quote).

colleges' decisions to go mixed. The men's colleges that were the first movers at Cambridge and Oxford tended not to be the richest or the most prestigious of their respective groups. Admitting women was seen as a way to gain advantage in the Tompkins and Norrington Tables, which ranked colleges at Cambridge and Oxford, respectively, on the basis of their graduating students' academic achievements. The women's colleges stood at the top of those tables. Admitting women would move a number of the very strongest students from the women's colleges to newly coeducational colleges; moreover, it would likely attract more accomplished male students who might otherwise have eschewed middling men's colleges for more prestigious choices.

Still, it was a considerable stretch to imagine mixed colleges at Cambridge. In May 1964, the Council of the Cambridge University Senate approved a provision whereby colleges that chose to admit men and women would no longer be ineligible for recognition from the university. Whether such recognition would ever come to pass was another question. In June 1964, the *Cambridge Review* opined both that mixed colleges were "necessary" and that "the prospect of them [was] so unlikely that if one said there would be an astronaut on the moon before women achieved parity in Cambridge this would not be a vainglorious claim but a safe bet." In fact it was a safe bet. The first moon landing came in July 1969, but parity between men and women undergraduates at Cambridge was not realized until 2005.[11]

Nonetheless, the unlikelihood of mixed colleges turned out not to be anywhere near as certain as the *Cambridge Review* predicted. In 1965 the University of Cambridge repealed its statute prohibiting mixed colleges. The immediate impact came at the postgraduate level, where the three new graduate colleges moved to admit women postgraduates and senior members.[12]

In a series of decisions taken between 1965 and 1970, three men's colleges—Churchill, Clare, and King's—admitted undergraduate

11 "1964—An important obstacle is removed," in *1972: Cambridge: Churchill, Clare, King's, Lucy Cavendish.*

12 J.R.C.H., Admission of Women: Note by the Bursar, Dec. 2, 1968, Churchill, CCGB/190/3.

women for the fall of 1972. In each case, two votes were required: a vote in favor of coeducation by the college's governing body (the fellows of the college) and a vote, also by the governing body, to repeal the college statute limiting enrollment to men. The latter decision was subject to approval by the Privy Council, the formal body of advisers to the Queen, generally drawn from current or former members of Parliament.

Initial Discussions in the Colleges

Churchill, Clare, and King's were united by their willingness to act in advance of other colleges, and they cooperated in important ways in planning and execution. But the decisions for coeducation at each college were taken independently and were rooted in local conditions, and the story of the coming of coeducation to Cambridge is best told by understanding the specific circumstances and decision-making processes at each of the three colleges. The story winds back and forth among the three, which acted roughly in parallel and in a similar time frame.

CHURCHILL

It was no surprise that Churchill College was one of the first to act. Founded to honor the great British prime minister, Sir Winston Churchill, and enrolling its first students in 1960, it was the newest college at Cambridge, with the briefest history, the fewest deeply rooted traditions, and the least consequential ties to alumni. The college fellowship had been assembled relatively recently; it was more flexible, nimble, and open to change than fellowships with long histories.

Churchill himself had been intimately involved in conceiving the plan for the new college. On a vacation trip to Sicily with his wife, Clementine, following his resignation as prime minister in April 1955, he struck up a conversation with two close colleagues who had accompanied them. One of them was Sir John Colville, one of Churchill's private secretaries. The other, Lord Cherwell— Frederick Lindemann—was an Oxford physicist, a longtime friend and confidant. As Churchill's principal scientific adviser, Cherwell, like other scientists, had expressed to the prime minister his concern that Britain was failing to produce an adequate number of specialists in science and technology. In the course of the conversation in Sicily, Churchill expressed regret that he had failed as prime minister to act on Cherwell's recommendation to do something about the deficit of technologists. Cherwell and Colville told him that it was not too late. Churchill himself had achieved a poor academic record in secondary school, and he had been educated at the Royal Sandhurst Military Academy, not at Cambridge or Oxford. But he admired the Massachusetts Institute of Technology, where he had given a speech in 1949, and during the conversation with Cherwell and Colville "the idea was born" of creating an institution in Britain similar to MIT. Colville volunteered to raise the funds.[13] The Churchill College Trust was established in 1958, under Sir Winston's chairmanship, to fund and build the new college of science and technology.

Women's organizations were quick to make the case for admitting women. There was a pressing need for more women in science, they said, and the planned college stood in a unique position to help meet it. In June 1958 the Open Door Council, an organization dedicated to "the economic emancipation of the woman worker," wrote to Sir Winston urging that the new college "accept both men and women students." With "the right training," they argued, women "could achieve great things equally with their fellow men."[14] Also in June, the president of the Women's Freedom League wrote requesting that Churchill use his influence in advancing the "revolutionary" proposal that the new college "become a pioneer co-educational college" in the interest of increasing the number of women scientists in Great Britain.[15] In July the British Federation of University Women urged "fuller opportunities . . . in the Universities for able and qualified women

---

13 Martin Gilbert, *Churchill: A Life* (New York: Henry Holt, 1991), pp. 943 (source of the quote), 951.

14 Mrs. C. M. Young to Sir Winston Churchill, June 5, 1958, Churchill, CCGB/210/2.

15 Marion Reeves to Sir Winston Churchill, June 11, 1958, Churchill, CCGB/210/2.

students."[16] Similar communications came from the National Federation of Business and Professional Women's Clubs and the Federation of Soroptimist Clubs.[17]

Churchill was personally sympathetic to the case for including women. His daughter, Mary Soames, told a story recounted to her by Colville: At one of the early meetings of the members of the Churchill Trust, Sir Winston had said, "My wife thinks women should be admitted to Churchill . . . and I think so too."[18] A "scribbled memo" in June 1958 noted "Winston's opinion that women should be admitted."[19]

But coeducation was a revolutionary concept at a time when university statutes still precluded women from being admitted to men's colleges. Churchill College had been planned as a national and Commonwealth memorial to Sir Winston, and funds for the new college had been raised on the promise that it would focus on education in science and technology and thus contribute to the national need for "an increased output of technologists."[20] That meant education for men. Proposing during the fund-raising process that the university permit the college to educate women as well as men would, one of Churchill's former private secretaries warned, "be like dropping a hydrogen bomb in the middle of the University."[21]

The members of the Churchill College Trust were aware of Churchill's views on the matter, however, and they did not want to offend him unnecessarily. "The reason why no reference was made to the sex of the inmates of Churchill in the Draft Statutes," one trustee wrote, "is because of Sir Winston's sensitiveness on this point!" Given the prohibition still in force against mixed colleges,

16 Kathleen Johnston to Lord Tedder, July 8, 1958, Churchill, CCGB/210/2.

17 Doris Smart to Lord Tedder, Aug. 19, 1958, and Miss P.A.B. Macdonald to the Secretary, Churchill College Trust Fund, Nov. 28, 1958, both in Churchill, CCGB/210/2.

18 Mary Soames, *Clementine Churchill: The Biography of a Marriage* (Boston: Houghton Mifflin, 1979), p. 619.

19 Mark Goldie, "Winston and the Women," *Churchill Review* 30 (1993): 9, Churchill.

20 J.R.C.H., Admission of Women: Note by the Bursar, Dec. 2, 1968, Churchill, CCGB/190/3.

21 Maria Tippett, "Twenty-Five Years of Women in Churchill, 1972–1997," *Churchill Review* 34 (1997): 44.

once the first male student was admitted to the college, the problem would be solved.[22] (Sir Winston's sensitivities notwithstanding, the final version of the statutes did include the usual prohibition against the enrollment of female students.)

As secretary to the Churchill Trust, A.F.W. Humphrys drafted responses to the women's organizations explaining why it was impossible to contemplate educating women at the new college. But Sir Winston rewrote the Humphrys draft in a less negative tone, partly to mollify the organizations, partly to leave the door slightly ajar.[23] As his letter to the president of the Women's Freedom League explained, the trust's executive committee had given sympathetic consideration to the league's views; although they would see what could be done for women students at Churchill, the league should understand that it might "not be possible to embody a fully co-educational college in the structure of Cambridge University."[24] The implication was clear: There was no intention to have any resident women students at the new college. The appeal for funds had been launched with the understanding that the college would be for men, and £2 million had already been raised. Changing direction to include women would risk upsetting those who had already contributed and likely prevent others from donating. However, there might be an opportunity for some women graduate students who could not find appropriate advisers in their own colleges to come to Churchill "for supervision of their work."[25]

With the repeal in 1965 of the University of Cambridge statute prohibiting mixed colleges, the possibility of educating men and women together was no longer unthinkable. A proposal to amend the Churchill College statutes to permit the admission of women was first approved by the college council in January 1965. It had still to be approved by the governing body, the sovereign body of

22 Letter from Lord Adrian, July 1, 1959, Churchill, CCGB/102/9.

23 Goldie, "Winston and the Women," p. 9.

24 Sir Winston Churchill to the President, Women's Freedom League, July 30, 1958, Churchill, CCGB/210/2. See also A.F.W. Humphrys to Doris Smart, Sept. 10, 1958, and Humphrys to P.A.B. Macdonald, Dec. 11, 1958, both in Churchill, CCGB/210/2.

25 A.F.W. Humphrys to Professor B. W. Downs, Nov. 17, 1958 (source of the quote), Churchill, CCGB/210/2; Goldie, "Winston and the Women," p. 10; Tippett, "Twenty-Five Years of Women in Churchill, 1972–1997," p. 44.

the college. Then, in a process extending from October 1965 until April 1966, Churchill went through the steps required to repeal its statute prohibiting women from enrolling, subject to approval by the Privy Council, which came in September 1966.[26]

That approval meant not that Churchill was ready to go mixed but that the governing body and the college council were ready to talk about it, and the college appointed a committee "to consider the pros and cons." One of the first steps was to meet with the heads of the three women's colleges at Cambridge to hear their views. Newnham and Girton were reported to be "quite sympathetic to the general case for the admission of women by Men's Colleges." What New Hall thought was yet to be determined. The committee would be reporting; there would be more discussion in the governing body and further consultations with the women's colleges.[27]

The subject was slated for discussion in the Churchill College governing body in September 1966. Admitting women was by no means a foregone conclusion. One member who could not attend the meeting opined that focusing on the admission of women seemed to be "a great failure in priorities." He said, "There is such a lot to be done, and wrangling or even agreeing about women seems to have no relevance."[28] The vice-master responded: "In the main I am completely with you on the undesirability <u>at present</u> of admitting women. . . . I would dearly like to see more women in Cambridge . . . and the only probable way to achieve this is for men's colleges to admit them. But I do not think Churchill is in a

---

26 College Council Minutes, Feb. 9 and Mar. 9, 1965, Churchill, CCGB/110; J.R.C.H., Admission of Women: Note by the Bursar, Dec. 2, 1968, Churchill, CCGB/190/3; "The Queen's Most Excellent Majesty in Council, Sept. 20, 1966," in *1972: Cambridge: Churchill, Clare, King's, Lucy Cavendish.*

27 In Churchill, CCGB/110, see College Council Minutes, Oct. 5 and Nov. 2, 1965, and Jan. 11, Feb. 1 and 15, Mar. 1, July 12, and Oct. 18, 1966. In Churchill, CCGB/190/2, see Master, Churchill College, to Miss R. L. Cohen [Principal, Newnham College], Oct. 7, 1965; Master, Churchill College, to Miss A. R. Murray [President, New Hall], Oct. 7, 1965; Master, Churchill College, to Mistress, Girton College [Mary Cartwright], Oct. 12, 1965; Cartwright to Master, Churchill College, Dec. 1, 1965; and Cohen to Master, Churchill College, Dec. 3, 1965. The quotes are from John Cockcroft, Master of Churchill College, to Lord Annan, Provost of King's College, May 10, 1966, Churchill, CCGB/190/2.

28 John [A. Oriel] to Kenneth [McQuillen], Sept. 25, 1966, Churchill, CCPP/1/6/10.

fit state to do this in the next five years at any rate. After that, on verra [we'll see]."[29]

CLARE

At Clare, as at Churchill, the mid-1960s brought the first serious consideration of the possibility of admitting women. Founded in 1326, Clare was the second-oldest college of the university. The master, Sir Eric Ashby, a distinguished botanist, had come to Clare in 1959 from the position of vice-chancellor of Queen's University, Belfast. Unusually, Ashby had no previous connection to Clare or to Cambridge. Perhaps because of that, he was more than ready to encourage and embrace change. Moreover, given his experience in university administration, he had the political savvy and management skill to lead Clare in challenging times.

Clare, Ashby said many years later, had been "very inbred." Recognizing that they were going to need to "face all the changes that were coming over the colleges," the fellows made the unprecedented decision to go outside the college and the university for a new master. "I think," Ashby reflected, "they wanted what you could call a breath of non-Cambridge air."[30] Ashby noted that Clare had been described to him "the best public school in Cambridge." He continued, "The Fellows wanted to turn it into the best College in Cambridge."[31]

Clare had a long history of admitting students from a small group of public schools—older, exclusive, fee-paying, independent schools like Eton and Harrow. When Ashby took up the mastership, more than 70 percent of the students came from these schools. At a time, he said, "when even Cambridge was a state-supported university it was no longer desirable to admit undergraduates of mediocre intellectual caliber . . . just because their fathers had been to Clare. My first job was to preside over a shift to a meritocratic admissions policy."[32] With Ashby's encouragement, the senior tutor, John Northam, a highly regarded Ibsen

29 [Kenneth McQuillen] to John A. Oriel, Oct. 4, 1966, Churchill, CCPP/1/6/10.
30 Ashby oral history, pp. 2–3.
31 Ashby, Biographical Notes, p. 62.
32 Ibid.

scholar, worked to achieve "a more diverse intake with stricter criteria for academic merit."[33] Ashby took no part in admission decisions, but he had an important role to play, both in "persuading grammar schools to send their boys to Clare" and in "pacifying indignant old Clare men who were outraged if their sons, with a row of C-level passes in GCE [the General Certificate of Education], were refused admission."[34]

The new admission policy was one part of what Ashby called "great changes": "a relaxation (some called it an abdication) of traditions (such as compulsory gowns at night), a much wider field for admissions, and a final withdrawal . . . from the century-long inbreeding which had produced scores of dons who had never been anywhere except at Cambridge since they came up."[35]

The greatest change during Ashby's mastership was the admission of undergraduate women. The motivating force behind the college's willingness to lead on this issue, he said, was the "grave and great inequality and injustice being done to women."[36] In the winter of 1966, on the initiative of John Northam, the governing body took up the possibility of admitting women to the college and set up a study group to look into the matter.[37] The study group "examined the options: increasing the size of women's colleges, building new co-residential colleges, admitting women to men's colleges." They investigated the implications of coresidence for academic standards, the balance of subjects likely to be studied, the college's cultural life and sporting activities, and the fellowship itself. They gathered information from universities that already had mixed residence halls and reported nearly unanimous testimony that "they succeed as communities, they do not inhibit good academic work, [and] in some cases they promote better standards of behaviour than are found in single-sex halls."[38]

33 Burges and Eden, "Eric Ashby (1904–1992)."
34 Ashby, Biographical Notes, p. 62.
35 Ibid., pp. 62–63.
36 Ashby oral history, p. 11.
37 Study Group, Interim Report, 1966, Clare, CCGB/4/8.
38 Ashby, "How Ever Did Women Get into Clare?," p. 9. The universities from which detailed information was collected included Aberdeen, Birmingham, Keele, Lancaster, and Imperial College, University of London. Their reports—appendixes to the 1966 Study Group report—are in Clare, CCGB/4/8.

The study group report came before the governing body in November 1968. In the meantime, there had been strong expressions of support for admitting women from the Clare junior combination room (JCR), the vehicle for undergraduate social and residential life and the body representing undergraduate interests in the college. The JCR wanted coresidence to be addressed; they also wanted the study group "upgraded to committee status," with undergraduates comprising half the members.[39] Ashby promised to take the proposal to the governing body.[40]

But Ashby followed up with some questions. The governing body would want to know why undergraduates were interested in coresidence. Was it "on national grounds"—because women accounted for so small a share of the student population of British universities? Was it that having women in the college would "promote its purpose . . . to foster learning and research?" Or was it "to provide an additional amenity for the social life of undergraduates?" Ashby also offered information to help the JCR prepare a persuasive document.[41]

The JCR submitted an extended commentary for the November 25 meeting of the governing body. The students thought that admitting women would likely raise the college's academic standards; among the women applicants would be a number who were "better qualified academically than some of the men presently admitted to Cambridge men's colleges." Also, mixed colleges might "have a better pick of highly qualified male students." Women would bring to bear intellectual perspectives different from those of men, which would enrich academic discussions and lead to "a more fruitful explanation of ideas." The presence of women would encourage men to pay more attention, work harder, and "think and speak more effectively."

Beyond the academic advantages of coresidence, the JCR argued, the "total life of the community" would benefit. Undergraduate extracurricular activities "would be enhanced"; "dining might

39 Dennis McQuillan [President of the Junior Combination Room] to the Master, Nov. 5, 1968, Clare, CCGB/4/8.

40 [Eric Ashby] to [Dennis] McQuillan, Nov. 5, 1968, Clare, CCGB/4/8.

41 Ibid., Nov. 8, 1968, Clare, CCGB/4/8.

well become more civilized"; students' emotional health would be improved by more normal interactions between men and women. All told, the JCR anticipated a "general civilizing effect."[42] Along with the JCR's commentary went 178 signatures from undergraduates (out of 193 people canvassed) in support of the motion: "We the undersigned . . . agree in principle that women be admitted into Clare on the same terms as men."[43]

The response of the governing body, by majority vote, was to reconstitute the study group as a committee of senior and junior members—five undergraduates and one graduate student, elected by their fellow students—"to outline the basic arguments for and against the admission of women to Clare College," to collect data, and to offer observations to help the governing body come to a decision. It was, Ashby made clear, "a committee to persuade, not to act." The decision on whether or not to admit women would be taken by the governing body.[44]

The Next Phase of Discussions

Just as the study group at Clare had proceeded slowly in reporting to the governing body, so the committee set up at Churchill to consider the pros and cons of admitting women deliberated but—for reasons that are not clear—delayed reporting.[45]

CHURCHILL

In October 1967, Churchill's senior tutor, R. H. Tizard, took matters into his own hands and made a personal report to the college council that he described as informed by the committee's deliberations and, he believed, consonant with its views. Tizard took seriously the charge to consider pros and cons. Two sections

42 JCR report to the Governing Body, untitled, n.d., but Nov. 1968, Clare, CCGB/4/8.
43 Dennis McQuillan to Master, Nov. 25, 1968, Clare, CCGB/4/8.
44 [Eric Ashby] to D. A. McQuillan, Nov. 26 and 28 (source of the quote), 1968, Clare, CCGB/4/8.
45 College Council Minutes, Apr. 25 and May 2, 1967, Churchill, CCGB/110.

of his report were titled "Why admit women?" and "Why not admit women?" The report also asked what information would be needed for a decision to be made, what problems might arise and what factors would have to be considered if women were admitted, and—if women were admitted—when that should happen.

Tizard's "pros" for admitting women encapsulated very well the considerations that would ultimately lead Churchill, Clare, and King's to go mixed. The first was increasing the number of women students in the university, which would be desirable for academic reasons, "either on the grounds that to do so would increase the average academic level of entrants, or on the grounds that teaching and learning would benefit." It would be desirable for social reasons on a national scale, "on the grounds that it is desirable to provide more women qualified for professions, or better educated mothers to benefit the next generation of sons, or on sex-egalitarian grounds." It would be desirable, too, for social reasons "on a domestic scale, on the grounds that it would improve the lot of the male undergraduate if there were more girls for him to meet." And, finally, it "might conceivably be a factor in encouraging more women into academical and professional life in certain subjects, especially engineering."

The argument for admitting women as a way to increase the average academic level in the college had multiple parts. If the total number of students at Churchill were to remain the same, it would be possible to substitute more qualified women for the "'tail-end' of the male applicants." Coeducation would make Churchill more attractive to boys in secondary schools, "increasing the competition for entry and giving us a larger number from which to select the best." And teaching men and women together would likely benefit "teaching and learning."

As for the social benefits, going mixed would make it "easier for undergraduates to meet girls, and to do so naturally in the ordinary course of living." Having women around on a regular basis would likely cause "standards of conduct, dress and behaviour amongst the men [to] rise." And the final argument for admitting women evoked the competitive streak so characteristic of decisions for coeducation in the United States: "Because we want to be modern and 'with it,' or because we do not want another College to do it first."

Tizard also outlined the reasons not to admit women. The women's colleges might object; academic standards could be threatened because the presence of women might distract men from their work; admitting women would run counter to the founding purpose of the college, to increase the number of scientists and engineers in the United Kingdom; coresidence would be an invitation to inappropriate behavior between the sexes; having men and women together all the time would be socially complicated. And there were other ways of increasing the number of women at Cambridge—by enlarging existing women's colleges or opening new ones.[46]

After considering Tizard's report, the college council decided to circulate it on a confidential basis, without making recommendations, to the members of the governing body, together with a summary of the council's discussion.[47] Further consideration of the matter remained on hold for nearly a year. The founding master of Churchill College, Sir John Cockcroft, a Nobel Prize–winning nuclear physicist, died suddenly in September 1967. With the vice-master, Kenneth McQuillen, in charge temporarily, it was no moment to look seriously at major institutional change. Cockcroft's successor, Sir William R. Hawthorne, a mechanical engineer specializing in jet engine technology who was heading the department of engineering at Cambridge, took up the mastership of the college in October 1968. Coresidence was far from the top of Hawthorne's agenda. Indeed, he had a reputation as an antifeminist; he was an accomplished magician, and one of the tricks of which he was proudest was to saw a woman in half. He was not reticent about making his views known. When Alison Finch, a scholar of French literature, took up her appointment to the fellowship in

46 R. H. Tizard, Admission of Women: Report to the College Council, Oct. 24, 1967, Churchill, CCGB/190/1.

47 College Council Minutes, Oct. 31, 1967; J.R.C.H., Admission of Women: Comments by the Council on the Report by the Senior Tutor, Nov. 15, 1967, both in Churchill, CCGB/190/1.

1972, virtually the first thing Hawthorne told her was, "Well, Miss Finch, I voted against the admission of women."[48]

But Hawthorne was not able to derail consideration of Churchill going mixed. The college fellowship had taken hold of the idea under Cockcroft's mastership, and Tizard, who was very much in favor, drove the process. As Hawthorne himself acknowledged, "The master has only one vote in spite of being the master." In effect, the fellowship overruled the master.[49]

In November 1968, after having discussed Tizard's report of the previous year, the governing body directed the college council to prepare a plan for the admission of women so that the governing body could come to a decision. The council empanelled a series of subcommittees to address the many aspects of the question: admissions, tutorial and decanal arrangements, facilities, finances, appointment of women fellows, cooperation with other colleges, and matters concerning statutes, ordinances, and regulations.[50]

By December, as the subcommittees began their investigations, Churchill was engaged in serious discussions internally, as well as with the women's colleges and other men's colleges considering going mixed. Three men's colleges were exploring the possibility: Clare, King's, and Gonville and Caius. Churchill and King's had already changed their statutes to permit the admission of women; that change would still need to be accomplished at Clare and Caius.[51]

KING'S

At King's, with more than five centuries of history as an all-male college, a major revision in the college statutes (submitted for royal approval in 1966) provided the opportunity to change "the

---

48 Alison Finch, in Nancy Weiss Malkiel conversation with Alison Finch, Archie Howie, and Mark Goldie, Oct. 28, 2013, Cambridge, England.

49 Hawthorne, quoted in ibid.

50 College Council Minutes, Oct. 29, Nov. 5, 12, and 26, and Dec. 3, 1968, and Feb. 4, 1969, Churchill, CCGB/110; Admission of Women: Report of the Council to the Governing Body, Feb. 26, 1969, Churchill, CCGB/190/1; W. R. Hawthorne to Governing Bodies of Churchill and other authorized Colleges, Nov. 21, 1968, Clare, CCGB/4/8.

51 Agenda, Meeting to Consider the Admission of Women, Dec. 11, 1968, Churchill, CCGB/190/3; Admission of Women: Report of the Sub-Committee on Action with Other Men's Colleges, Jan. 27, 1969, Churchill, CCAC/134/4/1, File 1.

female-exclusion clause in the statutes to an ordinance" so that it required only the college governing body rather than the Privy Council to revoke the exclusion. In other words, the college could now make its own decision on admitting women.[52] In March 1966 the governing body took up the motion "No woman shall be a member of the College whether on the Foundation or otherwise," which carried by a vote of "Ayes 42 and the Provost." The provost was Noel Annan, a member of the economics faculty and lecturer in politics who was about to take up a new post as provost of University College London.[53] In May, Annan told the master of Churchill that King's was "certainly not at the moment considering any change in the sexual composition of the College!"[54]

The turnaround at King's came with the election in 1966 of a new provost, Edmund Leach, a social anthropologist with a reputation as a "radical intellectual," a "militant atheis[t]," and an agent of change. As Leach wrote later, at Cambridge "the more intellectual among us were almost all of a radical, near communist, political persuasion. We were already coming to hate the social rigidities of the system in which we had been reared, the injustices of which were visible on every side."[55] Geoffrey E. R. Lloyd, a classicist who would serve as senior tutor at King's from 1969 to 1973, said of Leach: "What he stood for was a real openness of spirit and readiness to rethink educational issues, as well as himself giving great intellectual leadership."[56]

Leach turned out to be a very strong leader. He was fully in charge, and he proved to be less flexible than his supporters might have imagined. If he was on their side, his strength allowed him to accomplish their shared purposes. If he took an opposing position, he could be a formidable obstacle to progress. In such areas as

52 E-mail, Peter Jones [Fellow and Librarian, King's College] to Nancy Weiss Malkiel, June 5, 2013.

53 Quoted in Stanley J. Tambiah, *Edmund Leach: An Anthropological Life* (Cambridge: Cambridge University Press, 2002), p. 457, King's. As Tambiah notes, the minutes did not record negative votes or abstentions.

54 Lord Annan to Sir John Cockcroft, May 13, 1966, Churchill, CCGB/190/2.

55 Leach, quoted in Stephen Hugh-Jones, *Edmund Leach, 1910–1989: Provost, Emeritus Professor of Social Anthropology* (King's College, Cambridge, 1989), p. 9, King's. "Radical intellectual" and "militant atheist," Hugh-Jones's characterizations, are on p. 22.

56 Geoffrey E. R. Lloyd, quoted in Tambiah, *Edmund Leach*, p. 462.

student unrest and disciplinary matters, he proved to be dogmatic, even autocratic. Had he been on the wrong side of significant change in the life of the college, it might never have come to pass.[57]

But Leach did favor change, and under his leadership King's upended many of its traditions: "The Hall was turned back to front, the servery became a self-servery, the high table was made low, and English not Latin became the Provost's language in Chapel." Students gained "representation on the College Council and other administrative bodies."[58] May Week Balls, with tails and white waistcoats, gave way to informal discotheques, cabaret performances, folk and rock music, films, and barbecues.[59] Leach oversaw more substantive changes also. Building on a new admission policy instituted by Annan, who had seen King's as too much of a "seminary for young gentlemen," the college worked to recruit and admit more students from state, or maintained, schools, thus reducing the historic dominance of the independent schools.[60]

The decision to admit women was part and parcel of these changes. Lloyd put the case this way: "The main consideration that weighed with most of us that supported coresidence was the simple and stark statistic of the ratio between male and female undergraduates in Cambridge." Because the existing women's colleges could not "do much to redress that balance," only two options existed: founding a new college or colleges, which would be a hugely expensive venture, "or—far simpler—some of the male colleges should admit women." Another strong argument was based on equity: There were a great many bright, talented women, and it was only right that they should have their chance at a Cambridge education.[61]

57 Interview with Geoffrey E. R. Lloyd, Oct. 30, 2013, Cambridge, England.

58 Hugh-Jones, *Edmund Leach*, pp. 28–30 (the quotes are on pp. 28 and 30, respectively).

59 L. P. Wilkinson, *A Century of King's, 1873–1972* (King's College, Cambridge, 1980), pp. 148–49.

60 Annan, quoted in ibid., p. 142; Lloyd interview. On the fruits of what Wilkinson calls "the policy of widening the College's catchment area," see pp. 143 (source of the quote)–44.

61 E-mail, Geoffrey E. R. Lloyd to Nancy Weiss Malkiel, May 30, 2013.

It was no surprise that King's would be in the vanguard with respect to the admission of women. The college had a reputation for doing things differently, for being a bit pushy, for going its own way.[62] Moreover, Leach was strongly in favor of coeducation, as were the college tutors; students, too, were "very much interested."[63] In October 1968, the governing body received a report from the JCR urging King's to move to coresidence "as soon as possible."[64] The response of the governing body was to appoint a committee "to consider the advantages, disadvantages and feasibility of the admission of women" and to give the governing body information on which it could "form a considered judgment."[65]

Taking Action: Working toward a Final Decision

As King's was beginning deliberations, Churchill was moving forward. By February 1969 their deliberations had been concluded, the necessary work had been done, and the Churchill College council had a plan ready to submit to the governing body.

CHURCHILL

The Churchill proposal was grounded in these assumptions: Women would be admitted to the college at all levels, from undergraduates to fellows. The number of students in the college would not change, and a modest increase in the fellowship would accommodate the appointment of three women tutors. The ratios that had governed the composition of the student body—70–30 science/arts, 2–1 undergraduates/advanced students—would still obtain. Rules and regulations regarding student conduct would not change. Women would be housed, at least at first, in mixed as well as single-sex staircases. And Churchill would proceed to

---

62 Lloyd interview.
63 Wilkinson, *A Century of King's*, p. 152.
64 Council minutes, Oct. 25, 1968, with J.C.R. paper, "Co-Education and Co-Residence in King's: Proposals," Oct. 18, 1968, King's, KCGB/5/1/4/24.
65 Report of the Committee on the Admission of Women, May 1969, King's, KCGB/4/1/1/22.

admit women on its own schedule, without worrying about joint action with other colleges.[66]

Going mixed would require relatively modest expenditures: just over £59,000 in one-time costs for alterations to physical facilities and £5,700 in recurrent annual expenditures for the women tutors and a resident nurse. As for timing, once a decision to go mixed was taken, it would be at least twenty-seven months before women students could be in residence, a period dictated by the need to determine and advertise the admission procedure for women students.[67]

The vote in the Churchill governing body was set for March 8. The motion on the table called for the admission of women undergraduates beginning in October of 1972 or 1973, the schedule to depend on the development of "a suitable admissions procedure." Up to forty women might be admitted each year, assuming enough applicants "of sufficient merit." The same standards of admission would apply to women as to men. Funds should be raised to expand the size of the college by sixty to eighty students to minimize the reduction in the number of men.[68]

Not every member of the governing body could attend the meeting. An opponent wrote that if he could be present, he would vote against coresidence. He preferred "the creation of a fourth women's college and a contribution towards this," but he "doubt[ed] if such a proposal would stand a chance."[69] Another skeptic wrote, "My voice is old and my opinion old-fashioned! My instinct is against."[70] In contrast, a supporter wrote to say that if he were present, he would vote for the admission of women. Noting that it was bound "to come anyway," he said, "We may as well accept the inevitable with a good grace."[71]

---

66 College Council Minutes, Jan. 21 and Feb. 4, 11, and 25, 1969, Churchill, CCGB/110; Admission of Women: Report of the Council to the Governing Body, Feb. 26, 1969, Churchill, CCGB/190/1.

67 Admission of Women: Report of the Council to the Governing Body.

68 Motion to be placed before the Governing Body on Saturday March 8th, 1969, Churchill, CCGB/190/1.

69 Richard Adrian to the Master, [first week in March, 1969,] Churchill, CCAR/101/1/28.

70 George Mallaby to the Master, Mar. 3, 1969, Churchill, CCAR/101/1/28.

71 Lord Snow to the Master, Churchill College, Mar. 4, 1969, Churchill, CCAR/101/1/28.

The governing body's affirmative vote on March 8 was made public on March 17, giving the master and senior tutor time to inform people who needed to know in advance of the general announcement, from members of the Churchill Trust to major donors to headmasters of secondary schools.[72] With the announcement by Churchill, the other men's colleges that had been considering coeducation moved quickly to come to their own decisions. Gonville and Caius fell out; a motion that the college should alter its statutes to permit the admission of women failed by two votes to achieve the necessary two-thirds majority.[73] But Clare and King's were still on board.

CLARE

In a long report on coresidence dated February 27, 1969, the Clare College committee, set up by action of the governing body in November 1968, made the case for bringing women to Clare. The report began by rehearsing the statistics on the very small number of women in Cambridge in comparison with other universities. It was hard to see "any advantage in maintaining the present gross disparity between the sexes." Admitting women to men's colleges was the only way to increase "the proportion of women students in Cambridge."[74]

Drawing on extensive information from other universities that were already mixed, the report laid out the likely effects of coresidence on the balance of subjects studied, on students' academic quality and achievements, and on social life and behavior. It reviewed a number of practical matters, including accommodations, communal facilities, and tutorial arrangements.[75] The report also noted surveys done by the JCR. Women students in Cambridge (as determined by sampling students at Newnham, Girton, and New Hall) were overwhelmingly in favor of coresidence: 98 percent

72 For the early notifications, see, e.g., Lord Annan to W. R. Hawthorne, Mar. 10, 1969; Lord Todd to Hawthorne, Mar. 15, 1969; Master to Garfield Weston, Mar. 12, 1969; and R. H. Tizard to Headmaster, Mar. 15, 1969, all in Churchill, CCGB/190/1. For the public announcement, see Churchill College press release, Mar. 17, 1969, Churchill, CCGB/190/3.

73 Joseph Needham to W. R. Hawthorne, Mar. 24, 1969, Churchill, CCGB/190/6.

74 Report on Co-Residence, Feb. 27, 1969, p. 2, Clare, CCGB/4/8.

75 Ibid., pp. 3–17.

said that they would like to see more women students in Cambridge, and 92 percent said they would favor some men's colleges becoming coresidential. At Clare, 89 percent of undergraduates and graduate students favored coresidence.[76] The report concluded by stating the main advantages of coresidence: "an improvement in academic standards in certain subjects . . . and greater equity for women in admissions policy" and "a marked . . . improvement in the quality of life within the College as a society that is, in the widest sense, educational."[77]

In early March, a joint meeting gave the governing body and the committee on coresidence an opportunity to discuss the report in preparation for the special meeting of the governing body set for April 14 to come to a decision on the matter.[78] The March meeting also included a presentation from the JCR; it was the first time that student representatives had been invited to meet with the governing body. John Speed, chair of the JCR, described the opportunity to "put [the JCR's] case" for coresidence before the governing body as "typical of [Ashby's] inclusive approach." Speed said later: "I had come up to Clare from a mixed state grammar school on the Dorset coast, and found immediately that the social atmosphere of an all-male college lacked balance, the broader and more normal dimension of a mixed community was missing. . . . I did not think that it was right that the privilege of education in Clare should be closed to women."[79]

On March 17 Ashby sent a "strictly confidential" note to the members of the governing body. Because he would be in the chair on April 14, and thus constrained from speaking, he intended the note to convey his views on matters of procedure and on the substance of the issue. As a matter of procedure, it had been important

76 Ibid., p. 22. See also Clare Co-Residence Questionnaire Results, Feb. 1969, Clare, CCGB/4/8.

77 Report on Co-Residence, Feb. 27, 1969, p. 23.

78 E. A., Clare College Governing Body: Note from the Master, Mar. 5, 1969, and E. A., Summary of discussion on Co-residence Report, Mar. 10, 1969, both in Clare, CCGB/4/8.

79 "Co-residence in Clare: 40 Years Ago; Memories from John Speed," *Clare News* 31 (Summer 2013): 18, http://www.clarealumni.com/s/845/1col.aspx?sid=845&gid=1& pgid=348, accessed Jan. 6, 2014.

to consult Clare students because if they were not in favor of coresidence, it would be "unwise for the Governing Body to foist it on them or on their successors." But student views alone were not dispositive; nor were the views of Old Clare Men. It was the governing body's responsibility to take the long view: "Our decision must be made in the perspective of the rest of this century."

Ashby acknowledged that some fellows wanted more information before coming to a decision. But "the evidence for making a decision [could] never be complete," he said, and it was "a matter of judgment to decide when waiting for more evidence is wise, or when it is simply an excuse for procrastination." In this case, he said, waiting would be unwise; no further evidence could be brought to bear until some college actually tried coresidence. Short of that, waiting for more evidence would "give the impression that Fellows were dragging their feet, and this might well undermine the confidence and respect which I believe most junior members have in the Fellowship." He asked, therefore, that the governing body come to a decision, even though a decision was bound to "have some painful consequences." To decide would be "a sign of strength. Indecision would be interpreted as weakness."

Ashby listed for the governing body the reasons he believed that coresidence would spread to Oxford and Cambridge. "The history of women's education at Cambridge," he said, had "been marked by a succession of what now appear to have been overdue concessions." He continued, "It is reasonable to suppose that in the future the differentiation in treatment between men and women in Cambridge will continue to diminish." The university had voted to change its statutes, and coresidence was increasing in other universities and in secondary schools, even boarding schools. Whether or not these trends were desirable, they would "constitute a sustained pressure on single-sex institutions." The question was "more likely to be 'when' than 'whether': in 1972, or 1982, or 1992?" There were "advantages and drawbacks in being early in the field; and there are advantages and drawbacks in being late." The governing body had to decide "whether, on grounds of education in its widest sense, learning and research, and the stability of our society . . . the decision in principle should be made now or deferred into the future."[80] On April 14, by a two-thirds majority, the governing body voted to make Clare College coresidential "if satisfactory arrangements about admissions can be made."[81]

From the principal of Newnham College came a note of affirmation: "My College will certainly welcome the preliminary decision of Clare College to accept women, as we are so anxious to see more women undergraduates at Cambridge." How to handle admissions was a key question, of course, but those discussions were already underway. Newnham's biggest worry was the likely effect on women dons. If men's colleges going mixed appointed women fellows, women's colleges would be unable to compete, because men's colleges would pay higher salaries. If women's colleges were eventually forced to go mixed, they would need to appoint men as fellows, reducing the number of positions for academic women at Cambridge.[82]

A different kind of response came from the master of Trinity College, who wrote to Ashby, "We were hoping to have a quiet term." But "events in the Vice-Chancellor's College naturally have an effect here." The upshot, he predicted, would "undoubtedly [be to] stir up our left wing."[83]

The story at Clare was not finished. As we shall see in the next chapter, there would be much "stir[ring] up" there—from the right wing, not the left—before coresidence could go forward.

---

80 Note on co-residence from the Master to members of Clare College Governing Body, Mar. 17, 1969, Clare, CCGB/4/8.

81 Quoted in Ashby, "How Ever Did Women Get into Clare?," p. 11.

82 Ruth Cohen to the Master, Clare College, Apr. 17, 1969, Clare, CCGB/4/8.

83 R. A. Butler to the Vice-Chancellor, Apr. 16, 1969, Clare, CCGB/4/8.

22

Cambridge: "A Tragic Break with Centuries of Tradition"

After Clare's governing body voted in favor of coresidence, the college still needed to repeal the statute that prohibited the admission of women, an action that would require a two-thirds vote of the governing body at two meetings held at least one month apart. The proposed repeal would then go to the Privy Council for approval.[1] With the initial vote of the governing body for coresidence, the repeal should have been a simple matter. However, at a meeting called on May 5, 1969, to act on the repeal, the motion failed to get the necessary two-thirds majority.

Twists and Turns at Clare

One of the most senior fellows of the college, E. N. Willmer, a professor of histology elected in 1936, indicated the flavor of the opposition in a long memorandum he wrote to counter what he considered the "somewhat tendentious" report of the committee on coresidence. The statute, he said, was "a perfectly clear instruction" embodying "a reasonable custom that has been approved for 643 years." Statutes served "to ensure that erring generations do not interfere with the established system in order to satisfy their own whims." So long as Clare could be filled with "men of high intellectual ability and sound moral character," the fellows

---

1 Eric Ashby, copy of notice to be posted Apr. 15, 1969, Churchill, CCGB/190/3.

had a "plain and clear duty to obey the statutes, as we have promised to do."[2]

Although Willmer was correct that Clare had been all-male for 643 years, it was not the case that the college's statutes had mandated the exclusion of women from the time of Clare's founding. The statute in question dated only to 1926. So the argument that eliminating it would run counter to the will of the founder— appealing as it was to traditionalists—had no force.[3]

Willmer proceeded to make the case against "such a revolutionary change." It was "of the utmost urgency for this country to produce a generation of wise and learned men, who will stand some chance of being able to solve the incredibly complex problems" of the times. "Giving up any of our best educational places to those who, however brilliant, will in all probability only be able to be part-time workers" would be a waste. Moreover, admitting women would contravene the "fundamental physiological fact" that "woman is attractive to man and man to woman. . . . The proximity of women is inevitably a distraction to men, and, as such, is likely to interfere with their sustained study and mental effort."[4]

Whether or not Willmer's views were representative, enough fellows were skeptical, if not opposed, to block repeal of the statute. The grandson of one of them, Mark Harrison, himself a Clare man, told the story years later of his grandfather, W. J. Harrison, coming "out of retirement," traveling by train from the south coast of England to attend the meeting "and vote against." First named a fellow in 1907, Harrison, a mathematician, had served as bursar of the college from 1929 to 1949 and was strongly invested in Clare's traditions. Mark, an undergraduate at Clare at the time of the meeting, recalled "a cartoon in one of the student papers depicting [his grandfather] as wheelchair bound and foaming at the mouth." In fact, Mark said, his grandfather "was quite able to walk and he knew his own mind. Although he was one of the first Fellows

2 E. N. Willmer, Co-residence, n.d. [1969], Clare, CCGB/4/8.

3 Eric Ashby, "How Ever Did Women Get into Clare?," *Clare Association Annual*, 1986–87, p. 12, Clare, CCCS/4/5.

4 Willmer, Co-residence.

to marry and he married one of the first women to graduate from a Cambridge college, he just didn't think much of women." The meeting would be W. J. Harrison's last stand for Clare, for he died five weeks later at the age of eighty-five.[5]

The governing body's inaction caused considerable distress in the college. In the words of one of the fellows who favored repeal, "The narrow defeat of the statu[t]e leaves me very angry. It is a revolt of backwoodsmen who ought to have had the decency to do nothing."[6] Undergraduates were "most alarmed" at the governing body's failure to amend the statutes. Some two hundred of them signed a petition of protest, and the JCR passed resolutions asking opponents of coresidence "to explain their views at a meeting of the whole College" and expressing concern that members no longer active in college life could derail "the work of joint-don-student committees and thus damage don-student relations." Students believed that the forces of reaction had mobilized to prevent change, and they were angry that "people unconversant with the issues [were] able to take part in such voting."[7]

Sir Eric Ashby asked John Speed, chairman of the JCR, to assure his fellow students "that the overall position remains substantially as it was" at the time of the April 14 vote: "There is still a substantial majority of the Governing Body in favour of co-residence <u>provided</u> some very difficult problems about admissions, balance of subjects, and co-operation with other Colleges can be solved. These problems have not yet been solved, and there may well be some Fellows who are not willing to recommend that the Statutes should be amended until they are satisfied about the solutions to the problems." Resolving those problems, Ashby said, would "take time."[8]

---

5 Mark Harrison's story is recounted in "Forty Years On . . . Women at Clare 1972–2012," *Clare News* 30 (Autumn/Winter 2012): 8, http://www.clarealumni.com/s/845/1col .aspx?sid=845&gid=1&pgid=348, accessed Jan. 6, 2014. On W. J. Harrison's history at Clare, see "Obituaries: W. J. Harrison, Fellow 1907–69; Bursar 1929–49," *Clare Association Annual*, 1969, p. 56.

6 Jim Dickson to Master, May 5, 196[9], Clare, CCGB/4/8.

7 J.L.G. Speed to the Master, May 7, 1969, Clare, CCGB/4/8 (source of the quotes); interview with Speed, Oct. 26, 2013, London, England.

8 Eric Ashby to J.L.G. Speed, May 6, 1969, Clare, CCGB/4/8.

In a personal message to Speed, Ashby explained why retired fellows had standing to participate in decisions of major consequence: "The Governing Body of the College is all the Fellows. The retired ones have as much right to attend as any others. Moreover, they can claim to have had half a century of involvement and attachment to the College. I think, therefore, that the junior members of the College, whose involvement dates only from last October and who are likely to be as unfamiliar with the history (and purpose) of the College as the retired members may be unfamiliar with its present circumstances, have no cause for complaint."

Part of Ashby's purpose was to teach Speed how the college worked. The other part was to ask for trust from the students:

> Confidence between senior and junior members is absolutely essential for the welfare of the College. . . . We are going through an epoch of change which is difficult for both senior and junior members. A false step could do much damage. So let us base our mutual confidence on a simple proposition: that the dons will try to understand and appreciate the aspirations and enthusiasms of Clare students for the College, and to adopt those which are consistent with the purpose of the place; and, in return, the students will try to understand and appreciate the responsibility, and therefore necessary caution, which the Fellows have, as trustees of a society 6 centuries old, which has one clear purpose on which there can be no compromise: that it is dedicated to learning.[9]

Ashby acknowledged to a colleague that the outcome of the May 5 meeting was a real setback in terms of his efforts to build trust among undergraduates. The students had the mistaken impression, he said, that "the meeting was artificially 'packed' in order to prevent the two thirds majority which wanted to pursue the many problems associated with co-residence from getting on with its work."[10]

9 [Eric Ashby] to J.L.G. Speed, May 9, 1969, Clare, CCGB/4/8.
10 [Eric Ashby] to Professor Hutton, May 7, 1969, Clare, CCGB/4/8.

To another colleague who had strongly favored repeal of the statute, Ashby wrote more frankly and personally:

> It is only fair to tell you that many Fellows were surprised that two very senior Fellows, who had taken no part in any of the previous discussions, turned up at the meeting to vote. If they did this of their own initiative, this is of course perfectly understandable (though they have lost the respect of Fellows who think that it is more dignified when one has retired to keep out of controversial College matters). But if they were persuaded to come by Fellows actively in the College, then I think you should know that I have received several messages of anger and contempt for this (assumed) action. I can only reply that I don't know. If it is true, I share the anger and contempt. . . . I hope that Fellows who voted against the action will now help me (and the College) in the inevitable embarrassment.[11]

Speed later characterized Ashby as a remarkable leader: clear-thinking, charismatic, and highly respected. He knew that he needed to bring everyone along; he was very astute politically, and he had the skills to build consensus.[12] Speed's view was widely shared. The *Clare Association Annual* described Ashby as "dedicated to drawing the threads together and reconciling differences." Sir Brian Pippard, the first president of Clare Hall, observed that Ashby had "a genius for eliciting reform by consensus," talking over a problem "with anyone who had views on it, helping to polish up the good ideas and gently discouraging the bad."[13]

Solving the conundrum of the thwarted attempt at coresidence offered the perfect test of Ashby's ability to take a complicated situation and find a way forward. Ashby constituted a new committee

11 [Eric Ashby] to John ? [last name not given on the letter], May 6, 1969, Clare, CCGB/4/8.

12 Speed interview.

13 "Lord and Lady Ashby," *Clare Association Annual*, 1974–75, p. 8 ("drawing the threads together"); "Lord Ashby," *Clare Association Annual*, 1991–92, p. 7 ("reform by consensus," "polish up the good ideas").

to study the question again and make recommendations to a future meeting of the governing body.[14] The committee reported in November 1969. It laid out the principal arguments in favor of admitting women to Clare, considered alternative proposals (founding a new women's college or a new coresidential college, waiting to join the second wave of colleges embarking on coresidence), and addressed the various ways in which admissions might be handled and the practical changes in accommodations and physical facilities that would be required if a decision to admit women were to be implemented.[15]

At a meeting of the governing body held on December 8, only half of the fellows present spoke, which made it difficult to gauge "the feeling of the meeting." In a personal note to the governing body, Ashby conveyed his impressions: The doubters had not yet been persuaded. There was interest in the proposal that Clare might temporarily accommodate some Girton women while Girton was completing some new buildings; there was also interest in knowing whether other colleges might join with Clare in founding a new coresidential college. Ashby said that he would explore those options, but he noted that time was running out. If Clare was going to join the "first wave" of colleges going mixed, a formal decision would have to be taken soon. With his appointment as vice-chancellor (a position he held simultaneously with the mastership from 1967 to 1969) coming to an end, Ashby was getting ready to go abroad for a leave at the Institute for Advanced Study in Princeton, New Jersey. He wanted to know before he left, both for his own information and for the guidance of the acting master, W. B. Reddaway, recently elected to a professorship of political economy, whether it would be "sensible to have a formal meeting or not." He circulated a questionnaire to the fellows, asking for anonymous replies, to gauge their preferences.[16] Were the governing body to decide to hold a formal meeting during Ashby's time

14 Ashby, "How Ever Did Women Get into Clare?," p. 12.
15 Second Report on Co-Residence, Nov. 1969, Clare, CCGB/4/8.
16 E. A., Personal and Confidential to Members of the Governing Body, Dec. 10, 1969, Clare, CCGB/4/8. Reddaway's election is documented in *Clare Association Annual*, 1969, p. 15.

in Princeton, he planned to come back for the deliberations and the vote.[17]

Ashby approached the mistress of Girton, who said that the college would be interested in temporarily accommodating some of its students at Clare. And he wrote to the heads of nine other colleges asking whether they would be interested in joining together to found a new, "tailor made" coresidential college.[18] In early January he reported to the governing body that of forty-three replies received from fellows (out of a possible forty-four), thirty favored coresidence in the first wave. The remainder divided their preferences among a tailor-made coresidential college, temporary accommodation of Girton students, or no action.[19] Based on replies from other colleges, Ashby said, "a new college backed by a consortium of colleges" seemed unlikely.[20]

On January 12, 1970, the governing body rejected by a 3-to-1 majority a motion to postpone the whole issue for five years and set in motion plans for a formal meeting to consider a change of the statutes.[21] The first meeting was held on February 23, with Ashby having flown in from the United States. The acting master, Reddaway, presided. As Reddaway's son recalled, his father opened the meeting by asking, "'Does anyone believe that this change will not occur sometime?' No-one responded to this. So, Dad went on to say 'Well, we've thought through the practical issues, and found

17 Eric Ashby to Brian [Cooper, Bursar of the College], n.d., but Jan. 1970, Clare, CCGB/4/8.

18 Eric Ashby to Mistress of Girton, Dec. 8, 1969, and [Eric Ashby,] Text of letter sent to heads of nine Colleges, Dec. 10, 1969, both in Clare, CCGB/4/8.

19 E. A., Strictly Confidential to members of the Governing Body, Dec. 18, 1969, updated Jan. 1970, Clare, CCGB/4/8.

20 Ibid. The replies came from Gordon Sutherland, Master of Emmanuel College, Dec. 10, 1969; David Thomson, Master of Sidney Sussex College, Dec. 11, 1969; Keith Guthrie, Master of Downing College, Dec. 12, 1969; William Hodge, Master of Pembroke College, Dec. 12, 1969; Arthur [Armitage], President of Queen's College, Dec. 15, 1969; Alex [Todd], Master of Christ's College, Dec. 15, 1969; and Frank [Lee], Master of Corpus Christi College, Dec. 15, 1969, all in Clare, CCGB/4/8. Ashby reported confidentially on the views of the master of the ninth college in E. A., Postscript to papers circulated on co-residence issue, Dec. 20, 1969, Clare, CCGB/4/8. It turned out that one college was enthusiastic: Gonville and Caius. See Joseph Needham to W. B. Reddaway, Feb. 10, 1970; Needham to the Master, Clare College, Aug. 12, 1970; and Needham to the Provost, King's College, Aug. 12, 1970, all in Clare, CCGB/4/8.

21 Minutes of the Governing Body, Jan. 12, 1970, Clare, CCGB/4/8.

solutions to all of them. So, why don't we get on with it?'"[22] By more than a two-thirds majority, the fellows voted in favor of repeal of the relevant statute.[23] The second meeting, on May 18, with Ashby again having flown in, produced the same result. Accordingly, the college requested approval from the Privy Council to strike the prohibition against admitting women.[24]

What accounted for the turnaround? The documentary record is silent, but it is likely that Ashby played the critical role. He set in motion an elaborate process to reconsider the issue; he made plain his dismay that two retired fellows had sabotaged the previous effort; and he engaged in a host of private conversations to line up his troops. W. J. Harrison, one of the men who had blocked action the previous spring, died before the second meeting. The other man may have agreed to stand down from the deliberations. But whether the result was a function of who showed up at meetings or of changes of mind on the part of some fellows is not known.

On May 19, Reddaway wrote to Old Clare Men to inform them of the governing body's action and to offer anyone who was interested a copy of the report setting out the arguments for change.[25] In response, 132 Old Clare Men asked for the report. Of the 50 men who gave their views, 33 were in favor of the change and 17 were opposed.[26] Some correspondents were simply startled. A self-described octogenarian wrote, "One has got accustomed to the phrase 'the wind of change' but this surely is nothing less than a gale!"[27] Another said, "If Lady Clare herself had wanted it this way, she would have said so in the first place. . . . The College has managed quite successfully for over 600 years without women undergraduates. Why admit them now against the wishes of our foundress?"[28] Still another wrote, "Is it not another case of bend-

22 "Forty Years On . . . Women at Clare 1972–2012," 8.

23 W. B. Reddaway, College Statutes, Feb. 24, 1970, Clare, CCGB/4/8.

24 Amending Statute for Clare College, Cambridge, n.d., but 1970, Clare, CCGB/4/8.

25 W. B. Reddaway to all Old Clare Men, May 19, 1970, Clare, CCGB/4/8.

26 Analysis of Response of Old Clare Men to the Decision to Admit Women, n.d., but 1970, Clare, CCGB/4/8.

27 M. S. Evers to Senior Tutor, n.d., but 1970, Clare, CCGB/4/8.

28 D. H. Flint to W. B. Reddaway, June 4, 1970, Clare, CCGB/4/8.

ing over backwards in order to be 'mod'?"[29] Critics described themselves as "appalled," "shocked," and "saddened," expressing "dismay and distaste" at the "retrograde step of admitting women."[30] One Old Clare Man returned his rowing club blazer with a note: "I am appalled and disgusted at the decision of the College to admit women. After such a decision I have no wish to wear this blazer any more. I return it herewith."[31]

But others reacted favorably. A number of correspondents proclaimed that they were "delighted."[32] "At last," one man exulted, "Cambridge moves into the 20th century."[33] The decision was "courageous and . . . far-seeing," another opined.[34] Yet another wrote, "I think that this is a very good move, which will provide Clare with a head start in the years to come."[35]

Many Old Clare Men recognized that the move opened unexpected opportunities for their offspring. "My own daughter will be seeking university admission in 1972, and it could be that Clare might be her first choice," said one. "I trust . . . it will be possible to let me have two entry forms for my daughters, who I would like to put down for October 1976 and October 1978 respectively," said another.[36] But the fathers who responded so enthusiastically

29 E.T.L. Baker to the Senior Tutor, July 16, 1970, Clare, CCGB/4/8.

30 P. P. Whitmore to Dear Sir [W. B. Reddaway], May 26, 1970 ("appalled"); E. A. Marshall to Reddaway, June 2, 1970 ("shocked"); J.H.C. Gibb to Reddaway, July 5, 1970 ("saddened"); T. Bailey to Reddaway, July 8, 1970 ("dismay and distaste"); and T.P.N. Fawcett to Senior Tutor, May 28, 1970 ("retrograde step"), all in Clare, CCGB/4/8. There are many other letters of opposition; see, in the same collection, letters to Reddaway from J. Lendrum and J. Howard Freeboon, both May 22, 1970; Gordon Buxton, May 28, 1970; and Basil Engert, Aug. 25, 1970; as well as Laurence Edbrooke to [Charles] Feinstein, Sept. 9, 1970.

31 Quoted in Ashby, "How Ever Did Women Get into Clare?," p. 7.

32 For example, Rayner M. Mayer to Senior Tutor, June 21, 1970; A. S. Davies to W. B. Reddaway, June 15, 1970; and Gavin F. Anderson to Reddaway, May 27, [1970,] all in Clare, CCGB/4/8.

33 John Williams to Senior Tutor, June 13, 1970, Clare, CCGB/4/8.

34 W. C. Young to [Charles] Feinstein, May 24, 1970, Clare, CCGB/4/8.

35 Philip Rhodes to Eric Ashby, June 4, 1970, Clare, CCGB/4/8. On the same theme, in the same collection, see also D. M. Kellett Carding to W. B. Reddaway, July 3, 1970, and Ronald G. Stansfield to [Charles] Feinstein, May 26, 1970.

36 Derek Parsons to Dear Sir, May 25, 1970 ("my own daughter"), and E. N. Wilkinson to the Master, Clare College, June 1, 1970 ("two entry forms"), both in Clare, CCGB/4/8.

were not just those with daughters approaching college age. One wrote, "We have four daughters (5 and under) and I had regretfully come to the conclusion that my father and I would have no successor at Clare. Now—we might!"[37] Another said, "My nine year old daughter, who is named Clare for obvious reasons, vouchsafed to me the other day that she would go to Clare. I had to tell her that that would not be possible. Now, praise be, it may be on the cards."[38]

Taking Action: Working Out the Final Details

While Clare was caught up in an extended process to determine how to proceed, the report of the committee on the admission of women at King's, completed in May 1969, provided the context for deliberation and action.

KING'S LEADS THE WAY

The King's report began by noting the significant underrepresentation of women students at Cambridge in comparison with universities other than Oxford or Cambridge. It noted that standards for admission of women at Cambridge were higher than those for men, a situation that also obtained at Oxford. The committee had gathered information from mixed halls of residence at other British universities, and it made its findings—which attested to the success of coresidence—available to members of the governing body. It noted the prevailing view that "the atmosphere in mixed halls is easy and relaxed and that the advantage of co-residence is that it is more 'natural' and 'civilised.'" The committee also documented the availability of a strong pool of "high-calibre" women on which King's could draw for appropriate candidates for admission.[39]

---

37 C.P.W. Bryant to [Charles] Feinstein, May 23, 1970, Clare, CCGB/4/8. On the same theme, in the same collection, see also Roger Sawtell to W. B. Reddaway, June 7, 1970.

38 Philip Rhodes to Eric Ashby, June 4, 1970, Clare, CCGB/4/8.

39 Report of the Committee on the Admission of Women, May 1969, pp. 3–5, 7–12, 14–21, King's, KCGB/4/1/1/22. The quotes are on pp. 5 ("easy and relaxed") and 9 ("high-calibre").

The report laid out possible methods for admission of women to King's and recommended that the three men's colleges going mixed and the three women's colleges collaborate with respect to the selection of women, and that the mixed colleges admit men through the group system currently governing the admission of men at Cambridge. It concluded by recommending an intake of eighty men and thirty-five women undergraduates—enough men in comparison with the current ninety to a hundred but a small enough increase in the total student population not to threaten the basic nature of the college.[40]

The report urged prompt action by the governing body. With Churchill and Clare having already declared their intentions, and the knowledge in the public domain that King's was seriously considering the matter, it was important to "come to a decision . . . as soon as possible." It recommended a vote on a motion like this one: "That the Governing Body of King's College agree in principle to the admission of women to the College, the principle to be put into effect when a satisfactory method for admission of women has been worked out." The committee suggested that a straw vote be taken before "the formal and committing vote" was taken.[41]

As it turned out, there was a two-hour preliminary discussion without vote on May 17. To the question of how Old Kingsmen would react to a decision for coresidence, a story was told: When remarks on the prospect of admitting women were made at the last dinner of the King's College Association, "no due alarm and despondency had been evinced by the Old Kingsmen present." The provost, Edmund Leach, noting the fact that "King's has a reputation for innovation and enterprise," said, "In a major innovation such as this it would be quite out of character if King's were not in the lead." The discussion had been "so one-sided" in favor of accepting the recommendations of the committee that Leach feared that some members of the governing body might not show up for the vote on May 27. He urged his colleagues to attend. "This is the most important decision the College has had to take for over

40 Ibid., pp. 23, 25.
41 Ibid., p. 26.

a century, and it is most important that we are seen to take it in a serious and responsible manner."[42] On May 27 the governing body approved the motion proposed by the committee on the admission of women. The vote was 48 in favor, along with the provost; 5 opposed; and 6 abstentions.[43]

The intention, as the committee on the admission of women had proposed, was to "aim at an intake of 80 men and 35 women per year."[44] Leach explained that the college's decision "was based on the double conviction that Cambridge should be making a greater contribution to the education of women and that the admission of women to the College would provide an academic and social environment superior to that of a single-sex institution."[45]

Leach later told the story this way:

> We took things slowly and talked it out for a couple of years or perhaps more. The opposition were clearly in a minority, but we had to win by a two-thirds majority of the whole Governing Body (that is, all the Fellows, about 100 individuals). At the last minute, when I thought all was lost, the leader of the opposition got up and made a highly emotional speech to the effect that this was the most important vote that the College had faced during the last 500 years. He could see that his supporters were in a minority, so he asked them to change sides and let this historic decision go through on a unanimous vote. One splendid old boy refused to take that one and said he must abstain. So King's voted for the admission of women *nem. con.* [without dissent]!

"That could only have happened in King's," Leach continued. "But there was some anthropology in it, too. If I had not already begun to acquire the reputation of being much more conservative than my erratic predecessor, I doubt if we would have made

---

42 E. R. Leach, notes on preliminary discussion of co-education, May 18, 1969, King's, KCGB/4/1/1/22.

43 Governing Body minutes, May 27, 1969, King's, KCGB/4/1/1/22.

44 Edmund Leach to W. R. Hawthorne, May 27, 1969, Churchill, CCGB/190/6.

45 King's College press release, May 28, 1969, Churchill, CCGB/190/6.

it at all. I am no fisherman, but it was all rather like landing a salmon."[46]

DEVISING A SCHEME FOR THE ADMISSION OF WOMEN

Once Churchill, Clare, and King's agreed in principle to admit women, the biggest challenge was figuring out how to accomplish it. An intricate system governed applications, so that male students were required to opt for Cambridge or Oxford and were then expected to specify a college of choice instead of applying broadly. (Applicants who failed to win admission to the college of choice were put into a pool from which other colleges might then choose to offer admission.) Applicants also faced constraints on the numbers admitted in each field of study. How to make this system work with women required careful study. The prohibition against applying at both Cambridge and Oxford did not pertain to women, who normally applied to both institutions and were given the opportunity to decide where to go once they had their offers in hand. In addition, to avoid damaging the women's colleges, any new system needed to permit women to apply to women's colleges as well as mixed colleges.[47]

It was imperative, as Leach put it in a confidential letter to Sir William R. Hawthorne, the master of Churchill, "to devise an admissions system which [would] not damage the interests of the women's Colleges." The plan was to try to coordinate arrangements with the women's colleges as a group; in the short run, however, the women's colleges had been "unable to speak with a single voice." King's was eager to get going. Although they could act on their own, they "much prefer[red] a coordinated scheme." But if the women's colleges were unprepared "to produce a concerted scheme" so that the men's colleges "could negotiate possibilities," the tutors at King's were "likely to press the College to go ahead independently, though that is certainly not what we want to do,"

46 Adam Kuper, "An Interview with Edmund Leach," *Current Anthropology* 27 (Aug.–Oct. 1986): 382.

47 Admission of Women: Report of the Sub-Committee on Undergraduate Admissions, Jan. 24, 1969, Churchill, CCGB/111.

Leach said. The mood at King's was unmistakable: "Let's get a move on."[48]

Finally, the three men's colleges and the three women's colleges devised a joint admission procedure predicated on the understanding that women would no longer apply both to Oxford and to Cambridge and then make their choice once offers of admission had been made. Unlike in the men's system, however, there would be ways for a female candidate not accepted by the college of her first choice to be considered by other colleges at both universities. The Oxford women's colleges did not like some aspects of the plan. At various points in the negotiations, it was unclear whether they would accept the new arrangements under protest or demand that the existing system remain unchanged.[49]

After surveying headmasters and headmistresses for their views, and with concessions of various sorts made, agreement on "a new scheme of admissions" was finally reached with the Oxford colleges, to go into effect in January 1971, for candidates for admission in October 1972. For the admission of women at Cambridge, the three mixed colleges and the three women's colleges would constitute a group, with a common preliminary application form and opportunities for candidates to list up to six colleges in order of preference. For the admission of men, the mixed colleges would remain in the groups to which they had previously been assigned.[50]

The Coming of Coresidence

After years of planning, Churchill, Clare, and King's would admit their first women undergraduates in October 1972. By October 1971, the three colleges had begun interviewing women applicants.

48 Edmund Leach to W. R. Hawthorne, Nov. 3, 1969, Churchill, CCAR/101/1/28.
49 R. H. Tizard, Admissions: A Note by the Senior Tutor, Feb. 9, 1970, Churchill, CCGB/190/1; Tizard, Admission of Women, Apr. 23, 1970, with attached Proposals for a Scheme for the Admission of Women to Oxford and Cambridge, Apr. 1970, Churchill, CCAC/134/4/1, File 1; J. J. Turner (Admissions Tutor at King's), "Co-Residence— Admissions," May 2, 1970, King's, KCGB/4/1/1/22.
50 College Council Minutes, May 26 and July 28, 1970, Churchill, CCGB/110; R. H. Tizard, Admission of Women, July 27, 1970, with attached Admission of Women to Oxford and Cambridge, July 1970 (source of the quote), Churchill, CCAC/134/4/1, File 1.

R. H. Tizard, the senior tutor at Churchill, told a reporter for the *Daily Telegraph*, "I find that the girls are very well organised. They have studied the relevant information. If asked, they give good reasons for choosing the course they have applied for. Men are often vague on this point." The senior tutor at Clare, Charles Feinstein, said, "When I ask women applicants why they have chosen a mixed college, some say it's because they have been to a girls' school, some because they have been to a co-educational one."[51]

THE WOMEN ARRIVE

The academic year 1972–73 opened with thirty-two women undergraduates at Churchill, "almost equally divided between the sciences and the arts, and well distributed over all subjects."[52] The "spread of talent" among the women applicants, Tizard reported, had been "no different from that of the men." The college had expected the strongest women candidates to present themselves in the arts and the strongest men in the sciences, mathematics, and engineering, but the opposite proved true. Clearly the girls' schools had taken seriously Churchill's image as a scientific and technological college.[53]

At King's, 37 undergraduate women matriculated in 1972, along with 10 women graduate students. The next year, the annual report for the college said, "90 women are *in statu pupillary* [enrolled as students]." The year after, the report gave the number as 142. By the following year, 1975, the annual report made no mention of the number of women students.[54]

At King's, the first woman to be elected to the fellowship and appointed a tutor was Joanna Ryan, a psychologist, in the fall of 1970.[55] Clare elected its first woman fellow, Alison Sinclair, a

51 Quoted in Violet Johnstone, "When a College Goes Co-ed . . . ," *Daily Telegraph*, Oct. 13, 1971, clipping in Churchill, CCAC/134/4/1, File 2.

52 R. H. T[izard] to B. Little, July 10, 1972, Churchill, CCAC/134/4/1, File 2.

53 R. H. T[izard] to David Harrison, Nov. 28, 1972, Churchill, CCAC/134/4/1, File 2.

54 King's College, *Annual Report*, Nov. 1972, p. 15; Nov. 1973, p. 13; Nov. 1974, p. 15; Nov. 1975, King's.

55 E.R.L., The admission of women to College Fellowships, July 13, 1970, King's, KCGB/4/1/1/22.

scholar of modern Spanish literature and intellectual history, in the fall of 1971.[56] In the spring of 1971, Churchill elected Daphne Osborne, a plant physiologist, as a fellow and college lecturer in botany. The next year, she was appointed to a tutorship. Two other women fellows joined in 1972: Alison Finch in French literature and Patricia Wright in psychology. By 1973, Churchill had four women fellows, but progress in electing more women proved to be slow.[57] In 1981 Tess Adkins, a fellow in geography, was appointed senior tutor at King's, the first woman senior tutor in the previously male colleges.[58] In 2000 Polly O'Hanlon, a historian, was appointed the first woman senior tutor at Clare.[59] As late as 1985, the number of women fellows in mixed colleges at Cambridge was only 147, or 9.4 percent of the total.[60]

Churchill had gotten ready for the women students' arrival by making minimal alterations to facilities, mainly changes in plumbing, enlargement of the ladies' cloakroom, provision of an extra room in the sick bay, and installation of long mirrors.[61] Similar modifications were undertaken at King's and Clare. From the first year at King's, women's rooms were distributed in small clusters throughout the college.[62] At Clare and Churchill, students lived in selected all-female staircases; at Churchill, the college wanted to take stock of the experience of the first year and ask students their preferences before deciding on residential patterns going forward.[63]

56 "Forty Years On . . . Women at Clare 1972–2012," 8–9.

57 In Churchill, CCGB/190/6, see R. H. T[izard] to Principal of Newnham, Apr. 1, 1971. In Churchill, CCAC/134/4/1, File 2, see T[izard] to B. Little, July 10, 1972, and Tizard, Admission of Women to Churchill College, Cambridge, Dec. 12, 1973. See also Alison Finch, "The Fortieth Anniversary of the Admission of Women," *Churchill Review* 49 (2012): 65, http://issuu.com/churchillcollege/docs/review_2012?e=3143903/2750413, accessed Apr. 4, 2014.

58 L. P. Wilkinson, *A Century of King's, 1873–1972* (King's College, Cambridge, 1980), p. 152.

59 "Forty Years On . . . Women at Clare 1972–2012," 11.

60 Christopher N. L. Brooke, *A History of the University of Cambridge*, vol. 4, *1870–1990* (Cambridge: Cambridge University Press, 1993), p. 533.

61 R. H. T[izard] to David Harrison, Nov. 28, 1972, Churchill, CCAC/134/4/1, File 2.

62 Wilkinson, *A Century of King's*, p. 153.

63 R. H. T[izard] to B. Little, July 10, 1972, Churchill, CCAC/134/4/1, File 2.

Ample evidence indicated that the women were settling in without difficulty. Tizard described the Churchill women as "a splendid lot" who threw themselves enthusiastically into the life of the college, including taking up rowing, with significant success.[64] They participated in a wide range of other activities, from the JCR disco to the chapel committee; as Lesley Samuel, a woman in the first intake, reported, they held their own at the college bar and learned also to enjoy "the delights of table football and darts."[65] At Clare, women eagerly joined the boat club, jousting with male rowers for access to showers at the boathouse and regularly winning competitions, both among the colleges at Cambridge and between Cambridge and Oxford.[66] The male president of the JCR at King's, Anatole Kaletsky, described the women students there as very much at home and well integrated into the life of the college. "Every other university in the country—except Oxford—has been co-ed for some time," he said. "So there is nothing remarkable about what is happening here. We are just catching up."[67]

There was some awkwardness, to be sure, as men and women figured out how to interact with one another. Mary Simcock O'Toole, a member of the first intake at Clare in 1972, remarked on "the testosterone in the bar and TV room being such that, at first, few of us [women] dared to go in alone!" At drinks in the senior common room on the first night of coresidence, "the male undergraduates were encouraged to talk to the Fellows at one end of the room and the women were ushered down to the other end to talk to the Fellows' wives"—all "very well meant," Polly O'Hanlon, a member of the first female intake, recalled, "but somewhat disconcerting!" On the whole, however, as another woman in the first intake, Rachel Hood, recalled, "There was a tremendous sense of caring and the College was practical, sensitive and good at making the huge change occasioned by the arrival of women at Clare

---

64 R. H. T[izard] to David Harrison, Nov. 28, 1972, Churchill, CCAC/134/4/1, File 2.

65 Lesley Samuel, "Beauty amongst the Beasts," *Churchill Review*, 1973, p. 19, Churchill, CCRF/130/1.

66 "Forty Years On . . . Women at Clare 1972–2012," 10.

67 "Co-ed Colleges," *Oxford Mail*, Dec. 8, 1972, clipping in Bodleian, File 4.

work for all."[68] Two other women in that same intake, Sybil Del Strother and Alison Keightley, writing in 1973 in the *Clare Association Annual,* put it this way: "Co-residence—whatever was the fuss about? Nothing now seems more natural, and has since our arrival."[69]

To an inquiry from Cambridge's Emmanuel College, which was considering the admission of women, R. H. Tizard offered reassuring assessments: The life of the college was very much the same as before coresidence, the Churchill rugby club had not met its demise because of the arrival of the women, and social life generally had improved. "The one word which describes the community reaction to the change," he wrote, "is 'relaxed.'"[70] To the vice-master of St. Catherine's College, Oxford, he reported, "The girls are settling down well, seem to be a very sensible and level-headed lot, and are doing the men some good simply by their greater maturity."[71] Well into the second year of the women's presence in the college, Tizard noted, "My own opinion is that becoming co-residential has been highly successful."[72]

In the second year of coresidence, thirty-nine women were admitted to Churchill, and a woman, Lindsey Stevens, was elected the first female president of the JCR.[73] That fall, at the request of the JCR, the college council agreed to recommend to the governing body that the upper limit of forty women undergraduates a year be removed. Coresidence, the JCR opined, had been "an unqualified success," and there was no longer any reason to restrict the number of women students. With the knowledge that "the academic results of the women" in the first year had "not been significantly different from those of the men," and with Tizard's assurance that "removal of the restriction was very unlikely to cause a significant

68 "Forty Years On . . . Women at Clare 1972–2012," 11, 14.

69 "The First Year of Co-Residence," *Clare Association Annual,* 1973, pp. 13–14.

70 R. H. T[izard] to R. D. Gray, Nov. 13, 1973, Churchill, CCAC/134/4/1, File 2.

71 R. H. T[izard] to the Vice Master, St. Catherine's College, Feb. 12, 1973, Churchill, CCAC/134/4/1, File 2.

72 R. H. T[izard] to David Harrison, Mar. 21, 1974, Churchill, CCAC/134/4/1, File 2.

73 Women in Churchill, chronology of events compiled by College Archivist, 1997, Churchill.

change in the admissions pattern," the college council supported the request, and the governing body followed suit.[74]

Later a retrospective report made this case for the success of coresidence at Clare:

> Have academic standards suffered? On the contrary, standards have improved and Clare still holds a place at or near the top of the tripos awards. Have sporting activities suffered? In 1981–82 . . . there were nine men's VIIIs on the river and five women's IVs. Three Clare women . . . formed a fifth of the entire national women's rowing squad at the Moscow Olympics [in 1980]. Has the cultural life of the College suffered? Its reputation for music has never been higher. Has the level of morality sagged? If it has, the Tutors have not noticed it.[75]

ASHBY LOOKS TO THE WEST AND TO THE PAST

The decisions for coresidence at Cambridge were rooted in British society, and each of the three colleges that admitted women in 1972 acted from a mix of local imperatives. When fellows who participated in those decisions are asked whether they were aware of, even influenced by, what was going on at Princeton and Yale, they reject the notion out of hand. And yet the leader of one of those colleges was closely connected to the president of Yale and fully attentive to what was going on at Princeton.

Sir Eric Ashby and Yale's president, Kingman Brewster, were friends. They thought alike, and they enjoyed each other's company. Ashby thought of Brewster as a man who inspired great confidence. He admired Brewster's "great imagination" and "liveliness," as well as his "very quick response to . . . situation[s]."

74 David Banks and Chris Botten, Admission of Female Undergraduates, likely Nov. 6, 1973, Churchill, CCGB/190/1 ("unqualified success"); R. H. Tizard, Admission of Women to Churchill College, Cambridge, Dec. 12, 1973, Churchill, CCAC/134/4/1, File 2 ("academic results"); College Council Minutes, Nov. 20, 1973 ("removal of the restriction"); and Governing Body Minutes, Nov. 30, 1973, both in Churchill, CCGB/190/1.

75 Ashby, "How Ever Did Women Get into Clare?," p. 13.

Brewster's management of "the student problems" was particularly impressive. As Ashby told an interviewer, Brewster "was certainly the liveliest and most exciting of the university presidents." The two men "had a lot in common" and talked about many issues, but the discussions were "rather lighthearted," not "long [and] earnest." Ashby continued, "I can't remember anything he said, and he probably couldn't have remembered anything I said. We just got on. If we had been at neighboring universities, we would have been phoning one another and would have seen one another a lot. . . . It was a natural affinity." But affinity did not mean intense conversation about substantive issues. "We were both fellow fighters in a good fight," Ashby said, "and we were rather having the kind of talk two officers would have when off-duty in a bar." That meant that they compared notes on coeducation, but "didn't commune together" before they acted. Rather, they found the similarities in their experiences "in doing it."[76]

Ashby had no such close, easy, personal relationship with Robert Goheen, the president of Princeton. They were two quite different personalities, and Goheen was not the sort of person with whom Ashby would have compared notes while off duty in a bar. But Ashby learned from Princeton as he implemented coeducation at Clare. He had in his files at Clare a copy of Princeton's Patterson report—"'The Education of Women at Princeton': A Special Report," published in the *Princeton Alumni Weekly* in September 1968—along with a copy of *The Education of Undergraduate Women at Princeton: An Examination of Coordinate versus Coeducational Patterns*, the booklet published in March 1969 by the committee that made recommendations to the Princeton trustees about how coeducation should be implemented. How and when Ashby acquired the two Princeton reports is not known. But it was natural for him to turn to Princeton for information and guidance. He had previously requested Princeton publications of

76 Ashby oral history, pp. 15–18, 22, 31, 32. For correspondence attesting to the personal friendship, see, e.g., Eric Ashby to Kingman Brewster, June 15, 1970, Box 451, Folder 2; Ashby to Brewster, Mar. 23, 1971, and Brewster to Ashby, Apr. 5, 1971, Box 469, Folder 6, all in Brewster III.

various sorts.[77] He had visited the university a number of times; he knew well and had collaborated with Princeton faculty members; he knew both Goheen and the provost, William G. Bowen; and he was a personal friend of Goheen's predecessor, Harold W. Dodds, who called him "one of the greats—probably the greatest—among British university heads."[78]

That Ashby regarded the Princeton reports as consequential is suggested by the fact that they were retained in the otherwise very sparse collection of his papers in the Clare archives. How he used the reports is not well documented, but there is one good example of their influence. Upon his return from his sabbatical in Princeton in 1970, Ashby wrote a note in the *Clare Association Annual* to Old Clare Men to explain the events of the previous spring. He reported on the responses of the fifty-four Old Clare Men who had given their views on the decision to go mixed, "some of you with refreshing pungency." He noted that 65 percent of the respondents had favored admitting women—very like the majority required by the governing body for a change of statutes—and that "the only span of years which contained a majority opposed to admitting women was 1911–20."[79]

"The interest of these figures," Ashby pointed out, "is their close resemblance to a similar set of figures gathered from nearly 2,000 alumni by Princeton University, which recently decided to admit women not only to its classes but to its dormitories. The Princeton equivalent of the Clare Association Annual [that is, the *Princeton Alumni Weekly*, in its presentation of the Patterson report] devoted a special issue to the question, peppered with statistical tables." Ashby presented "the views of the Old Princetonians"

77 Eleanor H. Wright to Margaretta Cowenhoven, Apr. 16, 1964, Goheen, Box 138, Folder 2.

78 On Ashby's visits to Princeton, see, e.g., Robert F. Goheen to Eric Ashby, Nov. 6 and 21, 1963, and Mar. 31, 1964; Ashby to Goheen, Nov. 15, 1963, and Mar. 23, 1964; and Dan D. Coyle to J. Douglas Brown, Apr. 15, 1964, all in Goheen, Box 138, Folder 2. On Dodds and Ashby, see Ashby to Harold W. Dodds, July 16, 1962, Dodds, Box 81, Folder 1; Dodds to Brown, Oct. 10, 1963 (source of the quote), Dodds, Box 138, Folder 10; Dodds to Coyle, Mar. 27, 1964, Goheen, Box 138, Folder 2.

79 Typescript, "Notes from the Master," *Clare Association Annual*, 1970, p. 2, Bodleian, File 1. The published version is in Clare, CCCS/4/5.

(not mentioning that these were a subset of alumni, in the field of education) in tabular form, commenting, "It is interesting to see this similarity of opinion between the alumni of Princeton and the alumni of Clare."[80]

In addition to situating Clare in the context of Princeton, Ashby located the decision to go mixed in the context of an earlier change: the 1879 decision to remove the requirement that the tenure of a fellowship be "conditional upon either the taking of Holy Orders or on celibacy." That decision had meant that it was no longer "obligatory for one third of the Fellows of Clare to become ordained," and "no longer would Fellowships have to terminate with marriage." To catch his readers' attention, Ashby deliberately exaggerated the import of those changes, which he said had led to "a tragic break with five centuries of tradition" and "an irreparable secularization of college life—the loyalty of dons shared between the combination room and the marriage couch—the responsibility of being in loco parentis left in the hands of men who might preach and practice infidelity without restraint." Ashby continued, "Well, something like it, but far less revolutionary, has happened again," with the decision of the governing body to admit women to the college.[81]

The trends toward coeducation, Ashby said, were neither faddish nor new. Women's education at Cambridge had been evolving over the past century, with "a succession of what now appear to have been overdue concessions." He continued, "It was not exactly a reckless prediction to suppose that the differentiation in treatment between men and women in Cambridge would continue to diminish, and that co-residence—already a feature of a dozen British universities, not to mention Yale and Princeton—would spread to Cambridge."[82]

These trends, Ashby said, "are not passing fashions imposed upon us by the young; they are part of a long-term evolutionary change in the place of women in society." Of course there was

80 Ibid., pp. 2–3.
81 Ibid., p. 1.
82 Ibid., p. 3.

some risk to being out ahead of other colleges, but "when you are taking a calculated risk, the better place to be is in the vanguard, not in the rear." Ashby concluded, "In 90 years' time, or much sooner, it may appear to our successors to have been a change as natural, and as beneficial, as the abolition of celibacy for Fellows, made 90 years ago, now appears to us."[83]

Ashby's predictions proved prescient. The leaders of other men's colleges at Cambridge, together with their fellows, came to share the views that had prompted decisions for coresidence at Churchill, Clare, and King's. At the same time, students began pressuring the other men's colleges to go mixed. The pressure came partly from male students who wanted to go to school with women, but it came also from women who wanted to go to school with men. A poster advertising an antidiscrimination campaign led by women students made the case this way: "All Cambridge colleges admit women to make their beds, to clean their rooms, to cook their meals. Why don't they let us in to study?"[84]

Churchill, Clare, and King's were soon joined by other mixed colleges. The last of the men's colleges at Cambridge to admit women were Peterhouse in 1984 and Magdalen in 1988. Even the all-female Girton went mixed, admitting its first male undergraduates in 1979. Newnham and New Hall (renamed Murray Edwards College in 2008) remained single-sex, the only women's colleges remaining at Cambridge and Oxford.

83 Ibid., pp. 3, 5.
84 "Cambridge Target Is Men's Colleges," *Times Higher Education Supplement*, Mar. 22, 1974, clipping in Bodleian, File 4.

23

Oxford: "Our Crenellations Crumble, We Cannot Keep Them Out"

At Oxford the impetus for coeducation came alternately from students, fellows, and heads of colleges, each taking the lead in one college or another at different times and in different sequences. Initially, the colleges operated independently. Before long, they joined forces to explore their opportunities and lay their plans. At first, New College took the lead; over time, the initiative shifted to others. Unlike the decisions at Cambridge, however, the decisions at Oxford could not be made in the colleges alone. The university had a central role to play. The need to satisfy the requirements set by the university turned the colleges into a formal group, operating in concert to make decisions and set parameters for the new venture. Understanding the coming of coeducation to Oxford, then, requires following the not-always-linear twists and turns of deliberations in multiple colleges as well as in the larger university.

Early Discussions in the Colleges

The issue of coeducation came up first at New College in December 1963 in the course of a discussion by the governing body about Lord Robbins's call for more university places for women. One of the fellows of the college, a tutor who was also the college librarian, put forward a motion to admit twenty women undergraduates, whom he assumed might be housed in a college annex.[1] It

---

1 *Oxford Mail*, Mar. 10, 1964, clipping in Bodleian, File 1.

would be an experiment for one year, with the results to inform future action.

NEW COLLEGE LEADS OFF

The proposed experiment was a momentous step, for New College had been a men's college for almost six hundred years. In contrast with the middling standing of the first colleges to embrace coeducation at Cambridge, New College was one of the oldest, most prestigious colleges at Oxford. Since 1958 the college had been led by Sir William Hayter, who had been appointed to the position of warden after a long and successful career in the British diplomatic service.[2] On March 18, 1964, Hayter wrote the vice-chancellor of the university to say that the college's governing body had discussed coeducation and decided "to set up a committee to investigate the feasibility and implications to the College and to the University at large of the admission of women." Hayter also wrote to the heads of the women's colleges to let them know what was happening and to offer "to discuss the matter" when they were ready to do that.[3]

As the letter to the vice-chancellor suggests, Oxford was different from Cambridge in the statutory relationship of the colleges and the university. If Oxford colleges were to change their statutes, they would need the university's approval before they could seek the approval of the Privy Council. At Cambridge the colleges were free to go directly to the Privy Council without clearance from a central university body.

Noting the New College initiative, as well as discussions at Cambridge about removing the prohibition on colleges admitting students of both sexes, *The Times* commented, "Proposals of these kinds have been hawked round the older universities before, and it is a fair assumption that it will be some time before we see long-established Oxford and Cambridge colleges turned into

2 "Sir William Hayter," *The Independent*, Mar. 30, 1995, http://www.independent.co .uk/news/people/obituaries-sir-william-hayter-1613337.html, accessed Mar. 5, 2014.
3 William Hayter to the Vice-Chancellor, Mar. 18, 1964, Bodleian, File 1.

thorough-going co-educational establishments with male and female members of both Senior and Junior Common room living hugger-mugger together on the same staircase."[4]

On June 25, 1964, the New College governing body voted to amend the college statutes to permit the admission of women.[5] As one of the fellows, Geoffrey Ernest Maurice de Ste. Croix, a historian of ancient Greece, reported, the resolution passed "by appreciably more than the two-thirds majority required for a change of statute." The intention was to open college fellowships to women, offer places to women graduate students, and admit about thirty women undergraduates a year until women constituted a third of the undergraduate student body.[6]

"The argument in favour of our becoming a mixed college which weighed most with most of us," de Ste. Croix explained, "is that the proportion of women undergraduates at Oxford is far too small and that it cannot be substantially increased unless some men's colleges become mixed." A second argument of consequence was that "university education ought to be fully mixed: in the circumstances of Oxford, this means that the colleges themselves should be mixed." The third consideration was that "a wider field of choice of candidates should improve the quality of our admissions. No one will deny that some of the women who now have to be refused admission at Oxford are abler than many of the men who are accepted."[7]

The Times poked fun at the move:

The Warden's brow was sad
And the Warden's speech was low.
He gazed from Alma Mater's walls
Towards the female foe
That, wave on charging wave, advanced

---

4 "Coeducational Colleges?," *The Times*, Mar. 19, 1964, clipping in Bodleian, File 1.

5 John Grigg, "Not So Monkish," *The Guardian*, July 2, 1966, clipping in Bodleian, File 1.

6 G.E.M. de Ste. Croix, "The Admission of Women to New College," *Oxford Magazine*, Oct. 15, 1964, Bodleian, File 1.

7 Ibid.

And ebbed to charge anew
And for the many win a place
Reserved for far too few.

Out spoke the wise Librarian,
A master-man of ruse,
"Nuffield may think to *buy* them off.
It's not the slightest use.
To every man there cometh
The knowledge soon or late
That women are too much for him.
So, ope the College gate.

"Our crenellations crumble,
Our bastions are thin.
We cannot keep them out," he said,
"Well then, invite them in.
For what can we do better
To shorten fearful odds
Than share with ninety lovely girls
Our cloister and our quads?"

The Warden heaved a sigh
And flung the portal wide
And ninety maidens stared amazed,
Then fought to get inside,
The cream of all the maidens,
The toughest and the best.
O, dark and bitter were the thoughts
In Alma Mater's breast.

Then girlish laughter echoed
Up each New College stair,
Complacently the Warden sniffed
The bathsalts in the air.
But in the other S.C.R.s
What donnish teeth were ground.

They said, "Queer manners makyth man."
And gloomy port went round.
They blamed the wise Librarian,
Abused him and reviled.
But he picked up his Vogue and disingenuously smiled,
Because he numbered this among
His more successful ploys:—
A College that creams off the girls
Will (ergo) cream the boys.[8]

New College solicited the views of other colleges about its interest in going mixed. Support was limited or nonexistent. The governing body at Hertford, for example, instructed their principal, Sir Robert Hall, to write to Hayter "indicating that Hertford was in favor of increasing the number of women's societies within the University, but it was almost equally divided in its views on mixed men's colleges."[9] There was no division of opinion in the women's colleges, which feared that by "skim[ming] the cream," New College would "undermine their position." As Lady Margaret Hall put it in early 1965, "The opening of one of the ancient and famous men's colleges to a small number of women undergraduates . . . is likely to damage the existing women's colleges and the education of the majority of women at Oxford without proportionate gain to the small minority directly affected." Among other concerns, the women's colleges feared that they "would each lose a significant number of their ablest candidates."[10]

The Franks Commission weighed in as well. The commission was in the process of studying Oxford's role in the British system of higher education. Although it had not completed its work, it took note of the deliberations at New College. The college, it said, was free to act without waiting for the commission report. But if it were to go forward, with other men's colleges following suit, the change would likely "inflict great damage on the existing women's

---

8 "Selling the Pass," *The Times*, July 3, 1964, clipping in Bodleian, File 1.

9 Hertford Gov. Body, Feb. 17, 1965.

10 "Opposition to Mixed College Proposal," *The Guardian*, Feb. 23, 1965, clipping in Bodleian, File 1.

colleges." It was urgent that the men's and women's colleges reach agreement "on the extent and the timing of any proposed changes in the admission of the sexes to colleges in Oxford."[11]

At the next meeting of the New College governing body in June 1965, a motion to amend the college statutes to permit the admission of women failed on a vote of 17 in favor, 14 against, falling well short of the required two-thirds majority. Over the course of a year, then, in the face of opposition from the women's colleges, the college had reversed its course.[12]

But the challenge remained: how to open significantly more places in universities to women students. As an article in *The Times* put it in May 1966, the significant underrepresentation of women in British universities meant that Britain was "los[ing] much of her top brain power." The writer asked, "Have we perhaps come to a position where the interests of the women's colleges at Oxford and Cambridge, these great pioneers of women's education, no longer run parallel with interests of women's education?"[13]

Brasenose Takes Up the Discussion

In 1966 Brasenose became the second Oxford college to raise the possibility of admitting women students. Founded in 1509, Brasenose had been the first Oxford college to engage by statute in undergraduate education. The principal, Sir Noel Hall, a Brasenose graduate, was an economist who had been professor of political economy at University College London and a founder of the Henley Business School before returning to the college as principal in 1960. There was nothing to suggest that he had a personal interest in coeducation. But he had a group of young fellows who were very interested in it. Eight new fellows were elected at Brasenose between 1966 and 1968. They were distinguished both by their

11 Lord Franks to the Warden, New College, Mar. 15, 1965, Bodleian, File 1.
12 "Women at New College Move Fails," *Oxford Mail*, June 24, 1965, clipping in Bodleian, File 1.
13 E. M. Thomas, "A Problem of Talent," *The Times*, May 15, 1966, clipping in Bodleian, File 1.

youth and by their progressive inclinations.[14] The oldest, Laszlo Solymar, a thirty-six-year-old fellow in engineering science, who had come from Communist Hungary, regarded single-sex education as "unnatural." The younger fellows, most of them about thirty years old when they joined the college fellowship, thought about it the same way.[15] One of them, Graham Richards, a chemist who had been a postdoc at the Cité Universitaire in Paris, said that he found the mixed environment in Paris far superior to the single-sex culture he had known as an undergraduate at Brasenose. A supporter of the women's movement, he had a lot of women friends, and he liked successful women. It made good sense for him to spearhead the effort for coeducation.[16]

The possible admission of women students to Brasenose came to the fore because the college was planning new construction to provide additional accommodations. Richards circulated a paper arguing that new accommodations should be designed in a way that would permit, not prevent, the eventual admission of women. A special committee was appointed in November 1966 to consider the matter. Richards plotted the strategy so that the votes never addressed "the major question" of admitting women but were "phrased so that by voting yes, one did not rule out the possibility."[17]

When the special committee reported six months later, it was ready to confront the issue directly. The committee asked the Brasenose governing body whether "it would be prepared to amend the Statutes so as to allow women to become members of the College" and whether "it would be prepared to envisage the accommodation of women within the present curtilage of the College." The vote on the first question was 17 to 3 in favor; on the second, the division was closer, but it carried by a vote of 14 to 11. A committee of the principal and several fellows—the committee on membership of the college—was appointed to work on the matter.[18] Richards

14 J. Mordaunt Crook, *Brasenose: The Biography of an Oxford College* (Oxford: Oxford University Press, 2008), pp. 4, 13–14, 21–25, 396.

15 E-mail, Laszlo Solymar to Nancy Weiss Malkiel, Feb. 4, 2014.

16 Interview with Graham Richards, Feb. 19, 2014, Oxford, England.

17 Graham Richards, *50 Years at Oxford* (Bloomington, IN: AuthorHouse, 2011), p. 12.

18 Brasenose Gov. Body, Nov. 30, 1966, and May 24, 1967 (source of the quotes), GOV 3 A1/23.

described Hall as "quite terrified by what the old members of the College would think if news of our intentions got out. In fact he failed to register the salient fact that the old members would have an equal number of daughters as sons and so might be much less hostile than he envisaged." Clearly nervous about coresidence, Hall saw to it that the committee was called, simply, "membership of the college," evidence of his desire to keep the matter as quiet as possible.[19]

Recognizing that nothing could happen without some cooperation from the women's colleges, the Brasenose committee conducted an experiment in collaboration with Somerville "to admit female candidates from amongst those who had narrowly missed winning a place," but nothing came of the experiment.[20] They next met with the principals of the women's colleges. Solymar recalled the dinner conversation. The principals made clear that "mixed colleges [were] against the interests of the women's Colleges" and that they would oppose any move in that direction. Richards put it this way: The principals said that coeducation would come "over their dead bodies." The women's colleges provided jobs for women academics. If men's colleges were to go mixed, the jobs would go to men.[21]

Given the resistance of the women's colleges, the committee recommended, and the governing body agreed, that the college table further action until other men's colleges, along with at least two women's colleges, would be willing to join the initiative. Hall was authorized to communicate the decision to the heads of the women's colleges, along with a request to let them know "if or when any other men's college makes a similar overture."[22]

Later Discussions in the Colleges

By the latter part of the 1960s, the initiative had swung to the students. Beginning in 1968, with Wadham in the lead, one JCR after another passed resolutions favoring coeducation. By the spring of 1970, nineteen of twenty-three JCRs—including those at the five

19 Richards, *50 Years at Oxford*, p. 12.
20 Brasenose Gov. Body, Feb. 21, 1968, GOV 3 A1/23.
21 E-mail, Solymar to Malkiel; Richards interview.
22 Brasenose Gov. Body, May 1, 1968, GOV 3 A1/23.

women's colleges—had declared in favor of going mixed.[23] It was no surprise. With the student upheavals of 1968, the discussion of coeducation at Cambridge in progress, and the first steps toward coeducation having been taken at Princeton and Yale, "coeducation was in the air."[24]

WADHAM ENTERS THE LISTS

An account of the Wadham JCR resolution in the *Wadham College Gazette* sought to put the move toward coeducation in a context that old Wadham men might understand. The account was probably written by the legendary and long-serving warden, Sir Maurice Bowra. A scholar of ancient Greek literature, Bowra had announced plans to retire in August 1970 after a thirty-two-year tenure. He had championed the admission of grammar-school boys from state schools to balance Wadham's historic emphasis on students from independent schools. Whatever his private views, he understood that it was going to be necessary to admit women to the college.[25]

In his account of the JCR resolution, Bowra noted that the patterns familiar to old Wadham men no longer matched the experiences of students coming to the college in the 1960s: "A large proportion now come from day-schools, where they have lived at home and come into natural and frequent contact with the other sex. . . . Any restriction on the company of women, such as the Colleges impose by confining themselves to one sex, is so unfamiliar as to be wrong. This is entirely understandable, and there is no need to interpret a demand of co-education as yet another sign of our decadent age."[26]

Bowra knew that he had to tread carefully. Coeducation had the potential to be an enormously disruptive force to Oxford's

23 "Coeducation Is Favoured by Undergraduates," *Oxford Times*, May 29, 1970, clipping in Bodleian, File 1.

24 Interview with Raymond C. Ockenden, Feb. 21, 2014, Oxford, England.

25 Interview with Clifford S. L. Davies, Feb. 17, 2014, Oxford, England.

26 "Notes," *Wadham College Gazette*, no. 164, Michaelmas Term, 1968, p. 73, Wadham College Archives.

five women's colleges, which were accustomed both to educating highly capable women students and to having a staff of highly accomplished women fellows. The women's colleges stood at the top of the Norrington Table in their undergraduates' academic achievements, and they offered employment to the most outstanding women academics in Britain. Coeducation threatened both of those historic realities. Many of the best women graduating from secondary schools would undoubtedly be attracted to mixed colleges, and men's colleges going mixed were likely to hire very few women. Indeed, if women's colleges were forced to go mixed, they would almost certainly seek to balance their teaching staff by hiring men, and if women academics had to compete with men for jobs, prevailing prejudices would reduce their chances of academic employment.

These fears were well founded. As was the case at Cambridge, men's colleges at Oxford that admitted women were very slow to elect women fellows. Six years after the first five men's colleges went mixed in 1974, Brasenose still had no women fellows on staff. Jesus, more analogous to Churchill at Cambridge, had five. And the prognostication about the likely gender balance of fellows in women's colleges that went mixed also proved to be accurate. A year after they admitted male undergraduates, three of the erstwhile women's colleges at Oxford had already appointed significant numbers of men to their teaching staffs: at Lady Margaret Hall, seventeen men out of a teaching staff of forty; at St. Anne's, sixteen men out of forty; at St. Hugh's, twelve men out of forty.[27] As late as 1989, women constituted 14 percent of the academic staff and 3.3 percent of the professors at Oxford, with all colleges but two by then coeducational.[28]

Part of the challenge for Bowra, then, was to engage the women's colleges in thinking about how to handle the resolution of Wadham's JCR. With his retirement looming, Bowra knew that he

27 Marie Hicks, "Integrating Women at Oxford and Harvard, 1964–1977," in Laurel Thatcher Ulrich, ed., *Yards and Gates: Gender in Harvard and Radcliffe History* (New York: Palgrave Macmillan, 2004), p. 268, nn. 40, 41.

28 Judy G. Batson, *Her Oxford* (Nashville, TN: Vanderbilt University Press, 2008), p. 287.

had to avoid tying his successor's hands. To a Wadham alumnus unhappy about the JCR resolution, Bowra wrote, "You will agree that one cannot do anything but look into it very seriously and find out the problems and difficulties. . . . I am myself neutral, but in any case I am going in 1970 and it would be unjust for me to impose a new system on my successor. It would be fairer to let him work out the matter for himself."[29]

Bowra had two advantages in looking into the matter. Colleges especially inclined toward coresidence had either a fellowship with a longstanding sympathy for liberal causes or significant turnover among the fellowship in the 1960s, when a much younger generation of academics brought with them a worldview and a set of experiences that made them regard coresidence as a desirable norm. Wadham had both. The college had a reputation as "the home of left-wing causes." Most of the fellows were Labour supporters who prided themselves on being progressive. Moreover, three quarters of them were appointed in the 1960s. They were keen on coeducation, and their initiative played an important part in driving the idea forward.[30]

In the interest of looking into the proposal for coeducation at Wadham, Bowra corresponded with the heads of the five women's colleges.[31] He presented himself as being in fact-finding mode— "There is no harm in knowing what the situation is"—and as fully appreciative of the spot the women's colleges would be in: "I . . . think the whole operation exceedingly complicated and difficult."[32] He bent over backward to be sensitive to the women principals' concerns: "I agree with most of what you say, but . . . I am really a mere intermediary collecting information."[33] To the question of

29 Warden [Sir Maurice Bowra] to B[erick] Dale, Nov. 18, 1968, Wadham Co-Residence, Box 1.

30 Interview with Alan Ryan, Apr. 15, 2014, Princeton, NJ ("left-wing causes"); Davies interview.

31 Warden [Sir Maurice Bowra] to the Principal, St. Hilda's College, Nov. 22, 1968, Wadham Co-Residence, Box 1. Bowra sent the same letter to St. Anne's, Lady Margaret Hall, Somerville, and St. Hugh's.

32 Warden [Sir Maurice Bowra] to the Principal, St. Anne's College, Nov. 25, 1968, Wadham Co-Residence, Box 1.

33 Warden [Sir Maurice Bowra] to the Principal, St. Hilda's College, Nov. 30, 1968, Wadham Co-Residence, Box 1.

what his JCR had in mind, he responded, "I think my J.C.R., like other J.C.R.'s desire the change for the simple reason that most of them have been brought up at home with girls around them and find it very odd, if not unnatural, to be severed from them."[34]

For all of Bowra's sensitivity to the pressures on the women's colleges, he could not avoid acting on the JCR motion. The vehicle through which the issue was engaged was the college's liaison committee, a group established recently in response to student demand for a hand in running the college. Composed of undergraduates, graduate students, and dons, the liaison committee gave students opportunities to talk with the fellows about matters that were on their minds.[35] The suggestion to formally investigate coeducation came to the liaison committee. Bowra responded by creating a subcommittee to conduct the investigation. The members were two undergraduates, one graduate student, and the two youngest fellows in the college.[36]

As Ray Ockenden, one of those two very young fellows, recalled, four of the five subcommittee members were initially skeptical about coeducation.[37] But the group took its mandate seriously and investigated the question carefully. They "sounded out" the opinions of the fellows and distributed questionnaires to undergraduates and graduate students. Thirty-eight percent of Wadham students responded, with 91 percent of respondents in favor of increasing the proportion of women at Oxford, both to afford women equal academic opportunity and to improve the social life at the university. The preferred method of accomplishing those goals was for men's and women's colleges to go coed. A smaller number favored action only on the part of the men's colleges, and still fewer thought that expansion in the size of the women's colleges was the way to bring more women to the university. As for Wadham's best course of action, 61 percent thought the college

---

34 Warden [Sir Maurice Bowra] to the Principal, St. Hilda's College, Jan. 23, 1969, Wadham Co-Residence, Box 1.

35 A. F. Thompson, "The Bowra Years and After: 1938–1993," in C.S.L. Davies and Jane Garnett, eds., *Wadham College* (Wadham College, 1994), p. 86.

36 Ockenden interview; Davies interview.

37 Ockenden interview.

should go coed as soon as possible, and 69 percent said that it should go coed on its own if other colleges were not prepared to follow.[38]

The subcommittee investigated coeducation at other British institutions and talked to colleagues in the Cambridge colleges that had decided to admit women. They read and considered the implications of the Franks report. They talked to undergraduates at Wadham. By the time they were ready to write a report, they had become persuaded that embracing coeducation was the right thing to do. As Ockenden put it, "It was a demonstration of the fact that just thinking about something makes it possible."[39]

JESUS TAKES UP COEDUCATION

As Wadham deliberated, Jesus took up the issue. Jesus was widely understood to be "a liberal college," "socially unpretentious," where low "snob value" combined with high-powered academic achievement. The college was one-fourth to one-third Welsh, with a preponderance of students from Welsh grammar schools. The impediments to coeducation in a more conservative, more socially prestigious college were of less consequence at Jesus.[40] The principal, Hrothgar John Habakkuk, had taken office in 1967. An economic historian, he had published an important series of articles on English land ownership and the land market from the sixteenth to the eighteenth century, along with major books on the landed aristocracy in England and on American and British technology in the nineteenth century. A Welshman by birth, Habakkuk had tried unsuccessfully to win admission to Jesus and had instead gone on scholarship to St. John's College, Cambridge. His initial faculty appointment was as a fellow of Pembroke College, Cambridge. Upon his election to the Chichele chair in economic history at Oxford in 1950, he became a fellow of All Souls, a position he held until his

---

38 Interim Report of the Joint Sub-Committee on Co-Education, n.d., distributed to the college at the end of Trinity Term, 1969, Wadham Co-Residence, Box 1.

39 Ockenden interview.

40 Interview with John Walsh, Feb. 21, 2014, Oxford, England.

election as principal of Jesus. From 1973 to 1977 he served simultaneously as vice-chancellor of the university.[41]

Habakkuk's family background influenced his priorities as principal. As the historian Sir Keith Thomas said in his address at Habakkuk's memorial service, "His father's struggle to gain an education left him with an abiding conviction that opportunities should not be wasted. His mother's frustration at being forced to give up teaching when she married . . . helps to explain his own commitment to the higher education of women."[42]

In January 1969, the JCR at Jesus made their case for coeducation: "The aim of an educational institution is to prepare one best for life in society," they argued. "The present single-sex collegiate system is a result of the attempt in the past to provide best for existing society; this system does not provide best for ours." Coeducation would "remove the artificiality of present relations between men and women at the University and also many of the damaging psychological pressures. Academically, both men and women would benefit from the interaction between different intellectual approaches and the improved social atmosphere." Entrance to the College should be based not on gender but "on ability alone."[43]

The governing body at Jesus moved in January 1969 to "set up a Working Party" of fellows and students "to study and report on the problems and practical implications involved in admitting women to the College."[44] At its first meeting in February, the working party compiled an inventory of matters that would need to be attended to, including securing approvals for a change in statutes, decreasing the number of men in order to admit women, adapting existing facilities to accommodate women residents, deciding whether to admit candidates on merit or to fix a quota by gender,

41 "Obituary: Sir John Habakkuk," *Jesus College Record*, 2002, pp. 19–22, and Sir Keith Thomas, "Memorial Service for Sir Hrothgar John Habakkuk," *Jesus College Record*, 2003, pp. 31–39, both in Jesus College Archives.

42 Thomas, "Memorial Service for Sir Hrothgar John Habakkuk," p. 32.

43 G. M. Rees, J.C.R. Preliminary Report on Co-Education, Jan. 15, 1969, Habakkuk, File 3/3.

44 [H. J. Habakkuk] to P. R. Norton, Jan. 24, 1969, and [Habakkuk] to Andrew Hart and Gareth Rees, Jan. 25, 1969, both in Habakkuk, File 3/3.

balancing admissions in terms of subjects, and breaking "carefully nurtured links with schools which have sent us able boys" because fewer boys would be admitted. And there were other issues: the implications of a smaller number of men for organized college sports, the desirability of going mixed in conjunction with other colleges, and, as an alternative to coeducation, the possibility of a close partnership with a women's college.[45]

Jesus decided to explore this last possibility in conversations with St. Hugh's, an exploration that began in February 1969 and continued through the spring. Habakkuk and his counterpart at St. Hugh's, Kathleen Kenyon, agreed to convene a meeting of fellows of both colleges to pursue the idea without prior commitment on either side.[46] The meeting took place in late April. Jesus was ready to set up a joint committee to explore the idea, but St. Hugh's wanted to wait until the end of term to make sure that their JCR understood the implications of a partnership and would be enthusiastic about the prospect. As well, Keble, another men's college, had first suggested a partnership with St. Hugh's, which did not "want to be rude to them, or to one or two other colleges that have made murmurs of interest, by going too far at this moment."[47] Habakkuk responded that Jesus would await St. Hugh's decision "in the hope that it will be a favourable one."[48] By the end of term, though, it became clear that Habakkuk's proposal was more than St. Hugh's could manage.[49]

By the spring of 1969, most of the JCRs in the men's colleges had already passed resolutions in favor of coresidence. Balliol's

45 H. J. H[abakkuk], Working Party on Co-Education, Feb. 26, 1969, Habakkuk, File 3/3.

46 [H. J. Habakkuk] to the Principal, St. Hugh's College, Feb. 19 and Mar. 20, 1969; Kathleen M. Kenyon to the Principal, Jesus College, Mar. 3 and 13, 1969; H[abakkuk] to E. C. Thompson, G. T. Young, and D. Barlow, Apr. 16, 1969; and handwritten notes, [Habakkuk,] inaccurately titled Dinner, Feb. 18, 1969, but more likely spring or summer 1969, all in Habakkuk, File 3/1.

47 Kathleen M. Kenyon to the Principal, Jesus College, May 15, 1969, Habakkuk, File 3/1.

48 [H. J. Habakkuk] to the Principal, St. Hugh's College, May 23, 1969, Habakkuk, File 3/1.

49 Kathleen Kenyon to the Principal, Jesus College, June 20, 1969, and H. J. H[abakkuk] to the Principal, St. Hugh's College, Sept. 8, 1969, both in Habakkuk, File 3/1.

was typical of the others: "More women of high intellectual capacity are turned away from the University than men of the same standard, hence the general level of ability could be raised by an increase in the proportion of women . . . there are numerous social advantages to be gained from co-education . . . the first college(s) in Oxford to become co-educational would gain immediate and substantial increases in the number and quality of both men and women applicants."[50]

It was not only at the men's colleges where the JCRs took the lead in encouraging consideration of coeducation. At St. Anne's, one of the most venerable women's colleges, the JCR produced a report in March 1969 arguing the case for coresidence in the women's colleges, specifically St. Anne's. By providing "opportunities for fuller intellectual co-operation between men and women," coeducation would enrich students' educational experiences. The students had read Princeton's Patterson report, and they agreed with its arguments for the advantages of coeducation. They noted especially "the importance of the different viewpoints which could be brought to bear on subjects . . . by men and women." There was evidence, they said, that schoolgirls made more progress intellectually in coeducational rather than single-sex schools, and there was already some evidence that coeducation was having beneficial effects at the women's colleges at the University of London that had recently admitted men.[51]

In terms of life outside the classroom, the St. Anne's students cited the positive testimony of wardens and students who lived in mixed halls at other universities, like Aberdeen, Durham, and Leeds, and noted also the assessment in reports compiled at Cambridge that coeducation would have no inimical effects on morality and personal relationships. Coresidence, they argued, would have a positive effect on social life at St. Anne's and would help to break down the "artificial" division that existed "between [the] social and intellectual spheres of life."

50 Quoted in Co-Residence at St. Anne's, Mar. 1969, p. 1, Wadham Co-Residence, Box 1.

51 Ibid., pp. 3–4.

Underscoring the historic strengths of St. Anne's—"the college's high academic standard and its effectiveness as an educational institution"—the students argued that they were "being progressively jeopardized by the tensions that naturally arise through the existence of an all-female institution operating in an increasingly integrated society."[52]

HERTFORD BEGINS CONVERSATIONS

At Hertford the pressure to consider coeducation came from the fellows, many of them younger men appointed to the fellowship in the 1960s. They had two motivations: to increase the pool of good candidates for admission to what had been, at best, a middling college and to move the college away from single-sex education, which they believed was outmoded.

Hertford had long been impoverished. Unlike other men's colleges at Oxford, it had no endowments, and it had few resources to enable it to attract the most promising students. In the mid-1960s, a small group of fellows took steps to expand the college's reach by appealing to grammar schools that had not traditionally sent students to Cambridge and Oxford, a tactic that produced a number of better-qualified students than Hertford had seen before.[53]

Admitting women followed logically from the desire to improve the academic quality of Hertford students. According to Keith Mc-Lauchlan, who was elected to a fellowship in chemistry in 1965, "It was obvious that many clever women were not being admitted" to Oxford colleges; "we saw our chance to improve the quality of our entry. . . . At no time was anything approaching a feminist argument made—we simply wanted the most able students and realized that by being amongst the first to admit women the average ability was bound to improve."[54]

---

52 Ibid., pp. 4–5, 7, 11.

53 "Hertford College Goes Co-educational," attached to e-mail, Keith McLauchlan to Nancy Weiss Malkiel, July 18, 2014; "Hertford College, admission of women," attached to e-mail, John Torrance to Malkiel, July 21, 2014.

54 "Hertford College Goes Co-educational," attached to e-mail, McLauchlan to Malkiel.

In March 1969, with the physiologist Sir George Lindor Brown as principal, the Hertford governing body agreed to set up a committee of three fellows and three students "to discuss the problem of admitting women to the College as Junior and Senior members."[55] The joint committee reported in June. Recognizing the desirability of creating more places for women at Oxford and the probability that this could be done only if some men's colleges went mixed, the committee considered the pros and cons of Hertford being one of the colleges to take the lead. Going mixed would likely increase the pool of talented students available to the college. But given its economic situation, the college was "dependent on the goodwill of its old members," which might "be diminished if the College became mixed." Moreover, there was the question of whether the appointment of a woman fellow should precede the admission of women students. If so, it might be a long time "before the best candidate for a vacant fellowship proved to be a woman." Arguments could be made to mitigate both of these concerns. At best, they were "arguments for delay," not arguments against going mixed, and if other men's colleges decided to go mixed, it would be advantageous to be among the first movers, who would "reap more benefit than colleges making the change later."

The report made three recommendations: that the college statute limiting enrollment to men be revised "to legalize the admission of women to the College," that the college reach out to heads of mixed secondary schools, and that the college exchange with a women's college the credentials of their respective applicants to determine whether any of the rejected candidates would have found places at the other college.[56] In October the governing body agreed that the statute limiting enrollment to men "should be considered for revision when the College statutes were next revised." It was agreed, further, that there would be no official communication with anyone in the coming year "about the possibility of

55 Hertford Gov. Body, Mar. 15, 1969.

56 Admission of Women: Report of Joint Committee, June 18, 1969, Hertford unsorted, 71M1.

admitting women as members of the College."[57] Hertford, in short, was on hold.

WADHAM CONTINUES TO DELIBERATE

In March 1970, the joint subcommittee on coeducation appointed at Wadham College issued a report laying out the academic and social considerations pointing toward coresidence, along with the practical problems and difficulties that would need attention. The arguments were familiar. Despite the protestations of the women's colleges that they were "accepting all of their qualified applicants," the committee believed that "a reservoir of well qualified women" not currently applying and being admitted to Oxford "could be tapped to raise the academic standards" at the university. If the men's colleges admitted students on the basis of merit, more women would be enrolled at Oxford, and the university's overall academic standard would rise.[58]

As for social considerations, coeducation would lead to a radical alteration in the character of college life. Students would have the chance to form friendships with students of the opposite sex. Some of the least attractive "features of an exclusively male college," like "hooliganism and rowdy behavior," would gradually disappear. Although coeducation might have an adverse effect on the college's "sporting life," it would "be balanced against such advantages as might accrue to a college admitting women."[59] The committee said that it favored coeducation for Wadham, preferably in partnership with other men's colleges, but alone in the unlikely event that no other men's colleges chose to go mixed at the same time.[60]

There the matter stood until the new warden was installed in the fall of 1970. Maurice Bowra had thought it inappropriate to "preside over . . . a debate immediately before retiring from office," and the decision was made to hold the committee report over until the

---

57 Hertford Gov. Body, Oct. 29, 1969.

58 Report of the Wadham College Joint Sub-Committee on Co-Education, Mar. 12, 1970, pp. 2–4, Wadham Co-Residence, Box 1. The quotes are on p. 2.

59 Ibid., pp. 7–8.

60 Ibid., pp. 9–13.

beginning of the new term. In the search for Bowra's successor, the fellows applied an explicit test of the candidates' views on coresidence, a test that clearly shaped the final outcome. The two most compelling candidates were prominent philosophers, the logician A. J. Ayer, who held a chair in logic at Oxford, and the philosopher of mind and logic Stuart Hampshire, then on the faculty at Princeton University. (Hampshire's wife had previously been married to Ayer.) Ayer was believed (by himself as well as others) to be the leading candidate, but he made two mistakes: cultivating only the most senior fellows while ignoring the younger men and being dismissive about the admission of women. Ayer held the view that the college had operated very well as a men's college for more than 350 years, and no change was needed.[61]

In contrast, Hampshire was a strong proponent of coresidence at Wadham. He had seen coeducation in practice in its first year at Princeton, and he knew that it worked. In addition, he and his wife were well known for their liberal views. As department chair at Princeton, Hampshire had secured special fellowship support to enable the admission of women graduate students in philosophy at a time when the graduate school had not yet opened its doors fully to women students. Coresidence fit comfortably into Hampshire's view of the world, a significant part of the reason that the college elected him as master.[62]

Joint Discussions in the Colleges

One of the members of Wadham's joint subcommittee on coeducation, Ray Ockenden, wrote to Hampshire shortly after his arrival at Wadham asking that coeducation be put on the agenda for the first college meeting in October 1970. "You may feel you don't want to launch into such a major issue at your first session," Ockenden said, "but I think there are grounds for having a debate as soon

61 Davies interview; Ockenden interview.
62 Ibid. On the support for women graduate students, in Goheen, Box 14, Folder 1, see Stuart Hampshire to Robert F. Goheen, Apr. 29, 1966; Goheen to Hampshire, May 6, 1966; and Hampshire, Fellowship for a Woman Graduate Student in Philosophy, attached to memorandum, Hampshire to Goheen, June 3, 1966. In Goheen, Box 14, Folder 2, see Department of Philosophy, Confidential Report to the President for 1967–68.

as possible." Ockenden told Hampshire that he believed that "the rest of the University is waiting to see what this College is going to do."[63]

WADHAM RALLIES THE COLLEGES

Hampshire put the report on the agenda for the governing body, which set up a committee to investigate what would have to be done if the college decided to go mixed. Hampshire wrote to his fellow heads of colleges in early November to inquire about their thinking on coeducation. For the men's colleges, the questions were straightforward. Had they "taken any decision about the admission of women?" Would the college be "interested in exploring the arrangements which would be necessary or desirable if women were to be admitted to men's colleges?" If so, would the college be ready to cooperate with Wadham and other colleges that might be interested "in considering possible joint schemes for admissions"?[64]

For the women's colleges, Hampshire's approach was more delicate. He wrote that the committee wanted their opinions and wanted to know if "they might be ready to co-operate, particularly in respect of admissions, if Wadham College at some future date decided to admit women." Multiple schemes had been proposed for grouping colleges for admissions, and Wadham wanted their views on which ones might work. Wadham also wanted to know about ways beyond admissions in which the women's colleges would be affected by the adoption of coeducation.[65]

The responses came in due course.[66] Although the women's colleges were prepared to meet with the committee, they were plainly

63 Ray Ockenden to Warden [Stuart Hampshire], Oct. 11, 1970, Wadham Co-Residence, Box 1.

64 Letter from the Warden [Stuart Hampshire] to [Heads of Men's Colleges], Nov. 5, 1970, Wadham Co-Residence, Box 1.

65 Warden [Stuart Hampshire] to Principal, St. Anne's College, Nov. 5, 1970, Wadham Co-Residence, Box 1. The same letter went to the principals of the four other women's colleges.

66 For Hampshire's own summary of the responses, compiled before all responses had come in, see S. N. H[ampshire] to Members of the Co-Education Committee, Nov. 18, 1970, Wadham Co-Residence, Box 1.

nervous. As Lucy Sutherland, principal of Lady Margaret Hall, wrote to Hampshire, "The women's colleges are bound to watch these developments with some anxiety." Although they believed in "increasing the number of women at Oxford," the prospect of competition for women students from "the older (and more glamorous) [men's] colleges" was bound to make them "feel a little uneasy." The "dangers," Sutherland said, were that the men's colleges would take enough of the still-too-small number of science students away from the women's colleges, "leaving us in the position of Liberal Arts Colleges," and that "there might in the short term be even an over-all deficiency of suitable women candidates except in a few very popular subjects," like English and modern languages.[67]

From the principal at St. Hilda's, Mary Bennett, came some skepticism about the presumed case for going mixed. "It may be that clever girls are being kept out while stupid young men are being let in. But we have no really satisfactory evidence of this at present," she wrote, "and I think myself that it would be a pity for any of us to commit ourselves too far until such evidence is forthcoming." She added, "I don't myself think that we should allow ourselves to be too much influenced by the non-academic arguments for mixture. . . . I think that some men undergraduates (and some women dons) want simply more company of the opposite sex. But I do not think that this is any particular reason for transforming existing institutions. . . . The crux of the matter is really whether able young women are being kept out, or staying out, when they ought to be being brought in or attracted in."[68]

St. Hugh's, too, was skeptical "that there is a great pool of able schoolgirls unable to find places at Oxford."[69] The view at Somerville was the most encouraging in terms of willingness to entertain mixed colleges at Oxford. As the principal, Barbara Craig,

67 L. S. Sutherland to the Warden, Wadham College, Nov. 10, 1970, Wadham Co-Residence, Box 1.

68 Mary Bennett to the Warden, Wadham College, Nov. 11, 1970, Wadham Co-Residence, Box 1.

69 Kathleen M. Kenyon to the Warden, Wadham College, Dec. 4, 1970, Wadham Co-Residence, Box 1.

reported to Hampshire, "The College is eager to enable more women qualified to profit by an Oxford education to be admitted to Oxford." Although Somerville itself did not want to go mixed, it would "welcome an investigation of the possibility of having an alliance with one of the men's colleges" so that more undergraduates might be taught by "Senior Members of the opposite sex" and might have a chance, as well, at having "a member of the opposite sex as a tutorial partner."[70]

As for the responses Hampshire received from men's colleges, only University had decided firmly against coeducation.[71] Christ Church, Oriel, St. John's, St. Peter's, and Trinity reported that they were leaning against, or unlikely to embark on, coeducation, but that they would like to participate in the discussions.[72] Most of the other men's colleges were non-committal but willing to join in the discussions.[73] Brasenose was ready to go forward. It had been clear since 1967 that it had the votes for a two-thirds majority in favor of coeducation.[74] The other men's colleges most in favor of coresidence were Corpus Christi and New College.[75]

Many were puzzled about how the Wadham effort fit with an earlier initiative from Queen's, which had written to other colleges in September 1970 suggesting discussions about "devising joint arrangements for the entry of women." Queen's would have been a credible leader; founded in 1341, it was one of the wealthiest

70 Barbara Craig to the Warden, Wadham College, Nov. 16, 1970, Wadham Co-Residence, Box 1.

71 Master, University College, to the Warden, Wadham College, Nov. 11, 1970, Wadham Co-Residence, Box 1.

72 In Wadham Co-Residence, Box 1, see the following letters to the Warden, Wadham College: Henry Chadwick, Nov. 6, 1970; A. G. Ogsten, Nov. 7, 1970; Alec Cairncross, Nov. 9, 1970; Provost, Oriel College, Nov. 12, 1970; R. W. Southern, Nov. 30, 1970.

73 In Wadham Co-Residence, Box 1, see the following letters to the Warden, Wadham College: Walter Oakeshott, Nov. 16, 1970; Sir George Pickering, Nov. 13, 1970; R. E. Richards, Nov. 9, 1970; Dennis Nineham, Nov. 12, 1970; Sir Lindor Brown, Nov. 18, 1970; John Habakkuk, Nov. 12, 1970; Christopher Hill, Nov. 19, 1970; J.N.D. Kelly, Dec. 9, 1970; Rector, Exeter College, Dec. 10, 1970.

74 Brasenose Gov. Body, Oct. 14, 1970, GOV 3 A1/25; Richards interview; Noel Hall to the Warden, Wadham College, Nov. 20, 1970, Wadham Co-Residence, Box 1.

75 J. O. Urmson to the Warden, Wadham College, Nov. 7, 1970, Wadham Co-Residence, Box 1.

colleges in the university. But although a majority of the Queen's governing body favored engaging in discussions with other colleges, that majority fell short of the two-thirds that would be required to amend the college's own statutes.[76]

The Oxford colleges were not sure what to make of the two separate inquiries. Keble expressed "uncertain[ty] about the point of two such operations being carried on independently." Trinity said that it would be "desirable not to have more than one body discussing this question."[77] In fact, Hampshire had been in communication with Queen's; the plan was to coordinate the two efforts and to have a common meeting of the interested colleges later in the term, with Queen's as the convener.[78]

JOINT DISCUSSIONS BEGIN

The first "exploratory discussion" took place at Queen's on December 3, 1970. All eighteen men's colleges participated. The colleges were at different points in their consideration of admitting women. New College had initiated a proposal that had led to substantial discussion but had set it aside in the face of objections. Brasenose had taken initial steps in 1967 but had then declined to go forward until some other men's colleges, along with some women's colleges, were ready to participate. Hertford had empanelled a joint committee in 1969 but had proceeded no further on its recommendations. Wadham was perhaps furthest along, with the governing body having requested detailed schemes for the admission of women.

76 Secretary to the Governing Body, The Queen's College, Oxford, to Dear Sir, Sept. 1970, Wadham Co-Residence, Box 1.

77 Dennis Nineham to the Warden, Wadham College, Nov. 12, 1970, and A. G. Ogsten to the Warden, Wadham College, Nov. 7, 1970, both in Wadham Co-Residence, Box 1. On the theme of coordination, see also Sir Lindor Brown to the Warden, Wadham College, Nov. 18, 1970, Wadham Co-Residence, Box 1.

78 Warden, Wadham College, to the President, Trinity College, Nov. 9, 1970; Secretary to the Governing Body, The Queen's College, to the Warden, Wadham College, Nov. 17, 1970; Geoffrey Marshall to the Warden, Wadham College, Nov. 18, 1970; Warden, Wadham College, to the Principal, Hertford College, Nov. 19, 1970; Warden, Wadham College, to the Warden, Keble College, Nov. 18, 1970, all in Wadham Co-Residence, Box 1.

Each college gave an account of where it stood, and the group decided to constitute a "working party" of Brasenose, Magdalen, New College, St. Catherine's, and Wadham, to be convened by the warden of Wadham, to "devise an admission scheme or schemes to be shown to the women's colleges." Other colleges would be kept informed and could opt to join the working group.[79] Jesus soon asked to join; their governing body had "decided that it was in principle in favour of admitting women provided that suitable arrangements could be made with regard to accommodation and admissions procedure," and they wanted to take part in the feasibility study.[80] Before long, Balliol, Corpus Christi, Keble, and Lincoln signed on with similar understandings.[81] Hertford was not in a position to proceed. Its principal, Sir Lindor Brown, was ailing and frequently absent, and he would die in February 1971. The governing body had decided not to send a representative to forthcoming meetings but asked that the college be kept informed of subsequent discussions.[82] Queen's decided in the end to bow out. Because their governing body was "narrowly divided," sending a representative to the working party "might be misleading, and would be unfair to colleges which have 'advanced' further than we have."[83]

In preparation for the discussions, Hampshire set out to familiarize himself with other institutions' experiences with coeducation. He already knew about Princeton. He sought information from Cambridge about the scheme agreed to by Churchill, Clare, and King's.[84]

79 Minutes, meeting re Admission of Women Undergraduates, Dec. 3, 1970, Wadham Co-Residence, Box 1; Stuart Hampshire to the Master, St. Catherine's College (same letter to New College, Balliol, Corpus Christi, Brasenose, and Jesus), Jan. 5, 1971, St. Catz, Box XIID/B IV 14(f).

80 John Habakkuk to the Warden, Wadham College, Dec. 18, 1970, Wadham Co-Residence, Box 1.

81 Warden [Stuart Hampshire] to the Master, Balliol College, Jan. 5, 1971; minutes, meeting re Co-Residence, Jan. 21, 1971; Dennis Nineham to the Warden, Wadham College, Jan. 21, 1971; and M. P. Furmston to the Warden, Wadham College, Jan. 28, 1971, all in Wadham Co-Residence, Box 1.

82 Hertford Gov. Body, Dec. 5, 1970, and Jan. 16 and Mar. 13, 1971.

83 The Provost, Queen's College, to the Warden, Wadham College, Jan. 27, 1971, Wadham Co-Residence, Box 1.

84 Warden [Stuart Hampshire] to the Tutor for Admissions, King's College, Cambridge, Dec. 14, 1970; H[ampshire] to Members of the Committee on Co-Education, Jan. 8, 1971; and Admission of Women to Oxford and Cambridge, July 1970, all in Wadham Co-Residence, Box 1.

At the first meeting of the new working group, on January 21, 1971, the assembled representatives discussed "principles that might govern the admissions policy for mixed colleges," as well as the appointment of women fellows.[85] The second meeting, on February 4, brought together representatives of men's colleges interested in coresidence and representatives of the women's colleges. The women's colleges were asked for their views "both on the general questions of women's education in Oxford and on particular problems," including examinations, admissions, and possible subject quotas. It was agreed that a working group should be constituted to address "the main practical problem"—admissions.[86]

That group, chaired by the warden of New College, Sir William Hayter, reported in late April 1971. Its recommendation: In the first stage, a total of eighty to a hundred women should be admitted to three or four men's colleges. A second stage, with a larger group of men's colleges admitting women, might be considered in light of experience both at Oxford and at Cambridge.[87]

The larger group of representatives of interested colleges received the report in May. Although not everyone was persuaded by all of the working party's recommendations (among other things, it was believed that the working party was too sensitive to the views of the women's colleges and thus too conservative in its proposals), they agreed that the next step was to circulate the report to the colleges for consideration, both of "the principle of co-residence" and of "the practical proposals" in the report. They hoped that interested colleges might come to a judgment about how they wished to proceed by the beginning of the new term in October. After that, the colleges that wanted to go forward would "meet to work out common problems."[88]

---

85 Minutes, meeting re Co-Residence, Jan. 21, 1971; Warden [Stuart Hampshire] to the Warden, Keble College, Jan. 22, 1971 (source of the quote), both in Wadham Co-Residence, Box 1.

86 Minutes, meeting re Co-Residence, Feb. 4, 1971, Wadham Co-Residence, Box 1.

87 Report of the Working Party on Co-residence, Apr. 26, 1971, Wadham Co-Residence, Box 1.

88 Minutes, meeting re Co-Residence, May 13, 1971 ("principle," "practical proposals"); Co-Residence, May 17, 1971 ("common problems"); S. N. H[ampshire] to Members of the Committee on Co-Residence, May 12, 1971; H[ampshire], Committee on Co-Residence, n.d., all in Wadham Co-Residence, Box 1.

Jesus and Brasenose signed on right away.[89] Brasenose had already reiterated its May 1967 decision that it was prepared to amend the college statutes to allow women to become members, and in June 1971 it voted to do so by a margin of 24 to 8.[90] "Brasenose," *The Times* wrote, "thus becomes Oxford's new front-runner in what is proving a marathon run-up to co-education in Oxford colleges."[91] A mathematician, Bryan Birch, remembered that the majority of Brasenose fellows "simply felt . . . that the 'Men Only' Statute was out-of-date in principle."[92] A historian, Robert Evans, said that the push for coeducation reflected "the desire for the best students" on the part of a college that was "not brilliant academically."[93] A mathematical physicist, Simon Altmann, recalled the "crucial speech" by a very senior fellow, a professor of comparative law, who argued that the fellows were trustees of the college funds and that it was "wrong" to administer them "only for the benefit of men."[94]

Like Brasenose, Wadham was ready to go forward, given the history of deliberations there.[95] Balliol's position was also favorable; the college declared its intention to eliminate the statutory barriers to the admission of women, "with a view to admitting women at a later stage," but with qualifications: "if the Governing Body, after consultation with old members, so decided, and provided that the interests of the existing women's colleges were protected." In any event, Balliol "want[ed] to remain involved in the discussions as an actively interested party."[96]

89 In Habakkuk, File 3/3, see H. J. H[abakkuk] to All Members of the Governing Body, May 11, 1971. In Wadham Co-Residence, Box 1, see John Habakkuk to the Warden, Wadham College, June 16, 1971, and Noel Hall to the Warden, Wadham College, June 17, 1971.

90 Brasenose Gov. Body, Jan. 20 and June 16, 1971, GOV 3 A1/25.

91 "The Times Diary: Brasenose Takes Coeducational Lead," *The Times*, June 18, 1971, clipping in Bodleian, File 1.

92 E-mail, Bryan Birch to Nancy Weiss Malkiel, Dec. 8, 2013.

93 Telephone interview with Robert Evans, Dec. 17, 2013. Birch concurred; see his e-mail to Malkiel.

94 Interview with Simon Altmann, Feb. 18, 2014, Oxford, England.

95 Warden [Stuart Hampshire] to D. Pennington, June 7, 1971, Wadham Co-Residence, Box 1. Wadham voted on the overall principle on Oct. 20 and on specific amendments to its statutes on Nov. 24. H[ampshire], To All Fellows, Oct. 25, 1971, Wadham Co-Residence, Box 1.

96 D. Pennington to the Warden, Wadham College, June 3, 1971, Wadham Co-Residence, Box 1.

By October, the rest of the line-up was becoming clear. With a vote in the governing body of 23 in favor and 3 against, with 3 abstentions, St. Catherine's was on board.[97] St. Catherine's had originated in 1868 as St. Catherine's Society, which had allowed non-collegiate students who could not afford the cost of three or four years at college to study at Oxford and earn a degree. In 1962, as a result of a decade-long effort by the historian A.L.C. Bullock, then censor of the society, St. Catherine's—known familiarly as St. Catz—took its place as the newest college at Oxford.[98] Like Wadham, St. Catz had a reputation as "a left-wing, progressive place."[99] Bullock's background was a good match for St. Catherine's Society: His father worked as a gardener (and later as a Unitarian minister), his mother as a maid, and he had prepared for Oxford in a local grammar school. Bullock had read classics and modern history at Wadham and held his first faculty appointment at New College. He had become a prominent public figure as the author of the best-selling book *Hitler: A Study in Tyranny* (1952). By temperament as well as connections, he was well suited to the public engagement, diplomatic efforts, and major fund-raising required to establish a new college.[100]

Bullock, now master of the college, reminded members that the question of admitting women had been discussed when St. Catz opened as a college in 1962, but there was so much else to do then that they had "decided to let the matter rest as it was." Now, with the "general move towards the admission of women," it was time to join in. The main reason: "the desirability of making an Oxford education available on equal terms to women as well as to men."[101]

97 Handwritten notes on St. Catherine's College, Governing Body, June 9, 1971, Agendum 15: Co-Residence, and St. Catherine's College Governing Body, Oct. 5, 1971, both in St. Catz, Box XIID/B IV 14(f). See also minutes, Co-residence: Meeting of Colleges, Oct. 28, 1971, Wadham Co-Residence, Box 1.

98 Roger Ainsworth and Clare Howell, eds., *St. Catherine's, Oxford: A Pen Portrait* (London: Third Millennium Publishing, 2012), pp. 29–31.

99 Richards interview.

100 "Lord Bullock of Leafield," *The Guardian*, Feb. 3, 2004, http://www.theguardian.com/news/2004/feb/03/guardianobituaries.obituaries, accessed Mar. 10, 2014; Ainsworth and Howell, eds., *St. Catherine's, Oxford*, p. 45.

101 Alan Bullock and Wilfrid Knapp, The Admission of Women to St. Catherine's, Oct. 12, 1971, St. Catz, Box XIID/B IV 14(f).

Among other colleges, New College mustered "the necessary two-thirds majority to amend its Statutes . . . to permit the admission of women"—that is, to remove the existing ban on their admission—with the proviso that "any specific proposal for the first admission of women" would also require a two-thirds majority vote.[102] At Hertford, with an acting principal, Felix Markham (the college's senior fellow), in place following the death of the principal, the governing body decided by straw vote that "they would probably wish to change the Statute so as to permit the admission of women."[103]

In other men's colleges, various reasons were given for not going forward. With no chance of getting a two-thirds vote in favor of coeducation in their respective governing bodies, Corpus Christi, Keble, and Lincoln fell out.[104] Pembroke felt that the proposals of the working party offered insufficient security to the women's colleges.[105]

The larger group of interested colleges gathered for the last time on October 28, 1971, to take stock and determine next steps. The group agreed that the warden of Wadham would report to the vice-chancellor so that he and Hebdomadal Council (an elected body that functioned, in effect, as the university cabinet) "could decide to take appropriate action."[106] Hampshire told the vice-chancellor that he would receive proposed amendments to statutes from several colleges for action by council. It was now time for the university to "take the responsibility for constituting a body to

102 Warden, New College, to the Warden, Wadham College, Oct. 7 (source of the quote), Nov. 12, 1971, and Warden, New College, to the Vice-Chancellor, Nov. 17, 1971, both in Wadham Co-Residence, Box 1.

103 F.M.H. Markham to the Warden, Wadham College, Oct. 10, 1971 (source of the quote), and [Markham] to the Vice-Chancellor, Nov. 2, 1971, both in Wadham Co-Residence, Box 1.

104 Dennis Nineham to the Warden, Wadham College, Oct. 7, 1971; President, Corpus Christi College, to the Warden, Wadham College, Oct. 8, 1971; and Minutes, Co-residence: Meeting of Colleges, Oct. 28, 1971, all in Wadham Co-Residence, Box 1.

105 Sir George Pickering to the Warden, Wadham College, Oct. 20, 1971, and Pembroke College, Observations on the Admission of Women to Mixed Colleges, Oct. 25, 1971, both in Wadham Co-Residence, Box 1.

106 E-mail, Clifford S. L. Davies to Nancy Weiss Malkiel, May 5, 2014; minutes, Co-residence: Meeting of Colleges, Oct. 28, 1971, Wadham Co-Residence, Box 1 (source of the quote).

plan mixed admissions" and to make further arrangements necessary to advance the effort toward coeducation.[107]

As straightforward as that process may have sounded, the way forward, as the next chapter will make plain, turned out to be complicated, contested, and fraught with unexpected challenges.

---

107 Warden [Stuart Hampshire] to the Vice-Chancellor, Nov. 2, 1971, Wadham Co-Residence, Box 1.

24

Oxford: As Revolutionary as "the Abolition of Celibacy among the Dons"

Part of the complexity of implementing coresidence came from the bewildering array of committees involved in making decisions about it. Part came from the reality that colleges had different, sometimes incompatible, interests that were challenging, if not impossible, to adjudicate.

Enter the University

In November 1971, Hebdomadal Council received a report from a committee it had constituted "to advise on the University's position in the matter of the admission of women by men's colleges." The committee, composed of the heads of four colleges that were not considering coresidence, decided that it would be premature for council to intervene. Rather, the next step should be for interested men's colleges to talk to the women's colleges to settle on "an agreed method of proceeding." The committee proposed to help by sounding out the women's colleges, meeting with representatives of the interested men's colleges, and suggesting "how many and which men's colleges should reopen discussions with the women's colleges."[1]

Declining the offer, the men's colleges decided to work out their own arrangements for admitting women. Balliol voted not to be

---

1 Report of the Committee to advise on the University's position in the matter of the admission of women by men's colleges, Hebdomadal Council, Nov. 13, 1971, Wadham Co-Residence, Box 1. See also Vice-Chancellor A.L.C. Bullock to the Warden, Wadham College, Nov. 23, 1971, Wadham Co-Residence, Box 1.

part of the group, perhaps the result of a poll of its old members, which had revealed staunch opposition from the generations of the 1940s and 1950s but support from those of the 1960s—a generational division that the college did not want to accentuate.[2] Brasenose, Jesus, New College, St. Catherine's, and Wadham were still in, shortly to be joined by Hertford, which had already voted its intention to change its statutes and had a formal vote scheduled for the next term, by which time a new principal might be in place. The men's colleges still needed to consult with the women's colleges; a meeting was set for December, with Hrothgar John Habakkuk, principal of Jesus, in the chair.[3]

Recognizing that other colleges might be interested in amending their statutes and admitting women later, and that any major increase in the number of women would have broad implications, Hebdomadal Council decided to appoint yet another committee, including the vice-chancellor, the principal of Jesus and the provost of Queen's (both men's colleges), the principal of St. Anne's (a women's college), and others, "to consider the whole matter" and offer advice.[4]

At the December meeting, the colleges' committee on coresidence considered the issues raised in the report of the working party chaired by the warden of New College in April 1971. A subcommittee was appointed to "investigate the technical details" and report back in February 1972.[5] The subcommittee recommended that about a hundred women could be admitted, as many as six men's colleges might be involved, and October 1974 would be the

2 Keith Thomas, "College Life, 1945–1970," in Brian Harrison, ed., *The History of the University of Oxford*, vol. 8: *The Twentieth Century* (Oxford: Oxford University Press, 1994), pp. 209–10.

3 Warden [Stuart Hampshire] to Lady Margaret Hall, Somerville, St. Hugh's, St. Hilda's, St. Anne's, Nov. 22, 1971; Hampshire letter, presumably to heads of the interested men's colleges, Nov. 24, 1971; Report on Co-Residence, H[ampshire] to All Fellows, Nov. 30, 1971; Felix Markham (Hertford) to the Warden, Wadham College, Dec. 1, 1971; and minutes, meeting of the Colleges' Committee on Co-Residence, Dec. 16, 1971, all in Wadham Co-Residence, Box 1.

4 F. H. Sandford to the heads of all societies, Nov. 30 (source of the quote) and Dec. 7, 1971, Wadham Co-Residence, Box 1.

5 Minutes, meeting of the Colleges' Committee on Co-Residence, Dec. 16, 1971, Wadham Co-Residence, Box 1.

target date for the first women to matriculate. It recommended, too, that Oxford follow the Cambridge system with respect to admission groups, such that the mixed colleges would "remain in their present groups for men applicants but deal with women applicants as part of the women's group."[6]

In February 1972, the full committee resolved to circulate the subcommittee report to the colleges for review and comment. The committee stipulated a transitional period: If the first women matriculated at mixed colleges in October 1974, the arrangements that had governed their admission would remain in place for the next five years. A general review would take place as early as 1977, and its results might affect applicants for entrance in October 1979.[7]

HERTFORD MAKES ITS DECISION

The philosopher Geoffrey J. Warnock, who had been senior tutor at Magdalen, took office as the new principal at Hertford in January 1972. He had been extremely ill with pneumonia, and he was spirited into the principal's lodgings on a stretcher over the holiday break. It took him a long time to recover, and for some weeks his wife, the philosopher Mary Warnock, had to make excuses for his absence. Warnock's health was a particularly sensitive matter due to unusual instability in the Hertford principal's office. Sir Robert Hall had resigned abruptly after less than three years in office. He had been having an affair with a married woman; although both of them had divorced their spouses and they subsequently married, it was thought that a quiet exit would prevent scandal. Hall's successor, Sir Lindor Brown, fell ill with heart disease almost immediately after taking the principal's post and died after three and a half years in office, and the acting principal, Felix Markham, had been in office for almost a year by the time Warnock took over. The college needed stability and continuity. The college physician,

---

6 Colleges' Committee on Co-Residence, Sub-Committee on Admissions Procedure, Summary of Recommendations and Conclusions, Jan. 28, 1972, Wadham Co-Residence, Box 2.

7 Co-Residence, H. J. Habakkuk to Distribution, Feb. 8, 1972, Wadham Co-Residence, Box 2.

greeting Warnock upon his arrival in the principal's lodgings, exclaimed, "You simply can't die!"[8]

Given the state of Warnock's health, it was difficult for him to take leadership of the college's consideration of coresidence. The fellows were ready to act. The size of the college fellowship had doubled since the 1950s (there were twenty-one fellows by 1969). The men elected in the 1960s were predisposed toward coeducation, either from personal experience at other universities or because of their relative youth. In a departure from the bachelor-dominated fellowship of the 1950s, many of the new fellows were married. Political scientist John Torrance, one of the fellows elected in the 1960s, noted "belief in equality of opportunity" as a reason for his support for coeducation. Even some of those who had been elected to the fellowship in the 1950s, like Miles Vaughan Williams, a physiologist, favored admitting women "on the grounds of social justice." Vaughan Williams, who had two daughters, "felt strongly that women should have the same educational opportunities as men." The fellows in favor of coeducation believed that "women were far more serious and worked harder" than men. Hertford's male students were given to "high spirits, drinking and larking around," and it was difficult for tutors to get them "to take work seriously; women would change this atmosphere" for the better.[9]

Meeting in the absence of the principal, the fellows talked about the matter until it was clear that they would have a majority in favor of coeducation.[10] As chemist Keith McLauchlan recalled, there were two camps: in favor of coeducation, "all the more recently elected Fellows"; in opposition, "the rump of the Fellowship who had either graduated in Oxford themselves or had long been members of a Male College." Complicating matters, the acting principal and senior fellow, Felix Markham, was a bachelor who

---

8 Interview with Baroness Mary Warnock, Oct. 29, 2014, London, England.

9 "Hertford College, admission of women," attached to e-mail, John Torrance to Nancy Weiss Malkiel, July 21, 2014; notes, Charlotte Brewer interview with Miles Vaughan Williams, Aug. 5, 2014, Oxford, England, attached to e-mail, Brewer to Malkiel, Aug. 11, 2014. See also Vaughan Williams, "Admission of Women," *Hertford Revivals*, attached to e-mail, Vaughan Williams to Malkiel, July 30, 2014.

10 Notes, Brewer interview with Vaughan Williams.

had been at Hertford since 1932 and "largely identified Hertford with himself, so it was a big wrench for him" to contemplate co-education.[11] On February 2, 1972, the fellows were ready for the vote; the governing body agreed unanimously to change Hertford's statutes to enable women to become members of the college.[12]

The still-recovering Warnock circulated a memo for what was to be the decisive meeting on February 16. The plan being considered—for the admission of a hundred women across the colleges—was too restrictive, he argued. There would be too few women per college to make a difference; the "academic and social dividends would be pretty slight," as would "the contribution to the cause of equality for women." Would the gains be sufficient to justify the administrative complications, the likely "domestic turmoil and possibly expense," and the possibly negative effects on fund-raising? Would it be better to wait? It seemed neither "absolutely vital, [n]or even specially advantageous" to be among the pioneers.[13]

Warnock's memo led some fellows to believe that he was opposed to coresidence, or at least trying to slow it down. The explanation was presumed to be the influence of his wife. Mary Warnock had studied at Lady Margaret Hall and, beginning in 1949, had been a fellow and tutor in philosophy at St. Hugh's. From 1966 to 1972 she had been headmistress at the Oxford High School for Girls. She was then named a senior research fellow at Lady Margaret Hall, where she served from 1972 to 1976. It was assumed that she was sympathetic to the interests of the women's colleges and skeptical of the push for coeducation at Hertford.[14]

In recalling the situation many years later, Mary Warnock told a different story. She favored coeducation for Hertford, and so did

11 "Hertford College Goes Co-educational," attached to e-mail, Keith McLauchlan to Nancy Weiss Malkiel, July 18, 2014; notes, Brewer interview with Vaughan Williams.

12 Hertford Gov. Body, Feb. 2, 1972; G. J. W[arnock], Amendment of Statutes 1 and 15, Jan. 25, 1972, Hertford unsorted, 71H3.

13 G. J. W[arnock], Co-Residence, for the Governing Body, Feb. 16, 1972, Hertford unsorted, 72H5.

14 "Hertford College, admission of women," attached to e-mail, Torrance to Malkiel; e-mail, Toby Barnard to Nancy Weiss Malkiel, July 9, 2014; "Hertford College Goes Co-educational," attached to e-mail, McLauchlan to Malkiel; e-mail, Gerald Stone to Malkiel, Aug. 4, 2014. See also Vaughan Williams, "Admission of Women," *Hertford Revivals*.

Geoffrey. But they had some concerns about the college being part of the first cohort to go mixed; they did not want to risk failure in what was admittedly an uncertain experiment. Moreover, Geoffrey Warnock was just establishing his footing as leader of the college. The principal needed to build trust and support among the fellows. If he had announced his strong support for coeducation, he would have alienated the older members. Warnock's advice to his wife when she became mistress of the recently coeducated Girton College at Cambridge in 1986 mirrored the strategy he was following: "If you ever want something to happen, never let it be known that you want it." If Warnock had shown his hand on coeducation, he might have compromised his ability to achieve his objectives.[15]

Either way, it was clear that the fellows, who had come to their conclusion before Warnock took office, expected him "to carry out the wishes of the Fellowship." Once the motion was on the table, Keith McLauchlan recalled, Warnock "instantly acceded to our wishes."[16]

On February 16, 1972, by majority vote, the governing body decided that Hertford was prepared in principle to sign onto the "scheme for the admission of women" set out by the colleges' committee on coresidence, though it would prefer less restrictive conditions on the total number of women to be admitted and their distribution among the mixed colleges. When further negotiations with the larger group failed to secure concessions, the governing body voted, 11 to 7, to "continue to participate in the scheme for the admission of women." In May the governing body said that the college would abide by the arrangements agreed to by the larger group.[17] In short, Hertford was in for the first round.

THE JESUS GROUP ORGANIZES

Wadham signed on as a member of the colleges' committee on coresidence, now known familiarly as the Jesus group, even though

---

15 Warnock interview.
16 "Hertford College Goes Co-educational," attached to e-mail, McLauchlan to Malkiel.
17 Hertford Gov. Body, Feb. 16, Mar. 11, and May 10, 1972.

it had not yet taken the two separate votes necessary to agree formally to the admission of women.[18] The other members, in addition to Jesus, were Brasenose, Hertford, and St. Catherine's, along with the women's colleges.[19] New College was still participating in the discussions, though it, too, had not yet taken the necessary vote.

At a meeting held on March 2, 1972, Habakkuk told the assembled group that they would need to agree on a final scheme by March 17. Meeting that deadline would allow decrees approving the alterations of college statutes to be passed by the end of the next term, which would in turn allow planning to go forward for the admission of women in the fall of 1974. The women's colleges continued to take the position that the total number of women admitted to the men's colleges should be limited to a hundred, which the committee agreed on as "an essential part of the scheme." The colleges agreed, too, that the arrangements under discussion would apply only for a stipulated period, after which a general review would be conducted.[20]

On March 17 the Jesus group reached agreement on the final details of the plan to be submitted to Hebdomadal Council. Surprisingly, New College could not join the first round. The scheme had come up one vote short of the necessary two-thirds majority in the governing body, the accident of attendance at the meeting, with one fellow who favored coresidence away in the United States and a retired fellow, who opposed it, unexpectedly showing up to vote.[21]

The plan made these stipulations: The mixed colleges would stay in their present groups for the admission of men but deal with women applicants as part of the women's groups. Women

---

18 Minutes, College Meeting, Feb. 16, 1972; P.B.C., Co-residence, May 23, 1972; and Warden [Stuart Hampshire] to B.E.F. Fender, Mar. 1, 1972, all in Wadham Co-Residence, Box 2.

19 Gene Gordon to B.E.F. Fender, Feb. 22, 1972; G. J. Warnock to Fender, Feb. 22, 1972; and Minutes, the Colleges' Committee on Co-Residence, Mar. 2, 1972, all in Wadham Co-Residence, Box 2.

20 Minutes, meeting of the Colleges' Committee on Co-Residence, Mar. 2, 1972, Wadham Co-Residence, Box 2. See also W.G.F. and D.C.S., Co-Residence: Informal Report on the Meeting of the Colleges' Committee on Co-Residence, Mar. 2, 1972, Wadham Co-Residence, Box 2.

21 Minutes, meeting of the Colleges' Committee on Co-Residence, Mar. 17, 1972, Wadham Co-Residence, Box 2; interview with Alan Ryan, Apr. 15, 2014, Princeton, NJ.

applicants would list five colleges in order of preference, not more than two of them mixed. Women applicants not selected by any of their preferred colleges would go into a pool from which other colleges might make selections. The number of women admitted to mixed colleges from the preference lists would be limited to a hundred. Scholarship awards would be given to women only by their first-choice college. In some of the subjects in which the women's colleges considered themselves "particularly vulnerable to competition," the mixed colleges would not advertise or offer awards for women, and in others, the women's colleges would have first pick from the pool. The first entry of women would come in October 1974, and no formal review of the agreed-upon arrangements would begin before 1977, for candidates matriculating in 1979.[22]

THE UNIVERSITY COMMITTEE HAS ITS SAY

The committee appointed by Hebdomadal Council to offer advice about coresidence reported in April 1972. They spoke not to the proposal from the Jesus group but rather to the larger question of Hebdomadal Council's responsibility in a world in which the women's colleges had long had a monopoly on the admission of women undergraduates but were now facing a situation in which they alone could not correct the imbalance between women and men at Oxford. Going forward, there would surely be more pressure from men's colleges to admit women. Council needed to give the women's colleges time to figure out how to adjust to this new reality. For that reason, it was essential that "the present operation should be regarded as a closed experiment." After five years, a general review should be conducted to take stock of the experience thus far and make plans for the future. Council should make sure that the five colleges were following the rules, and it should make plain that during the closed experiment it would not approve changes in statutes of other men's colleges. The plan should be regarded

22 Co-Residence: Report on proposals by Brasenose, Hertford, Jesus, St. Catherine's, Wadham, Lady Margaret Hall, St. Anne's, St. Hilda's, St. Hugh's, and Somerville Colleges sent to Hebdomadal Council, Mar. 17, 1972, Wadham Co-Residence, Box 2; H. J. Habakkuk to the Registrar, Mar. 17, 1972, Habakkuk, File 3/3.

as a genuine experiment; doubtless many details would need to be tweaked or changed altogether. The review, which would commence in 1977, should be "a real review," not just an examination of "ways in which the arrangements [could] be improved and expanded to other colleges."[23]

COUNCIL APPROVES THE CHANGES IN COLLEGE STATUTES

On April 24, Hebdomadal Council adopted the recommendations of the university committee on coresidence.[24] The university registrar then wrote to the men's colleges that had submitted requests for changes in statutes to allow for the admission of women. He told them that the changes were approved, provided that they agreed to abide by the rules of the closed experiment.[25] Once assurances were given, the amendments to the college statutes would be submitted to the Privy Council for final approval.[26]

Not everyone was supportive of the plan, and an attempt was made to derail it. The naysayers were a group composed of colleges opposed to coresidence and colleges in favor of coresidence but opposed to the scheme put forward by the Jesus group. The effort came to a head in Congregation, the assembly of all academic employees of the university and the body where authority in the university ultimately rested.[27] On May 30, 1972, four resolutions were introduced asking council to annul its previous approval of changes in college statutes and approve what was billed as an

23 Report of the Committee on Co-residence, Hebdomadal Council, vol. 272, Apr. 21, 1972, pp. 9–18, Wadham Co-Residence, Box 2.

24 F. H. Sandford to the heads of all societies, Apr. 25, 1972, Wadham Co-Residence, Box 2.

25 F. H. Sandford to the Warden, Wadham College, Apr. 28, 1972, Wadham Co-Residence File, Box 2. See also University of Oxford, *Report of the Committee on Co-residence,* Supplement No. 6 to the *University Gazette* 102 (May 1972): 1–12, Wadham Co-Residence, Box 2.

26 F. H. Sandford to the Warden, Wadham College, June 19, 1972, Wadham Co-Residence, Box 2. For the letter from Wadham offering those assurances, see Warden [Stuart Hampshire] to the Registrar, June 21, 1972, Wadham Co-Residence, Box 2. For St. Catz, see unsigned letters, likely from the master or the vice-master, to the Registrar, Apr. 27 and May 2, 1972, St. Catz, Box XIID/B IV 14(f).

27 E-mail, Clifford S. L. Davies to Nancy Weiss Malkiel, May 5, 2014.

improved scheme. Some of the proponents were conservatives deeply opposed to coresidence; others were looking out for the interests of their own colleges.

The first resolution was proposed by R.F.S. Hamer of Christ Church and seconded by C. A. Caine of St. Peter's College.[28] One scholar has aptly characterized them as "the last ditchers"— conservatives who "wished to prevent co-residence from taking place."[29] The resolution asked for "a full and public debate" on the issue, which, the authors alleged, had "nearly slipped through unquestioned." The proposed scheme would likely be very expensive, and no provisions had been made for paying for it. Moreover, it depended on the notion of "vast untapped deposits of women more able than the less able men we at present take," an assumption supporters of the resolution believed to be unfounded. Finally, supporters questioned the premise that the approved scheme was truly a limited experiment. Once in effect, they argued, it would become permanent, both in the colleges authorized to go forward and in others eager to follow.[30]

The second and third resolutions were proposed mainly by fellows from Merton and Lincoln Colleges, but also supported by a group of fellows from Corpus Christi and individual fellows from Worcester, Lady Margaret Hall, and St. Anne's. They wanted to allow colleges to amend their statutes to permit coresidence before the promised review in 1977. In other words, the resolutions challenged the monopoly on coresidence given to the first five entrants in the field.[31] The fourth resolution, put forward by Balliol and New College, said that colleges that had already changed their statutes to permit the admission of women, as they had, should be permitted to go ahead with that admission no matter how the 1977 review turned out.[32]

28 "Co-Residence: Verbatim Report of Debate in Congregation," *Oxford University Gazette*, Supplement (3) to No. 3510, June 7, 1972, pp. 1053–55, Bodleian, File 3.

29 Jason Leech, "*First of the Last*: Wadham College and the Decision for Co-Residence in 1974," p. 41 (unpublished thesis, Wadham College, n.d.), Wadham Co-Residence, Box 1.

30 "Co-Residence: Verbatim Report of Debate in Congregation," pp. 1053–55.

31 Ibid., pp. 1059–64; Leech, "*First of the Last*," p. 41.

32 "Co-Residence: Verbatim Report of Debate in Congregation," pp. 1064–65; Leech, "*First of the Last*," p. 41.

Although the second, third, and fourth resolutions may have sounded relatively benign, they were not. Had they been approved, the Jesus plan would have been scuttled and implementation of coresidence postponed indefinitely.[33] After lengthy debate in Congregation, the four resolutions were defeated—the first by a vote of 200 against, 66 for; the second, by 153 against, 89 for; the third, by 129 against, 88 for; and the fourth, by 102 against, 57 for.[34] In the hope of overturning these decisions, proponents called for a postal vote among all members of the academic staff in the university, but the postal ballot confirmed the rejection of the resolutions.[35] Planning could now proceed for the admission of women to the five men's colleges in the fall of 1974.[36]

The Coming of Coresidence

In a speech given in June 1972 at the Jesus College Gaudy, the college's annual celebratory reunion dinner, the principal, Hrothgar John Habakkuk, endeavored to explain to Old Members why the college was pursuing coeducation. As Sir Eric Ashby had done in his message to Old Clare Men, Habakkuk set the context by reminding Old Members of another change at Jesus that had appeared to threaten the very nature of the college. "A little less than a century ago," he said, "the Fellows of this College were facing a most difficult question. Should they revise the Statutes of the College so as to allow Fellows to marry without surrendering their Fellowships? To our predecessors in the nineteenth century the answer was much more debatable than it might appear today. The scholarly zeal of a Principal might survive matrimony; but, for the rest, it was doubtful whether devotion to wife and family would

33 The Co-residence Scheme—Congregation 30.5.72, memorandum from E. E. to Warden and Fellows, May 27, 1972, Wadham Co-Residence, Box 2.

34 "Co-Residence: Verbatim Report of Debate in Congregation," pp. 1059, 1064, 1066.

35 "Go-Ahead for Mixed Colleges," *Oxford Mail*, June 17, 1972, Bodleian, File 3.

36 In Wadham Co-Residence, Box 2, see John Habakkuk to the Warden, Wadham College, Nov. 21, 1972, and Feb. 27, 1973. In Habakkuk, File 3/3, see minutes, meeting on Co-Residence, Dec. 5, 1972, and Warden [Stuart Hampshire] to the Principal, Jesus College, Feb. 6, 1973. In Habakkuk, File 3/2, see E. A. Baskerville letter to Headmaster/Headmistress re Admission of Women by Mixed Colleges at Oxford, 1973.

be compatible with devotion to scholarship and to the College." As with the abolition of celibacy, it was impossible to predict the consequences of coeducation. Given the uncertainties, why had the college decided to go forward?

Habakkuk pointed first to "the desire, on grounds of public policy, to correct the imbalance in the numbers of men and women at Oxford." The second consideration, he said, was that many "able sixth-formers" (who were coming increasingly from coeducational schools) were put off by a university consisting solely of single-sex undergraduate colleges. Third, the college wanted to choose "the undergraduates best able to avail themselves of the particular education which Oxford offers and not to be subject to a constraint"—gender—"which is not relevant to the ability to use these opportunities." Then came the clinching argument: "We look forward to welcoming as candidates the daughters of Jesus men no less warmly than their sons." "What the consequences of the change will be we cannot be sure," Habakkuk concluded. "My own belief is that we shall take it in our stride and that in ten years' time no one will give it a second thought. Searching in the two histories of the College, I could find no mention of the abolition of celibacy among the dons. So it will be with co-residence."[37]

"IT WAS JUST NORMAL"

At Oxford, as at Cambridge, the coming of coresidence was in many ways anticlimactic. When asked, "What was it like when Hertford became coeducational?," Gerald Stone, a fellow in Slavonic languages who had joined the college in 1972 after teaching at Nottingham University, answered, "Well, it was just normal."[38] When the first women students arrived in the fall of 1974 at the five Oxford colleges going mixed, Oxford experienced none of the commotion attendant on the coming of coeducation to American universities like Princeton and Yale. At Brasenose, the college

---

37 "A Speech Given at the College Gaudy by the Principal," June 23, 1972, *Jesus College Record*, 1972, pp. 6–8, Jesus College Archives.

38 E-mail, Stone to Malkiel.

magazine, *The Brazen Nose*, called the "advent" of the women "as undramatic as it has been welcome." The magazine declared, "The changing social climate, not only of Oxford but of the whole society, has made it a non-revolutionary event."[39]

Some modest preparations had been made for the women: Plumbing was renovated as necessary, shower curtains and long mirrors were installed, and some drying and ironing rooms were created. The bursar at St. Catherine's, Tony Gye, said, "There has been a gentle feminisation, the rooms have been redecorated and smartened up with full length mirrors, an ironing room and an extra bedroom."[40] As one of the first women at St. Catz recalled, "The male students promptly said that they wanted shower curtains and full-length mirrors too."[41] At Jesus, mirrors were hung for the women. As one of the first women recalled, the college staff "may have felt a little anxious about the dreadful hordes that were about to descend on them, but they knew one thing for sure. Women need mirrors!"[42] But not every college took special steps; as the domestic bursar at Wadham, James D. Lunt, put it, "In this age of equality of the sexes we feel there should be equal and equivalent accommodation for men and women."[43]

The question of housing provoked considerable discussion and division. At Hertford the women students "were housed in small rooms at the top of the Principal's lodgings—rooms not nearly as good as those available to men," until one woman "protested and had to be allowed a proper room," whereupon "the system broke down" and women were housed in accommodations comparable to men's.[44] In some colleges women were housed in separate staircases; in others, the staircases were mixed from the outset. At

39 *The Brazen Nose*, 1975, p. 7, Brasenose College Archives.

40 Quoted in "More Mirrors to Welcome the Ladies," *Oxford Times*, Oct. 4, 1974, clipping in Bodleian, File 4.

41 Harriet Sergeant, "Women in College—The First Intake," in Roger Ainsworth and Clare Howell, eds., *St. Catherine's, Oxford: A Pen Portrait* (London: Third Millennium Publishing, 2012), p. 172.

42 Fiona Greig, "25th Anniversary of the Admission of Women: A Woman's View," *Jesus College Record*, 1999, p. 49, courtesy of John Walsh.

43 Quoted in "More Mirrors to Welcome the Ladies."

44 Notes, Brewer interview with Vaughan Williams.

Wadham, Lunt was responsible for dealing with student accommodations. The governing body, he said, "was at sixes and sevens regarding how and where the women should be accommodated," so he made the decisions himself: "I gave it up and contented myself with putting locks on all the lavatories; and where the bathrooms had only head-high partitions between the baths, I raised them to the ceiling, ensuring thereby that only someone on stilts would be able to satisfy his natural curiosity. I then scattered the women all over the College and waited for the storm to burst."[45]

At Hertford an excess of zeal to treat women and men evenhandedly (the controversy over accommodations notwithstanding) had amusing repercussions in the first weeks of school. "Wishing not to discriminate between the sexes in any way all the toilets and bathrooms were simply labelled as such," Keith McLauchlan remembered. "During the first Governing Body meeting of the term the main quadrangle became full of men demonstrating. We went to see why and they complained that they could hardly ever get into the bathrooms and if they did they were full of women's underclothes drying." Appropriate designations by sex were introduced.[46]

Male students in the colleges looked out for "their" women. Miles Vaughan Williams said of Hertford, "Once women had arrived the male undergraduates were very protective of them—no one from other colleges was to bother 'our girls.'"[47] The social life of the colleges became more spontaneous and more relaxed. The male president of the Wadham JCR in 1974 said, "Parties tend to be more civilised and natural without the usual preponderance of males."[48] One of the first women to come to Wadham recalled,

45 James D. Lunt, "A Memory," *Wadham College Gazette*, New Series 4, no. 3 (Jan. 2000), p. 53 ("sixes and sevens"); Lunt, "I Remember, I Remember . . . ," *Wadham College Gazette*, New Series 3, no. 9 (Jan. 1994), p. 62 ("I gave it up"), Wadham College Archives.

46 "Hertford College Goes Co-educational," attached to e-mail, McLauchlan to Malkiel.

47 Notes, Brewer interview with Vaughan Williams.

48 Mark Gore, "President of the J.C.R.," *Wadham College Gazette*, New Series 1, no. 1 (Hilary Term, 1975), p. 9. The next JCR president made a similar observation about the improvement in the social life. See John Instance, "J.C.R.," *Wadham College Gazette*, New Series 1, no. 2 (Michaelmas Term, 1975), p. 7.

"Whenever any event took place in College, it was felt to be mandatory that the women should be represented, so that the 29 of us kept being invited to drinks parties and so on."[49] The same was true at Brasenose, where the women "were invited to more than [their] fair share of parties."[50] One notable feature of the evolving social life at Wadham involved staircase parties, a form of socializing that had not been imagined when the residents of those staircases were all men.[51]

At Brasenose, the presence of the women students ("Nosewomen") led to "a greater level of conversation at breakfast"— "for good or ill," the male leaders of the JCR remarked, "depending on one's temperament"—and, more generally, "a civilised atmosphere," with "no more stale dinner rolls being thrown around at dinner."[52] Women participated in establishing a college events committee, which sponsored Sunday evening discussions with distinguished guests.[53] And women began to assume leadership roles in college activities.[54]

WOMEN BECOME REGULAR MEMBERS OF THE COLLEGES

Male journalists had some fun with the arrival of the first women students. Writing in the *Times Higher Education Supplement* in October 1974, one reporter described the scene this way: "It only needed a beginning of term stroll through the porters' lodges where Habitat bags and vanity cases were piled up against the usual trunks to reveal that things were going to be very different." He told the story of the Hertford student who had brought along a wardrobe, dressing table, and cooker, alarming the domestic bursar,

49 Julie Curtis, "The First Generation of Women in Wadham—1974," *Wadham College Gazette*, New Series 4, no. 3 (Jan. 2000), p. 50.

50 Nancy Hulek, Reminiscences, Brasenose College Archives.

51 Ray Ockenden, "Some Reminiscences of the Coming of Co-Residence to Wadham," *Wadham College Gazette*, New Series 4, no. 3 (Jan. 2000), p. 55; interview with Ockenden, Feb. 21, 2014, Oxford, England.

52 J. M. Fletcher and R. A. Kyprianou, "Junior Common Room Report for 1975," *The Brazen Nose*, 1975, p. 62; Hulek, Reminiscences ("civilised atmosphere," "stale dinner rolls").

53 Fletcher and Kyprianou, "Junior Common Room Report for 1975," p. 62.

54 *The Brazen Nose*, 1976, p. 10, 1977, pp. 8–9, 69, 72.

who had "hitherto regarded requests" for "an extra chair . . . as a major nuisance."[55]

The women students had their own take on their first days in college. Daphne Dumont arrived at Wadham early, on September 28, 1974, the first female student to arrive at any of the five colleges. "On my way back across the quadrangle," she recorded in her diary, "I was nearly run down by a man on a bike, a professor who knew who I was. 'You're her,' he said, 'the FIRST WOMAN!'" Dumont and another woman were later stopped by a professor at St. John's who noticed their Wadham scarves. "He wished us all the luck in the world—very nice of him. So many people seem to have our best interests at heart."[56]

Julie Curtis, who also entered Wadham in October 1974, recalled:

> At the Freshers' Dinner we were slightly taken aback when the Warden, Stuart Hampshire, welcomed the new intake without referring to the fact that any major change had taken place. We later came to appreciate that this was a shrewd way of making it clear to all that we were to feel ourselves normal members of the College, rather than guinea-pigs. One person . . . who had clearly not taken the point was the College Doctor, who requested that the young men leave the Hall . . . before he spoke to us about contraception![57]

It had been widely assumed that one of the costs of admitting women would be some diminution in the success of sporting activities. Rowing and rugby were thought to be in particular peril, and indeed the fortunes of the Jesus rugby team plummeted.[58] To

---

55 Ian Bradley, "Women Breach Oxford Defences," *Times Higher Education Supplement*, Oct. 25, 1974, clipping in Bodleian, File 4.

56 Quoted in Rachel O'Connell, "The Admission of Women to Wadham—A Tradition of Transformation," *Wadham College Gazette*, New Series 4, no. 3 (Jan. 2000), p. 48.

57 Curtis, "The First Generation of Women in Wadham," p. 50. For a similar story at Hertford, see "Gullivers or Guinea Pigs? Some Reflections on the First Two Years of an Hertford Lady," *Hertford College Magazine* 63 (Sept. 1976): 7, Hertford College Archives.

58 Interview with John Walsh, Feb. 21, 2014, Oxford, England.

the surprise of the colleges, however, women proved to be keen on rowing. In the competitions in Eights' Week in 1976, the Wadham women's eight claimed head of the river, a source of considerable pride.[59] Their success continued; as the warden noted in reporting on the events of 1978–79, the Wadham oarswomen were "once again comfortably head of the river."[60] At Brasenose, where some of the more conservative fellows had welcomed coeducation as a way of diminishing the college's "hearty, sporty" image, it turned out that the women were eager to form boats of their own (indeed, the Brasenose women mustered more eights than the men) and were very successful in competing with other colleges.[61] At Jesus, women students distinguished themselves in intercollegiate competitions in squash. Jesus women also represented Oxford in sports competitions with Cambridge and won major awards in cricket and squash.[62]

By all counts, women held their own academically. Brasenose reported that "there is every indication that the women have taken their place in the academic community without prejudice to their identity, and that their contribution to the life of the College is of the highest value."[63] Some fellows remarked on differences in learning styles between men and women. One Wadham fellow said that "the women brought a new attitude with them into college, a questioning attitude that had not been stifled by the strictness of boys' public schools." Another noted that "the traditional Oxford tutorial technique, based on an adversarial and aggressive public school manner, did not work at all well with his new women students."[64]

59 O'Connell, "The Admission of Women to Wadham," p. 49; Curtis, "The First Generation of Women in Wadham," p. 50. See also "Sports and Societies, 1975–6," *Wadham College Gazette*, New Series 1, no. 3 (Hilary Term, 1977), p. 13, and "Warden's Notes," *Wadham College Gazette*, New Series 1, no. 4 (Hilary Term, 1978), p. 6.

60 "The Warden," *Wadham College Gazette*, New Series 1, no. 5 (Hilary Term, 1979), p. 4.

61 Interview with Graham Richards, Feb. 19, 2014, Oxford, England. See also *The Brazen Nose*, 1976, pp. 9–10, and 1977, p. 73.

62 "Editorial," *Jesus College Record*, 1977, p. 2, and "Speech Given at the College Gaudy by the Principal, Sir John Habakkuk," June 23, 1978, *Jesus College Record*, 1978, p. 8.

63 *The Brazen Nose*, 1976, p. 3.

64 O'Connell, "The Admission of Women to Wadham," p. 49.

Fellows who had opposed coresidence either kept their counsel or admitted that they had been mistaken. In Jesus, for example, a classics don who referred to himself as "the college fossil" freely acknowledged after his first women students arrived, "I was wrong, terribly wrong."[65] There is no evidence of fellows and tutors treating women students as any less able and serious than men and no evidence of the ham-handed interactions in which faculty members at American colleges and universities asked their new women students for the woman's point of view. That does not mean that such interactions never happened, but there are no sources that capture sexist behavior. And there is no evidence that Oxford men treated Oxford women (or that Cambridge men treated Cambridge women) in ways that made Princeton, Yale, and especially Dartmouth so awkward for, and at times so deeply inhospitable to, women students.

Of course mixing the sexes was not uncomplicated. Harriet Sergeant, a member of the first intake at St. Catz, told a story that captured very well the more innocent interactions between men and women:

> We broke into the room of the captain of the football team and made him an apple-pie bed. The next evening I emerged from the shower to find my room empty. Everything—desk, clothes, bedding, books and posters—had been carried downstairs and set up on the lawn in the middle of the quad. The sight of me, hair dripping wet, wrapped only in a towel and running around the quad on a cold, February night, mollified even the football captain. The next day he presented me with a bunch of daffodils. . . . The lads, he said diffidently, would really like it if I watched a game.[66]

This encounter is qualitatively different from the interactions between men and women that made life so difficult for women at some American colleges and universities. John Torrance's

---

65 Walsh interview.
66 Sergeant, "Women in College—The First Intake," p. 172.

observation that coeducation made Hertford "more civilised" could never have been said of Dartmouth, for example.[67] The absence of evidence of more problematic interactions does not mean that none of those occurred at Oxford and Cambridge, but if troubling behavior on the part of men had been as extensive there as it was at some American colleges and universities, it would surely have made its way into the written record or oral recollections.

Why did the inclusion of women in these venerable male colleges go so smoothly? For all the novelty of mixed colleges at Cambridge in 1972 and at Oxford in 1974, Cambridge and Oxford had educated women students for almost a century. Women had sat in lectures with men, very occasionally participated in tutorials with men, and engaged in routine social interactions with men who lived and studied nearby. The schools had sponsored mixed dances; men and women had sung together, debated one another, participated in the same religious groups, and belonged to the same theater, journalism, and political clubs.[68] Although the colleges had not been mixed, the universities had, and women and men were sufficiently accustomed to encountering one another in a range of settings to make coresidence a less dramatic change than coeducation at single-sex colleges and universities in the United States.

Moreover, the intense animus from alumni that fueled unrest over coeducation in the United States was not part of the picture in the United Kingdom. Alumni were a much less powerful force in the United Kingdom, in significant measure because of different funding arrangements; annual giving had not yet become a major feature of the expected support for colleges at Oxford and Cambridge. And alumni were quick to recognize that coeducation had advantages for them. As the *Hertford College Magazine* reported shortly before the first women undergraduates matriculated in the fall of 1974, "Several old members have already brought their young daughters to look the place over!"[69]

---

67 "Hertford College, admission of women," attached to e-mail, Torrance to Malkiel.
68 Janet Howarth, "Women," in Harrison, ed., *The History of the University of Oxford*, vol. 8: *The Twentieth Century*, pp. 361–62, 365, 367.
69 "College News," *Hertford College Magazine* 61 (Sept. 1974): 4.

The Aftermath: Achieving Full Coeducation

As had been agreed when the five colleges went mixed, a committee to review coresidence was empanelled in the early fall of 1976. Whether a sensible review could be accomplished was debatable. As Geoffrey Warnock had written the previous winter, "The 'experimental' scheme" had operated "on so relatively tiny a scale" that it was not possible "to know what actually happens to a men's college when it [be]comes . . . a college [fully] open to both men and women." Rather, what could be observed was "what happens to a men's college when, because of special restrictions, a small minority of its junior members are women, and, because of the short period of time involved, practically all its senior members . . . are men. And what happens then is, of course, very nearly nothing—the institution remains, obviously and overwhelmingly, a men's college, of which a rather inconspicuously small number of women are junior members." Similarly, it was not yet possible to know how the women's colleges would fare—whether they could "survive as such—in straight competition with the rest of the University for both junior and senior members." In short, Warnock said, "we shall not really have had much useful experience by the time the question comes up for re-examination."[70]

Warnock's arguments notwithstanding, a review was required, and the committee began work a year earlier than originally anticipated to provide time to prepare for admission for the fall of 1979.[71] The committee first asked which of the colleges that had not already done so would want to begin admitting women within the next few years.[72] If there were only a few, they might be able to agree on an order and timing for going mixed.[73] If there were more, more work would need to be done centrally. Among the men's colleges, Keble, Magdalen, and New College wanted to go

70 G. J. Warnock, "The Co-Residence Question," *American Oxonian* 63 (Apr. 1976): 168–69. The article is reprinted from *Oxford*, Dec. 1975.

71 Report of the Committee to Review Co-residence, Hebdomadal Council, Jan. 28, 1977, pp. 233–40, Bodleian, File 5. The report was published in the *Oxford University Gazette*, Supplement (1) to no. 3686, Feb. 3, 1977, also in Bodleian, File 5.

72 Geoffrey Caston to the Principal, Hertford College, Sept. 30, 1976, Bodleian, File 4.

73 Minutes, meeting of Committee to review co-residence, Sept. 30, 1976, Bodleian, File 4.

mixed as soon as possible. Balliol, Exeter, St. John's, and University were likely to want to do so in the next few years. Among the women's colleges, St. Anne's and St. Hugh's were ready to act.[74] Collegial agreement on order and timing would not work.

The committee reviewed statistics on the admission of women to the university and concluded that "the interests of the women's colleges" had not "been damaged." It reviewed the balance of subjects in the mixed colleges and found no concerns. It forecast that the number of women applicants to Oxford would likely grow, and the proportion of women at Oxford likely increase to approximate the national average, "without any lowering of . . . standards."[75]

There was no reason not to anticipate more colleges going mixed. The question was whether Hebdomadal Council "should take the initiative in securing an orderly increase in the number of mixed colleges." The committee concluded that too many colleges were ready to act, and "any attempt by the University to impose on the colleges a further 'controlled experiment' would give rise to many problems." There was "need for some restraint," but "such restraint must be voluntary and its limits agreed amongst the colleges themselves."[76]

Hebdomadal Council agreed to consult Congregation "on the proposition that the University should no longer seek to control the extension of arrangements for the admission of women undergraduates and graduates to further men's colleges by withholding consent to changes in the statutes of such colleges, and that responsibility for ensuring restraint in this matter should rest with the colleges themselves."[77] On March 8, 1977, on a closely divided vote of 88 in favor, 85 against, Congregation approved the resolution.[78] Some opponents exercised their right to call for a postal

74 Committee to Review Co-Residence: Colleges' intentions in the matter of co-residence, Nov. 26, 1976, Bodleian, File 4.

75 Report of the Committee to Review Co-residence, Hebdomadal Council, Jan. 28, 1977, pp. 234, 236.

76 Ibid., p. 236.

77 Ibid., pp. 239–40.

78 University Acts, Congregation, 8 March, *Gazette*, 107, Mar. 10, 1977, p. 571; "Co-Residence: Verbatim Report of Debate in Congregation," *Oxford University Gazette*, Supplement (2) to no. 3691, Mar. 16, 1977, pp. 589–94, both in Bodleian, File 5.

vote among all members of the academic staff.[79] The resolution carried by a much more decisive margin of 744 in favor, 355 against.[80] The conversation then shifted to a proposal that the colleges agree on "a voluntary scheme for an orderly increase in the number of mixed colleges," with a first round in 1979 in which a fixed number of additional colleges would go mixed, followed by a subsequent round, without restriction, in 1983.[81] But too many colleges were ready to go mixed, and there was little appetite for another controlled round. In addition, with the passage in Parliament in 1975 of a Sex Discrimination Act outlawing discrimination on the basis of sex in employment and education, it was not clear that the university any longer had the authority to block colleges from going mixed. As it turned out, sixteen colleges, two of them women's colleges, announced that they would admit men and women for the fall of 1979. With the five that had gone mixed in 1974, twenty-one of Oxford's twenty-eight colleges would be coresidential as of 1979.[82] By 1985, all of the men's colleges and three women's colleges had gone mixed.[83] Somerville went mixed in 1994 and St. Hilda's in 2008, effectively ending single-sex education at the University of Oxford.

79 "Mixed Colleges Put to the Vote," *The Guardian*, Mar. 9, 1977, clipping in Bodleian, File 5.

80 Hebdomadal Council, May 2, 1977, Bodleian, File 5.

81 Report by the Sub-Committee of the Management Committee of the Admissions Office on Co-Residence, May 19, 1977, Habakkuk, File 3/2.

82 Judy G. Batson, *Her Oxford* (Nashville, TN: Vanderbilt University Press, 2008), pp. 286–87; "Colleges Go Mixed," *The Guardian*, Oct. 24, 1977, clipping in Bodleian, File 5.

83 Michael Brock, "The University since 1970," in Harrison, ed., *The History of the University of Oxford*, vol. 8: *The Twentieth Century*, p. 746.

Part V

Taking Stock

25

Epilogue

The decisions for coeducation chronicled in this study were part of—indeed, helped to unleash—a flood of similar actions at other colleges and universities. Watching closely what was occurring at Princeton and Yale, many other men's colleges in the United States went coed in this same period: for example, Kenyon and Trinity in 1969; Williams, Wesleyan, the University of Virginia, Johns Hopkins, Caltech, and Colgate in 1970; Brown, Bowdoin, and Rutgers in 1971; Davidson in 1972; Amherst in 1975. The same thing happened in Catholic colleges and universities: Georgetown went coed in 1969, Boston College in 1970, Notre Dame and Holy Cross in 1972. And women's colleges, watching Vassar, followed suit: Connecticut, Bennington, and Sarah Lawrence in 1969, Skidmore in 1971. The military academies—West Point, the Naval Academy, the Coast Guard Academy, and the Air Force Academy—admitted women in 1976. There were a few stragglers: Haverford in 1980, Columbia in 1983, Washington and Lee in 1985, Goucher in 1986, Wheaton in 1988, and The Citadel and Virginia Military Institute in 1993 and 1997, respectively. And as we have seen, at Cambridge and Oxford, coeducation was the norm by the close of the 1980s. By 2015 four men's colleges remained in the United States: Hampden-Sydney, Morehouse, Wabash, and Deep Springs (although the last was engaged in a contentious battle to coeducate). Although the Seven Sisters remained strong, the number of women's colleges had declined significantly, with repeated decisions for coeducation or decisions to close for lack of enrollment. In the United Kingdom, three women's colleges remained at Cambridge.

The Accomplishments of Coeducation

What has coeducation accomplished? And what has it not accomplished? The one incontrovertible point is that coeducation has opened educational opportunities for women that had not previously existed. Being able to attend previously all-male colleges has given women access to a broader range of educational opportunities. Women now have full access, as men do, to the best university education in the Anglo-American world: to faculty members at the cutting edge of their respective disciplines, as well as to the best libraries, laboratories, and other educational facilities. And women students have the opportunity to profit from the intellectual stimulation and interchange, as well as the social interactions, fostered in mixed-sex educational environments. Going to school together means learning to live and work together. In the early twenty-first century, most college-bound students see coeducational environments as more "normal" than environments segregated by sex.

At Oxford, both the number of applications and the acceptance rates are now nearly comparable for men and for women. In 2014 the gender balance among undergraduates was 54.6 percent male, 45.4 percent female.[1] The student bodies of previously all-male colleges and universities in the United States, so skewed toward men in the early years of coeducation, now tend to be evenly balanced. If anything, given that the college-going population has been 55 percent or more female for more than two decades, the issue for so many colleges is to maintain roughly equal numbers of men and women students.[2]

---

1 "University of Oxford Applications Statistics," https://public.tableau.com/views /UoO_UG_Admissons2/AcceptanceRate?%3Aembed=y&%3Adisplay_count=yes& %3AshowTabs=y&%3AshowVizHome=no, accessed Mar. 28, 2016, courtesy of Charlotte Brewer (under "Select UCAS Cycle," enter 2014; under "Select Demographic (Columns)," enter Sex); "Student Numbers 2014," University of Oxford, *Gazette Supplement*, Jan. 28, 2015, http://www.ox.ac.uk/gazette/statisticalinformation/studentnumberssupplements/, accessed Mar. 10, 2015, courtesy of Brewer and Christopher McCloskey, Hertford College.

2 Total fall enrollment in degree-granting postsecondary institutions, by attendance status, sex of students, and control of institution: Selected years, 1947 through 2012, Table 303.10, National Center for Education Statistics, *Digest of Education Statistics*, http://nces.ed.gov/programs/digest/d13/tables/dt13_303.10.asp, accessed Jan. 9, 2015.

As for the impact of coeducation on colleges and universities, the first point to be made is that coeducation did not mean revolution. Women (or, in the case of Vassar, men) were added to the mix, which in itself had a transformative aspect. But the institutions themselves proved to be remarkably durable, and women (or men) generally accepted or embraced traditions rather than upending them. In both the United States and the United Kingdom, women (or men) were included, assimilated, accepted; colleges and universities were flexible enough to accommodate them but not so flexible that the institutions became unrecognizable compared with their former selves. To take three examples: Princeton and Dartmouth have gained gender-neutral alma maters, but the eating clubs at Princeton and the fraternities at Dartmouth continue to exercise outsized, problematic influence on campus social life, which, in the second decade of the twenty-first century, bears a surprising similarity to what it was more than forty years earlier. At Princeton and Yale, the last of the all-male eating clubs and secret societies finally admitted women in 1991 and 1992; at Harvard, Spee Club, the first of the nine all-male final clubs to admit women, did so only in 2015.[3] At King's College, Cambridge, and Hertford College, Oxford, the discourse about the coming of coeducation was framed identically in describing the women admitted to each of the colleges as "honorary men." Anniversary celebrations at those colleges illustrate the ongoing complexity of the change. At King's, celebrating the twentieth anniversary of coeducation, women students covered the portraits of men in the dining hall with brown paper on which they wrote feminist slogans.[4] At Hertford, celebrating the fortieth anniversary of coeducation, portraits of men were removed from the dining hall and photographs of women associated with the college were hung instead—an action that drew widespread attention in the international press and provoked some controversy among

3 "With an Invitation, a Gender Barrier at Harvard Falls," *New York Times*, Sept. 12, 2015, p. A15.
4 Interview with Melissa Lane, Nov. 6, 2014, Princeton, NJ. Lane earned her M.Phil. and Ph.D. at King's and was a fellow of the college for fifteen years, including a stretch of time as women's tutor.

alumni/ae of the college.[5] Coeducation is not so settled a venture that it no longer commands attention.

The second important point is that coeducation accompanied, but did not cause, more profound social transformations in these colleges and universities. In both the United States and the United Kingdom, the push in the 1960s to admit students from a broader range of backgrounds and schools preceded, indeed paved the way for, coeducation. In the United States, in the late 1960s and 1970s student populations at elite institutions became more diverse in terms of race and ethnicity—changes that operated in parallel with the new diversity in terms of gender. Elite education became less aristocratic and more democratic/meritocratic—again, in parallel with, but not as a result of, coeducation.

With respect to the impact of coeducation on women's colleges, one key point should be made. Deciding to go coed was much, much tougher for women's colleges than for men's institutions. Prestige and reputation play a large role in such matters. For an alumnus of Yale or Princeton, Clare or Wadham, having the opportunity for a daughter to matriculate at the father's alma mater is a huge point of pride. Whether the issue is a matter of prejudice or perceived status, having a son enroll at what was previously a women's college is a more ambiguous proposition. Even today, many male students are still just a little uncomfortable about going to what often continues to be seen as a women's school.

We have seen the positive effects of coeducation on the number of applications at prestigious men's colleges and universities, reversing the slippage that had begun to occur in the late 1960s and stoking the ablest high school students' interest in those schools. For the men's schools that admitted women, coeducation essentially served to stabilize the academic quality of the undergraduate student body. Princeton SAT data shown in table 25.1 illustrate the point.[6]

---

5 On the display of photographs, see www.hertford.ox.ac.uk/portraits, accessed Oct. 28, 2014, courtesy of Claire Blake, Hertford College; on the controversy, see http://www .theguardian.com/commentisfree/2014/jun/21/oxbridge-co-ed-40-years-women-feminism -arts and http://www.theguardian.com/commentisfree/2013/dec/15/gender-segregation -unacceptable, accessed July 10, 2014, courtesy of Emma Smith, Hertford College.

6 Princeton University Admission Office data, in the possession of Nancy Weiss Malkiel.

TABLE 25.1. PRINCETON, MEAN SAT SCORES,
FIVE-YEAR INTERVALS, 1965–90

Class Years	Verbal	Math
1965–69	651	696
1970–74	644	685
1975–79	644	681
1980–85[a]	638	676
1986–90	644	692

[a]Six-year interval.

Coeducation has been a much more difficult proposition for Vassar, the most prestigious of the women's colleges to go coeducational, than for the equally prestigious men's colleges that admitted women. In contrast to Princeton, the presenting credentials of incoming Vassar students declined after coeducation, as shown in table 25.2, especially when large numbers of women began enrolling in previously all-male colleges. What cannot be determined is the cause of the decline; it is impossible to disaggregate the effects of adding men to the Vassar student body and having to compete for students with the range of newly coeducational men's colleges and universities.[7]

More than four decades after the coming of coeducation, Vassar is consistently 55 percent female, 45 percent male, a ratio very like those of many other private colleges and universities. Vassar's closest peers, in terms of overlapping applications and acceptances, are Wesleyan, Brown, Penn, and Oberlin—by any measure, a strong set of coeducational institutions.[8]

The road forward for women's colleges that have remained single-sex has been complicated. The strongest women's colleges took a hit when leading men's schools coeducated. To give a simple illustration: Some three quarters of freshmen at Smith and

7 SAT Mean Scores: Vassar and The Nation, internal annual report from the Office of Admission, provided by the Office of Institutional Research, Vassar College.

8 Telephone interview with Catharine Bond Hill, Dec. 15, 2014.

TABLE 25.2. VASSAR MEAN SAT SCORES,
FIVE-YEAR INTERVALS, 1965–85

Class Years	Verbal	Math
1965–69	647	618
1970–74	651	627
1975–79	596	596
1980–85[a]	577	584

Note: The scores for the classes of 1984 and 1985 represent students who actually enrolled in the fall. Scores for some of the previous years may have been estimated in the spring on the basis of planned matriculations. SAT data for the classes of 1986–90 are not available.
[a]Six-year interval.

Wellesley had typically been in the top 10 percent of their high school graduating classes; over time, those colleges came to report a little more than four-fifths of incoming freshmen in the top *20 percent*.[9] As at Vassar, SAT scores at Smith peaked in the period 1965–74. As table 25.3 shows, the decline at Smith was less precipitous than at Vassar through 1980–85, but Smith SAT scores continued to drop through 1986–90.[10]

The population of students interested in women's colleges has shrunk dramatically. Fewer than 5 percent of high school girls say that they are willing to consider going to a women's college. Their primary reason is that they do not want to be separated from men. In addition, many students (and parents) are leery of the image of women's colleges as institutions especially hospitable to lesbian students, a perception that arose in the 1980s and 1990s and has

9 Susan F. Watts, ed., *The College Handbook* (New York: College Entrance Examination Board, 1975), p. 490; Watts, ed., *The College Handbook* (New York: College Entrance Examination Board, 1977), p. 533; Maureen Matheson, ed., *The College Handbook, 1979–80* (New York: College Entrance Examination Board, 1979), p. 662; Matheson, ed., *The College Handbook, 1981–82* (New York: College Entrance Examination Board, 1981), pp. 620, 628.

10 SAT medians, Smith College classes of 1958–91, Office of Admission data, courtesy of Debra Shaver.

TABLE 25.3. SMITH MEDIAN SAT SCORES,
FIVE-YEAR INTERVALS, 1965–90

Class Years	Verbal	Math
1965–69[a]	653	625
1970–74	665	639
1975–79	627	618
1980–85[b]	601	600
1986–90	585	593

[a]Four-year interval; one year's data missing.
[b]Six-year interval.

not dissipated. Whether an accurate description or a pejorative stereotype, the image has had some effect on admissions and alumnae attitudes. So, too, has the more recent issue of how women's colleges handle transgender students, both as applicants and as matriculated students.[11]

A large proportion of the ablest high school girls used to aspire to attend women's colleges; now they aspire to attend the most prestigious coeducational schools. Women's colleges have needed to adjust accordingly, and the readjustments have sometimes been challenging. Today Smith and Wellesley are thriving, albeit not with the same population of students that they used to have (the presenting credentials are more modest than they were before coeducation, when the credentials of applicants to the Seven Sisters closely tracked those of applicants to the best all-male colleges) but rather with new groups: international students, first-generation immigrants, first-generation

11 Ruth Padawer, "When Women Become Men at Wellesley," *New York Times Magazine*, Oct. 15, 2014, http://www.nytimes.com/2014/10/19/magazine/when-women-become -men-at-wellesley-college.html, accessed Jan. 11, 2015; "Wellesley College to Accept Transgender Women," *Boston Globe*, Mar. 5, 2015, http://www.bostonglobe.com/metro /2015/03/05/wellesley/1a3eDzywpzF4QAznRuOw3L/story.html, accessed Mar. 9, 2015; Admission Policy Announcement, Smith College, May 2, 2015, http://www.smith.edu /studygroup, accessed May 31, 2015; "Barnard College, after Much Discussion, Decides to Accept Transgender Women," *New York Times*, June 5, 2015, p. A22.

college students, religiously observant students. Although the incoming credentials are different, there is good reason to believe that these colleges are continuing the work that has long distinguished them: producing talented graduates who take up positions of leadership in the professions and in their communities.

And yet, before 1969–74, when the most elite of the men's colleges and universities opened their doors to women, the most prominent, highest-achieving women were typically graduates of women's colleges. Vassar alumnae include Katharine Graham, publisher of the *Washington Post*, and actress Meryl Streep. Television broadcasters Barbara Walters and Diane Sawyer are alumnae, respectively, of Sarah Lawrence and Wellesley. Wellesley is also the alma mater of two of the three women who have served as U.S. secretary of state, Madeline Albright and Hillary Rodham Clinton. Smith is the alma mater of chef, author, and television personality Julia Child and of two women who led the women's movement of the 1960s and 1970s, Betty Friedan and Gloria Steinem. Bryn Mawr is the alma mater of Hanna Holborn Gray, president of the University of Chicago, and Drew Gilpin Faust, president of Harvard University. In the United Kingdom, novelist Iris Murdoch and British prime minister Margaret Thatcher were both graduates of Somerville. Novelist Margaret Drabble is a graduate of Newnham. Biographer Antonia Fraser and playwright Caryl Churchill are both graduates of Lady Margaret Hall.

Since the coming of coeducation, the most prominent, highest-achieving women have more often been graduates of coeducational colleges and universities. Harvard-Radcliffe alumnae include Benazir Bhutto, prime minister of Pakistan; Amy Gutmann, president of the University of Pennsylvania; and Emily Mann, theater director and playwright. Novelist Zadie Smith is an alumna of King's College, Cambridge, actress Felicity Jones of Wadham College, Oxford. Yale alumnae include Maya Lin, designer of the Vietnam Veterans Memorial in Washington, D.C.; Jodie Foster, actress, film director, and producer; and Amy Klobuchar, U.S. senator from Minnesota. Kirsten Gillibrand, U.S. senator from New York, is an alumna of Dartmouth. Princeton alumnae include the actress Brooke Shields; Meg Whitman, chief executive officer, successively, of eBay and Hewlett-Packard; and two justices of the U.S. Supreme Court, Sonia Sotomayor and Elena Kagan. Other Princeton alumnae include Queen Noor of Jordan (the former Lisa Halaby) and Michelle Obama, first lady of the United States.

Remaining Challenges

For all the gains realized through coeducation, it is important to be clear about what coeducation has not done—and should not have been expected to do.

Coeducation has not resolved longstanding complexities in the relations between men and women. Colleges and universities in the second decade of the twenty-first century are struggling with problems of sexual harassment and sexual assault, problems no more under control after more than four decades of coeducation than they were when men and women first started going to college together.

Coeducation has not resolved the perplexingly gendered behaviors and aspirations of female students. Consider studies undertaken at Duke University in 2002–3 under the leadership of then-president Nannerl O. Keohane and at Princeton University in 2010–11 at the instigation of then-president Shirley M. Tilghman—at Duke to assess the overall climate for women at the university, at Princeton to understand patterns of engagement, leadership, and achievement on the part of women undergraduates. Duke had become formally coeducational in 1972 with the merger of the women's and men's colleges; 47 percent of undergraduate students were women in 2003. Yet the Women's Initiative found that in many respects, the university was not yet truly coeducational. The study revealed that women and men came to Duke with "a fairly well-developed set of cultural expectations about how women and men should behave," expectations that were "powerfully reinforced" at the university. These norms tilted against equal participation of men and women "as members of a community of scholars"; they were "strongly gender-specific, in terms of everything from what one should eat or how one should dress to romantic and sexual encounters, even reaching into what is regarded as appropriate in terms of intellectual assertiveness or interest in leadership." In so many ways, women and men were "pattern[ed]" and "channel[ed] . . . into sex-stereotypical slots." The social norms were "suffocating" for many women undergraduates, who strove, above all, for what they described as "effortless perfection": "the expectation that one would be smart, accomplished, fit, beautiful, and popular, and that all this would happen without visible effort."[12]

At Princeton, the Steering Committee on Undergraduate Women's Leadership sought, in the words of its charge from Tilghman, "to understand how undergraduate students perceive and seize the opportunities available to them to assert leadership both inside and outside the classroom" and to suggest some answers to "the critical question of whether women undergraduates are realizing their academic potential and seeking opportunities for leadership at the same rate and in the same manner as their male colleagues."[13] The motivation for the committee's formation came from discussions on campus about "disparities between men and women in visible positions of campus leadership," as well as what appeared to be disparities in the highest levels of academic achievement. The committee found that there were real differences *between the ways most Princeton female undergraduates and most male undergraduates approach their college years, and in the ways they navigate Princeton when they arrive.*" Women students consistently undersold themselves and declined to put themselves forward for major leadership positions. And they felt "intense pressure to behave in certain socially acceptable ways."[14]

In short, coeducation has not eliminated still-gendered patterns of behavior on college campuses that have enrolled women and men for many decades. Nor has coeducation alleviated the

12 Duke University, *Report of the Steering Committee for the Women's Initiative*, 2003, pp. 7, 8, 10, 12, http://universitywomen.stanford.edu/reports /WomensInitiativeReport.pdf, accessed Jan. 11, 2015.

13 "The President's Charge to the Steering Committee on Undergraduate Women's Leadership," in Princeton University, *Report of the Steering Committee on Undergraduate Women's Leadership*, Mar. 2011, p. 110, http://www.princeton.edu/reports/2011/leadership/, accessed Jan. 11, 2015.

14 Princeton University, *Report of the Steering Committee on Undergraduate Women's Leadership*, pp. 11, 13, 88.

still-gendered patterns of academic achievement at institutions that enroll women and men. At Oxford and Cambridge, men continue to receive a much higher proportion of "firsts" than women do.[15] At Princeton, more men than women achieve at the very highest levels; the same is true at a number of other coeducational universities in the United States. As the Steering Committee found, women were often "more reticent [than men] about speaking up" in the classroom. And although they "outpace[d] men in academic achievement," they did not do so "at the very highest levels."[16]

And coeducation has not resolved the conundrum of gendered fields of study, especially the persistent underrepresentation of undergraduate women in such fields as computer science, economics, mathematics, and physics. At Yale, for example, among graduating seniors in the years 2009–14, men accounted for 5.2 times as many majors as women in computer science, 2.0 times as many in economics, 2.8 times as many in mathematics, and 2.4 times as many in physics.[17] At Princeton, among graduating seniors in the years 2010–14, men accounted for 3.7 times as many majors as women in computer science, 1.9 times as many in economics, 6.0 times as many in mathematics, and 2.8 times as many in physics.[18] And this was true at a time when the ratio of undergraduate men to women at both of these institutions was roughly 1 to 1.

Nor has coeducation balanced the highly skewed gender patterns among college and university faculty members and graduate students. In terms of faculty, men still hold a major edge over women, especially in the tenured ranks. At Princeton in 2014–15, women accounted for 24.6 percent of tenured faculty members in the arts and sciences and engineering and 44.2 percent of non-tenured

15 "Final Honour Schools, Bachelor of Fine Art and Bachelor of Theology, 2014," University of Oxford, *Gazette Supplement*, Jan. 21, 2015, Table 2, http://www.ox.ac.uk /gazette/statisticalinformation/#d.en.6207, accessed Mar. 10, 2015, courtesy of Charlotte Brewer and Christopher McCloskey, Hertford College.

16 Princeton University, *Report of the Steering Committee on Undergraduate Women's Leadership*, ch. 3 and pp. 87–88 (source of the quotes).

17 Yale College Undergraduate Junior and Senior Majors by Gender, 2008–9 to 2013– 14, Office of Institutional Research, Yale University.

18 Undergraduate Degrees Conferred, 2009–10 to 2013–14, Office of the Registrar, Princeton University.

faculty members.[19] At Yale, women accounted for 23.8 percent of the tenured faculty in arts and sciences and 40.4 percent of the non-tenured faculty.[20] Among graduate students, the gender imbalance shows up especially, though not exclusively, in the hard social sciences, the physical sciences, and engineering. To illustrate the point: Nationally, in 2013, at the most research-intensive universities, women earned 35.2 percent of the doctorates in economics, 29.0 percent of the doctorates in the physical sciences, and 22.9 percent of the doctorates in engineering.[21]

Just as coeducation has failed to achieve gender balance among university faculty members and graduate students, so too it has failed to ensure that women alumnae can expect professional careers that parallel those of men. Despite the ample supply of female graduates of prestigious previously all-male institutions, women continue to face challenges in finding leadership positions and professional advancement. Pressing issues also remain in the area of work-family balance. Witness the controversy generated in October 2003 by "The Opt-Out Revolution," an article in the *New York Times Magazine* by Lisa Belkin, Princeton '82, who documented the withdrawal from the workforce of highly educated women who gave up, at least temporarily, on maintaining demanding careers to stay home to raise their children. "I don't want to be on the fast track leading to a partnership at a prestigious law firm," said a woman lawyer. "Some people define that as success. I don't." A theater artist and teacher added, "I don't want to be famous; I don't want to conquer the world; I don't want that kind of life. Maternity provides an escape hatch that paternity does not. Having a baby provides a graceful and convenient exit." Belkin noted that in the Stanford class of 1981, 57 percent of mothers "spent at least a year at home caring for their infant

19 Total Faculty Composition Data (excluding visitors), as of Nov. 1, 2014, Office of the Dean of the Faculty, Princeton University, courtesy of Toni Turano.
20 Yale University Tenured and Term Faculty (Headcounts) by Gender, 2014–2015, http://oir.yale.edu/node/79/attachment/, accessed Mar. 6, 2015.
21 Data compiled by Gilda G. Paul from the National Center for Education Statistics, http://nces.ed.gov/ipeds/datacenter/InstitutionList.aspx. The data are drawn from 108 institutions in the Research University (very high level of research activity) Carnegie classification.

children in the first decade after graduation," and "one out of four have stayed home three or more years." She referenced, too, a survey of women graduates of the Harvard Business School in the classes of 1981, 1985, and 1991, which found that only 38 percent were working full-time. "This was not the way it was supposed to be," Belkin observed. "Women—specifically, educated professional women—were supposed to achieve like men."[22]

Consider another variant of the same theme: the highly publicized debate in the second decade of the twenty-first century about whether or not women can manage high-powered careers and meet their family responsibilities. The debate took place between two highly accomplished graduates of Princeton and Harvard. The first was Princeton alumna Anne-Marie Slaughter, former dean of the Woodrow Wilson School of Public and International Affairs at Princeton, director of policy planning at the State Department, and now president of the New America Foundation. The second was Harvard alumna Sheryl Sandberg, chief operating officer of Facebook and before that, vice president of global online sales and operations at Google and chief of staff to U.S. Secretary of the Treasury Lawrence Summers. In a TED talk in 2010, "Why We Have Too Few Women Leaders," Sandberg said, "Women are not making it to the top of any profession anywhere in the world." Women need to stop dropping out, she argued; they need to claim their places at the table, share family responsibilities with their partners, and "lean in" to their professional responsibilities rather than leaning out. When a woman starts thinking about marrying and having children, Sandberg said, "she doesn't raise her hand anymore. . . . She starts leaning back." That was a mistake: "Don't leave," she admonished, "before you leave."[23]

Sandberg followed up her TED talk with a highly publicized commencement address on the same theme at Barnard College in 2011 and in a 2013 book, *Lean In: Women, Work, and the Will*

22 Lisa Belkin, "The Opt-Out Revolution," *New York Times Magazine*, Oct. 26, 2003, http://www.nytimes.com/2003/10/26/magazine/26WOMEN.html, accessed Jan. 9, 2015.

23 Transcript, Sheryl Sandberg, "Why We Have Too Few Women Leaders," TED-Women 2010, video filmed Dec. 2010, http://www.ted.com/talks/sheryl_sandberg_why_we _have_too_few_women_leaders/transcript, accessed Jan. 9, 2015.

to Lead, which spent many weeks on the best-seller list. Women should be more ambitious, she said, asking "What would you do if you weren't afraid?" Gender biases in the workplace notwithstanding, Sandberg argued, women have the capacity to determine their own futures by believing in themselves, working as hard as they can, "lean[ing] in," and not missing out on professional opportunity and success by doubting their ability to combine work and family.[24]

Not so simple, Slaughter rejoined. Sandberg's focus on the ways in which women hold themselves back needed to be supplemented by a hard look at the ways in which demanding workplaces have to change.[25] In the summer of 2012, in a long article titled "Why Women Still Can't Have It All" in *The Atlantic*, Slaughter, who had stepped down after two years as director of policy planning at the State Department, talked bluntly about how hard it was for women "to combine professional success and satisfaction with a real commitment to family." Slaughter gave a highly personal account of why she had found it impossible, in such a high-powered job, to be "both the parent and the professional I wanted to be." She argued that "the decision to step down from a position of power—to value family over professional advancement, even for a time—is directly at odds with the prevailing social pressures on career professionals in the United States." It was essential, she said, to change the culture of work; to allow women (and men) to go home at a decent hour to have dinner with their families; to allow them to do some of their work from home after children go to bed, on days when children are out of school, or on weekends; and to value family commitments as part of a professional's daily life. Institutions also needed to "redefin[e] the arc of a successful career," recognizing that women are likely to "stair-step their careers" rather than follow a direct linear path, "taking time out periodically, [and] pursuing an alternative path during crucial parenting

24 Sheryl Sandberg with Nell Scovell, *Lean In: Women, Work, and the Will to Lead* (New York: Alfred A. Knopf, 2013).

25 Anne-Marie Slaughter, "Yes, You Can: Sheryl Sandberg's *Lean In*," *New York Times Book Review*, Mar. 7, 2013, http://www.nytimes.com/2013/03/10/books/review /sheryl-sandbergs-lean-in.html, accessed Jan. 9, 2015.

or parent-care years." With such changes, women would be better able "to be both mothers and top professionals."[26]

In the final analysis, coeducation at the most elite colleges and universities did not solve, and could not have been expected to solve, such persistently challenging personal and social issues. Colleges and universities changed with the coming of coeducation, but not so much as they might have. And norms, assumptions, stereotypes, and prejudices in American and British society also changed, but—again—not so much as they might have. Educating men and women together does not mean that their experiences have become identical. Nor does it mean that gender has become irrelevant, neutral, or less consequential as a determinant of choices made or opportunities taken. Still, much has been accomplished in the past half-century; one hopes that the next half-century will bring continued progress.

26 Anne-Marie Slaughter, "Why Women Still Can't Have It All," *The Atlantic*, July 2012, http://www.theatlantic.com/magazine/print/2012/07/why-women-still-can't-have -it-all/309020/, accessed Jan. 9, 2015. For the perspective of Slaughter's husband, see Andrew Moravcsik, "Why I Put My Wife's Career First," *The Atlantic*, Oct. 2015, http:// www.theatlantic.com/magazine/archive/2015/10/why-i-put-my-wifes-career-first/403240, accessed Sept. 14, 2015.

Manuscript Collections and Oral History Transcripts: Abbreviations

Manuscript Collections

Adams	Ruth M. Adams Papers, ID89, Wellesley College Archives
Admission Office	Admission Office Records, AC152, Princeton University Archives, Department of Rare Books and Special Collections, Princeton University Library
AYA	Association of Yale Alumni Records, 1826–1977, RU792, Accession 19ND-A-336, Manuscripts and Archives, Yale University Library
Bodleian	UR6/W/12, Admission of Women to Men's Colleges, Bodleian Library, Oxford
Bowen president	Office of the President Records, William G. Bowen, AC187, Princeton University Archives, Department of Rare Books and Special Collections, Princeton University Library
Bowen provost	Office of the Provost Records, William G. Bowen, AC195, Princeton University Archives, Department of Rare Books and Special Collections, Princeton University Library
Brasenose Gov. Body	Vice Principal's Register (Governing Body minutes), Brasenose College Archives, Brasenose College, Oxford
Brewster I	Kingman Brewster, Jr., Presidential Records, RU11, Series I, Manuscripts and Archives, Yale University Library
Brewster II	Kingman Brewster, Jr., Presidential Records, RU11, Series II, Manuscripts and Archives, Yale University Library

Brewster III	Kingman Brewster, Jr., Presidential Records, RU11, Series III, Manuscripts and Archives, Yale University Library
Bunting	Mary Ingraham Bunting-Smith, Records of the President of Radcliffe College, 1960–72, RG11, Radcliffe College Archives, Arthur and Elizabeth Schlesinger Library on the History of Women in America, Radcliffe Institute for Advanced Study, Harvard University
CAP	Concerned Alumni of Princeton Papers, AC305, Princeton University Archives, Department of Rare Books and Special Collections, Princeton University Library
Chinoy	Faculty Papers, Ely Chinoy, Smith College Archives
Churchill	Churchill College archive, Churchill College Archives Centre, Churchill College, Cambridge
Clare	Clare College Archives, Clare College, Cambridge
Cmsn. Future College	Records of the Commission on the Future of the College, 1F, Wellesley College Archives
Coed II	Coeducation II, Vertical Files, Rauner Special Collections Library, Dartmouth College
Coed III	Coeducation III, Vertical Files, Rauner Special Collections Library, Dartmouth College
Conant	Records of the President of Harvard University, James Bryant Conant, UAI5.168, Harvard University Archives, Pusey Library, Harvard University
Dean of College/Faculty	Dean of College/Dean of Faculty Records, Vassar College Archives
Dean of Students	Dean of Students Records, Vassar College Archives
Dickey	John Sloan Dickey Papers, DP-12, Rauner Special Collections Library, Dartmouth College
Dodds	Office of the President Records, Harold W. Dodds, AC117, Series 15, Princeton University Archives, Department of Rare Books and Special Collections, Princeton University Library

EVP	Executive Vice President Papers, 1ED, Wellesley College Archives
Gilbert	Helen Homans Gilbert Papers, SC75, Radcliffe College Archives, Arthur and Elizabeth Schlesinger Library on the History of Women in America, Radcliffe Institute for Advanced Study, Harvard University
Goheen	Office of the President Records, Robert F. Goheen, AC193, Princeton University Archives, Department of Rare Books and Special Collections, Princeton University Library
Habakkuk	Principal Habakkuk Papers, Jesus College Archives, Jesus College, Oxford
Heller	Julie M. Heller, The Impact of Coeducation on Yale's Alumnae, 1973–83, RU96, Manuscripts and Archives, Yale University Library
Hertford Gov. Body	Minutes of the Governing Body, Hertford College, Oxford, in bound volumes in the principal's office
Hertford unsorted	Hertford College Archives, Unsorted File, Hertford College Governing Body Papers, 1968–75, Hertford College, Oxford
Horner	Matina Horner, Records of the President of Radcliffe College, 1972–89, RG11, Radcliffe College Archives, Arthur and Elizabeth Schlesinger Library on the History of Women in America, Radcliffe Institute for Advanced Study, Harvard University
Horton	Arthur J. Horton Collection on Coeducation, AC039, Princeton University Archives, Department of Rare Books and Special Collections, Princeton University Library
Jahnige	Special Programs, Jahnige Social Science Center, Smith College Archives
Keller	Suzanne Keller Papers, privately held, Princeton, NJ
Kemeny	John G. Kemeny Presidential Papers, DP-13, Rauner Special Collections Library, Dartmouth College

Kemeny personal	John G. Kemeny Personal Papers, MS-988, Rauner Special Collections Library, Dartmouth College
King's	King's College Archives, Archives Centre, King's College, Cambridge
May	Records of the Dean of Yale College, Georges May, RU126, Manuscripts and Archives, Yale University Library
Mendenhall	Smith College, Office of President, Thomas Corwin Mendenhall Files, RG32, Smith College Archives
Middle States	Middle States Association Records, Vassar College Archives
ODUS	Records of the Dean of Undergraduate Students, AC136, Princeton University Archives, Department of Rare Books and Special Collections, Princeton University Library
Patterson	Committee on the Education of Women at Princeton Records, AC184, Princeton University Archives, Department of Rare Books and Special Collections, Princeton University Library
Princeton publications	Princeton University Publications, AC364, Princeton University Archives, Department of Rare Books and Special Collections, Princeton University Library
Princeton trustees	Board of Trustees Records, AC120, Princeton University Archives, Department of Rare Books and Special Collections, Princeton University Library
Pusey	Records of the President of Harvard University, Nathan Marsh Pusey, UAI5.169, Harvard University Archives, Pusey Library, Harvard University
PUWO	Princeton University Women's Organization Papers, AC172, Princeton University Archives, Department of Rare Books and Special Collections, Princeton University Library
Raushenbush	Esther Raushenbush Papers, Sarah Lawrence College Archives

Rose	Peter Rose Papers, Smith College Archives
Sarah Lawrence trustees	Board of Trustees Records, Sarah Lawrence College Archives
Simpson	Alan Simpson Papers, Vassar College Archives
Smith faculty	Faculty Meeting Minutes, Smith College Archives
Smith trustees	Board of Trustees Records, Smith College Archives
St. Catz	St. Catherine's College Archives, St. Catherine's College, Oxford
Subject Files Princeton	Historical Subject Files, AC109, Princeton University Archives, Department of Rare Books and Special Collections, Princeton University Library
Subject Files Radcliffe	Radcliffe College Archives Subject Files, RG24, Arthur and Elizabeth Schlesinger Library on the History of Women in America, Radcliffe Institute for Advanced Study, Harvard University
Subject Files Vassar	Vassar Subject Files, Vassar College Archives
Vassar faculty	Vassar College Faculty Minutes, Vassar College Archives
Vassar trustees	Vassar College Trustee Minutes, Vassar College Archives
Vassar trustees (E)	Vassar College Trustee Executive Committee Minutes, Vassar College Archives
Vassar-Yale	Vassar-Yale Joint Study Group Records, RU526, Manuscripts and Archives, Yale University Library
Vassar-Yale (V)	Vassar-Yale Records, Vassar College Archives
Wadham Co-Residence	Wadham College Archives, 2B/1, Co-Residence File, 1968–73
Wasserman I	President's Office, Records of the Office on the Education of Women, RU821, Accession 19ND-A-086, Manuscripts and Archives, Yale University Library
Wasserman II	President's Office, Records of the Office on the Education of Women, RU821, Accession

2006-A-213, Manuscripts and Archives, Yale University Library

Wellesley trustees

Board of Trustees Records, Wellesley College Archives

Wilkie

John Wilkie Papers, Vassar College Archives

Wilson

Linda S. Wilson, Records of the President, Radcliffe College, 1989–99, RG11, Radcliffe College Archives, Arthur and Elizabeth Schlesinger Library on the History of Women in America, Radcliffe Institute for Advanced Study, Harvard University

Women at Dartmouth

Women at Dartmouth Collection, DO-61, Rauner Special Collections Library, Dartmouth College

Oral History Transcripts

Adams oral history

Ruth Adams interview, Hanover, NH, May 29, 1996, DOH-18(1), Rauner Special Collections Library, Dartmouth College

Ashby oral history

Sir Eric Ashby interview, June 19, 1991, Griswold-Brewster Oral History Project, RU217, Series I, Box 1, Folder 3, Manuscripts and Archives, Yale University Library

Beinecke oral history

William Sperry Beinecke interview, Aug. 19, 1991, Chatham, MA, Griswold-Brewster Oral History Project, RU217, Series I, Box 1, Folder 5, Manuscripts and Archives, Yale University Library

Bok oral history

Derek Curtis Bok interview, Mar. 9, 2000, Oral History of Radcliffe College during the Horner Years, MC796, R.A.T-129, Arthur and Elizabeth Schlesinger Library on the History of Women in America, Radcliffe Institute for Advanced Study, Harvard University

Bowen oral history

William G. Bowen interviews, June 9 and 25, July 21, and Sept. 18 and 28, 2009, Princeton, NJ, Princeton University Presidents Oral History Collection, AC318, Series 3, Princeton University

Archives, Department of Rare Books and Special Collections, Princeton University Library

Brewster oral history

Kingman Brewster interview, n.d., Griswold-Brewster Oral History Project, RU217, Series I, Box 2, Folder 16, Manuscripts and Archives, Yale University Library

ML Bundy oral history

Mary Lothrop Bundy interviews, June 15 and July 12, 2005, Oral History of Radcliffe College during the Horner Years, MC796, R.A.T.-129, Arthur and Elizabeth Schlesinger Library on the History of Women in America, Radcliffe Institute for Advanced Study, Harvard University

WP Bundy oral history

William P. Bundy interviews, May 10, 1991, and Apr. 24, 1992, Princeton, NJ, Brewster-Griswold Oral History Project, RU217, Series I, Box 2, Folders 24–25, Manuscripts and Archives, Yale University Library

Bunting oral history

Mary Ingraham Bunting oral memoir, Sept.–Oct. 1978, Radcliffe College Archives, Arthur and Elizabeth Schlesinger Library on the History of Women in America, Radcliffe Institute for Advanced Study, Harvard University

Burr oral history

Francis Hardon Burr interview, Nov. 4, 1999, Oral History of Radcliffe College during the Horner Years, MC796, R.A.T-129, Arthur and Elizabeth Schlesinger Library on the History of Women in America, Radcliffe Institute for Advanced Study, Harvard University

Clark oral history

R. Inslee Clark, Jr., interviews, Apr. 8, 1993, Riverdale, NY, and May 13, 1993, New Haven, CT, Griswold-Brewster Oral History Project, RU217, Series I, Box 3, Folders 33–34, Manuscripts and Archives, Yale University Library

Dilworth oral history

J. Richardson Dilworth interview, Mar. 16, 1991, Princeton, NJ, Griswold-Brewster Oral History Project, RU217, Series I, Box 4, Folder 47, Manuscripts and Archives, Yale University Library

Dunlop oral history

John Thomas Dunlop interview, Mar. 10, 2000, Oral History of Radcliffe College during the Horner Years, MC796, R.A.T-129, Arthur and Elizabeth Schlesinger Library on the History of

	Women in America, Radcliffe Institute for Advanced Study, Harvard University
Emden oral history	Ronnie-Gail Emden '74 interview, July 20, 2008, Portland, OR, Princetoniana Committee Oral History Project Records, AC259, Box 2, Princeton University Archives, Department of Rare Books and Special Collections, Princeton University Library
Fields oral history	Sally Ann Fields '73 interview, July 21, 2014, Princeton, NJ, Princetoniana Committee Oral History Project Records, AC259, Box 4, Princeton University Archives, Department of Rare Books and Special Collections, Princeton University Library
Gilbert oral history	Helen Homans Gilbert interview, Helen Homans Gilbert Papers, SC75, Folder 1, Radcliffe College Archives, Arthur and Elizabeth Schlesinger Library on the History of Women in America, Radcliffe Institute for Advanced Study, Harvard University
Goheen oral history	Robert F. Goheen interviews, Oct. 21 and 26 and Nov. 4, 2004, and Jan. 6, 2005, Princeton, NJ, Princeton University Presidents Oral History Collection, AC318, Series 1, Princeton University Archives, Department of Rare Books and Special Collections, Princeton University Library
Graham oral history	Patricia Albjerg Graham interview, Oct. 13, 2000, Oral History of Radcliffe College during the Horner Years, MC796, R.A.T-129, Arthur and Elizabeth Schlesinger Library on the History of Women in America, Radcliffe Institute for Advanced Study, Harvard University
Haskins oral history	Caryl Haskins interview, Oct. 5, 1990, Washington, DC, Griswold-Brewster Oral History Project, RU 217, Series I, Box 5, Folder 70, Manuscripts and Archives, Yale University Library
Horner oral history	Matina Horner interview, Aug. 13, 1999, Oral History of Radcliffe College during the Horner Years, MC796, R.A.T-129, Arthur and Elizabeth Schlesinger Library on the History of Women in America, Radcliffe Institute for Advanced Study, Harvard University

Horowitz oral history

William Horowitz interview, May 7, 1991, New Haven, CT, Griswold-Brewster Oral History Project, RU217, Series I, Box 6, Folder 74, Manuscripts and Archives, Yale University Library

Howe oral history

Harold Howe II interview, Oct. 23, 1990, Cambridge, MA, Griswold-Brewster Oral History Project, RU217, Series I, Box 6, Folder 77, Manuscripts and Archives, Yale University Library

Jean Kemeny oral history

Jean Alexander Kemeny interview, June–July 1996 and Nov. 2000, Etna, NH, DOH-32(1), Rauner Special Collections Library, Dartmouth College

John Kemeny oral history

John G. Kemeny interview, 1984, DOH-2, Rauner Special Collections Library, Dartmouth College

Kemper oral history

Dorothy Kemper '72 interview, Nov. 9, 2007, St. Louis, MO, Princetoniana Committee Oral History Project Records, AC259, Box 3, Princeton University Archives, Department of Rare Books and Special Collections, Princeton University Library

Kernan oral history

Alvin Kernan interview, May 10, 1991, Princeton, NJ, Griswold-Brewster Oral History Project, RU217, Series I, Box 6, Folder 81, Manuscripts and Archives, Yale University Library

Kurtz oral history

Agnes Bixler Kurtz interview, July 24, 1997, Hanover, NH, DOH-13(1), Rauner Special Collections Library, Dartmouth College

Lindsay oral history

John V. Lindsay interview, Mar. 12, 1992, New York City, Griswold-Brewster Oral History Project, RU217, Series I, Box 7, Folder 89, Manuscripts and Archives, Yale University Library

Lyman oral history

Susan Storey Lyman interview, June 25, 1999, Oral History of Radcliffe College during the Horner Years, MC796, R.A.T-129, Arthur and Elizabeth Schlesinger Library on the History of Women in America, Radcliffe Institute for Advanced Study, Harvard University

May oral history

Georges May interview, Apr. 22, 1992, New Haven, CT, Griswold-Brewster Oral History

Project, RU217, Series I, Box 8, Folder 99, Manuscripts and Archives, Yale University Library

Miller oral history

J. Irwin Miller interview, Dec. 18, 1991, Columbus, IN, Griswold-Brewster Oral History Project, RU217, Series I, Box 8, Folder 103, Manuscripts and Archives, Yale University Library

Nelson oral history

Mary Nelson '77 interview, Oct. 8, 2009, St. Louis, MO, Princetoniana Committee Oral History Project Records, AC259, Box 3, Princeton University Archives, Department of Rare Books and Special Collections, Princeton University Library

Obertubbesing oral history

Carol Obertubbesing '73 interview, May 30, 2008, Princeton, NJ, Princetoniana Committee Oral History Project Records, AC259, Box 3, Princeton University Archives, Department of Rare Books and Special Collections, Princeton University Library

Pforzheimer oral history

Carol Koehler Pforzheimer interview, Feb. 7, 2001, Oral History of Radcliffe College during the Horner Years, MC796, R.A.T-129, Arthur and Elizabeth Schlesinger Library on the History of Women in America, Radcliffe Institute for Advanced Study, Harvard University

Raushenbush oral history

The Reminiscences of Esther Raushenbush, Feb. 19–May 3, 1973, Oral History Research Office, Columbia University, copy (OH-36) in Arthur and Elizabeth Schlesinger Library on the History of Women in America, Radcliffe Institute for Advanced Study, Harvard University

Scranton oral history

William Warren Scranton interview, July 16, 1992, Scranton, PA, Griswold-Brewster Oral History Project, RU217, Series I, Box 10, Folder 124, Manuscripts and Archives, Yale University Library

Soifer oral history

Aviam Soifer interview, Sept. 6, 1991, Boston, MA, Griswold-Brewster Oral History Project, RU217, Series I, Box 10, Folder 131, Manuscripts and Archives, Yale University Library

Solomon oral history

Barbara Miller Solomon interview, Mar. 1989, Radcliffe College Archives, RA.A/S684, Arthur and Elizabeth Schlesinger Library on the History of Women in America, Radcliffe Institute for Advanced Study, Harvard University

Taylor oral history

Kathy Taylor '74 interview, Oct. 27, 2009, Princeton, NJ, Princetoniana Committee Oral History Project Records, AC259, Box 4, Princeton University Archives, Department of Rare Books and Special Collections, Princeton University Library

Wasserman oral history I

Elga Ruth Wasserman interview, May 7, 1992, New Haven, CT, Griswold-Brewster Oral History Project, RU217, Series I, Box 12, Folder 145, Manuscripts and Archives, Yale University Library

Wasserman oral history II

Elga Wasserman interview, May 24, 2007, Waltham, MA, Oral Histories Documenting Yale University Women, RU1051, Box 1, Manuscripts and Archives, Yale University Library

Zaharko oral history

Wendy Zaharko '74 interview, May 30, 2008, Princeton, NJ, Princetoniana Committee Oral History Project Records, AC259, Box 4, Princeton University Archives, Department of Rare Books and Special Collections, Princeton University Library

Interviews

Simon Altmann, Feb. 18, 2014, Oxford, England
Marilyn Austin-Nelson, Jan. 29, 2015, by telephone
William J. Baumol, Oct. 3, 2010, by telephone
Alison Bernstein, Feb. 9, 2015, by telephone
Halcyone H. Bohen, Jan. 30, 2015, by telephone
Derek Bok, Jan. 21, 2015, by telephone
Caroline W. Bynum, Jan. 13, 2015, Princeton, NJ
Henry Chauncey, Jr., Apr. 13, 2012, New Haven, CT
Giles Constable, Jan. 16, 2015, Princeton, NJ
Clifford S. L. Davies, Feb. 17, 2014, Oxford, England
Robert Evans, Dec. 17, 2013, by telephone
Alison Finch, Oct. 28, 2013, Cambridge, England
Margaret Skelly Goheen, Mar. 9, 2012, Princeton, NJ
Mark Goldie, Oct. 28, 2013, Cambridge, England
Hanna Holborn Gray, Nov. 18, 2014, New York, NY
Philip Green, Apr. 20, 2013, by telephone
Robin Herman, Mar. 10, 2015, by telephone
Catharine Bond Hill, Dec. 15, 2014, by telephone
Matina Horner, Feb. 9, 2015, by telephone
Archie Howie, Oct. 28, 2013, Cambridge, England
Melissa Lane, Nov. 6, 2014, Princeton, NJ
Nancy LeaMond, Apr. 26, 2013, by telephone
Mary Lefkowitz, Aug. 23, 2013, by telephone
Marsha Levy-Warren, Mar. 9, 2015, by telephone
Geoffrey E. R. Lloyd, Oct. 30, 2013, Cambridge, England
Carol Mann, Nov. 7, 2014, New York, NY
Evangeline Morphos, Aug. 15, 2014, by telephone
Daniel M. Nelson, Feb. 4, 2015, by telephone
Raymond C. Ockenden, Feb. 21, 2014, Oxford, England
Geneva Overholser, Nov. 15, 2013, New York, NY
Philip Phibbs, Sept. 3, 2013, by telephone
Graham Richards, Feb. 19, 2014, Oxford, England
Donald Robinson, Apr. 11, 2013, by telephone
Peter Rose, Apr. 4, 2013, by telephone
Alan Ryan, Apr. 15, 2014, Princeton, NJ
Neil Rudenstine, Feb. 9, 2015, Princeton, NJ
Cornelia Mendenhall Small, Nov. 12, 2014, by telephone
John L. G. Speed, Oct. 26, 2013, London, England
M. Christine Stansell, Jan. 20, 2015, New York, NY
Carol J. Thompson, Apr. 24. 2012, Cambridge, MA
Miles Vaughn Williams (conducted by Charlotte Brewer),
    Aug. 5, 2014, Oxford, England
John Walsh, Feb. 21, 2014, Oxford, England
Baroness Mary Warnock, Oct. 29, 2014, London, England

Index

Page numbers in italics refer to tables.